THE WORLD
AN ILLUSTRATED
HISTORY

Edited by
GEOFFREY PARKER

HARPER & ROW, PUBLISHERS, New York

Cambridge, Philadelphia, San Francisco, London

Mexico City, São Paulo, Singapore, Sydney

1817

Editorial direction	Andrew Heritage Barry Winkleman
Design and art direction	Ivan Dodd
Page design and layout	Vivienne Hookings Abigail Dodd Ian Smith
Map design and artwork	James Mills-Hicks and Malcolm Swanston of Swanston Graphics, Derby Alison Ewington
Text editors	Ailsa Heritage Elizabeth Wyse
Historical research	Jane Ohlmeyer
Picture research	Sharon Buckley Caroline Lucas
Place names and index	P. J. M. Geelan

This book is a companion volume to the South Carolina Educational Television series "The World: A Television History," presented to PBS stations.

FIRST U.S. EDITION

LIBRARY OF CONGRESS CATALOG CARD NUMBER: 86 45133
ISBN: 0 06 015502 7

86 87 88 89 90 10 9 8 7 6 5 4 3 2 1

CONTENTS

THE CONTRIBUTORS

Edited by
GEOFFREY PARKER
Professor of History
University of Illinois
formerly
Professor of Early Modern History
University of St Andrews, Scotland

Principal Consultants
GEOFFREY BARRACLOUGH
Late Chichele Professor
of Modern History
University of Oxford
President, The Historical Association,
1964-67

NORMAN STONE
Professor of Modern History
University of Oxford

CHRIS SCARRE
Faculty of
Archaeology and Anthropology
University of Cambridge

Contributing Historians
W.S. ATWELL
Associate Professor of History
Hobart & William Smith Colleges

IRIS BARRY
Formerly Research Student
Institute of Archaeology
University of London

CHRISTOPHER BAYLY
Reader in History
University of Cambridge
Fellow of St. Catharine's College

A.D.H. BIVAR
Lecturer in Central Asian Archaeology
School of Oriental and African Studies
University of London

HUGH BROGAN
Senior Lecturer
Department of History
University of Essex

D.A. BULLOUGH
Professor of Medieval History
University of St Andrews, Scotland

JILL COOK
Deputy Keeper
Department of Prehistoric and
Romano-British Antiquities
British Museum

JOHN FERGUSON
Former President
Selly Oak Colleges
Birmingham

JONATHON ISRAEL
Professor of
Dutch History and Institutions
University College, London

JOHN KEEGAN
Defence and Military Correspondent
Daily Telegraph, London
formerly Senior Lecturer in War Studies
Royal Military College, Sandhurst

BRUCE LENMAN
Reader in Modern History
University of St Andrews, Scotland

WOLFGANG LIEBESCHUETZ
Professor of Classical and
Archaeological Studies
University of Nottingham

DEREK McKAY
London School of Economics

WILLIAM McNEILL
Robert A. Millitin
Distinguished Services Professor
of History
University of Chicago

R.J. OVERY
Lecturer in History
King's College, London

D.W. PHILLIPSON
Curator
Museum of Archaeology and
Anthropology
University of Cambridge

J.C. RANKIN
Former Principal Lecturer
in Religious Studies
West Sussex Institute of Higher
Education

H.W.F. SAGGS
Former Professor of Semitic Languages
University College, Cardiff

G.V. SCAMMELL
Pembroke College
University of Cambridge

ANDREW SHERRATT
Assistant Keeper of Antiquities
Ashmolean Museum
Oxford

PETER SLUGLETT
Lecturer
in Modern Middle Eastern
History
Durham University

NINIAN SMART
Professor of Religious Studies
University of Lancaster and
University of California, Santa Barbara

MALCOLM TODD
Professor of Archaeology
University of Exeter

D.C. TWITCHETT
Professor of East Asian Studies
Princeton University, New Jersey

D.S.M. WILLIAMS
Lecturer in the History of Asiatic Russia
School of
Slavonic and East European Studies
University of London

INTRODUCTION

This book has grown out of the 26-part series *The World: A Television History*, produced by Network Television for Goldcrest and Bricomin Films. Each of the twenty-six chapters of this volume corresponds to a programme in the series, and the texts are based upon the scripts that were broadcast. But they are not identical, for what is effective as television is not always effective in print, and vice versa. There is, accordingly, much material here that will not be found in the series – although most of it has been provided by the same contributing historians who wrote the original scripts, according to the general plan laid down by the late Geoffrey Barraclough.

Professor Barraclough's principal concern in writing world history, whether in print or for the screen, was to avoid telling the whole story in terms of the rise of the West. He believed that, at least until 1750, the role of Europe is usually exaggerated. Before that date (and arguably for some further decades afterwards), the achievements of the great civilizations of Asia were far superior to those of Europe: while those of Africa and the Americas were often comparable. Barraclough argued that a true world history should cover, wherever possible, what was important *then* rather than what seems important *now*; and that 'in the world as constituted today, the histories of India, China and Japan, and of other countries in Asia and Africa, are as relevant as the history of Europe'.

This global approach also lay behind *The Times Atlas of World History (Times Books, 1978)* – conceived by Barry Winkleman, planned and edited by Geoffrey Barraclough – which provided the original inspiration for Network's television series.

Nevertheless, the present work is intended to stand on its own feet. In such a compact format, it cannot – must not – attempt to provide a total history. Nor does it seek to chronicle major developments in a random selection of individual countries, for world history is more than just the sum of various national histories. Instead, it tries to chart the relations and interactions between different regions, and to analyze the broad influences that affected several areas at once. And within that framework (like any other work of analytic history), it attempts to distinguish what changed from what stayed the same, and to separate the trends from the aberrations. It offers, for what it is worth, a general account of the outlines of human history from the beginnings, when Man's ancestors first emerged from the tropical forests of Africa, to the complexities of the modern world.

I am grateful to a number of people without whom this book would never have been completed. Firstly, Nancy Wood who produced numerous drafts of the chapters, swiftly and accurately. Secondly, the various contributors who gracefully accepted my efforts to edit their texts, and courteously corrected my errors and misconceptions. Thirdly, the editorial team at Times Books who gave expert guidance, assistance and encouragement at all times. Finally, the team at Network Television who brought this monumental project to life on the screen: executive producer Nicholas Barton, who conceived the series; the producer/directors, Taylor Downing, David Wright and John Selwyn Gilbert; the creative consultant Colin Millward; associate producers Leontine Ruette and Jenifer Millstone; researchers Sally Spencer and Sharon Buckley and finally the production assistants Diana Sprot, Janni Perton, Sarah Tatham and Alison Baigent. My thanks to them all.

GEOFFREY PARKER
MAY 1986

A CHRONOLOGY OF WORLD HISTORY

ASIA EXCLUDING THE NEAR EAST	EUROPE	NEAR EAST AND NORTH AFRICA	OTHER REGIONS
		c.9000-8000 Domestication of animals and crops (wheat and barley), the 'Neolithic Revolution', in the Near East; beginning of permanent settlements **8350-7350** Jericho founded: first walled town in the world (10 acres) **c.7000** Early experiments with copper ores in Anatolia **6250-5400** Çatal Hüyük (Anatolia) flourishes: largest city of its day (32 acres)	**c.9000** Hunters spread south through Americas
	c.6500 First farming in Greece and Aegean; spreads up Danube to Hungary (c.5500), Germany and Low Countries (c.4500) and along Mediterranean coast to France (c.5000). Farmers cross to Britain c.4000	**c.6000** First known pottery and woollen textiles (Çatal Hüyük) **c.5000** Colonization of Mesopotamian alluvial plain by groups practising irrigation **c.5000** Agricultural settlements in Egypt	
c.6000 Rice cultivation (Thailand)		**c.4000** Bronze casting begins in Near East; first use of plough	
c.3500 Earliest Chinese city at Liang-ch'eng chen (Lung-shan culture)	**c.3500** Construction of Megalithic tombs and circles in Brittany, Iberian peninsula and British Isles (Stonehenge c.2000)	**c.3500** Invention of wheel and plough (Mesopotamia) and sail (Egypt) **c.3100** Pictographic writing invented in Sumer **c.3100** King Menes unites Egypt; dynastic period begins	
c.3000 Use of bronze in Thailand	**c.3000** Spread of copper-working **3200-2000** Early Cycladic civilization in Aegean	**c.3000** Development of major cities in Sumer **c.2685** The 'Old Kingdom' (pyramid age) of Egypt begins (to 2180 BC)	**c.3000** Arable farming techniques spread to central Africa **c.3000** First pottery in Americas (Ecuador and Colombia)
c.2750 Growth of civilizations in the Indus valley		**c.2590** Cheops builds great pyramid at Giza	
c.2500 Domestication of horse (central Asia)	**c.2000** Indo-European speakers (early Greeks) invade and settle Peloponnese; beginnings of 'Minoan' civilization in Crete **c.2000** Use of sail on seagoing vessels (Aegean)	**2371-2230** Sargon I of Agade founds first empire in world history **c.2000** Hittites invade Anatolia and found empire (1650) **c.1800** Shamshi-Adad founds Assyrian state	**c.2500** Desiccation of Saharan region begins **c.2000** First metal-working in Peru **c.2000** Settlement of Melanesia by immigrants from Indonesia begins
c.1600 First urban civilization in China, Shang Bronze Age culture **c.1550** Aryans destroy Indus valley civilization and settle in N. India	**c.1600** Beginnings of Mycenaean civilization in Greece	**c.1750** Hammurabi founds Babylonian Empire **c.1567** Kamose and Amosis I expel Hyksos invaders and inaugurate Egyptian 'New Kingdom' (to 1090 BC)	
c.1500 Ideographic script in use in China **c.1450** Development of Brahma worship; composition of Vedas (earliest Indian literature) begins	**c.1500** 'Linear B' script in Crete and Greece **c.1450** Destruction of Minoan Crete	**c.1500** Hittite cuneiform in Anatolia **c.1370** Akhenaten enforces monotheistic sun worship in Egypt **c.1200** Collapse of Hittite Empire **c.1200** Jewish exodus from Egypt and settlement in Palestine	**c.1300** Settlers of Melanesia reach Fiji, later spreading to Western Polynesia
	c.1200 Mycenaean civilization in Greece collapses	**c.1200** Beginning of Jewish religion (worship of Jahweh) **1166** Death of Ramesses III, last great pharaoh of Egypt **c.1100** Spread of Phoenicians in Mediterranean region (to 700 BC)	
c.1027 Shang dynasty in China overthrown by Chou; Aryans in India expand eastwards down Ganges valley	**c.1000** Etruscans arrive in Italy **776** First Olympic Games held in Greece **753** Traditional date for foundation of Rome **c.750** Greek city states begin to found settlements throughout Mediterranean	**c.1100** Phoenicians develop alphabetic script (basis of all modern European scripts) **c.1000** King David unites Israel and Judah **c.840** Rise of Urartu	**c.1150** Beginning of Olmec civilization in Mexico **c.900** Foundation of kingdom of Kush (Nubia)
c.800 Aryans expand southwards in India **800-400** Composition of Upanishads, Sanskrit religious treatises **771** Collapse of Chou Feudal order in China	**c.750** Homer's *Iliad* and Hesiod's poetry first written down **c.700** Scythians spread from central Asia to eastern Europe **c.700-450** Hallstatt culture in central and western Europe: mixed farming, iron tools	**814** Traditional date for foundation of Phoenician colony at Carthage **c.750** Amos, first great prophet in Israel **721-705** Assyria at height of military power	
c.660 Jimmu, legendary first emperor of Japan **c.650** Introduction of iron technology in China	**c.650** Rise of 'Tyrants' in Corinth and other Greek cities	**671** Assyrian conquest of Egypt; introduction of iron-working **c.650** First coins: Lydia (Asia Minor) and Greece (c.600)	

ASIA EXCLUDING THE NEAR EAST	EUROPE	NEAR EAST AND NORTH AFRICA	OTHER REGIONS
	c.650 Rise of Greek lyric poetry (Sappho born c.612)	**612** Sack of Nineveh by Medes and Scythians; collapse of Assyrian power	
	585 Thales of Miletus predicts an eclipse: beginnings of Greek rationalist philosophy	**586** Babylonian captivity of the Jews	
528 Traditional date for death of Mahavira, founder of Jain sect	**c.530** Pythagoras, mathematician and mystic, active	**558** Zoroaster (Zarathustra) begins his prophetic work	
520 Death of Lao-tzu (born 605), traditional founder of Taoism	**510** Foundation of Roman Republic	**550** Zoroastrianism becomes official religion of Persia	
c.500 Sinhalese, an Aryan people, reach Ceylon	**c.505** Cleisthenes establishes democracy in Athens	**c.550** Cyrus II (the Great) of Persia defeats Medes and founds Persian Empire	
c.500 Caste system established in India		**c.540** Deutero-Isaiah, Hebrew prophet, at work during exile in Babylon	
486 Death of Siddhartha Gautama, founder of Buddhism	**490** Battle of Marathon: Persian attack on Athens defeated	**521** Persia under Darius I (the Great) rules from the Nile to the Indus	
	480 Battles of Salamis and Plataea (479): Persian invasion of Greece defeated	**c.520** Darius I completes canal connecting Nile with Red Sea	**c.500** Iron-making techniques spread to sub-Saharan Africa
479 Death of Confucius	**479-338** Period of classical culture. Poetry: Pindar (518-438); drama: Aeschylus (525-456), Sophocles (496-406), Euripides (480-406), Aristophanes (c.440-385); history: Herodotus (c.486-429), Thucydides (c.460-400); medicine: Hippocrates (c.470-406); philosophy: Socrates (469-399), Plato (c.427-347), Aristotle (384-322); sculpture: Phidias (c.490-417), Praxiteles (c.364); architecture: Parthenon (446-431)	**c.500** Achaemenid Persians transmit food plants (rice, peach, apricot, etc.) to western Asia	**c.500** First hieroglyphic writing in Mexico (Monte Albán)
		494 Persians suppress Ionian revolt	**500-AD200** Period of Nok culture in northern Nigeria
	478 Foundation of Confederacy of Delos, later transformed into Athenian Empire		
	c.450 La Tène culture emerges in central and western Europe		
403-221 'Warring States' period in China	**431-404** Peloponnesian War between Sparta and Athens		
350-200 Great period of Chinese thought: formation of Taoist, Legalist and Confucian schools; early scientific discoveries	**356** Philip II, king of Macedon		
322 Chandragupta founds Mauryan Empire at Magadha, India	**338** Battle of Chaeronea gives Macedon control of Greece	**334** Alexander the Great (of Macedon) invades Asia Minor; conquers Egypt (332), Persia (330) reaches India (329)	
	290 Rome completes conquest of central Italy	**323** Death of Alexander: empire divided between Macedon, Egypt, Syria and Pergamum	
277 Death of Ch'ü Yüan (born 343), earliest major Chinese poet	**241** First Punic War (264-241) with Carthage gives Rome control of Sicily	**312/11** Start of Seleucid era; first continuous historical dating-system	
262 Asoka, Mauryan emperor (273-236), converted to Buddhism	**218** Second Punic War (218-201): Hannibal of Carthage invades Italy	**304** Ptolemy I, Macedonian governor of Egypt, founds independent dynasty (to 30 BC)	
221 Shih Huang-ti, of Ch'in dynasty, unites China (to 207)	**206** Rome gains control of Spain	**c.290** Foundation of Alexandrian library	
202 Han dynasty reunites China; capital at Changan		**247** Arsaces I founds kingdom of Parthia	
185 Demetrius and Menander, kings of Bactria, conquer north-western India	**168** Rome defeats and partitions Macedonia	**149** Third Punic War (149-146): Rome destroys Carthage and founds province of Africa	
	146 Rome sacks Corinth; Greece under Roman domination		
	142 Completion of first stone bridge over river Tiber		
141 Wu-ti, Chinese emperor, expands Han power in eastern Asia	**133-122** Failure of reform movement in Rome, led by Tiberius and Gaius Gracchus		
c.138 Chang Chien explores central Asia			
130 Yüeh-chih tribe (Tocharians) establish kingdom in Transoxania	**89** All Italy receives Roman citizenship		**100** Camel introduced into Saharan Africa
c.112 Opening of 'Silk Road' across Central Asia linking China to West	**49** Julius Caesar conquers Gaul	**64** Pompey the Great conquers Syria; end of Seleucid Empire	
79 Death of Ssu-ma Ch'ien, Chinese historian	**47-45** Civil war in Rome; Julius Caesar becomes sole ruler (45)	**53** Battle of Carrhae: Parthia defeats Roman invasion	
	46 Julius Caesar reforms calendar; Julian calendar in use until AD 1582 (England 1752, Russia 1917)		
	31 Battle of Actium: Octavian (later Emperor Augustus) establishes domination over Rome	**30** Death of Antony and Cleopatra: Egypt becomes Roman province	

ASIA EXCLUDING THE NEAR EAST

5 Building of national shrine of Ise in Japan
AD9 Wang Mang deposes Han dynasty in China
AD25 Restoration of Han dynasty; capital at Loyang
c.AD60 Rise of Kushan Empire
AD78-102 Kanishka, Kushan emperor, gains control of north India
AD91 Chinese defeat Hsiungnu in Mongolia
AD105 First use of paper in China
c.125 Third Buddhist conference: widespread acceptance of the sculptural Buddha image
150 Earliest surviving Sanskrit inscription (India)
c.150 Buddhism reaches China
184 'Yellow Turbans' rebellions disrupt Han China
c.200 Indian epic poems: *Mahabharata, Ramayana and Bhagavad Gita*
220 End of Han dynasty: China splits into three states
245 Chinese envoys visit Funan (modern Cambodia), first major South-East Asian state
271 Magnetic compass in use (China)
285 Confucianism introduced into Japan
c.300 Foot-stirrup invented in Asia
304 Hsiungnu (Huns) invade China; China fragmented to 589
320 Chandragupta I founds Gupta Empire in northern India
c.350 Hunnish invasions of Persia and India
350 Buddhist cave temples, painting, sculpture (to 800)

413 Kumaragupta; great literary era in India

480 Gupta Empire overthrown

c.520 Rise of mathematics in India: Aryabhata and Varamihara invent decimal system
c.550 Buddhism introduced into Japan from Korea

589 China reunified by Sui dynasty

EUROPE

31-AD14 The Augustan Age at Rome: Virgil (70-19), Horace (65-27), Ovid (43-AD17), Livy (59-AD17)
27 Collapse of Roman Republic and beginning of Empire
AD43 Roman invasion of Britain
c.AD90-120 Great period of Silver Latin: Tacitus (c.55-120), Juvenal (c.55-c.140), Martial (c.38-102)
AD117 Roman Empire at its greatest exent
165 Smallpox epidemic ravages Roman empire

c.200-250 Development of Christian theology: Tertullian (c.160-220), Clement (c.150-c.215), Origen (185-254)
212 Roman citizenship conferred on all free inhabitants of Empire
238 Gothic incursions into Roman Empire begin
274 Unconquered Sun proclaimed god of Roman Empire
293 Emperor Diocletian reorganizes Roman Empire

313 Edict of Milan: Christianity granted toleration in Roman Empire
330 Capital of Roman Empire transferred to Constantinople
370 First appearance of Huns in Europe
378 Visigoths defeat and kill Roman emperor at Adrianople

404 Latin version of Bible (Vulgate) completed
406 Vandals invade and ravage Gaul and Spain (409)
410 Visigoths invade Italy, sack Rome and overrun Spain
449 Angles, Saxons and Jutes begin conquest of Britain
476 Deposition of last Roman emperor in West
486 Frankish kingdom founded by Clovis
493 Ostrogoths take power in Italy
497 Franks converted to Christianity

529 Rule of St Benedict regulates Western monasticism
533 Justinian restores Roman power in North Africa and Italy (552)
534 Justinian promulgates Legal Code
538 S. Sophia, Constantinople, consecrated
c.542 Bubonic plague ravages Europe
563 St Columba founds monastery of Iona: beginning of Irish mission to Anglo-Saxons

568 Lombard conquest of north Italy
590 Gregory the Great expands papal power

NEAR EAST AND NORTH AFRICA

c.AD30 Jesus of Nazareth, founder of Christianity, crucified in Jerusalem

AD44 Mauretania (Morocco) annexed by Rome
AD46-57 Missionary journeys of St Paul
AD70 Romans destroy the Jewish Temple in Jerusalem
AD116 Roman Emperor Trajan completes conquest of Mesopotamia
132 Jewish rebellion against Rome leads to 'diaspora' (dispersal of Jews)
c.200 Completion of *Mishnah* (codification of Jewish Law)
224 Foundation of Sasanian dynasty in Persia

276 Crucifixion of Mani (born 215), founder of Manichaean sect

426 Augustine of Hippo completes *City of God*
429 Vandal kingdom in North Africa

531 Accession of Chosroes I (died 579): Sassanian Empire at its greatest extent

OTHER REGIONS

c.AD50 Expansion of kingdom of Axum (Ethiopia) begins

c.150 Berber and Mandingo tribes begin domination of the Sudan

c.250 Kingdom of Axum (Ethiopia) gains control of Red Sea trade

c.300 Rise of Hopewell Indian chiefdoms in North America and of Maya civilizations in Mesoamerica; large civilized states in Mexico (Teotihuacán, Monte Albán, El Tajín)
c.300 Settlement of eastern Polynesia
325 Axum destroys kingdom of Meröe (Kush)

c.600 Apogee of Maya civilization

ASIA EXCLUDING THE NEAR EAST

607 Unification of Tibet
607 Chinese cultural influence in Japan begins
617 China in state of anarchy
624 China united under T'ang dynasty
c.640 Empire of Sri Harsha in northern India
c.645 Buddhism reaches Tibet (first temple 651)
645 Fujiwara's 'Taika Reform' remodels Japan on Chinese lines
658 Maximum extension of Chinese power in central Asia; protectorates in Afghanistan, Kashmir, Sogdiana and Oxus valley
665 Tibetan expansion into Turkestan, Tsinghai
676 Korea unified under Silla
c.700 Buddhist temples built at Nara, Japan
700 Golden age of Chinese poetry: Li Po (701-62), Tu Fu (712-70), Po Chü-i (772-846)
712 Arabs conquer Sind and Samarkand
c.730 Printing in China
745 Beginnings of Uighur Empire in Mongolia
751 Battle of Talas River: sets boundary of China and Abbasid caliphate
751 Paper-making spreads from China to Muslim world and Europe (1150)
755 An Lu-shan's rebellion in China
794 Japanese capital moved to Kyoto from Nara
c.800 Temple at Borobudur (Java) constructed by Shailendra kings
c.802 Jayaxarman II etablishes Angkorean kingdom (Cambodia)
836 Struggle for control of Indian Deccan
840 Collapse of Uighur Empire
842 Tibetan Empire disintegrates
853 First printed book in China
c.890 Japanese cultural renaissance: novels, landscape painting and poetry
907 Last T'ang emperor deposed
916 Khitan kingdom in Mongolia founded
918 State of Koryo founded in Korea
939 Vietnam independent of China
947 Khitans overrun northern China, establish Liao dynasty with capital at Peking
967 Fujiwara domination of Japan begins

979 Sung dynasty reunites China

c.1000 Great age of Chinese painting and ceramics

1018 Mahmud of Ghazni sacks Kanauj and breaks power of Hindu states
1018 Rajendra Chola conquers Ceylon

EUROPE

610 Accession of East Roman Emperor Heraclius; beginning of Hellenization of (East) Roman Empire, henceforward known as Byzantine Empire
680 Bulgars invade Balkans
687 Battle of Tertry: Carolingians dominate Frankish state

711 Muslim invasion of Spain
722 St Boniface's mission to Germany
725 Bede (673-735) introduces dating by Christian era
732 Battle of Poitiers halts Arab expansion in western Europe
751 Lombards overrun Ravenna, last Byzantine foothold in northern Italy
774 Charlemagne conquers northern Italy
782 Alcuin of York (735-804) organizes education in Carolingian Empire: 'Carolingian renaissance'
788 Great mosque in Córdoba
793 Viking raids begin

800 Charlemagne crowned emperor in Rome; beginning of new Western (later Holy Roman) Empire
843 Treaty of Verdun: partition of Carolingian Empire
862 Novgorod founded by Rurik the Viking
863 Creation of Cyrillic alphabet in eastern Europe
865 Bulgars and Serbians accept Christianity
871 Alfred, king of Wessex, halts Danish advance in England
882 Capital of Russia moved to Kiev

910 Abbey of Cluny founded
911 Vikings granted duchy of Normandy
929 Abdurrahman III establishes caliphate of Códoba
955 Otto I defeats Magyars at Lechfeld
959 Unification of England under Eadgar
960 Miesko I founds Polish state
962 Otto I of Germany crowned emperor in Rome
972 Beginning of Hungarian state under Duke Geisa
983 Great Slav rebellion against German eastward expansion
987 Accession of Capetians in France

1014 Battle of Clontarf breaks Viking domination of Ireland
1016 Cnut the Great rules England, Denmark and Norway (to 1035)
1018 Byzantines annex Bulgaria (to 1185)
1031 Collapse of caliphate of Córdoba

NEAR EAST AND NORTH AFRICA

611 Persian armies capture Antioch and Jerusalem and overrun Asia Minor (to 626)
622 *Hegira* of Mohammed; beginning of Islamic calendar
625 Mohammed begins his prophetic mission
632 Death of Mohammed: Arab expansion begins
636 Arabs overrun Syria
637 Arabs overrun Iraq
641 Arabs conquer Egypt and begin conquest of North Africa
c.690 Arabic replaces Greek and Persian as language of Umayyad administration
692 Completion of Dome of Rock in Jerusalem, first great monument of Islamic architecture
718 Arab siege of Constantinople repulsed
750 Abbasid caliphate established
760 Arabs adopt Indian numerals and develop algebra and trigonometry

809 Death of caliph Harun al-Rashid

935 Text of Koran finalized
936 Caliphs of Baghdad lose effective power

969 Fatimids conquer Egypt and found Cairo

1020 Death of Firdausi, writer of Persian national epic, *The Shahnama*

OTHER REGIONS

c.700 Rise of empire of Ghana

c.800 First settlers reach Easter Island and New Zealand (850) from Polynesia
c.850 Collapse of Classic Maya culture in Mesoamerica

c.990 Expansion of Inca Empire (Peru)
c.1000 Vikings colonize Greenland and discover America (Vinland)
c.1000 First Iron Age settlement at Zimbabwe (Rhodesia)

ASIA EXCLUDING THE NEAR EAST

1020 Completion of *Tale of Genji* by Lady Murasaki
1021 Cholas invade Bengal
1038 Tangut tribes form Hsihsia state in north-west China
1044 Establishment of first Burmese national state at Pagan
c.1045 Moveable type printing invented in China

1094 Composition of old Javanese *Ramayana* by Yogisvara

1126 Chin overrun northern China; Sung rule restricted to south
c.1150 Hindu temple of Angkor Wat (Cambodia) built

1170 Apogee of Srivijaya kingdom in Java under Shailendra dynasty
1175 Muizzuddin Muhammad of Ghazni, founds first Muslim empire in India
c.1180 Angkor Empire (Cambodia) at greatest extent
1185 Minamoto warlords supreme in Japan
1193 Zen Buddhist order founded in Japan
1206 Mongols under Genghis Khan begin conquest of Asia
1206 Sultanate of Delhi founded
c.1215 Islamic architecture spreads to India
c.1220 Emergence of first Thai kingdom
1234 Mongols destroy Chin Empire

1264 Kublai Khan founds Yüan dynasty in China
1275 Marco Polo (1254-1324) arrives in China
1279 Mongols conquer southern China

1333 End of Minamoto shogunate: civil war in Japan

c.1341 'Black Death' starts in Asia
1349 First Chinese settlement at Singapore; beginning of Chinese expansion in South-East Asia
1350 Golden age of Majapahit Empire in Java
c.1350 Japanese cultural revival
1368 Ming dynasty founded in China

EUROPE

1054 Schism between Greek and Latin Christian churches begins
1066 Norman conquest of England
1071 Fall of Bari completes Norman conquest of Byzantine Italy
1073 Gregory VII elected Pope: beginning of conflict of Empire and papacy

c.1100 First universities in Europe: Salerno (medicine), Bologna (law), Paris (theology and philosophy)
1125 Renewal of German eastwards expansion
1154 Accession of Henry II: Angevin Empire in England and France
1154 Chartres Cathedral begun; Gothic architecture spreads through western Europe
c.1160 Development of European vernacular verse: Chanson de Roland (c.1100), El Cid (c.1150), Parzifal, Tristan (c.1200)
1198 Innocent III elected Pope
1198 Death of Averroës, Arab scientist and philosopher

1204 Fourth Crusade: Franks conquer Byzantium and found Latin Empire
1212 Battle of Las Navas de Tolosa
1215 Magna Carta: King John makes concessions to English barons
1226 Death of St Francis of Assisi
1236 Mongols invade and conquer Russia (1239)
1241 Mongols invade Poland, Hungary, Bohemia
1242 Alexander Nevsky defeats Teutonic Order
1250 d. of Emperor Frederick II; collapse of Imperial power in Germany and Italy
1261 Greek empire restored in Constantinople
1274 Death of St Thomas Aquinas: his *Summa Theologica* defines Christian dogma
1290 Spectacles invented (Italy)
1291 Beginnings of Swiss Confederation

1309 Papacy moves from Rome to Avignon
1314 Battle of Bannockburn: Scotland defeats England
c.1320 Cultural revival in Italy: Dante (1265-1321), Giotto (1276-1337), Petrarch (1304-71)
1325 Ivan I begins recovery of Moscow
1337 Hundred Years War between France and England begins
1339 Building of Kremlin (Moscow)
1348 Black Death from Asia ravages Europe
1360 Peace of Brétigny ends first phase of Hundred Years War
1361 Ottomans capture Adrianople
1378 Great Schism in West (to 1417)
1386 Union of Poland and Lithuania

NEAR EAST AND NORTH AFRICA

1037 Death of Avicenna, Persian philosopher
1055 Seljuk Turks take Baghdad
1056 Almoravids conquer North Africa and southern Spain
1071 Battle of Manzikert: defeat of Byzantium by Seljuk Turks
1096 First Crusade: Franks invade Anatolia and Syria, and found crusader states

c.1100 Omar Khayyam composes *Rubaiyyat*
1111 Death of al-Ghazali, Muslim theologian
1135 Almohads dominant in north-western Africa and Muslim Spain

1171 Saladin defeats Fatimids and conquers Egypt
1188 Saladin destroys Frankish crusader kingdoms

1228 Hafsid dynasty established at Tunis

1258 Mongols sack Baghdad; end of Abbasid caliphate

1299 Ottoman Turks begin expansion in Anatolia

1377 Death of Ibn Battuta (born 1309), Arab geographer and traveller

OTHER REGIONS

1076 Almoravids destroy kingdom of Ghana

c.1100 Toltecs build their capital at Tula (Mexico)

c.1150 Beginnings of Yoruba city states (Nigeria)

c.1200 Rise of empire of Mali in west Africa
c.1200 Emergence of Hausa city states (Nigeria)
c.1200 Aztecs occupy valley of Mexico

c.1250 Mayapan becomes dominant Maya city of Yucatán

c.1300 Kanuri Empire moves capital from Kanem to Borno
c.1300 Emergence of empire of Benin (Nigeria)

1325 Rise of Aztecs in Mexico: Tenochtitlán founded

ASIA EXCLUDING THE NEAR EAST	EUROPE	NEAR EAST AND AFRICA	NEW WORLD
1370 Hindu state of Vijayanagar dominant in southern India	**1387** Lithuania converted to Christianity		
1380 Timur (Tamerlane) begins conquests	**1389** Battle of Kosovo: Ottomans gain control of Balkans	**1392** Death of Hafiz, Persian lyric poet	
1392 Korea becomes independent	**1397** Union of Kalmar (Scandinavia)		
1394 Thais invade Cambodia; Khmer capital moved to Phnom Penh			
1398 Timur invades India and sacks Delhi	**1400** Death of Chaucer, first great poet in English	**1402** Battle of Ankara: Timur defeats Ottomans in Anatolia	
c.1400 Establishment of Malacca as a major commercial port of S.E. Asia	**1410** Battle of Tannenberg: Poles defeat Teutonic Knights	**1406** Death of Ibn Khaldun, Muslim historian	
1405 Chinese voyages in Indian Ocean	**1415** Battle of Agincourt: Henry V of England resumes attack on France	**1415** Portuguese capture Ceuta: beginning of Portugal's African empire	
	1428 Joan of Arc: beginning of French revival	**1430** Construction of great stone enclosure at Zimbabwe (Rhodesia)	
1428 Chinese expelled from Vietnam	**1445** Johannes Gutenberg (1397-1468) prints first book in Europe	**1434** Portuguese explore south of Cape Bojador	
	1453 England loses Continental possessions (except Calais)	**c.1450** Apogee of Songhay Empire; university at Timbuktu	
	1453 Ottoman Turks capture Constantinople: end of Byzantine Empire		
1471 Vietnamese southward expansion: Champa annexed	**1475** Burgundy at height of power (Charles the Bold)		**1470** Incas conquer Chimú kingdom
	1478 Ivan III, first Russian tsar, subdues Novgorod and throws off Mongol yoke (1480)		
	1492 Fall of Granada: end of Muslim rule in Spain; Jews expelled from Spain	**1492** Spaniards begin conquest of North African coast	**1492** Columbus reaches America: discovery of New World
	1494 Italian wars: beginning of Franco-Habsburg struggle for hegemony in Europe		**1493** First Spanish settlement in New World (Hispaniola)
			1493 Treaty of Tordesillas divides New World between Portugal and Spain
1498 Vasco da Gama: first European sea-voyage to India and back			**1497** Cabot reaches Newfoundland
1500 Shah Ismail founds Safavid dynasty in Persia	**c.1500** Italian Renaissance: Leonardo da Vinci (1452-1519), Michelangelo (1475-1564), Raphael (1483-1520), Botticelli (1444-1510), Machiavelli (1469-1527), Ficino (1433-99)		**1498** Columbus discovers South America
		1505 Portuguese establish trading posts in east Africa	
	1509 Watch invented by Peter Henle (Nuremburg)	**c.1510** African slaves to America	
1511 Portuguese take Malacca	**1519** Charles V, ruler of Spain and Netherlands, elected emperor		**1519** Cortés begins conquest of Aztec Empire
1516 Ottomans overrun Syria, Egypt and Arabia (1517)	**1521** Martin Luther outlawed: beginning of Protestant Reformation		**1520** Magellan crosses Pacific
	1521 Suleiman the Magnificent, Ottoman sultan, conquers Belgrade		
	c.1525 Introduction of potato from South America to Europe		
1526 Battle of Panipat: Babur conquers kingdom of Delhi and founds Mughal dynasty	**1526** Battle of Mohács: Ottoman Turks overrun Hungary		**1532** Pizarro begins conquest of Inca Empire for Spain
1539 Death of Kabir Nanak, founder of Sikh religion	**1534** Henry VIII of England breaks with Rome		
	1541 John Calvin founds reformed church at Geneva		
	1543 Copernicus publishes *Of the Revolution of Celestial Bodies*		
1550 Mongol Altan-khan invades northen China; Japanese 'pirate' raids in China	**1545** Council of Trent: beginning of Counter-Reformation	**1546** Destruction of Mali Empire by Songhay	**1545** Discovery of silver mines at Potosí (Peru) and Zacatecas (Mexico)
1557 Portuguese established at Macao (China)	**1556** Ivan IV of Russia conquers Volga basin		
	1559 Tobacco first introduced into Europe		**c.1560** Portuguese begin sugar cultivation in Brazil
1565 Akbar extends Mughal power to Deccan	**1562** Wars of religion in France (to 1598)	**1571** Portuguese create colony in Angola	**1571** Spanish conquer Philippines
1581 Yermak begins Russian conquest of Siberia	**1571** Battle of Lepanto: end of Turkish sea power in central Mediterranean	**1578** Battle of Al Kasr al Kebir: Moroccans destroy Portuguese power in north-western Africa	
1584 Phra Narai creates independent Siam	**1572** Dutch Revolt against Spain	**1591** Battle of Tondibi: Moroccans destroy Songhay kingdom	
1598 Shah Abbas I creates imperial capital at Isfahan	**1588** Spanish Armada defeated by English		
	1598 Time of Troubles in Russia		

11

ASIA	EUROPE	AFRICA	NEW WORLD
c.1603 Beginnings of Kabuki theatre, Japan	**1600** Foundation of English and Dutch (1602) East India Companies	**c.1600** Oyo Empire at height of power	
	1607 Monteverdi's *La Favola d'Orfeo* establishes opera as art form		**1607** First permanent English settlement in America (Jamestown, Virginia)
1609 Beginning of Tokugawa shogunate in Japan	**1609** Dutch Republic becomes independent		**1608** French colonists found Quebec
	1609 Telescope invented (Holland)		
	c.1610 Scientifc revolution in Europe begins: Kepler (1571-1610), Bacon (1561-1626), Galileo (1564-1642), Descartes (1596-1650)		
	1616 Death of Shakespeare (born 1564) and Cervantes (born 1547)		
1619 Foundation of Batavia (Jakarta) by Dutch: start of Dutch colonial empire in East Indies	**1618** Outbreak of Thirty Years War		**1620** Puritans land in New England (*Mayflower*)
	1620 First weekly newspapers in Europe (Amsterdam)	**1628** Portuguese destroy Mwenemutapa Empire	**1625** Dutch settle New Amsterdam
	1630 Gustavus Adolphus of Sweden intervenes in Thirty Years War		
	c.1630 Apogee of Netherlands art: Hals (1580-1666), Rembrandt (1606-69), Vermeer (1632-75), Rubens (1577-1640)		
1638 Russians reach Pacific			**1636** Foundation of Harvard College, first university in North America
1641 Dutch capture Malacca from Portuguese	**1642** English Civil War begins		
1644 Manchus found new dynasty (Ch'ing) in China	**1648** Peace of Westphalia ends Thirty Years War		**1645** Tasman circumnavigates Australia and discovers New Zealand
1649 Russians reach Pacific and found Okhotsk	**1649** Execution of Charles I of England; republic declared		
c.1650 Beginnings of popular literary culture in Japan (puppet theatre, kabuki, the novel)	**1652** First Anglo-Dutch War: beginning of Dutch decline	**1652** Foundation of Cape Colony by Dutch	
1653 Taj Mahal, Agra, India, completed	**1654** Ukraine passes from Polish to Russian rule		
	1656 St Peter's, Rome, completed (Bernini)		
	1658 Peace of Roskilde: Swedish Empire at height	**1659** French found trading stations on Senegal coast	
	c.1660 Classical period of French culture: drama (Molière, 1622-1673, Racine, 1639-1699, Corneille, 1606-1684), painting (Poussin, 1594-1665, Claude, 1600-1682), music (Lully, 1632-1687, Couperin, 1668-1733)		
	1662 Royal Society founded in London and (1666) Académie Française in Paris	**1662** Battle of Ambuila: destruction of Kongo kingdom by Portuguese	
	1667 Beginning of French expansion under Louis XIV		**1664** New Amsterdam taken by British from Dutch (later renamed New York)
1674 Sivaji creates Hindu Maratha kingdom	**1683** 'Glorious Revolution'; constitutional monarchy in England		
	1687 Isaac Newton's *Principia*		**1684** La Salle explores Mississippi and claims Louisiana for France
1689 Treaty of Nerchinsk between Russia and China	**1689** 'Grand Alliance' against Louis XIV		
1690 Foundation of Calcutta by English	**1690** John Locke's *Essay concerning Human Understanding*		**1693** Gold discovered in Brazil
1697 Chinese occupy Outer Mongolia	**1699** Treaty of Carlowitz: Habsburgs recover Hungary from Turks		
	1700 Great Northern War (to 1720)	**c.1700** Rise of Asante power (Gold Coast)	
	c.1700 Great age of German baroque music: Buxtehude (1637-1707), Handel (1685-1759), Bach (1685-1750)		
	1703 Foundation of St Petersburg, capital of Russian Empire (1712)		
1707 Death of Aurangzeb: decline of Mughal power in India	**1707** Union of England and Scotland		
	1709 Battle of Poltava: Peter the Great of Russia defeats Swedes		
	1709 Abraham Darby discovers coke-smelting technique for producing pig-iron (England)		
	1713 Treaty of Utrecht ends War of Spanish Succession		**1728** Bering begins Russian reconnaissance of Alaska
c.1735 Wahabite movements to purify Islam begins in Arabia	**1730** Wesley brothers create Methodism	**c.1730** Revival of ancient empire of Borno (central Sudan)	
1736 Safavid dynasty deposed by Nadir Shah	**1740** War of Austrian Succession: Prussia annexes Silesia		

12

ASIA

1747 Ahmad Khan Abdali founds kingdom of Afghanistan
1751 China overruns Tibet, Dzungaria and Tarim Basin (1756-9)
1751 French gain control of Deccan and Carnatic
1755 Alaungpaya founds Rangoon and reunites Burma (to 1824)
1757 Battle of Plassey: British defeat French
1761 Capture of Pondicherry: British destroy French power in India

1796 British conquer Ceylon

1817 Foundation of Hindu college, Calcutta, first major centre of Western influence in India
1818 Britain defeats Marathas and becomes effective ruler of India
1819 British found Singapore as free trade port

1824 British begin conquest of Burma and Assam
1825-30 Java war: revolt of Indonesians against Dutch
1828 Foundation of Brahmo-samaj, Hindu revivalist movement
1830 Russia begins conquest of Kazakhstan (to 1854)

EUROPE

1756 Seven Years War begins
c.1760 European enlightenment: Voltaire (1694-1778), Diderot (1713-84), Hume (1711-76)
1762 J.J. Rousseau's *Social Contract*
c.1770 Advance of science and technology in Europe: J. Priestley (1733-1804), A. Lavoisier (1743-94), A. Volta (1745-1827). Harrison's chronometer (1762), Watt's steam engine (1769), Arkwright's water-powered spinning-frame (1769)
1772 First partition of Poland (2nd and 3rd partitions 1793, 1795)
1774 Treaty of Kuchuk Kainarji: beginning of Ottoman decline
1776 Publication of *The Wealth of Nations* by Adam Smith (1723-90) and *Common Sense* by Tom Paine (1737-1809)
1781 Immanuel Kant's *Critique of Pure Reason*
1783 Russia annexes Crimea
1789 French Revolution begins; abolition of feudal system and proclamation of Rights of Man
c.1790 Great age of European orchestral music: Mozart (1756-91), Haydn (1732-1809), Beethoven (1770-1827)
1791 Russia gains Black Sea steppes from Turks
1792 French Republic proclaimed; beginning of revolutionary wars
1792 Cartwright invents steam-powered weaving loom
1793 Decimal system introduced (France)
1793 Attempts to reform Ottoman Empire by Selim III
1796 Jenner discovers smallpox vaccine (UK)
1798 Malthus publishes *Essay on the Principle of Population*
1799 Napoleon becomes First Consul and (1804) Emperor of France

1805 Napoleon defeats Austria and (1806) Prussia
1805 Battle of Trafalgar: Britain defeats French and Spanish fleets
1807 Abolition of serfdom in Prussia
1812 Napoleon invades Russia
1812 Cylinder printing press invented, adopted by *The Times* (London)
1815 Napoleon defeated at Waterloo, exiled to St Helena
1815 Congress of Vienna
c.1820 Romanticism in European literature and art: Byron (1788-1824), Chateaubriand (1768-1848), Heine (1797-1856), Turner (1775-1851), Delacroix (1798-1863)
1821 Greek war of independence
1821 Electric motor and generator invented by M. Faraday (Britain)
1822 First photographic image produced by J-N. Niepce (France)
1825 First passenger steam railway: Stockton and Darlington (England)
1830 Revolutionary movements in France, Germany, Poland and Italy; Belgium wins independence

AFRICA

1798 Napoleon attacks Egypt

1804 Fulanis conquer Hausa

1806 Cape Colony passes under British control
1807 Slave trade abolished within British Empire
1811 Mohammed Ali takes control in Egypt

1818 Shaka forms Zulu kingdom in SE Africa

1822 Liberia founded as colony for freed slaves

1830 French begin conquest of Algeria

AMERICAS AND AUSTRALASIA

1760 New France conquered by British: Quebec (1759) and Montreal (1760)

1768 Cook begins exploration of Pacific

1775 American Revolution begins
1776 American Declaration of Independence

1783 Treaty of Paris: Britain recognizes American independence
1788 British colony of Australia founded
1789 George Washington becomes first President of United States of America

1793 Eli Whitney's cotton 'gin' (US)

1803 Louisiana Purchase nearly doubles size of US

1808 Independence movements in Spanish and Portuguese America: 13 new states created by 1828

1819 US purchases Florida from Spain

1823 Monroe Doctrine

13

ASIA	EUROPE	AFRICA	AMERICAS AND AUSTRALASIA
1833 Death of Rammohan Roy (b.1772), father of modern Indian nationalism	**1832** Death of Goethe (born 1749) **1833** Formation of German customs union (*Zollverein*) **1833** First regulation of industrial working conditions (Britain) **1836** Needle-gun invented (Prussia), making breech-loading possible **1837** Pitman's shorthand invented **1838** First electric telegraph (Britain)	**1835** 'Great Trek' of Boer colonists from Cape, leading to foundation of Republic of Natal (1839), Orange Free State (1848) and Transvaal (1849)	**1834** First mechanical reaper patented (US)
1842 Opium War: Britain annexes Hong Kong **1843** British conquer Sind **1845-9** British conquest of Punjab and Kashmir	**1840** First postage stamp (Britain) **1845** Irish famine stimulates hostility to Britain and emigration to US **1846** Britain repeals Corn Laws and moves towards complete free trade **1848** Revolutionary movements in Europe; proclamation of Second Republic in France **1848** Communist Manifesto issued by Marx (1818-83) and Engels (1820-95) **1849** Death of Chopin (b.1810); apogee of Romantic music with Berlioz (1803-69), Liszt (1811-86), Wagner (1813-83), Brahms (1833-97), Verdi (1813-1901)		**1840** Britain annexes New Zealand **1845** Texas annexed by US **1846** Mexican War begins: US conquers New Mexico and California (1848) **1846** Oregon treaty delimits US-Canadian boundary **1850** Australian colonies and (1856) New Zealand granted responsible government
1850 Taiping rebellion in China – (to 1864), with immense loss of life	**1851** Great Exhibition in London **1852** Fall of French republic; Louis Napoleon (Napoleon III, 1808-73) becomes French emperor		
1853 First railway and telegraph lines in India **1854** Perry forces Japan to open trade with US **1857** Indian Mutiny **1858** Treaty of Tientsin: further Treaty Ports opened to foreign trade in China	**1853** Haussmann begins rebuilding of Paris **1854** Crimean War (to 1856) **1856** Bessemer process permits mass-production of steel **1859** Sardinian-French war against Austria; Piedmont acquires Lombardy (1860); unification of Italy begins **1859** Darwin publishes *The Origin of Species*	**1853** Livingstone's explorations begin	**1859** First oil well drilled (Pennsylvania, US)
1860 Treaty of Peking: China cedes Ussuri region to Russia	**c.1860** Great age of European novels: Dickens (1812-70), Dumas (1802-70), Flaubert (1821-80), Turgenev (1818-83), Dostoyevsky (1821-81), Tolstoy (1828-1910) **1861** Emancipation of Russian serfs **1861** Pasteur evolves germ theory of disease	**1860** French expansion in West Africa from Senegal	**1861** Outbreak of American Civil War **1861** Women first given vote (Australia)
1863 France establishes protectorate over Cambodia, Cochin China (1865), Annam (1874), Tonkin (1885) and Laos (1893)	**1863** First underground railway (London) **1864** Prussia defeats Denmark: annexes Schleswig-Holstein (1866) **1864** Russia suppresses Polish revolt **1864** Foundation of Red Cross (Switzerland) **1866** Prussia defeats Austria **1867** Establishment of North German confederation and of dual monarchy in Austria-Hungary **1867** Marx publishes *Das Kapital* (vol. 1)		**1864** War of Paraguay against Argentina, Brazil and Uruguay (to 1870) **1865** End of American Civil War; slavery abolished in US **1867** Russia sells Alaska to US **1867** Dominion of Canada established
1868 End of Tokugawa Shogunate and Meiji Restoration in Japan	**1870** Franco-Prussian war **1870** Declaration of Papal infallibility **1871** Proclamation of German Empire, beginning of Third French Republic: suppression of Paris commune **1874** Emergence of Impressionist school of painting: Monet (1840-1926), Renoir (1841-1919), Degas (1834-1917) **1875** Growth of labour/socialist parties: Germany (1875), Belgium (1885), Holland (1877), Britain (1893), Russia (1898)	**1869** Suez Canal opens **1875** Disraeli buys Suez Canal Company shares to ensure British control of sea route to India	**1869** Prince Rupert's Land, Manitoba (1870) and British Columbia (1871) join Canada **1869** First trans-continental railroad completed (US) **1874** First electric train (New York); telephone patented by Bell (US 1876) **1876** Porfirio Díaz (1830-1915) gains control of Mexico (to 1911)
1877 Queen Victoria proclaimed Empress of India			

ASIA	EUROPE	AFRICA	AMERICAS AND AUSTRALASIA
	1878 Treaty of Berlin: Romania, Montenegro and Serbia become independent, Bulgaria autonomous		
1879 Second Afghan War gives Britain control of Afghanistan	**1878** First oil tanker built (Russia) **1879** Dual alliance between Germany and Austria-Hungary **1884** Maxim gun perfected	**1881** French occupy Tunisia **1882** Revolt in Egypt leading to British occupation	**1879** War of the Pacific (Chile, Bolivia, Peru) **1879** F. W. Woolworth opened first '5 and 10 cent store'
1885 Foundation of Indian National Congress **1886** British annex Upper Burma **1887** French establish Indo-Chinese Union **c.1890** Beginnings of modern literature in Japan on western models **1891** Construction of Trans-Siberian railway begun **1894-5** Sino-Japanese War: Japan occupies Formosa	**c.1885** Daimler and Benz pioneer the automobile (Germany) **1888** Dunlop invents pneumatic tyre **1890** Dismissal of Bismarck; Wilhelm II begins new course **c.1890** Europe – realistic drama: Ibsen (1828-1906), Strindberg (1849-1912), Chekhov (1860-1904), Shaw (1856-1950) **1894** Franco-Russian alliance **1895** Röntgen discovers X-rays (Germany); Marconi invents wireless telegraphy (Italy); first public showing of motion picture (France)	**1884** Germany acquires SW Africa, Togoland, Cameroons **1885** King of Belgium acquires Congo **1886** Germany and Britain partition East Africa **1886** Gold discovered in Transvaal; foundation of Johannesburg **1889** British South Africa company formed by Cecil Rhodes, begins colonization of Rhodesia (1890)	**1882** First hydro-electric plant (Wisconsin, US) **1885** Completion of Canadian Pacific railway
	1896 Herzl publishes *The Jewish State* calling for Jewish National Home	**1896** Battle of Adowa: Italians defeated by Ethiopians	
1898 Abortive 'Hundred Days' reform in China	**1898** Germany embarks on naval building programme; beginning of German 'world policy' **1898** Pierre and Marie Curie observe radioactivity and isolate radium (France) **1899** Howard's *Garden Cities of Tomorrow* initiates modern city planning	**1898** Fashoda crisis between Britain and France **1899** Boer War begins	**1898** Spanish-American war: US annexes Guam, Puerto Rico and Philippines
1900 Boxer uprising in China	**1900** Planck evolves quantum theory (Germany) **1900** Freud's *Interpretation of Dreams,* beginning of psychoanalysis (Austria)	**1900** Copper-mining begins in Katanga	
1904 Partition of Bengal: nationalist agitation in India **1904-5** Russo-Japanese War; Japanese success stimulates Asian nationalism **1906** Revolution in Persia	**1904** Anglo-French entente **1905** Revolution in Russia, followed by Tsarist concessions **1905** Norway independent of Sweden **1905** Einstein's theory of relativity (Germany) **1907** Anglo-Russian entente **1907** Exhibition of Cubist paintings in Paris: Picasso (1881-1973), Braque (1882-1963)		**1901** Unification of Australia as Commonwealth **1903** Panama Canal Zone ceded to US **1903** First successful flight of petrol-powered aircraft (Wright Brothers, US) **1907** New Zealand acquires dominion status
	1908 Young Turk revolution: Ottoman sultan deposed **1908** Bulgaria becomes independent; Austria annexes Bosnia and Herzegovina	**1908** Belgian state takes over Congo from King Leopold	
1910 Japan annexes Korea **1911** Chinese Revolution: Sun Yat-sen first President of new republic **1914** German concessions in China and Colonies in Pacific taken over by Japan, Australia and New Zealand	**1910** Development of abstract painting: Kandinsky (1866-1944), Mondrian (1872-1944) **1912-13** Balkan wars **1914** Outbreak of First World War **1917** Revolution in Russia: Tsar abdicates (March), Bolshevik take-over (Nov); first socialist state established	**1910** Formation of Union of South Africa **1911** Italy conquers Libya **1914** Britain proclaims protectorate over Egypt **1914-15** French and British conquer German colonies except German East Africa	**1910** Mexican revolution begins **1910** Development of plastics **1913** Henry Ford develops conveyor belt assembly for production of Model T automobile (Detroit, US) **1914** Panama Canal opens **1916** First birth control advice centre opened (New York)
1917 'Balfour Declaration' promises Jews a National Home in Paletine	**1917** First use of massed tanks (Battle of Cambrai) **1918** Germany and Austria-Hungary sue for armistice: end of First World War **1918** Civil war and foreign intervention in Russia		**1917** US declares war on Central Powers **1918** President Wilson announces 'Fourteen Points'

EUROPE	AFRICA	AMERICAS AND AUSTRALASIA

1919 Amritsar incident; upsurge of Indian nationalism
1919 May 4th movement in China; upsurge of Chinese nationalism
1920 Mustafa Kemal (Atatürk) leads resistance to partition of Turkey; Turkish Nationalist movement
1921 Reza Khan becomes leader and takes power in Persia, becomes Shah (1925) and introduces reform
1921-2 Washington Conference attempts to regulate situation in East Asia
1922 Greek army expelled from Turkey; last Ottoman sultan deposed; republic proclaimed (1923)

1919 World-wide influenza epidemic reaches Europe
1919 Rutherford (1871-1937) splits atom (UK)
1919 Bauhaus school of design started by Gropius at Weimar (Germany)
1920 League of Nations established (headquarters Geneva)
1922 Mussolini takes power in Italy
1922 Irish Free State (Eire) created
1923 French occupy Ruhr; runaway inflation in Germany
1923 Development of tuberculosis vaccine (France)
1924 Death of Lenin
1924 Thomas Mann (1875-1955) publishes *The Magic Mountain*; apotheosis of the novel with Proust (1871-1922), Joyce (1882-1941), Lawrence (1885-1930)
1925 Locarno treaties stabilize frontiers in West
1925 Franz Kafka (1883-1924) publishes *The Trial*, Adolf Hitler publishes *Mein Kampf*

1919 Nationalist revolt in Egypt

1921 Battle of Anual: Spanish army defeated by Moroccans

1919 First crossing of Atlantic by air (Alcock and Brown)

1920 US refuses to ratify Paris treaties and withdraws into isolation
1920 First general radio broadcasts (US and UK)
c.1920 Emergence of jazz in US: Louis Armstrong (1900-71), Duke Ellington (1899-1974), Count Basie (1904-1984)
1921 US restricts immigration

1923 General Motors established: world's largest manufacturing company

1926 Chiang Kai-shek (1886-1975) begins reunification of China

1931 Japanese occupy Manchuria
1932 Kingdom of Saudi Arabia formed by Ibn Saud
1934 'Long March' of Chinese Communists begins
1936 Japan signs anti-Comintern pact with Germany
1936 Arab revolt in Palestine against Jewish immigration

1937 Beginning of full-scale war between Japan and China

1926 General Strike in Britain
1926 Salazar takes power in Portugal
1928 First Five-Year Plan and collectivization of agriculture in Russia
1931 Spain becomes a Republic
1933 Hitler made Chancellor in Germany; beginning of Nazi revolution
1936 German reoccupation of Rhineland
1936 Spanish Civil War begins
1936 Keynes publishes *The General Theory of Employment, Interest and Money*
1936 First regular public television transmission (UK)
1937 Jet engine first tested (UK)
1938 Germany occupies Austria
1938 Munich conference: dismemberment of Czechoslovakia
1939 German-Soviet non-aggression pact; Germany invades Poland; Britain and France declare war on Germany
1939 Development of penicillin (UK)
1939 Development of DDT (Switzerland)
1940 Germany overruns Norway, Denmark, Belgium, Netherlands, France; Italy invades Greece but is repulsed
1940 Battle of Britain

1926 Revolt of Abd-el Krim crushed in Morocco

1934 Italian suppression of Senussi resistance in Libya
1935 Italy invades Ethiopia
1936 Anglo-Egyptian alliance; British garrison in Suez Canal Zone

1940-1 Italians expelled from Somalia, Eritrea and Ethiopia

1927 Emergence of talking pictures. Rise of great film makers: D.W. Griffith (1874-1948), Chaplin (1889-1977), John Ford (1895-1973), Eisenstein (1896-1948), Clair (1898-1981), Hitchcock (1899-1980), Disney (1901-66)
1929 Wall Street Crash precipitates world Depression
1930 Military revolution in Brazil; Vargas becomes president
1932 Chaco War between Bolivia and Paraguay (to 1935)
1933 US President Franklin D. Roosevelt introduces New Deal
1935 Cárdenas president of Mexico: land redistribution and (1938) nationalization of oil
1936 Pan-American congress; US proclaims good neighbour policy

1937 Invention of nylon (USA)

1939 US proclaims neutrality in European War

1941 US begins 'lend-lease' to Britain

1941 Japan attacks US at Pearl Harbor
1942 Japan overruns SE Asia
1942 Battle of Midway; US halts Japanese expansion

1945 US drops atom bombs on Japan, forcing surrender

1946 Civil War in China (to 1949)
1946 Beginning of Vietnamese struggle against France (to 1954)

1947 India and Pakistan independent

1941 Germany invades Russia; declares war on US
1943 German VI army surrenders at Stalingrad; Italian capitulation
1944 Anglo-American landing in Normandy; Russians advance in E. Europe
1945 Yalta Conference, beginning of Cold War
1945 Defeat of Germany and suicide of Hitler
1947 Intensification of Cold War; Truman Doctrine enunciated
1947 Greek Civil War (to 1949)
1947 Marshall Plan for economic reconstruction in Europe

1941 Germans conquer Cyrenaica and advance into Egypt (1942)
1942 Battle of el-Alamein; German defeat and retreat
1942 Anglo-American landings in Morocco and Algeria

1941 US enters war against Germany and Japan

1942 Fermi builds first nuclear reactor (US)

1944 Perón comes to power in Argentina

1945 United Nations established (headquarters New York)
1945 Atom bomb first exploded (US)

1946 First electronic computer built (US)

1947 First supersonic flight (US)

16

ASIA	EUROPE	AFRICA	AMERICAS AND AUSTRALASIA
1948 Establishment of state of Israel; first Arab-Israeli war	**1948** Communist takeover in Czechoslovakia and Hungary; Berlin Airlift		**1948** Organization of American States established
1949 Communist victory in China	**1949** Formation of NATO alliance	**1949** Apartheid programme inaugurated in S Africa	**1948** Transistor invented (US)
1949 Indonesia independent	**1953** Death of Stalin	**1952** Beginning of Mau Mau rebellion in Kenya	**1951** Australia, New Zealand and US sign Anzus Pact
1950 Korean War begins	**1955** Warsaw Pact signed	**1952** Military revolt in Egypt; proclamation of republic (1953)	**1951** First nuclear power stations (US and UK)
1954 Geneva conference: Laos, Cambodia and Vietnam become independent states	**1956** Polish revolt, Gomulka in power; Hungarian revolt crushed by Russians	**1954** Beginnings of nationalist revolt in Algeria	**1952** Contraceptive pill developed (US)
1955 Bandung Conference	**1957** Treaty of Rome: Formation of European Economic Community and (1959) of European Free Trade Association	**1956** Suez crisis: Anglo-French invasion of Canal Zone	**1956** Beginning of rock and roll music (US): Elvis Presley (1935-77)
1956 Second Arab-Israeli war		**1957** Beginning of decolonization in sub-Saharan Africa: Gold Coast (Ghana) becomes independent	
1957 Civil war in Vietnam	**1957** First space satellite launched (USSR)	**1960** 'Africa's year'; many states become independent; outbreak of civil war in Belgian Congo	**1959** Cuban Revolution
	1958 Fifth Republic in France: de Gaulle first President		
1960 Sino-Soviet dispute begins	**1961** East Germans build Berlin Wall		
1961 Increasing US involvement in Vietnam	**1961** First man in space: Gagarin (USSR)	**1961** South Africa becomes independent republic	
	1961 Structure of DNA molecule (genetic code) determined (UK)	**1962** Algeria becomes independent	**1962** Cuba missile crisis
1962 Sino-Indian war	**1962** Second Vatican Council reforms Catholic liturgy and dogma	**1965** Rhodesia declares itself independent of Britain	**1963** President Kennedy assassinated
1964 Publication of *Thoughts of Chairman Mao*	**1968** Liberalization in Czechoslovakia halted by Russian invasion	**1967** Civi war in Nigeria (secession of Biafra) (to 1970)	**1964** US Civil Rights Bill inaugurates President Johnson's 'Great Society' programme
1965 Indo-Pakistan war	**1968** World-wide student protest movement		
1965 Military take-over in Indonesia			**1966** Eruption of Black American discontent; growth of Black Power
1966 Cultural Revolution in China	**1969** Outbreak of violence in N. Ireland		**1968** Assassination of Martin Luther King
1967 Third Arab-Israeli war (Six-Day War)	**1970** Polish-German treaty; *de facto* recognition of existing frontiers		**1969** First man lands on moon: Armstrong (US)
1971 People's Republic of China joins UN	**1973** Britain, Eire and Denmark join EEC		**1970** Allende elected president of Chile (killed 1973)
1971 Indo-Pakistán war leads to break-away of East Pakistan (Bangladesh)	**1974** End of dictatorship in Portugal	**1974** Emperor Haile Selasse deposed by Marxist Junta	
1973 US forces withdraw from South Vietnam	**1974** Turkish invasion of Cyprus	**1975** Portugal grants independence to Mozambique and Angola	**1971** US President Nixon and Secretary of State Kissinger initiate policy of detente with China and USSR
1973 Fourth Arab-Israeli war	**1975** Death of Franco; end of dictatorship in Spain		**1971** USA abandons the Gold Standard and depreciates the dollar
	1975 European Security Conference, Helsinki; recognition by W. Germany of post-war states of E. Germany and Poland		**1973** Major recession in US
1975 Civil war in Lebanon			
1975 Communists take over Vietnam, Laos and Cambodia	**1976** 1st supersonic transatlantic passenger service begins with Concorde	**1976** Morocco and Mauritania partition Spanish Sahara	**1974** President Nixon resigns following Watergate affair
1976 Death of Mao-Tse Tung; political re-orientation and modernization under Deng Xiao-Ping	**1977** Democratic election held in Spain, first in 40 years	**1976** Establishment of Transkei, first Bantustan in S. Africa	
1977 President Sadat visits Jerusalem; Egypt/Israeli peace talks culminating in Camp David Peace Treaty (1978)	**1978** Election of John Paul II, first Polish pope		
1977 Pakistan military coup by Zia ul-Haq; former president Bhutto executed in 1979	**1980** Death of Marshal Tito	**1979** Tanzanian forces invade Uganda, and expel President Amin	**1979** Civil War in Nicaragua, President Somoza overthrown
1979 Fall of Shah of Iran, establishment of Islamic Republic under Ayatollah Khomeini	**1980** Creation of independent Polish trade union Solidarity; martial law (1981)	**1980** Black majority rule established in Zimbabwe (Rhodesia)	**1979** Military junta established, continuing civil war (El Salvador)
1979 Afghanistan invaded by USSR	**1981** Mitterand elected 1st Socialist President of France since World War II	**1981** President Sadat of Egypt assassinated	**1980** Ronald Reagan President of USA
1979 Sino-Vietnamese War			**1980s** Computer revolution; spread of computers in offices and homes in the Western world
1979 Vietnam invades Cambodia expelling Khmer Rouge government	**1981** Widespread demonstrations against stationing of further nuclear missiles in Europe		
1980 Military coup in Turkey, power assumed by General Evren	**1981** Greece joins EEC		**1981** First re-usable shuttle space flight (USA)
1980 Outbreak of Iran/Iraq War	**1981** IRA hunger strikers die in Northern Ireland		
1982 Israel invades Lebanon, expulsion of PLO from Beirut	**1982** Death of USSR President Brezhnev, succession of Y. Andropov		**1982** Argentina occupies South Georgia and Falkland Is.; surrenders to UK Task Force June 15th
1982 Israel withdraws from Sinai peninsula	**1984** Death of Andropov, succession of K. Chernenko as USSR leader		**1983** Democracy restored in Argentina
1984 Indira Gandhi assassinated following suppression of Sikh revolt at Amritsar	**1985** Mikhail Gorbachov inaugurates new generation of USSR leaders		**1983** Coup in Grenada; US invades
1984 Britain and China agree on return of Hong Kong and New Territories to China in 1997.	**1985** Live Aid charity concerts reach largest ever TV audience		
	1986 Spain joins EEC		
	1986 Chernobyl nuclear reactor disaster	**1986** Widespread communal violence in S. Africa	**1986** US bomb Libya in retaliation for terrorist actions

17

Pacific
Ocean

135

South China Sea

120

Choukoutien
Lantien

Niah

Mal'ta

105

Sangiran
Modjokerto
Ngandong
Trinil

Novoselovo

A   S   I   A

Krutaya

E   U   R   A   S   I   A

90

Sungir

Siwalik

Kostienki

Teshik-tash

INDIA

Pushkari
Mezin

Kiik Koba

Bilzingsleben   Ehringsdorf
Brünn   Predmost
Shanidar

tnewydd   Neanderthal
aviland   Engis   Obercassel
Swanscombe   Ganovce
2   Spy   Mauer   Vértesszöllös
1   4   16   15   Steinheim
3   5   13   14   Krapina
7   6   12   Saccopastore   Petralona
8   9   10   11
Montmaurin   Monte
Cova Negra   Circeo
bes Quarry
Ternifine

Mount Carmel
Amud
Jebel Quafza
Ubeidiya

ARABIA

Indian   Ocean

75

Mediterranean
Sea

Red Sea

Afalou
Mechta

Sidi Abder Rahman
Jebel Ighoud

A   F   R   I   C   A

Hadar

Asselar

Omo
East Rudolf

60

Lothagam
Kanapoi
Kanam and Kanjera   Fort Ternan
Elmenteita
Peninj
Olduvai

Laetolil

Broken Hill

45

Atlantic

Ocean

Makapan

Kromdraai
Sterkfontein
Swartkrans   Springbok Flats
Taungs   Boskop   30
Florisbad
Matjiesriver
Klasies River Mouth
Saldanha   Fish Hoek
Cape Flats

Rift   Valley

CHAPTER 1

HUMAN ORIGINS
8,000,000–8000 BC

The evolution of the human species is a long and complicated story covering some eight million years. At present, unfortunately, by far the greater part of that story remains obscure and uncertain, for all we have to go on are scattered, fossilized human remains found by archaeologists in locations that are usually both remote and far removed from one another. But the presence in Africa today of Man's two nearest primate relatives, the gorilla and the chimpanzee, suggest that it is indeed in the forests of tropical Africa that we should seek the origins of our species, and most early human remains so far recovered have come from there. The critical divergence of the evolutionary lines leading to humans and to apes took place in this region between about eight and five million years ago, but despite sustained research still very little is known about this early period, or what triggered the emergence of the first humans. However, it seems that by four million years ago our earliest ancestors were firmly established.

The earliest humans already differed significantly in physique from their cousins the apes. First of all, whereas apes travel either by using their arms and legs or (more unusually) by swinging from branch to branch, the earliest human skeletons show differences in the pelvis, spine, knees, hips and toes which made it possible for them to walk upright. The consequences of this were dramatic: it freed their hands for other tasks such as carrying, manipulating and, eventually, making things. At the same time the jaw and snout, no longer needed to seek out and grasp food, became less prominent. And finally, the brain cavity both increased and changed shape. Manual dexterity, walking upright, and expanding intellectual ability were to contribute significantly to the adaptability and success of the human species.

An almost complete fossil skeleton from Hadar in Ethiopia gives a clear picture of the appearance of a female who lived nearly three million years ago. Nicknamed 'Lucy', she was less than five feet tall and weighed probably only about 58 pounds. Her face would have been lightly set, although her jaw was prominent; and her skeleton shows that she was adapted to walking upright on two legs. This is not the oldest evidence showing that early humans walked upright, for at Laetoli in Tanzania the fossilized footprints were found of two adults and possibly a child – a family group? – who had been walking together, probably holding hands, some 3,750,000 years ago. The trail, extending for nearly 30 metres, was preserved by a fall of volcanic ash and offers a rare glimpse of our distant ancestors in motion. But 'Lucy' remains the earliest known skeleton.

Creatures like Lucy, commonly called Australopithecines (which means 'Southern apes') are at present known to have inhabited at least

The distribution of fossils of early man *left*. The earliest direct ancestors of modern man are the 'Australopithecines' or 'Southern Apes' *above*. These inhabited tropical Africa from 5 million to 1 million years ago, and remains of several species have been found in the east and south. Around 2 million years ago a more advanced hominid known as *Homo habilis* developed, and then around 1.5 million years ago *Homo erectus*. *Homo erectus* was the first type of hominid to spread outside Africa, and his remains have been recovered from scattered sites in Europe and as far east as Java and northern China.

- ● fossil hominoids (apes)
- ◉ Australopithecus uncertain
- ◐ Australopithecus africanus
- ○ Australopithecus robustus
- ○ early Homo (habilis and E.R.1470)
- ◐ Homo erectus
- ◐ Rhodesian man
- ● Solo man
- ○ early modern people
- ● classic Neanderthals
- ○ fully modern people

1 Biache-St-Vaast	9 La Ferrassie
2 St Brelade's Bay	10 Arago
3 Abri Saurd	11 Lazaret
4 St Césaire	12 Grimaldi
5 Fontéchevade	13 Le Monstier
6 La Quina	14 Laugere-Basse
7 Combe Capelle	15 La Chapelle-aux-Saints
8 Cro-Magnon	16 Chancelade

'Lucy', the most complete fossil of an early hominid yet to have been discovered *below*. Study of the pelvis and limb bones have shown that this Australopithecine was already walking upright c.3 million years ago. Striking evidence of this comes from Laetoli in Tanzania *right*, where footprints of early hominids in the mud of an ancient lake bed around 3.7 million years ago confirm that early hominids were walking on their hind legs, a development which freed their hands for activities such as tool-making. They also enable archaeologists to estimate the height of these early hominids (4.5ft), a calculation based on the length of the strides.

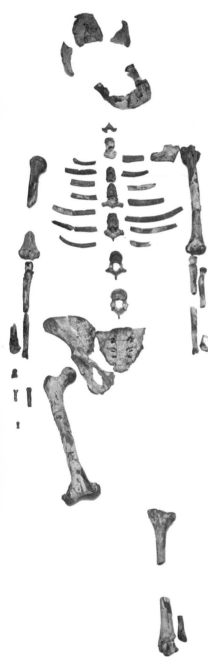

two regions of Africa: the Rift valley in the east, and the high plateaux in the south. In the former, they lived beside lakes and along rivers at the bottom of the great valley; in the latter, we cannot be sure of their habitat because most of their remains have been found in caves among the jettisoned refuse of leopard kills. Lacking both tools and fire, these small, lightweight scavengers were very much at the mercy of the larger predators.

The Australopithecines do not seem to have spread outside Africa; and, even there, the last of them died out about a million years ago. But long before that they had been replaced as the most successful hominid by more advanced species who are known collectively as *Homo*: man. Australopithecus had a brain capacity of only 700 cubic centimetres, not much different from that of the modern ape; and his immediate successor, *Homo habilis*, represented only a modest increase, with a brain size of around 800 cubic centimetres. But during the following stage, that of *Homo erectus*, it increased to 1,000 and sometimes more. All the while, the physiognomy of these creatures was also becoming more 'human', with a flatter face and a more upright stature. But it was not until some 50,000 years ago that we get skeletal remains indistinguishable in any way from those of modern man; and the cranial capacity had by then attained today's average of 1,500 cubic centimetres.

This increase in brain size was a decisive factor in hominid success and in the development of modern man. The genus *Homo* was the first

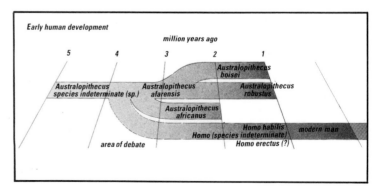

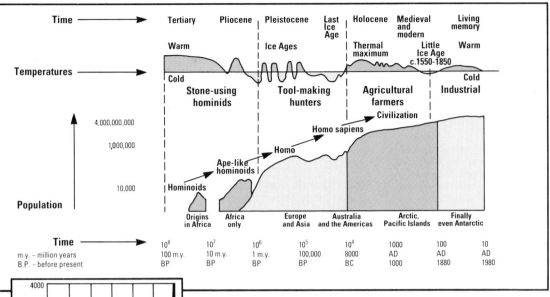

Time ➤	Tertiary	Pliocene	Pleistocene	Last Ice Age	Holocene	Medieval and modern	Living memory
Temperatures ➤	Warm		Ice Ages		Thermal maximum	Little Ice Age c.1550-1850	Warm
	Cold						Cold
	Stone-using hominids		Tool-making hunters		Agricultural farmers		Industrial

4,000,000,000
1,000,000
10,000

Population

Origins in Africa | Africa only | Europe and Asia | Australia and the Americas | Arctic, Pacific Islands | Finally even Antarctic

Time ➤
m.y. – million years
B.P. – before present

	10^8	10^7	10^6	10^5	10^4	1000	100	10
	100 m.y. BP	10 m.y. BP	1 m.y. BP	100,000 BP	8000 BC	AD 1000	AD 1880	AD 1980

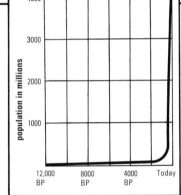

Climatic change and population growth *above*. The chart, on a logarithmic scale, plots population and climatic variation during the pleistocene; the lower diagram indicates the explosive growth of population during the last 200 years.

The ancestors of modern man *left*. The Lucy skeleton is the most complete example of *Australopithecus afarensis*, the oldest fossil type yet known, which disappears from the fossil record c.2.8 million years ago. *Africanus*, on the other hand, is evident until c.2 million years ago, although restricted to finds in southern Africa so far. Two other Australopithecines – *boisei* and *robustus* – despite their hardy build, substantial molars and impressive chewing muscles, became extinct c.1 million years ago, a genetic dead end. *Homo habilis* is the first example of the *Homo* genus, distinguished from the Australopithecines by a larger brain capacity and a smaller facial area – his appearance coincides with evidence of the first primitive stone tools. *Homo erectus* was the first hominid to control fire, and had a brain capacity of 1000 millilitres (that of modern man is 1330).

to specialize in mental rather than physical power; and his mental skills account for man's inventiveness, for his capacity for learning, communication and co-operative action, and for his ability to adapt to physical conditions far beyond the original homeland in Africa – across Asia and Europe into the Americas and Australasia. Many other animals were more fleet of foot; many were stronger and more agile. But thanks to their intelligence, the human race eventually prevailed over them; and the first unmistakable sign of that intelligence is the widespread use of tools and weapons.

Chimpanzees use sticks to probe ant-hills, and eagles use stones to break the shells of tortoises, but mankind is the only species which modifies natural materials and actually *makes* tools. The oldest recognizable man-made tools are pebbles with irregular sharp edges created by using one stone as a hammer to chip a series of flakes off another. Both the chipped stones and the flakes could be used as implements, and tools of this sort dating back to about 2,000,000 BC have been found at Olduvai gorge, associated with remains of *Homo habilis*.

The emergence of tools is certainly a reflection of the superior mental ability of the larger-brained hominids over their Australopithecine forebears; but it may also be associated with an important change in diet. The Australopithecines were probably vegetarians, but the manufacture of tools made it possible for *Homo habilis* to cut meat from carcases and, indeed, early tools are often found alongside the remains of butchered animals. It is unlikely, however, that these small and defenceless hominids were themselves able to hunt and kill the large animals such as horse and antelope with which their tools are sometimes associated: *Homo habilis* probably obtained most of his meat by scavenging from the abandoned kills of lion and other predators. The manufacture of tools and weapons nevertheless marks an important step in human evolution, because it both widened the range of foodstuffs and enabled materials such as wood, bark, reeds and hides to be cut and sharpened into useful everyday items. With these skills, humans were eventually to learn how to construct shelters and make clothing – both essential if man was to spread beyond Africa to cooler environments.

The first humans to set foot outside Africa belonged to the next major group in the evolutionary sequence: *Homo erectus*. The first

Olduvai Gorge in the East African Rift Valley *below*, one of the most famous localities in recent studies of early man. The main gorge and side gorge have cut into the landscape to a depth of up to 90m, exposing a series of strata dating back over more than 2 million years.

The earliest recognizable tools consist of crudely chipped pebbles and choppers from sites in Africa *below left*. It was with the aid of these tools that early hominids were first able to add meat to their diet, using them to cut flesh from the carcases of dead animals. At Olduvai Gorge, butchery sites have been preserved, and early tools are found among the skeletons of animals, including both large species such as elephant, hippopotamus and antelope and smaller species such as tortoise and rodents.

skeletons of this type are a little over one and a half million years old, and were found in Africa; their descendants colonized parts of Asia and Europe between about eight hundred and five hundred thousand years ago. These people had larger brains and they were more adept at tool manufacture: their principal tool, the handaxe, remained in use (in a variety of forms and sizes) for over a million years. More important still, they were the first users of fire. The earliest hominids, it must be remembered, were sub-tropical or equatorial creatures, adapted for life in the warm African grasslands and unable, without artificial heat, to extend their range far beyond. Fire opened the way to migration. But it provided much more: besides offering some protection against other predators, a means of cooking, and a valuable aid in the working of materials such as wood, the ability to control and, eventually, to make fire gave man a new and revolutionary means of mastering his natural surroundings.

The earliest hearths, found in places as far apart as Britain, Hungary and China, date from the period known as the Ice Age, when temperatures on earth fluctuated sharply, sometimes falling 10 to 15°C lower than those of the present day. The climate began to cool about 38 million years ago, and pack-ice formed around the Antarctic; but temperatures only began to decline rapidly some 14 million years ago, and thereafter the southern pack-ice grew prodigiously. By three million years ago, ice-sheets had formed around the North Pole as well, and in about 1,500,000 BC the first full-scale glaciation occurred, with temperatures falling to well below their present level and the ice-sheets advancing far to the south. Finally, after some tens of thousands of years of cold conditions, temperatures recovered again and the ice-sheets retreated.

This pattern of alternating glacial advance and retreat has become the dominant feature of our environment. At roughly regular intervals of between 80,000 and 100,000 years, temperatures on earth fall dramatically and ice-sheets cover much of the earth; in between come warmer periods known as interglacials, characterized by temperatures

The tools made by early man probably included many of organic material such as wood and plant fibre, but save for a very few exceptions it is only the more durable implements of stone and bone which have survived to the present day. A variety of stones were used, including obsidian, chert and quartzite, but in Europe the dominant material was flint. This has the advantage of splitting in a regular manner, allowing the shape of the tool to be carefully controlled during manufacture. The basic technique *above* is to remove flakes from a lump of flint (the core) by striking it with a piece of stone or bone (the hammer).

With the appearance of Homo erectus around 1.5 million years ago, an elaborate tool technology developed, the hand-axe *above left* being one of its finest products. Hand-axes were prominent in many parts of the Old World until the beginning of the last Ice Age c.75,000 years ago. Hand-axes vary greatly in size and shape, and were probably used for a range of tasks, including the cutting of meat from carcasses. The prevalence of the same basic tool-type for over a million years indicates the slow rate of cultural and behavioural innovation by early man.

similar to those of the present day. The most recent ice age ended around 10,000 years ago, and we are now living in an interglacial similar to those separating earlier phases of intense cold. It is likely that in due course – though not perhaps for several thousand years – the ice-sheets will advance once again and a further ice age will ensue.

At the height of the glacial periods, ice-sheets covered large areas of northern Europe, Asia and North America, bringing harsh, cold conditions which prevented human settlement. Further south, however, milder conditions prevailed and the tropical regions remained hot, although much drier than today. With every ice advance, the animals suited to temperate conditions were obliged to move southward as the forests gave way to vast expanses of frozen, treeless tundra along the edges of the ice-sheets. Now only species specially adapted to the cold, such as mammoth, woolly rhinoceros and reindeer were able to survive there, feeding off the lichens and dwarf shrubs which constituted the sole vegetation. Such conditions were highly unfavourable to any species of tropical origin, such as man, and it is one of the most striking success stories in the history of human development that, over the course of several hundred thousand years, he was able to develop the skills, equipment and behavioural patterns that enabled him to live – and indeed to thrive – in such inhospitable environments.

The spread of man beyond his African homeland was a gradual process, rapid during interglacial periods, but halting or reversing during the periods of most intense cold. Nevertheless, with the aid of tools, fire and (almost certainly) clothes, these early colonists of Asia and Europe were able to adapt to the new conditions with considerable success. A key ingredient in this was finding shelters from the cold. In some cases, caves were used, as at Choukoutien (Zhoukoudian) near Peking where the inhabitants warmed themselves some 400,000 years ago before a hearth fire. But the popular image of early man as an habitual cave-dweller is misleading, for in most known cases he lived in the open and built tents or simple houses for shelter from the elements. As these would be made largely from perishable materials which leave no trace in the ground, very little is known about them; but one rare example comes from the site of Terra Amata on the Mediterranean coast of modern France. Here, some 300,000 years ago, people

23

taking advantage of the resources of the seashore constructed small houses from branches, with stones around the base. Inside there were hearths for heating, and work-places with chipped stone instruments.

The diet of *Homo erectus* is something of an enigma. Vegetable foods no doubt formed a large part of it, even though the gathering of fruits and plants has left virtually no trace. But he was also a meat-eater, as finds of tools and animal bones around his settlements show; and probably on a larger scale than any earlier hominid. However, the tools found – above all hand-axes – would have been useful for butchery but not for killing: they would not have been able to penetrate the hide of an animal if thrown. At first sight this is surprising, but the evidence shows that methods of hunting were being used which did not require projectiles such as arrows or spears. It is true that pointed wooden objects with fire-hardened tips have been found at Clacton in southern England and Lehringen in Germany, but they too would not have been able to kill an animal if thrown. Instead, animals were probably run down or mired, and then despatched by stabbing at close range; or else stampeded into pits armed with pointed stakes. A similar strategy was employed at La Cotte de St. Brelade in Jersey, where rhinoceros were driven over a cliff and butchered at the bottom. Such techniques, in addition to scavenging, may have been the most common (and least dangerous) means of obtaining meat: they did not require specially designed weapons. They did, however, demand a considerable degree of co-operation and, though we know little about social organization at this remote period, nor if fully human speech was by then developed, some method of effective communication must have existed. Something like speech has thus existed for at least the last 300,000 years.

The most recent Ice Age began some 80,000 years ago, and ended only about 10,000 years ago. When temperatures were at their lowest, the continental ice-sheets extended far south of the Baltic, and also covered much of the British Isles. As before, the areas adjacent to the ice were too inhospitable for human settlement, but further south conditions were somewhat better. In these areas human life continued to flourish.

By the beginning of the last Ice Age *Homo erectus* had been replaced by more advanced species characterized by a still larger brain size. In Europe and western Asia the dominant type was Neanderthal man, with a brain the same size as modern man's (around 1,500 cubic centimetres), but with a different skull shape and sturdier limb bones. The first evidence of a spiritual awareness among humans is associated with the Neanderthals. At several sites in Europe and Asia intentional burials have been found, in which the male graves were provided with offerings of animal bones (originally joints of meat) and unusually well-made stone tools. The inclusion of grave-goods suggests belief in an after-life. In addition, some skeletons bear marks of previous injury or of a disabling disease which would have made them unable to fend for themselves; so they must have been cared for by other members of the group. The Neanderthals were thus the first society to show such a high level of concern for the elderly and the sick, and it is clear that although they differed anatomically from modern man in several important respects, they already had some of the feeling we regard as fundamentally human.

The first fully modern humans – *Homo sapiens sapiens* – developed around 40,000 years ago, and during the 30,000 years that followed they spread throughout the whole of the inhabited world. With these new people, bone and antler spear tips, harpoons, and beautifully decorated spearthrowers appeared for the first time, along with finely made stone points for spears, and possibly also for arrows. The artefacts reveal a

In order to colonize the colder parts of the globe, man had to devise ways of keeping warm; fire, clothes, shelter. In southern Russia, the remains of ingenious huts have been found constructed of mammoth bones covered by branches and reeds or animal hides. At Mezhirich in the Ukraine several collapsed mammoth bone huts have been uncovered *above*.

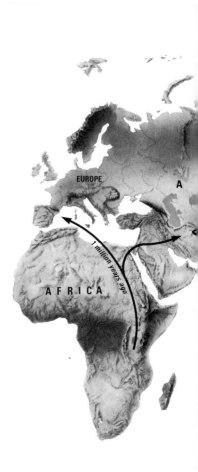

It was only during the last Ice Age, 20,000-15,000 years ago, that man began to develop the kind of sophisticated hunting equipment such as spears or javelins and bows and arrows, that we associate with hunting peoples of recent times. Bone harpoons *left* were developed for use in the rivers of south-western France, which during the last Ice Age were probably rich in fish. The first evidence of these new kinds of hunting equipment — and the first evidence of fish as an important part of the human diet — comes only after c.40,000 BC.

The spread of man from his original homeland in Africa to cover every continent of the globe *below* took over three quarters of a million years. Colonization was dependent on the regular variations in climate caused by a sequence of ice ages which started 1.5 million years ago. The advance and retreat of the ice-sheets and the consequent rise and fall of the sea levels, which produced land bridges, both restricted movement and enabled it — man reached America by crossing the Bering Straits land bridge which emerged when the sea level reached its lowest point at the height of the last Ice Age.

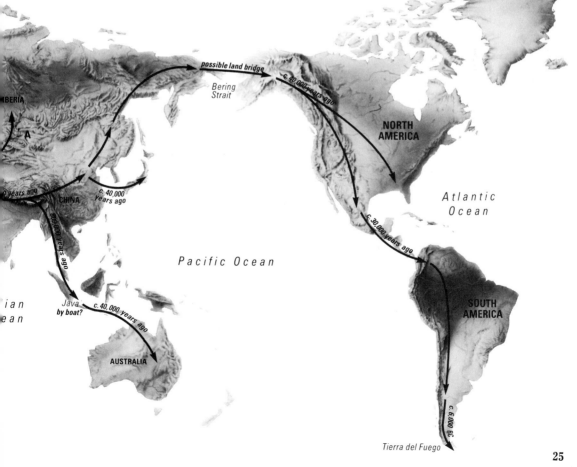

possible land bridge

Bering
Strait

c. 40,000 years ago

IBERIA

A

NORTH
AMERICA

0 years ago

CHINA   c. 40,000
years ago

800,000 years ago

Atlantic
Ocean

c. 30,000 years ago

Pacific Ocean

ian
ean

Java
by boat?   c. 40,000 years ago

SOUTH
AMERICA

AUSTRALIA

c. 6,000 BC

Tierra del Fuego

society which, for the first time, practised hunting with projectiles that could kill or disable an animal some distance away. The success of the new equipment is illustrated by sites such as Predmost (in modern Czechoslovakia), with a mass kill of mammoth, or Solutré (in France), where there were remains of thousands of horses. The hunters of the last Ice Age seem often to have concentrated on one particular animal in this way, and it is possible that this was because they followed the herds on their annual migrations. The hunters no doubt learned to control some of the species on which they preyed, and in some cases they may have tamed or domesticated a few individual horse or reindeer.

The improvements in hunting weapons and strategies were extremely important because they gave people a much more effective means of exploiting animals; and their success in this may have been one reason for the extinction of some of the larger species, such as mammoth and woolly rhinoceros, before the end of the last Ice Age. Further evidence of cultural advance is to be found in the artistic activity of these late Ice Age hunters and gatherers. Cave art, some of it dating back 30,000 years, is a remarkable sign both of the artistic ability and the imaginative powers of early man – so remarkable, indeed, that for a long time the paintings were written off as modern forgeries. The subject matter is nearly always animal: the cave art of Europe teems with wildlife – perhaps a natural obsession for communities which relied heavily on hunting. Some of the animals are shown with distended bellies, as if pregnant; and, indeed, ensuring the fertility of the herds may have been one of the principal reasons for the paintings. But some pictures are found in the least accessible recesses, deep inside the caves, far beyond any of the parts which may have been regularly occupied, and

The most important artistic achievements of this period were the masterly cave paintings of south-west France and northern Spain, dating from the end of the last Ice Age between 15,000 and 10,000 years ago. Some of the animals are shown pierced by spears and arrows, and it seems certain that these life-like representations of the animals which were hunted during this period had ritual or magical significance connected with the great hunt. The caves themselves were probably used as a backdrop for ritual ceremonies, perhaps the initiation of young hunters. *Above left* bison from Altamira cave, Spain, and *above right* horses and hands from the principal gallery at Pech-Merle, France.

The 'Venus of Willendorf' *right*, limestone figurine c. 25,000 BC from a Paleolithic settlement. Unlike cave art which is restricted to parts of Spain and France, Venus figurines are found throughout Europe between 25,000 and 23,000 years ago. The figurines may be of ivory or stone, but all have accentuated sexual characteristics and only a token or schematic rendering of face and arms. This concentration on sexual features at the expense of other details suggests that the figurines had a fertility role and perhaps represented a mother goddess.

26

it is clear that these served as a background for sacred or ritual ceremonies. People rarely appear in the paintings and, when they do, they are represented schematically and can either be regarded as hunters attacking their prey, or as sorcerers performing magic rites in animal costumes. Stone lamps have also been found, shallow bowls which (filled perhaps with animal fat and provided with a wick) would have been the only means by which many of the paintings could have been seen. In some of the caves, footprints preserved in the muddy floor of inaccessible galleries show that groups of people, including children, visited the paintings, perhaps – though this is pure speculation – as part of mystical initiation ceremonies which the young hunters had to undergo. A particularly bizarre element is the representation of human hands, outlined in paint which was presumably sprayed from the mouth: in three cases the hands appear to be mutilated, lacking parts of the fingers, though whether as the result of frostbite in these harsh arctic conditions, or because of some curious ritual of the cave artists, it is not possible to say.

Though much attention has been focused on their spectacular cave art, the late Ice Age communities of Europe and western Asia also produced many fine sculptures of bone, ivory and antler. The female figurines are the most notable of these sculptures. The exaggerated breasts, stomachs, buttocks and thighs have led some writers to label them Venus figurines, and they may indeed have served as fertility symbols. At any rate, marks of wear suggest that the figurines were frequently handled. Alongside these human figures are many representations of animals, which were perhaps used as talismans for hunting. More tantalizing lengths of bone with a series of notches cut into them have also been found, and have been interpreted by some as evidence that these early communities had already developed a system of numbering and recording (for example, for counting the number of animals in a herd, or for marking off the stages of the lunar cycle). Be that as it may, these advances in technology, culture and art show that, towards the end of the last Ice Age, modern man had achieved an intellectual ability that was impressively different from anything that had gone before.

Homo erectus had spread from Africa to colonize Europe and Asia, but it was left to *Homo sapiens sapiens* to complete the process by occupying the remaining continents of Australasia and the Americas. In this, the harsh climate of the last Ice Age proved, paradoxically, to be an ally. The periods of intense cold caused large quantities of water to be frozen at the poles. As a result, sea levels were lowered all over the world and land-bridges appeared, linking most mainland areas and many islands. Australia and Tasmania formed one territory, joined across what is now the Torres Strait to New Guinea; and New Guinea

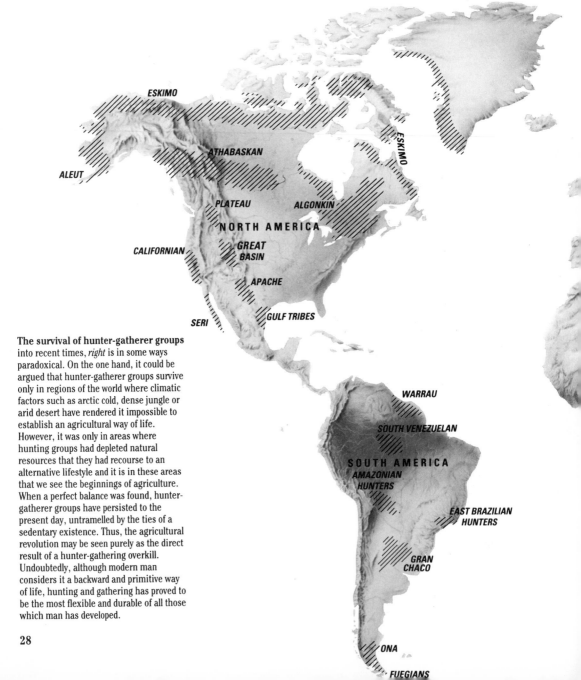

The survival of hunter-gatherer groups into recent times, *right* is in some ways paradoxical. On the one hand, it could be argued that hunter-gatherer groups survive only in regions of the world where climatic factors such as arctic cold, dense jungle or arid desert have rendered it impossible to establish an agricultural way of life. However, it was only in areas where hunting groups had depleted natural resources that they had recourse to an alternative lifestyle and it is in these areas that we see the beginnings of agriculture. When a perfect balance was found, hunter-gatherer groups have persisted to the present day, untramelled by the ties of a sedentary existence. Thus, the agricultural revolution may be seen purely as the direct result of a hunter-gathering overkill. Undoubtedly, although modern man considers it a backward and primitive way of life, hunting and gathering has proved to be the most flexible and durable of all those which man has developed.

was linked in its turn with the Philippines and Indonesia, thus reducing considerably the width of open sea separating Australia from the south-east Asian mainland. Using boats, people crossed these waters more than 40,000 years ago, to become the first inhabitants of Australia. Around 40,000 years ago, another period of intense cold led to the emergence of a land-bridge from Korea which allowed the colonization of Japan, while, further north, there was a similar connection across the Bering Strait linking eastern Asia with Alaska. Across this bridge to America poured animals of all sorts – giant bison with a six-foot horn spread, horses, sloths, moose, large cats and mammoths; and, hard on their heels, followed man the hunter. Within a few thousand years, people had traversed the entire continent and established colonies in Chile and on Tierra del Fuego, its southernmost tip. As the last Ice Age came to an end, some 10,000 years ago, man was established almost everywhere. He had already become, beyond all question, the world's most widespread and successful animal.

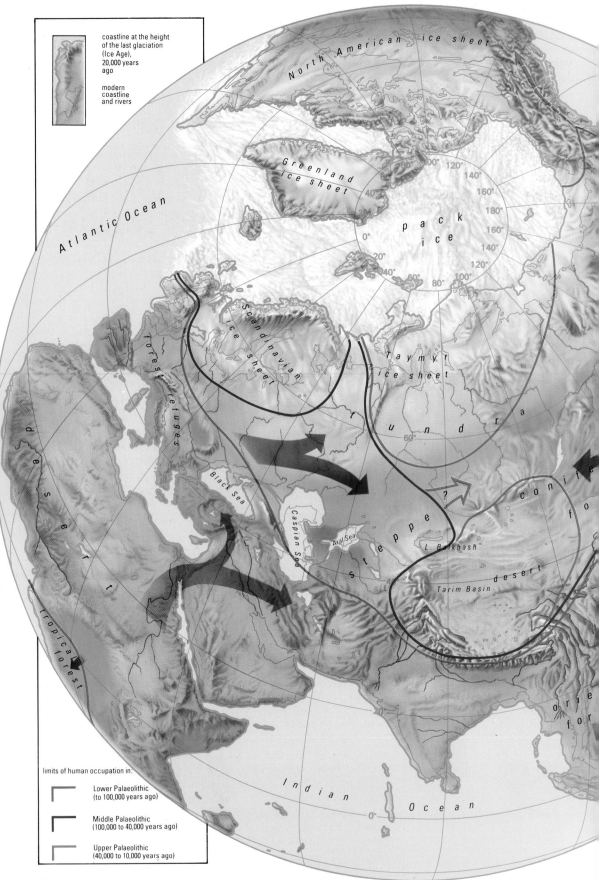

coastline at the height of the last glaciation (Ice Age), 20,000 years ago

modern coastline and rivers

North American ice sheet

Atlantic Ocean

Greenland ice sheet

pack ice

Scandinavian ice sheet

Taymyr ice sheet

t u n d r a

forest refuges

Black Sea

Caspian Sea

Aral Sea

s t e p p e

L. Balkhash

Tarim Basin

desert

conife

for

?

desert

tropical forest

orie
for

Indian Ocean

0°

limits of human occupation in:

Lower Palaeolithic
(to 100,000 years ago)

Middle Palaeolithic
(100,000 to 40,000 years ago)

Upper Palaeolithic
(40,000 to 10,000 years ago)

100° 120° 140° 160° 180° 160° 140° 120° 100° 80°

40° 0° 20° 40° 60° 80°

60°

The World 20,000 years ago was in the grip of the last Ice Age, and vast ice sheets covered much of the northern hemisphere. As the temperature went up and the ice melted, more land became available for human colonization. This led after 10,000 BC to the first experiments with agriculture, and soon afterwards the first farming villages appeared in the Near East, marking one of the most important advances in human history.

Pacific Ocean

Sea of Japan

CHAPTER 2

THE AGRICULTURAL REVOLUTION
8000–5000 BC

About 20,000 years ago, the last Ice Age was at its height. Outside the tropics, temperatures were as much as 15°C lower than today, and vast ice-sheets covered almost one-quarter of the earth's present land surface: in the northern hemisphere, they reached as far south as Berlin, London and Chicago. The huge quantities of water locked up in these ice-sheets were no longer available to fall as rain, and about half the land between the tropics of Capricorn and Cancer became arid desert. At the same time, and for the same reason, the sea-level was dramatically lowered.

These severe conditions persisted for several thousand years, but at length the ice-sheets began to retreat as average temperatures slowly rose. By 10,000 BC a climate not unlike today's had returned, and it persisted. As the ice-sheets and glaciers melted, the sea rose again and by 5000 BC had reached almost its present height. In the process, large areas of formerly dry land were drowned, but the milder temperatures more than compensated for this, in human terms, by encouraging an increasing abundance of plant and animal food. Forests, with their accompanying wildlife, recolonized much of the former arctic wastes while grasslands, likewise teeming with game, replaced the deserts around the equator. For *Homo sapiens* this was a period of new possibilities and broadened opportunities, and in several parts of the world human societies grasped these opportunities by developing a completely new way of life, based on farming.

But, at first, numbers were small and resources sparse. Some 10,000 years ago, as the Ice Age ended, the global human population was probably less than 5 million people, living for the most part in natural shelters such as caves, or in the open. Their material wealth amounted to little more than could be easily carried about, and their economy was based – as it had been for thousands of years – on hunting and gathering. There was no need for anything more: although these people lived in close contact with their natural environment, and were acutely aware of the manner of reproduction of their plant and animal food sources, the earth provided them with adequate food of its own accord, and there was no need to take on the arduous work of sowing, weeding and harvesting. But this situation could not last indefinitely. In the favourable conditions immediately following the end of the last Ice Age, many of these communities grew rapidly in size until their needs could no longer be satisfied by hunting and gathering. A new subsistence strategy had to be adopted: farming.

The new strategy had two aspects. On the one hand there was agriculture – the deliberate alteration of natural systems in order to produce an abundance of a particular variety of plants. On the other

31

During the last Ice Age and in the period which followed the melting of the ice, human communities began to develop a more complex relationship with the animals they killed for meat; controlling the number of animals they killed to ensure that the hunting potential of the herd was not exhausted, and following herds on their annual migrations, as the Lapps of present-day Scandinavia follow the herds of wapiti (elk) *below*. It is possible that the antler frontlet from the hunters' camp of Star Carr *below right* (c.7500 BC) which was worn as headgear, may have been used in rituals connected with the fertility of the red deer herds.

With a more settled lifestyle, food could be processed and stored. Quernstones *below left* were essential for grinding the hard cereal grains to make flour; a quantity of grain was scattered on the quernstone and ground with the 'rubber' – a second, smaller stone.

came the domestication of useful animal species to provide meat, milk, hides or wool, and (equally important in pre-industrial societies) a vital source of power for ploughing and other agricultural processes. It seems likely that both plant and animal husbandry may have begun on a small scale before the end of the last Ice Age. The remains of many early hunting camps in Europe show a concentration on reindeer which suggests that the hunters had developed a special relationship with a particular herd; and some groups may have followed the reindeer on their annual migrations, like the Lapps in more recent times. Such a strategy could easily and naturally lead on to domestication. In the same kind of way, plants may have been tended and perhaps re-seeded in order to increase or safeguard their yields.

Thus the full-scale agriculture which developed in the Near East around 8000 BC, and a little later in the Far East and Mesoamerica, was not entirely without precedent. But it was both quantitatively and qualitatively different: not just a peripheral tinkering with the natural environment by small groups of hunters and gatherers, but a wholesale reliance on cultivated plants and animals by substantial sedentary communities. In addition, the species domesticated by the early farmers have remained the mainstay of agricultural economies to this day – such as wheat and barley, rice and millet, maize, beans and the potato.

Religion and ritual played an important part in the life of early farming communities as they continue to do among many agricultural societies today. Special rites and observances were carried out to encourage and ensure the success of crops and livestock. This group of clay figures and model furniture from the Bulgarian farming village of Ocharovo *above right*, probably had a ritual purpose. The tables and chairs give a vivid picture of the type of furniture in use at this period.

Halafian bowl from the Mesopotamian village of Arpachiyah, c.5000 BC *above*. Pottery is a common feature of many early farming settlements, and such high quality vessels, made by craftsmen and fired in high temperature kilns, are clearly luxury goods which advertized the status of the owner. The manufacture of non-utilitarian items marks an important transition towards a materialist society where an individual's standing with his community is invariably bound up with the quality and quantity of his possessions.

These changes were revolutionary, for they marked the development of a completely new way of life. The immense impact of agriculture, vastly increasing the number of people who could be fed and clothed, and in the process transforming the face of the earth, makes it one of the most important developments in the history of mankind.

The first economies to be based on the husbandry of modern animal and plant staples came into being in the Near East as the melting of the ice-sheets released water that had been frozen, and thus increased overall humidity and rainfall. In the hills and mountains of the Near East – the Zagros, Taurus and Palestinian uplands – moister conditions led to the spread of open woodland, and of associated large-seeded grasses: the ancestors of modern wheat and barley. These grasses, with their nutritious and easily-stored grain, naturally attracted the attention of local hunter-gatherers, who used flint-bladed reaping knives to harvest them. In doing so, they were automatically selecting those plants in which the grains were held tightly in the ear, since loosely-held grains would already have fallen to the ground, or would immediately do so when the stems were cut. They would also naturally have chosen plants with bigger heads, containing more grain. After the harvest had been brought home, it was these genetically determined characteristics which were reproduced among the descendants of these plants, as they sprouted the following year on rubbish heaps and in the phosphate-rich areas around the houses. So, coincidentally, people improved the yield of these wild grasses, as well as introducing them to new types of habitat. The best evidence for this intensive collection of wild cereals comes from Palestine where, around 10,000 BC, small villages of circular stone-walled huts developed, whose inhabitants lived from both the hunting and herding of gazelle and the harvesting of wild emmer wheat.

The next stage in the process, the sowing of cereals outside their natural habitat, is first found at sites in northern Syria around 9000 BC. Here the species concerned was einkorn, another variety of wheat, which grew wild in the foothills of the Taurus and Zagros mountains to the north and east; but its appearance at Mureybat and Tell Abu Hureyra, on the banks of the river Euphrates, where it would never have been found in the natural state, indicates that the inhabitants of these settlements must have been cultivating the plant intentionally,

33

although the einkorn remained wild in form with a seed head which shattered readily on ripening. Shortly afterwards, around 8500 BC, the first fully domesticated, non-shattering cereals made their appearance at Jericho in the Jordan valley, probably cultivated on muddy ground around a perennial spring. By this stage, the explosive potential of the new economy had been realized, for Jericho was no small farming village but a town of 10 acres, surrounded by a substantial stone wall, fronted by a rock-cut ditch and guarded by towers (chapter 3). By 7000 BC, wheat and barley cultivation was widely established throughout the Near East, from Anatolia to the Zagros mountains and it spread, shortly afterwards, to Greece and to the Indus valley.

But plant husbandry was only one part of the story. Man is an omnivore, and normally requires a range of both vegetable and animal foods for a balanced diet. In almost all parts of the world, the cultivation of plants has been accompanied by intensification in animal husbandry, developing techniques of livestock management which originated tens of thousands of years ago. Animals, however, are less efficient converters of energy to food: an acre of farmland under cereals feeds between 10 to 20 times as many people as the same area under livestock. Accordingly, as populations grew, less and less space was available for animals. This problem dates back to the early millennia of agriculture when, under pressure from an increasing density of population, the area of land under cultivation expanded. Hunting and loose-herding were consequently no longer possible in many areas and so new strategies of animal husbandry were required. Most of the early Levantine farming sites relied for meat principally on gazelle, herded in a domesticated (or at least semi-domesticated) state. In southern Palestine, however, goats were being herded instead and, as a more efficient user of grazing, they had largely replaced gazelle by around 7000 BC. From there they spread in domesticated form throughout the Near East. Sheep, close cousin to the goat, had already been domesticated in the Zagros mountains of Mesopotamia, perhaps as early as 9000 BC, and other important meat species soon followed: pig in southern Turkey by 7000 BC; cattle in the Aegean region before 6000 BC. In addition to meat, these animals could also provide milk, wool and manure for fields. With the introduction of the plough and the wheeled cart shortly after 4000 BC cattle also took on an important role as draught animals.

Rock painting from the Tassili area of the central Sahara *above*, (c. 6000-3500 BC) showing herdsmen and cattle at the time when parts of the Sahara were grassland. The domestic livestock of the early farmers and herders have been transformed by specialized spreading. Soay sheep *above right* are the nearest present-day equivalent to those of the first European farmers, while a primitive form of pig has been bred on an experimental farm.

The beginning of farming was closely followed by an increase in the number of people to match the greater productive potential of the new economy: more and more land was brought into cultivation to feed the ever larger populations. But there came a point in many areas at which no further good farming land was available. Community size continued to increase, however, and so it became necessary either to intensify the methods of farming, in order to extract a larger crop yield from the same amount of land, or to bring marginal land into use by means of special techniques. In the Near East, the principal technique was irrigation: by digging canals and constructing dams, rain and river water could be collected and channelled to semi-arid land on the fringes of the desert. Many of the early agricultural communities of the Near East could not have survived without irrigation.

Another solution to land shortage was for a section of the community to move to a new area where farming had not yet become established and where fertile land was still available. It was this which provided the driving force behind the agricultural colonization of, for example, much of Europe. Farming was introduced to Greece and Bulgaria around 6500 BC and by 5500 BC, agricultural communities had grown up along the banks of the river Danube. From this point, the

Aerial photographs of a neolithic enclosure at Semussac in western France *above* c.3000 BC. Such enclosures are common in Europe; they may have been used to keep herds of livestock, or have been places where the local community gathered for protection against enemies. Many of these sites have been discovered by aerial photography. In the enclosure ditches the soil is deeper and wetter than in the rest of the field, so that the crop grows taller and ripens later. From the air, this difference in height or colour clearly reveals the plan of the enclosure ditches. Infra-red photography sometimes produces a still better image.

Jericho *below* an early farming settlement in the Jordan valley c. 8500 BC. The settlement grew rapidly, reaching 10 acres, and a powerful protective wall and ditch, with at least one massive circular tower, were ample testimony to its prosperity and the envy of its neighbours.

spread was rapid, reaching the Paris basin in little more than 500 years (c.5300-4750 BC), a rate of advance of over one mile per year. The pottery and houses of the earliest farmers of the Paris basin are similar to those of early agricultural communities in Hungary, indicating that it was probably farmers from the latter area who colonized the new lands.

In time, European farmers also began, like their Near Eastern counterparts before them, to experience the difficulties caused by a shortage of suitable agricultural land to feed a growing population. The solution they adopted was not irrigation – temperate Europe has never been short of rainfall – but the introduction, around 4000 BC, of the plough. This device required the maintenance of draught oxen, a costly business, but provided a much more efficient way of breaking the ground than the previous methods based on hoes and spades; and it allowed new areas to be farmed that would not otherwise have been economic.

The development of plant cultivation in the Near East can be paralleled in many other parts of the world, though at slightly later dates. In Mexico, good conditions of preservation have yielded large amounts of organic food remains at many ancient sites, and the study of these has demonstrated that the transition from hunting and collecting to farming was very gradual. Thus in the Tehuacán valley, a few locally available plants such as chili, avocado and bottle gourd may have begun to be cultivated before 6500 BC; but only about a thousand years later did new crops appear which were not found wild in the valley. Th   included maize, which later became the staple New World cereal.

he gradual impact of agriculture is illustrated by the fact that, as la e as 4500 BC, over 2,000 years after the first cultivation, only an e timated 10 percent of the food consumed in the Tehuacán valley by the local population came from their domesticated plants and, 1,500 years later, only 30 percent. The rest still derived from hunting and the collection of wild plant foods. Settlements continued to consist of small hamlets little more substantial or permanent than those of the pre-agricultural period. It was only around 2000 BC that full-scale agriculture developed; for only then did genetic modification in maize make it, for the first time, significantly more productive than wild plants. Thus the earliest settled villages of pottery-making farmers in highland Mexico developed over 5,000 years later than those of the Near East (chapter 16.)

Mesoamerica suffered from a scarcity of animals suitable for domestication. Apart from the turkey, the early agricultural peoples of Mexico continued to rely on hunting for their meat. In Peru, however, the second principal centre of New World cultivation, more suitable animals were available. In the high Andes, the llama and alpaca were domesticated before 5000 BC; and, though eventually they came to be used exclusively as pack animals, they may at first have been eaten. The wooded valleys of the Andes were the home of the guinea-pig, and this too was domesticated at an early date. It is still common in Peru today to keep guinea-pigs, which are allowed to roam freely as household scavengers until they are needed for a meal. Alongside these animals, the Peruvians cultivated a range of important plants, including maize, beans and potato. As in Mexico, the transition to a fully agricultural way of life was gradual, taking place over several thousand years; but by 3000 BC large, stable villages had developed.

Plants and animals were independently domesticated in many other parts of the world. In northern China millet, another cereal, began to be cultivated on the great loess plain around the Yellow River and its tributaries in about 5000 BC. It remained the staple crop of

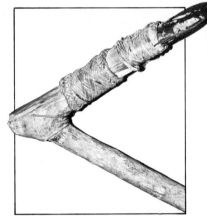

One of the first tasks for the early cultivators in forested areas such as temperate Europe, was the creation of clearings in which crops could be planted and livestock pastured. Forest clearance was carried out using axes and adzes of flint *above* and hard stone, often ground and polished to give a sharp cutting edge.

South American peasant farmers with their potato harvest *right*. The ability to manipulate the natural environment and its plant and animal food sources often led to heavy reliance on a single particularly productive crop or species. This tendency to monoculture led to an increase in health problems and deficiency-related diseases.

Early farmers had to rely solely on human muscle power to work their fields, but in the Old World the potential of domesticated animals was soon realized. The ox-drawn plough was introduced c.4000 BC, allowing heavier soils to be cultivated and making it economic to farm less fertile areas. Plough marks have been preserved under later burial mounds or barrows, and miraculously intact ploughs have been retrieved from Danish bogs. Ploughs and ploughing scenes often feature in Scandinavian and Alpine rock art, and in Egyptian tomb paintings and models *below*.

northern China for many centuries. Further south the principal cereal was rice, first cultivated in the Yangtze delta before 4000 BC, and independently domesticated in south-east Asia perhaps at an even earlier date. Rice proved to be one of the world's most successful food plants, and it spread rapidly from these early centres: by the first century AD it was being grown in places as far apart as Japan and Persia. Tropical Africa, too, had its indigenously domesticated crops, notably the yam, a tuber, in the west African woodland belt; and the cereals sorghum and finger millet, cultivated around the confluence of the Blue and White Niles perhaps as early as 4000 BC. The Indus valley appears to have been the home of the earliest cultivated cotton, in about 5500 BC; but a related species of the same plant was independently domesticated in Mexico one thousand years later. Nor, in the New World, were Peru and Mexico the only places where important modern cultivated plants were first domesticated. Manioc, one of the most productive and least demanding crops ever grown by man, and still a staple foodstuff in many parts of South America, was originally cultivated in the tropical lowlands of the Amazon basin some time before 1500 BC. Thus, far from being an unusual event, restricted to one place and period, domestication appears to have occurred entirely independently in many places, at different times, as a natural development in man's relationship with the plants and animals on which he depends.

The development and spread of farming had profound consequences, not just for food procurement and diet, but for all aspects of life. Modern studies show that, in general, hunting and gathering can-

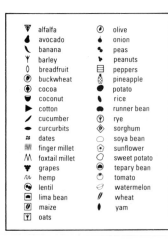

alfalfa		olive	
avocado		onion	
banana		peas	
barley		peanuts	
breadfruit		peppers	
buckwheat		pineapple	
cocoa		potato	
coconut		rice	
cotton		runner bean	
cucumber		rye	
curcurbits		sorghum	
dates		soya bean	
finger millet		sunflower	
foxtail millet		sweet potato	
grapes		tepary bean	
hemp		tomato	
lentil		watermelon	
lima bean		wheat	
maize		yam	
oats			

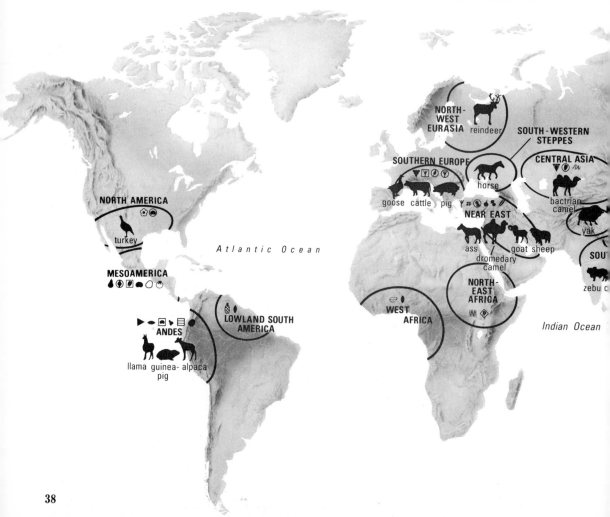

The introduction of farming resulted in population growth which led in turn to the development of more efficient and intensive methods of cultivation. These new methods varied depending on the nature of climate and terrain, but almost all entailed the dramatic modification of the natural landscape. Paddy-field cultivation of rice *right* dates back in parts of eastern China to before 5000 BC. This system of farming allows the growing crop to feed on the rich nutrients carried by the water. In the mountainous terrain of Peru *below* the need to expand the amount of land available for cultivation was met by the construction of elaborate systems of terracing. Sophisticated networks of irrigation canals were also an important feature of ancient Peruvian farming, as in the Near East.

With the growth of travel and communications, most of the plants and animals on which we rely today have been carried beyond their original centres of domestication *below* to other parts of the world. Near Eastern wheat and barley arrived in China before 2000 BC, while in more recent times maize, tobacco and potatoes have spread from the Americas to Europe, Africa and parts of Asia. Few animals were domesticated in the New World, however, and most of the livestock herded in the Americas today are of Old World origin.

CHINA
M ○

SIA

Pacific Ocean

water
buffalo

SOUTH PACIFIC
○ ●

not support permanent, all-year-round settlements of any size, as there are insufficient natural resources within range of any one site. Human groups are consequently obliged to move on at frequent intervals, consuming the produce of each area in turn in an annual cycle. But communities relying on the cultivation of crops such as wheat, rice and maize, on the other hand, normally reside in permanent farms, villages and towns.

This greater size and permanence of farming settlements may be explained in several ways. In part, it is a direct result of the exceptional productivity of the major cultivated species, sufficient to feed large concentrations of people on a year-round basis. Critical to this is the ability of the plant foods to survive storage over many months, allowing the community to stay in one place living off the previous harvest while a new crop grows and ripens. Cereals are particularly suitable for such long-term storage. Another explanation of the sedentary character of early farming settlements is the need for the farmers to be near their fields, both to protect them against human and animal predators and to minimize the travel and transport involved in preparing the ground, in weeding and in harvesting. A further factor may have been the natural human desire, circumstances permitting, for the richer social life which villages and towns permit.

The new way of life clearly had many advantages but, like most changes, it had its disadvantages too. Amongst the most important of these was an increase in the incidence of disease. The new diet was not one to which mankind was necessarily well-suited physiologically, and

agriculture sometimes encouraged communities to rely on too narrow a range of foodstuffs. Deficiency diseases were the inevitable consequence. Higher densities of population will also have led to an increased incidence of infectious disease such as measles and tuberculosis, from which the sparse and scattered hunter-gatherer groups had been largely exempt. Further health hazards were presented by the farming of areas high in agricultural potential but less suitable for human settlement in certain other respects. In East Asia, the paddy-field cultivation of rice brought the serious risk of infection from waterborne parasites such as the liver-fluke. At Çatal Hüyük in Turkey, the bones of the early farmers gave evidence of porotic hyperostosis, a thickening of the blood-carrying parts of the skull, probably caused by malaria in this marshy lowland basin. Disease must have been a principal cause of the low life expectancy among the inhabitants of Çatal Hüyük – around 30 years for women and 35 years for men – and among early farmers generally.

A further important consequence of the inception of agriculture was a general increase in the amount and variety of material goods and equipment. Among nomadic hunters and gatherers, possessions are kept to a minimum since everything must be carried around. Sedentary communities are freed from this constraint and produce a wide range of items, some utilitarian, others of a more ritual nature. One of the commonest finds among all excavated remains is pottery. Because of its weight and fragility, pottery was of little use to nomadic peoples, but sedentary groups employed it for a wide variety of containers: cooking vessels, drinking cups, storage jars. Other substances worked by these early farming communities included stone, wood, shell and metals; and many of the items produced were as much for ornament and display as for utilitarian purposes. This was particularly true of copper and gold, which began to be worked in parts of Europe and the Near East between 7000 and 5000 BC.

The use of these new raw materials brought in their wake further consequences. Often they were not available locally and so trade networks, sometimes extending over several hundred kilometres, needed to be established to supply them. And then the task of working them, especially the metals, gave rise to increasingly sophisticated craftsmanship. Finally, the new metalwork played an important role in the rise of a new social élite, serving as a visible symbol of the rank and status of the more powerful individuals and families; the settled villages and towns, with their larger populations, required more complex organization and regulation than most hunter-gatherer communities. The systems of authority which developed are reflected in impressive works of communal labour, such as the megalithic tombs of Atlantic Europe or the irrigation canals of Mesopotamia. Those people who rose to positions of power in the new agricultural society also gained control of a larger than average share of resources. Objects placed with the dead in graves illustrate a growing discrepancy between rich and poor in the period following the establishment of farming villages; items of gold and copper are normally found only with the wealthiest burials. The rich no doubt controlled the trade in raw materials and provided the economic support which increasingly freed craftsmen from agricultural work and gave them the opportunity to work full-time on specialist manufacture. The pace of change was accelerating, and around 3000 BC a new threshold was reached, a further critical stage in man's progress towards the modern world: the emergence of the first cities, and of the first ordered civilizations.

Megalithic chambered tomb of La Frébouchère in western France *right* Such tombs frequently contain remains of several individuals, perhaps community leaders, and frequently the bodies were exposed elsewhere and the skeletons were placed in the tombs in disarticulated form. The communal nature of the burials and the considerable effort that must have been involved in the construction of these tombs, indicates a growing degree of social organization. Megalithic tombs are a characteristic feature of the early farming societies of Atlantic Europe, from 4500 to 2500 BC, but were also built in other parts of the world at widely differing periods, as recently indeed as the 19th century in Madagascar.

Interior of neolithic house at Skara Brae, Orkney, c.2500 BC centre. Most early houses were built of perishable materials which have left little trace. However at Skara Brae the walls and fittings of the houses were all built of stone, including the central hearth, built-in cupboards, and raised moss-lined beds.

Stonehenge in southern Britain *below* is one of the most impressive prehistoric monuments of western Europe. Dating from the Early Bronze Age, c.1900 BC, it consists of a series of stone settings, up to 29 feet tall, within a circular bank and ditch. Some of the smaller stones were brought, probably by sea and river over 134 miles from South Wales. It is estimated that Stonehenge took over 2 million man-hours to complete. Stonehenge is aligned so that the midsummer sunrise can be seen along the axis of the monument.

ANATOLIA
farming
communities,
sophisticated
bronze-use and
incipient
urbanization

KAZAKHSTAN
early horse-based pastoralism
and metallurgy

TURKESTAN
walled cities and irrigated
agriculture villages

IRANIAN PLATEAU
scattered cities supported by
long-distance trade and
irrigated agriculture

ARABIA
maritime trading cities in contact
with Mesopotamia and
the Indus Valley

DECCAN
temporary hunting camps
and cattle-herding pens
replaced by farming
villages

DESERT NOMADS

MESOPOTAMIA

Arctic Ocean

STEPPE

Black Sea

Caspian Sea

Aral Sea

L. Balkhash

Mediterranean Sea

Red Sea

Arabian Sea

Persian Gulf

INDIA

INDUS PLAIN

Hindu Kush

Pamirs

Caucasus Mts

Zagros Mts

Taurus Mts

Ural Mts

R. Ob
R. Ural
R. Volga
R. Dneiper
Syr Darya
Amu Darya
R. Nile
R. Euphrates
R. Tigris
R. Indus
R. Godavari

Troy
Çatal Hüyük
Mycenae
Knossos
Crete
Cyprus
Sinope
Hattushash
Tell Brak
Tepe Gawra
Habuba
Ashur
Tell Asmar
Ebla
Mari
Ugarit
Sippar
Babylon
Kish
Shuruppak
Umma
Susa
Nippur
Tello
Lagash
Abu Salabikh
Uruk
Ur
Eridu
Heliopolis
Memphis
Kahun
Abydos
Thebes
Hieraconpolis
Edfu
Elephantine
Buhen
EGYPT

Mundigak
Rahman Dheri
Rana Ghundai
Harappa
Rupar
Alamgirpur
Kalibangan
Mohenjo-Daro
Kot Diji
Nindowari
Amri
Sutkagen Dor
Balakot
Allahdino
Desalpur
Surkotada
Lothal
Rangpur

30°   40°   50°   60°   70°   80°

The circular stone tower of Jericho *far left* is one of the most spectacular remains from the oldest walled settlement in the world, dating from 8000 BC. The permanence of agricultural settlements, remaining in the same place over hundreds or even thousands of years, and the more substantial buildings they contained, led in the course of time to the accumulation of considerable mounds of debris, as mud brick houses collapsed and new ones were built on their ruins. These artificial settlement mounds or tells, *left* are a distinctive feature of the Near East and often contain hundreds of individual occupation layers. At Jericho the growth of the tell eventually engulfed the stone tower.

CHAPTER 3

THE BIRTH OF CIVILIZATION
6000 –2000 BC

A decisive revolution in human history occurred about five thousand years ago when, in four separate areas of intense agricultural activity, a number of dispersed farming villages evolved first into towns, and then into cities. From these centres eventually arose the first civilizations, all of them located in broad river valleys: the Tigris and Euphrates in Mesopotamia, the Nile in Egypt, the Indus in India, and the Huang Ho (or Yellow River) in China. There were, however, some precursors: notably the settlements at Jericho in the Jordan valley and at Çatal Hüyük in southern Anatolia.

The ten-acre site at Jericho, not far from the Dead Sea, was first occupied around 8500 BC. Perhaps its most remarkable feature was a ring of impressive fortifications: a stone wall over twelve feet high,

The first civilizations of the Old World *left*. Around 3500 BC the first cities developed in Mesopotamia, followed shortly afterwards by similar developments in the Nile and Indus valleys and a little later on the Yellow River, China. Each of these urban literate civilizations was centred on a major river valley which had the agricultural potential needed to support a dense population. In other regions, such as Europe and south-east Asia, farming communities remained scattered, although there was an increasing use of bronze at this period, and more complex hierarchical societies were developing.

▨	fertile land
—	centres of urban civilization
▬▬▬	areas of pastoral nomadism

fronted by a ditch cut in the rock, and punctuated by defensive towers (the surviving one standing over thirty feet high). The existence of these defences – the first known anywhere in the world – is significant for two reasons. Firstly, it demonstrates the ability of this early farming community to organize considerable numbers of people to work together on collective enterprises; secondly, it attests the accumulation of wealth to the point where permanent, static defences were considered necessary. The settlement of Çatal Hüyük was founded around 6500 BC This town was far larger than Jericho: thirty-two acres of tightly-packed brick and stone buildings, unseparated by streets or alleyways. Access to each house was gained by crossing the roofs to the stairways leading down into each interior and some of the houses were decorated with frescoes. Many appear to depict hunting scenes, but others were almost certainly of a ritual nature: for example, the juxtaposition of wall-paintings of bulls, clay platforms bearing cattle horn remains, and the plastered skulls of wild oxen set into walls, suggests the existence of a cattle cult. This, however, is hardly surprising for Çatal Hüyük, though no doubt a regional centre of some kind, was still essentially a farming community.

By 5500 BC, when Çatal Hüyük was abandoned, numerous communities were living in permanent villages all over the Near East. It was not long before some of them developed into towns. One of the earliest, at Tell es-Sawwan in central Mesopotamia, became a walled settlement in about 5350 BC. At much the same time, a little further south at Choga Mami, the earliest Mesopotamian irrigation system was built. It was

Wall paintings from Çatal Hüyük *left*, the largest settlement of its period in the Near East, c.6500 BC, show a town of close-packed rectangular houses at the foot of a volcano. The houses at Çatal Hüyük were built against each other without intervening streets or passages, and access to the individual dwellings must have been across the roofs. The volcano may be one of those from the region of eastern Turkey which supplied Çatal Hüyük with obsidian, a volcanic glass used as a substitute for flint, which was widely traded throughout the Mediterranean and Near East.

The Warka vase *below left*, c.3400 BC, a finely carved ritual vessel from the early Mesopotamian city of Uruk, depicts scenes from the New Year festival: in Spring, the cities of Mesopotamia enacted a sacred marriage between the patron deities of each city to ensure the fertility of the land. Men are shown bearing gifts of agricultural produce to the goddess.

A man-made sacred mountain, the ziggurat of Ur in southern Mesopotamia *below*, c.2100 BC, was built of baked brick standing three storeys high. Trees may once have grown on the terraces, while the summit was crowned by a temple where the symbolic annual marriage between city deities may have been consecrated.

This group of figurines from a temple at Tell Asmar *below right*, the ancient city of Eshnunna in Mesopotamia, date from the early 3rd millennium BC. The two taller figures are deities – represented symbolically by their stature, the size of their eyes, and the emblems inscribed at the base of the statues. These figurines were placed in the temple by worshippers as a gesture of devotion.

fairly simple, with transverse trenches diverting streams into neighbouring fields; and they were intended only as an insurance policy, for in most years these areas already received adequate rainfall to support agriculture. But around 5000 BC, for the first time, farmers from northern and central Mesopotamia moved down into the alluvial plain of the Tigris and the Euphrates rivers.

These were immensely fertile lands with enormous potential, but to realize that potential there were two major requirements: firstly, an irrigation system capable of controlling and spreading the copious but unpredictable floodwater of the rivers had to be constructed; secondly, a continous supply of raw materials – stone, metals and wood above all – with which to construct and maintain the settlements, canals and dams of the plain had to be organized. To master all this called for a high degree of co-ordination, and this was only forthcoming, after about 3500 BC, with the emergence of a number of larger settlements possessing most of the characteristics of cities. Under their aegis, harvest yields of sixty, seventy and even eighty grains for each grain sown are recorded; and on this surplus the earliest of all known civilizations arose – Sumer.

Sumerian civilization was based upon some twelve city-states and, at first, pre-eminence passed from one to another. But the higher concentrations of people on the fertile plain called for greater management than a single city could provide. Eventually, in 2371 BC, a centralized authority spanning the whole valley was established by the first of a series of semi-legendary conquerors: Sargon of Agade. Before long his power extended far beyond Mesopotamia to Elam and the Zagros mountains in the south-east, and all the way to Syria and the Mediterranean coast in the north-west. But Sargon's empire proved to be short-lived and its collapse, due both to external invasions and to internal strains, was followed by a renaissance of the Sumerian city-state system in which Ur was the dominant force, its hegemony stretching from the Persian Gulf to Nineveh. But Ur also fell, around 2000 BC, creating a power vacuum in which Amorites from the western desert created fresh city-states, among the most important being Mari on the upper

Euphrates and Babylon further south. Under her powerful King Hammurabi (1792-1750 BC), Babylon created another empire that covered the whole of southern Mesopotamia; but, once more, it did not long survive its founder.

Even before Sargon unified Mesopotamia, Egypt was brought under the sway of a single ruler. Civilization there depended upon the annual flood of the river Nile, which covered the alluvial plain with a layer of fertile mud and provided floodwaters which could be trapped in artificial basins and cisterns for later use. Until 3100 BC, there had been an upper and a lower kingdom in the Nile valley, but around that time they were unified (according to some traditions), by Menes, the founding pharaoh, of the first of the thirty-one dynasties which were to rule Egypt for over 2,500 years. This continuity, although not unbroken, stood in marked contrast to the evolution in Mesopotamia. The two civilizations also differed in other respects. Firstly, because of the annual flood, there was no need for irrigation canals and dams in the Nile valley; secondly, although Egypt possessed some major cities, they lacked the geographical concentration found in southern Mesopotamia, so that the leaders who emerged tended to be rulers of rural regions rather than the lords of city-states. However, from the new capital at Memphis, created to mark the junction of the upper and lower kingdoms, the pharaohs dominated the Nile valley from the first cataract at Aswan to the Mediterranean coast, a cultivable and populated area of some 15,000 square miles.

The earliest civilization of the Indian sub-continent emerged in the Indus valley around 3000 BC. It included over seventy towns, and two large cities (Mohenjo-Daro and Harappa) which, between them, dominated by far the largest area of any of the ancient civilizations: roughly half a million square miles. Because of the limited nature of the written records associated with these sites, very little is known about them. It is not clear, for example, whether the entire valley was divided into a number of city-states; or whether there were only one or two large kingdoms. Some have even suggested that Harappa and Mohenjo-Daro were the successive capitals of a single state. Nor is the nature of these urban societies clear. Of course there were merchants, craftsmen and farmers, for no dense concentrations of people could exist without them; and there must also have been a political élite, who ensured the construction of the high citadels, solid buildings, uniform grids of streets and elaborate drainage systems which distinguished the various cities. Perhaps, also, there was a priestly class, on the Egyptian or Mesopotamian model: the Great Bath inside the citadel at Mohenjo-Daro, and the foot-basin at the entrance, have been interpreted as evidence of a stress on ritual purity with the citadel perhaps reserved for a ritually pure priesthood. But on this, the sparse surviving records (most of them still undecyphered) are silent. If priests existed, they disappeared with the rest of the Indus civilizations around 2000 BC.

The rise of civilization in China was different again. The first Chinese farmers began to cultivate the rich, well-drained soils of the Yellow River valley around 5000 BC. After 2500 they began to establish walled settlements and to work jade, metals, and other materials with great skill. Then, about 1700 BC, the whole region came under the rule of a dynasty known as the Shang.

Traditionally, the Shang are supposed to have come from Asia and conquered northern China; but, if so, they quickly adopted the culture of their new subjects, for the old ways continued and virtually the only novelties associated with the 'conquerors' were, on the one hand, the use of bronze (also from about 1700 BC) and, on the other, the writing of 'oracle bones'. The existence of these bones in large numbers, each

Statue of a god or priest-king c.2100 BC, from the Indus city of Mohenjo-Daro *below*. Surviving texts show that specialized priesthoods were an important feature of early civilization in both Mesopotamia and Egypt. The situation is less clear in the Indus, as few texts have been deciphered, but the Great Bath on the citadel at Mohenjo-Daro suggests that purification rituals were important, and it was probably used by a priestly élite.

Seated statue of Chephren *left*, ruler of Egypt c.2500 BC and builder of the second pyramid at Giza. Behind the king perches the falcon-god Horus, protective deity of the Egyptian kings. Artistic conventions relating to dress, pose and proportion were strictly observed – the statue represents an ideal of god-like majesty.

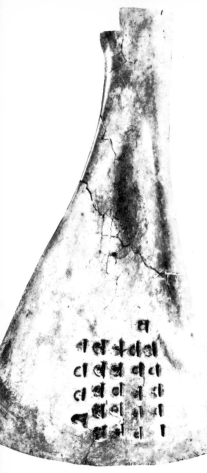

bearing several pictograms (clearly the ancestors of modern Chinese characters) and numerous heat-cracks, suggests that Shang China possessed a priestly class which interpreted the cracks and recorded the messages or auguries. It is true that no religious temple has so far been positively identified; but such rituals as were practised may have been performed in private houses and palaces. There were certainly plenty of palaces, for the Shang kings changed their capital six times. Two of them – at Chengchow and Anyang – have been excavated, revealing the existence of a court, royal functionaries, and craftsmen who made fine bronze vessels and superb carvings of stone and ivory. The Shang state covered an area of over a quarter of a million square miles, with its core in the Yellow River valley and outposts as far south as the Yangtze basin. It also had trade relations with steppe peoples to the north and west. In the eleventh century BC, however, one of these peoples, the Chou, conquered the Shang and also subjugated most of the area between the Yellow River and the Yangtze, bringing the unification of China measurably nearer and helping to assimilate the numerous ethnic groups of the area into a distinctive, unified Chinese civilization.

It seems beyond doubt that, except perhaps for the idea of writing, these various civilizations developed independently of one another; and yet the similarities between them are both numerous and striking, marking them all off from the farming communities out of which they sprang. One of their most obvious common features was the great cities. They were far larger than anything that had gone before – larger, indeed, than many that came after. Jericho, as already noted, was exceptional for its time; yet it covered no more than ten acres. Mohenjo-Daro and Harappa, however, each occupied over 100 acres, and the early Sumerian cities were larger still. Uruk, for example, in 3000 BC

Shang oracle bones *above* were used for divinations which were performed on behalf of the king. The ancestors of the monarch were consulted on a wide range of subjects from matters of state, such as military campaigns and payment of tribute, to more everyday concerns – the vagaries of the weather, the outcome of future hunting expeditions, the interpretation of dreams. The inscriptions on the bones which record the outcome of these predictions provide a comprehensive and evocative picture of Shang culture.

Bronze vessels *right* are the most outstanding products of Shang China and indicate a high level of specialist craftsmanship. Casting in ceramic moulds, unique to China, enabled complex shapes and elaborate decorations to be produced. Some of the finest Shang bronzes are wine vessels *far right*, and wine-drinking was extremely popular among the aristocracy.

The centre of the ancient city of Uruk in southern Mesopotamia *left*, contained three temple complexes. To the left is the temple of Anu, the principal Sumerian deity, and his consort, while in the background is the temple of Inanna, fertility goddess and patron deity of Uruk. By the end of the 4th millennium, Uruk covered an area of 1,400 acres and was enclosed by a protective wall 6 miles long.

covered some 1,400 acres. Temples and palaces dominated all these cities: visible symbols of the power of the priesthood and the kings who, in some places and periods, were regarded as divine. The early Sumerian temples at Nippur and Uruk were adorned with brightly painted frescoes, and at Uruk also with a colonnade, each column measuring 9 feet in diameter. It has been calculated that the massive building at Uruk known as the White Temple would have taken 1,500 men, each working a ten-hour day, five years to complete. The monuments of the pharaohs of Egypt, above all the pyramids, were even larger – so vast, indeed, that whole villages were built to house the labourers working on them.

The stepped pyramid of King Zoser at Saqqara *below left* was the first pyramid to be built in Egypt in c.2630 BC, the result of a number of changes to the original design, which was for a low, flat-topped tomb. Below the pyramid the mummified body of the king rested in a burial chamber of granite. The pyramid design proved popular, rapidly reaching its apotheosis in the famous pyramid complex at Giza *below*. The great pyramid of Khufu (c.2530 BC) is 146m high and consists of c.2.3 million stone slabs – the enormous communal effort involved in constructing such a monument was the ultimate testament to the control exercized over the Egyptian people by one individual.

The Vulture Stele from the Mesopotamian city of Telloh *left*, showing king Eannatum, ruler of the city-state of Lagash, with serried ranks of soldiers, armed with helmets, shields and spears. The city-states of the Near East were engaged in constant struggles for supremacy during the 3rd and 2nd millennia BC, and were able to support armies of trained soldiers, often with tens of thousands of combatants.

All this monumental architecture was meant to impress: to mark the gulf that divided the ruling hierarchies from the common people and to stress the exalted, divine character of the rulers. It used to be thought that the early Sumerian city-states were run by the temple priests, but the decypherment of further records has discredited this view. It now seems that the temples only controlled around 30 percent of the land, with the rest in private ownership; and that the earliest rulers were not priests, but patricians elected by a council of the leading families. In any case, though, under their stewardship, the food surpluses made possible by increased agricultural production were accumulated and used to finance the great ceremonial buildings and monuments and to support the specialized craftsmen – masons, metalworkers, sculptors, painters – engaged on constructing and embellishing them. The neolithic farmer had, to a large extent, been a jack of all trades – required to produce not only his own food, but also his own clothes, his own pottery and his own tools. But once society became more complex, and particularly when cities grew up, this had to change.

Early specialists to be released from direct subsistence labour included the priests, freed from other tasks in order to conduct magical ceremonies to placate the gods, control the crops and ensure adequate water; and also skilled craftsmen, such as potters and metalworkers. Although many specialized tasks doubtless continued to be performed on a part-time basis, gradually a distinct class of craftsmen grew up. But many of them remained dependent upon raw materials imported from outside, since the alluvial plains where the first civilizations arose were almost totally devoid of minerals, timber and other requirements

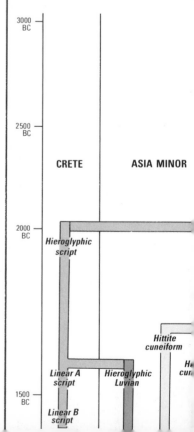

CRETE   ASIA MINOR

3000 BC

2500 BC

2000 BC

Hieroglyphic script

Hittite cuneiform

Linear A script   *Hieroglyphic Luvian*

1500 BC

Linear B script

Seals from the Indus city of Mohenjo-Daro *below left* were probably the marks of individual merchants impressed on clay to indicate the ownership of merchandise and guarantee the integrity of contents. The seals were used in trade and are sometimes found in Mesopotamia, indicating the scale of trading contacts.

The development of writing *below*. The invention of writing around 3000 BC was of fundamental importance in the development of civilization. The chart shows the chronological development and geographical dissemination of the principal scripts. The spread of writing, largely from the two main stems, Mesopotamian cuneiform and Egyptian hieroglyphics, is a good index of the spheres of influence of the two dominant centres, and of the dissemination of civilization from them.

A scribe's training was long and arduous *below right*, but those who persevered were held in high esteem. As the Egyptian scribe Mahu wrote to a discouraged pupil: "Do not be a silly fellow, with no learning. The night is spent training you, and the day teaching you; but you do not listen to any instruction, but go your own way. The ape understands words, and it is brought from Kush [Nubia]. Lions can be trained, and horses broken, but beyond you there is none of your kind in the whole inhabited land. Consider that!"

of civilized life. This led to the early appearance of still another class: the professional merchants. They are specifically mentioned in the earliest temple accounts from Lagash, in southern Mesopotamia, in about 2350 BC; and, before long, every city of Mesopotamia and the Indus valley seems to have had a special sector reserved for craftsmen and traders, and some of them created trading colonies in the distant areas that supplied the raw materials: thus the Assyrians maintained outposts, circa 1900 BC, in Anatolia to secure metal ores; and the Egyptians sent expeditions to quarry copper and turquoise from Sinai. The trade of Babylon in the time of King Hammurabi was so lively that his celebrated law-code (circa 1760 BC) devoted a section to regulating interest rates and customs tariffs for merchants.

One of the advantages enjoyed by the merchants of these advanced societies was their ability to keep written records of their business. Some early clay tablets with writing, found recently at Tell Brak in northern Mesopotamia, have been dated to 3200 BC (which would make them the earliest written inscriptions in the world); and there are more from the city of Uruk of about 3000 BC. They are no more than lists, however, and consist of simple pictograms of cows, fish, grain and so on. But by about 2800 BC the representation of these and other items had been reduced to conventional symbols made on a flat clay tablet with wedge-shaped strokes, and known as cuneiform script (from *cuneus*, the Latin for 'wedge'). Compared with modern alphabetic scripts, using a relatively small number of symbols, cuneiform signs were cumbersome; but they constituted an enormous step forward, for writing proved to be an important vehicle for the cultural integration of the different early civilizations. The pictographic script of the Sumerians may perhaps have influenced the subsequent development of writing elsewhere – in Persia, India, Egypt, Crete, even China; but, if so, it was only the concept which spread, for the signs used in the various cultures were all different. It is equally possible that, as in the Americas, the idea was born independently as each civilization reached the

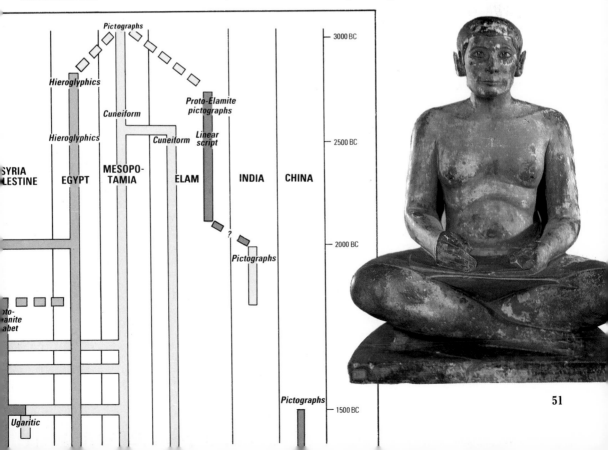

Pictographs

3000 BC

Hieroglyphics

Proto-Elamite pictographs

Cuneiform

Hieroglyphics   Cuneiform   Linear script

2500 BC

SYRIA PALESTINE   EGYPT   MESOPO-TAMIA   ELAM   INDIA   CHINA

Pictographs

2000 BC

Proto-Canaanite alphabet

1500 BC

Pictographs

Ugaritic

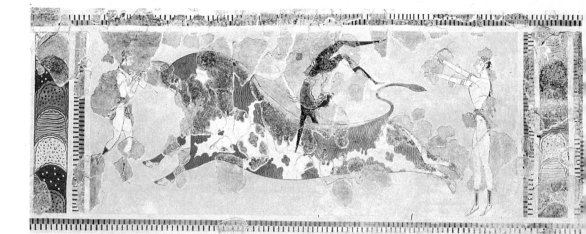

stage where it became necessary, whether for trade and administration or for religion. But writing, in Sumer and elsewhere, soon came to be used for other things besides business: to preserve religious traditions, which thereby became sacred books; to register social customs, which thereby became codes of law: and to hand down myths, which thereby became history and literature.

The invention of literacy was not the only outstanding achievement of these early civilizations, however. Hardly less valuable was the measurement of time and the creation of the calendar. From the Sumerians we inherit the division of the hour into sixty minutes and of the minute into sixty seconds; and the twenty-four hour day comes from a combination of Mesopotamian and Egyptian time-measurement. The 365 day calendar also originated in Egypt and, although adjusted slightly by Julius Caesar and Pope Gregory XIII, is still in use today.

These calculations, like accounting and estate management, required a knowledge of mathematics; and, for this, the Sumerians and Babylonians, who had already standardized weights and measures, evolved appropriate rules and formulae. By about 1800 BC the temple clerks had drawn up multiplication tables, could work with fractions, and were able to solve quadratic equations. They were already the masters of an exact science: the foundations of modern mathematics and geometry had been laid.

All in all, the 'urban revolution' of the fourth millennium BC marks the beginning of a new phase in world history. True, not all areas were affected by it: Australasia, Africa and large parts of Asia had no cities; the first civilizations of the Americas did not emerge until about 1500 BC and, when they did, owed nothing to ideas introduced from outside (chapter 16). Europe, at this stage, also lagged far behind: it was still a land of scattered farmers and dispersed villages, and the one exception – the Minoan civilization in Crete after about 2000 BC – had closer links with the world of Egypt and western Asia than with later European cultures. But in the Near East, in the Indus valley and along the Yellow River, the growth of the first great cities with their monumental architecture and their class divisions marked a turning-point. It also gave rise to a period of great and lasting technological advance. Writing, mathematics and the calendar were witnesses to a sudden burst of creativity. But in the second millennium BC, the equilibrium of these early civilizations began to change. Technological developments (notably the working of iron), an increasing rivalry for territorial and political control, and the developing threat presented by nomadic groups on the fringes of the civilized world combined to produce a new historical dynamic: the imperial impulse.

Minoan Crete takes it name from the legendary king Minos, who dwelt in a palace where the double-axe or *labyrys* was a sacred symbol. Palaces such as Knossos were not only royal households, but also centres for a flourishing rural economy; agricultural produce was collected, stored and redistributed, and resident craftsmen produced pottery, metalwork and carved ivory of great sophistication. Palaces were also ritual and ceremonial centres and the dangerous sport of bull leaping, *above*, was probably a common spectacle in palace courtyards. On Minoan frescoes men are shown red, women white, an artistic convention borrowed from contemporary Egypt; just one example of the many links, both commercial and cultural, which bound the eastern Mediterranean together.

Bronze head of an Akkadian king *right*, possibly Sargon (2371-2316 BC). Born of humble origin, he was the cup-bearer to the king of Kish, whom he eventually overthrew. He founded a dynastic capital at Agade and pursued a relentlessly expansionist military policy in Mesopotamia, temporarily uniting disparate city-states under his rule when he conquered Elam in the east and Syria in the west. His reign ended in general revolt; and it fell to his son, Rimush, to re-establish Akkadian authority. However, his empire was the first to be established in the Near East and it provided a model to which later rulers aspired.

On the map:

Great Wall

Yellow Sea

(Yellow River)

Loyang

R. Yangtze

Hsienyang

C H I N A

MIN-YUEH

NAN-YUEH

20°

South China Sea

R. Mekong

CHAMPA

Legend:

Achaemenid empire at its greatest extent c.512 BC

Persian Royal Road

Ch'in territory before 300 BC

other major states with dates of conquest by Ch'in

new areas conquered by Ch'in after unification

Chandragupta Maurya's empire 297 BC

Asoka's empire 232 BC

▲ rock and pillar edicts

Indian Royal Highway

From 500 BC the history of the Old World *above* was dominated by the rise and fall of a series of powerful empires larger than any that had previously been seen.

Assyrian bas relief from the palace of Ashurbanipal at Nineveh *left*, showing the cavalry and archers of the Assyrian army. In an increasingly militarist era, subject peoples were reminded of their humiliation by fiercely propagandist palace reliefs, and victory monuments. The Assyrians in particular were renowned for their cruelty and gloated over their atrocities. One king (Ashurnasirpal 884-859 BC) recalled 'I built a pillar over against the city gate and I flayed all the chiefs that had revolted and I covered the pillar with their skin'.

CHAPTER 4

THE AGE OF IRON
2000 BC–AD 200

Sargon of Agade (2371-2316 BC), is commonly regarded as the first great empire-builder in history, for he managed to extend his authority over an extremely large area: the whole of Mesopotamia, together with parts of Anatolia, Syria and Persia (chapter 3). Over the next two millennia, several other conquerors established imperial dynasties: the pharaohs of the New Kingdom in Egypt and beyond, the kings of Assyria in the Near East, the Chou emperors in China. But then, after about 600 BC came empires of a size and cohesion never previously seen: the Achaemenids and Parthians in Persia; Mauryans in India; Ch'in and Han in China; Alexander the Great and his successors over almost the entire Near East.

Each of these later empires was also a great regional civilization, and by the third century BC they spanned almost the whole of Asia, from the Aegean in the west to the shores of the Pacific in the east. This remarkable expansion in political power was the product, in large measure, of new techniques of government, and improved ways of administering and defending the vast imperial territories. Asoka (272-232 BC), the unifier of most of India, commanded a standing army of 700,000 men with 9,000 elephants and 10,000 chariots; while the Persian kings had a crack regiment of heavy infantry, the famous 10,000 Immortals. In China, the first Ch'in emperor, Shih Huang-ti, linked together the various fortifications along the northern frontier and, with the labour of about 500,000 pairs of hands, created a continuous barrier running 2,000 miles, known today as the Great Wall. These and other security measures made possible economic growth on an unprecedented scale, boosting agriculture, manufacturing and long-distance trade. Further, major public works also helped. In Persia, a great Royal Road ran for 1,677 miles from Susa, north of the Persian gulf, to Sardis in Asia Minor, not far from the Aegean coast. In India, a similar Royal Highway ran all the way from the Ganges delta to Taxila, near the Khyber Pass, where it connected with caravan routes west to Persia and the Middle East, and north to central Asia. In China there was an elaborate network of roads centering on the capital, Changan (a city of a quarter of a million inhabitants) and also an elaborate system of canals, linking present-day Shanghai with the interior, and present-day Canton with the Yangtze valley.

All this implied a greatly increased efficiency of government; and efficient government was, in fact, a characteristic of all the new empires. In Persia, Darius the Great (522-486 BC) reorganized his domains into twenty provinces or satrapies under unified control, with a comprehensive code of law, equitable taxes and a stable currency. Han China, about 150 BC, was governed by some 130,000 salaried civil

55

servants, arranged in provincial hierarchies, each responsible to the imperial administration in Changan.

The extension and strength of these major empires is all the more surprising when it is contrasted with the eclipse and decline of so many of the preceding Bronze Age civilizations. But the wealth and luxury of their cities had presented an irresistible temptation to the surrounding tribesmen, and an influx of peoples from the steppe began around 2000 BC. The earliest groups moved into Asia Minor from north of the Black Sea, among whom the most prominent were the Hittites: by 1600 BC they had established a powerful kingdom in Anatolia which afterwards extended into northern Syria. The Hittite invasions seem to have triggered the migration of other peoples whose origins and early history lie shrouded in mystery: the Hyksos, who overran Egypt for about a century after 1720 BC; the Kassites, who conquered Babylon in about 1600; and the Hurrians, who founded a kingdom in Syria in about 1475 and occupied Assyria for about half a century after that.

These invaders introduced a new and devastating military weapon: the horse-drawn chariot. The idea of a mobile battle-wagon was not new, for the Royal Standard of Ur, dating from about 2500 BC (chapter 3), shows a heavy cart with solid wheels, towed into action by onagers. But the light war chariot, with two spoked wheels, pulled by horses which one warrior steered, while the others fired a hail of arrows, was something quite different. Even with only a handful of chariots, victory over unsupported infantry formations was easy, for the typical Bronze Age warrior was the foot soldier armed with club, axe, spear and shield. Against chariots, he was almost helpless unless, as in a battle mentioned in the Old Testament, the elements came to his aid: according to the *Book of Judges*, on one occasion the Israelites wiped out an army which included 'nine hundred chariots of iron' when the power of prayer diverted the river Kishon into their path. After that 'the land had rest forty years'.

The fate of the early civilizations of Europe and India was very different. Already by 1350 BC (at the latest) the flourishing palace-based Minoan culture in Crete (named after Minos, the legendary king of Knossos) had been taken over by a wave of Greeks, probably from Mycenae in the Peloponnese, who adopted and developed the civilization which they found there. Mycenaean civilization had developed on mainland Greece in the sixteenth century BC, largely independent of the Minoans. However, this too was overthrown. A series of local insurrections, possibly coupled with attacks from the peoples of northern

Detail from the 'war' side of the standard of Ur *far left* (c.2500 BC), showing a four-wheeled battle waggon drawn by onagers.

Sculpture of an armed god *left* from a gateway of the Hittite capital of Boğhazköy. During the 13th century BC control of the Levant was contested between the rival imperial powers of Egypt and Hittite Anatolia. Both made extensive use of the war chariot in their campaigns. Boğhazköy, with its powerful walls and gates, is one of the most strongly fortified sites in the Near East, intended to provide a secure base for imperial expansion.

According to legend, at the time of the Trojan war the kingdom of Mycenae was the residence of Agamemnon, the overlord of all Greece, and the Mycenaeans were portrayed as enterprising sailors and heroic warriors. The warrior vase *right*, found at Mycenae shows a line of marching soldiers carrying the military equipment typical of late Mycenaean Greece – spear, circular shield, plumed helmet, and what may be leather tunics.

Mohenjo-Daro *below* and Harappa were the two largest cities of the Indus civilization and may either have been the capitals of separate states, or successive capitals of a single Indus state. The regularly laid out streets of the city and other features such as the provision of municipal drains testify, together with Mohenjo-Daro's size (40 ha), to the presence of a central governing authority. After the decline of Indus civilization in 2000 BC, no cities appeared in India for over 1,000 years, although it was during this period that the Aryan invasions recorded in Vedic literature must have taken place.

Greece, led to the destruction of the palaces and citadels of the Mycenaeans. Their trading activities, which had extended to southern Italy (and probably also Sardinia) in the west, and to Cyprus and the coast of Palestine in the east, now ceased; and a dark age ensued from about 1200 BC until foreign trade and colonization resumed some four centuries later (chapter 5).

The fate of the Indus civilization in about 2000 BC was equally catastrophic and mysterious. When the ruins of Mohenjo-Daro were excavated in the 1920s, skeletons were found in the streets, suggesting that some disaster had occurred, but its immediate cause has been the subject of some controversy. Soil exhaustion through over-cropping, fluctuations in river courses which left the land around the cities desiccated, and flooding caused by changes in the level of the river Indus have all been suggested; and one or more of these, coupled perhaps with a famine or epidemic which left the cities vulnerable to attack, may indeed have been to blame. But the records are silent. Certainly the next series of archaeological remains in the area belong to a very different people, who bred horses (unknown in Harappa and Mohenjo-Daro) and buried their dead in the same way as the tribes who lived

beyond the Hindu Kush. Even if they did not destroy the cities, these invaders – known to history as the Aryans – spread their culture into the Ganges basin and beyond.

Of all the ancient civilizations, that of Egypt survived longest. Most of the country was, it is true, overrun by the Hyksos in the eighteenth century BC; but these intruders were expelled 150 years later by a new native dynasty who proved to be as adept at chariot-warfare as the invaders. In the sixteenth century BC, and again under Pharaoh Tuthmosis III (1504-1450 BC) the Egyptian army pursued the invaders northwards until it reached the upper Euphrates and the borders of Anatolia. Never before had Egypt acquired an Asiatic empire. But it could not be held: after the death of Tuthmosis, the Hittites and other northern states drove the Egyptians back into Palestine. And then, some two centuries later, Egypt herself was attacked by the 'Sea Peoples' – presumed to contain a large Greek element, possibly including Mycenaeans and Sardinians; but both Pharaoh Merneptah in 1232 BC, and Ramesses III in 1191 BC, inflicted decisive defeats on the invaders. Finally, in the seventh century, Assyria conquered the Nile delta, penetrating as far south as Thebes.

Assyria succeeded in large measure probably because her empire rested upon the power of iron. The Assyrians did not themselves invent iron-working – the earliest evidence of the ability to smelt iron comes from Alaça Hüyük in Turkey around 2500 BC – but in about 1900 BC tablets stored at the Assyrian trading post of Kültepe in eastern Anatolia mention iron as a principal traded commodity, and iron was regarded, at this time, as five times more valuable than gold. For about

Rock-cut temple of Ramesses II (1290-1224BC) *below* overlooking the Nile at Abu Simbel in Lower Nubia. Here and elsewhere Pharaoh Ramesses II used colossal size to convey Egyptian imperial might, even though by his reign the power of Egypt had passed its peak.

The Assyrians 800-625 BC were masters of imperial propaganda, decorating the walls of their palaces with scenes showing victories, court ceremonials and lion hunts, obviously designed to impress visitors with the might of Assyrian arms. The bronze decorations from the Balawat Gates *above right* at the palace of Shalmaneser III (883-824 BC) vividly illustrate the story of the king's wars and the tribute which he exacted. Stone reliefs on the walls of palaces, *centre right* demonstrate Assyrian ingenuity in the arts of war. In open battle they used infantry cavalry, and chariots manned by a driver, shield-bearer and lancers.

Glazed-brick dragon *below right*, a low relief figure from the imposing Ishtar Gate at Babylon. After the fall of Assyria, Babylon took over its Near Eastern empire under king Nebuchadnezzar (604-562 BC). Nebuchadnezzar rebuilt Babylon, and a 6th-century account by the Greek historian, Herodotus, evokes a picture of a magnificent city surrounded by walls so wide that a 4-horse chariot could be driven along them.

a millennium, iron continued to be treated as a precious metal, and its use was correspondingly small: a gold-hilted dagger with an iron blade from the tomb of Pharaoh Tutankhamun (c.1350 BC); small amounts of iron from late Mycenaean sites (c.1200 BC); occasional iron objects in northern Europe (c.1500 – c.1100 BC). A regular iron-working industry only developed about 1100 BC in the lands around the eastern Mediterranean: Cyprus, Phoenicia, coastal Greece, the Aegean islands and (after 1000 BC) Italy. By the seventh century BC iron-smelting was also widespread north of the Alps, and it began soon afterwards in Egypt, at the Greek colony of Naucratis, founded c.620 BC.

At that time, the power of Assyria was at its height. She had recovered quickly from the unrest of the twelfth to tenth centuries, and in the ninth began to extend her frontiers dramatically. First Babylonia was conquered; and then the foothills of the Zagros and Taurus mountains, rich in horses, metals and timber – tools of empire which the Assyrians levied as tribute. By 650 BC, from their capital at Nineveh on the Tigris, they ruled the whole of Mesopotamia, Syria and Palestine, and even extended, nominally, to northern Egypt. They possessed iron technology, a well-disciplined army, and an efficient bureaucracy; they appeared, to the Old Testament prophets at least, to be invincible. And yet, for all that, Assyria was destroyed in 612 BC by a coalition of her enemies: the Babylonians and the Medes, aided by Scythian horsemen from the steppe. Nineveh was sacked and abandoned for ever. After nearly seventy years of subsequent control by the Babylonians, whose most famous ruler was Nebuchadnezzar, the Fertile Crescent fell to Cyrus the Great (550-530 BC), who united the Medes and the Persians to create the nucleus of the powerful Achaemenid empire in modern Persia. Finally, in 525 BC, his successors conquered most of Egypt too.

These momentous political changes involved far less discontinuity than might have been expected. In the first place, Assyria was strongly influenced by Babylon: although Assyrian was the official dialect of the

empire, Babylonian was used for literary composition; they collected and preserved the literature of the Mesopotamian past; they developed an art which owed much to Babylonian antecedents; and they worshipped the old Babylonian gods. Later on Cyrus the Great, in his turn, made a point of encouraging the continuance of existing institutions after his conquests had been achieved. In Babylonia, the same officials sometimes remained in office before and after the Persian take-over.

Iron, unlike copper and tin, was available in large quantities in almost every region so that, once the technology of smelting was mastered, it could spread almost anywhere. Indeed, the extensive development of iron technology was possibly provoked by the disruption in the traditional trade in copper and tin during the general disturbances at the end of the second millennium BC. The widespread distribution of iron ore meant that iron technology was not much affected by the disruption of trading networks. On the other hand, Phoenician colonists introduced iron metallurgy to north-west Africa in the ninth and eighth centuries BC, and from cities like Carthage and Leptis the new technology spread south of the Sahara: iron was being produced at Taruga, in modern Nigeria, from about 450 BC. At much the same time, there was a limited spread of iron-working down the Nile to Meroë in the Sudan, which had become an important centre of production by 500 BC.

Whether or not the use of iron in India was influenced by the discoveries in the Near East is more difficult to say. But between 1300 and 1000 BC, small quantities of worked metal are found in a few northern areas; and over the next five hundred years iron gradually came into general use throughout most of India, with several centres of production in the Ganges valley. This area had only been colonized from about 800 BC, quite possibly because the thick forests and heavy soils of the region could only be mastered with the use of iron. But, once broken in, it was farmed in a new and different way: wet-rice cultivation. Rice had been grown by the people of the Indus civilization, but only as one crop amongst several. During the first millennium BC, however, it became the dominant cereal in the middle and lower Ganges valley, and this permitted a rapid expansion of the area's population. By 600 BC there were some sixteen well-articulated political units on the Gangetic plain, several boasting major walled cities. Over the next two centuries, to the despair of many observers (such as Gautama Siddhartha, the founder of Buddhism), the major states engaged in almost continuous conflicts to secure hegemony in the area. The eventual winner, Magadha – its capital at Pataliputra (modern Patna), on the Ganges, boasting a river frontage of more than nine miles – formed the nucleus of a great empire founded in 322 BC by Chandragupta Maurya and extended by his famous grandson, Asoka, who brought almost the whole of the Indian peninsula under his rule (chapter 6).

The Iron Age in China presents so many contrasts with the experience of other societies that, almost certainly, it was an independent process. Towards the end of the Shang period, in the thirteenth and twelfth centuries BC, bronze axes with cutting edges made from meteoric iron have been found. But the use of iron developed only slowly under the Shang and their successors the Chou (1027-771 BC). The Chou presided over a form of feudal state: they invested their leading supporters with fiefs, and these feudatories gave land to their own followers, and so on. At the base of the social pyramid, as in medieval Europe, was the peasant family which provided labour services, food and clothes for their lord. But in 771 BC, the Chou capital at Hao (near Changan) was sacked by western invaders and the chief

Lion-headed pillar capital from Sarnath, India *below*. These pillars were erected as imperial propaganda by the Mauryan ruler Asoka (272-232 BC) after his conversion to Buddhism. The shafts carry royal edicts propounding the Asokan principle of Dhammavijaya, a code of social responsibility intended to unify the disparate peoples of his extensive realm. The edicts were distributed throughout the Mauryan empire, especially in the cities of the Ganges plain and near the imperial frontiers, and emissaries travelled as far as the Hellenistic kingdoms and Ceylon to preach the doctrine of peace. The idea of inscriptions in public places and the use of animal-headed pillars were derived from Achaemenid Persia.

Silver rhyton (drinking horn) from Erzinan in Armenia *left*, with foot in the form of a horned griffin. The frequent occurrence of animal motifs in Persian art, a feature shared with the Steppe people to the north, may reflect the nomadic origins of the Persian aristocracy. Spectacular finds of rich metalwork are amongst the gifts of tribute brought to the Persian king by delegations of subject peoples portrayed in the relief sculptures at the great palace of Persepolis *below* built by Darius (521-486 BC). Achaemenid Persia was a vast empire extending from Asia Minor to the Indus valley, and the tribute offered by the various delegations reflects the national resources of each country – lions from Susa, antelopes from Ethiopia, horses from Scythia, camels from Arabia and gold from India. This was the first truly cosmopolitan empire the world had yet seen; inscriptions at Persepolis itself record that people from all over the empire were involved in its construction, and the architectural styles are eclectic, ranging from Greek columns to Egyptian cornices.

feudatories seized the opportunity to break away and establish their own independence. Although the Chou dynasty continued to rule from a new capital at Loyang, their state was now one amongst many: over 100 separate states are known to have existed in China in the five centuries following 770.

Making historical sense of such complexity clearly poses major problems. Traditionally, the period has been divided into two halves: the years down to 481 BC, during which the old feudal order collapsed; and from then until 221 BC, when a new order was gradually established which culminated in the unification of the whole of China under a single ruler.

The chief agent of change in both processes was war: not for nothing is the latter era known as the Warring States period. But the nature of the conflicts changed considerably. In the first place, wars became less common. Between 722 and 464 BC, there were only 32 recorded years of peace; but between then and 221 there were 89. On the other hand, as time passed wars, though less frequent, tended to last longer, to cover a wider area, and (above all) to involve far more troops. In the eighth century BC, battles had usually been fought between hundreds of chariots, each containing a select band of noble warriors; but by the fourth century, the leading states were each able to

Bronze model of a two-wheeled horse-drawn carriage with parasol *below*, from a Han tomb at Wuwei, Kansu, 2nd century AD. The Han ruled a united China for over four centuries. During this period of stability, China grew extremely prosperous, with an efficient bureaucracy, an extensive road and canal network, and a growing number of large towns. The model illustrates the great skill of the Chinese metalworkers, and gives an impression of the lifestyle of the Han aristocracy – graves from this period further reinforce the impression of a cultivated, leisurely ruling class, with finds of delicate lacquer tea-sets and richly woven silk wall-hangings, gowns and slippers.

Early Chinese coinages *below* developed around 500 BC and took a variety of forms, including 'knife', 'spade' and 'disc', until the last was established as the sole official coin in Han times. Before the unification of China in 221 BC, each independent kingdom had its own coinage, and differences in form were one way of maintaining the distinctions between the kingdoms. The spade and knife coins suggest that in earlier times actual spades and knives were used as units of value.

support standing armies (mainly conscripted) of one million men, mostly infantry but with some cavalry. Battles involving 100,000 men were not unknown, and major sieges might last several months and tie down hundreds of thousands of men. It has been suggested that the size of the Chinese armies increased ten-fold over this period (a phenomenon not paralleled in Europe until the sixteenth century AD: chapter 17).

Clearly, military changes on this scale presupposed equally great changes on the part of the peoples and governments who waged the wars. In the first place, a major increase in the size of the population was required. Data before the great imperial census of AD 2 is lacking, but the total population then was given as 59.5 million; and it has been suggested that it may not have been much smaller four centuries before. Certainly there were notable improvements in agriculture in the fifth century BC, above all the sudden appearance of cast-iron tools, of a fairly uniform design, all over China, and of iron tips and cutting edges added to wooden implements. At the same time, major irrigation works were undertaken, such as the Tuchiang dam in Szechwan, built in the third century BC and still in use today, which may have increased crop yields in the area five-fold. Elsewhere fertilizers also improved harvest size. But the surpluses thus created did not long remain in the hands of the producers. The endless wars resulted in the destruction of most of the states formed after 770, and most annexations were accompanied by the demotion of the defeated nobles. Instead of labour services to a lord, the peasants of these areas now paid taxes to the conqueror. By the time of the philosopher Confucius (551-479 BC), the standard rate of tax was about 20 percent. These were the sinews of war.

The new states also prospered from taxes levied on trade, and here too they reaped (in part) the fruit of their own policies. On the one hand, they encouraged the growth of cities, where goods were both manufactured and exchanged; on the other their innovations for the sake of improving military efficiency – such as building roads and canals – and minting bronze coins at the same time helped to promote trade. Above all, the creation of a few large, integrated states in place of many smaller ones (and by 300 BC there were only seven), together with the replacement of hereditary nobles by salaried professional administrators greatly assisted the development of trade, by extending the area in which merchants could safely travel.

Coinages in the ancient world originated in Lydia, Turkey, in the 7th century BC *above*. This Lydian *stater, centre* (560-546 BC) is decorated with a lion and a bull to represent royal power. The Achaemenids of Persia established a standard gold coinage, as a means of unifying the empire, and the gold daric *below* (c.500 BC) was a month's pay for a Persian soldier. The Phoenician *shekel, top* (385-72 BC) shows the great king of Persia in a chariot, reflecting the extent of Persian control.

Finally, in 318 BC, the westernmost of the seven large states – Ch'in – which had managed to stay out of many earlier conflicts and thus build up its strength, began to attack and annex her immediate neighbours. In 256 BC, Loyang, the imperial capital of the Chou, was taken and from 246 Prince Cheng, the able young ruler of Ch'in, launched an all-out attack on the other states and destroyed them one by one. By 221 the whole of China acknowledged his authority. Cheng thereupon took the name Shih Huang-ti (meaning 'first emperor') and immediately extended the system of government perfected in his own state to the rest of the country: the population was organized into groups of families, who were made collectively responsible for keeping the peace and performing their duties; a strict penal code was made binding on all; heavy demands for men to serve in the army and on public works were made. Chief among the latter were the Great Wall, which claimed the lives of so many labourers that it gained the nickname of 'the longest cemetery in the world', and the imperial mausoleum, now in the process of excavation near his capital at Hsienyang (near Sian). Larger than the pyramids of Egypt, it took 700,000 conscript labourers some 36 years to build.

Shih Huang-ti also ordered the construction of a national network of roads and canals, centered on the new capital; he introduced a uniform coinage whose distinctive shape (circular with a square hole in the centre) remained standard until 1911; and he took steps to standardize the written language throughout the empire. Small wonder that 'China' got her name from his dynasty. Admittedly Ch'in rule, harsh and exacting, provoked revolts; but in 202 BC central control was firmly re-established by a new dynasty, the Han, and China emerged as one of the great world powers.

But the age of iron did not only permit the spread of empires: it also allowed the extension of farming to heavier soils wherever crops could grow. By the first century BC, a series of populous communities arose in the river valleys and coastal plains of south-east Asia, all the way from southern China to Bengal, using both bronze and iron. In the mountains of southern India and in Ceylon, small independent kingdoms with advanced religious, political and economic structures of their own likewise flourished.

In Europe, on the other hand, civilizations of a considerably greater complexity were beginning to emerge on the shores of the Mediterranean. To the north, central and western Europe were occupied during the Iron Age by the Celtic peoples, whose warlike activities are reflected in hillforts and chariot burials. In the fourth and third centuries BC the Celts engaged in a series of raids and invasions, spreading into eastern Europe and the Mediterranean lands. They sacked Rome in 390 BC and the Greek shrine of Delphi in 279 BC. Relations with the Greeks and Italians were not always hostile, however, for the Celtic chieftains developed a taste for wine and Greek tableware, and wine amphorae are found in their graves. A taste for luxury is also reflected in Celtic art, a distinctive style used for drinking vessels, mirrors, swords and bracelets. During the third to the first centuries BC, the Celtic tribes began to form themselves into kingdoms, and hillforts were replaced gradually by large earthwork enclosures with residential and craft areas, the earliest towns of temperate Europe.

It was here, in Europe, that the Iron Age peoples met their match, for as the classical cultures of the Mediterranean littoral developed and expanded, so these warlike peoples were pushed increasingly to the far-flung, inhospitable corners of the continent, swept on before the inexorable power and vision of the classical world of Greece and her successor, Rome.

Maiden Castle *above* is an impressive Celtic hillfort in Dorset, southern Britain, with multiple lines of defensive ditches and ramparts, and complex entrance-works. Hillforts were a common feature of Iron Age Europe. The defenders of these hillforts were skilful slingers, but such methods were insufficient to resist the Roman armies and a war grave by the gate contained remains of 38 defenders. Maiden Castle and some 20 other hillforts in south-western England were captured by a Roman army under Vespasian in AD 44.

Horse-drawn chariot with charioteer *above right*, detail of relief frieze on the great bronze krater found in the grave of a Celtic princess at Vix in eastern France. The krater, a large vessel for mixing wine, was made in Greece or in a Greek colony in southern Italy around 525 BC. Its discovery in a Celtic grave illustrates the importance of Greek trade north of the Alps, which had a major impact on the development of Celtic society.

Pottery army of Shih Huang-ti *right*, the Chin emperor who was the first to create a unified China. The army was found in a great pit a mile to the east of the huge imperial mausoleum at Hsienyang and consisted of 6,000 soldiers armed with spears, swords, bows and crossbows. The figures are modelled to represent individual soldiers from real life and it is possible that an entire division may have been fortunate enough to sit for their portraits rather than being buried alive. The pit gives us a unique insight into the appearance of the Chin armies which conquered rival states and unified China in 221 BC.

Colonization in the Mediterranean World *below*. The Phoenicians, were able seamen who established trading posts and colonies in northern Africa and southern Spain — areas rich in natural resources such as silver, iron, lead and copper. Many Greek cities from c.750 BC onwards also sent out both trading and agricultural colonists to seek new homes overseas; When established, the colonies became independent states. By the 2nd century BC the western basin was dominated by Carthage and Rome.

The gold mask *right* was found in a shaft grave at the citadel of Mycenae in Greece by the German Heinrich Schliemann, who pioneered the excavations of Mycenae and Troy. He immediately sent a cable to the Kaiser 'I have gazed upon the face of Agamemnon' — the ruler who led the Greek attack on Troy narrated in Homer's *Iliad*. In fact the mask dates from the 16th century BC, 400 years before the Trojan War.

The voyage of the Greek leader Odysseus, at the end of the Trojan War, was a series of legendary episodes commemorated in an epic poem attributed to Homer, the *Odyssey*. Its continuing popularity with later generations is reflected in the mural from Pompeii *below right* painted in the 1st century AD, which shows Ulysses (the Latin name of Odysseus) tied to the mast of his galley in order to resist the call of the Sirens, spirits of death who lured less resolute mariners to their death on the rocks.

	Greece and Greek settlement c.750 BC
	Phoenician settlement c.550 BC
	border of Carthaginian empire c.264 BC
	border of Roman empire c.133 BC
□	Phoenician or Punic city
●	Greek city
◆	Greek colony
■	Philistine city

North Sea

EUROPE

GAUL   R. Rhine   GERMANY

R. Rhône

IBERIA   Massilia   CELTS

Pyrenees   Nicaea   Alps   R. Po

Saguntum

Gades   Hemeroscopium   Alalia   Corsica   ETRUSCANS

Balearic Is.

Sardinia   ○Rome   Adriatic Sea   ILLYRIA   Carpathian Mts

MAURETANIA   NUMIDIA

Atlas Mts   Pithecusa   ITALY

MAGNA   Neapolis

Utica   Selinus   Lilybaeum   GRAECIA   Tarentum   Epidamnus

Carthage   Panormus   Apollonia

Malta   Sicily   Nexos   Messana   Croton   Aulon   R. Danube

SCYTHIA

Syracuse   Corcyra   MACEDONIA

Olbia

Leucas   EPIRUS   Apollonia

TRIPOLIS   Mediterranean   Achaea   Thasos   THRACE

Leptis Magna   Corinth   Chalcis   Abydus   Byzantium   Heraclea   Chersonensus

Megara   Eretria   Phocaea   Dascylium   Pontica   CRIMEA

PELOPONNESUS   Athens   Lesbos   PHRYGIA   Panticapaeu

GREECE   MYSIA   LYDIA   BITHYNIA   Black Sea

Aegean   Samos   CARIA   ASIA   MINOR   PAPHLAGONIA

Euhesperides   Sea   Thera   Miletus   Xanthus   Anatolia   Sinope

Cyrene   Rhodes   LYCIA

PAMPHYLIA   PONTUS

Side   Taurus Mts   Tra

Paphos   Cyprus

Citium   Salamis

Nauciatis   PERSIA

EGYPT   EMPIRE

R. Nile   Byblos

Joppa   Sidon

Ascalon   Tyre

Red Sea   Gaza   Ashdod

AFRICA NOVA

AFRICA

CYRENE

CHAPTER 5

GREECE AND ROME
1200 BC–AD 200

The earliest advanced civilization of Europe, 'Minoan' Crete, flourished from about 2200 to about 1400 BC. Towards the end of this period Mycenaean civilization, indebted to Crete, became established on the mainland and, around 1450, seems to have taken over its parent culture (chapter 4). But in the twelfth century BC both were wiped out and, for the next four hundred years, south-eastern Europe entered what has been called the 'Greek Dark Age'. The area remained a backwater of small farming communities and local chiefdoms, dominated by various Greek-speaking tribes. Little reliable written evidence about them has survived, but archaeologists are gradually amassing information from excavated burial sites and settlements. This suggests that some significant changes began after about 800 BC. By then, the main city-states had been founded, population was increasing fast and settlements of Greeks were to be found around the Aegean – on the islands of Lesbos, Chios and Samos, and on the Anatolian coast at Ephesus and Miletus.

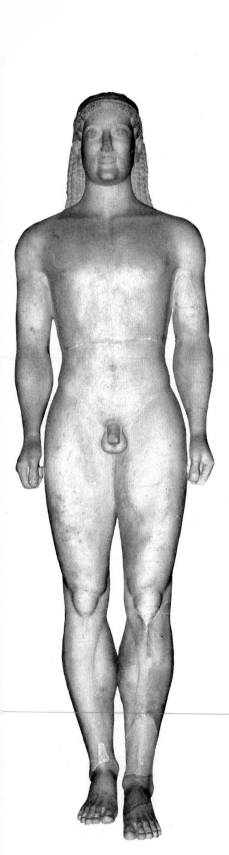

The foundations of Greek civilization were also already apparent in many fields – the first temples date from the eighth century – and Greek settlements also soon appeared around the Black Sea as well as along the Mediterranean coasts of Italy, France and Spain.

The principal motive for expansion was probably land-hunger. Since Greece itself was unable to support a large population – four-fifths of the peninsula is rock and mountain, and the coastal plains are the only areas suitable for arable farming – the emerging city-states encouraged emigration by their citizens. But the economic insufficiency of the cities also stimulated expansion in another way: they had long exchanged the products made by their craftsmen for supplies of tin, copper and iron; now they also exchanged them for corn. Some of the oldest colonies were established along metal or grain trade-routes.

The Greeks enjoyed notable advantages as merchants. First, they could boast a long tradition of successful seamanship. As early as the thirteenth century BC, the legendary voyage of Jason and the Argonauts in search of the Golden Fleece indicated that ancient twenty-oared galleys probably traded successfully over long distances. Geographically, the Greeks were especially well-placed for seaborne commerce: they could supply trading partners not only with their own produce, but also with the luxury goods of the Near East. Furthermore, from these more sophisticated markets they acquired more sophisticated techniques: coins were adopted around 600 BC from Asia Minor (where they had recently been invented, chapter 4) and an alphabetic script from the Phoenicians, which they adapted to their own language; this made possible the preservation of far more than commercial data: the

epic stories about their ancestors, attributed to the bard Homer, were also written down at an early date. Finally, when it came to war, the Greeks possessed superior weapons, made of iron, and advanced tactics both by land and by sea.

But iron swords, swift galleys, coins and an alphabet were not enough to forge an empire. Greece continued to be divided into numerous, belligerent, intensely nationalistic states: the principal political unit remained the *polis* – a compact city-state, usually dominating one of the small, isolated coastal plains. Even the greatest *polis*, Athens, which ruled the relatively large and fertile plain of Attica, never increased much beyond 250,000 free citizens. But, on the other hand, whereas the larger and initially more prosperous cities of the Anatolian coast had to contend with great principalities on their doorstep, those of mainland Greece were left free to follow their own destinies, for the most part unhindered by foreign interference. Within their narrow, fragmented compass developed the first – and perhaps the most influential – of the western civilizations that came in time to dominate the entire globe.

Athens had been a major centre since the eighth century, but after 500 BC it became both the most advanced and the richest state in mainland Greece. It was also culturally the most productive. Fifth-century Athenians could enjoy the drama of Aeschylus, Sophocles, Euripides and Aristophanes, as well as the history of Herodotus and Thucydides. They could also admire a set of public buildings which demonstrated to all the world the taste, wealth, power and piety of Athens: in 447 BC work began on the Parthenon, and before long the

The Acropolis or high point of the Greek city was both a natural stronghold and the home of the gods (the meeting-point of earth and heaven). The Acropolis at Athens *below centre* was ravaged in the Persian Wars and in the mid-5th century it was rebuilt on a monumental scale by the statesman Pericles. Approached by a processional entrance or *propylaea*, the acropolis is over 1000 feet long and rises 325 feet over the surrounding plain. It is crowned by the Parthenon, Athens' greatest temple (to the right), begun in 447 BC. Built of marble, it measures c.288 feet by 101 feet on the podium, with 8 columns to the front and back and 17 along the sides. It is decorated by a remarkable frieze which depicts the procession which was the climax of the Panathenaea, Athens' greatest religious festival. The famous sculptor Phidias supervised its execution, and himself produced the majestic central statue of Athene in gold and ivory.

On land the core of Greek armies were the heavily armed infantry, or *hoplites*, like the soldier with the plumed helmet depicted on the red-figure vase *below left*, poised beneath his great shield to plunge a spear into his enemy.

high ground at the centre of Athens (the Acropolis, or 'high city') was crowned by a monumental gateway and spectacular temples.

Fifth-century Athens was dominated by a spirit of scientific inquiry which derived its confidence from the advances in speculative thought and mathematics achieved in many centres of the Greek world, from Ionia to southern Italy. Where the Babylonians had observed eclipses, the Greeks developed astronomical geometry to trace the movements of the heavenly bodies; where the Egyptians had used triangles with sides in the proportion of 3:4:5 to construct right angles, Pythagoras devised his famous theorem to prove the mathematical principle on which it was based. He also discovered that there is a connection between numbers and music.

The cultural triumph of Athens was achieved under the aegis of the first democratic government in recorded history. True, the system was not universal democracy, for only male citizens were allowed to participate. But in 431 BC there were about 65,000 male citizens (as against perhaps as many slaves, and three times as many women and children); and all of the former might exercise their political rights directly. This is a great deal more 'democratic' than our modern political systems (which the Athenians would have dismissed as 'elec-

tive aristocracies', not democracies at all), for all power in their state lay with the Assembly, in which every citizen had the right to speak and to vote. The executive council of 500, serving in committees of fifty for a tenth of the year, was chosen by lot, as were most magistrates and humbler officials; any citizen might become president of the republic – but only for one day. Military commanders alone were chosen not by lot but by election. They held their command for a year at the end of which – like all other officials – they had to satisfy the scrutiny of the People's Courts. In the words attributed to the great fifth-century orator, Pericles: 'Our Constitution is called a democracy because power is held by the majority, not a minority. But our laws ensure equal treatment for all in private disputes; and public opinion values an individual for his personal qualities, not for sectional reasons…We do not call a man who does not share in public life politically quietist; we call him politically useless…All in all, I am claiming our city as an education to Greece'.

But this open society was not without its problems. The curse of Greece was political conflict: war between the states, and civil strife within them. In Sparta, the great rival of Athens which depended on a serf-based agriculture, the fear of rebellion by the *helots* (an entire

Pericles (c.495-429 BC) *below* dominated Athenian politics from 461 to 429 BC. An aristocrat with democratic policies at home and imperialist ambitions overseas, Thucydides preserves for us something of his vision of Athens. 'Our polity is called a democracy because it favours the majority rather than the minority. The laws provide equality for all in private disputes. Advancement in public life depends on merit not on class consideration … In a word I assert that as a city we are an education to Greece, and our citizens, man for man, yield to none in many-sidedness of achievement, flexibility, the graces of life and self-reliance, physical and mental'.

The Peloponnesian War *below* was fought between Athens and Sparta and their respective allies for the supremacy of the Greek world. It lasted from 431 to 404 BC, when Athens, having lost two armies through her imperialist ambitions in Sicily, and recovered with extraordinary resilience, was eventually forced to capitulate.

Under Alexander the Great the Macedonian conquests *below right* stretched to the limits of the known world and beyond, taking Hellenistic civilization decisively beyond the Mediterranean and turning European minds and energies for the first time to the east; they probably also made it more vulnerable to the implacable Roman drive from the west.

people reduced to the condition of slaves of the state) more or less turned Sparta into a military camp, forced to exalt the virtues of austerity and discipline in order to survive. In Athens, too, wealth was unevenly distributed, albeit far less than in most other states. After the early sixth century, when the moderate statesman Solon helped to reduce the problem of debt among the peasantry, the general condition of agriculture (upon which perhaps three-quarters of all Athenian citizens depended) improved markedly. In addition, the wages paid for discharging public office, for attending the public assembly or the law-courts, and (in time of war) for service as soldiers or oarsmen, all helped to redistribute income more uniformly among the mass of the citizens, and enabled them to share in the growing wealth of the state. But war steadily eroded that wealth, for Athens was rarely at peace.

In the early fifth century BC, the great enemy was the Persian empire which, having suppressed a revolt by the Greeks of Asia Minor, mounted a punitive expedition in 490 against the cities across the

The Peloponnesian War, 431–404 BC
left inset

- Spartan confederacy
- neutral states
- Athens, members of the Delian League and allies
- ✕ Athenian victory
- ⊗ Spartan victory

Aegean which had supported the rebels; and then, ten years later, Persia made a determined attempt to conquer the Greek mainland itself. The celebrated defeats of the invaders at Marathon (490), Salamis (480) and Plataea (479) in fact bought less than a quarter-century of relative peace. For between 461 and 404 BC Athens and Sparta, with their respective allies, fought each other bitterly in the two Peloponnesian wars, which left the whole of Greece exhausted and divided. There was, as yet, no cultural collapse, for fourth-century Athens could still boast the philosophical genius of Plato and Aristotle; but wars continued to sap the strength of the city-states until, later in the fourth century, they all fell before the might of Macedon.

The well-trained Macedonian army subdued Greece during the reign of King Philip II (359-336 BC), but the conqueror promptly associated the vanquished with his ambitious policies in a Hellenic League formed in 338. All the states except Sparta were represented in the League, of which the king of Macedon was president and supreme

Alexander the Great (356-323 BC) *below* king of Macedon. One of the greatest of all military commanders, he was a notable founder of cities, a restless, charismatic, heroic, figure, perhaps convinced of his own divine calling.

CHORASMII **SCYTHIA**

Aral Sea

L. Balkhash

R. Oxus

R. Jaxartes

DAHAE **MASSAGETAE**

Sea

Amol
Rhagae (Teheran)

HYRCANIA

Hecatompylos
Thara

Caspian Gates

PARTHIA

Susia

Salt Desert

ARIS (ARIA)

Artacoana

Persia

Alexandria (Merv)

Bukhara

Maracanda (Samarkand)
Nautaca (Karshi)

Bactra (Balkh)

Derbent
Cyropolis

Alexandria Eschate

Sogdian Rock (besieged 328)

SOGDIANA

BACTRIA

Drapsaca

Alexandria Areion (Herat)

Alexandria Prophthasia

CENE

PERSIS

Persian Gates

Pasargadae

Persepolis

CARMANIA

DRANGIANA

Ned-i-Ali

SEISTAN

Alexandria Arachoton (Kandahar)

Alexandria (Ghazni)

ARACHOSIA

Alexandria ad Caucasum
Nysa

Hindu Kush

Nicaea

Aornos
Taxila

326

Bucephala
Nicaea

Sangela

R. Ravi

R. Sutlej

KINGDOM OF ABHISARA

KINGDOM OF OMPHIS

KINGDOM OF PORUS

R. Indus

R. Jhelum

Quetta

Multan

Alexandria Opiana

Harmozia

Pura

GEDROSIA

Gwadar

Pashi

Kokala

Las Bela

Alexandria

Pattala

City of the Brahmans

INDIA

Indian Desert

sian Gulf

empire of Alexander

route of Alexander the Great

✕ Alexander's major battles

commander; and its first collective objective was declared to be a war against Persia. Although Philip was assassinated before he could organize the campaign, the task was enthusiastically taken on by his extraordinary twenty-year-old son, Alexander.

The imperial achievements of Alexander the Great are so stunning that they almost defy explanation. In the spring of 334 he crossed into Asia Minor with an army of some 35,000 men, both Greeks and Macedonians. Within two years he had defeated the main Persian armies and occupied Anatolia and Palestine. In 332 he annexed Egypt virtually unopposed; he then rapidly conquered the rest of the Persian empire and in 327-325 he campaigned in India. When he died in 323 – still only 32 years old – he had led his army over 12,000 miles, victorious all the

Alexander's victory over the Persians at Issus in 333 BC *right* soon passed into legend. In this Roman mosaic from Pompeii, copied from an earlier painting, the young king is shown bare-headed, wild-eyed and in shining armour, as he furiously attacks the bodyguard of the terrified Persian king. But behind the spectacular victories lay meticulous and minute preparation. To lead a force which reached a maximum fighting strength of 45,000 infantry and 7000 cavalry far into Central Asia and back through north-west India required the provision of 120 tons of food, plus water, and fodder for the horses, each and every day. Yet so admirable was Alexander's supply system that his army sometimes covered 19 miles a day, and his cavalry 46, without running dangerously short of provisions.

way. It was an extraordinary strategic and logistical triumph. It also caused a marked increase in long-distance trade – fostered by the unprecedented unification of such a large area, and encouraged by the foundation of numerous cities in the wake of the conquests.

Those cities helped to preserve prosperity after the loss of unity. For, after Alexander's death, his empire fragmented into several divisions: Syria, ruled by the Macedonian general Seleucus Nicator and his successors (the Seleucids); Egypt, governed by another general, Ptolemy Soter (founder of a dynasty made up almost entirely of monarchs of the same name: thirteen Ptolemies and seven Cleopatras); and Macedon itself, under a third general, Antigonus (initially as regent for Alexander's children, whom he later had murdered). Under these

The Alexander sarcophagus from Sidon *below* was one of seventeen sarcophagi found in a Royal Cemetery. It is dated to the last decade of the fourth century BC and was perhaps the burial place of Abdalonymus, the last king of Sidon. It is called the Alexander sarcophagus because it portrays on one side a battle between Greeks and Persians, and the mounted Greek to the left with the lion's head helmet has been identified with Alexander, though this is not certain. The carving is vigorous and in high relief, carefully composed with a base of dead and dying figures, and well conveying the intensity of battle. On the other side is a lion-hunt. Substantial traces of colour – violet, brown, red, yellow and blue remain.

Hellenistic states Greek civilization, hitherto confined to the Mediterranean, was extended far to the east. Alexander himself founded at least sixteen Alexandrias (tradition said over 70), of which all except Alexandria in Egypt and Alexandretta on the border of modern Turkey and Syria were in the east. The Seleucids, too, built many cities on the Greek model, which they filled with Greek army veterans, merchants, artists and administrators. A hybrid form of Greek, known as Koine, spread throughout the Middle East as a common language.

Hellenic influence outside the older Greek settlements, however, remained confined to the cities – and even there to the upper classes, who adopted Greek manners and amusements, bought and sold goods in the impressive new market places, or went to Greek plays and spectacles in the great open-air theatres. The peasantry of the countryside, taxed to provide a splendour in which they could not share, remained outside. The ordinary town-dwellers, too, were often excluded. Formerly, the *polis* had been the sole focus of law, morality and religion; but in the world of great territorial empires decisions affecting the inhabitants might be made in a distant capital and men had to accept that their city was but a small part of a vastly greater world. Intellectuals sought guidance in cosmopolitan philosophies: the Stoics, with their moralizing fatalism; the Epicureans, with their withdrawal into the simple life; the Cynics, with their flouting of convention and their assertion of individual liberty and independence. Others sought refuge in the Hellenized religions of the Orient, which often involved ceremonies that were more emotive and theatrical than those of the old cults of Greece.

Nevertheless, the Hellenistic world did not crumble because of some deep moral crisis, but through simple military inferiority. The

Post-classical Greek art and architecture *below left* is illustrated by the beautiful remains of the circular tholos, of unknown purpose, in the sanctuary of Athene Pronaia at Delphi. It dates from 380-375 BC. In the Hellenistic Age Pergamum became a political and cultural centre of major importance. In 241 BC Attalus I defeated the Gauls or Celts who had crossed over from Europe and were raiding and pillaging. Among the monuments to this victory was a huge Baroque circular offering to Athene consisting of bronze figures of the defeated Gauls. Some think that this wonderful study in inner courage in the face of death is a marble copy of one of those figures *below*. The Romans much admired the purity of Greek architecture and sculpture and many of the pieces which survive today are in fact Roman copies of Greek originals.

The Roman Empire from Augustus to c.AD 280 *below.* Augustus settled with Parthia, annexed Egypt, Galatia (25 BC) and Judaea (AD 6) and advanced over the Alps to the Danube and the Rhine, adding the provinces of Rhaetia, Noricum, Pannonia and Moesia. Settlement of colonies continued until Hadrian (d.138), after which 'colonia' became a title for privileged *municipia*. Syria and Cappadocia were extended under the Flavians (69-96) and the German frontier advanced to the Black Forest (Agri Decumates). Trajan, whose reign marked the end of the empire's significant territorial additions, fought wars for the annexation of Dacia (106), Armenia and Assyria (114), and Mesopotamia (116), to join Arabia Petraea, already taken in 106. His successor, Hadrian, decided to abandon these eastern acquisitions, apart from Arabia and Dacia, and to consolidate the frontiers of the empire.

	Roman empire in AD14
	provinces added after AD14

fragmentation of the empire created by Alexander left each of the successor states without the resources to resist the power of Rome, exercised by men who were prepared to be ruthless in exterminating those who opposed them. In the stinging comment, attributed to a defeated British chieftain by the Roman historian Tacitus: 'To plunder, butcher and steal are the activities they misname "empire"; they make a wilderness, and they call it "peace"'. The Britons were not the only ones to experience the truth of this.

Rome's rise to power was rapid and seemingly inexorable. In the sixth century BC, the city was just a small fortress-town in central Italy commanding both the lowest crossing-point on the river Tiber, and a salt-route between the mountains and the sea. But by exploiting quarrels with their neighbours, the Roman Republic emerged as the dominant power first in central Italy and then in the whole peninsula. By 270 BC the entire area south of the river Arno was in Roman hands, and in 264 its army crossed into Sicily. This marked the beginning of Roman imperialism, for Sicily was one of the dominions of Carthage, at the time the greatest sea-power of the Mediterranean, with colonies in North Africa, Spain and Sardinia as well as Sicily. For more than a century, the two empires remained locked in a conflict known as the Punic wars. Although the brilliant campaigns of the Carthaginian general Hannibal almost brought Rome to her knees in 217-216, in 201 Carthage admitted defeat: Spain and the Mediterranean islands were surrendered, and the Carthaginian fleet was destroyed.

Henceforth, Rome unscrupulously sought pretexts in order to expand. First she turned on those who had supported Hannibal: the Celts of northern Italy were resubjugated; the Seleucid king's military power was broken and he was forced to cede territory; Macedonia was

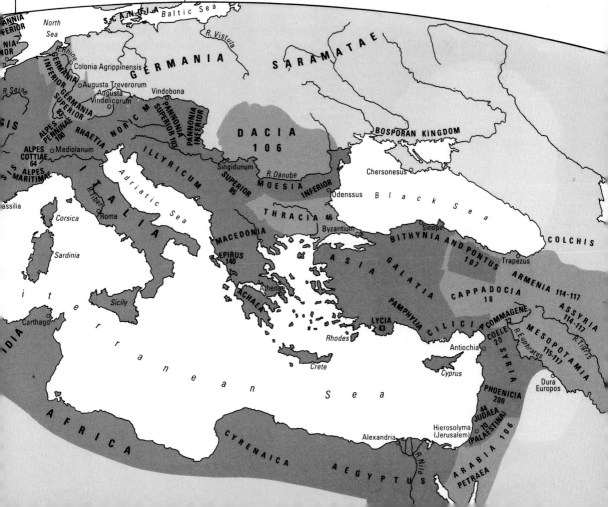

Gaius Julius Caesar (100-44 BC) *below* began his military career in 81 BC in Asia, and continued it in Spain and Gaul. But between his campaigns, he built up a popular following in Rome and held numerous public offices (including *Pontifex maximus* – chief priest – in which role he introduced in 45 BC the 'Julian Calendar' which lasted until AD 1582). Following his brilliant conquest of Gaul between 58 and 49 BC (which included a brief invasion of Britain) he used his army to seize power in Rome. After five years, however, he was stabbed to death in the Senate by a group of disaffected aristocrats. Caesar had not brought peace to the Roman world. His rise to power was accompanied by civil war, fought in Italy, Greece, Egypt, Africa and Spain, and his death provoked an armed struggle for ascendancy.

After the restoration of peace by Augustus, artists working for upper-class patrons developed a style of landscape painting which captured the tranquillity of rural life, and suffused the whole scene with an idyllic reverence, as in the picture *right* of the villa of Agrippa Postumus near Pompeii. Horace, along with Virgil and Ovid one of the great poets of the Augustan age, voices the same sentiments; 'O country home, when shall I look on you again! When shall I be allowed, between my library of classics, and sleep, and hours of idleness, to drink the sweet draughts that make us forget the troubles of life?'.

defeated, partitioned, and eventually occupied as a Roman province. Rome next embarked on further expansion in the east, securing step by step the whole eastern seaboard of the Mediterranean, a policy triumphantly concluded with the conquest of Egypt from the last descendant of Ptolemy Soter, Cleopatra VII, in 30 BC.

These acquisitions were for a long time treated primarily as a source of booty. Roman provincial government was extortionate – so much so that, after a campaign in Macedonia in 167 BC the wealth flowing in from the conquered provinces (coupled with the income from the state-run mines) made it possible to abolish direct taxation altogether for Roman citizens. The number of these was constantly increasing at a great rate. In about 80 BC, there were some 463,000 citizens; eighty years later there were no less than 4,233,000 (out of a total population in the empire of perhaps 50 million); and in AD 212 citizenship was granted to virtually every free man and woman living in the empire.

By then, Roman rule extended far beyond the Mediterranean basin. This expansion began in 49 BC when Julius Caesar, a dissolute, ambitious but able aristocrat, launched an attack on Gaul, hoping (and managing) to line his pockets with the spoils of conquest. The frontier was soon advanced to the Rhine and Danube. Later, during the first century AD, much of England and Wales was added; and, during the second century, Romania too. In the east, further gains for a time carried the frontier almost to the Caspian Sea, but expansion there was decisively halted by the Parthians, who had taken the place of the Seleucids as the leading power in the Middle East: against the mounted archers of this redoubtable adversary, despite repeated attempts, the legions could not prevail.

But their achievements were considerable enough as they stood, and they created a host of problems. Above all, how could the political apparatus appropriate to a small city-state be adapted to govern half the world? For a time, power remained in the hands of male members of the city's aristocracy, who passed through a series of administrative posts before becoming one of two consuls, the supreme office held for only one year at a time. They would then serve a further year as proconsuls, governing a province overseas. The Senate, which retained effective control over the state, was dominated by those who had already held public office. But in the first century BC the machinery began to creak: there was inadequate supervision, leading to corruption and incompetence. There was also economic tension, as great estates (usually worked by slave labour) swallowed up the plots of the peasant-farmers. Eventually, in periods of crisis, ambitious generals seized power for themselves by main force, bending the constitution and breaking the rules: Marius of the left wing, Sulla of the right; Pompey the would-be dictator, Caesar the successful autocrat. After Caesar's assassination in 44 BC, there was a further period of civil war until in 31 BC his great-nephew, known to history as Augustus, achieved sole power.

Augustus was a brilliantly successful pragmatist. He is called emperor, but that is merely the English form of the Latin word *imperator*, meaning 'commander-in-chief'. In fact, his several powers were strictly republican; but he accumulated them and in practice, if not in law, he held them in perpetuity. His justification was that he brought peace to the Roman world, and the Augustan age of peace was indeed celebrated in both literature – with the poetry of Virgil, Horace and Ovid – and in stone – with aqueducts, bridges, monuments and other splendid public buildings.

Over the next four hundred years, the size of the Roman empire

Roman settlements were built to last
above. Even the eruption of Vesuvius in AD
79 did not destroy the streets of Pompeii.
Not only the buildings — streets of houses,
gardens, public baths, theatres, shops and
taverns — were preserved in their entirety,
but also their contents — wall-paintings,
statues, cooking utensils and toilet articles,
all perfectly preserved beneath a layer of
volcanic ash. Here, modern archaeology
had its beginnings — the town was lost
until the 18th century when local workmen
accidentally uncovered some of the
remains. Excavations over the ensuing 250
years have revealed a town frozen at the
moment of its destruction; dozens of
skeletons and even a chained dog have
been discovered in mid-flight, engulfed and
smothered by the torrent of ash and
pumice. Pliny the younger recounted the
disaster in his eye-witness account.
Confronted with inexplicable disaster
'many sought the aid of the gods, but still
more imagined that the universe was
plunged into eternal darkness for
evermore'.

varied little. There were some losses in the mid-third century, when the
empire was near collapse, but stability was restored (and most of the
losses were recovered) under three powerful rulers: Aurelian (270-
275), Probus (276-282) and Diocletian (284-305). Perhaps the greatest
achievement of Rome was to give to a larger area of the globe a longer
period of relative peace than at any other time in human history, either
before or since. This was largely with the consent of the governed: the
whole of North Africa, for example, from the borders of Egypt to the
Atlantic, was policed by a single legion (nominally 6,000 men) together
with auxiliary units. A network of roads centred on Rome, a single
coinage, and a single language and legal system all assisted the interchange of goods and peoples so that it was safe for trade to take place
by both land and sea anywhere in the empire, which formed a vast,
almost self-sufficient area uncluttered by political frontiers.

The achievements of Roman rule were most apparent in the towns.
Even relatively modest urban centres were decked out with an impressive array of theatres, triumphal arches, baths and fountains –
indeed the provision of reliable drinking water and higher standards of
hygiene was one of Rome's main contributions to Western civilization.
Also, the Romans improved rural areas by introducing irrigation and
drainage systems, as well as better agricultural tools and techniques.
The proliferation of 'villas' (country farms) is an index of increased
productivity and prosperity in the countryside. Of course not all members of the rural population were wealthy: the peasants remained, for
the most part, poor, illiterate and heavily taxed – in the province of
Africa, the standard tax rate for peasant farmers was one-third of their
production plus six days' labour service. But their position was safeguarded by a powerful corpus of law which gradually offered more

Petra in Jordan *above right* was the capital city of Nabataea, an Arab state which had prospered on the profits of the incense trade. The future Dean Burgon described it as 'A rose-red city, half as old as time'. Much of the rock is red, and the pious student thought that time began in 4004 BC. Carved out of a cliff-bound valley, crossed by numerous *wadis*, Petra occupied a key point on the overland routes linking the classical cities of the Mediterranean with the incense traders of Arabia, and from there the Indian Ocean. Its position is accountable for the strong Hellenistic influences visible in the classical facades of many of the temples which were carved out of the solid rock. Ed Deir *above right* is the largest of the rock-cut monuments of Petra — its facade is 130 feet high. The Romans annexed Petra in AD 106, and added a theatre and other buildings.

Jerash in northwest Jordan *right* was originally a Hellenistic city, later incorporated into the Roman province of Syria. Its imposing ruins are mainly of the Roman period and demonstrate a successful synthesis of Hellenistic and Roman architectural styles. They include an Arch of Hadrian, a remarkable oval forum, an elaborate theatre and a temple of Zeus.

Trajan's column in Rome *left* standing an imposing 100 feet high, is covered by a spiralling frieze, over 650 feet long, carved in relief with more than 2,500 figures representing scenes from Trajan's Dacian wars, which resulted in the annexation of Dacia as a Roman province in AD 107. It originally stood in a colonnaded court flanked by two libraries — from the upper tiers of these buildings viewers could see the carvings at close range.

The Romans developed their own styles of portraiture. Their stone portrait busts are outstanding; in the Republican and early Imperial period the subjects were portrayed with candid realism *below*, and the style was adopted by all classes of Roman society from artisans to senators. In the later Imperial period, however, a tendency towards idealized representation developed, which bore more resemblance to Roman ideals of deity than to the uncompromisingly realistic portraits of earlier times. In Pompeii, the walls of many of the buildings were decorated with medallions – panels with a central portrait in relief. Among these is a charming realistic picture of a pensive young girl *right* holding a stylus and a wax tablet.

protection to the poor. Eventually the law even protected slaves against wanton cruelty. Roman law (although not fully codified until the reign of Justinian in the sixth century AD) made a contribution to the legal and social systems of all subsequent European nations that it would be hard to exaggerate.

But in other respects, Rome was more notable as an imitator than as an innovator. One of her greatest strengths was the power to assimilate and adapt the achievements of others. Already in the first century BC, many of the Republic's political and cultural leaders came from northern Italy (which the Romans called 'Gaul on this side of the Alps'). By the first century AD, many of the leading figures came from Spain; in the second, from Africa and in the third from Syria and the Balkans. But, in terms of culture, Rome always took most of her inspiration from

Greece. The Latin poets sometimes claimed that their greatest original-
ity was to introduce some aspects of Greek literature to the Latin
tongue, and even Roman philosophy was, for the most part, Greek
philosophy in Latin. Roman art, similarly, was often no more than the
work of Greek craftsmen, as the murals of Pompeii remind us; and even
its architecture, in design at least, was imitated from Greek originals.
But there were differences. The portrait-bust of the Roman noble was a
new and attractive genre, while the employment of brick and concrete
for imperial buildings – of which the most impressive surviving example is the Pantheon in Rome – was entirely original. Likewise, the
Romans developed a new, narrative style of art to commemorate their
achievements, such as Trajan's column (a sort of lapidary newsreel of
the Dacian wars); and they also developed the art of mosaic decoration

to an astonishingly high standard, as can be seen in the excavated floors of even relatively isolated provincial villas. But undoubtedly Rome's principal achievement in this field lay in engineering: the various Roman roads and bridges (some still carrying traffic in Renaissance times), or the great aqueducts (such as the one at Nîmes, spanning a windswept valley and built of freestone masonry without cement or mortar), are tangible monuments to the skill and vision of the architects and administrators who made them.

Roman civilization, then, spread as an alien, superimposed culture; but it nevertheless made a lasting impact. In central Europe, the frontier of the Roman empire could still be identified by the cultural and linguistic differences still traceable on either side until relatively recently. To the areas it ruled in the west, Rome transmitted the intellectual discoveries made by the Greeks, together with the Christian religion, and the language, laws and literature of the empire. Thus, for example, the English language may not be descended from Latin, yet more than half its vocabulary has grown from Latin roots, and Rome remains the capital of the world-wide organization of the Catholic church, which has existed continuously from Roman times to the present day. Elsewhere the eventual legacy was far less, not least because the East Roman empire of Byzantium ironically survived the violent irruptions of Germanic tribes which destroyed the Western empire, only to be finally eradicated by a new and powerful force: Islam.

The Pont du Gard *top* in southern France combined grace and proportion with useful function. It was built in 19 BC by Roman engineers to carry drinking water, as well as a road, to the nearby city of Nîmes: three tiers of arches, 880 feet long and 155 high, bore the water conduit across the river Gard. Monumental arches were built simply for display, like the Arch of Constantine *above* erected at the entrance to the Forum in Rome c. AD 312 to celebrate the new emperor's victory over his rival Maxentius. The great arch incorporates sculptures and stones from several earlier buildings; it may be that Constantine asserted his claims to the succession by placing this emphasis on historical continuity.

The remarkable Roman road network consolidated power throughout the empire, enabling messages to be carried quickly to remote outposts, and allowing the Roman armies to respond promptly to threats of invasion or insurrection, and carrying a considerable volume of commercial traffic. The Appian Way *right* begun in 312 BC linked the capital with Brindisi, the port which connected Italy with Greece.

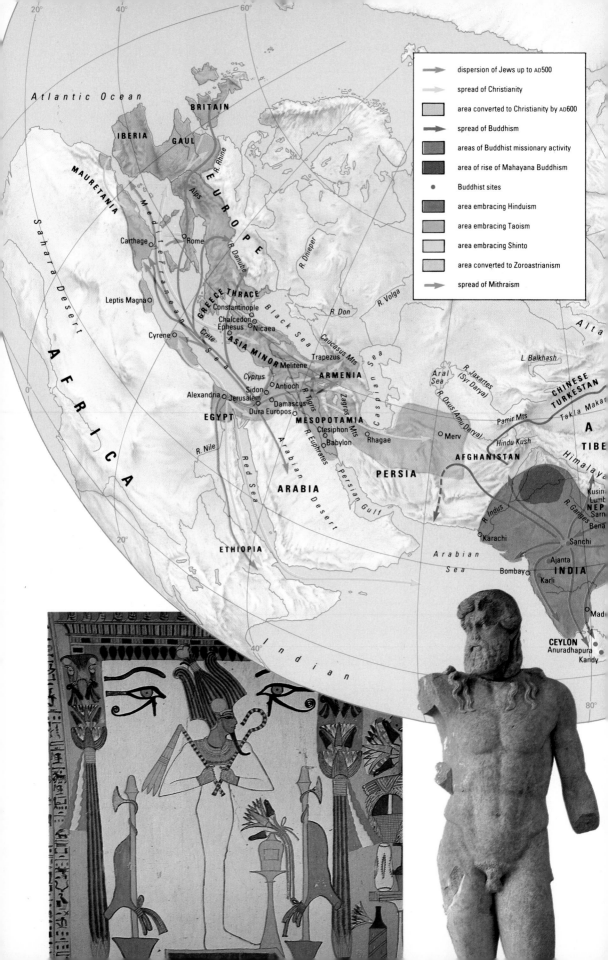

Atlantic Ocean

BRITAIN

IBERIA

GAUL

MAURETANIA

EUROPE

R. Rhine

Alps

R. Danube

Carthage

Rome

Mediterranean Sea

Leptis Magna

GREECE THRACE

Sahara Desert

AFRICA

Cyrene

Crete

Constantinople

Chalcedon

Ephesus Nicaea

ASIA MINOR

Melitene

Cyprus

Sidon

Alexandria Jerusalem

Damascus

Dura Europos

EGYPT

R. Nile

Red Sea

Arabian Desert

Black Sea

Trapezus

Antioch

Caucasus Mts

Zagros Mts

R. Tigris

Ctesiphon

Babylon

ARMENIA

MESOPOTAMIA

R. Euphrates

R. Dnieper

R. Don

R. Volga

Caspian Sea

Aral Sea

R. Jaxartes (Syr Darya)

R. Oxus (Amu-Darya)

Rhagae

Merv

PERSIA

AFGHANISTAN

L. Balkhash

Alta

CHINESE TURKESTAN

Takla Makar

Pamir Mts

Hindu Kush

Himalaya

A

TIBE

Kusin

Lumb

NEP

Sarn

Bena

Sanchi

Ajanta

INDIA

Karli

Bombay

Mad

CEYLON

Anuradhapura

Kandy

ARABIA

ETHIOPIA

Arabian Sea

R. Indus

Karachi

R. Ganges

Persian Gulf

Indian

20°

40°

60°

20°

0°

20°

40°

80°

R. Amur

Sea
of
Japan

Pacific
Ocean

JAPAN

Kyoto
Nara

L. Baikal

KOREA

Kyongju

160°

Gobi Desert

Peking

Wutai Shan

Yellow River

Puto Shan
Tientai Shan
Chiuhua Shan

Wanfohsiu
Tunhwang

CHINA

A

Formosa

140°

R. Yangtze

Omei Shan

S   I   A

PHILIPPINES

South China Sea

Lhasa

R. Brahmaputra

ANNAM

R. Mekong

BURMA

Sukhothai   Angkor

Pagan   Prome
Pegu
Rangoon

SIAM

BORNEO

120°

tta

Bay
of
Bengal

MALAYA

SUMATRA

Borobudur

100°

Ocean

O

The diffusion of world religions *left*.
The development of the great world
religions is frequently associated with the
four riverine civilizations of Egypt,
Mesopotamia, the Indus and the Yellow
River, and expansion generally followed
trade routes. Religions were exported by
traders, soldiers, administrators, and
ordinary travellers, sometimes with a
deliberate missionary purpose, naturally
using the same routes. Buddhism spread
along the coast of south-east Asia and also
by the silk route through central Asia. The
Roman and Chinese empires were points o
attraction, and peaceable governments
helped religious diffusion. Christian
writers claim that the peace brought by
Rome was providentially designed for the
spread of Christianity.

CHAPTER 6

THE WORLD RELIGIONS
600 BC–AD 500

All of the major world religions originated in Asia, and three of them –
Judaism, Christianity and Islam – sprang up in much the same region
and even came to regard the same city (Jerusalem) as holy. Equally
remarkably, several of them were either established or radically reformulated, under the influence of great leaders, at much the same
time: the outstanding prophets and reformers of Hinduism, Buddhism,
Judaism, Confucianism and Taoism all lived in the sixth century BC.

This remarkable concentration in both time and space requires
explanation. After all, the world was not devoid of religions before the
sixth century. On the contrary, every tribe and separate community in
early times seems to have possessed its own hierarchy of deities and
supernatural powers. Some revered spirits – spirits powerful for good
or evil, spirits which inhabited the dark forests that surrounded them,
or the spirits of ancestors. Others, usually in more complex cultures,
worshipped gods and goddesses who were thought to watch over a
particular aspect of human or natural affairs: Osiris, the Egyptian god
who controlled the flooding of the Nile; Aphrodite, the Greek goddess
of love; and so on. But the new religions were different. Most of them
tended to move away from a pantheon of gods and spirits towards the
concept of a single spiritual reality, valid for all mankind. All were also,
to some extent, moral systems: they offered salvation to the righteous

The peoples of the Ancient World each
possessed their own pantheon of gods and
goddesses. The Egyptians believed that
Osiris *far left* was the god of vegetation,
responsible for the annual flooding of the
Nile. He was perpetually opposed by his
brother Seth, represented as a war between
the desert and fertile land and between
darkness and light. The Greeks revered a
more patriarchial hierarchy of deities,
presided over by the Great Zeus *left*, god of
the sky and 'the father of the gods and
men'. In Greek mythology, Zeus is the
father of Athene, Artemis, Apollo, Aries,
Dionysus and innumerable other children.

87

and the good. In primitive religions, the basic concept is power, a power that is usually amoral; in polytheism, the gods are superior to humans (for example, through being immortal), but not necessarily morally better; but in the new religions, the Divine Being acts in rational, intelligible ways that require right conduct from the believer.

Most of these new religions had, or came to have, some association with one of the great empires of the ancient world – Zoroastrianism with the Persian empire of Cyrus and Darius the Great; Buddhism with the Indian empire of Asoka; Confucianism and Taoism with China under the Chou dynasty; Christianity with the later Roman empire – and the reason for this can only be guessed at. Perhaps as powerful states grew, embracing not only larger areas but also many disparate peoples and customs, a need developed for a broader and more sophisticated system of belief and behaviour than the legion of different tribal gods could provide. Be that as it may, the transition from a multitude of local polytheistic cults to half-a-dozen universalist religions seems to have been the work of only a handful of remarkable reformers; in Persia, Zarathustra (or Zoroaster); in India, Mahavira and Gautama Siddhartha; in China, K'ung Fu-tzu (or Confucius, as he is known in the West) and Lao-tzu; and, among the people of Israel, a nameless prophet who is called the second (or Deutero) Isaiah.

Little is known – in some cases practically nothing – about these men personally; but it seems likely that all were reacting to the tensions of their age, to the oppression and extortion of the great warring

Zoroastrianism, named after the prophet Zoroaster, was the state religion of three successive Persian empires, the Achaemenid, Parthian and Sassanian. Zoroaster has been called the first monotheist, teaching that Ahura Mazda the 'wise lord' and 'the Creator of all things by the Holy Spirit' embodied ultimate good, eternally opposed by Angra Mainyu the spirit of ultimate evil. Man was free to choose between good and evil, and if he chose righteousness he would be rewarded. In their emphasis on the idea of heaven and hell, resurrection and final judgement, the teachings of Zoroaster had a profound influence on later religions – Judaism, Christianity and Islam. In a sculpture from Persepolis, *bottom left*, Ahura Mazda is shown as a venerable bearded figure with symmetical wings and a bird's tail. He is presenting the emperor Ardashir I with his diadem, thereby strengthening his claim to be the legitimate successor to the throne. Ahura Mazda's horse tramples Angra Mainyu, whose malignant features are shown on the gold medallion, *right*.

empires with their armies and their tax-gatherers, which exposed the inadequacy of the old beliefs and traditions. They were all at work independently, in widely separated regions; but it was their common sense of frustration, their search for a new synthesis, that gave birth to the various new faiths.

Zoroaster, of whom virtually nothing is known (estimates of his dates vary from 1800 to 500 BC), was the author of a rigorous intellectual creed which, under Darius the Great (521-486), became the official religion of the Persian empire. Zoroaster's message, expressed in old Iranian texts known as the *Gathas*, was highly abstract. He saw life as a battleground between the forces of light and order, represented by a supreme, incorporeal and universal deity, Ahura Mazda (The Wise Lord), locked in continual conflict with Angra Mainyu (The Adversary), malign and ignorant. On the side of Ahura Mazda were the powers of light, the sun and fire; those who followed his precepts would attain immortality. The obdurate, however, would on the Day of Judgement be smitten by a bolt from heaven.

Although today only the Parsees of India and a few believers in Iran still follow the teachings of Zoroaster, before the rise of Islam they commanded a far larger following. Apart from successive Persian dynasties down to the Sassanians, all of whom made Zoroastrianism their state religion, the cult spawned imitators and offshoots, some of which spread far and wide in the later Roman empire in the form of Mithraism. Altars to Mithras, erected by imperial soldiers, have been found from Hadrian's wall in northern England to frontier outposts in Germany, as well as in the Near East and North Africa. The teachings of Zoroaster also had a marked impact upon the religion of the Jews after their Temple in Jerusalem was destroyed, and they were sent to weep by the waters of Babylon by King Nebuchadnezzar in 586 BC. Later Judaism, and Christianity after it, saw the struggle between good and evil, as well as the symbolic figures of angels and demons and the promise of a Last Judgement, in much the same terms as Zoroaster.

Judaism, however, was affected by the Babylonian captivity in other ways. That it was a monotheistic faith was made clear by the famous Covenant of Moses with Yahweh (Jehovah, or God), after the Exodus from Egypt: 'Thou shalt have no other gods before me...for I the Lord thy God am a jealous God'. But in its early phase, it was also an exclusive religion: the tribal or national cult of the people of Israel, with an ethical code enshrined in the Torah or Law (including the familiar Ten Commandments) and a sacred centre in the Temple of Jerusalem. But when the Jews were carried off into exile, they lost touch with Jerusalem, and therefore with the Temple, its priests and its ritual; and although they were permitted to return in 538, and some did so, others remained behind in Babylon. Furthermore, the religious leaders who sustained the faith in exile – particularly the unknown prophet who wrote the *Book of Isaiah*, chapters 40-59 – interpreted the traditional teachings in new ways, switching the emphasis from observance and sacrifice to morality and right conduct. Through his words, God called on His people to loose the fetters of injustice, free the oppressed, share food with the hungry, and clothe the naked. This was the way to appease Jehovah and win salvation: temples and sacrifices were no longer essential.

Judaism thus emerged from the crucible of exile and affliction as a powerful moral force. It also lost some of its exclusiveness: Jehovah was no longer just the god of the Jews. The Jews might still be the people chosen by Him for special purposes, but Jehovah was the Lord of all mankind. As He said to Israel, 'I will make you a light to the nations, so that my salvation may reach to the earth's farthest bounds'. Thus, as a Jewish scholar has said, 'nationalism merged into universalism and religion became a matter of righteous living rather than of ritual practice'.

The ritual of early Hebrew religion, in the period building up to the first century AD, centred on temple worship, and sacrifice. Sacifices were conducted in the open air on stone altars *left* which were considered to represent the deity. In the 7th century BC, King Josiah abolished these altars (high places) and decreed that sacrifices should only be offered in the central sanctuary at Jerusalem. With the destruction of the second temple in AD 70, the sacrificial cult was abandoned, and there was a shift in emphasis towards communal synagogue worship.

Scenes from the life of Christ are frequently portrayed in Christian art, as in this ivory book cover *left* commissioned for the Bishop of Metz in 855. The best-preserved artefacts from the Carolingian period (c. 768-900) are ivories and illuminated manuscripts, which are amongst the first masterpieces of Medieval Christian art.

The Last Supper is frequently portrayed in Christian art either as a factual representation, or with a symbolic emphasis placed on the sacramental nature of the event. In this wall painting (c.1200) *below* from the rock-cut church of Karanlik Kilise in Turkey, the scene is treated symbolically – the fish is a common early Christian symbol used to represent Christ. It was not until the 15th century that the eucharistic interpretation of the scene becomes explicit with the appearance of the chalice and wafer.

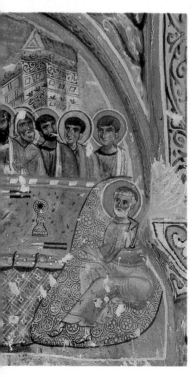

The Babylonian exile, and the sack of Jerusalem, thus helped Judaism to become a world religion. Though it was not such a proselytizing or missionary faith as, say, Buddhism, there were nevertheless converts; and by the end of the first century BC, communities of Jews were to be found throughout the Mediterranean world. But then, in 64 BC, Judaea was overrun by the Romans and, before long, religious, political and nationalist tensions threatened to make the province ungovernable. Several protest movements grew up – some of them withdrawn and ascetic, such as the Essenes; others militantly political, such as the Zealots. This was the backcloth for a new faith: Christianity.

When, some time between AD 27 and 30, Jesus of Nazareth began to preach that 'the kingdom of God is at hand', it was a message for which many Jews were anxiously waiting. After the Babylonian exile, Messianism (the expectation of an 'anointed' Deliverer and Ruler) had become part of the Jewish faith; and, for his followers, Jesus was indeed seen as the Messiah, Liberator or Saviour, whose coming the prophets had foretold. But after an initial, short-lived success, Jesus's popular following declined; and three years after his ministry began, he was seized by the Jewish authorities, who were frightened of possible disorder and its consequences, and handed over to the Roman governor, Pontius Pilate, who had him crucified as a revolutionary. Even his closest disciples were discouraged; but their faith was restored when two days later (and on a number of other occasions over the next few weeks), they experienced the presence of Jesus, apparently resurrected from the dead. Now they began to proclaim Jesus as Messiah (in the Greek, 'Christ') and Lord, and invited their hearers to repent, be baptized, receive forgiveness and, with it, the spirit of God.

At this stage Christianity was still exclusively a Jewish cult, and it was to their fellow Jews that the disciples initially addressed

The Early Christian churches *below*.
Starting with the journeys of St. Paul in
Greece and Anatolia, Christian churches
sprang up throughout the Roman world. By
the time of the Roman emperor
Diocletian's persecutions (304), they were
thickly clustered around the
Mediterranean, and scattered as far apart
as Britain and the Nile.

North Sea

Atlantic Ocean

Mediterranean Sea

Armagh
Down
Eburacum
Lindum
Cashel
Louth
Verulamium
Trajectum
Ardmore
Bancorna
Colonia Agrippina
Cloyne
Menevia
Legionum
Augusta Treverorum
Llandaff
Urbs
Cantuaria
Parisii
Remi
Rotomagus
Civitas Senonum
Turones
Bituricae
Augstodunum
Andegavum
Lugdunum
Vesontio
Aguntum
Poetovio
Pictavi
Mediolanim
Grado
Emona
Aquileia
Trieste
Sirmium
Valentia
Augusta
Ravenna
Burdigala
Arausio
Taurinorum
Ariminum
Salonae
Ratiaria
Nemausus
Vasio
Florentia
Naissus
Telosa
Biterrae
Reii
Scodra
Scupi
Marcianopolis
Arelate
Massilia
Pisa
Stobi
Serdica
Adrianopolis
Caesaraugusta
Narbo
Pons Milvius
Amphispolis
Apollonia
Constant.
Asturica
Barcino
Rome
Thessalonica
Neapolis
381
Puteoli
Beroea
Cyzicus
Bracara
Carales
Neapolis
Larisa
Troas
Lampsacus
Assos
Pergamun
Vivarium
Nicopolis
Mytilene
Thyatira
Toletum
Messina
Chois
Smyrna
Sardes
Olisipo
Corduba
Hippo
Carthage
Rhegium
Athens
Ephesus
Philadel
Illiberris
Regius
Syracusa
Corinth
Samos
Miletus
Laodic
Hispalis
Carthago
Milev
Melita
Cos
Nova
Tipasa
Cirta
Sicca
Rhodes
Tingis
Veneria
Gortyna
Sabrata
Oea
Leptis Magna
Ptolemais
Cyrene
Ale
Berenice

areas strongly Christian by 325

areas largely Christian by 600

○ sites of churches founded by 600

▲ patriarchate

■ archbishopric

● bishopric

Jerusalem *left* is a unique holy city, held in special veneration by three of the world's main religions, Judaism, Christianity and Islam. In c.1000 BC it became capital of the small kingdom of Israel under King David, and the First Temple was built under his son Solomon. The inhabitants of Jerusalem were taken into captivity by the Babylonian king Nebuchadnezzar in 586 BC, but were restored to freedom by Cyrus, the Persian emperor, in 537 BC, and the Second Temple was built there in 516 BC. In AD 67-70, when a revolt against the occupying Roman army was brutally suppressed, the Temple was destroyed and part of it – the Wailing Wall – remains an object of Jewish veneration today. Christ was crucified by the Roman governor, Pontius Pilate, at Jerusalem, and the Church of the Holy Sepulchre sanctifies the place of his entombment, and has become an object of Christian pilgrimage. The Koran refers to a journey made by the prophet, Mohammed, to Solomon's temple, and the Dome of the Rock was built on this site in AD 691 by the Caliph Abdul al-Malik, ensuring that, for Muslims too, this would remain a holy place of pilgrimage. The photograph shows the Dome of the Rock in the centre, below it the Wailing Wall and, in the top right, the Garden of Gethsemane.

themselves. They met with some hostility from the authorities and, in the event, most converts in Judaea were wiped out by Roman forces after a Jewish rebellion in AD 70. But by then the Christians, as they came to be called, had reached out to non-Jews. The process began with Paul, a Hellenized Jew from the city of Tarsus in Asia Minor, formerly a persecutor of Christians. His missionary journeys – to Anatolia, to Greece and eventually to Rome – were a turning-point in the history of Christianity. Paul denied that Jesus was sent merely to redeem the Jews; rather, he preached, a loving Father had sent his only Son to atone for the sins of all mankind. Christianity was henceforth not merely a Jewish sect: the Church of Christ was a community for Gentiles as well as for Jews.

Paul's message found a responsive audience. Everywhere people were longing for a Saviour, but few were willing to accept the ritual obligations of Judaism (particularly circumcision). Now, converts to Christianity did not have to conform to Jewish law: faith in Christ leading to a reformed life as a member of a Christian community was enough. The result, of course, was a breach with Judaism; but it was a breach that opened the new faith to millions of Gentiles. By severing its ties with Judaism, Christianity became a world religion, spreading throughout the Roman empire in spite of intermittent persecution. But it was not confined to Roman dominions alone. Although it is hard to credit a Christian mission (supposedly led by St Thomas) to India in the first century, there was certainly expansion to Armenia, Assyria and Persia, and the Goths and Vandals from central Europe were already evangelized before they overran the Roman empire. But the principal stronghold of Christianity still lay within the Mediterranean basin and the Near East.

A major turning-point came when the Roman emperor Constantine, in AD 312, not merely granted the Christians toleration but furthered their cause in other ways. By 392, Christianity had become the state religion of the Roman empire, and all rival cults were suppressed. The

93

The Hindu religion, enshrined in the sacred Vedas, recognises over 3 million deities ranging from village-gods and cults to the two major gods, Vishnu – frequently worshipped as Krishna or Rama – and Shiva. Vishnu *left* is the pillar of the universe, the eternal and omnipresent spirit. With his many arms he stands for motion and pervasiveness. Siva *right* represents the unpredictable side of divinity and emphasizes the transitory nature of this world. He is known as 'the destroyer' and, in this Mughal miniature of c.1570, he spears with his flaming lance the demon Andhaka. Kali Ma, the black mother, is the most fierce and bloodthirsty form assumed by Siva's consort, although she is also venerated as the mother goddess. She is shown *below* naked to the hips, with a necklace of skulls, and a girdle of two rows of human hands. She holds the head of a giant.

faith that had once been the preserve of humble people now became an organized church with an elaborate hierarchy closely identified with the Roman state, and its predominance in the Mediterranean area would continue until Islam, the last of the global religions, burst upon the world in the seventh century (chapter 8).

The basic elements of the religion called Hinduism, which today has some 530 million Indian followers, can first be detected with the arrival of the Aryan invaders in India around 1500 BC (chapter 4). But it was not until some time afterwards that the Sanskrit religious verses known as the *Vedas* were composed, giving Hinduism its distinctive devotional formulae; and not until almost a millennium later that the notion of caste established the fundamental social patterns which have shaped life in India ever since.

Hindus worship a number of gods, the most important of whom are Vishnu and Shiva. Vishnu has many incarnations, including the heroes Rama and Krishna; Shiva is both the destroyer and the yogi; and Shiva's wife, the mother goddess, also appears both as the gentle Parvati and the fierce Kali. Hindu society is strictly divided into hereditary social classes, or castes. It is believed that the caste system owes its origin to a fourfold division of society which originated in the body of the creator, Brahma: the Brahmans, or priestly and learned class, from Brahma's mouth; the Kshatriyas, noblemen and soldiers, from his arms; the Vaisyas, farmers and merchants, from his thighs; and the Sudras, peasants and labourers, from his feet. Those outside this caste system were known as the 'Untouchables'. Through a series of reincarnations, a soul may improve its position by means of right actions or *karma*, or lower it for lack of them.

Thus, many cults with widely differing practices exist within the faith side by side. As well as worshipping a number of gods, Hinduism

offers various approaches to the ultimate – through physical discipline, knowledge, personal devotion, good works, or contemplative discipline. Always more than a religion, it is a complete way of life.

But in the sixth century BC, at least, it was not a faith without critics. Mahavira and Gautama Siddhartha, two of the most important reformers of Hinduism, were both noblemen by birth. Both were alienated by the suffering and distress they saw about them, and both abandoned their wealth and position in society in favour of poverty and an itinerant life. Mahavira was the founder of the religion we call Jainism, a rigorously ascetic creed – so ascetic, indeed, that its following was always limited. Nevertheless there are a million Jains living in western India today, and Mahavira's central doctrine of non-violence (or *ahimsa*) to both men and animals was later adopted by Hinduism, and exercised a powerful influence on (for example) the life and works of Mahatma Gandhi.

The influence of Gautama, a Kshatriya Hindu born in about 563 BC in north-east India, and known to posterity as the Buddha or 'the Enlightened One', spread far wider than that of Mahavira. He preached that all life is suffering; that all suffering comes from desire; and that the way to destroy suffering is therefore to end desire through improved attitudes and actions. Unlike other religions, the Buddha's message did not centre upon a god, but rather upon deliverance from suffering and the

The Jains of western India believe that release from the endless cycle of death and rebirth can be achieved by a righteous and ascetic devotion to enlightenment. A reformed Hindu cult, a fundamental tenet of Jainism is the belief that souls are trapped in all matter – even winds, stones and fire – and they are devoted to ideals of non-violence. Strict vegetarians, devout Jains must carry a small brush as they walk along the road to remove insects before they are crushed beneath their feet, and even wear veils to avoid killing a fly by accidentally swallowing it. Mahavira, the founder of the sect, is thought to be a contemporary of the Buddha. In this 18th century icon, punched into a brass plate, a just man's spirit is released.

**Buddhism is one of the great
missionary religions**, practised widely
throughout southern Asia and the Far East.
When, in c. 1st century AD, a division in
Buddhist teaching and practice developed,
the more conservative Theravada tradition
spread to Burma, Thailand and Ceylon,
while the Mahayana tradition – more open
to local cults and beliefs, spread throughout
China, Tibet, Mongolia, Korea, Japan, and
Indochina. The Buddha is usually
represented as looking like the inhabitants
of the country in which he is revered;
although all the images hold certain
features in common – for example the hand
positions (*mudras*) which are used to
show whether the Buddha is meditating,
giving his blessing, subduing the forces of
evil, or teaching. When Buddhism reached
Afghanistan, an Indo-Hellenistic tradition
developed, Gandharan, which has many
recognizably western characteristics such
as this carved figure of a preaching Buddha
from Hoti-Mardan, *right*, and the carved
Gandharan pediment *below* (c.2nd century
AD).

The impressive city of Angkor in Cambodia, capital of the Khmer empire between the 9th and 13th centuries, represents an interesting fusion between Hindu and Buddhist beliefs. The Hindu religion was probably brought to the Khmer by Indian traders, and originally Angkor was an eloquent monument to Hinduism – the temple of Angkor Wat (c.1113-1150), the largest and best-preserved, is adorned with many thousands of feet of continual bas-relief showing narratives from the Hindu Myths of Vishnu, Rama and Krishna. However, when in 1177, Angkor was attacked by a vassal state, the Khmer king Jayavarman II rejected the religion that had abandoned him to ill-fortune, and dedicated his main capital Angkor Thom to the Buddhist faith. When the Khmer dynasty ended in the 16th century, even Angkor Wat, dedicated to Vishnu, became a Buddhist shrine *centre right*.

attainment of *Nirvana* – the blessed state reached when the flame of desire has been totally extinguished.

Ever since Gautama's death in 483 BC, his teachings have been kept alive by followers who live together in monastic communities. But it was the conversion in about 257 BC of Asoka, the greatest of the Mauryan emperors of India – moved (as he himself said) by remorse at the slaughter and misfortune he had caused – that made Buddhism into a major force. In edicts inscribed on rocks and pillars scattered throughout India, Asoka spread the Buddhist virtues of compassion, tolerance and respect for all forms of life; and it was under his rule that Buddhism began its missionary vocation, eventually spreading in the form known as Theravada, conservative and traditionalist, to Sri Lanka, Burma and Thailand. Equally important was the diffusion of the new faith northwards to the Kushan kingdom (in modern Afghanistan), for here and in India a new form of Buddhism took shape, known as Mahayana (meaning 'the Great Vehicle', which would bear all mankind to salvation). Mahayana Buddhism was more open to popular practices and local beliefs: one of its distinctive features was the *bodhisattvas*,

semi-divine beings who could help ordinary mortals to salvation and
eternal life. This innovation gave a great impetus to Buddhism, which
now spread rapidly through central Asia, reaching China in the first
century AD and moving on from there to Korea in the fourth century
and to Japan in the sixth (chapter 12).

The early peoples of China had practised ancestor cults and worshipped nature spirits. K'ung Fu-tzu, or Confucius, born in 551 BC, did
not doubt the reality of this traditional spiritual world; but his principal
concern was with the conduct of Man. Confucianism was not so much a
religion as an ethical code which was concerned with propriety in
human relations, based on love and respect for one's fellows. 'If you do
not know about the living', wrote Confucius, 'how can you know about
the dead?' Born at a time when the Chou empire was beginning to
disintegrate, Confucius's reactions sprang from the same concern with
the disorders and injustices of his day – how can a good man live well
in a wicked world? – that inspired his Indian contemporaries, Gautama
and Mahavira. Confucius was concerned to show that to be a gentleman, one of those upon whom the burden of administration rested, was

Confucius (551-479 BC) *above* came from an impoverished noble family and served for a time as a government accountant and administrator before he became a teacher after 517 BC. Thereafter his informal school achieved fame by teaching ethics, history, literature and statecraft to all who aspired to be civil servants, and the philosopher emphasized the need for government to act through moral example and persuasion rather than by force. A man who lives according to Confucian standards is a *chün-tzu* or gentleman, unlike the small man, or knave, who rejects these values. Good-manners, education, moral rectitude – all these attributes, Confucius believed, could be found in members of any class, and were not conferred by birth. Hence the examination system, through which the bureaucracy was recruited, was open to all classes; Confucius had opened a gate by which any low-born young man could obtain high office with ability and hard work.

a matter not of birth but of training. In the second century BC, Confucianism was declared the official ideology of the empire, and so it remained until the fall of the Manchu dynasty, more than 2000 years later, in 1911. But it was always an upper-class code, with limited popular appeal. Too much was left out, such as the mysteries of nature and the depths of human passion. These could be found in Taoism.

This ancient creed was founded upon a book, the *Tao-te-ching* (The Way-Power Book), in which the essence of the Tao, 'the Way', is explained in parables and metaphors. It is attributed to Lao-tzu, a shadowy contemporary of Confucius, supposedly a civil servant at the Chou court who, despairing at the anarchy and corruption about him, abandoned his job and went off alone into the distant countryside. Taoism later became a more complex system, including demons and magic; but there was nothing of that about Lao-tzu's teachings. His is a call to virtue by following the way of the universe, without ulterior motive, selfish purpose, or ambition, in order to live in harmony with 'the Way' in humility and passivity. There are obvious parallels here with the teaching of the Buddha, and also with the later ideas of Christianity. But unlike Christianity, Taoism did not offer the consolation of an after-life.

The impact of these few religious leaders was indeed remarkable. Although all of them set out merely to be reformers – seeking to purify and update traditional religions rather than to create new ones – in fact they presented mankind with a different type of faith. For they offered salvation. At first it was reserved for the righteous, but in time the great missionary creeds – Buddhism and Christianity – also began to press that salvation upon those who did not initially see the need for it so that, contrary to all that their founders had willed and believed, religions conceived in love and peace became a source of discord and conflict. The phase of proselytizing, however, did not occur within the lifetime of those founders: rather it arose in subsequent periods of exceptional upheaval and uncertainty. Thus Buddhism made its greatest progress in China during the chaotic period when the Han empire was collapsing; and the advance of Christianity in the Roman empire increased in step with the disastrous setbacks – inflation, civil war, extortionate taxation – which set in after about AD 250. They coincided, in short, with the calamitous end of the ancient world which swept away the great empires but left the religions relatively intact.

Lao-tzu *below* is thought to have been a contemporary of Confucius, and the *Tao Te Ching*, the most important Taoist philosophical text is ascribed to him. Compiled in around the 4th century BC, it expounds in a series of aphoristic sayings the concept of the *tao* or way. *Tao* was the fundamental base of all being – to become united with *tao* the disciple must strive for a state of *wu-wei* (non-being), emptying himself of all worldly desires and intentions through silence and tranquillity. A new attitude to nature became apparent during this period; *wu-wei* could be reached by 'folding one's hands in silence amidst the mountains and forests' and Chinese paintings reflect the awe and tranquillity which man can achieve confronted by the sublime beauty of Nature. In the Taoist landscape painting *right* humans and their dwellings are dwarfed by the majesty of the landscape.

Immense quantities of raw materials and finished goods were transported by sea and river in the Roman empire. Transport by road was much more expensive, and the costs became prohibitive over long distances. Goods and commodities transported in great bulk included grain from Egypt which was exported from Sicily and North Africa to Rome under the direction of the emperor's own agents, stone and marble for public buildings, wine and pottery. Not only traders prospered; those engaged in the provision of ships and waggons also benefited from more extensive trading contacts. This 1st-century AD wall painting *left* from the Roman spa and summer resort at Stabiae, on the bay of Naples, shows the lighthouse, the quays and the bustle of a typical busy Roman harbour under the *Pax Romana*.

Atlantic Ocean

Picts and Scots attack Hadrian's Wall

451 Huns withdraw from Gaul
452 Huns invade Italy
453 death of Attila, retreat of Huns

Hadrian's Wall

ANGLES, SAXONS, JUTES

562 Avars invade Frankish lands

from 370 Goths displaced by Huns, settle in West Roman empire

GERMANY

EUROPE

Alps

ITALY

Rome

601 Avars defeated by Byzantines

North African limes

Carthage

Constantinople

Black Sea

370 Black Huns appear in Europe

R. Don

R. Volga

Ural Mts.

R. Ob

R. Yenisey

R. Lena

L. Baik

ASIA

550 Juan-juan (Avars) driven westwards out of Mongolia by Blue (Celestial) Turks

L. Balkhash

SINKIANG

M

Aral Sea

R. Jaxartes (Syr Darya)

Athens

ASIA MINOR

Anatolia

Mediterranean Sea

Berbers, attack Roman empire in north Africa

Syrian limes

R. Tigris

R. Euphrates

Zagros Mts

Caspian Sea

R. Oxus (Amu Darya)

Takla Makan

1st century AD Hsiungnu broken by Han China and move westwards

Hindu Kush

Kabul

expansion of Tibetans

TIBET

Himalayas

Alexandria

EGYPT

Ctesiphon

484 White Huns (Ephthalites) kill Sassanian emperor, but Persian empire survives.

PERSIA

R. Indus

Mathura

Pataliputra

R. Ganges

Sahara Desert

R. Nile

AFRICA

Red Sea

Persian Gulf

480 White Huns destroy Gupta empire

Arabian Desert

INDIA

Indian Ocean

40

80°

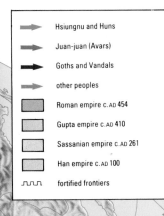

The collapse of the ancient world, *below*. All the great civilizations of the classical world came under pressure from the barbarian peoples of northern and central Europe and from pastoral nomads who formed confederacies of mobile cavalry armies. The most dramatic fall was that of the Roman empire in the west, but China north of the river Yangtze was equally devastated. Persia was weakened, and Gupta rule in India collapsed.

→	Hsiungnu and Huns
→	Juan-juan (Avars)
→	Goths and Vandals
→	other peoples
▨	Roman empire C. AD 454
▨	Gupta empire C. AD 410
▨	Sassanian empire C. AD 261
▨	Han empire C. AD 100
⌐⌐⌐	fortified frontiers

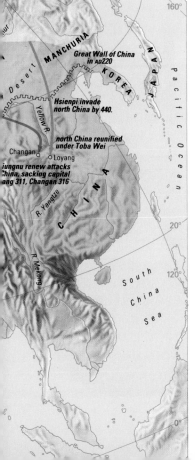

CHAPTER 7

THE END OF THE ANCIENT WORLD
AD100–600

Two thousand years ago, about the time of Christ, a continuous web of complex, advanced societies stretched across the southern half of the continents of Europe and Asia. In the west, Rome had imposed its rule and imprint on the whole Mediterranean world from Asia Minor, through North Africa and southern Europe, to the Strait of Gibraltar, and was in the process of further extending its dominion beyond the Alps and Pyrenees to the Rhine, the Danube and Britain. The whole structure was integrated by an imposing network of roads, and communications by sea and river. Meanwhile in China, the Han ruled a state that equalled the Roman empire in population and territorial extent. Just as Julius Caesar and Augustus had carried Roman power far to the north, so the Chinese emperor Wu-ti in the first century BC had carried the power of the Han dynasty to the Tarim Basin of central Asia, far to the west. Separating these two superpowers were two other important states: the Kushan empire, which straddled the mountain passes of Afghanistan and extended south into the Punjab and northern India; and the Parthian empire, which dominated Persia and Mesopotamia.

The existence – or rather the co-existence – of these great empires meant that vast areas of the Old World enjoyed internal peace and efficient government, conditions which made possible the growth of trade on a scale never seen before. For the most part it was internal trade, between one province and another. In the west, for example, Italy supplied wine, pottery, oil and metalware to Spain, Gaul, Britain and the western Balkans. But there was also long-distance trade by land and sea. China was famous for its export of silk. India produced large quantities of textiles (calico, muslin, linen and cotton) for both domestic and foreign markets; other exports included pepper, spices, ivory and precious stones. In return, gold and silver, mostly in coins, moved eastwards from the Roman empire; also clothing, wine, glass, coral and metals. In between, on the land routes, the Kushan and Parthian empires both fostered this interchange – maintaining and garrisoning the roads, protecting the caravans, and thriving on the tolls. By the second century AD, trade routes covered Eurasia.

Of special importance was the so-called Silk Road, stretching for 2,500 miles across inner Asia. From the Han capital of Changan, the route proceeded north-west to the frontier town of Tunhwang. This was the starting point of the 'Silk Road', a series of caravanserais dotted through arid deserts and windswept mountains until the convoy reached Kushan territory at Merv. From there it ran south of the Caspian Sea, through Parthia and the Roman empire, to the shores of the Mediterranean. As its name implies, the main traffic along this route was Chinese silk, which probably comprised 90 percent of China's

Extensive commercial and cultural links *right* between the major classical civilizations of Eurasia have been traced by archaeological finds. The picture revealed is one of complex international relations: the major sea routes (often determined by monsoon patterns) and overland routes, such as the Silk Road linking Loyang in China with Merv in northern Persia, were the conduits for commerce and the exchange of ideas. At times they proved less beneficial, for example when major infectious diseases were spread by travellers. Nevertheless, the extensive disruption of the overland routes during the 4th and 5th centuries AD dealt a catastrophic blow to the ancient world, and inaugurated a period of regional dislocation and isolation.

— trade route

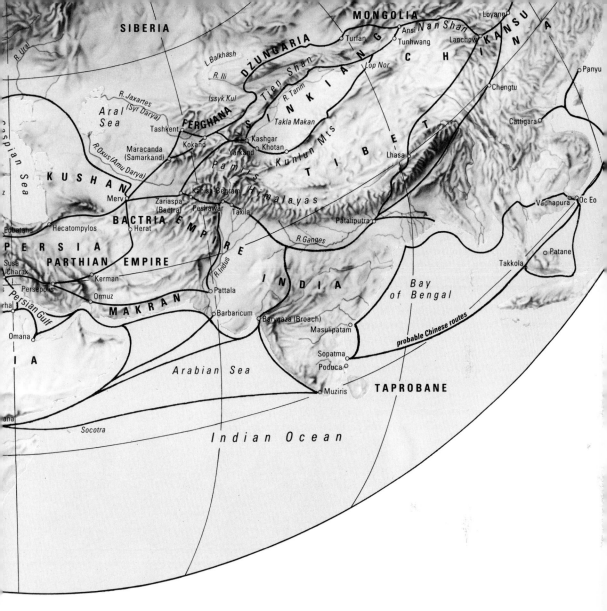

The following place names and labels appear on the map:

SIBERIA · MONGOLIA · *Nan Shan* · Loyang · Ansi · Turfan · Tunhwang · Lanchow · KANSU · CHINA · DZUNGARIA · L.Balkhash · R.Ili · R.Tarim · Lop Nor · Panyu · R.Jaxartes (Syr Darya) · *Aral Sea* · Issyk Kul · Tien Shan · SINKIANG · Chengtu · FERGHANA · Tashkent · Kashgar · Takla Makan · Cattigara · Maracanda (Samarkand) · Kokand · Khotan · Kunlun Mts · R.Oxus (Amu Darya) · Yarkand · Pamirs · T I B E T · Lhasa · KUSHAN · Merv · Kapisa·Begram · Himalayas · Vadhapura · Oc Eo · Zariaspa (Bactra) · Peshawar · Taxila · *Caspian Sea* · BACTRIA · EMPIRE · Pataliputra · Hecatompylos · Herat · R.Ganges · Patane · Ecbatana · R.Indus · P E R S I A · Lhasa · Takkola · PARTHIAN EMPIRE · I N D I A · Bay of Bengal · Susa · Charax · Kerman · Persepolis · Ormuz · MAKRAN · Pattala · Masulipatam · Omana · Barbaricum · Barygaza (Broach) · *probable Chinese routes* · I A · *Arabian Sea* · Sopatma · Poduca · Socotra · Muziris · TAPROBANE · *Indian Ocean*

The dhow *left* with its distinctive lateen sail, has been the traditional sailing vessel of the Indian Ocean from the legendary days of Sinbad until the present. Due to its simple rigging it requires a relatively small crew and can carry a large payload of either passengers or cargo, as this illustration from a Baghdad manuscript of 1238 shows. The boat shown here is steered by a stern-post rudder, which was invented in China in the 1st century AD, at about the same time as the magnetic compass. Both inventions spread only slowly westwards, being adopted firstly by Arab traders, and then passed by them to the Europeans.

exports at this time and was much prized in Rome, where the secrets of silk manufacture were still unknown.

Nevertheless, the overland trails were in general not as important as the sea routes. On the one hand, the rudimentary and very expensive nature of land transport (largely restricted to mules, camels and oxen was a severe handicap: it was cheaper, for example, to ship grain right across the Mediterranean than to carry it fifty or sixty miles inland. On the other, any overland itinerary obviously depended upon political stability along the way, and in fact the collapse of the Kushan empire in the third century AD fatally disrupted the Silk Road. But, by that time, long-distance travel by sea had been revolutionized by the discovery of the cycle of monsoon winds in the Indian Ocean. Instead of hugging the coasts, mariners found they could sail rapidly and directly from India to Arabia in the winter months, and back again just as speedily in the summer. Egypt was now only four months away from India, and by the first century AD over 100 ships, some of them with a carrying capacity of 500 tons, were regularly exploiting the monsoons to ply between the Red Sea and the mouth of the Indus. The centre for the redistribution of oriental goods in the west was Alexandria, a city of perhaps 700,000 inhabitants by the third century AD, when the disruption of the Silk Road made it the principal centre of east-west trade and the second most important city in the Roman empire.

The effects of these far-flung trading links were not merely commercial. They also resulted in significant cultural interactions. Thousands of people – sailors, camel-drivers, merchants, porters – made a living by travelling through the bazaars of Asia, from China to the Caspian Sea and from southern India to Syria. Some of them came from the West, for it is known from Indian sources that a few Greek and Syrian merchants settled permanently in Gujerat; but only rarely did they venture further. Oriental wares, mainly silks and spices, were normally bought in the Far East by Indian merchants, who then shipped them to the port-cities of western India where they were purchased by European traders. It is impossible to estimate their number, but their impact is clear enough: the transplantation of Indian civilization to the maritime areas of south-east Asia, and the formation there of the first organized states, Khmer and Champa on the mainland and Srivijaya in Sumatra, was in large part the work of Indian merchants. The trade routes were also the vehicle for the expansion of the great missionary religions (chapter 6): Buddhism spread from India towards the Far East; Christianity was implanted in southern India (the so-called 'Church of Saint Thomas') and in central Asia (the Nestorian church).

Thus by about AD 100, economically advanced and relatively prosperous societies stretched from China across to the Atlantic seaboard, directly linked by a complex chain of commercial and cultural interchange. Yet, four centuries later, almost all of the major civilizations – West Rome, Han China, Parthia, Kushan – were in ruins, and the transcontinental trade was at an end.

Borobudur in Java *below* was one of the many magnificent temples erected in the Indonesian archipelago by its Buddhist rulers. Built between AD 750 and 850, of dark grey volcanic stone, the large square base bears six smaller square terraces, with receding levels rather like a stepped pyramid. Each is decorated with intricate panels in the bas-relief showing aspects of the Buddha's life and teaching. In addition, some 500 images of the Buddha are included in niches around the terraces or in the *stupas* on top. The magnificent complex seems to have been abandoned about AD 1000, perhaps because subsidence damaged the structure, and it remained overgrown with vegetation until restored by Dutch archaeologists in 1907-11.

Gandhara occupied a strategic position on the upper Indus and successively formed part of the empires of Achaemenid Persia, Hellenistic Greece under Alexander the Great and Mauryan India. Its craftsmen and artists were thus open to both Hellenistic and Buddhist influences. Greek imports such as metalwork, coins and even sculpture, may have aided the spread of western styles in the representation of the human figure. Whether western artists and craftsmen found their way to the Indus valley is not certain, but by no means impossible. As part of the Kushan empire, in the 1st and 2nd centuries AD, Gandhara craftsmen produced a rich variety of sculptures of the Buddha *right* in a distinctively Greco-Roman style. This figure, carved from grey-blue mica schist, was originally painted and gilded.

武皇帝劉秀

The Han emperor Wu-ti (140-87 BC) *left*, whose title means 'the martial emperor', was a man accustomed to command. The ruler of some 59 million subjects, he extended Chinese power into Asia and strengthened the empire's defences against its nomadic neighbours to the west.

The light horseman *below* was one of the most dangerous enemies of the empires of Rome and Han China. Mounted on a small but sturdy steppe horse, armed with a lance (or more effectively with a composite bow) and protected by a simple leather jerkin, such riders formed fast-moving skirmishing detachments which could harry and cut off slower-moving imperial infantry, proved more agile and ingenious than the imperial heavy cavalry, and *en masse* could deliver lightning attacks against unsuspecting cities.

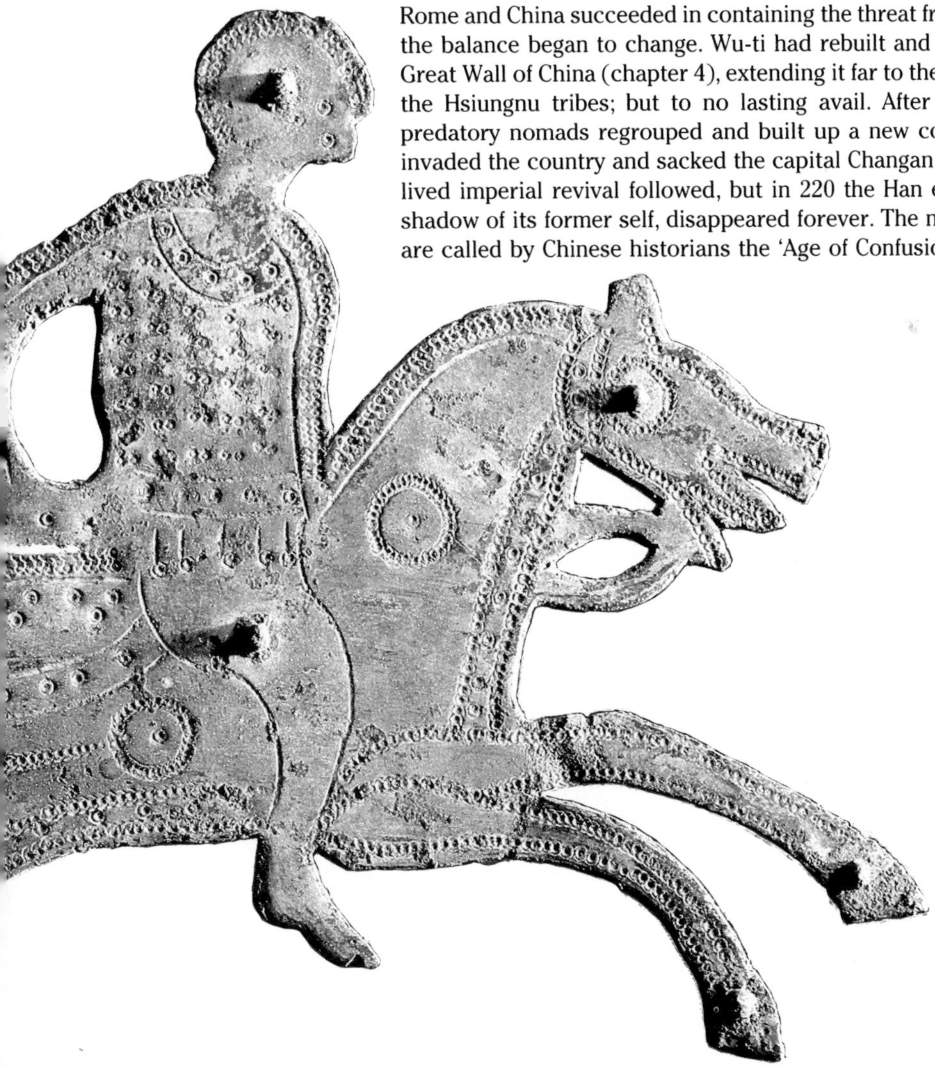

Part of the explanation for this sudden collapse lies in the fact that the greater part of the 'civilized world' in these centuries was only a narrow belt, flanked to the north by the domain of fierce nomadic tribesmen. They lived on horseback, as their descendants still do, following their sheep and cattle from one grazing ground to the next on the arid plateaux and inhospitable mountainsides of central Asia. As long as adequate pasture could be found, all was well. But if there were too many animals for the available grass, or if the climate changed for the worse, conditions for the nomads quickly became desperate. They were forced either to move into the neighbouring areas of more settled farming society, or die. The margin between subsistence and starvation was narrow and, without warning, raiders from the steppes could appear, plundering and destroying everything in sight.

But this menace was nothing new. China had been exposed in the second century BC to the depredations of the Hsiungnu, an Asiatic people who were probably the ancestors of the Huns; and it was against them that the emperor Wu-ti launched the expeditions which carried Chinese power far into central Asia. The Roman empire in the west faced similar pressures, this time from the settled German tribes beyond the Rhine and Danube. Yet until the second century AD both Rome and China succeeded in containing the threat from outside. Then the balance began to change. Wu-ti had rebuilt and strengthened the Great Wall of China (chapter 4), extending it far to the west to keep out the Hsiungnu tribes; but to no lasting avail. After their defeat, the predatory nomads regrouped and built up a new confederacy which invaded the country and sacked the capital Changan in AD 23. A short-lived imperial revival followed, but in 220 the Han empire, by now a shadow of its former self, disappeared forever. The next few centuries are called by Chinese historians the 'Age of Confusion'.

After the Roman emperor Trajan (AD 98-117) had conquered Dacia (modern Romania), he commissioned a commemorative stone column which portrayed episodes of the Dacian wars rather in the manner of a modern newsreel *right*. The reliefs illustrate many of the problems involved in the occupation of newly conquered territory and the summary justice which could be expected by opponents and trouble-makers.

The emperor Constantine I (AD 305-337) *below* commemorated his achievements in a somewhat different but nonetheless traditional way, by a triumphal arch in which sculpted reliefs two centuries old were incorporated. Although the son of the western emperor, his succession was bitterly opposed by rival claimants for several years. Once established as sole ruler (in 324), he constructed a new capital at Constantinople (modern Istanbul) to reflect the shift in the centre of Roman power to the richer East. The last of the emperors to rule effectively over the whole empire, Constantine was baptized a Christian on his death-bed, having earlier acknowledged the Christian faith as the offical religion of the State.

In the west, the turning point came in AD 117 after the death of the emperor Trajan. Thenceforth, expansion ceased and most of Trajan's successors went over to the defensive. In Britain, the emperor Hadrian (117-138) built the Roman Wall which runs seventy-three miles, more or less in a straight line, from the Solway to the Tyne, to protect the country from the hostile Caledonians; his successor Antoninus Pius built a short-lived second fortified front-line, the 'Antonine Wall', further north between the Forth and Clyde. Other defences were constructed elsewhere: between the Rhine and the Danube against the Germans; in Syria against the Persians; in North Africa against the Berber tribesmen marauding from their home in the Atlas mountains and the high plateaux and mountains to the south of the coastal plain, in present-day Algeria. But a largely defensive policy had obvious drawbacks, for there was no hope of manning these long artificial borders from end to end. In 167 the German tribes pushed across the Danube in force and reached Aquileia, the gateway to north-east Italy; in 170 they poured into Greece and almost captured Athens.

These were dramatic events. The Han empire and the Roman empire had once seemed invincible; for centuries they had beaten off the marauders on their frontiers. But, in time, the strain of this military effort began to tell. So long as the armies were successful, so long as new lands were conquered, foreign tribute helped to pay the immense costs of empire; but when expansion ceased, as it did in Rome during the second century AD, the process went into reverse. The legions, which had provided slaves and booty during the period of expansion, became a burden during the period of contraction. Historians of the day clearly described the results as they were seen in Rome: the exhaustion produced by excessive taxation; the ruin of the middle class; the decline of morale in the army, rebellious when it was not paid. It was much the same in China. Extortionate taxation squeezed the peasants, and there were great rebellions in the south, such as the 'revolt of the yellow turbans' which began in 184, lasted for thirty years and brought down the dynasty.

Depreciation of the currency and inflation added to the general distress in both imperial China and in Rome, but in the latter they were exacerbated by an adverse trade balance producing a chronic drain of gold to the east. Already in the first century AD Pliny complained that the import of Indian goods such as spices and jewels, was costing the Romans 55 million sesterces a year in gold, and imports from India, China and Arabia ran to 100 million: 'our women and our love-affairs are so expensive!' he lamented. It could not go on. Before long, inflation reached drastic levels, even by present-day standards. A measure of wheat which cost 6 drachmae in Egypt during the first century rose to 200 in 276, to 9,000 in 314 to 78,000 in 334 and, later on, to more than 2 million. Not surprisingly, anti-tax revolts became endemic. Even desertion to the barbarians across the frontier might be resorted to. As if these miseries were not enough, there was also plague. A devastating epidemic began in the east in AD 162 and spread along the transcontinental trade routes until it struck the Mediterranean world in 165.

Certainly, one must not write off the Roman empire too soon. Marcus Aurelius, the emperor at the time of the plague, still managed to lead his legions to victory beyond the Danube – achievements duly commemorated on his triumphal column erected in the imperial capital. But in the ninety years that followed his death there were no less than eighty emperors, as one military power-group after another tried to place their own candidate on the throne. And when at last, in the third century, one of them (Diocletian, 284-305) succeeded in defeating all his rivals, he found that the empire could only be ruled effectively

by dividing it into two halves. In the year 330, his successor Constantine I founded a massive new city on the Bosporus, transforming the ancient Byzantium into Constantinople, which quickly became the empire's eastern capital. Within 150 years it had become the empire's only capital, for Rome, like the rest of Italy, fell under barbarian control.

At first sight, the destructive power of the nomadic peoples of Eurasia seems surprising, for they were primarily sheep and cattle farmers. But they were highly mobile and heavily armed, enviably adept with bow, lance and sabre: their speed and striking power could seldom be matched by their more settled neighbours. In effect they formed vast confederacies of self-contained cavalry units.

Their dramatic expansion began in earnest with renewed invasions of China by the Hsiungnu. In 304 they broke through the Great Wall and within a decade had reached the Yellow River, sacking the ancient Han capitals of Loyang (311) and Changan (316). This successful invasion opened the way for other Asiatic peoples, Mongols and Turks, and for the next 280 years northern China was dominated by a succession of invaders from the steppes.

At the same time another branch of the Hsiungnu, the Huns, swept south-westwards through Asia from the Altai mountains: Europe, Persia and India were all to suffer devastation at their hands. Europe first. The arrival of the Huns in about 370 threw the whole Germanic world along the Black Sea and the Danube into turmoil. To escape them the Visigoths, perhaps 80,000 strong, forced their way into the Balkan provinces of the Roman empire and settled there. In 378, in a pitched battle outside Adrianople, their army of not more than 10,000 men under their chief, Alaric, defeated and slaughtered a large Roman force under the personal command of the emperor Valens. It was a shattering blow to Rome's pride and powers of resistance, and the victorious invaders advanced into Italy. For a time the legions, and diplomacy, held them back, but at last the Visigoths broke through and in 410 they amazed the world by capturing and sacking Rome itself. Moving on again, they established a kingdom, covering much of Spain and southern France, which lasted for three centuries.

Attila the Hun *top left* advanced into Italy in 452 but according to legend, was persuaded to spare Rome through the personal intervention of Pope Leo I – the Renaissance painter Raphael piously captured the encounter in this imaginative fresco in the Vatican – but, even so, he failed to dissuade the Vandals, who devastated the city in 455. The Vandals, however, chose to see themselves in a positive light. The mosaic from Carthage, their capital *above*, made in about AD 500, shows a Vandal warrior leaving his country villa just as if he were the heir, rather than the destroyer, of Roman civilization.

Throughout the history of the Roman empire its frontiers were assailed almost continuously in one region or another by raiding parties of barbarians *left*, who aimed to amass as much plunder as possible before returning home. On occasion the imperial government would admit entire peoples within the frontier, but was careful to split them up and deny them the possibility of concerted military action. But in AD 376, 405 and 455 came large-scale invasions by peoples whom the Romans were unable to disperse and control. The irruption of the Asiatic Huns caused the severest disturbance by impelling previously settled German tribes (Goths and Vandals) to pour through the boundaries of the empire.

113

Several of the major Germanic peoples
had embraced Christianity before they
entered the Roman empire in the 4th and
5th centuries. Others were converted *en
masse* following the baptism of their
leaders. The close alliance between the
later Visigothic rulers of Spain and the
Church is illustrated by the elegant votive
crown of gold, dedicated by King
Recceswinth (649-72) *far right*. The
Visigoths also constructed numerous
churches, the style surviving in the church
of San Miguel de Lillo, built in the Asturias
around 850. In Italy, a helmet plaque *below
right* shows an Ostrogoth ruler flanked by
angels, who are ushering Christian
worshippers into his presence.

The Mausoleum of Theodoric the Great
in Ravenna *below* shows how swiftly the
barbarian invaders of Rome came to terms
with their new political and artistic
heritage. In 481 Theodoric, one of the
Ostrogothic chiefs who threatened
Constantinople, had been made a consul by
the Byzantine emperor Zeno, in order to
placate him. Then in 488, having
introduced his new colleague to Roman
ways, Zeno sent him (and his 100,000
turbulent followers) to restore imperial
control over Italy — lost since 476. This he
did, ruling both Ostrogoths and Romans
with an even hand until his death in 526,
preferring to be buried like a Roman
patrician rather than a Germanic chief.

While Rome's main army was defending Italy, other Germanic tribes seized the opportunity to cross the Rhine. The Vandals, the Alans and the Sueves invaded Gaul in 406 and plundered it for three years before passing on to do the same in Spain. Next, in 429, the Vandals penetrated Roman North Africa – Carthage fell in 439 – and in 455 they sailed across to Rome which, like the Visigoths before them, they captured and looted. Once again, the empire's northern frontiers were left unguarded; once again Gaul was invaded – this time by the Burgundians and Alemanni, who settled in the east, and by the Franks, who occupied most of the north. Meanwhile, Roman Britain also came under attack. The army there was weakened by the need to defend Gaul and, although it was never withdrawn, when pay failed to arrive the units seemingly melted away, leaving the remaining Romanized inhabitants to deal as best they could with attacks by Picts from Scotland in the north and by marauders from the continental coastlands in the east. Their ultimate fate is unknown for certain; but a Gaulish chronicler noted under the year 441-2 that Britain, after various misfortunes, had finally succumbed to the Saxons.

On other fronts, the emperors of West Rome made concessions and even paid bribes to the barbarians in order to buy a temporary truce. Their only success came in 451 when, with the aid of earlier invaders (the Franks and Visigoths), a Roman army opposed another great onslaught from central Europe led by Attila the Hun. At the Catalaunian Fields, near Châlons in Gaul, the Huns were heavily defeated and, after a brief foray into Italy, Attila died and his hordes moved on. But the Roman empire in the west was doomed. In the second half of the fifth century, the Franks, Visigoths and Burgundians ruled most of Gaul; small Anglo-Saxon states were installed in south-eastern England; the Visigoths dominated Spain; the Vandals governed north-west Africa; and the Ostrogoths held Italy. In 476 the last emperor in Rome was deposed by the local German chieftain, Odovacar.

But there were still Roman emperors: now, however, they ruled from the eastern capital – Constantinople or Byzantium. For a moment, under the first great Byzantine emperor, Justinian, it seemed as if the empire might be restored in the west. At the time of his accession, in

The emperor Justinian, Archbishop Maximian, and priests and bodyguards of Byzantium, as the East Roman empire founded by Constantine became known, look down with approval on the altar of the church of San Vitale at Ravenna *below*. The mosaic, completed soon after Ravenna was regained by Byzantine forces in 540, testifies to the success of the eastern emperor in restoring imperial authority in the west. Ravenna remained the capital of Byzantine Italy until 751, when the Lombards captured the city and made it part of their short-lived kingdom in northern Italy.

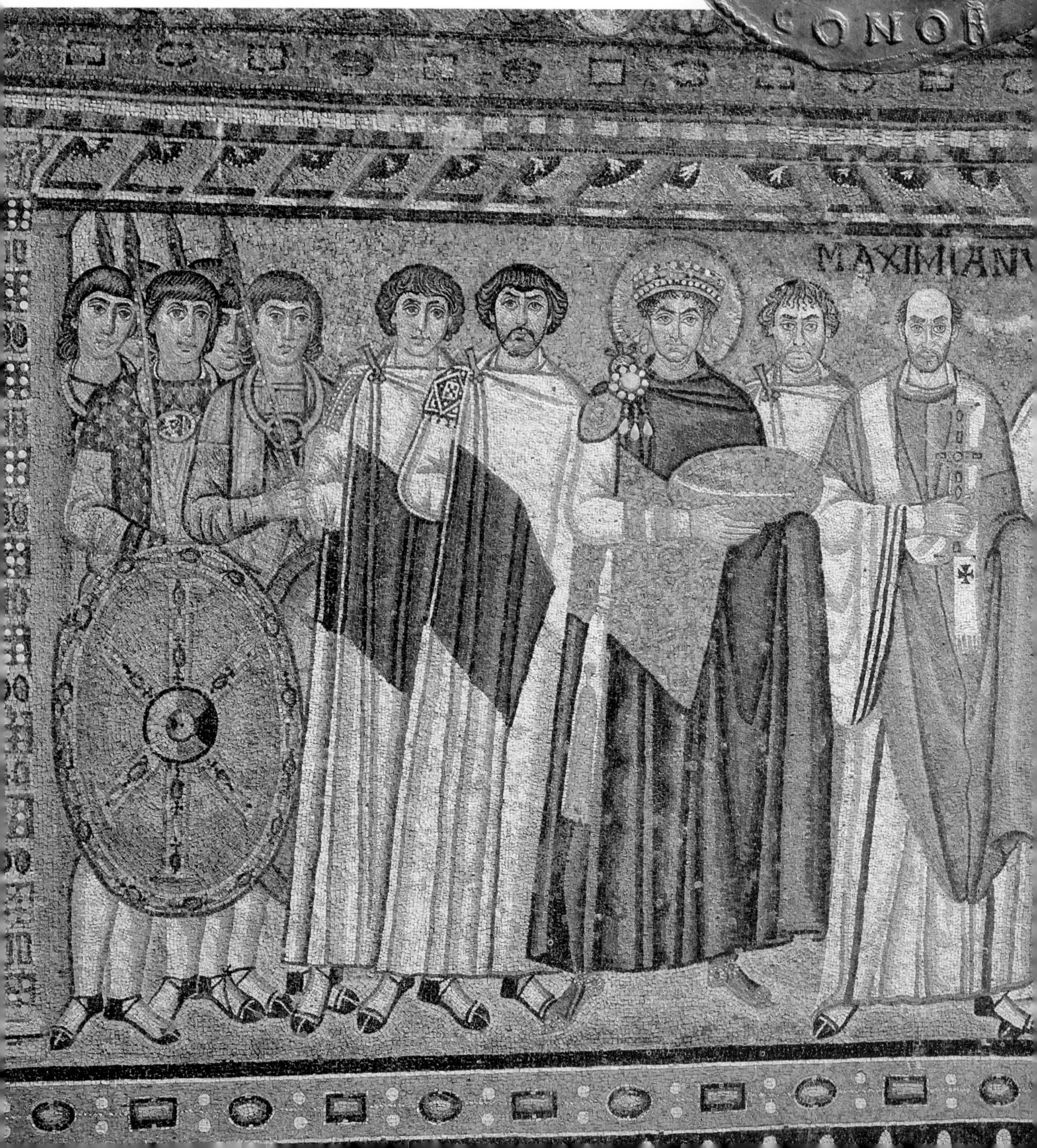

Coinage in the ancient world served two functions. First, of course, it was used as a medium of exchange and as payment for armies; but it also offered an opportunity for propaganda. Some coins simply announced, through a well-struck portrait, the succession of a new emperor; *far left* a gold solidus of Emperor Honorius, 393-423. Others however, were more specific: *left*, Justinian celebrated his reconquest of the Vandal kingdom of Africa in 534. This technique of realistic portraiture on coins was never fully mastered by the barbarian rulers. The silver coin of King Mihirakula of the White Huns (500-528) *far right* bears no comparison with Justinian's, and the gold solidus of the Romanized Theodoric the Great *right* minted in Rome c.510 is a poor imitation of earlier imperial issues.

527, Byzantine possessions were confined to the eastern Mediterranean. By the year of his death in 565, however, his forces had reconquered North Africa, the islands of the western Mediterranean and much of Italy. But it did not endure, for a last wave of Asiatic peoples entered Europe. First, in the 550s, the Avars sowed a new path of desolation through Gaul, Italy and the Balkans. Then, in their wake, came other warlike tribes who carved out and settled large areas of the old Roman world: the Slavs in the Balkans as well as in eastern Europe; the Lombards in northern Italy; and the Bulgars who colonized what is today still called Bulgaria.

The destruction caused by these successive 'barbarian invasions' was not, however, confined to Europe. India, too, was gravely affected. The subcontinent was divided at the time among a number of separate kingdoms – as it had been since the collapse of Asoka's empire (chapter 6) – but after AD 320 rulers of the Gupta dynasty, at first based in Asoka's capital at Patna on the Ganges, established their sway over much of the north. Chandragupta II (375-415) ruled an empire that stretched from the Indus to the Bay of Bengal, and from the Himalayas to beyond the Krishna river. Amid conditions of peace and prosperity, a major Hindu literature in Sanskrit developed – including the definitive versions of India's national epics, the Mahabharata and the Ramayana. Even more impressive, it was probably under the Gupta that Indian scholars formulated the decimal numerical system (using ten as a base, presumably because people counted on their fingers), and a simple new method of writing the numbers down (which we call 'Arabic numerals' only because they came to the west via Arab merchants and scholars: their inspiration was entirely Indian). The real revolution was devising a symbol for zero, which made it possible to represent symbolically the empty column of the abacus. The importance to mankind of these mathematical innovations has been ranked with the invention of the wheel, the alphabet, or the compass.

However, all of these achievements were seriously threatened after 455 by the invasions of other nomadic peoples, the Ephthalites or White Huns. The strain of continuous wars and devastation fatally undermined Gupta power and by the middle of the sixth century their empire was no more: India lapsed into a tangle of warring states, some native and some alien, for more than five hundred years.

After ravaging India, the Huns turned their attention to Persia; but there they failed. Since AD 240 the empires of Kushan and Parthia had been merged into a single Persian realm under the powerful Sassanian dynasty. By the end of the fourth century, Sassanian rule stretched

from the Indus to the Euphrates, and within those boundaries there was great prosperity and intense economic activity. The empire successfully resisted all efforts by the Huns to invade: although in 484 a Persian ruler was defeated and killed by them, in the 550s the tables were turned and the Sassanian frontier was advanced to the river Oxus at the expense of the barbarians.

Nevertheless, by the year 600, the Eurasian world was vastly changed. Its great cities – Changan, Loyang, Rome – which had been the proudest symbols of the classical civilizations, were prostrate, while the empires which they had once ruled, and which had seemed so firmly established some four centuries earlier, had perished. Only Sassanian Persia had weathered the storm. China – particularly north China which had been the heartland of the Han empire – suffered terribly: even the use of money disappeared in some areas and there was a reversion to a barter economy. And yet, in spite of the devastation, when China was finally reunited after 581 under the Sui and T'ang dynasties, a surprising amount of classical civilization survived. The

Originally nomads from the shores of the Caspian Sea, the Parthians entered Seleucia in 141 BC and established a Persian empire which was to last until AD 226. The only state able to resist the elsewhere invincible Roman legions, much of their success was due to their great skill in mounted battle, in particular their invention of heavy cavalry. This graffiti from Dura-Europos on the Euphrates *above centre* shows a warrior (*cataphract*) mounted on a heavy horse capable of carrying a rider, lance and chain-mail armour. The Sassanians succeeded the Parthians as controllers of the Iranian plateau threatening to the eastern Roman world and resistant to invaders from the north and east. The silver dish *above left* shows the Sassanian King Ardashir III (628-30) hunting.

imagohominis

MACHEUS HATHEUS

The Lindisfarne Gospels *above right* were copied and illustrated in the late 7th century AD on Lindisfarne, Holy Island, off the Northumberland coast of England. The richly illuminated Bibles and the sculpted stone crosses of Dark Age Britain show the extent to which the advance of Christianity in the north and west of the islands revitalized native art: scribes, painters and sculptors found their patron in the Church. Learning and literature, as well as the graphic arts, were also fostered by the Church, notably through its monastic schools. In such centres great scholars such as Bede and Alcuin kept learning alive.

reason for this was that, although the north was overrun, the south escaped; indeed, vast numbers of Chinese fled to the south. Furthermore, the invaders in the north were forced to adopt native methods of government and to co-operate with the local gentry, in order to keep the administration going. They were thus absorbed into the Chinese system, taking on its customs and culture as they did so. The same was true in India. The Rajputs, the descendants of the Hun invaders of the fifth century who still inhabit Rajputana in north-east India, soon became assimilated to local social and religious practices and were easily absorbed into the Indian warrior caste. It was the victors who adopted the civilization of the vanquished, and not vice versa.

So India, like China, emerged from its time of troubles with a classical heritage that was impaired but not extinguished. It was very different in Europe: classical civilization there was shattered beyond recall, despite repeated attempts at restoration. For a time the West still lived in the shadow of Rome – that is, of East Rome or Byzantium – and the unity of the Mediterranean, which all along had been the basis of Rome's ascendancy, was still a fact. But no carts or chariots, and no legionaries, now travelled along the Roman roads; the bridges and aqueducts were left to fall into ruins; and the great forum of the capital itself became desolate and silent. Of course life continued, and farming remained the basis of societies and states alike; but the units were small, and knowledge of classical culture was confined to a handful of monasteries.

And then, in the seventh century, the ancient world suffered a final, shattering blow: the rise of Islam. By destroying the Sassanian empire and absorbing its riches, by robbing Byzantium of its wealthiest provinces, and by advancing to the Chinese frontier in central Asia, Islam completely changed the balance of power in the Old World. The disciples of Mohammed did finally drive back the nomads of the steppe; but the Muslim states they erected in their place constituted an equally formidable barrier to cultural interchange. Furthermore, by gaining control of the Mediterranean, Islam severed the last tenuous links between western Europe and Byzantium. The West was now isolated from the Greek world which had once moulded its culture, and was left to rely upon its own resources alone. For the present, and for a long time to come, the centre of political power shifted elsewhere.

Rome was a target for various groups during the 5th and 6th centuries AD. It was sacked twice (410 and 455) and the last emperor of the west was deposed there in 476. But still the Roman ways endured: the Senate continued to sit, the central administration continued to function; and the victorious Ostrogothic leaders, first Odovacar and then Theodoric, claimed to rule as agents of the Byzantine emperors. Only after the capture of the city by the Goths in 546 did this change, when the victors decided to expel all the inhabitants. From now on, grass grew in the Forum *right*. The Temple of Castor and Pollux (on the right), built at the foundation of the Republic in about 500 BC, collapsed; the triumphal Arch of Titus (AD 81) commemorated victories that now seemed hollow; and no more spectacles were staged in the Colosseum (at top left).

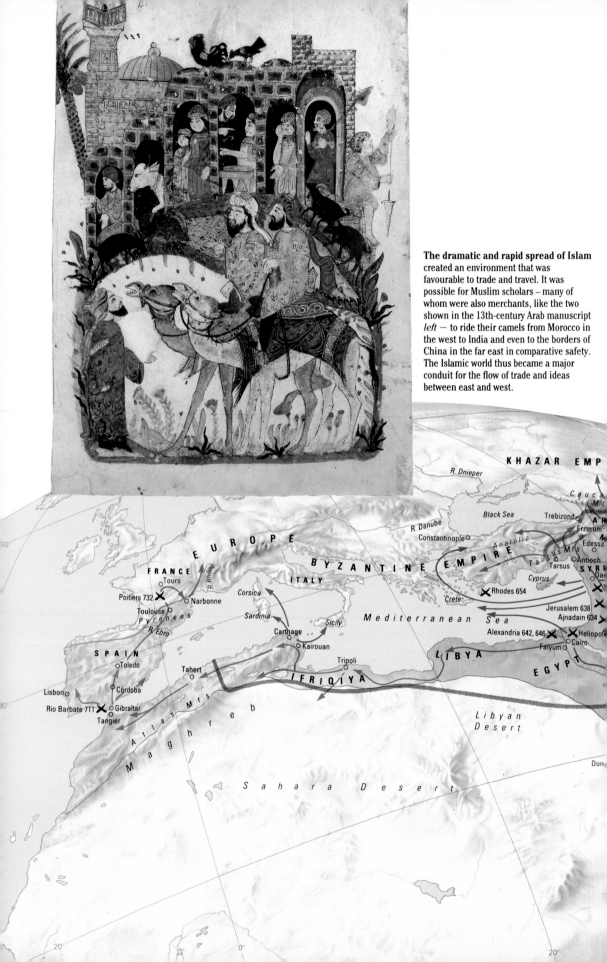

The dramatic and rapid spread of Islam created an environment that was favourable to trade and travel. It was possible for Muslim scholars – many of whom were also merchants, like the two shown in the 13th-century Arab manuscript *left* – to ride their camels from Morocco in the west to India and even to the borders of China in the far east in comparative safety. The Islamic world thus became a major conduit for the flow of trade and ideas between east and west.

CHAPTER 8

ISLAM
600–1200

The rise and expansion of Islam was perhaps the most important development in world history between the fall of Rome and the Europeans' discovery of America. Within a remarkably short time, a new world religion created the dynamic civilization which now embraces about one-seventh of the present global population. There are today over 600 million Muslims in the world, from Morocco in the west to Indonesia in the east, and from as far north as Siberia to Zanzibar in the south.

Two questions are immediately posed by this dramatic success story. First, why did a new religion of such immense vigour spring to life during the seventh century in the sparsely populated Arabian peninsula? And, second, how was it that, within a century, the inhabitants of that arid peninsula were able to impose their authority and faith on half – or rather more than half – of the Eurasian world?

The starting-point was, perhaps, the sudden emergence of Arabia as a centre of transcontinental trade. The wars between the Persian and Byzantine empires disrupted the main trade routes between Europe and Asia across what is now Turkey and Iran in the late sixth century.

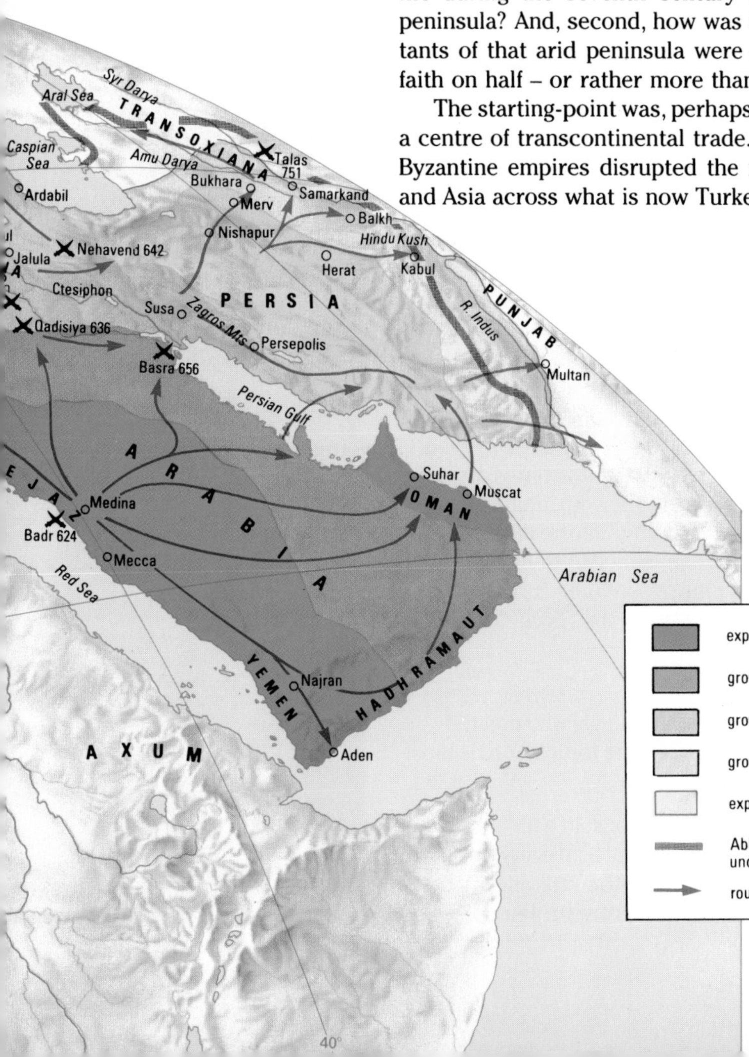

The **spread of Islam** outside the Arabian peninsula *left* began almost immediately after the Prophet's death in 632. By 711 Arab armies were simultaneously attacking Sind in north-eastern India and preparing for the conquest of the Iberian peninsula. In general, the conquests in the east exceeded those in the west in size and importance. By 750, when the Abbasids ousted the Umayyad dynasty, the empire to which they succeeded was the major civilization west of China.

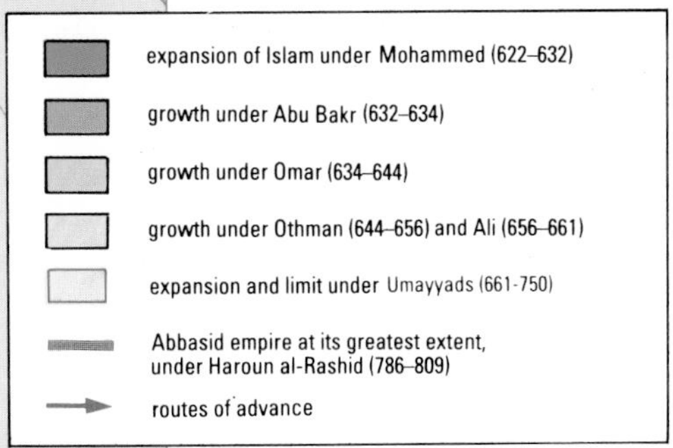

Map labels:
Aral Sea, Syr Darya, TRANSOXIANA, Caspian Sea, Amu Darya, Talas 751, Ardabil, Bukhara, Samarkand, Merv, Balkh, Nishapur, Hindu Kush, Jalula, Nehavend 642, Herat, Kabul, Ctesiphon, PERSIA, PUNJAB, Qadisiya 636, Susa, Zagros Mts, Persepolis, R. Indus, Basra 656, Multan, Persian Gulf, ARABIA, Suhar, Muscat, OMAN, HEJAZ, Medina, Badr 624, Mecca, Red Sea, Arabian Sea, YEMEN, HADHRAMAUT, Najran, AXUM, Aden

Map legend:
expansion of Islam under Mohammed (622–632)
growth under Abu Bakr (632–634)
growth under Omar (634–644)
growth under Othman (644–656) and Ali (656–661)
expansion and limit under Umayyads (661-750)
Abbasid empire at its greatest extent, under Haroun al-Rashid (786–809)
routes of advance

So the produce of Asia began to come to the ports of Arabia and was transported thence by camel trains up the peninsula to the Mediterranean. The towns along this route prospered, but the new prosperity, which attracted many migrants from the countryside, was accompanied by a new differentiation between rich and poor and a gradual rejection of the traditional tribal values of honour, magnanimity and the protection of the weak.

By 570, when the Prophet Mohammed was born, Mecca had long been an important centre of pilgrimage. The local tribes had come to worship the idols at the shrine of the Black Stone, the Kaaba or cube, which contained some 360 sacred stones, statues and other objects. However, monotheism was not unknown in the Arabian peninsula: scattered Christian and Jewish communities had long been established there, and it is clear that Mohammed himself grew up in an atmosphere in which pagan beliefs were being questioned and yearnings towards a more sophisticated religious and political order were being expressed in the society around him.

Orphaned as a small child, Mohammed grew up in relative poverty, from which he was rescued by his marriage to a woman considerably older than himself, when he was about 25. Little information has survived about his early life, but in middle age he began to retreat to the mountains outside Mecca to spend time in solitary contemplation. About the year 610, Mohammed saw a vision of the Angel Gabriel.

'Recite,' commanded the angel.
'What shall I recite?' enquired Mohammed.
'Recite in the name of thy Lord who created all things, who created man from a clot of blood,' replied the angel. 'Recite for thy Lord is most generous.'

Mohammed was to experience many further visions, in which the angel revealed to him messages from God and made him repeat every word. The various messages, which Muslims believe to be the utterances of God transmitted through Mohammed, were subsequently written down and now form the Koran, the Holy Book of Islam. It contains guidance on how the faithful should live – habits and hygiene, marriage and divorce, commerce and politics, law and order, peace and war are all covered – as well as on what they should believe. The Koran required both the recognition of the unity and supreme power of Allah (God the Creator) and of Mohammed's role as His prophet, and the performance of certain rituals: daily prayers at prescribed times; fasting from dawn until dusk during the month of Ramadan; the generous giving of alms in the name of Allah; a pilgrimage to Mecca for every believer, if at all possible, at least once. These obligations, together with the assertion of the main tenet of Islamic belief, 'I bear witness that there is no God but Allah, and Mohammed is the Messenger of Allah', are known as the Five Pillars of Islam. Islam, which means 'submission to the will of God', was thus not only a religion; it was also a political creed and a social code. It offered to its followers both a precise theology and a distinctive pattern of public and private behaviour.

Mohammed was not intolerant of all other creeds; indeed Muslims are specifically enjoined to protect the 'people of the book', that is, adherents of monotheistic religions with written scriptures. Thus Mohammed accepted the authenticity of several Jewish prophets, including Abraham and Moses, and he recognized Christ, too, as a prophet (though not as the son of God). But he was opposed to the idolatry and polytheism of traditional Arab religion, and he spoke out against them. The conservative élite of Mecca saw this as a threat to the prosperity they derived from

God's revelations to the Prophet Mohammed were collected and copied into the Koran (which means 'reading' or 'recitation'), the Holy Book of Islam and the most outstanding work of Arabic prose. It is not a long work – about the same length as the New Testament in the Christian Bible – but infinite care was taken over the preparation of individual manuscript copies of the text, which is regarded by Muslims as the word of God. All of them are written in Arabic – indeed Muslim authorities believe that the Koran cannot be translated without losing its Divine authority. Their appearance often varies from the elaborate stylization of the 9th-century gold-on-black kufic script produced in Kairouan in Tunisia *below centre* to the beautifully illuminated text *far left* produced in Egypt in the 14th century.

The volume of prayers *above* is known as the *Dala'il al-Khayrat* (Guide to the Virtues) composed in the 15th century by the Moroccan mystic Al-Jazuli. Like all the religious writings of Islam, it was not illustrated, for the depiction of human figures in a religious context was condemned by Mohammed and his followers as idolatry (although, as the illustrations on the next page show, the prohibition was not universally observed).

the steady influx of pilgrims coming to worship at the Kaaba, and Mohammed and his followers came under attack. In 622, in the face of mounting local hostility, they decided to withdraw from Mecca to the town of Medina, 180 miles to the north, whose inhabitants had invited Mohammed to arbitrate in a dispute between local rival clans. It did not seem a major step at the time – the Prophet was followed by less than 100 disciples, several of them members of his immediate family – but his migration, known as the Hejira, marks the beginning of the Islamic calendar, the precise point at which the Mohammedan era commenced.

For it was in Medina that the first Muslim state was established and the first mosque built (on the site now occupied by the Mosque of the Prophet, where Mohammed is buried). Once the Arabs of Medina had accepted the new faith, Mohammed organized attacks on the Mecca caravans and distributed the spoils to his followers. News of his successes attracted a considerable body of supporters until, by 630, the Muslims could field an army of 10,000 men. In that year they decided to attack Mecca itself, led by Mohammed in person. He was allowed to enter the city and demanded the keys to the Kaaba; they were surrendered, and at once the pagan idols within were smashed. But Mohammed knew how to build as well as how to destroy, and was keenly

Depictions of Mohammed are rare, as figurative representation in general is proscribed by Islamic law. These depictions of the Prophet come from a late 14th-century Turkish illuminated book, but there too the face of Mohammed is obscured. The Prophet is shown with the Archangel Gabriel *below left* and reciting the God's message before the Kaaba *below right*, and in both images his head is surrounded by a flame, not dissimilar to the halo of Christian art.

The Kaaba in Mecca *above* measuring 40 feet long by 33 feet wide and 50 feet high, is the most sacred sanctuary of Islam, the place towards which Muslims face while praying. Until 630 it housed the sacred stones and other objects venerated by the tribes of Arabia, in an inner chamber, but all except the 'Black Stone' (said to have been brought by the Archangel Gabriel to Abraham while he was constructing the Kaaba) were removed by Mohammed when his forces took the city. Thereafter the purified Kaaba became the centre of the Muslim world. Around it runs a track along which each of the millions of pilgrims who visit Mecca make a sevenfold circuit of the sanctuary. For most of the year the Kaaba, which now stands at the centre of the Great Mosque of Mecca, is covered by an enormous black brocade cloth, adorned with verses from the Koran.

aware of the importance of emphasizing the elements of continuity between the old religion and the new. Thus he immediately ordered his *muezzin* (or prayer leader) to climb to the roof of the Kaaba and call the faithfull to prayer in words which are still heard today from the minaret of every mosque throughout the world:

'God is most great. I testify that there is no God but Allah. I testify that Mohammed is God's apostle. Come to prayer, come to security. God is most great.'

Ever since that day, the Kaaba in Mecca has been the centre of the Islamic world, and every Muslim, wherever he happens to be, turns towards Mecca to pray. Every year, millions of believers make a pilgrimage to worship at the holy city and its principal shrine.

As a prophet, Mohammed was unusual, for he became a temporal as well as a spiritual leader. He replaced the many tribal gods of the Arabs with the omnipotent Allah, yet at the same time he galvanized the military potential of the tribes themselves. Many joined him in expectation of booty as well as of salvation, for raiding and conquest acquired an element of sanctity under the banner of Islam (since the conquered territories were also won for the faith). So by the time of his death in 632, Mohammed ruled a state which included the Hejaz, Yemen and Oman, and seemed poised to take over the rest of Arabia.

But at first this empire appeared likely to end with the death of its founder, especially as Mohammed had not laid down any guidelines as to how the Islamic community should choose his successor. Several of the tribes which had accepted his authority considered that his death effectively terminated the alliance, but the new leader of Islam, Abu Bakr, Mohammed's father-in-law, quickly defeated them and forced them back into the Muslim fold. For a time, at least, the crisis was over. Abu Bakr, who died in 634, took the title of caliph (or 'deputy'), because he was regarded as principal defender of the new faith and secular chief of Mohammed's community. He was succeeded by Omar, the husband of one of Mohammed's daughters, under whom the expansion of Islam began in earnest, with Syria, Mesopotamia and Egypt annexed by the time of his death ten year later.

Just before his death, Mohammed had authorized the first of the expeditions outside the Arabian peninsula which were to be continued with such spectacular effect under his successors. The Islamic conquests were undertaken partly out of religious enthusiasm, and partly out of political necessity. In the first place, the early caliphs were worried that the tribes which had briefly withdrawn their allegiance in 632 might try to do so again, so they planned a series of expansionist campaigns in the hope of securing sufficient booty to encourage the continued loyalty of the volatile Bedouin. In addition, the Arab cavalry was found to be formidably effective in battle: in particular, their camels could travel routes and cross deserts that horse-borne armies found impossible. And yet determined resistance might still have checked them, or at least reduced their booty, for their numbers were not great – fewer than 10,000 men captured the whole of Lower Egypt in 640. However, the early warriors of Islam were also sustained by the conviction that God was with them and that they were fighting for His cause. 'I risked my life for the idols of Mecca', said one who had been a leading opponent of Mohammed before his conversion. 'Why should I hold back now from risking it for God?' But here another factor came into play: Persia and Byzantium, like Egypt, were quite unable to resist the attacks of the Arabs, for the two empires had spent most of the previous century locked in debilitating wars of attrition. In 636, attacking in the midst of a sandstorm, the Arabs routed a Byzantine army at the Yarmuk river and occupied the rich province of Syria; the following year, from this strategic base, they conquered Mesopotamia. In both areas they secured vast booty which attracted a new wave of Bedouin reinforcements to the cause. The tide of conquest now seemed irresistible. Under Omar and his successor Othman (644-56), Persia was conquered: the only classical civilization to survive the barbarian invasions from the east now succumbed to the onslaught of nomads from the west. The last Sassanian emperor was killed in battle in 651.

But then came a hiatus, during which the succession to the caliphate was disputed between Ali, the Prophet's cousin and son-in-law, and the Umayyads, relatives of Othman, who enjoyed support from the merchants of Mecca. By 661, the latter had won and, for almost a century, members of the Umayyad family were recognized as caliphs. But it was not a complete victory: many Muslims regarded Ali and his descendants as the lawful heirs of the Prophet, because of their status as members of Mohammed's family, calling themselves Shi'ites (from *Shi'at Ali*, 'the party of Ali'). Their more numerous opponents, who acknowledged the authority of the Umayyads and subsequently of their successors the Abbasids, were known as Sunnites (because they accepted the *Sunna* or 'traditions of the Prophet'). In general, largely because they tended to inhabit different geographical areas, an uneasy peace has characterized relations between the two sects ever since.

The Umayyad caliphs who ruled from Damascus in Syria, were nevertheless able to advance the frontiers of Islam still further. To the east they conquered Afghanistan in 664 and Sind in 712: both have remained Muslim ever since. Further north they pressed beyond the Oxus river into central Asia until they reached the frontiers of the Chinese empire. At the Talas river in 751 their troops defeated a major Chinese army and the domination of Islam as far as the Pamirs was established for good. Meanwhile, in the west, the Arabs advanced steadily along the African shore of the Mediterranean, finding converts among the Berber tribesmen. Carthage fell in 698, only a century and a half after Justinian's forces had regained it for Rome (chapter 7). Next they occupied Morocco and in 711 invaded Spain, defeating the Visigoths and driving the Christians into the mountains in the north-west of the Iberian peninsula. Although an attempt to expand north of the Pyrenees was defeated by the Franks at the battle of Tours in 732, the Umayyads had now extended their empire to the Atlantic.

	Byzantine empire c. 930
	reconquered by Byzantines by 1070
	limit of area controlled by Seljuk Turks c. 1080
	limit of area controlled by Seljuk Turks in early 13th century

Mohammed died without leaving clear guidance on how his successors should be selected. The first three Caliphs were all Companions of the Prophet from the earliest days of his preaching in Mecca. Abu Bakr (632-4), Omar (634-44) and then Othman, who was murdered in 656. After Othman's death Ali, the Prophet's cousin and son-in-law, *below* succeeded, but his authority was soon challenged by Othman's relatives, the Umayyad family, led by Mu'awaya the powerful governor of Syria. Ali himself was murdered in 661, and most Muslims accepted the Umayyads as the legitimate Caliphs, and subsequently became known as Sunnites. However, some Muslims regarded the descendants of Ali (the Imams, who were the direct descendants of the Prophet) as the true leaders of Islam. They became known as Shi'ites, and now account for about one-fifth of the world's Muslims.

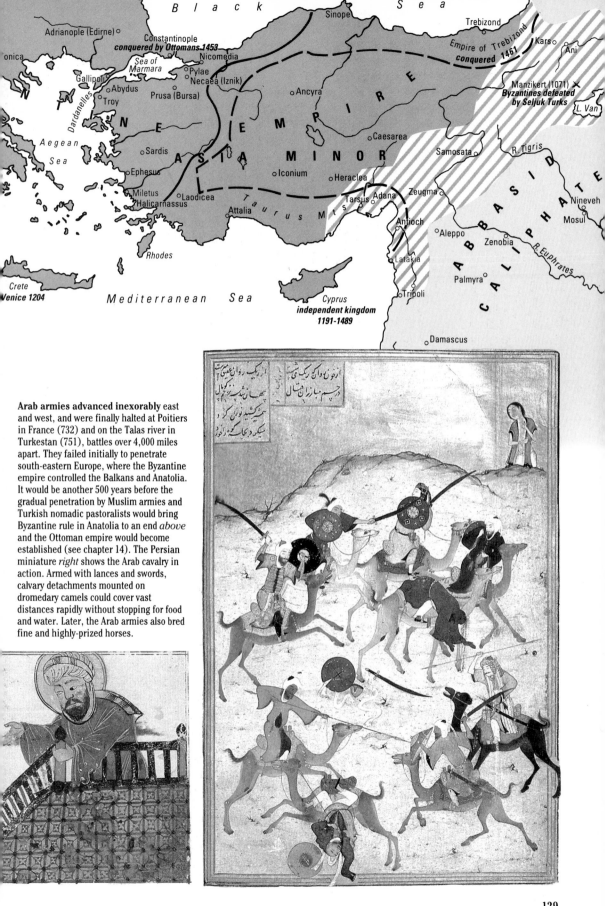

Black Sea

Sinope

Trebizond

Adrianople (Edirne)

Constantinople
conquered by Ottomans 1453

Nicomedia

Empire of Trebizond
conquered 1461

Kars

Ani

onica

Sea of
Marmara

Pylae

Gallipoli

Necaea (Iznik)

Ancyra

Manzikert (1071) ✕
**Byzantines defeated
by Seljuk Turks**

Abydus

Troy

Prusa (Bursa)

L. Van

Dardanelles

BYZANTINE EMPIRE

Caesarea

ASIA MINOR

Aegean
Sea

Sardis

Samosata

R. Tigris

Ephesus

Iconium

Heraclea

ABBASID

Nineveh

Miletus

Laodicea

Tarsus Adana

Zeugma

Mosul

Halicarnassus

Attalia

Taurus Mts

Antioch

Aleppo

Zenobia

CALIPHATE

R. Euphrates

Rhodes

Latakia

Palmyra

Crete
Venice 1204

Mediterranean Sea

Cyprus
**independent kingdom
1191-1489**

Tripoli

Damascus

Arab armies advanced inexorably east
and west, and were finally halted at Poitiers
in France (732) and on the Talas river in
Turkestan (751), battles over 4,000 miles
apart. They failed initially to penetrate
south-eastern Europe, where the Byzantine
empire controlled the Balkans and Anatolia.
It would be another 500 years before the
gradual penetration by Muslim armies and
Turkish nomadic pastoralists would bring
Byzantine rule in Anatolia to an end *above*
and the Ottoman empire would become
established (see chapter 14). The Persian
miniature *right* shows the Arab cavalry in
action. Armed with lances and swords,
calvary detachments mounted on
dromedary camels could cover vast
distances rapidly without stopping for food
and water. Later, the Arab armies also bred
fine and highly-prized horses.

Islamic learning was recorded in books, much as in Europe; but Muslim libraries, such as the one shown in this later 13th-century Persian manuscript *left*, tended to be divided into pigeon holes, rather than shelves. The books were arranged in subject piles, rather than stacked horizontally. In the foreground, a group of students listen attentively to a turbanned figure, who is in fact the notorious trickster Abu Zaid. This illustration is taken from the *Maqamat* (or Book of Assemblies) by Al-Hariri of Basra (1054-1122), one of the most popular prose works in Arabic, which relates the adventures of Abu Zaid, who travelled the Muslim world earning a living from his clever talk and his wits.

But one objective escaped them: Byzantium. Weakened by wars against the Persians and the Slavs, the eastern Christian empire had lost Syria (636), Cyprus (648) and Rhodes (654) to the Arabs whose fleets, fitted out in the dockyards of Alexandria, were now formidably effective. But in 673-8 they failed to force the surrender of Constantinople, largely because the Byzantine navy used a new deadly weapon – 'Greek fire' or naptha – which kept the enemy's warships at bay. A second siege in 717-18 was also unsuccessful, preserving Anatolia and the Balkans in Christian hands and thereby exposing the heart of Islam to the threat of Byzantine counter-attack.

Nevertheless, the expansion of Islam in the century following Mohammed's triumphant return to Mecca was astonishing: the theocratic rule of the Umayyads stretched across nearly one third of the globe. But, as yet, it did not penetrate very deep. The Arab conquerors were everywhere, but usually only as a tiny minority entrenched within heavily-defended cities, dependent for their livelihood on the taxes they raised from their non-Muslim subjects. In effect, Islamic rule meant that a small number of Arabs, mostly soldiers and officials, grew rich on the skills and industry of millions of conquered peoples, many of them heirs to higher and older cultures. Not surprisingly, the conquered peoples resented it – especially after the faith of the political overlords had been widely adopted, without bringing any access to power and privilege. The growing number of non-Arab Muslims, known as *Mawali*, who were concentrated chiefly in the cities where they could prosper from the trade of the Arab élite, now became a powerful pressure group, seeking to gain a political status commensurate with their economic power.

The *Mawali* seized their chance when, in 744, the succession to the caliphate was disputed by various Arab factions. Once the last of the Umayyads had been killed, in 750, the caliphate was seized by the leader of the Abbasid family, descendants of Abbas the Prophet's uncle, whose adherents, mainly from the province of Khurasan, consisted largely of those who had been banished from Mesopotamia by the Umayyads to guard duty on the north-eastern frontier of the Islamic empire. The caliph now ceased to be an Arab sheikh defended by his

Many visitors to Islamic countries commented on the frequency and elaboration with which Muslims bathed themselves. Here *right* the Abbasid caliph Al-Mamun (813-33) is shown at his toilet: on the top floor he takes a shower (powered by an ox outside); on the middle floor his hair is trimmed; finally, at the foot of the illustration he relaxes during a massage. For many in the West, in subsequent centuries, the major Islamic contribution to civilization remained the 'Turkish' bath.

tribal warriors; instead he became an autocrat on the Sassanian model, ruling through a salaried bureaucracy (mostly Persian) and a standing army (soon mainly Turkish). In 762 Caliph Al-Mansur (754-775) symbolically turned his back on the Mediterranean by moving his capital to Mesopotamia, where a fabulous new city, Baghdad, the 'city of peace' was built on a circular plan that measured almost two miles in diameter.

The new dynasty ruled a truly multi-racial empire. Although Arabic remained the universal language, a multitude of peoples and nations shared a common culture, united by their belief in Allah and their respect for the Koran. Baghdad was the centre of that culture, and Al-Mansur's successors were notable patrons of learning and education. Caliph Al-Mamun (813-33), for example, built an observatory in Baghdad, and next to it erected a special 'House of Learning' where scholars studied algebra and astronomy, and translated the works of Euclid, Galen and Aristotle from Greek into Arabic. Baghdad became the principal repository of classical culture. At the same time, distinctive forms of Islamic art were created. Partly because it was forbidden to represent human figures in a religious context – Muslims denounced this as idolatory – a rich repertoire of calligraphic forms developed. Religious texts, richly ornate and vividly coloured, became the principal decoration of palaces, mosques, pottery, glassware and even fabrics; and so they have remained to this day.

The economy, too, flourished under the Abbasids. Textiles – especially cotton, linen and silks – and carpets of high quality were produced in large quantities, and were traded over large distances. Other items of international commerce included ivory, gold and slaves from Africa; spices and ceramics from the Far East; and furs, amber, wax and more slaves from Scandinavia. Islamic coin hoards recently found in all three locations confirm the scale of these contacts. And to finance trade and industry, a full banking service grew up, emulated much later in Europe, with loans, clearing and cheques: it became possible to take out a bank draft in Mecca and cash it in Merv or Marrakesh.

Yet the new regime was never entirely secure. Even the most famous of the Abbasid caliphs, Harun Al-Rashid (786-809), the contemporary of Charlemagne whose court was the setting for *The Thousand and One Arabian Nights*, was not obeyed throughout the Islamic world. Both Spain, ruled by Umayyad princes, and Morocco refused to recognize his authority. From 910 a Shi'ite dynasty, the Fatimids, also claimed to be the rightful caliphs and gradually extended their power from Yemen to Egypt, North Africa and Sicily. In 929 the Spanish ruler, Abd Al-Rahman II, likewise declared himself caliph. By this time there were other semi-autonomous dynasties in Morocco (the Idrisids),

When Mohammed began to preach in Mecca, his forthright message of the uniqueness of God was considered a threat to the prosperity of the city, which depended upon its status as a pilgrimage centre. Accordingly Mohammed sent some of the early converts to Ethiopia, where they sought sanctuary at the court of the Christian emperor, the Negus. The *World History* compiled around 1300 at Tabriz in northern Iran by Rashid al-Din records the incident *below*. On the left, turbanned envoys from Mecca plead for the return of the refugees; the Negus, in the centre, patiently inclines his ear. He finally refused. Ethiopia acquired an almost legendary status as an outpost of Christianity, and some medieval European scholars identified the kingdom with that of the legendary African ruler, Prester John.

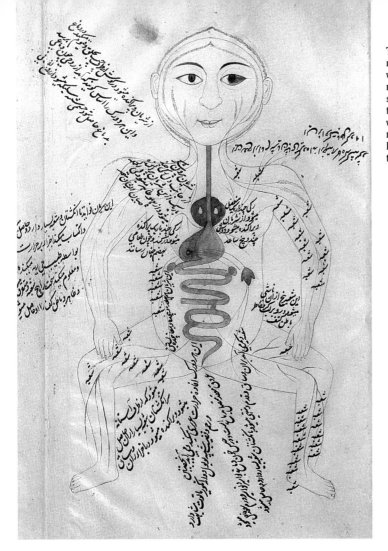

The sciences, and not least the study of medicine, were advanced in the Islamic world. This 17th-century Persian manuscript, entitled *A medical treasury*, *left*, shows that the internal human organs and the method by which the blood circulated were clearly understood. This illustration is more or less contemporary with the European discovery by William Harvey of the circulation of the blood.

Tunisia (the Aghlabids), Transoxiana (the Samanids) and Afghanistan (the Ghaznavids). Finally, from the middle of the tenth century, the caliphs in Baghdad came under the control of Turkish troops, and were restricted to the performance of their religious functions alone. Although the caliphate continued until the Mongol conquest in 1258, henceforward it was a mere shadow of its former self.

With so much political fragmentation, the historian is bound to wonder why the power and influence of Islam should have continued more or less unabated in the centuries that followed. In part, the explanation lies in the weakness of its neighbours: Europe was little more than a mosaic of warring states, and so was India, while the energies of imperial China, after the T'ang, were concentrated on withstanding renewed barbarian attacks (chapter 7). The religious toleration of the Islamic states also played its part: the 'peoples of the book' – the Jews, Christians and Zoroastrians who worshipped one God and revered His written revelations – were protected and left to practise their faith unmolested. They were no 'fifth column'.

But in the main, Islam remained powerful because its component states, though smaller, were still strong in comparison with their neighbours – especially the Fatimids in Egypt, the Ghaznavids in Afghanistan, and the Almohads in Spain. The Fatimid Al-Muiz (952-75), for example, ruled from the Euphrates to the Atlantic, and founded the city of Cairo as his capital, endowing it in 971 with the university of Al-Azhar (a full three centuries before any such centre of learning appeared in Christian Europe). Slightly later, Mahmud of Ghazni (998-1003) ravaged the Punjab and extended his rule from the Oxus to the Indus, making his capital of Ghazni one of the most glittering centres of the Islamic world. Later still, in Spain, the Almohads managed to hold the Christian reconquest a little south of the Tagus and gathered together the leading philosophers of the age, including Maimonides, a Jew born in Córdoba in 1132, and the great Aristotelian scholar, Averroës. Theirs was also a golden age of Muslim architecture, which can still be admired in the great mosque of Seville with its towering minaret, known today as 'La Giralda', and in the magnificent Alhambra, the 'red citadel' of Granada, with its courtyards, pavilions, gardens and richly decorated galleries. Seville, which the Almohads made their capital, was outstanding among the European cities of its day for its brilliant intellectual life, its elegant pottery and glassware, and its fine weapons and metalwork. Only the great Christian victory at Las Navas de Tolosa, in 1212, ended the days of Moorish splendour.

The Alhambra (or Red Fort) was built on a hill overlooking Granada in southern Spain between 1238 and 1354. It is the finest example of late Moorish architecture in Europe, comprising a citadel, a palace (Granada was the capital of the Moorish rulers of Spain) and the quarters once used by the royal officials. The halls and chambers surround a series of open courtyards, such as the Court of Lions *right* with arcades resting on 124 white marble columns, and a fountain at the centre supported by white marble lions. The Court of Myrtles *above* is famous for its delicate honeycomb vaults, decorated with marble, glazed tiles, and moulded plaster.

The fusion of Seljuk and Persian art is reflected in this fine polychrome bowl made in the 13th century in the Near East. It shows the Seljuk army — horse archers supported by artillery in the shape of a giant catapult — defeating a rival tribe. Exquisite glazed pottery, with both figurative and abstract designs, is among the finest achievements of medieval Islamic culture.

Meanwhile, at the heart of the Islamic world, the backbone of the caliphate was stiffened by the rise to power of the Seljuk Turks, who established themselves in Baghdad in 1055, their leader taking the title 'sultan'. This initiated a remarkably successful partnership between the 'men of the sword', mainly of Turkish origin, and the 'men of the Law' (the administrators) who were Persian and Arab in culture. In 1071 the Seljuks routed a Byzantine army at Manzikert and drove the Christians out of most of Asia Minor: the important Greek outpost of Antioch fell in 1084. It is true that this reverse attracted a major counter-attack by the Christian west, known as the Crusades (chapter 9), which recovered Antioch (1098) and Jerusalem (1099); but the Seljuks managed to keep the invaders pinned down to the coastal plain until, less than a century later, an army from Egypt under Saladin (successor to the Fatimid dynasty) reconquered almost the entire Levant. Jerusalem, the third holiest place of Islam (after Mecca and Medina) was regained; and

the Dome of the Rock, its fine seventh-century mosque, was restored to Muslim worship for good.

'There is no God but Allah and Mohammed is his Prophet,' says the Koran; and by 1200 that message was proclaimed not only in Jerusalem, Mecca and Medina, but from the Atlantic to the Himalayas. Over the next three centuries, it began to be heard even further afield. In the east, merchants and missionaries carried it to the Malay peninsula and then on to the Indonesian archipelago, Borneo and the southern Philippines. In Africa, Muslim traders travelled across the great caravan routes of the Sahara, bringing Islam to the kingdom of Mali as early as 1350, and later to the Hausa states in what is now Nigeria. They also travelled from Egypt to Ethiopia and down the Swahili coast to Sofala.

From its cradle in Arabia, Islam first became the opportunistic creed of a horde of Arab conquerors, and then the passionately-held faith of millions of non-Arab adherents. And it was by capturing the hearts and souls of the conquered peoples that it entered on the inheritance of the ancient world and became its heir. The purely Arab contribution to Islamic culture is easily exaggerated: it was the more civilized peoples of Egypt, Syria, Mesopotamia and Persia who, after their conversion to Islam, made the real impact. Few of the writers, philosophers and thinkers whom we associate with the flowering of Islamic civilization were Arabs by origin. The transmission of Greek learning comes from Alexandria and other ancient centres of classical culture. Nevertheless, for a thousand years after the birth of Mohammed, Islam was the leading civilization of the western hemisphere. Its neighbours – whether in central Asia, Africa or Europe – long remained underdeveloped and impoverished in comparison; and when, eventually, their intellectual achievements matched those of the Muslims, much of it was due to the traditions and inspiration of the world of Islam.

Islam today numbers some 400 million adherents, about one-seventh of the world's population, and Islamic culture has set an indelible print on about one-fifth of the earth's surface. The great mosques and minarets dominate the skyline of Islamic towns from southern Spain to south-east Asia. They remain singular in style and immediately recognisable. The Dome of the Rock in Jerusalem *above* is one of the oldest surviving Islamic monuments, completed in 691. The mausoleum of Tamerlane *left* at his capital Samarkand, in modern Russia, dates from 1405; it is, predictably, less well maintained than the slightly later and more modest dome at Mahan in central Iran *above left*.

137

Legend

——	Frankish empire 814	→→	routes of Magyar invasions
- - -	Byzantine empire c. 1025	▢	areas of Viking settlement and penetration
▢	areas of Muslim settlement and penetration	→	Viking routes

GREENLAND

Arctic Ocean

White Sea

to Greenland 982,
America c. 1000

ICELAND

870

Faroe Is.

Shetland Is.

Orkney Is.

Bergen
Stavanger

SCANDINAVIA

Uppsala

Björkö

Baltic Sea

Staraya Ladoga

Novgorod

KIEVAN
RUSSIA

North Sea

IRELAND
Dublin
Limerick
Waterford
Wexford

York

BRITAIN

London
Winchester

Ribe
Hedeby

Hamburg

✗ Süntel (782)

R. Elbe

R. Vistula

R. Dnieper

Kiev

R. Dniester

Carpathian Mts.

Cologne

Aachen ✗ Tertry (687)
Rouen
Paris
Chartres

FRANKISH

R. Rhine

HUNGARY

R. Danube

Black Sea

✗ Lechfeld (955)

Atlantic Ocean

844

Santiago de
Compostela

Roncesvalles
(778)

Pyrenees

Bordeaux

Toulouse

EMPIRE

R. Rhône

Arles

ALPS

Venice

Pavia

Bologna
Ravenna

Constantinople

BYZANTINE

✗ Poitiers (732)

Barcelona

R. Ebro

Corsica

ITALY

Rome

Taranto

EMPIRE

Anatolia

CALIPHATE

O F

CORDOBA

Cordoba
Seville

859

Balearic Is.

Sardinia

Sicily

Crete

Mediterranean Sea

Tunis

Kairouan

NORTH AFRICA

70

30

10

CHAPTER 9
EUROPE
RECOVERS
800–1250

On Christmas Day in the year 800, at Mass in St Peter's Basilica at Rome, Charles, King of the Franks and Lombards – better known to us as Charles the Great or Charlemagne – was acclaimed Emperor and crowned by the Pope. For the first time since the fall of the Roman empire (chapter 7), a ruler had emerged who was strong enough to unify Western Europe. Yet when Charlemagne was born, less than sixty years before, his father was not even a king – only the power behind the throne in a kingdom that was effectively limited to northern and central France, the Low Countries and the Rhineland. Between his accession in 768 and his imperial coronation in 800, Charlemagne secured the legitimacy of his dynasty (which was to rule for more than a century and a half), established his rule throughout Gaul, and extended his territorial authority from the Elbe to the Ebro and from the North Sea to Rome. His imperial coronation by the Pope was an unequivocal sign that, after 400 years of chaos, Europe was on the way to recovery.

But Charlemagne's concern lay not solely with conquest. Many scholars and artists came to court under his patronage: the Northumbrian Alcuin, a gifted teacher of young adolescents in the clerical community serving York cathedral, from England; the Lombard Paul the Deacon, a poet, grammarian and historian, from Friuli in Italy; the East Frankish Einhard, one of the few literate laymen of the period and author of the first biography of Charlemagne, from Germany. These men, and others like them (often their pupils), rescued classical Latin learning from oblivion and ensured its transmission to later generations. They also added distinctive innovations of their own – such as a new, clear script for the text of their books, now known as 'Carolingian minuscule'. It seems familiar to us because the first printers of the Italian Renaissance, some six centuries later, chose examples of it as the model for lower case type.

Charlemagne's throne c.805, and tomb 1215, at Aachen his imperial capital, offer a strong contrast in styles. Although the emperor was one of the most powerful rulers of his day, his marble throne *below right*, modelled on descriptions of that of Solomon, was still simple and austere. By the thirteenth century, however, his successors spared no expense in celebrating and honouring his memory when adorning this tomb *above* with jewels and gold. No verifiable likeness of Charlemagne exists, and later artists and craftsmen presented idealized images.

The invasions *left* No part of the Christian West was immune from external attack in the 9th and 10th centuries. From their base in the Hungarian Plain the Magyars traversed vast distances, but as they moved fast the disruption they caused was short-lived. Arabs and Vikings established bases in the west and were consequently a more persistent threat; the Arabs were eventually expelled, but the Norwegian and Danish invaders were in time assimilated, as were the Swedes, who penetrated eastern Europe and Russia, establishing trading contacts as far as Constantinople and, eventually, Baghdad.

Beatissimo papae Damaso
Hieronimus

Nouum opus me facere cogis ex uetere · ut post exemplaria scrip
turarum toto orbe disperса · quasi quidam arbiter sedeam
& quia inter se uariant quae sint illa quae cum greca consent
ant ueritate decernam · Pius labor · sed periculosa praesump
tio · Iudicare de ceteris ipsum ab omnibus iudicandum · senis muta
re linguam · & canescentem mundum ad initia retrahere paruu
lorum · Quis enim doctus pariter uel indoctus cum in manus suo
lumen adsumpserit · & a saliua quam semel in bibit uiderit discre
pare quod lectitat · Non statim erumpat in uocem me falsarium
me clamans esse sacrilegum quia audeam aliquid in ueteribus
libris addere mutare corrigere · Aduersus quam inuidiam du
plex causa me consolatur · Quod & tu qui summus sacerdos es
fieri iubes · & uerum non esse quod uariat & male dicorum

The Carolingian Renaissance, however, did not last long. Charlemagne's only surviving son, Louis 'the Pious', succeeded him peacefully in 814; but even before his death, in 840, first quarrels and then wars had broken out among his heirs. This forced his subjects to give their allegiance to one claimant and reject the others, bringing armed conflict to most of the Frankish heartland. Gradually, a distinction began to emerge between the lands to the east of the Rhine that became the nucleus of Germany and those in the west that became the core of France; the unity established by Charlemagne was shattered for ever. No single ruler would dominate the entire continent again for another thousand years.

But no doubt, sooner or later, the enormously long frontiers would have proved impossible to defend effectively for, shortly after Charlemagne's death, Europe came under heavy attack from outside. In the north and west the Scandinavian peoples, the Vikings, were on the move – at first raiding by sea, but then acquiring land-bases around convenient estuaries, and learning to fight and conquer from horseback. Important Viking colonies were established in the west, around the river Humber in England, where numerous Yorkshire and Lincolnshire villages with names ending in -by reveal the scale of Scandinavian settlement; around the Seine estuary in Normandy, which was ceded to the Vikings by the Carolingian ruler of France in 911; and on the islands off the northern and western coasts of Scotland, and in Ireland (with their capital at Dublin). In the east, other Scandinavian groups penetrated Russia, where they created in the ninth century a series of small states based on such centres as Novgorod and Kiev. One of these bands already called themselves the Rus, from which the entire country was to take its name; and their leader, Rurik, was regarded as the ancestor of all the tsars.

Meanwhile a second, separate group of invaders attacked Christian Europe from the south. Muslim Arabs from Africa overran Spain,

Carolingian minuscule c.880 *above left* was developed and used by scholars at the court of Charlemagne and his successors, as in these 9th-century Gospels from France. Gradually it spread from the imperial court to other centres. The first printers of the Renaissance, six centuries later, chose examples of it as the model for their 'lower case' type: the appearance of the printed *Gutenberg Bible* of 1455 (chapter 17) is therefore not much different from this manuscript text.

Byzantine silk c.1000 *above* from the imperial workshops of Basil II. This heavy silk and twill fabric, decorated with heraldic designs like several others of similar date, was no doubt originally intended as a hanging for the walls of a palace; but it was eventually placed in a tomb in St Germain at Auxerre in France. Byzantine works of art were keenly sought in western Europe, and Charlemagne himself invited Byzantine artists and scholars to work at his court.

Viking silver at Björkö, 10th century
right The bracelets and brooches from Britain and the hoard of silver coins from the Middle East reflect the prosperity which came through trade and piracy to the Vikings in the 9th and 10th centuries. These items came from some of the town's 3000 excavated graves.

attacked southern France, raided what little shipping there was in the western Mediterranean, and in the late ninth and tenth centuries wrested Sicily and parts of southern Italy from the Byzantine Empire (chapter 8). Finally, in the late ninth century, a previously unknown nomadic people from central Asia, the Magyars, launched destructive raids on central and southern Germany and penetrated deep into Italy. At last, in 955, King Otto I of Germany won a decisive victory over the Magyars at a battle on the river Lech, in what is now Bavaria, after which they retreated and began to settle on the plain of Hungary.

So, by the middle of the tenth century, the tide of invasion had been halted. The Vikings had become assimilated by the societies they had defeated: those in Normandy, for example, soon adopted the language, institutions and religion of the rest of northern France. The Muslims were kept south of the Pyrenees. The Magyars remained in Hungary. The preservation of an independent western civilization was symbolized in 962 by the coronation in Rome of Otto I of Germany, the victor over the Magyars, as Emperor of the West, the successor of Charlemagne. For more than seven centuries, the imperial title would be associated with German dynasties, their lands called (from 1254 onwards) the 'Holy Roman Empire'.

Meanwhile, in the east, the Byzantine empire too was recovering from a long period of weakness. The failure of the Muslim siege of the capital, Constantinople, in 717-718 (chapter 8) did not end the threat of further Islamic assaults. For almost two hundred years, the eastern empire remained on the defensive, recovering only in the midtenth century with the campaigns by land and sea of a brilliant Byzantine commander, Nicephorus Phocas, who briefly became emperor (963-69). Under him, Crete, Cyprus and Syria were regained for Christendom. With their eastern frontier thus secured, the emperors turned their attention northwards to Bulgaria, whose rulers had long exploited Byzantium's preoccupation with Islam in order to exact tribute and exert pressure. Basil II (966-1025) campaigned successfully – and ruthlessly – against the Bulgars: after one battle, in 1014, for example, he blinded 15,000 prisoners and sent them home with 150 'guides' who had had only one of their eyes put out. By 1018 he had conquered all of Bulgaria, pushing the imperial frontier back to the Danube, and earning himself the title 'Basil the Bulgar-slayer'. In the wake of these conquests came missionaries. The Greek Orthodox Church had already gained many converts in south-eastern Europe, thanks to the efforts of men like Saint Cyril and Saint Methodius, whose religious allegiance was to Constantinople, not Rome. Now, during the tenth century, their successors also won over Kievan Russia, giving it both the Orthodox religion and the distinctive 'Cyrillic' alphabet and script that survive today.

Whereas the Byzantine empire was a centralized state, divided into some thirty provinces, known as *themes*, with a single bureaucracy, army and legal system, in western Europe effective political authority remained fragmented. Men with titles such as duke, marquis, or count – who had originally led armies and presided over courts of justice in their king's name – now acknowledged only a distant allegiance to their monarch, and passed on title and powers to a son or other descendant, mostly without challenge. They and their families also controlled bishoprics and monasteries and regarded themselves as the 'owners' of lesser churches. Some, like Duke William of Normandy, who defeated the last native English king at the battle of Hastings in 1066, even went on to conquer a whole kingdom.

Lesser landowners too – known usually as *milites* or knights – were busily extending their properties, maximizing the return from their lands, and increasing their power over those who cultivated them. Estates were consolidated; increased labour services and higher rents were exacted. The area of land under cultivation also expanded. In the Po valley and along the North Sea coasts, for example, marshes were drained to become arable land or pasture; inland, further inroads were made into the already much-diminished natural forest, sometimes by peasants seeking new opportunities for themselves, but more often by the agents of a royal or noble landlord. In almost all areas, the general trend over two or three centuries was one of marked increase in population, until a peak was reached about the year 1300, when Europe may have had 80 million inhabitants, two or three times as many as 300 years previously.

The Norman Conquest of England in 1066 was a major military operation. Duke William of Normandy led his uniformly mail-clad warriors across the Channel *right* to the south coast of England, where a single battle, near Hastings, brought Saxon rule to an end. Shortly afterwards, the principal episodes of the campaign, and its antecedents – such as William's meetings with the Saxon leader, Harold, were embroidered on the 'Bayeux Tapestry' *above*, forming a band of linen over 70 metres long. The continuous strip of action is accompanied by a Latin narrative and decorative borders, illustrating scenes from everyday life, which reflect and comment on the story, and which together form a remarkable piece of political propaganda.

Pope Urban II at Cluny in 1095 *left* Since the days of Charlemagne, the Roman church had fallen increasingly under the control of laymen. But in the early 11th century pressure grew from within to improve clerical standards and loosen the dependence of churchmen on their lay patrons. At first, the reform movement was led by the abbots and monks of convents like Cluny, in Burgundy, but it soon won the active support of the papacy. Here Pope Urban II (1088-99), himself a former prior of Cluny, attended by cardinals, consecrates the third church at the Abbey. On the right stand the abbot and his monks.

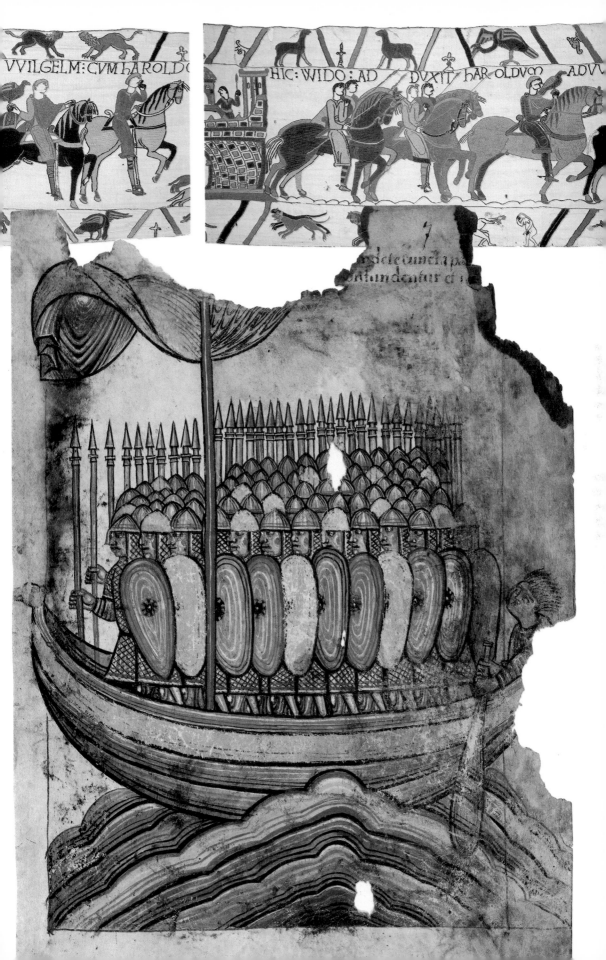

Everywhere, the towns stood out as centres of growth. Some were new settlements, developing in the eleventh and twelfth centuries around fortresses constructed to resist the Vikings or other invaders. Others dated from Roman times, steadily increasing their populations until they spilled out beyond existing limits. At Cologne, for example, in western Germany, three new circuits of walls were constructed within 180 years, more than doubling the size of the town. Lübeck on the Baltic was rebuilt and fortified in 1143 by the local Count and, according to the chronicler Helmold:

'Because the land had been deserted, he sent messengers to every country, to Flanders and Holland, Utrecht, Westphalia and Friesland to invite anyone who was suffering from land-hunger to come with his family to receive a very good land and a large one, fertile, well-stocked with fish and flesh and good pasture for cattle.'

The multitude of various peoples who responded to the Count's invitation provided the solid economic base for the subsequent prosperity of Lübeck and other towns further east. But the wealth of Lübeck was also due to a series of treaties made with other towns both to reduce conflict and to facilitate access to each other's markets. In time, these alliances grew into the Hanseatic League, under Lübeck's leadership, which linked towns and cities from London in the west to Novgorod in the east, and from Bergen in the north to Cologne in the south. The League dealt on equal terms with the rulers of all the lands through which their commercial convoys passed, and was able to supply all Europe with timber, furs, fish and grain.

Even more spectacular developments were taking place around the north-western shores of the Mediterranean. First, Arab bases along the coast – above all the stronghold at Fraxinetum – were regained; then the islands – Corsica, Sardinia, Sicily, Malta – were reconquered by the Christians. Italian seafarers from Genoa, Pisa, Venice and Amalfi were able to trade extensively in the Mediterranean which, for almost three centuries, had been under Muslim control. The merchants of Genoa and Pisa sailed mainly to Spain and North Africa; those from Venice and Amalfi to Constantinople and the Levant. All these cities began to serve as an entrepôt where the goods of Europe could be readily exchanged for the exotic wares of Asia and Africa, with the Italians growing rich on the profits. Wool, iron, furs and other raw materials were brought over the Alps; silks, sugar, spices and wine were taken back. Although this commerce was already gathering momentum in the tenth century, it underwent a further dramatic expansion after 1100, thanks to the achievements of the Crusading movement.

In 1095 Pope Urban II called upon kings, nobles and knights – as well as ordinary people – to 'Rise up and remember the manly deeds of your ancestors, the prowess and greatness of Charlemagne', and to 'take up the cross' and recover the Holy Places in Palestine for the Faith. The response of ordinary Christians in the West was remarkable. Tens of thousands set out: lords and servants, peasants and townsmen, spilled out of Europe and descended on the Middle East.

Many Crusaders were moved by pious zeal. Some of them sought forgiveness for their sins by helping to expel the infidel; others, especially the humblest who went first on the 'People's Crusade' (and mostly died on the way), confused the heavenly and the earthly Jerusalem they had heard about in sermons. But not all the Crusaders were moved by piety. Stephen, Count of Blois, took up the cross primarily to escape a nagging wife (and when he found the siege of Antioch was even worse, he hurried back home). Bohemond, younger son of the ruler of Naples, took up the cross specifically to carve out a principality

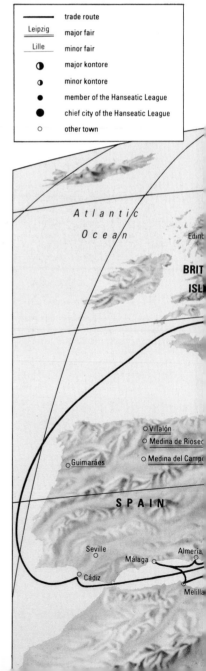

European trade *below* 14th-century Venice and the Hanseatic League provided sea-links between the Mediterranean and northern Europe in the later Middle Ages. Venetian galleys brought spices, silks, wines and fruit; Hanseatic counting houses (*kontore*) held ready stocks of metals, fish, textiles and Russian furs. Their meetings in Flanders joined two huge zones of commercial activity and the resulting trade-flows brought great profit to Italy's merchant-financiers. Genoa, like Venice, had a long history of trade in the Mediterranean and across Europe, and by the end of the Middle Ages her trading network had established Genoa as the major commercial rival to Venice.

——	trade route
Leipzig	major fair
Lille	minor fair
◑	major kontore
◔	minor kontore
●	member of the Hanseatic League
⬤	chief city of the Hanseatic League
○	other town

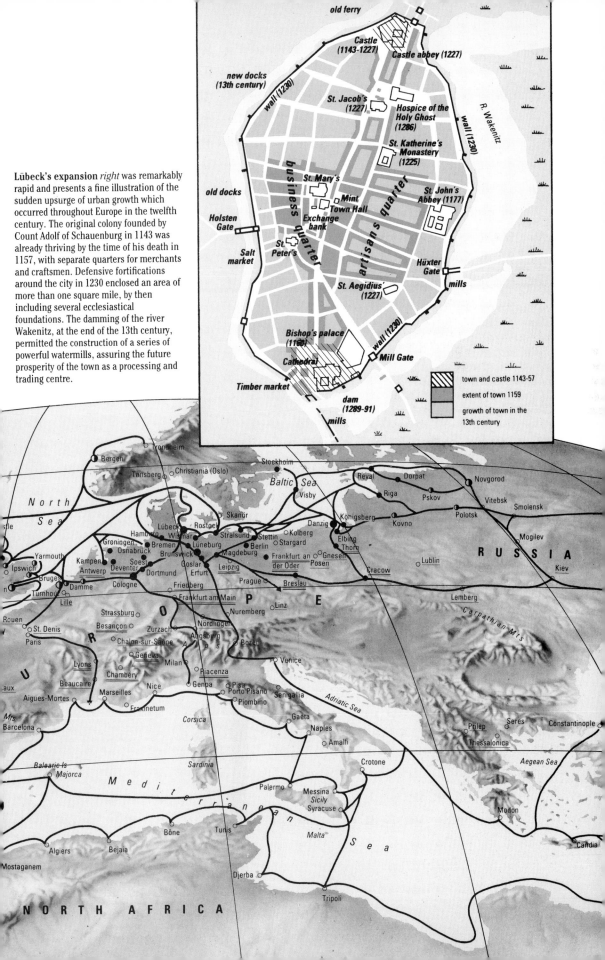

Lübeck's expansion *right* was remarkably rapid and presents a fine illustration of the sudden upsurge of urban growth which occurred throughout Europe in the twelfth century. The original colony founded by Count Adolf of Schauenburg in 1143 was already thriving by the time of his death in 1157, with separate quarters for merchants and craftsmen. Defensive fortifications around the city in 1230 enclosed an area of more than one square mile, by then including several ecclesiastical foundations. The damming of the river Wakenitz, at the end of the 13th century, permitted the construction of a series of powerful watermills, assuring the future prosperity of the town as a processing and trading centre.

old ferry

Castle
(1143-1227)

Castle abbey (1227)

new docks
(13th century)

wall (1230)

St. Jacob's
(1227)

Hospice of the
Holy Ghost
(1286)

R. Wakenitz

wall (1230)

St. Katherine's
Monastery
(1225)

business quarter

old docks

St. Mary's

Mint
Town Hall

St. John's
Abbey (1177)

Holsten
Gate

Exchange
bank

artisans quarter

Salt
market

St.
Peter's

Hüxter
Gate

mills

St. Aegidius
(1227)

Bishop's palace
(1160)

wall (1230)

Mill Gate

Cathedral

Timber market

dam
(1289-91)

mills

town and castle 1143-57

extent of town 1159

growth of town in the
13th century

for himself in the east (and did so at Antioch). Together these minor western rulers, and others like them, gathered with their followers at Constantinople in 1096, swore an oath of allegiance to the Byzantine emperor and set out to regain the lands lost to Islam. Aided by temporary disunity among the Muslim states opposing them, they recaptured Nicaea in 1097, Antioch in 1098 and – in an orgy of bloodletting against Jews as well as Muslims – Jerusalem in 1099.

At once the Crusaders, who by now numbered perhaps only ten thousand, created states of their own at Antioch, Edessa, Jerusalem and Tripoli. To defend them they built magnificent castles such as the Krak des Chevaliers, which still stands today in what is now Syria; and, as garrison troops, they employed mainly members of military orders – the Knights Hospitallers and the Knights Templar – which were specially formed to keep the Holy Land in Christian hands. Meanwhile the Crusader barons themselves lived ostentatiously in the coastal cities, where their needs could more easily be supplied by merchant fleets from Italy. They had become a colonial élite, isolated behind their massive fortifications from both the native population and from their peers in the west.

This isolation contributed significantly to the Crusading movement's eventual failure. For nearly a hundred years the Crusaders held on to their possessions in the Levant, but already in the latter half of the twelfth century the Muslims surrounding them recovered their strength. Powerful leaders like Saladin of Egypt led them in a *jihad*, or holy war, against the Christian invaders. In 1187, less than a century after its recapture, the Christians lost Jerusalem (chapter 8). From this time forward, the Crusader states were doomed.

Part of their problem was simple logistics: the journey to the Near East was a hazardous one at the best of times. Relatively few were prepared to contemplate it, whilst those who did arrive safely often became homesick and, like Stephen of Blois or Bohemond of Antioch, soon decided to return. Not all of them made it. Some were captured by the Saracens – like Louis IX of France, after his abortive attempt to conquer Egypt in 1250. He was lucky: most of his army was killed. Others simply got lost, like Count Hugh of Vaudémont, who began his return in 1249, but did not reach home for fourteen years and he died

The Crusaders take Antioch in 1098
below according to the chronicle of William of Tyre (1130-85), chancellor and historian of the Latin kingdom of Jerusalem. This illustrated manuscript copy, completed in France around 1280, contains an imaginative representation of the first major success of the First Crusade.

The Crusaders sack Jerusalem in 1099
right from a mid-14th century version of William of Tyre's chronicle. The Crusading chronicles were among the first popular works of European secular literature, and their colourful and inventive illustrations reflect something of the myopic European view of the wider world.

Krak des Chevaliers *below left* in modern Syria is one of the masterpieces of military architecture and a formidable example of medieval engineering. Built in 1131 by the Crusading order of the Knights of St John (Hospitallers), it was designed to withstand extensive sieges. Two concentric towered walls, separated by a wide moat, surmount a naturally inaccessible outcrop, and could garrison up to 2,000 men. It was held by the Christians until 1271.

Saladin defeats the Crusaders in 1187
below right from the Great Chronicle of Matthew Paris. The Muslim reconquest of the Holy Land was achieved by Saladin (1138-93), the ruler of Syria and Egypt, whose victory at Hattin in July 1187 was so complete that not enough Crusaders were left to defend the fortified strongholds of the Latin kingdom. The Great Chronicle of Matthew Paris, compiled in England in the mid-13th century, portrayed the loss of Jerusalem and its priceless Christian relics, such as the True Cross, as a major disaster.

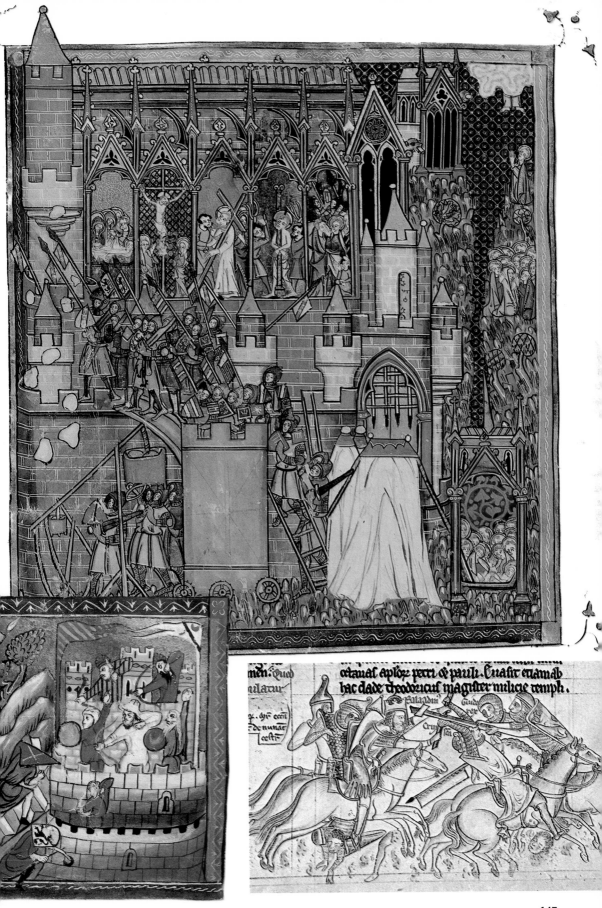

Knights Hospitallers at Rhodes c.1480
right Also known as the Knights of St John, the Hospitallers were one of the most important of the Crusading orders. They cared for sick Crusaders and pilgrims as well as defending Christian outposts against Muslim attack. From 1309 to 1522 they garrisoned the island of Rhodes and after its loss to the Ottoman Turks (chapter 14) they moved to Malta.

shortly afterwards. Such experiences must have discouraged many potential Crusaders from setting forth; and, in the end, the Crusading kingdoms failed, essentially, through lack of manpower.

In the chronicles compiled by Muslims, the Crusades are scarcely mentioned: the Islamic world considered them insignificant. But this view is unjust. In the Near East, a Christian presence was maintained on the mainland until the fall of Acre in 1291, and offshore until the fall of Rhodes and Cyprus in the sixteenth century. Even today, parts of the lands once dominated by the great Crusading castles are still inhabited by Maronite Christians who are the direct heirs of those Arabs who became followers of the Church of Rome in the twelfth century. And in parts of the west, the impact and legacy of the Crusades was far greater. A sustained offensive by the Christians in Spain steadily drove back the Muslims until by 1275 only the kingdom of Granada was in Arab hands. In north-eastern Europe, the Christian states in what are now Germany, Poland and Hungary zealously conquered and converted their pagan neighbours further east. This movement was spearheaded by the Teutonic Knights who came to control the lands on the southern coast of the Baltic Sea. Subject populations were held down by a network of fortresses constructed with all the refinements of design learnt

St Francis of Assisi *above* preaching to the birds as depicted by Giotto (c.1267-1337). The austere life-style and love of nature displayed by St Francis (c.1181-1226) had attracted some 5000 disciples by the time of his death, and the religious order he founded continued to expand rapidly. About a century later, the Italian artist, Giotto, famous for the innovatory naturalism of his style, was commissioned to paint leading scenes from the founder's life.

from Byzantium and the Arabs in the Near East. Like the Hospitallers and the Templars, the Teutonic Knights observed a strict code of celibacy and maintained rigorous self-discipline. But they also earned a reputation for ruthlessness. For them, salvation was to be won not only by self-sacrifice but by bringing others to Christ, if necessary by force. Thousands were butchered in the northern Crusades.

It was a very different kind of crusade that the Italian monk St Francis of Assisi preached in the first quarter of the thirteenth century, initially in the face of indifference and outright hostility. His message of peace and compassion to all forms of life won many converts but offered a remarkable contrast to the more aggressive methods employed by the Knights. And yet spreading the word of God on the point of the sword was not as incongruous then as it appears to us today. For, by the time of St Francis, knighthood was both a way of life and an integral part of the institutional structure of all western kingdoms. Its most visible expressions were the stone castles which became common all over western Europe. Although many were built to defend an open frontier against an enemy – as in Normandy between the duke and his suzerain the king of France, or in Spain between the Christian states and the Moors – elsewhere castles were built simply to impress or overawe one's subjects and neighbours. The knights who owned them became landlords and administrators, rather than frontiersmen.

The knightly class, and especially its younger sons, also became an important source of recruitment to the growing class of professional lay administrators in the service of kings, dukes and counts: they worked side by side with the clerics who were still largely responsible for the written records of central administration. In England in particular, they were even more important at a local level, playing a key part in the administration of justice and later in the assessment and collection of taxes. But the knights and barons were not always passive vassals, blindly strengthening the authority of their king at the expense of their own traditional privileges. From time to time, royal attempts at centralization provoked civil wars which forced monarchs to issue promises, even formal guarantees like England's Magna Carta of 1215, that they would in future respect the rights of their leading subjects.

It was the constitutional victories of the barons that led kings, in the thirteenth century, to call into being assemblies representing their non-noble subjects as a counter-balancing force. But, even so, in the 'Parliaments' (as they were called in England and Scotland), the different status of the two groups was clearly recognized: the nobles, summoned as individuals, formed one chamber; elected knights, together with representatives of the towns, formed another. This bicameral Parliamentary system was found in the British Isles, Scandinavia, and eastern Europe – the areas surrounding the old Carolingian

The English Parliament 1295 *right* first assembled under Edward I (1272-1307), shown here surrounded by lords, clerics and commons. Note also the seats formed from bales of wool, forerunners of the Woolsack, the official seat of the Lord Chancellor today. However, the attendance of the rulers of Scotland and Wales, shown flanking Edward, is misleading; both rulers in reality rejected England's claims to sovereignty.

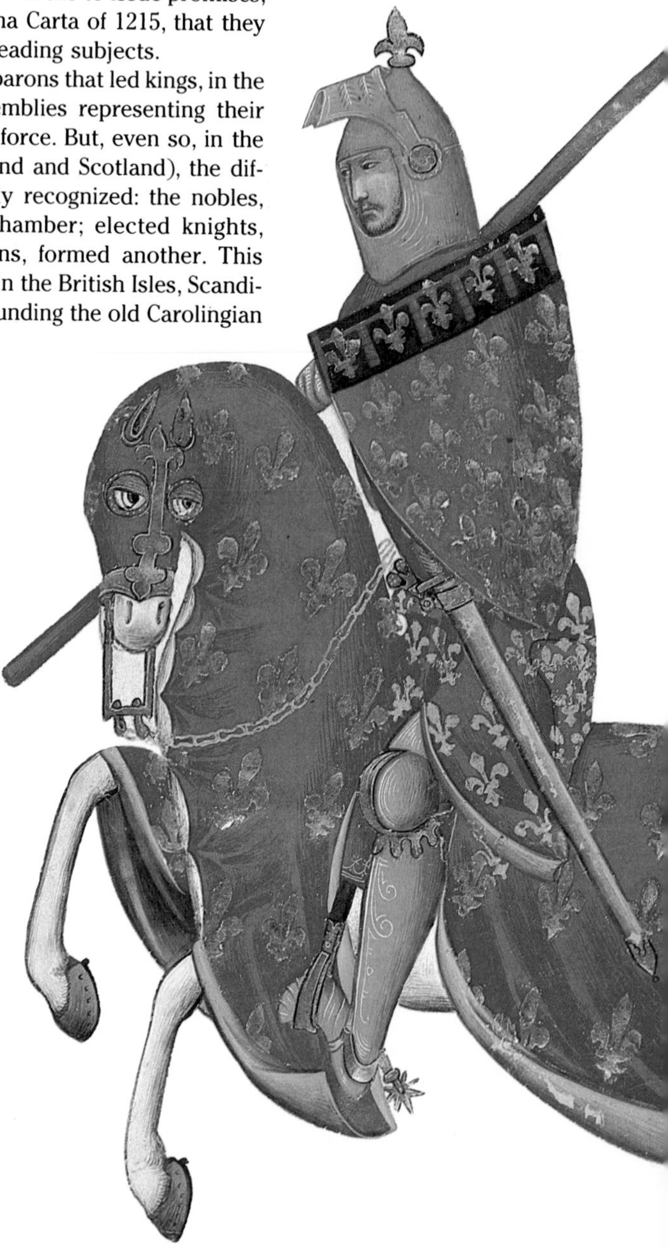

The European knights of the 14th century *right* were very different from those of earlier times. Where the warriors of Charlemagne and William of Normandy had worn chain-mail, those of later centuries were protected by an interlocking carapace of steel plates. The extra weight of these made it necessary to breed horses that were both larger and stronger than before, and often they went into battle carrying armour plating of their own. This French warrior, however, on his richly decorated charger, is in full heraldic dress ready for some local pageant or court function.

150

longtain voiage: quil souffira de porter seulemet vng
las de soye a vng ymage de sainct george pendat a icellui.
Aussi se ledit colier dor auoit besoings de reputacion il pora
estre mis en la main de sounier iusques a ce quil soit
repure. Lequel colier aussi ne pourra estre enrichy de
pierres ou daultres choses/ reserue les ymage qui pourra
estre garny au plaisir du cheualier. Et aussi ne pourra
estre ledit colier vendu engaigte donne ne aliene pour
necessite ou cause quelconque que ce soit

Alexander Rex
Scotox

lewellin
princeps
vvallie

The Domesday Book 1086 *below* compiled for William the Conqueror by seven or eight teams of royal commissioners, recorded the pattern of landholding throughout England south of the river Tees. All over the country they convened juries of local men and questioned them about the ownership, value, production and assets of each manor. The data was then reorganized and copied down so that the holdings of the King and his leading vassals in each county could be seen at a glance. Here the holdings of various churches in the county of Gloucester are summarized, starting with Archbishop Thomas of York and his predecessors *top left*, and working through the Bishop of Worcester and Hereford to the abbeys of Glastonbury and Malmesbury. In terms of thoroughness, clarity and speed of compilation, the Domesday Book had few equals in medieval Europe.

empire. But within the Carolingian heartland – France, the Low Countries, and western Germany – and also in Spain and Italy, representative assemblies developed later, and normally possessed three chambers rather than two: clergy, nobles and towns.

All these developments were accompanied by – and indeed depended upon – a massive extension of written records. In 1066 Duke William of Normandy conquered England. Twenty years later he ordered the compilation of a massive village-by-village survey of the whole kingdom, recording who owned the land at the time, who had owned it immediately after the conquest, and who had held it just before. The survey, known as the Domesday Book, bristled with information on the population, wealth, and property of each community.

It was soon joined by other volumes of government records: 'Pipe Rolls' recording the king's income and expenditure; 'Assize Rolls' reporting legal cases heard by judges who toured the country regularly from the middle of the twelfth century; 'Plea Rolls' registering cases decided by the central courts which already met, as they still do, at Westminster. Similar records were preserved by other European states from the twelfth century onwards: England may have been the most highly centralized of the western kingdoms, but it was not unique.

The administration of government and justice required the services of a class of literate laymen, several of whom had attended one of the institutions of higher learning which in the twelfth and thirteenth centuries grew out of cathedral schools or developed from a spontaneous assembling of 'masters' in one place and were eventually to be known as 'universities' – Paris, Oxford, Bologna, Salamanca and so on. At Paris, students at the beginning of the twelfth century could hear the stimulating lectures of Peter Abélard, who adopted the techniques of courtroom lawyers to establish the truth about theology and philosophy. His book *Sic et non (Yes and no)* attempted for the first time to found the Christian faith on the methods developed by other disciplines. A century and a half later, Thomas Aquinas from Naples produced two massive treatises, the *Summae*, which endeavoured to reconcile the Scriptures with ancient philosophy in general and with Aristotle (newly translated from Greek into Latin) in particular. Aquinas was convinced that there was no true contradiction between reason and revelation – or, where it appeared to exist, that it was due to some error by either the philosopher or his interpreter. 'Wisdom', he

Medieval education in Europe centred at first on the schools attached to important monasteries and cathedrals. In Paris *left*, Hugh of St Victor (1096-1141) advised his pupils 'Learn everything, and you will see that nothing is useless'. Here he comments upon the Bible, while a young monk follows the lesson in his own manuscript copy. Two centuries later *below*, teaching techniques had hardly changed. Master Brunet, a Latin teacher, instructs his students, not all of them tonsured monks. Some of them would go on to university, where Latin was the language of instruction throughout Europe until the sixteenth century.

wrote, 'by its very nature implies an abundance of knowledge, which enables a man to judge all things; for everyone has the capacity to judge what he fully knows'. Aquinas's views have a surprisingly modern ring to them, and they were quickly adopted as the touchstone of Catholic orthodoxy.

So by the end of the thirteenth century, western Europe had developed a unique culture, an expanding economy, and a distinctive form of state organization. Each was the result of a fusion of east and west – of Greek, Latin and Arab influences. Only the powerful position of the Church was distinctively European: but it was crucial. From the eleventh century, there was a single church for the whole of Latin Christendom, ruled from Rome: a glance at the correspondence of Pope Innocent III (1198-1216) shows that papal authority by then extended over the entire continent, from Iceland to Italy and from Sweden to Spain. But there were other unifying factors, too: monasteries, prelates and (from the 1220s) friars were found all over western Europe. Even the churches built in the twelfth and thirteenth centuries, in the Gothic style, were remarkably similar from one state to another. Yet, for a long time, these and other institutions of the Christian life remained confined to Europe. The Crusading states mostly crumbled within a century; the attempts to transplant the western system to the Baltic lands and the east European and Hungarian plains proved to be a slow and painful processs. And, in any case, before long, most of those areas were overwhelmed by an irresistible attack which threatened for a time the entire Christian world: the Mongol onslaught.

Gothic cathedrals appeared all over Europe in the 13th century. Perhaps their most distinctive element was the rib-vault, which enabled builders to construct far larger churches than ever before: the skeletal rib-vault dispersed the weight and stress of greater spans and taller elevations and permitted a greater wall area to be pierced with windows. The impressive late 12th-century nave at Bourges, in central France *right* is an early example of the new style. At the same time the façades of the new cathedrals became more ornate and irregular, festooned with sculptures and other features which, as at Wells, in England *below*, served to instruct as well as to impress the observer. The great churches and cathedrals of medieval Europe remain remarkable feats of organization and engineering as well as triumphs of design.

The Mongol horseman *left* was master of the plains, due to his immense versatility in the saddle. Whether rounding up horses or shooting arrows accurately at the gallop, the Mongols could operate at high speed with complete confidence. This tradition of horsemanship is preserved today among the herding tribes of Afghanistan, seen here playing Royal Buskashi, a forerunner of the game of polo.

The *yurt* below right still serves, in parts of Afghanistan, as the dwelling of nomad families. Made of skins or handwoven textiles stretched over a wooden frame, and decorated with brightly coloured rugs, it offers some protection against the fierce cold of the Asian steppe in winter, and the style has changed little since the days of Genghis Khan.

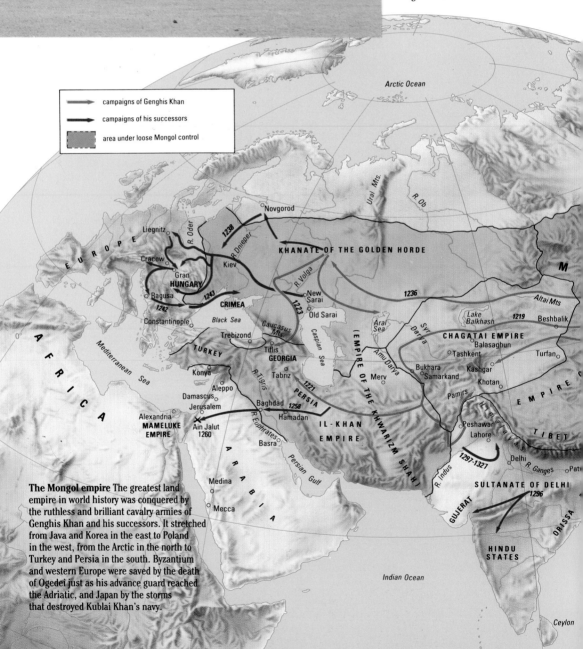

campaigns of Genghis Khan

campaigns of his successors

area under loose Mongol control

Arctic Ocean

Novgorod

1238

R. Oder

R. Dnieper

KHANATE OF THE GOLDEN HORDE

Ural Mts.

R. Ob

M

Liegnitz

Cracow

Kiev

R. Volga

1236

Altai Mts

EUROPE

Gran
HUNGARY

1243

New Sarai

Lake Balkhash

1219

Beshbalik

Ragusa

1242

CRIMEA

1223

Old Sarai

Aral Sea

CHAGATAI EMPIRE

Constantinople

Black Sea

Caucasus Mts.

Caspian Sea

Syr Darya

Balasaghun

Turfan

AFRICA

Trebizond

Tiflis

GEORGIA

Amu Darya

Tashkent

EMPIRE O

Mediterranean Sea

TURKEY

Tabriz

Merv

Bukhara

Kashgar

Khotan

Konya

R. Tigris

1221

Samarkand

Aleppo

PERSIA

Pamirs

TIBET

Damascus

Jerusalem

Baghdad

1258

IL-KHAN

Peshawar

Lahore

Alexandria
MAMELUKE
EMPIRE

Ain Jalut
1260

R. Euphrates

Hamadan

EMPIRE

1297-1321

Delhi

R. Ganges

Pat

Basra

ARABIA

Persian Gulf

R. Indus

SULTANATE OF DELHI

Medina

GUJERAT

1296

ORISSA

The Mongol empire The greatest land empire in world history was conquered by the ruthless and brilliant cavalry armies of Genghis Khan and his successors. It stretched from Java and Korea in the east to Poland in the west, from the Arctic in the north to Turkey and Persia in the south. Byzantium and western Europe were saved by the death of Ogedei just as his advance guard reached the Adriatic, and Japan by the storms that destroyed Kublai Khan's navy.

Mecca

HINDU STATES

Indian Ocean

Ceylon

CHAPTER 10

THE MONGOL ONSLAUGHT
850–1300

Geographically, the vast continent of Asia falls broadly into four divisions: the northern forest or *taiga*; the steppe, or prairie grassland; the desert; and the great river valleys of the south – the Yellow River and Yangtze, Ganges and Indus, Euphrates and Tigris. The last, the great river valleys, provided the life-blood of the early civilizations of China, India, and Mesopotamia; but the second, the steppe, was the home of the pastoral nomad. From northern China to Hungary, a distance of some 5,000 miles, pastoral nomads had lived on the steppe for centuries by raising animals, mainly horses and sheep, spending their lives wandering from place to place with their herds as they followed the pasture and the seasons.

Nomadic societies had always been both patriarchal and predatory – organized into clans which spent most of their time contesting the best grazing lands with their neighbours, or combining to plunder the fields and cities of the more sedentary people around them. So, by the very nature of his society, the nomad was compelled always to be ready for war. Since his livelihood – his herds of livestock – his home (a felt tent or *yurt*) and his family all had to move with him, there could be no walls for defence. Security depended on constant vigilance, readiness and, above all, mobility. Once the nomad had adopted the horse, the stirrup and the bow, he became a skilful horse-archer, the most formidable cavalryman in the world until modern times, with rider and horse both able to survive on the meagre resources of the wind-swept, thinly-populated steppe through even the most severe winter.

Life on the vast, open grasslands of Asia is hard and cruel. Summer lasts only three months, when from June to August the steppe blossoms into a carpet of grass and flowers. By September the cold is fierce. In October the plateaux are swept by blizzards; by November the rivers are frozen; and until the following March, snowfalls are frequent and the bare plain is swept by ferocious winds; and yet, from this harsh environment the Mongols staged their sudden, devastating and brief irruption into world history.

Mongol siege warfare c. 1310 *right* as seen by Rashid al-Din a Jewish physician (1247–1318) who converted to Islam and entered the service of the Mongol rulers of Persia at Tabriz. Eventually he became chief minister, and directed the compilation of the first true history of the world. From his colleagues he learnt about Genghis Khan; from a Catholic monk he acquired knowledge about Europe; from a Kashmiri Buddhist he found out about India. In this original version of his manuscript, covering the Indian campaigns of Mahmud of Ghazni in the early 11th century, a series of miniatures illustrate leading events – but in contemporary dress. Here Mahmud's troops, dressed like Mongol warriors, undertake a siege with a catapult, advised by an Arab specialist (bottom right), while the army's commanders (seated top right) look on.

Genghis Khan holds court c. 1220 *left* The rapid expansion of the Mongol empire is reflected in this 13th-century miniature. The manuscript it is taken from is Persian; some of the advisers wear the distinctive Chinese mandarin costume; the refreshments are served in Chinese porcelain. But the ruler is still unmistakably a nomad: his 'palace', although richly decorated, is still a *yurt* (a nomad tent), and the essential symbols of his authority are the yak-tails that fly outside it.

Theirs was not the first empire of the steppe. In the seventh century AD, in the wake of the upheavals that destroyed the ancient world (chapter 7), a confederation of Turkish tribes had managed to dominate the grasslands from the Great Wall of China to the Black Sea; but by 750 their rule had been undermined by feud and faction. For the next four centuries, no single tribe or confederation gained supremacy over the steppe. It was into this turbulent, unstable society that, about the year 1167, Temujin, the son of the chief of the Mangkhol tribe from which the Mongols take their name, was born.

At first the young man did not seem destined to be a world conqueror. After his father's murder by rivals, Temujin, his mother and six siblings were forced to fend for themselves in a country where those who could claim no tribal protection almost invariably perished. But the group somehow survived and, as Temujin grew to manhood, the renown of his exploits and achievements – which all displayed to a high degree the qualities required from a clan leader – began to attract followers. Gradually he established himself as a minor chief and, making the most of his descent from the legendary Khans of Mongolia as well as of his military prowess, he steadily extended his authority over more and more tribes, Turkish as well as Mongol. Eventually, in 1206, at a *kuriltai* (or full assembly) of the tribes, held in the heart of Mongolia on the banks of the river Onon, Temujin was proclaimed supreme ruler 'of all who dwell in tents of felt' and assumed the name Genghis Khan, 'prince of all that lies between the Oceans'. The palace of this great ruler might have been a tent; but from it, plans were laid to conquer the world.

Genghis looked first to the East. China was, at this time, divided between two hostile dynasties: the Chin, themselves formerly nomads from the steppes, in the north; and the highly civilized Sung in the south. In 1211, the Mongols attacked. After mounting a series of raids deep into the country south of the Great Wall, they decided that more was to be gained by conquest than by plunder. Three armies advanced into Chin territory and occupied large tracts of territory. But, at first, they found the defences of the Chin cities unassailable: the walls of Peking, for example, stretched for eighteen miles and were forty feet wide and forty feet high. Only when a corps of engineers, skilled in siegecraft, had been created from Chinese prisoners could Peking be blockaded and captured in 1215. It was the first of many populous capitals to feel the savage fury of fierce nomads who feared and hated a way of life they could not understand: its buildings were looted and burned; its inhabitants were enslaved or slaughtered.

After the fall of Peking, Genghis was compelled to lead his armies towards the west against the Islamic state of Khwarizm, which stretched from the Caspian Sea to the Pamir Mountains. Under its ambitious ruler, Mohammed Shah, Khwarizm had expanded considerably while the Mongols were tied down in China. Now, in 1218, Genghis demanded that Mohammed should acknowledge him as Great Khan and overlord; when he refused, and murdered the Mongol ambassadors, Genghis took the offensive and commenced a three-year campaign of sustained devastation during which most of the Khwarizmian towns were totally destroyed. At Bukhara, for example, which the Mongols reached in 1220, they first set the wooden buildings on fire and drove the inhabitants before them – as cover – in an all-out attack on the citadel. Fire-bombs and rocks were hurled in, and assaults of increasing ferocity were launched against the walls until, finally, the citadel was taken. The 30,000 defenders were slaughtered and their women and children taken as slaves, while all buildings were razed to the ground. Eventually, the Great Khan climbed into the pulpit of the city's mosque and delivered an admirably terse sermon to the surviving population: 'Oh people, know that you have committed great sins...If you ask me what proof I have for these words, I say it is because I am the punishment of God. If you had not committed great sins, God would not have sent a punishment like me upon you!'

Genghis remained in the west until 1223, mopping up resistance. It was his last effective campaign. He invaded China again in 1226, but was already an old man and seriously ill: he died the next year, aged 73, at Chen-jung, a little south of the Great Wall. On his death bed, the Khan told his courtiers, 'I die without regrets, but my spirit wishes to return to my native land'. After a brief period of mourning, his corpse was carried in state across the desolate steppes of Asia to his homeland in Mongolia, where he was buried on a mountain spur. But every living thing that crossed the procession's path was slain, with the words: 'Depart for the next world and there attend upon your dead lord'. The Mongol leader died as he had lived: amid desolation and massacre.

Genghis Khan preaching at Bukhara from the 'Book of Kings' c. 1350 *below*
The Persian rhyming history of Genghis and his successors known as the *Shahanshad Nameh* was composed and illustrated for the Mongol rulers of Persia in the early 14th century. This episode from the history illustrates the Great Khan's sermon to the surviving population of Bukhara after its sack in 1220.

As a conqueror, Genghis ranks with Alexander the Great, Napoleon and Hitler. In twenty years he had extended his rule from the Pacific Ocean to the Caspian Sea – a remarkable achievement indeed. But how can it be explained? The question is easy to pose, but hard to answer, because there are so few surviving contemporary records. Before Genghis, the Mongols were a non-literate society, and only one chronicle written in their language is known to us: the anonymous *Secret History of the Mongols*, compiled in about 1240, which tells the story of Genghis. But even that source has only survived in a much later Chinese transcription and we depend, for most of our knowledge, upon the accounts written by scholars from nations conquered or attacked by the Mongols. Naturally, these were biased. For example, the detailed biography of Genghis, *The History of the World Conqueror* written in the 1250s by the Persian civil servant Juvaīnī, is both illuminating and revealing; but it must be remembered that its author spent his entire life under Mongol rule. He could not afford to be too outspoken or critical. Nevertheless, Juvaīnī does offer a plausible explanation for the Mongol's amazing military success. The first thing to remember, he wrote, was their sheer weight of numbers:

'The troops of the Great Khan were more numerous than ants or locusts, being in their multitude beyond estimation or computation. Detachment after detachment arrived, each like a billowing sea.'

Nor was that all. Lightly equipped, fast moving, agile and efficient, the Mongols were able to cover over 100 miles a day. They were also masters of deception. Sometimes they stampeded riderless horses into the enemy to confuse them; sometimes they tied stuffed sacks to their horses to appear more numerous. They had also perfected techniques of feigned withdrawal, luring the enemy into ambush. But beyond these

The mounted archer *below* was the most formidable fighting unit before the modern age. This Chinese drawing captures the two essential elements of the Mongol cavalry: the small, compact horse, able to withstand intense cold and capable of great speed for short periods, and the lightly-armoured rider, bearing a quiver of arrows capable of penetrating armour.

tactical devices, the Mongol rules of war were simple. Those who surrendered instantly became their slaves; those who did not were massacred.

At a general assembly of Mongol leaders in 1229, the third son of Genghis, Ogedei, was elected Great Khan. He was not an outstanding soldier like his father, nor yet a gifted administrator: rather, he was chosen because his popularity and political skills made his authority acceptable to the numerous and powerful descendants of Genghis. Conquest was left to his generals, and during the reign of Ogedei the frontiers of the Mongol empire were significantly advanced in three directions: against the Chin empire in China, against the remnants of Khwarizmian power in Persia, and into Europe.

The Chin were finally overthrown by the Mongols in 1234 (chapter 12), and in the next year Ogedei planned an invasion of Europe, which was to be led by Batu, a grandson of Genghis, who became viceroy of the westernmost parts of the empire. Batu had at his disposal about 150,000 troops, at a time when no European power could muster much more than 20,000. Not surprisingly, there were frenzied attempts by rulers near the Mongol line of advance to find allies, but all of them proved vain. The Mongols' first European target was Russia and a campaign was launched over the winter of 1237-38, the frozen rivers serving as highways for the advancing cavalry. The unprepared and disunited principalities of southern Russia were unable to offer effective resistance. One by one they were destroyed, and all was laid waste (chapter 21). Batu's achievement is all the more remarkable when we consider the fate of the winter campaigns against Russia directed by Napoleon or Hitler. His was, in fact, the only successful winter invasion of Russia in history.

The campaign was renewed in 1240 with the storming of the city of Kiev, which was rendered as desolate as Bukhara or Peking. Then followed a two-pronged assault against Poland and Hungary. The river Oder was passed at Ratibor and the Mongol army swept northwards up the river valley. Breslau was bypassed and on 9 April 1241 a combined German-Polish army was annihilated at Liegnitz. After the defeat of the other Christian army in Hungary at Mohi, a few days later, an eye witness reported: 'During a march of two days, you could see nothing along the roads but fallen warriors, their dead bodies lying about like stones in a quarry'. He might have added that the Mongols also used

The sack of Kiev 1240 *right* as portrayed in the city's medieval chronicle, was a bloody event involving the death or mutilation of the entire native population, as the impassive Mongol riders looked on. The destruction of the city was equally thorough. Six years later, when a papal envoy passed through on a mission to the Mongol Khan, he reported that only 200 houses still stood in Kiev, once the capital of Russia.

A cavalry attack *below* portrayed in Rashid al-Din's World History. Although the incident is meant to portray the army of the Buyid dynasty of Persia in the 10th century, they are equipped with the armour and the weapons favoured by the Mongol rulers whom the author served. They are also shown suddenly turning to attack as they apparently retreat, a ruse often employed by the Mongol cavalry to confuse their enemies.

Mongol groom leading a Chinese horse 1347 by Chao Yung *below* Many Chinese painters worked for the Mongol (Yüan) dynasty between 1279 and 1368. Their work demonstrates the gradual absorption of their Mongol overlords into the traditional Chinese way of life. Here, something of the process is reflected in the replacement of the Mongol light pony by the heavier Chinese horse.

The sack of Baghdad 1258 *right* marked a clear turning-point in Islamic history, for the Mongol troops of Hülegü destroyed the sole authority capable of holding together the Muslim world. The magnificent city, built in 762 as the capital of the caliphs, was laid waste; the last Abbasid caliph was slain and 800,000 inhabitants were said to have perished.

性是龍媒形
鳳姿于里左
立控鞚霜貢
呈咨薩圅常
非短奇
事乃信王孫
甲申新春
御題

the severed heads of the vanquished to ornament beacons warning enemies of the fate that awaited them unless they surrendered. The invaders swept through Budapest and Gran, nearly reaching Vienna before swinging southwards along the Adriatic and into the Balkans.

However, in the winter of 1242-43, Batu unexpectedly led his troops back to the Volga. The Mongols had held Europe at their mercy: they seemed poised to conquer Europe as easily as they had subjugated Asia. Why, then, did they not press home their advantage? Most authorities agree that only the death of the Great Khan Ogedei, in December 1241, halted the Mongols' westward advance, for it unleashed disputes over the succession which persuaded Batu to return eastwards in order to safeguard his own position.

Eventually, Ogedei's ambitious nephew Möngke was elected Great Khan, and the Mongol chieftains decided to abandon the conquest of Europe in favour of simultaneous campaigns against the Sung empire in southern China and the Islamic states of the Near East 'as far as the borders of Egypt'. Möngke himself was to take charge of the Chinese war, while the campaign in the west was entrusted to his younger brother Hülegü. Both operations were planned with the usual Mongol thoroughness. On New Year's Day 1256, a powerful army made the passage of the river Oxus, heading for the Islamic heartland. The key to the campaign was the capture of Baghdad and the city fell early in 1258. The palace of the caliph, the Great Mosque, the tombs of the Abbasids and other public buildings were all burnt: much of the cultural accumulation of five centuries was destroyed, and a blow was struck at Arabic civilization from which it never recovered. Never had the fortunes of Islam stood at such a low level. It no longer had a recognized head or centre of unity; ferocious pagans were in occupation of its plundered metropolis, and no Muslim prince reigned east of the Tigris save by their permission and as their slave. Worse yet, Hülegü had been ordered to subdue 'all the lands of the West', and it seemed that even the holy cities of Mecca and Medina might not be safe from the sacrilegious enemy.

The line of succession *below* to Genghis
Khan led initially to the division of his
great empire among his four sons. Later
succession became increasingly complex,
and Kublai's assumption of the title Great
Khan was disputed by his brother Arigböge
and his cousin, Kaidu. Further, Kublai
Khan's effective power was limited to the
Chinese section of the empire, and after
his death imperial cohesion disintegrated
considerably.

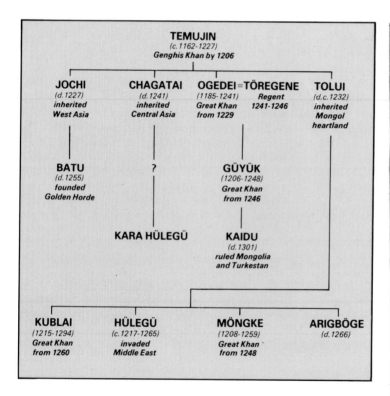

TEMUJIN
(c.1162-1227)
Genghis Khan by 1206

JOCHI	**CHAGATAI**	**OGEDEI**=**TÖREGENE**	**TOLUI**
(d.1227)	*(d.1241)*	*(1185-1241)* *Regent*	*(d.c.1232)*
inherited	*inherited*	*Great Khan* *1241-1246*	*inherited*
West Asia	*Central Asia*	*from 1229*	*Mongol*
			heartland

BATU
(d.1255)
founded
Golden Horde

?

GÜYÜK
(1206-1248)
Great Khan
from 1246

KARA HÜLEGÜ

KAIDU
(d.1301)
ruled Mongolia
and Turkestan

KUBLAI	**HÜLEGÜ**	**MÖNGKE**	**ARIGBÖGE**
(1215-1294)	*(c.1217-1265)*	*(1208-1259)*	*(d.1266)*
Great Khan	*invaded*	*Great Khan*	
from 1260	*Middle East*	*from 1248*	

But the situation was transformed once again by a distant and
unexpected event. At his camp near Aleppo, early in 1260, Hülegü
received the news that his brother Möngke had died in China the
previous August. Just as Christian Europe was saved by the death of
Ogedei in 1241, so the death of Möngke saved Muslim Asia. A succession dispute broke out between the late Khan's youngest brother, Kublai, and a faction supporting one of his cousins. Hülegü therefore withdrew his army from Syria and set out for the Mongol heartland, leaving
only a skeleton force in the Near East. This soon became known in
Cairo and the sultan of Egypt marched to the defence of Islam. At Ain
Jalut, near the Sea of Galilee, on 3 September 1260, the Mongols were
decisively defeated by the superior Egyptian army: the battle was a

turning point in world history, for the spell of Mongol invincibility was shattered and their westward advance was never seriously renewed.

Nevertheless, it is possible to exaggerate the importance of Ain Jalut. Certainly it set a limit to Mongol influence in the west; but its verdict was never subsequently challenged because the short-lived unity of the Mongol empire really came to an end with the death of Möngke. Kublai was eventually successful in the struggle for power and was proclaimed the fifth (and last) Great Khan. But almost the whole of his long life was spent in China; and, although never forgetting that he was the grandson of the world-conqueror, his primary objective became the restoration of the unity of the Chinese realm, which had been shattered by the fall of the T'ang dynasty in AD 907. In the 1270s, after more than a decade of conflict, he achieved this aim by overthrowing the Sung empire south of the Yangtze (chapter 12). But outside China, Kublai exercized only a nominal suzerainty over the other Mongol dynasties established to the west: the Il-Khans of Persia, descended from Hülegü (who died in 1265); the Khans of the Golden Horde in Russia; and the rulers of the Mongol heartland.

Hülegü pauses for refreshment c. 1260, Iran *below* The conqueror of Mesopotamia and destroyer of Baghdad was also a keen hunter. Here, with furrowed brow, he relaxes on the chase. The dynasty he established continued to rule Persia until 1353.

Kublai Khan goes hunting c. 1290 *left*
Although already old, the ruler Marco Polo described as the 'most powerful man since Adam' enjoyed hunting game. Here, dressed in ermine, he watches an archer shoot at birds on the wing, while his dog waits to retrieve them. A train of camels in the background carry merchandise.

Towers of skulls c. 1400, India *right*
Mongol brutality in war did not end with Kublai Khan and Hülegü. Their successors and imitators continued to punish and intimidate their enemies with such practices as building gruesome cairns of severed heads either to celebrate a victory or to frighten others into surrender. In this late 16th-century Mughal miniature, the troops of Timur the Lame (Tamerlane), a Mongol descendant, are shown demolishing the fortress of Mikrit in the Hindu Kush, some 200 years before, and using the debris to erect a tower of skulls.

It is hard to reconcile the history of the civilized ruling élites of Kublai's China or Hülegü's Persia with the rapacious savages portrayed in western sources such as the 'Great Chronicle' of Matthew Paris, composed at St Albans in England in the 1240s and 1250s: 'Mongols are inhuman and beastly, rather monsters than men, thirsting for and drinking blood, tearing and devouring the flesh of dogs and men'. Yet this was not mere fantasy. The Arab historian Ibn al-Athir waited for many years before writing his history of Genghis Khan because (he told his readers) the events he had seen were too horrible to record. The Mongol conquest was, he protested, the greatest calamity that had ever befallen mankind. However, the Mongols did give the Eurasian world almost a century of peace, which permitted the exchange of goods and ideas between the far east and the far west on an unprecedented scale.

The 'Silk Road' of ancient times was revived: silver and gold from Europe reached China; Chinese porcelain circulated in Europe. But the Mongols themselves had little positive to offer, and it is not easy to trace any substantial social and cultural legacy of their shattering intervention in world history. They entirely failed to match the achievements of the Arabs, who also began as illiterate nomads, but quickly absorbed the learning of their subject peoples and created an enduring civilization. Rather, the Mongol conquests can be seen as the end of an epoch. From the dawn of civilization, city-dwellers and the cultivators of the soil had been menaced by assaults from the fierce riders of the steppe. But during the life of the Mongol empire came the development of firearms: no longer would battles be decided solely by endurance, resourcefulness and speed. During the succeeding centuries Russia and China, the two nations which had suffered most from nomad aggression, steadily moved in to contain once and for all the recalcitrant herdsmen of the steppes. The Mongols were the last nomadic people to hold the civilized world to ransom.

The Mongol peace c. 1340, central Asia
right The 'Silk Road' was little more than a chain of widely-spaced towns and oases spread out across the inhospitable terrain of central Asia. In between, travellers were forced to bivouac on the steppe, at the mercy of bandits and nomads. Regular trade between Europe and China was therefore only possible when the security of itinerant merchants could be guaranteed. Here a party of traders, following the footsteps of Marco Polo, sleep beside their camels, secure in the peace that a hundred years of Mongol rule had established from the Pacific Ocean to the Black Sea. It was one of the few times in history that uninterrupted overland trade across the continent was possible.

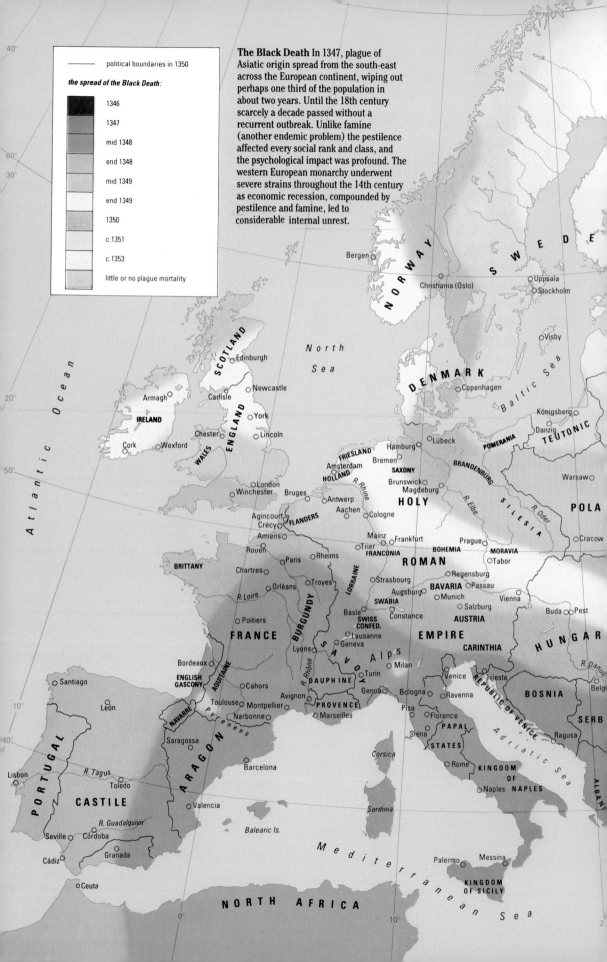

The Black Death In 1347, plague of Asiatic origin spread from the south-east across the European continent, wiping out perhaps one third of the population in about two years. Until the 18th century scarcely a decade passed without a recurrent outbreak. Unlike famine (another endemic problem) the pestilence affected every social rank and class, and the psychological impact was profound. The western European monarchy underwent severe strains throughout the 14th century as economic recession, compounded by pestilence and famine, led to considerable internal unrest.

political boundaries in 1350

the spread of the Black Death:

1346
1347
mid 1348
end 1348
mid 1349
end 1349
1350
c.1351
c.1353
little or no plague mortality

On the map: RUSSIAN STATES, Novgorod, PRINCIPALITY OF MOSCOW, Smolensk, R. Dnieper, LITHUANIA, Kiev, UKRAINE, KHANATE OF THE GOLDEN HORDE, R. Dniester, MOLDAVIA, Bucharest, LLACHIA, Black Sea, BULGARIA, BYZANTINE EMPIRE, Adrianople, alonica, Constantinople, OTTOMAN TURKS, Aegean Sea, Smyrna, DUCHY OF ATHENS, Athens, Rhodes, Crete, 30°

CHAPTER 11

THE EXPANSION OF EUROPE
1250–1500

By the end of the thirteenth century, the relentless advance of the armies of the Mongol Great Khan had created an empire stretching from the borders of Hungary to the Sea of Japan; and yet, such was Mongol power, that the routes that ran through their immense possessions were 'perfectly safe by day or night' (chapter 10). It is a curious paradox that although the Mongols ruthlessly slaughtered all who opposed them, after the conquest they were relatively tolerant, and intensely curious to learn about what little of the world there remained to be subdued. For example, from the 1240s onwards, European churchmen were allowed to travel eastwards in an attempt to convert the invaders to Christianity. They met with some success, and the Pope appointed a succession of Archbishops to Peking who gradually built up a small congregation of believers in China. At the same time, European merchants, chiefly from Genoa and Venice, were allowed to penetrate to the furthest east in search of those luxuries (notably silks and spices) that they had formerly purchased in the Levant, at markets from which they were increasingly excluded after the collapse of the Crusading states. The best route to the east started from the shores of the Black Sea, where the Italian maritime republics already had footholds. One itinerary led to the mouth of the Persian Gulf, and thence eastwards by a long and arduous sea voyage. Far better were the ancient overland routes passing through the steppe of central Asia right into China. How many Europeans travelled with the caravans, wending their way across the immense Eurasian landmass, it is difficult to estimate. Some returned to beguile poets and scholars with their tales; some became famous, like Marco Polo. But others prudently refrained from disclosing how and where the wealth of the Orient was to be found.

Yet the total number of western merchants travelling through Asia must have been substantial, for detailed guidebooks were prepared to help them on their way. The most comprehensive, written in 1340 by Francesco Balducchi Pegolotti, manager of the Cyprus branch of a large Italian banking firm, provides a fascinating insight into what the successful European merchant should look out for on his way to China, and what he should avoid. Pegolotti had learnt about both the main routes – via the Persian Gulf and overland – 'from the merchants who had journeyed along them' and he assured his readers that, when in convoy, travellers 'would be as safe as if they were in their own home'.

But Pegolotti was writing in a void. His valuable compilation remained unpublished for three centuries; and, although some details from his manuscript were used in later medieval manuals of trade, the

175

Niccolo and Matteo Polo leave Venice
left from a manuscript of c.1400. The Polo family were the most famous Europeans to travel along the Silk Road to China. In the 1260s, Niccolo and Matteo travelled right across Asia and back by land. In 1271, they returned to the East, accompanied by Niccolo's son, Marco, who wrote a fascinating account of the twenty years he spent in the lands of Kublai Khan. Marco became one of the emperor's most trusted advisors, charged with delicate and confidential missions to distant parts of the empire. After his return to the West in 1295, Marco wrote about his experiences, and his *Book of Marvels* becoming popular reading, being translated into many tongues. Many of his accounts were seen as fanciful, but his description of the court of Kublai Khan, its splendour and leisurely pursuits *right*, did much to inspire the European urge to explore the wider world.

material on Asia was always omitted. There were several reasons for this neglect. In the first place, the century of Mongol peace came to an end almost before the ink was dry on Pegolotti's manuscript. The successors of Kublai Khan (who died in 1294) failed to retain a grip on areas outside China; then, in 1368, they were driven out of China altogether and the 'Silk Road' was closed to Europeans.

This was not a total disaster for the West. Trade swung back to other, older routes, like that through the Red Sea and Egypt, whose capricious Muslim rulers the well-organized Venetian state soon learned to handle. And both Venice and her age-old rival Genoa turned to exploit more fully the opportunities of Asia Minor and the Levant, exporting to the west caviar from Russia, sugar from their colonies, and the sweet and heady Malmsey wine of Greece. But there was no commerce more financially rewarding than that, hotly disputed between Venice and Genoa, in slaves from the shores of the Black Sea. Men were sent to serve in the armies of the sultans of Egypt; girls, especially the blond and striking Circassians, were despatched into domestic servitude and prostitution in both Muslim and Christian areas of the West. Neither the popes nor the Venetian Senate proved able to stop this callous trade in human life. It was only interrupted, along with everything else in Europe, by an unparalleled calamity which began in the year 1347: the Black Death.

Millions died of the Black Death in Europe alone. The victims included the merchant Pegolotti; one-third of the College of Cardinals; three archbishops of Canterbury within a year; and Giovanni Villani, the greatest historian of his day, who perished in the midst of an unfinished sentence which began, 'And this plague lasted until…' Many towns saw half their population die; some monasteries lost all but one or two of their monks; some settlements were entirely wiped off the map, to become the 'deserted medieval villages' whose ridge-and-furrow fields are all that now remain. The chronicler Froissart, writing soon after the event, believed that 'a third of the world died'. Agnolo di Tura, writing his chronicle in Siena while the horror still lasted, was more alarmist still: 'This,' he wrote, 'is the end of the world'.

Venice in 1486 *below* from Bernard of Breydenbach's *Peregrenatio in terram sanctam*. Although it was no longer possible after about 1350 for Europeans to journey overland all the way to China, many still sought to visit the Holy Land. For them, travel-guides were composed which suggested the best itineraries and gave advice on what to see and where to stay along the way. For most pilgrims, as for the Polos, the prosperous and populous merchant city of Venice was the point at which they took ship for the Orient.

The plague strikes Rome *below* from the *Book of Hours* of the duke of Berry. Although the Black Death seemed a special scourge from God to contemporaries, it was known that similar plagues had afflicted Europe before. The clerics in this sumptuous painting may be wearing late 14th century costumes, but they represent Pope Gregory the Great (590-604) and his cardinals, leading a procession to plead for an end to one of the earlier epidemics.

Considering the scale of the catastrophe, it seems curious that there is still no agreement on how it started. Certainly it came to Europe from Asia, and the most likely theory is that the first European carriers were a group of Genoese who returned to the west after the siege of their fortress at Kaffa in the Crimea. They reported that the Mongol besiegers suddenly began to die of a strange disease that gave its victims black swellings that oozed blood and caused unbearable pain until they died. In desperation, the Mongols hurled the rotting corpses of their own dead over the city walls by giant catapult. So when, in 1347, a small party of Genoese survivors managed to escape from Kaffa, the terrible plague raged amongst them too until, by the time they reached Sicily, most of them were dead. Having travelled remorselessly across Asia, the Black Death now arrived in Europe. Before the end of the year, it had spread to the mainland: first to Pisa and Genoa, then to Marseilles. In 1348 it moved northwards into France and eastwards into Spain; then in relentless sweeps it travelled to the far corners of the continent and to the furthest islands beyond. Only a handful of places escaped: central Poland, Silesia, Milan. By 1353, when the pestilence finally abated, perhaps 20 million Europeans had been claimed by the epidemic.

The Triumph of Death c.1400 *below* by an anonymous Sicilian artist, offers a sharp contrast in style to the illustration opposite, composed for the French duke of Berry by the three Limbourg brothers (also c.1400). Whereas the former is literal and linear, with a meticulous attention to detail reminiscent of an illuminated manuscript, the Italian picture is imaginative, vigorous and lively. Both, however, emphasize that the plague did not discriminate but struck down rich and poor alike without warning.

The impact of the Black Death was felt by all peoples throughout Europe. This unsophisticated 15th-century Flemish illumination reflects the way in which sudden death became an accepted, everyday phenomenon; indeed, in both Chaucer's *Canterbury Tales* (c.1387) and Boccaccio's *Decameron* (c.1353), Death is personified as a mysterious wayfarer, ever ready to strike up an acquaintance with an unfortunate traveller.

It is generally agreed that the disease was bubonic plague, and that it was spread by deadly parasites carried in the stomach of a flea that was attracted both to house rats and to men. The best defence against it therefore was to kill all rats and to avoid all places – such as houses – where they lived. But instead, most people killed all dogs and cats, in the belief that they were the source of infection, and the rats multiplied still further; and instead of travelling into the countryside and sleeping rough like the sensible storytellers in Boccaccio's *Decameron* (set during the plague), most people stayed at home like the writer's mistress Fiammetta. And, like her, they died. 'How many brave men and fair ladies', wrote the poet disconsolately, 'whom any physician would have pronounced in the soundest of health, ate breakfast with their kinsfolk, comrades and friends in the morning; and when evening came shared supper with their forefathers in the other world'.

The Black Death was by no means the only disaster to strike Europe during the fourteenth century. By the year 1300, the continent was almost certainly over-populated: a century or more of unbroken economic growth had produced a rapid increase in population, especially in the cities, and it became increasingly hard to feed them. Between 1315 and 1319, a run of bad harvests caused famines, epidemics and heavy mortality in many areas. As the century advanced, harvest fai-

The Garden of Earthly Delights *left* completed by 1500, forms part of a dark vision of things to come by the Dutch painter Hieronymus Bosch. The psychological and cultural impact of the vicissitudes of the 14th century were greatest north of the Alps; there was a renewed religious fervour stocked by glimpses of a terrestrial Hell, which often found expression in the widespread development of heretical sects and millennialism, forecasting the Day of Judgement. This detail from the right-hand panel of the triptych shows the fate of the ungodly in Hell. Devils torment the damned with their former pleasures: minstrels are tortured by the instruments they used to play; the soldier is eviscerated by a pack of satanic hounds; one gambler's hand is impaled while another is battered to death with his own backgammon board.

lures became more frequent, leading the starving masses to eat whatever they could lay their hands on – dogs, cats, grass, even (it was said) their own children. But if there were perhaps too many people in Europe before the great plague, there were certainly too few afterwards. Harvests were abandoned in the fields and industrial production slumped: all areas experienced an acute shortage of labour which pushed wages up and caused a further fall in the demand for goods. Recovery from the recession was delayed by almost a century.

Yet in spite of depression and plague, there still seemed to be enough people left to wage wars. Few years passed in the fourteenth century without a battle being fought somewhere in Europe; and some wars lasted for generations. The struggle between England and France that began in 1337, popularly known as 'The Hundred Years' War', in fact lasted until 1453 and spilled over into Scotland, Portugal, Spain, Italy and the Low Countries. In the 1360s, for example, both the English (under their king's eldest son, Edward 'the Black Prince') and the French (under their equally famous leader Bertrand du Guesclin) campaigned in Castile, deposing the king and causing widespread devastation; and in 1385, more English troops aided the Portuguese to maintain their independence of Spain at the great battle of Aljubarrota, fought at the spot where the ornate monastery of A Batalha – 'the

Chronicles of war were more popular in later medieval Europe than any other form of literature, and their authors achieved international acclaim. Both Jean Froissart (1337-1410) and, later, Jean Wavrin (1400-71) were allowed to cross frontiers in order to collect information for their accounts of the great wars of western Europe, and manuscript copies of their works were equally popular in France, England and Spain. Wavrin, although French, presented a magnificently illuminated copy of his *Chronique d'Angleterre* to King Edward IV of England. From this come the scenes of English forces fighting victoriously at the siege of Mortagne, in the Low Countries, in 1340 *right*, and at Aljubarrota, in Portugal, in 1385 *below*. One of Froissart's chronicles described an unsuccessful French expedition to North Africa in 1390 *below right.* Setting off in July, the knights sweltered in their armour as they strove to starve out fortified towns. Not surprisingly, losses on such expeditions were heavy, more from disease than actual combat, but this unacceptable face of war was deliberately played down, in favour of chivalric hyperbole, by Froissart.

battle' – now stands in commemoration. When the war abated in the west, the unemployed warriors merely moved to Italy, where they fought in 'Free Companies' for any state that would employ them. There, too, they destroyed, looted and pillaged over a wide area. In the face of so many dangers and disasters, it is hardly surprising that Christian civilization, which in the thirteenth century had witnessed St Thomas Aquinas's triumphant marriage of Catholic orthodoxy with Aristotelian philosophy, came to be dominated in the fourteenth by despairing melancholy and bitter satire.

It was while dispirited Europe was beset by recession, plague and wars that the south-eastern parts of the continent fell under Muslim rule at last. Where the Arabs had repeatedly failed, the Ottoman Turks now succeeded. These fierce warriors of Islam had been moving steadily westward since the thirteenth century. In the 1320s they captured all the surviving Byzantine strongholds in Anatolia; in the 1340s they crossed into Europe and began to strangle all overland contacts between the surviving fragments of Byzantium (chapter 14). The fall of the venerable East Roman Empire, which had endured for a thousand years, was now only a matter of time. In 1389 the Ottoman army routed Byzantium's Serbian allies at the battle of Kosovo; seven years later, in 1396, a relief army of perhaps 100,000 Crusaders from the west was destroyed at Nicopolis. The 'Nicopolis Crusade' distracted the Turks and helped to save Constantinople for a few more years, but its ultimate fate could not be seriously in doubt. Nevertheless when, after a long siege, the city fell in 1453, it dealt a shattering blow to Christian pride: Constantinople, built by the first Christian emperor of Rome in 330, now became a Muslim city. It also dealt a considerable reverse to Christian trade. Within thirty years the western merchants had lost almost all of their trading outposts and colonies around the Aegean and the Black Sea.

The Arsenal at Venice *above*, pictured in this watercolour plan by Antonio di Natale, was (as the Venetian Senate itself said in 1509) 'the heart of the state'. From here, Venetian control of the eastern Mediterranean was effected. It was the largest industrial complex in Europe, employing some 5000 workers, and it was capable of sheltering 150 galleys. More galleys still were stored in warehouses around the main dock, their planks and spars all numbered for immediate assembly should the Venetian Republic be attacked.

The Venetian Republic was the most exposed and vulnerable of the European powers in this long contest between Islam and Christianity. As a maritime community overwhelmingly dependent on the trade in spices and exotic goods from the east, Venice needed an equitable relationship with the Islamic world in order to survive: she required the Islamic world to see her not as an eastern outpost of Christendom, but as a neutral middleman. For a time, this precarious policy paid off, but as the Turkish advance continued, criticism of the Republic mounted. 'Alas, Venetians', wrote Pope Pius II in 1463, 'how your ancient character is debased! Too much trading with the Turk has made you friends of the infidel!' '*Siamo Veneziani, poi Cristiani*', retorted the Venetians: 'We are Venetians first, and Christians afterwards'. But it could not last. To keep the Turks out of Venetian waters, extensive and expensive fortifications along the Adriatic were built; and to avoid total commercial dependence on the Sultan, trade was carried on with his enemies in the Levant: the Mameluke rulers of Syria and Egypt. But when they too fell victim to Ottoman conquest after 1514, Venetian trade with the east temporarily collapsed.

Venice's traditional rival in the trade with the Orient, the Republic of Genoa, reacted to the rise of Ottoman power in a totally different way. Her merchants, many of them refugees from their own strife-torn city, shifted their wealth into the opportunities presented by Spain and Portugal. They lent money to kings and nobles, ran lucrative monopolies and, more importantly, backed voyages of exploration beyond the shores of Europe.

The spectacular achievements which culminated in the discovery of a sea-route from Europe to India began with a crusade rather like the ill-fated Nicopolis expedition. In 1415, the king of Portugal led an army to conquer the Moorish pirate base of Ceuta, just across the straits of Gibraltar. It was successful. Among those present at the capture was one of the king's sons, Henry.

The prince was head of the largest Crusading order in Portugal. But he was also a younger son, excluded from politics, chronically short of money and imbued with the expensive ideals of contemporary chivalry. Within a few years of the capture of Ceuta, seamen in his service – and others, too, who being less influentially backed have left little trace – began to sail along the Atlantic coast of Africa. Islands to the west of the landmass were soon discovered when ships were obliged to stand out to sea by the prevailing winds, or as they searched for realms sited in these waters by medieval imagination: the uninhabited Madeira (c. 1420), the Azores (1427), the Cape Verde Islands (1456-60). All were soon populated and brought under cultivation, with the help of Genoese capital, to become highly profitable producers of sugar. And eventually Prince Henry's apparently pointless and fruitless insistence on the exploration of the African coast, opposed by many, was vindicated by the discovery that gold and slaves could be obtained on the shores of Guinea. So the pace and scale of Portugal's endeavour increased, and in 1460 her explorers first heard the thunder-storms whose roar lead them to call the highlands behind the Windward Coast 'Sierra Leone' – Lion Mountains. Henry the Navigator's captains had travelled 2,000 miles down the coast of West Africa.

The Republic of Genoa *below* could boast nothing to match the Arsenal of Venice but, as this oil-painting by a local artist in 1481 clearly shows, it was no less prosperous. Trading galleys, merchantmen and coastal craft almost choke the outer harbour, while numerous small boats ferry cargoes to and from the wharves. Genoa was the principal trading force in the western Mediterranean, although at this date the population of Genoa was about 60,000, and that of the city of Venice about 100,000.

The Adoration of the Magi *left* by Albrecht Dürer (1471-1528) with its naturalistic detail and close observation, reveals also that by the beginning of the 16th century Blacks were undoubtedly familiar to northern Europeans. The model of Dürer's gift-bearing king was probably a slave.

By now, the explorers' primary motive was no longer religion or curiosity, but commercial gain. In 1445 a great slave auction, the first in Europe to involve west Africans, was held at Lagos, in the Algarve. In the words of the chronicler Azurara:

'Some held their heads low with their faces bathed in tears;…others stood very dolorously, looking up to the height of heaven and crying out loudly as if asking help from the Father of Nature; others still made their lamentations in the manner of a dirge, after the custom of their country. And though we could not understand the words of their language, the meaning was clear enough…And then, to increase their suffering still more, those who had charge of the division of the captives now arrived, and began to separate one from another. They parted husbands from wives, fathers from sons, brothers from brothers. No respect was shown either to friends or relations. It was a terrible scene of misery and disorder…'

But slavery was an almost universal fact of life in the fifteenth century. There were European slaves in the Middle East; Moorish slaves in Europe; and a well-established slave-system in Africa, where servitude was the normal punishment for crime (chapter 15). Portugal merely exploited the existing structures, importing and redistributing first hundreds and later thousands of black slaves every year.

The profits from this activity were substantial, and so the voyages of exploration continued. After the death of Prince Henry in 1460, they were patronized by the Portuguese government and during the 1470s the explorers discovered the 'Gold Coast', the 'Slave Coast' and the 'Ivory Coast' – places whose very names revealed their principal products. Still they pressed onwards until in 1488 Bartolomeu Dias rounded the Cape of Good Hope. At his furthest landing-place, on a promontory at the mouth of the Great Fish River, Dias erected a large stone cross bearing the arms of Portugal, as he and his predecessors had done throughout their voyages: Portuguese crosses, or *padrões*, now dotted the African coast for 7,000 miles.

The last stages of the exploration had yielded less profit than before: beyond the Slave river, nothing was found to match the gold and the negroes of Guinea. But the desire to continue was unaffected by reduced profits, because the Portuguese now hoped to find, beyond the tip of Africa, a sea-route to India.

It is hard for someone living in the twentieth century to imagine how the world looked to Dias's contemporaries. Well over a thousand

Prince Henry of Portugal (1390-1460)
left, nicknamed 'the Navigator' in the
19th century, was the driving force behind
the voyages of exploration that sailed
southwards down the coast of Africa. This
portrait, copied from a contemporary
Portuguese manuscript, reveals little about
its subject – the prince gazes out
enigmatically – and historians have been
likewise confused by Henry's motives for
sponsoring so many costly voyages. Was it
merely a continuation of the Crusading
urge, to spread Christianity beyond the
confines of the known world, or rather reap
the rewards of trade, not least those of
African slavery?

The *Geography* of Claudius Ptolemy
who lived in Egypt in the 2nd century AD,
was rediscovered by Europe in the early
15th century. It proved an immediate
success, and numerous copies – at first
manuscript but later printed – were made,
many of them accompanied by maps.
Below a 1486 woodcut *Geography*,
published in Germany, shows the limits of
cartographical knowledge on the eve of the
great discoveries. It depicts only half the
globe, yet it showed a substantial continent
joining Africa with south-east Asia. Thus,
in Ptolemy's view, a sea-route to India was
not possible. Moreover, the continent of
Asia ran off the edge of Ptolemy's map,
making the Indian Ocean a landlocked sea.

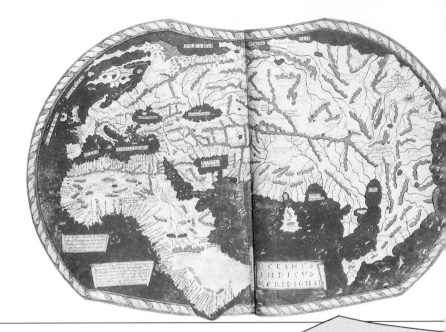

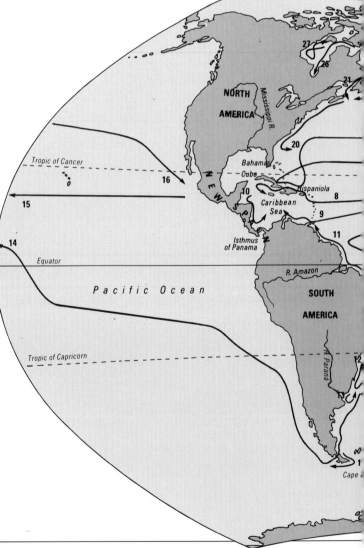

Voyages intended for southern Asia by a south-east route:

1. Dias 1487/88 to Cape Agulhas
2. Vasco da Gama 1497-99 to India
3. Cabral 1500 to India via Brazil
4. First Portuguese voyage to Malacca 1509
5. Abreu 1512-13 to Molnccas
6. First Portuguese voyage to China 1514

Voyages intended for China and southern Asia by west or south-west route:

7. Columbus 1492-93 to Bahamas
8. Columbus 1493-94 to Cuba
9. Columbus 1498 to Venezuela
10. Columbus 1502-04 to Panama
11. Ojeda and Vespucci 1499-1500 to R. Amazon
12. Coelho and Vespucci 1501 to Uruguay
13. Solis 1515 to R. Plate
14. Magellan and Elcano 1519-22 first circumnavigation
15. Saavedra 1527 from Mexico to Moluccas
16. Urdaneta 1565 eastwards across Pacific
17. Schouten and Le Maire 1616 around Cape Horn

Voyages intended for Asia by north route:

18. Cabot 1497 to Newfoundland
19. Corte-Real 1500 to Greenland
20. Verrazzano 1524 to North America
21. Cartier 1534 and 1535 to St. Lawrence River
22. Willoughby and Chancellor 1553 to Archangel
23. Frobisher 1574 to Baffin Island
24. Davis 1587 to edge of ice
25. Barents 1596-97 to Noaya Bay
26. Hudson 1610 to Hudson Bay
27. Button 1612 to Hudson Bay
28. Baffin and Bylot 1616 to Baffin Bay

The world map of Henricus Martellus 1490 *left* represented an advance on Ptolemy in two respects. First, he clearly showed the sea washing round the entire southern shore of Africa. Second, his map covered three-quarters of the globe, yet still portrayed Asia running off the edge – which suggested that the islands of eastern Asia (such as Japan) were not too far from the islands off western Europe (such as the Canaries or the Azores). This misconception was shared by Christopher Columbus, and played a major part in stimulating his accidental discovery of America.

years before the Portuguese exploration of West Africa began, the Roman geographer Strabo had drawn a map of the known world, stretching from northern Britain across Europe and north Africa to India. He had guessed that the African continent was surrounded by water; but his 'Africa' was no larger than Libya. The Egyptian, Ptolemy, working in the second century AD, drew upon a slightly expanded area of the known world, and he disagreed with Strabo about Africa: Ptolemy showed a vast continent running right off the bottom of the map, joined to Asia by a southern land bridge. For more than a thousand years, the works of these classical geographers were simply lost to the West, a victim of the upheavals that desolated Europe; and when they were rediscovered, in the early fifteenth century, it was the theories of Ptolemy that commanded greater support. But by sailing round the southern tip of Africa, Dias had proved Ptolemy wrong. The map drawn by the German cartographer Henricus Martellus around the year 1490 shows the western coastline of Africa sweeping down to the Cape, together with a continuous sea-route to India and the East. The voyage of Dias resolved the most pressing geographical dilemma of the day.

His success could not be followed up at once. He had, said a con-

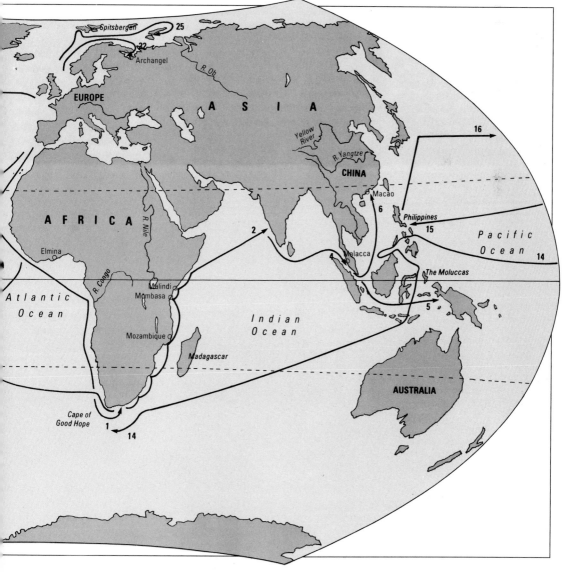

189

temporary, been prevented like Moses from entering the Promised Land; but he had sighted the southern tip of Africa, naming it 'Good Hope, for the prospect it gave of the discovery of India'. Money, however, was short. Portugal was locked in dispute with Spain over spheres of influence, following discoveries in the west, and there was strenuous opposition at court to the diversion of energies away from Africa. Only through the determination of King Manuel I (1495-1521) was exploration resumed: in 1497 a new fleet, fitted out under the supervision of Dias and commanded by the fiery aristocrat Vasco da Gama, sailed from Lisbon. After rounding the Cape of Good Hope it turned up the East African coast to reach the flourishing but squabbling Arab trading centres north of the Zambezi. From Malindi, guided by a local pilot, the expedition sailed to western India along the routes normally followed by native seamen. Within two years the remnants of the fleet were back home, having lost more than half its complement, but with a rich cargo of pepper and cinnamon. And though da Gama misunderstood much of what he encountered – taking the Hindus for errant Christians, and so on – he certainly appreciated that the trade the Portuguese sought was firmly under Muslim control. To the fervently Catholic and intensely rapacious Portuguese, it seemed their clear duty to divert such wealth into their own Christian hands by 'cruel war with fire and sword'. So in 1500, a fleet of fourteen vessels under Pedro Alvares Cabral (which accidently discovered Brazil on the way) entered the Indian Ocean to set about the destruction of Muslim seaborne commerce.

But there was already, by this time, another European who claimed to have discovered a sea route to Asia and who bore the proud title 'Admiral of the Ocean Sea'. His name was Christopher Columbus. In 1492 he sailed west from Seville in Spain, via the Canaries and, after four weeks' navigation over uncharted seas, discovered several Caribbean islands, which he thought to be the islands of Japan. In his later voyages, he believed he had discovered a new continent lying to the

A Portuguese carrack *below*
by Cornelis Anthoniszoon of Amsterdam (1500-54) captures the two essential elements of this type of vessel: its size – for some carracks, at 2,000 tons, were the largest wooden ships ever built; and its artillery – heavy naval guns poke out of ports specially cut into the lower deck, a new invention of the time. These were the ships which, in the phrase of the Portuguese poet Camoës, 'sailed the oceans none had sailed before', and brought back the silks and spices of the Orient.

south-west of Asia; in fact, he had found South America.

The reasons for Columbus's mistake are as remarkable as his reasons for making the daring four-week voyage into the unknown. He was one of the many Genoese who entered Portuguese service in the fifteenth century. About the year 1487, when he was thirty-six years old, Columbus became convinced that 3,000 miles west of Lisbon, a persistent explorer would discover East Asia. Two major errors underlay this miscalculation. First, Columbus accepted an estimate of the earth's size which was about 20 percent too small: he therefore thought that the continents lay closer together than they really do. Second, he placed too much reliance on the distances between the cities of Asia visited and recorded by Marco Polo. Columbus possessed a copy of Polo's journal, and his numerous annotations show that he meticulously added up all the distances to find how far it was from Venice to Peking. It was a clever idea; but unfortunately Polo, though an accurate observer, had only a vague idea of how far he had travelled. He thought he had covered 16,000 miles (instead of only 7,000), and therefore situated China far further to the east of Venice than it really is. But that, of course, placed China far closer to *western* Europe by sea. So Columbus calculated from these two mistaken concepts – a smaller world plus a larger Asia – that China was in fact only about 4,000 miles away from Lisbon. The islands of Japan, he reasoned, would be even closer. Small wonder, then, that when he had sailed his 3,000 miles due west and came upon the coast of Cuba, the 'Admiral of the Ocean Sea' at once assumed it was Cathay and sent an embassy ashore to find the representative of the Great Khan. Small wonder, too, that he should have named many capes and rivers of the Caribbean after the places described in the book of Marco Polo. Even today, following Columbus, we perversely refer to the Caribbean islands as the 'West Indies'.

But in 1487 all these discoveries lay in the future. In that year, Columbus's calculations were solemnly discussed by the Portuguese

Christopher Columbus (1451-1506)
below grew up in Genoa and became the agent of a company that engaged in maritime trade. In their service he sailed to Portugual, Iceland, England, the Azores, Cyprus and West Africa. However strange his ideas about geography may have been, his skills as a navigator were the fruit of a long apprenticeship and they enabled him, once he had reached the New World, to explore and chart the unfamiliar coasts with great accuracy. This woodcut, however, from a late 16th-century popular work on European overseas expansion, portrays Columbus in the Americas as a decadent courtier. It does little justice to his remarkable achievements as Admiral of the Ocean Sea.

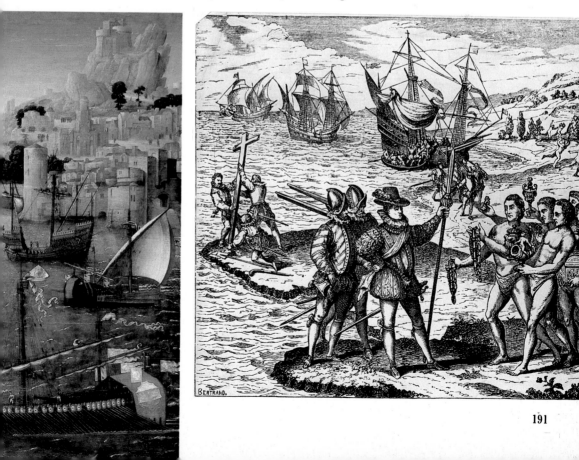

The printed world map of Martin Waldseemüller 1507 *above* covered all 360° of the earth's surface for the first time, and both on the main map and on another projection in the small cartouche above it the size of Asia is reduced in order to leave room for a new continent, which Waldseemüller christened 'America', after his friend the explorer Amerigo Vespucci. This was the first map to include either the continent or the name, and the elegance of its compact design did much to popularize both.

council of state, and were – quite correctly – rejected as ridiculous. The Portuguese had invested their money in an eastward sea-route to India; they did not see any reason to back Columbus's rival theory as well, and the triumphant return of Bartolomeu Dias the following year seemed to justify their caution. For the next five years Columbus, disappointed, toured the capitals of western Europe trying to persuade some other ruler that he was right. Henry VII of England was not convinced; the government of France was impoverished; the rulers of Spain, Ferdinand and Isabella, were too busy reconquering the Muslim kingdom of Granada, the last Islamic outpost in western Europe. No one would finance the Genoese adventurer. But in January 1492 the citadel of Granada itself fell and, almost at once, Isabella gave Columbus three ships with which to sail to 'the Indies'. His return in 1493, with gold and Indians, stupefied Europe. Everyone had to accept that the garrulous, eccentric Admiral had discovered a 'New World'.

In the mid-fifteenth century, to European eyes Africa south of the Sahara was still shrouded in uncertainty; the Far East comprised a mass of often contradictory legend; and America remained totally unknown. Yet within half a century, a handful of explorers from the Iberian and Italian peninsulas had linked these hitherto divided regions of the world into an enduring global system. In 1519 a Portuguese pilot in Spanish service, Ferdinand Magellan, led an expedition that, for the first time, eventually sailed right round the world (chapter 18). Now Europeans, Africans, Asians and Americans all came into contact with each others' products, beliefs and prejudices. But it was an exchange that was by no means to everyone's advantage. Even Europe may have lost as much as she gained during the first century after the 1490s, the great decade of discoveries; and for those who were 'discovered', for the Africans and the Americans in particular, the gains were few, if any, and the losses were catastrophic.

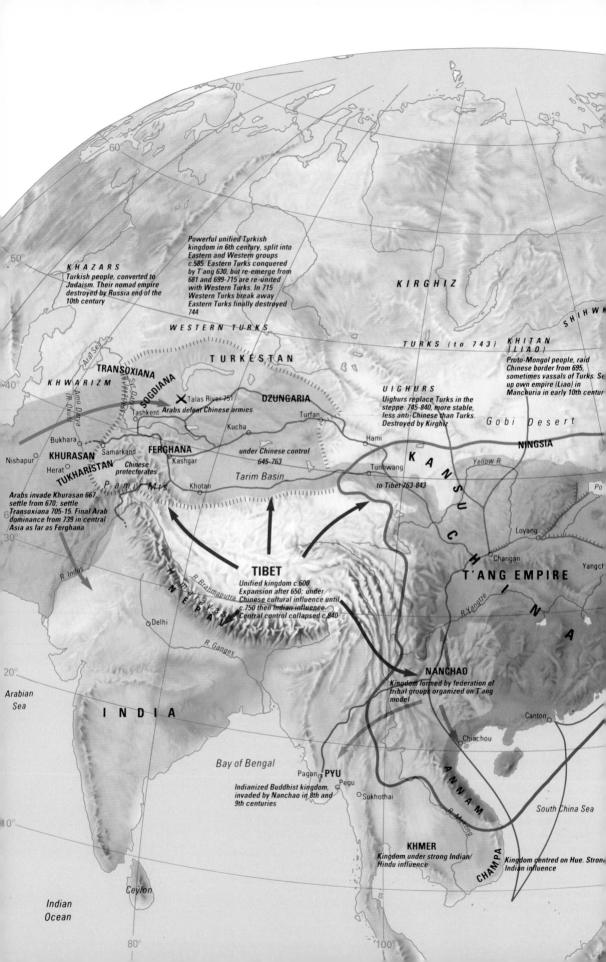

KHAZARS
Turkish people, converted to Judaism. Their nomad empire destroyed by Russia end of the 10th century

Powerful unified Turkish kingdom in 6th century, split into Eastern and Western groups c.585. Eastern Turks conquered by T'ang 630, but re-emerge from 681 and 699-715 are re-united with Western Turks. In 715 Western Turks break away. Eastern Turks finally destroyed 744

KIRGHIZ

SHIHW

WESTERN TURKS

TURKESTAN

TURKS (to 743)

KHITAN (LIAO)
Proto-Mongol people, raid Chinese border from 695, sometimes vassals of Turks. Se up own empire (Liao) in Manchuria in early 10th centur

TRANSOXIANA

KHWARIZM

SOGDIANA

DZUNGARIA

✕ Talas River 751
Arabs defeat Chinese armies

UIGHURS
Uighurs replace Turks in the steppe. 745-840, more stable, less anti-Chinese than Turks. Destroyed by Kirghiz

Aral Sea

Amu Darya R. Oxus

Syr Darya R.

Tashkent

Turfan

Kucha

Hami

Gobi Desert

NINGSIA

Bukhara

Samarkand

FERGHANA

Kashgar

under Chinese control 645-763

Yellow R.

Nishapur

KHURASAN

Herat *TUKHARISTAN*

Chinese protectorates

Pamir Mts.

Tarim Basin

Tunhwang

to Tibet 763-843

K A N S U

C H I N A

Loyang

Arabs invade Khurasan 667, settle from 670; settle Transoxiana 705-15. Final Arab dominance from 739 in central Asia as far as Ferghana

Khotan

Changan

Yangch

T'ANG EMPIRE

R. Indus

TIBET
Unified kingdom c.600. Expansion after 650; under Chinese cultural influence until c.750 then Indian influence. Central control collapsed c.840

H i m a l a y a s

R. Brahmaputra

N E P A L

R. Yangtze

Delhi

I N D I A

R. Ganges

NANCHAO
Kingdom formed by federation of tribal groups organized on T'ang model

Canton

Chiachou

Arabian Sea

Bay of Bengal

Pagan *PYU*
Pegu
Indianized Buddhist kingdom, invaded by Nanchao in 8th and 9th centuries

Sukhothai

A N N A M

South China Sea

0°

KHMER
Kingdom under strong Indian/Hindu influence

CHAMPA
Kingdom centred on Hue. Stron Indian influence

Ceylon

Indian Ocean

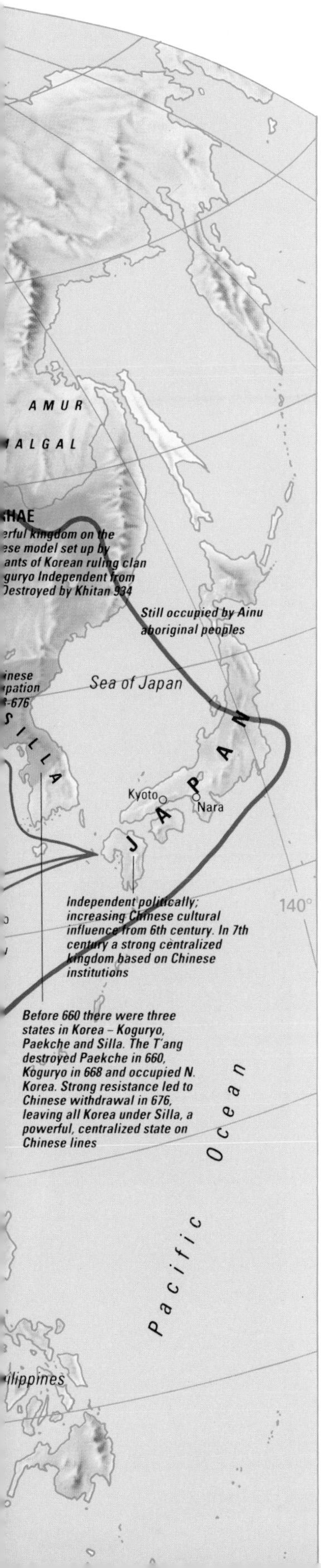

CHAPTER 12

CHINA IN TRANSITION
581–1279

The collapse of the Han dynasty in AD 220 ushered in a period of unusual confusion in Chinese history. For more than three centuries, much as in Europe (chapter 7), political power was fragmented between a number of independent states. Although at first there were only three (Wei, Shu and Wu), by the fourth century there were many more – each of them unstable, and many of them vulnerable to attack by nomads from the northern steppes. The country was only reunified at the end of the sixth century when a high-ranking general of the state of Chou, based on Changan, first usurped the throne (581) and then proclaimed himself the founding emperor of the Sui dynasty. In 589 he conquered his southern neighbour, the Chen. What is known as China's second empire had begun.

The impact of the Sui dynasty on the subsequent development of Chinese civilization was enormous. The ruling family belonged (like their successors the T'ang) to the Turko-Chinese aristocracy that ruled the north-west, and they were not fully familiar with the traditional Chinese system. Instead, they imposed on the entire empire a set of

A M U R

A L G A L

HAE
erful kingdom on the
ese model set up by
ants of Korean ruling clan
guryo Independent from
Destroyed by Khitan 934

Still occupied by Ainu
aboriginal peoples

inese
pation
-676

Sea of Japan

SILLA

JAPAN

Kyoto
Nara

Independent politically;
increasing Chinese cultural
influence from 6th century. In 7th
century a strong centralized
kingdom based on Chinese
institutions

140°

Before 660 there were three
states in Korea – Koguryo,
Paekche and Silla. The T'ang
destroyed Paekche in 660,
Koguryo in 668 and occupied N.
Korea. Strong resistance led to
Chinese withdrawal in 676,
leaving all Korea under Silla, a
powerful, centralized state on
Chinese lines

Pacific Ocean

ilippines

�	area under permanent T'ang civil administration
	area of temporary occupation during 7th century
	area under Chinese military control
	zone of Chinese cultural dominance
	Islamized areas by 750
	Islamic penetration
	trade routes
	canals

The Chinese world *left* During the 660s and 670s Chinese military power reached a peak, and briefly extended the power of the T'ang from Sogdiana to north Korea. The Chinese remained in control of the Tarim Basin and Dzungaria until 756; the Tarim and parts of north-west China fell to the Tibetans in 763-783, after Chinese garrisons were withdrawn. Chinese institutions and literary culture extended over parts of the Far East which were never formally controlled by China, but became parts of the Chinese ecumene. By the 9th century, however, Chinese power was considerably contained, by Islamic forces to the west, by a number of small Hindu-Buddhist states to the south, and by the increasingly restless movements of the steppe peoples to the north.

administrative measures that had been devised to control the north of China, with its multi-racial population (resulting from repeated foreign invasions in the fourth and fifth centuries), and its comparatively backward economy. But the Sui also encouraged Confucian learning – a conservative philosophy that emphasized the advantages of education, order and moral persuasion (chapter 6) – and they revived the Confucian-oriented civil service examination system. This system, and the cultured bureaucrats it produced, were to be two of the distinguishing features of Chinese civilization for the next 1300 years. Like others both before and after them in Chinese history, the Sui understood that while 'you can conquer China on horseback, you cannot rule it on horseback'.

The new dynasty also improved the communications of their vast empire by constructing a system of 'grand canals' which served to bring the produce of the rich agricultural lands in the south within easy reach of the government and the army, which were both based in the north. By 609, when the network was completed, the government was able to collect its revenues in grain and move them in bulk to supply the huge standing armies which defended the northern frontier. Although altered and repaired many times subsequently, some of these canals are still in use today.

But the cost of all this construction proved prohibitive: canals, roads and other public works were expensive in both taxes and labour services. They exhausted the population. Worse still, the second Sui emperor, Yang-ti, also indulged in major military expeditions designed to bring the outlying dominions once ruled by the Han dynasty back under Chinese control. Expensive operations were launched in the

south against Annam, (now Vietnam), in the north-east against Korea and in the north-west against the tribes of central Asia. All were disasters, and the constant levies of men and supplies caused widespread uprisings until, by 617, support for the dynasty had crumbled and rebellions were rife throughout the empire. The emperor Yang-ti was assassinated in 618 and his dynasty came to an ignominious end.

The T'ang, who eventually emerged as the new unifiers of China after almost a decade of civil war, were members of the same north-

The armies of the T'ang were enormous. Their campaigns against Korea in the 660s, for example, involved 150,000 troops, and the major battles were fought by 30-40,000 men. Few opponents could match the massed charge of well-disciplined, armoured lancers like the one modelled *right* in glazed pottery, now in the British Museum.

Under the Sui dynasty (581-618) a period of economic recovery began. The emperor distributed relief to the peasantry, reduced taxation and shortened military service. He set a personal example of thrift, eschewing silk clothing and gold or jade ornament. These traditional tomb guardian figures *far left* are simply carved in soapstone.

The Chinese élite remained remarkably consistent in clothing and bearing over time: the costumes of T'ang times were not notably different from those of the earlier Han, or later Sung and Ming periods. This T'ang painted pottery figure *left* with its extraordinary bird-hat and remarkably low-cut dress, comes from an excavated tomb.

197

T'ang T'ai-tsung *right* emperor of China 626-649 and founder of the T'ang dynasty, skilfully consolidated the power of the new dynasty at home and extended it abroad. In addition, under his enlightened rule, China established stimulating contacts with Persian and Indian civilizations; foreign visitors from all areas were welcomed, while the arts and letters flourished. With a humility uncommon among great rulers, T'ai-tsung compared himself to a ship, and his subjects to the waters that can either support it or let it sink.

western aristocracy as the Sui, to whom they were related by marriage. Thus the T'ang victory did not bring about any sweeping changes in the ruling group, or in the machinery of government. Essentially, the new regime consolidated the institutions founded by the Sui, refined them, and extended them throughout the empire by means of an improved system of local administration under firm central control.

Much of the credit for the T'ang's early success is usually given to its second emperor, T'ai-tsung, who reigned from 626 to 649. A tough and able military commander, T'ai-tsung also proved to be a brilliant administrator and has long been reputed one of the two or three greatest rulers in Chinese history. During his long reign, the government was efficiently and honestly run, the economy recovered from the disasters of the late Sui period, and peace and stability returned to the countryside. But T'ai-tsung also resumed the expansionist policies of his Sui predecessors, and by 640 a T'ang army had reached Turfan in what is now the far north-west of China. Over the next several decades the T'ang consolidated their power in this region and even established protectorates in modern Uzbekistan and Afghanistan. At the same time, Chinese armies also intervened in India and established protectorates in Sogdiana, Ferghana and eastern Persia, while in the north-east they briefly occupied northern Korea. Direct Chinese political influence would never extend so far again.

Indeed, it has been argued that the T'ang overreached themselves, and that it was for this reason that they were soon under pressure from various neighbours. Korea easily shook off Chinese rule and, in the north, the nomadic tribes from the steppes mounted increasingly heavy assaults on the T'ang defences. Then, in the early eighth century, fresh enemies emerged to the west: the militant forces of Islam and the newly unified and increasingly warlike kingdom of Tibet both began to press against the borders of the Chinese empire. The T'ang responded by increasing their expenditure on defence and by devolving wide economic and administrative powers to the frontier commanders; by 750, more than half a million men were serving on the frontiers; but it

The Uighurs *below* of the northern steppe pay homage to a Chinese general in 765; but, in reality, the survival of T'ang rule depended by the late 8th century on the support received from the tribes north of the Great Wall. This ink drawing of the 11th century shows General Kuo Tzu-i, unarmed but authoritative, persuading the uncivilized tribesmen, whose exotic appearance has been purposefully exaggerated, to join him in attacking the Tibetans.

was still not enough. In 751 a major Chinese army was routed by Islamic forces at the Talas river, delivering central Asia to Muslim control; and, four years later, one of the frontier generals, An Lu-shan, marched on the capital, Changan, with 160,000 men. It was captured in 756. Although the rebel leader was assassinated after only a few months, the revolt which he began lasted for several years and devastated huge areas of north-central China. The Tibetans exploited these developments to the full, expanding eastwards until in 763 they were within a hundred miles of the imperial capital.

In that year, the T'ang government was able to restore internal order, but it was forced to pay a heavy price. At home, wide powers had to be devolved to a new group of provincial administrators – some of whom were surrendered rebels who retained their private armies and ruled their lands with little reference to the capital. In 780, when a new emperor tried to regain ascendancy over the provincial governors, a fresh civil war broke out, ending in virtual stalemate. This weakness at home was paralleled by weakness abroad. In the seventh century, the T'ang emperors had been recognized as suzerain by many of the tribes and states of Asia. But by the ninth century, China was surrounded on all sides by powerful, independent, well-organized neighbours, all with literate cultures: Silla in Korea, Parhae in Manchuria, the Uighurs in Mongolia, the Tibetans to the west, and the Nanchao kingdom in modern Yunnan. The emperors could only manage to keep their frontiers

Buddhism entered China in the 1st or 2nd century AD, and became widely established by the 6th century (chapter 6). After a short period of repression, the Sui dynasty revived the popularity of the faith, and during Wen-ti's reign more than half a million statues were restored, more than 100,000 created *below* and nearly 4000 temples were constructed. Buddhism continued to thrive under the T'ang dynasty, despite the official patronage of Taoism and Confucianism as well.

intact thanks to an alliance with the Uighurs. The 'golden age of the T'ang' was over.

Even so, the dynasty survived for another 150 years and T'ang China remained one of the political and economic wonders of the medieval world. Perhaps nowhere was more spectacular than Changan which, for most of this period, ranked as the largest city on earth. Begun by the Sui on a historic site in the Wei river valley (now occupied by the modern city of Sian), Changan grew at an extraordinary rate during the seventh century. By the eighth century there may have been a million people living within the walls, with another million in the surrounding metropolitan area. (By contrast, the population of London or Paris at this time was only a few thousands and did not top the million mark for another 1,100 years.) The vast majority of Chang-an's residents were Chinese, but there was a sizeable foreign community as well. As the historian Edward Schafer has put it:

'There were Indian Buddhists in abundance, but also Persian priests…Turkish princelings pondered the ways of gem dealers from Oman; Japanese pilgrims stared in wonder at Sogdian caravaneers. Indeed, hardly any imaginable combination of nationality and profession was absent. All these travellers brought exotic wares into China, either as sovereign gifts, or as saleable goods, or simply as appendages to their person.'

China under the T'ang dynasty welcomed visitors from all over the world, and Chinese artists captured their distinctive, unfamiliar appearance in paintings, drawings and in pottery figures *right*. This foreign trader with his big nose, on his Bactrian camel, probably travelled from the Middle East along the Silk Road of central Asia in search of exotic goods.

These exotic wares helped to give T'ang China an amazingly cosmopolitan character, one that was reflected in the painting, architecture, literature, music, entertainments, and even the fashionable dress of the day. China would never again be open to such a wide variety of foreign cultural influences until modern times.

Of all the foreign imports, none was more important in T'ang life than Buddhism. Having reached China from India during the first century AD, Buddhism worked its way into the fabric of Chinese civilization over the next several hundred years – a slow process because of the vast linguistic and cultural differences that existed between China and India (chapter 6). But by the sixth century, Buddhism had become the dominant religion in both north and south China; and when the Sui and T'ang reunified the country after 589, they championed the faith partly because they believed that it would be an effective instrument for knitting together the various different sub-cultures which had grown up during the centuries of political disunion. Their hopes were largely realized. All over the empire, pagodas and temple complexes sprang up; and many visitors from afar were reassured to find the temple bells rung and the sutras chanted in the capital just as they were at home.

Although very little of this temple architecture remains in China today, at least some idea of its splendour can be gained from the magnificent early temples in Japan, all of which date from approximately the same period. Japan, like Korea, was heavily influenced by China and particularly by Chinese Buddhism, and Japanese artists and craftsmen faithfully copied the work of their continental counterparts between the seventh and the ninth centuries. Only after the imperial capital was moved from Nara to Kyoto, in 794, did Japan break free of the pervasive cultural, political and economic influence of China; but by then, Chinese Buddhism had made an indelible mark on its neighbour.

However, Buddhist influence in T'ang China itself was not confined to art and architecture. Due to tax and other privileges granted by the

Sung T'ai-tsu ('Great ancestor of the Sung') *below* usurped power as ruler of the state of Chou in 960. However, his official portrait on silk stresses his legitimacy and clear 'mandate of heaven' to govern. By the time of his death in 976, he had managed to reunite most of China under his sway.

The Great Buddha Hall *right* of the Todaiji Temple at Nara, the ancient Japanese imperial capital, is currently the largest wooden building in the world. It was based on Chinese prototypes, and is now one of the few remaining examples of early medieval Chinese construction techniques. It measures 187 feet long, 164 feet wide and 161 feet high (an earlier structure on the site, destroyed in 1180, was even larger). It was constructed to house a gigantic bronze Buddha, cast in 749, standing 71 feet high and weighing 551 tons. It is the largest bronze statue in the world – even the Buddha's thumb measures 5 feet 3 inches – and remains perhaps the most venerated object in Japanese Buddhism.

state, some Buddhist temples became powerful landowners, operated pawnshops and other money-lending institutions, organized famine relief, carried out public works projects, and took an active interest in education. Also, the dissemination of Buddhism was closely associated with the development of woodblock printing in China and thus helped to make the country one of the most literate of all pre-modern societies. The oldest surviving printed book in the world, dated to 868, is a Buddhist text in Chinese. However, this text, known as the 'Diamond Sutra', was printed when Buddhist influence in China was already on the wane. In 843-845 the emperor Wu-tsung launched a campaign of savage persecution, hoping that the seizure of temple lands and wealth would solve his pressing financial problems. 40,000 Buddhist shrines and temples were closed, 260,000 monks and nuns were returned to lay life, and huge tracts of monastic land were confiscated and sold. At the same time, Zoroastrianism and Christianity were also outlawed.

Although the suppression itself was short-lived, it was a blow from which none of these churches entirely recovered. Never again would any religion occupy such a central place in Chinese economic and cultural life as Buddhism had done. But whereas some temples, at least, survived, the T'ang dynasty did not. A combination of border wars, climatic disasters and devastating epidemics led to revolts in the 870s which caused even greater destruction and left the emperors as mere puppets in the hands of the warlords who controlled northern China.

The T'ang finally fell in 907. There ensued more than half a century of political disunion in which a series of five military regimes dominated the north of the country while the south was divided among eight or nine smaller states until, in the late tenth century, one of the northern dynasties – the Sung – reunited most, but not all, of the empire again. The northern portion of Annam, which had been under direct T'ang control, became independent; and in the north-west there was

The Diamond Sutra *below* is the oldest surviving printed book in the world. It is a collection of Chinese Buddhist prayers printed from wood-blocks (not movable type) with black ink onto a roll of paper. One reason for the survival of these and other works is the almost immutable form of Chinese calligraphy: the characters drawn by T'ang scholars are almost the same as those drawn by scholars under the Ming and Manchu, so that early texts could be easily read by later generations.

political confusion which was eventually ended by the emergence of a unified state called the Hsi-hsia, dominated by a Tibetan-speaking people known at the Tanguts. More significantly, in the north-east the Mongolian-speaking Khitans (from whom the word Cathay is derived) established a dynasty called the Liao which overran the northern portion of the north China plain. The area around Peking would not be under Chinese rule again for more than four hundred years.

But if Sung China was smaller than its predecessors in area, it was larger in population and resources. In the middle of the eighth century, for example, there were probably about 60 million Chinese, more than half of whom lived in north China. By 1100, the population was well over 110 million, two-thirds of whom lived in central and southern China. This massive movement of people, fleeing from the devastation in the north, began the economic dominance of the Yangtze valley and the south which persists to this day. To feed these extra millions required major advances in agricultural technology: the construction of literally thousands of new irrigation networks, and the sophisticated use of new and faster-maturing strains of rice. It was the resulting sharp increase in agricultural productivity that made possible the very substantial population growth of T'ang and Sung times.

Industry also boomed in Sung China, and cities began to break away from the more tightly circumscribed administrative roles of earlier days. Kaifeng, for example, was chosen to be the headquarters of the dynasty because of its commercial potential: it was not selected, like

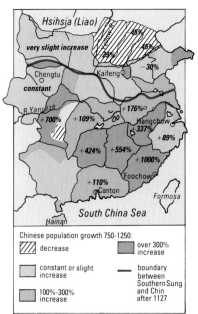

Chinese population growth 750-1250:

▨ decrease	▦ over 300% increase
□ constant or slight increase	— boundary between Southern Sung and Chin after 1127
▧ 100%-300% increase	

Chinese population growth *left* The period from 750 to 1250 saw a very rapid growth in the Chinese population, which probably doubled. At the same time, the distribution of the people completely changed. In the 7th century 73 percent of the population lived in the north-east and on the lower reaches of the Yellow River. By the 13th century the situation was reversed, and China's economic centre of gravity had shifted to the Yangtze valley.

The Spring Festival Scroll *below* drawn in about 1120 by Chang Tse-tuan, depicts everyday scenes in the Sung capital, Kaifeng. The city was recorded as having 260,000 households at this time, and the scroll portrays many aspects of its bustling everyday life. Here, in front of a maze of small shops and restaurants, rich men in sedan chairs pass mandarins on horseback and labourers hurrying with their burdens. Long-distance traders with carts and camels reflect the commercial character of the capital, placed at the eastern end of the Silk Road, and linked to the Pacific coast by a series of canals.

earlier capitals, for historical associations or strategic importance. Kaifeng, and other cities like it, became busy centres of commercial activity as trade and industry became an increasingly important source of Sung government revenues. Merchants and artisans began to play a more visible and significant role in Chinese cultural life.

Important changes were also taking place in the way China was governed. Although the examination system had been revived and used by the Sui and T'ang, it had not entirely broken the power of the old aristocracy which had ruled China since Han times. But by the tenth century that power was gone, and the state came to rely more and more heavily on the examination system to recruit its bureaucrats. Under the Sung, China became a meritocracy. Moreover, these bureaucrats, trained in a revitalized Confucianism that prized education highly and was committed to public service as the most noble of all careers, helped to spread high cultural values throughout society more thoroughly than ever before in Chinese history. Artistically, this fact is reflected in the gradual turning away from more exotic themes and techniques – such as the impressionist 'ink-splash' paintings which tried to convey immediacy and action rather than permanence or beauty – towards a reaffirmation of established Chinese ways and methods. It is generally considered, for example, that it was under the Sung that the tradition of Chinese landscape painting reached its zenith. At the same time, other well-educated subjects of the Sung were building schools, writing histories, studying classics, collecting

antiques, and exploring their country's past with a skill and enthusiasm that would be unknown in other parts of the world for some time to come.

During the eleventh and twelfth centuries, then, Sung China was undoubtedly the richest, best-governed, and most cultured of the world's states. But that does not mean that it lacked problems. First, there were the hostile Liao on the northern frontier whom the Sung, despite the maintenance of a huge standing army, could not dislodge from territories that had formerly been Chinese. Indeed, the emperors even agreed to pay indemnities to the Liao in order to keep the peace. In the early twelfth century they tried to end this humiliation by entering into an alliance with another northern state, the Chin from the area of modern Manchuria. The Chin duly helped to destroy the Liao, but then they turned on the Sung and overran most of northern China. In

Public works under the Sung dynasty took many forms, although among the most significant was the construction of widespread irrigation networks which did much to transform the Yangtze river valley into an efficient agricultural region, capable of supporting a considerable increase in population in the area. Here the emperor inspects the (labour intensive) flooding of an irrigation dyke.

1126 they took Kaifeng and forced the Sung to regroup around their so-called 'temporary capital' at Hangchow to the south-east. But the move proved to be anything but temporary. The Sung never regained their lost territory, a fact which undoubtedly helped to intensify the feelings of xenophobia and paranoia about the outside world that had been growing since the ninth century. By 1200 Sung China was a nation on the defensive, both militarily and psychologically. The receptivity to foreign ideas and influences that had characterized T'ang times was replaced by a beleaguered, fortress mentality.

Even reduced to two-thirds of its former size, however, the Southern Sung, as they were now known, remained a formidable economic and political power. They still controlled the richest parts of the old empire; and, despite military burdens which would have crushed lesser states, trade and industry flourished, great works of art continued to be

Classical Chinese landscape painting became fully established under the Sung dynasty. The complexity of such detailed panoramas in which the majesty of Nature overwhelmed the significance of man was heavily influenced by Taoist philosophy. In *Sleeping Hermit*, by Ma Yuan (active 1190-1225) *left* the style reached a point of sublime simplicity. Landscape painting, like poetry, was regarded as a worthy courtly pursuit *below*, and the Sung emperors were often accomplished poets, essayists, calligraphers and painters, as well as statesmen.

produced, and literature, history, and philosophy were still studied and written. The printing press was widely used for everything from Buddhist scriptures to banknotes. Hangchow, with its beautiful West Lake, quickly replaced Kaifeng as the greatest city in east Asia, if not in the world. Yet even as the pleasure craft were gliding back and forth across the lake in the early thirteenth century, and restaurants in Hangchow were serving a glittering array of delicacies, events were happening elsewhere in Asia which would change the course of Chinese history. For the residents of Hangchow, as for many other peoples from Japan to Germany, the Mongols were coming.

Impressionistic sketches drawn from life *above* were another important feature of Sung dynasty art. Economic in style and possibly influenced by the increasing use of printing, this art form remained uniquely Chinese until its discovery by European artists in the 19th century.

The West Lake at Hangchow *right* was a famous beauty-spot outside the Sung 'temporary capital'. For over a century after Kaifeng was abandoned in 1126, traditional Chinese life continued here and, according to Marco Polo, a voyage on the lake offered 'more refreshment and delectation than any other experience on earth'. The boats in this peaceful 13th-century painting appear just as Polo described them: 'Roofed over with decks on which men stand with poles, which they thrust into the bottom of the lake to propel the barges'. For a moment, art and reality seemed to become one in Sung China.

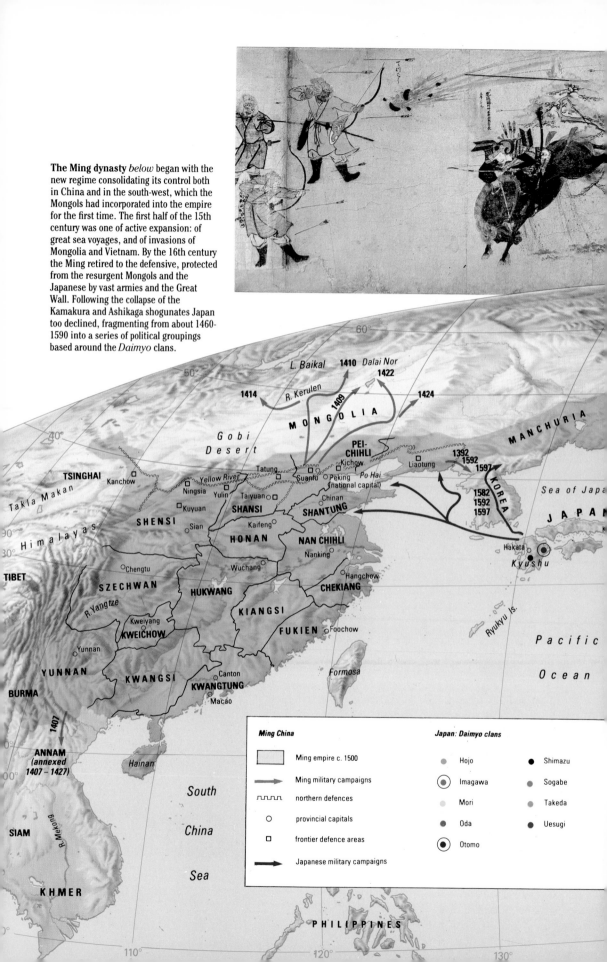

The Ming dynasty *below* began with the new regime consolidating its control both in China and in the south-west, which the Mongols had incorporated into the empire for the first time. The first half of the 15th century was one of active expansion: of great sea voyages, and of invasions of Mongolia and Vietnam. By the 16th century the Ming retired to the defensive, protected from the resurgent Mongols and the Japanese by vast armies and the Great Wall. Following the collapse of the Kamakura and Ashikaga shogunates Japan too declined, fragmenting from about 1460-1590 into a series of political groupings based around the *Daimyo* clans.

L. Baikal · 1410 · Dalai Nor · 1422
1414 · R. Kerulen · 1409 · 1424
MONGOLIA
Gobi Desert
PEI-CHIHLI
Kichow
1392
1592
1597
MANCHURIA
Liaotung
KOREA
1582
1592
1597
Sea of Japan
JAPAN
TSINGHAI · Kanchow
Takla Makan
Tatung · Suanfu · Peking (national capital) · Po Hai
Yellow River
Ningsia · Yulin · Taiyuan · Chinan
SHANSI · SHANTUNG
Kuyuan
Himalayas
SHENSI · Sian · Kaifeng
HONAN
NAN CHIHLI
Nanking
Hakata
Kyushu
TIBET
Chengtu · Wuchang
SZECHWAN
R. Yangtze · Kweiyang
HUKWANG
Hangchow
CHEKIANG
KIANGSI
Ryukyu Is.
Yunnan
KWEICHOW
FUKIEN · Foochow
Pacific Ocean
YUNNAN
KWANGSI · Canton
KWANGTUNG
Macao
Formosa
BURMA
1407
Hainan
ANNAM (annexed 1407 – 1427)
South China Sea
SIAM
R. Mekong
KHMER
PHILIPPINES

Ming China
Ming empire c. 1500
Ming military campaigns
northern defences
○ provincial capitals
□ frontier defence areas
Japanese military campaigns

Japan: Daimyo clans
● Hojo
◉ Imagawa
● Mori
● Oda
◉ Otomo
● Shimazu
● Sogabe
● Takeda
● Uesugi

The Mongol invasion of Japan in 1281 was meticulously recorded in an illustrated scroll composed for one of the victors some ten years later. In the initial phase of the campaign *left*, the Japanese experienced difficulty in confining the invaders to the beaches they had occupied. Their warriors were shot down by arrows, lances and primitive firearms. But the *samurai* counter-attacked *bottom right*, and several junks were captured. It was, however, the destruction of almost the entire invasion fleet by a typhoon, two months later, which probably saved Japan from Mongol occupation.

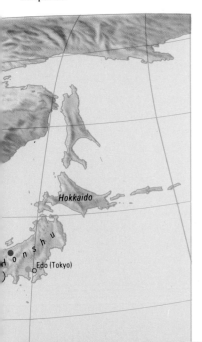

Hokkaido

Honshu

Edo (Tokyo)

CHAPTER 13

CHINA AND JAPAN
1279–1600

In 1274, a full five years before he completed the conquest of China, the Mongol ruler Kublai Khan sent an army of 30,000 men to invade the southern Japanese island of Kyushu. The army was met by a much smaller force of Japanese warriors who, although outnumbered, were determined to defend their homeland to the death. But before most of them had the chance to do so, a storm blew up which forced the Mongol invaders to return to their ports of embarkation in Korea. Japan was saved. Seven years later, Kublai tried again, this time with a mixed force of 140,000 Mongols, Koreans, and Chinese in one of the greatest amphibious assaults in pre-modern history. When these troops arrived in Japan, however, they were quickly hemmed in on a narrow beach-head near the modern city of Hakata. A battle then raged for nearly two months until, in August 1281, a violent typhoon struck the area, destroying much of the Mongol fleet at anchor and forcing the rest to withdraw. Many of the invading troops had to be abandoned and were killed by the victorious *samurai*. The Japanese called the storm *kamikaze*, or 'divine wind'. For the second time in less than a decade, severe weather had helped to defend Japan, leaving its people with the conviction that their country was uniquely favoured by the gods, who could be relied on to send another 'divine wind' to save the archipelago whenever need arose. For many centuries after the defeat of the Mongols, Japan went her very separate way.

山房臨碧海一天
紫翠上飛鳧島松月
中開鳳笙朮烟生石
窟竹雪瀾前橋誰見
陳高士熙夷善養生
八月廿日為州平畫紫
英山房尚廿眺五言楷

Landscape, c.1350 by Ni Tsan *right*
Although some Chinese artists were
prepared to work for the foreign Yüan
dynasty, many others were not. The painter
Ni Tsan (1301-74), who specialized in ink
monochromes, was one of the latter. His
most famous masterpieces were simple yet
austere landscapes, often with large areas
of the paper left blank and usually – like
this one – containing a rustic hut and a few
trees, but no other signs of life.

Sung celadon vessel, 12th century from Shensi *left* The kilns of Shensi province began to produce, under the southern Sung dynasty, high-quality imitations of the bronze vessels of ancient times. This distinctive tripod cooking-vessel, known as a *ting*, which resembles Shang bronze work (chapter 4) in both shape and decoration, reflects the general revival of interest in ancient art during the southern Sung dynasty. This sense of continuity maintained the fabric of Chinese culture, notwithstanding foreign invasions and incursions.

Kublai Khan may have failed to conquer Japan, but he could console himself with the fact that his empire was the greatest the world had ever known. His conquest of southern China during the 1270s gave him direct access to the silks, porcelains, and other luxury goods which Marco Polo and Ibn Batuta described with such enthusiasm in their famous travelogues, and which European and Middle Eastern merchants journeyed thousands of miles to acquire. Even more important to Kublai were the taxes he collected in south China which enabled him to build up his military strength and to fend off all threats to his position as Khan of Khans, the greatest of the Mongol chieftains. When he died in 1294, few would have challenged Marco Polo's assessment that Kublai was 'the most powerful man since Adam'.

For the first time, all of China had been placed under foreign rule. Interestingly enough, however, although far from enthusiastic about the quality of Mongol rule in general, most Chinese adjusted to it surprisingly quickly and came to see their foreign rulers as a legitimate, and sometimes even admirable, dynasty. Admittedly this feeling was less pronounced in the north of the country, which had suffered terrible devastation during the conquest of the 1230s; but in the south, the Mongol triumph over the Southern Sung forty years later caused relatively little economic dislocation, and Chinese ways soon began to reassert themselves in many aspects of cultural, economic and even political life. In the cultural sphere, for example, styles and standards in landscape painting developed which were to dominate Chinese art for centuries to come. Similarly, there were important innovations in popular literature: the writing of fiction flourished, and dramatic works were produced which are recognized as among the finest ever composed in China.

But although Kublai brought a measure of peace and stability to China, after his death there were coups and counter-coups as rival claimants fought for control of the imperial throne. Then, during the 1340s and '50s, much as in Europe at the same time (chapter 11), the process of dynastic decline was accelerated by floods, droughts and outbreaks of epidemic disease which, together with increasing discontent with the quality of Mongol rule, touched off a series of uprisings against the government. The most serious of these occurred in central and south-eastern China and, in 1368, the most powerful of the southern rebels, Chu Yüan-chang, proclaimed the establishment of a new dynasty called the Ming, with their capital in the great walled city of Nanking. Within a few years, the Mongols were driven back to the steppe and the Ming controlled all China.

Chu Yüan-chang 1328-98 *left* founder of the Ming dynasty, began life as a peasant. In 1344 he became a monk and soon joined a bandit gang. Gradually Chu became the leader of a considerable rebel army, with which he seized Nanking in 1356. Twelve years later he proclaimed himself the founder of a new imperial dynasty and took the title 'Hung-wu' (meaning 'mightily martial'). By 1382 his forces had pushed the Mongols back beyond the Great Wall. Chu had made many enemies on his rise to power. One of them must have commissioned the caricature portrait of the emperor *far left*.

The Yung-lo emperor 1360-1424 *right* was the most powerful ruler of his day. Yet, like his father, Chu Yüan-chang, he usurped the imperial throne: he rebelled against his young nephew in 1399 and, after a civil war, seized Nanking in 1402 and took the imperial name 'Yung-lo', meaning 'eternal joy'.

Chu Yüan-chang, the first Ming emperor, was a rarity in Chinese history: a pauper who founded an imperial dynasty. Born into grinding poverty in the year 1328, Chu spent the next forty years working his way to the top of the Chinese political world. Along the way he became a Buddhist monk, a bandit and a military commander. Perhaps this unstable background explains why, as emperor, he saw plots on every side. Such was his fear of a coup that in 1380 Chu dismissed all his chief advisers, taking over personal responsibility for virtually all executive functions of government. Such a system worked well for Chu, and for some of his more energetic successors; but when less able or less dedicated men were on the throne, operations of government could be brought to a virtual halt for lack of central direction.

After Chu's death in 1398, at the age of seventy, there was a succession dispute from which his fourth son eventually emerged victorious and became known as the Yung-lo emperor. During his father's lifetime, Yung-lo had been in charge of Peking, the former Mongol capital in the north. Now he made it the Ming capital, employing 200,000 workmen to rebuild the mud and straw walls with brick and stone for the first time, creating most of what is today called 'The Forbidden City', which became his headquarters. Yung-lo also launched a series of campaigns against the Mongols, in an attempt to create an effective shield against the tribesmen of the steppe. But he failed to capture any of their leaders and so new defensive walls were built and the northern garrisons strengthened. To feed these troops, and the residents of his capital, he improved and extended the Grand Canal, which now stretched 1,000 miles from Hangchow to just south of Peking, turning it into one of the wonders of the world. It carried some 200,000 tons of grain northwards every year, due to the numerous locks, the 20,000 barges and the 160,000 guards maintained by the Ming dynasty to secure this lifeline of their empire.

The Great Wall of China *right* is the only
man-made object that can be seen from
space. It runs 1500 miles from the Pacific
shore to the deserts of central Asia, with an
average height of 30 feet. It was originally
begun after 221 BC by the first emperor of a
united China, Shih Huang-ti (chapter 4),
who conscripted millions of workers to link
the existing northern defences of his
empire into a single system, fortified by
watchtowers. So many people died in its
construction that the Great Wall came to be
called 'the longest cemetery in the world'.
The wall in its present form was largely
constructed under the Ming, who
considerably extended and strengthened
the system.

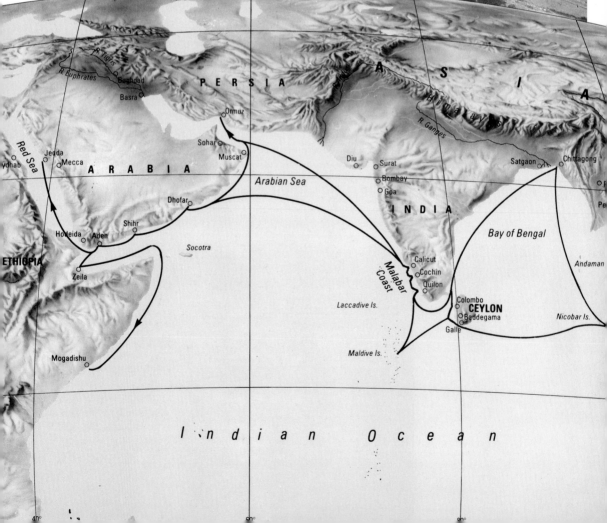

Yung-lo did not confine his expansionist policies to the north. He also sent his armies into Annam (Vietnam) where, although they managed to annex the northern parts for a time, they soon became involved in an indecisive guerrilla war. Rather more successfully, Yung-lo also set about extending his influence by sea. At his command, huge fleets of 'treasure ships' were built at Nanking and sent on a series of seven voyages to South-East Asia, India, Ceylon, Arabia and even the east coast of Africa. Designed in part to show the Ming flag and advertise Yung-lo's position as the world's greatest ruler, these maritime expeditions were truly colossal in scope. The fourth voyage, in 1413-15, consisted of sixty-three or more large vessels and almost 28,000 men, and the others were no less impressive. (By contrast, the Portuguese navigator Vasco da Gama, entered the Indian Ocean in 1498 with only four small ships and scarcely 500 men!) The Chinese fleets, commanded by the Muslim eunuch Cheng Ho, brought back valuable tribute, submissive foreign rulers (including, in 1411, the king of Ceylon) and rarities such as giraffes, lions and exotic spices.

But much as these voyages may have flattered Yung-lo's vanity and roused his curiosity, their cost far exceeded the value of the tribute they brought back. Not long after his death in 1424 they, together with colonies such as Annam, were abandoned.

Almost immediately, the empire's resources had to be redeployed to meet a new threat from the north. In 1449, Yung-lo's descendant Cheng-t'ung, a young emperor with delusions of grandeur and an entourage of poor advisers, led a military expedition north of Peking that ended in disaster. He was ignominiously captured by the Mongols not far from the capital and was deposed by his outraged subjects. The Mongols now ended the tribute they had paid to the Ming and instead made a succession of economic and political demands upon the Chinese. When these were not met, raids were launched into the empire – some of which reached the suburbs of Peking. The imperial government eventually responded by renovating and extending what we now call the 'Great Wall', until it achieved the impressive dimensions that we see today, stretching for almost two and a half thousand miles. It certainly provided eloquent proof of the Ming dynasty's logistical and technological abilities; but, for all that, it did not always keep the Mongols out. From this time forward, the dynasty was often on the defensive.

Nor was the northern frontier Ming China's only trouble spot. After the ocean voyages ended in the 1430s, coastal defence was neglected and all overseas trade banned, except under strict government control. Not surprisingly, by 1500 smuggling had become a commonplace problem in the south-eastern provinces of Chekiang, Fukien and Kwangtung. By 1550, the seas around China were infested by heavily-armed bands of smugglers and pirates who terrorized the coastal regions of the country. These men are generally referred to, in Chinese sources, as 'Japanese pirates', but most were, in fact, Chinese seafarers whose livelihoods had been threatened by government policies. For the first time in Chinese history, the south-eastern coast became a frontier of crucial military importance.

Important developments were also taking place across the China Sea. The Kamakura shogunate had ruled Japan since the twelfth century, and had successfully organized the nation's defence against Kublai Khan's army in the thirteenth. But in 1333 it collapsed – the victim of political intrigue, its own outdated policies, and the gradual erosion of the old ties of personal loyalty upon which the Kamakura feudal system had been based.

Its successors, shoguns from the Ashikaga family, never managed to

The seven voyages of Cheng Ho 1405-33 *below* brought back to Ming China tribute and gifts from no less than 37 rulers around the Pacific and Indian oceans. But the reason for undertaking them remains obscure. Perhaps they originated in Yung-lo's fear that the nephew he deposed in 1402 had fled abroad to prepare a counter-attack; but this cannot explain why the later expeditions ranged as far as Arabia, and sailed down the coast of east Africa almost as far as Zanzibar. It is more probable that the emperor, like his contemporary Henry the Navigator of Portugal (chapter 11), was motivated mainly by curiosity about the distant parts of the world in which he lived.

establish effective control over the entire country. Indeed, for much of the period between 1350 and 1600 Japan was plagued by local and provincial wars and the last century of Ashikaga rule is known, quite aptly, as the 'Era of the Warring States'. Local rulers in the south and west made a fortune from trade and piracy – mostly at Chinese expense – and lords in the central areas gradually usurped more and more of the power once exercised by the central government. By about 1560, some ten leading families had formed clan alliances that covered most of Japan, and competed openly for supreme power: Oda in the centre, Takeda and Hojo to the north, Otomo and Shimazu to the south.

But in many ways, the most important single place in Japan was still the city of Kyoto. Originally built at the end of the eighth century, Kyoto remained the Japanese imperial capital for 1,000 years. It was both the home of the emperor and of the Ashikaga shoguns, and the crucible of

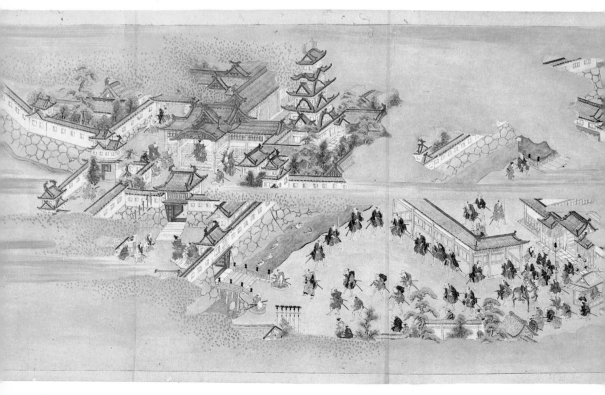

The Dragon Peace Temple or *Ryoanji* of Kyoto *left* was constructed in the turbulent late 15th century by Zen Buddhists, with lavish out-buildings and a rock garden. When, in the 1790s, the temple burned down, it was rebuilt with the rectangular garden – the only part of the original complex to survive – at the centre. It is surprisingly small (102 × 50 feet), with just fifteen stones set in raked gravel, but possesses a curiously restful beauty and epitomizes Zen aestheticism.

Japanese culture – a culture that was now heavily influenced by Buddhism, and particularly by the Buddhist school known in its Japanese form as Zen.

Although elements of Zen thinking had been present in Japanese Buddhism for generations, it was only formally introduced into the country from China in the twelfth and thirteenth centuries. Combining as it did an insistence upon rigorous self-discipline and the need for self-understanding through meditation (rather than through textual studies), Zen proved very appealing to the unlettered warriors of the Kamakura and Ashikaga periods. Zen ideas and particularly Zen aesthetics also found favour at the imperial and shogunal courts. It was important in the refined rituals of the tea ceremony, in landscape painting, in calligraphy, and in architecture.

Disruption in Japan reached its peak in the mid-sixteenth century,

The elegant Golden Pavilion Temple or *Kinkakuji* *left* was built in 1394 by the third Ashikaga shogun, Yoshimitsu. The small Pavilion, entirely covered with gold foil, is set amid gardens, lakes and the splendour of nature on the outskirts of Kyoto, the old imperial and religious capital of Japan. A testament to classical Japanese taste and balance it miraculously survived the period of civil wars in the 15th and 16th centuries; and (like the rest of Kyoto) the bombings of World War II: but in 1950 it was burnt to the ground. The present structure is an exact replica.

Japanese namban screen c.1600 *left* depicting the arrival of a Portuguese ship at Nagasaki. In the late 16th and early 17th centuries, Japanese Christian artists produced paintings influenced by Western styles, often (like this one) mounted on screens. Certain features of the southern barbarians or *namban* (as the Japanese referred to their visitors) were caricatured: the big noses, tall stature and baggy breeches of the *fidalgos*; the black dress of the tall priests; the great size of the carracks, compared with the Asian junks. Once Christianity was prohibited in Japan in the 1630s, this type of art ceased.

Himeji castle, Hyogo *left* was one of over 200 massive and elaborate stone castles built throughout Japan in response to the European challenge between 1570 and 1630. It says much about Japanese culture that these buildings, (like Japanese armour, swords and war scrolls) retain an exquisite balance between refined elegance and the practical arts of war.

just at the moment when the first Europeans arrived in Japan. They brought with them Christianity, preached by missionaries like St Francis Xavier, and firearms, which the Japanese soon learned how to make. The diffusion of the western-style guns swiftly revolutionized warfare in Japan, as it had done in Europe, making it necessary to build massive castles of stone in order to resist bombardment. Between 1570 and 1630, some 200 new fortresses – all with bastions, citadels and moats – were erected from the north of Honshu to the south of Kyushu, many of them stunningly beautiful.

Ironically, it was at precisely this time that the age of internal warfare came to an end, thanks to the work of three remarkable unifiers. In 1568, Nobunaga, leader of the Oda clan, captured Kyoto, the imperial capital. In 1573, he deposed the last Ashikaga shogun and by the time he was assassinated by a jealous rival, in 1582, he had forced almost all the other lords to accept his orders. Within a decade, his ablest general, Toyotomi Hideyoshi – though born a peasant – had consolidated Nobunaga's work, reorganizing the tax system and redistributing the land to provide sufficient funds for his ambitious policies. He died in 1598, undisputed master of the whole of Japan. But there is a Japanese saying: 'Nobunaga made the loaf; Hideyoshi baked it; but Ieyasu ate it' – because it was another of Nobunaga's generals, Tokugawa Ieyasu, who in 1603 established the dynasty of shoguns that ruled Japan until the nineteenth century. Under the Tokugawa there was peace in all the islands for two and a half centuries – an achievement unparalleled in any other advanced society. But it was only secured at

221

The unification of Japan under Toyotomi Hideyoshi and the Tokugawa dynasty depended upon the brutal exploitation of the peasantry, which was required to pay a substantial portion of its rice production to the local lords. In the 1590s, Hideyoshi organized a detailed survey of land to establish how much rice was being produced, and therefore how much each lord should receive. In this 17th-century scroll, *below* on the right women are depicted harvesting and preparing the year's rice crop while, on the left, the farmers pay over the lord's share – which might amount to as much as 50 percent of the total. Not surprisingly, peasant revolts against such extortionate demands were common, especially in the earlier 17th century.

a price. On the one hand, life for the majority of the population was extremely hard, with strict government control of thought and deed at all levels and a draconian legal system. On the other, Japan was shielded from all contact with much of the outside world. Although in the early years of the seventeenth century, a number of Japanese-built merchant ships sailed every year to the major ports of south-east Asia, from the 1630s it was made illegal for any subject of the shogun to trade with or visit foreign countries. At the same time, trade by foreigners with Japan was also restricted. The English, who had once maintained a factory in Nagasaki and provided Tokugawa Ieyasu with an esteemed adviser, Will Adams, were refused permission to return; the Portuguese and the Spaniards were expelled. Only the Dutch were allowed to handle the trade between Japan and Europe, and even they were closely confined to a small, secluded island in Nagasaki bay.

Just as Japan was finding peace and unity, China lost them. In 1393 the first Ming emperor had ruled over some 60 million subjects; but by

大明隆慶庚午年造

1580, the total had more than doubled to perhaps 130 million. To meet the increased demand for food, more and more land was brought under cultivation and new crops began to change the agricultural balance: sweet potatoes, maize and tobacco, for example, were introduced from the New World. To clothe the multitudes, cotton, which had become common under the Mongols, was widely grown and spun in the Yangtze delta. And for export, Chinese craftsmen produced many exquisite luxury goods, above all the blue and white 'Ming porcelain' that has been a collector's item ever since. Some of these goods went to traditional markets. The museums of South-East Asia – Thailand, Burma, Indonesia and the Philippines – are all filled with late Ming pottery: indeed porcelain is often their principal exhibit. But the silks and ceramics of China were also exchanged at Manila for Spanish silver from Mexico and Peru, which helped to satisfy China's monetary needs and was a significant factor in the vigorous economic growth which characterized the last few decades of the sixteenth century.

Ming Blue-and-white ware *left* was highly prized in its day, and has remained the popular yardstick of excellence in fine porcelain ever since. It was hand-produced in large quantities mainly at the imperial factory in Ching-te-chen, both for export to the West and to supply the imperial court. Surprisingly the finish is often quite crude, the glazes sometimes have minor defects, and the pieces themselves, such as this fishbowl, are commonly large in scale. On the other hand, the dexterity and robust confidence in handling form and decoration remain unparalleled by the more delicate and perfectly finished products of the later Ch'ing dynasty, or contemporary Japan.

Yet while some prospered, many suffered. The years after 1580 saw a deterioration in the climate, with numerous harvest failures, droughts and famines. There were also severe outbreaks of epidemic disease. At the same time, Ming China faced new and increasingly serious military problems. In 1592, and again in 1597, Hideyoshi sent his armies into Korea, where they sacked its capital, Seoul, and apparently laid plans for an invasion of China: having conquered the whole of Japan, he seems to have dreamed of ruling the whole of East Asia. But in the face of the powerful Japanese attacks, the Koreans appealed to Peking for aid, and a large Chinese army duly arrived and drove the invaders back. For some years they remained as an army of occupation, lest the Japanese should return; but their victory was illusory. Firstly, it was expensive, and the extra taxes levied in China to pay for the army caused uprisings in many major cities. Secondly, it diverted much-needed troops from the north-eastern frontier, where a new power was emerging among the peoples of the forest and the steppe: the Manchus.

A well-organized confederation of tribes in Manchuria, the Manchus, attacked Korea in 1606. They were repulsed. But in 1618 they turned their attention to China and invaded and occupied Chinese-held territory, north-east of the Great Wall. In 1621, they captured Shenyang, or Mukden, and soon made it their capital: Ming China, weakened by increasingly frequent army mutinies and peasant revolts, was unable to stop them. So, under their able leader Nurhaci, the Manchus were able to build up their military strength until in 1636, Nurhaci's son proclaimed himself founder of a new imperial dynasty, the Ch'ing, and intensified his pressure on the Chinese frontier. The Ming were now trapped: unless they deployed their army along the Great Wall, Peking would fall to the Manchus; but if they withdrew their forces from the capital, it might fall to the rebels. In April 1644, this is precisely what happened: the army of one of the rebel leaders, Li Tzu-ch'eng, reached Peking. As his forces closed in on the Forbidden City, the last Ming emperor hanged himself in a small pavilion near his palace. But before a new Chinese dynasty could be established, the Manchus advanced beyond the Great Wall and drove Li Tzu-ch'eng out of Peking. Within a few years, all vestiges of resistance had been eradicated and once again, as in Mongol times, the whole of China was ruled with an iron hand by foreigners from the north. It was to stay that way until 1911. With the Tokugawa firmly established in Japan, and the Ch'ing in China, a new age in east Asian history had begun.

The Manchu Tai-tsu shih-lu *right* was a detailed visual record of Nurhaci's invasion of China and defeat of the Ming. Like the Norman Bayeux Tapestry, it was a popular and successful piece of political propaganda; it went through several editions. Here we can see the Manchu cavalry armed, like their Mongol forebears, with composite bows, long arrows in quivers, and swords, routing the prolific Ming artillery, sweeping the light mounted cannon aside with considerable ease.

The Ottoman advance *below* Until the mid-15th century, Ottoman expansion was largely directed into the Balkans; by 1389 substantial areas of mainland Europe had fallen under Ottoman control. After the Mongol invasion in 1402, progress was halted for a number of years, but by 1453, and the capture of Constantinople, the Ottomans were definitively established as the major power in the eastern Mediterranean. The defeat of the Safavids at Çaldiran in 1514 led to the absorption of the Mameluke empire in Egypt 1517 and opened the way to the Red Sea and the north African coast. Although defeat at Lepanto in 1571 effectively limited Ottoman naval power, control of eastern Europe was to expand steadily, culminating in the assaults on Vienna of 1529 and 1683.

Orkhan 1324-60 *right* the second Ottoman Sultan, regarded himself as the foremost warrior of Islam. Nevertheless he married a Christian, the Byzantine princess Theodora, and surrounded himself with Christian advisors, shown here to the right of his throne. However, his campaigns considerably extended Ottoman incursions into Christian territory. In 1356 his troops captured Gallipoli and began the Turkish advance into mainland Europe that eventually took them to the gates of Vienna.

growth of the Ottoman empire

- Ottoman conquests 1389
- Ottoman conquests to 1402 (incl. vassalages)
- Ottoman empire 1620

(1289) date of incorporation into Ottoman empire

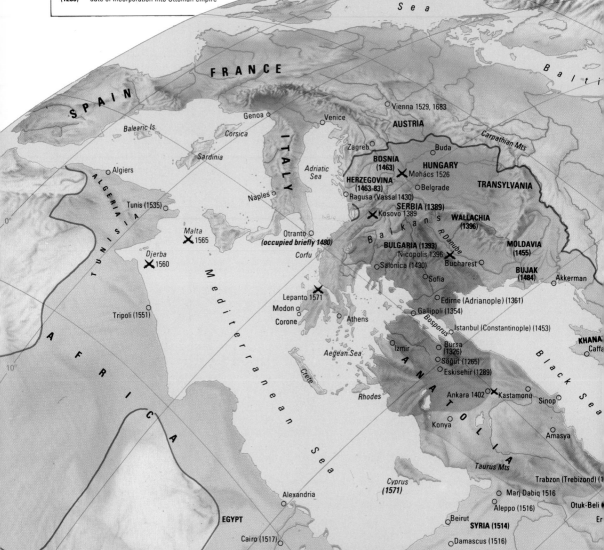

North Sea

Balti

SPAIN

FRANCE

Vienna 1529, 1683

AUSTRIA

Genoa   Venice

Balearic Is.

Corsica

Zagreb   Buda   Carpathian Mts

ITALY   BOSNIA (1463)   HUNGARY

Sardinia   Adriatic Sea   HERZEGOVINA (1463-83)   ✕ Mohács 1526   TRANSYLVANIA

Algiers   Belgrade

ALGERIA   Ragusa (Vassal 1430)   SERBIA (1389)   WALLACHIA (1396)

Tunis (1535)   Naples   ✕ Kosovo 1389

Malta ✕ 1565   B a l k a n s   R. Danube   MOLDAVIA (1455)

Djerba ✕ 1560   Otranto   BULGARIA (1393)   Nicopolis 1396   BUJAK (1484)

Corfu   *(occupied briefly 1480)*   Bucharest   Akkerman

Salonica (1430)

Sofia   Lepanto 1571 ✕   Modon   Edirne (Adrianople) (1361)

Tripoli (1551)   Corone   Gallipoli (1354)   KHANA

A F R I C A   Athens   Istanbul (Constantinople) (1453)   Caffa

Izmir   Bursa (1326)   Black Sea

Aegean Sea   Söğüt (1265)   B a l k a n s

10°   Eskisehir (1289)

Crete   Ankara 1402 ✕ Kastamonu   Sinop

Rhodes   A N A T O L I A

Konya   Amasya

Taurus Mts

Cyprus (1571)   Trabzon (Trebizond) (1

Alexandria   Marj Dabiq 1516   Otuk-Beli

EGYPT   Aleppo (1516)   Er

Beirut   SYRIA (1514)

Cairo (1517)   Damascus (1516)

CHAPTER 14
THE OTTOMAN EMPIRE
1280–1683

In 1258, the Abbasid caliphate, the ailing but nevertheless supreme symbol of unity and authority for the majority of Muslims, was overthrown in Baghdad by the vastly superior forces of the Mongols (chapter 10). Although the concept of the caliphate was to be revived by the Ottomans in the early sixteenth century, the events of 1258 mark a clear turning-point in Islamic history. After that date, no single universal Islamic authority was ever able to assert itself successfully: although the Mongols and their successors either were or quickly became Muslims, and presided over a considerable expansion in the territorial extent of the Islamic world, the states which they ruled were essentially political entities – great powers with their own individual policies and interests – and not theocracies. The Ottoman empire was soon to become one of these new-style Islamic states.

During the sixth century, the Turks were one of the many nomadic peoples of Central Asia. Moving steadily westwards, they gained control of the silk bazaars of Samarkand, and later advanced to the borders of Anatolia. There were many tribes of Turks. Some of them became Muslims as they spread westwards and, from the eighth century, Turkish troops formed the core of the armies of the caliphs of Baghdad. By the eleventh century, the Seljuk Turks, based at Konya (in the heart of modern Turkey), virtually controlled the caliphate and, following their victory over a Byzantine army at Manzikert (1071), they emerged as the dominant power in Anatolia and Persia. But their hegemony lasted less than two centuries. In 1243, the Seljuks were routed at the battle of Kösedağ by the advancing Mongols, which seriously weakened their power.

However, after their defeat at Ain Jalut (chapter 10), the Mongols withdrew into Persia, leaving a power vacuum in Anatolia. In earlier centuries, Byzantium might have been expected to take advantage of this development; but the sack of Constantinople by Crusaders from the West in 1204, and the creation of a rival Latin empire in Greece and the Balkans, had fatally weakened Byzantine power. Thus the no-man's-land between Byzantium and the Mongols soon came to be filled by small Turkish states, about ten in all, each vying with the others for political supremacy in the area; all justified their existence by the claim that they were *ghazis*, Warriors for the Faith, seeking to wrest lands from non-Muslims and bring them into the Islamic fold. One of these small warrior states was ruled, at the start of the fourteenth century, by a chief named Osman (Uthman in Arabic), from whom the dynastic name 'Ottoman' is derived.

Under Osman (1281-1324) and his son Orkhan (1324-1360), the Ottoman state gradually expanded at the expense of both its Muslim

CRIMEA (1475)

Caucasus Mts

Caldiran 1514

Sultan Mehmed I 1402-13 was buried in the Green Mosque, built at his command in Bursa. His massive yet simple tomb *left*, topped by his turban, was decorated with ceramic tiles bearing inscriptions in golden characters on an azure background adorned with flowers and arabesques. It was one of the earliest examples of a distinctive style in Ottoman art.

and its Christian neighbours. One of their greatest successes was the capture in 1326 of the Byzantine city of Bursa after a five-year blockade: the Ottomans at once made it their capital, and all the early sultans are buried in magnificent tombs within the city's Green Mosque. The Ottoman élite turned Bursa into a centre of art and learning, for the Turks were becoming settlers as well as nomads and their leaders were becoming rulers as well as chiefs. Orkhan, indeed, began to mint his own coins, a sure sign of independence and permanence; and he recruited Christian administrators to help him run the state.

As the Ottomans became better organized, the services of their successful troops were soon in demand. In 1346, Orkhan loaned some 5,500 of his soldiers to a Byzantine nobleman, John Cantacuzenus, who wished to become emperor. He succeeded in this, and in return the sultan was given the new emperor's daughter as a bride. This partnership also enabled Orkhan to establish himself and his followers on the European side of the Bosporus, a development which was to be crucial for the further expansion of Ottoman power. The Turks occupied Thrace and the useful port of Gallipoli on the European side of the Bosporus, and Orkhan hastily sent large numbers of his tribesmen to settle in the rich new European lands he had acquired, in order to 'Turkify' it. When he died in 1360, he had doubled his inheritance. But it was still small: at 30,000 square miles, the Ottoman state was about the same size as Ireland, or the state of Maine.

However, Orkhan's son Murad I, the third sultan, immediately increased his hold over Europe. In 1361 he captured Adrianople, second only to Constantinople in importance as a Byzantine city; Murad renamed it Edirne and made it his capital. This advance of Islam within Europe provoked unease among the Christian states of the Balkans and beyond. In 1389 a large army was assembled by the king of Serbia and his allies, but the Ottomans wiped it out in the decisive battle of Kosovo. Although Murad was killed in the mêlée, his son and successor Bayezid I exploited the victory to the full. Within a few years the kingdom of Bulgaria had been annexed (1393), a large crusading army from the West had been massacred at Nicopolis (1396), and most of the independent emirates in Anatolia had also been absorbed into the Ottoman state, which now stretched from the Carpathians to the Taurus mountains and covered some 267,000 square miles.

Already, under Bayezid, the empire displayed many of the hallmarks for which it was later famous. At the heart of the system was the sultan and his family, for the tribe of Osman remained at the core of the state. They were surrounded by a sort of court aristocracy made up of members of the old Turkish élite, and were served by viziers, the sultan's deputies who supervised his administration. But there were also innovations. The Turkish court functioned according to an elaborate

The battle of Nicopolis in 1396 marked a high point in the reign of Bayezid I, the Thunderbolt. His invasion of Hungary and blockade of Constantinople in 1395, and his continual pressure on Venetian holdings in the eastern Mediterranean, led to a major European crusade, organized by the Hungarians. A coalition army besieged Nicopolis, the main Turkish stronghold on the Danube, but was rapidly destroyed by superior Turkish cavalry tactics. Christian losses were heavy, and Bayezid executed the majority of prisoners, thereby discouraging any future European task forces.

etiquette, introduced from Byzantium (and probably beginning with Orkhan's Greek wife), while in the army the free *ghazi* raiders of Osman and Orkhan were replaced by highly-trained troops specially recruited from among youths captured during the Balkan wars. These were called the 'New Force': the *yeniçeri*, known in English as the 'janissaries' and easily recognizable in action by their tall plumed hats. Murad also conscripted Christian boys from the Balkans and trained them in the Turkish language, law and faith, so that they could enter the Ottoman administration.

This conscription of likely Christian boys for military or government service, known as *devşirme*, was made easier by the dislocation that accompanied the Turkish conquests. Not only were prisoners taken in battles and raids: the threat of war, the destruction of property, and the Black Death (which affected Eastern as well as Western

Bayezid's court *right* was regulated by strict ritual which stressed the Sultan's exalted status. He was attended by members of the hereditary Turkish aristocracy, by the traditional élite of his conquered territories, and by the administrators and advisors that he himself had elevated from obscurity, as depicted in this contemporary miniature.

Europe after 1347), all caused considerable movement of populations. The fourteenth century was indeed a 'time of troubles' which favoured military recruitment. But, to most of the subject peoples, the Ottoman conquest brought much-needed peace and stability, for the Turks followed the traditional Islamic policy of toleration towards the 'peoples of the book' – that is, Christians and Jews who accepted the same one God. Indeed, Ottoman rule in the Balkans was normally less oppressive than the system it superseded, in which feudal dues and labour services weighed far more heavily on the population than the sultan's taxes. This continued to be true in later periods: peasants living under Habsburg rule bore far more onerous burdens than their contemporaries in the Ottoman lands.

But in Asia, Ottoman expansion was less popular. In the 1390s, Sultan Bayezid, nicknamed *Yildirim* – 'Thunderbolt' – on account of his rapid campaigns, began to attack his eastern neighbours, demanding that they switch allegiance from their existing overlord to himself. Those rulers who would not were deposed. Unfortunately for him, this overlord was Timur the Lame, known to us as Tamerlane, a descendant of Genghis Khan, commander of vast armies and conqueror of an empire that stretched from Persia to India. In 1402 he outmanoeuvred Bayezid and began to sack Ankara, chief city of Anatolia; when the Sultan's forces approached, they were wiped out and Bayezid himself was captured. The Ottoman dominions in Asia Minor were systematically ravaged, and those whom Bayezid had deposed were restored to their possessions.

The catastrophe at Ankara might have spelled the end of Ottoman rule but, ironically, the Turks were rescued by their enemies: in return for a suitable remuneration, Italian merchantmen ferried survivors from the battle across to safety in Europe. Moreover, Timur died in 1405, before he had managed to create any successor states in Anatolia capable of matching the Ottoman enclaves left intact. Nevertheless, there followed an eleven-year hiatus, between 1402 and 1413, when the Balkan states and the Anatolian emirates took advantage of the opportunity provided by the Mongol victory to shake off Ottoman rule. Bayezid himself died in captivity the year after his defeat, and his four sons fought viciously for control of the remnants of his empire. By 1406 the eventual winner, Mehmed II, was in control of all parts of Asia Minor still loyal to the Ottomans; by the time of his death in 1413 he also reigned supreme in Turkish Europe. But his empire was reduced to some 110,000 square miles, less than half the area ruled by his father. It was only under Mehmed's son Murad I (1413-1451) and his grandson Mehmed II (1451-81) – nicknamed *al-Fatih*, 'the Conqueror' – that the Ottoman empire became a world power, extending even beyond the frontiers of Bayezid's day. It had grown larger than any of its neighbours and possessed an almost irresistible power.

This expansion took place equally in Europe and Asia Minor. In a series of bold strokes, the independent states of Anatolia were once again weakened, defeated and finally annexed, bringing the Ottoman empire to the Black Sea and the borders of Syria. In Europe, great gains were made by exploiting the civil wars that beset the numerous Christian states of the Balkans and Greece. Serbia was annexed in 1459; Bosnia in 1463; Albania in 1478; Herzegovina in 1483. A series of campaigns against Venice (1462-79) gradually forced all of the Republic's strongholds on the Greek mainland to surrender, and in 1480 the Turks even took Otranto in southern Italy – although they could not hold it.

The most spectacular of Mehmed's conquests was, of course, the capture of Constantinople in 1453. Its great walls – over 100 feet in height – had previously withstood many sieges (seven at the hands of

Timur the Lame (Tamerlane) 1336-1405 *above* claimed to be descended from Genghis Khan; he created an empire which stretched from the river Ganges in India to the Black Sea, with his capital at Samarkand. He was the last of the Mongol invaders to penetrate as far west as Anatolia, and his defeat and capture of the Ottoman Sultan Bayezid at Ankara in 1402 was as celebrated in its day as Hülegü's sack of Baghdad more than a century before. Although this miniature merely shows Bayezid kneeling before his conqueror, contemporary tradition has it that the defeated Sultan was kept in a small cage, so that Timur could gloat over him.

The Fall of Constantinople 1453 *right* came as no surprise to observers in the east. The previous year, Sultan Mehmet II had managed to close the Bosporus by building castles at its narrowest point; Constantinople was now cut off both from western naval assistance and from its traditional sources of food and supply. When the final siege began, on 6 April, there were only some 10,000 Christian defenders to resist an Ottoman army of more than 100,000. After a prolonged artillery bombardment, several Turkish ships managed to penetrate the inner harbour (known as the Golden Horn, at the centre of the picture) and on 29 May a general assault was ordered. The city was taken within a few hours.

The artillery of Mehmet II, the Conqueror *above* was massive. Where west European gunfounders concentrated on casting artillery that was mobile and quick-firing, their Ottoman counterparts tried to make guns of the greatest possible power. This cannon, known as the 'Dardanelles Gun', cast in bronze and capable of firing a 676 lb shot at targets up to a mile away, was so large that it had to be made in two pieces, with a breech chamber which had to be screwed into place before firing.

After the Turkish conquest the Christian churches of Constantinople became Islamic mosques – including the basilica of St Sophia *left*, built between 532 and 537, during the reign of the great Byzantine emperor Justinian. All its Christian monuments and icons were removed, and minarets were added to call the faithful to prayer in what had once been the largest church in Christendom.

the Ottomans themselves). But Mehmed was able to concentrate against these ancient defences, originally built a thousand years before, the greatest military innovation of the Renaissance: a battery of siege guns. Some of them, like the 'Dardanelles Gun', presently on view at the Tower of London, measured over 20 feet in length and hurled stone shot weighing 676 pounds. On 5 April the Turkish army of about 150,000 men stood before the capital of Constantine, defended by a mere 8,000 troops; on 29 May, at the third assault, the city finally fell to the Turks.

It was a victory of great importance. On the religious plane, it fulfilled a call by the Prophet Mohammed himself, that one day the forces of Islam would conquer Constantinople. On the political plane, it gave the Turks a new imperial capital, which they renamed Istanbul and proceeded to beautify. But the Byzantine buildings were also carefully preserved. Even during the sack of the city, it is said, when the sultan discovered one of his soldiers trying to remove part of the marble floor at St Sophia, perhaps the greatest church of Christendom, Mehmed struck the man with his sword, saying: 'For you, the treasures and the prisoners are enough. The buildings are mine'.

Mehmed II's eighteen victorious campaigns had carved out a state that was as vast as the Byzantine empire at its height. But his death brought a temporary halt to these advances, for a disputed succession severely weakened the position of his son Bayezid II (1481-1512). Nevertheless, during his reign the Ottomans built up a powerful fleet, which they used to defeat the Venetians and capture the last Christian toe-holds in Greece – Modon, Corone and Lepanto – and to extend their control over the entire Black Sea littoral – even the Khanate of the Crimea, a last remnant of the Mongol invaders of Russia, acknowledged Ottoman suzerainty.

The Ottoman empire did not expand only at the expense of Christendom. The Sultans also subjugated other Muslim states including the Arab lands, Egypt and the north African littoral. They only failed against Persia, ruled from 1501 by a new dynasty – the Safavids – who used their distinctive Shi'ite form of Islam (chapter 8) to rally support for their continued (and usually successful) resistance to the Sunnite Turks *below*. War between the two states continued intermittently for three centuries.

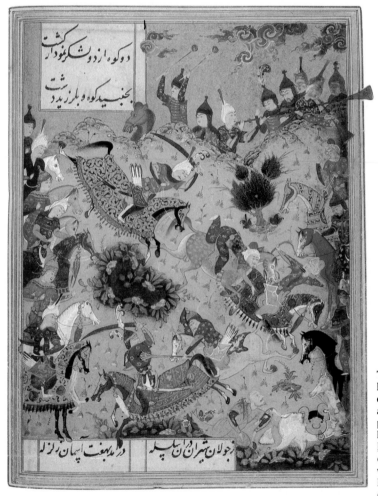

The Turkish threat in the Mediterranean was considerable. The capture of Constantinople and its naval arsenal allowed the Ottomans to become as powerful by sea as they were already by land. Following the capture of the island of Rhodes *above* in 1522, by the Janissaries of Sultan Suleiman (the Janissaries are wearing their distinctive white-plumed hats), the Ottoman navy dominated the eastern basin of the Mediterranean. Until the resounding defeat of Lepanto in 1571 *right* it also threatened the security of the western basin.

The last years of Bayezid II's reign, and most of that of his successor Selim I (1512-1520), were largely taken up with events in the east: in Persia, Egypt and the Fertile Crescent. The sudden rise of the Safavid dynasty in Persia after 1500, created a state both militarily strong and ideologically hostile to the neighbouring Ottomans. Shi'ism, the form of Islam favoured by the Safavids, was also attractive to dissident forces and groupings within the Ottoman state, who eagerly lent their support to the new dynasty and engineered a series of Shi'ite-inspired risings among the Turkish tribes near the Persian frontier. It was to end this threat that Selim led out his army against the Safavid Shah Ismail,

inflicting a crushing defeat at Çaldiran in 1514 which both secured the eastern frontiers and removed the threat of religious separatism for a time. But it also brought the Ottomans into direct contact with the Mameluke empire. Over the next two years Selim managed to destroy the Mamelukes politically and militarily, conquering Aleppo and Damascus in 1516, and taking Cairo in 1517. This campaign not only added new territories – Syria, Palestine, Egypt and most of Arabia; it also added all three holy places of Islam – Mecca, Medina and Jerusalem. The prestige and authority of the Ottoman dynasty were thus enormously enhanced.

The tide of conquest continued. Under Selim's son Suleiman, known in the West as Suleiman the Magnificent (1520-1566), the Ottoman empire reached its greatest extent, stretching from Budapest to Basra, from the Crimea to Cairo, and from Algiers to Arabia. It covered a million square miles and its capital, Istanbul, was by far the largest city in Europe, with 500,000 inhabitants. An inscription of 1538 found in Romania, gives some indication of Suleiman's power:

'I am God's slave and sultan of this world. By the Grace of God I am head of Mohammed's community. God's might and Mohammed's miracles are my companions. I am caliph in Mecca and Medina. In Baghdad I am the shah, in Byzantine realms the Caesar, and in Egypt the sultan; who sends his fleets to the seas of Europe, North Africa and India. I am the sultan who took the crown and throne of Hungary and granted them to a humble slave…'

It is true that there were some interruptions to Ottoman progress. Perhaps the most famous was the battle of Lepanto, in 1571, in which the Turkish fleet was caught at its anchorage off the Greek coast and 200 of the 230 Turkish warships present were either sunk or captured by a Christian fleet mobilized by Spain, Venice, Naples, Sicily, Genoa and the Papacy. Senior Turkish officers, sailors and craftsmen captured at Lepanto were all executed following the battle. Certainly it was a great victory, but it was not followed up. Nor did it restore to Venice the prosperous island of Cyprus, captured by the Turks in the same year. Life in Istanbul continued unaffected for, as the Grand Vizir told the Venetians: 'You have singed our beard, but it will soon grow again; but we have cut off your arm, and you can never find another'.

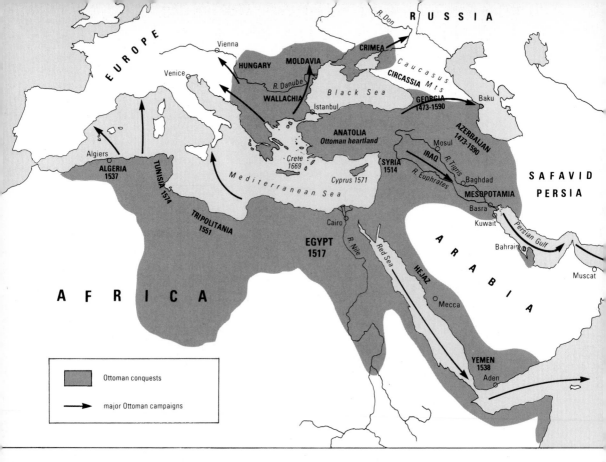

The Ottoman sultans who followed each other in direct descent from Osman to Suleiman the Magnificent were all rulers of unusual ability. Orkhan, the second sultan, may have been premature in his claim of 1337 to be 'marcher lord of the horizon and hero of the world' but his descendants – especially Bayezid 'Thunderbolt', Mehmed 'the Conqueror' and Suleiman 'the Magnificent' – were all statesmen of outstanding talents in both war and peace. However, after Suleiman's death there were few sultans who stood out as great commanders; and it has been suggested that the lack of inspired leadership caused the empire to decline. The quality of the rulers was affected, it is argued, by their style of life, always dwelling among their concubines in the large harem of the Topkapi palace in Istanbul. But, by this time, the government of the Ottoman empire had become so complex that the personality of the sultan was less important than it had been. Even under a deranged psychopath like Mehmed III, whose first public act in 1595 was to have his nineteen brothers strangled to prevent any succession dispute, the Ottoman army still inflicted major defeats on the Christians in Hungary.

The impact of domestic problems on the efficiency of the empire after Lepanto has also been somewhat exaggerated. Peasant revolts in Anatolia, palace revolutions in the capital, and roaring price inflation following the influx of silver from America certainly happened; but their impact was not noticeably worse in the Ottoman lands than elsewhere, for civil wars, depositions and the price revolution were also endemic in Christian Europe. However, the Ottoman state had derived much of its momentum from constant expansion; and, when the conquests slowed down after the capture of Cyprus in 1571, increasing administrative corruption set in. In addition, the Ottomans failed to introduce the technological innovations possessed by their contemporaries, and this gradually reduced their capacity for effective resistance.

The Ottoman empire at its greatest extent *above* emerged as the principal Islamic world power, and retained this role for several centuries. Encompassing the Islamic heartland of Arabia and the Near East, the Ottomans consolidated Islamic power in northern and eastern Africa, and established an enduring Islamic imprint in southern Russia, the Caucasus and south-eastern Europe. Paradoxically, their expansion eastwards was contained by the Shi'ite Safavid state in Persia, and elsewhere Ottoman influence was increasingly confined by the thrusting ambitions of the rapidly expanding Christian European powers.

Selim II (1566-78) *right* has always had a bad press from historians, who nicknamed him 'Selim the Sot', and suggested that he was a slave to passion, spending all his time on women and wine. This 17th-century Turkish miniature proves that such a view is not new. Selim's achievements as a statesman and soldier suggest otherwise. He conquered and held the important Christian island of Cyprus in 1571, settling it with thousands of Turkish families from Anatolia to ensure its loyalty; and, although his fleet was defeated that year at Lepanto, by 1574 he had constructed another one which finally recaptured Tunis from a powerful Spanish garrison.

The arresting of Ottoman expansion was thus not so much the result of increased internal weakness as of growing external opposition. Timur had destroyed so many states, putting nothing comparable in their place, that it proved impossible to organize effective resistance to the Ottomans in the Near East. Both the Mamelukes and the Safavids stood alone against Selim; and alone they fell. But under Shah Abbas the Great (1587-1629), the builder of Isfahan, the Persians secured assistance from both Russia and the Christian West in order to drive the Turks out of Mesopotamia and much of the Caucasus. They even tried to coordinate their campaigns with the Habsburgs in Hungary. Nevertheless, after the death of Abbas, the Ottomans recovered much of their lost ground. Although their troops surrendered Baghdad in 1624, they regained it in 1638.

It was much the same story in the west. Lepanto was won in 1571 because, for a brief moment, three major Christian states of the Mediterranean – Venice, Spain and the Papacy – pooled their resources. But within two years the Venetians concluded peace and the Turks were able to make good most of their losses. It was over a century before another alliance of western states proved capable of halting a major Ottoman offensive, in 1683. For three months, an Ottoman army of 200,000 men held Vienna, capital of the Austrian Habsburgs, under siege. But they failed to fortify their own camp and, on 12 September, a force of 80,000 Poles, Germans, Spaniards, Portuguese

Suleiman the Magnificent *right* on his last campaign is shown in this contemporary miniature receiving Christian vassals as his army besieges the Hungarian town of Szigetvár. Shortly afterwards the Sultan died, his army mutinied, and his son Selim II faced a succession struggle that prevented him from continuing the conquest of Hungary.

Gentile Bellini (1429-1507) was sent by the Venetian republic to Constantinople in 1480 to paint Mehmed the Conqueror. From that point onwards, many artists specialized in producing pictures depicting scenes from Turkish life. His *Venetian ambassador visiting the Sultan, left* clearly implies a meeting of equals: Western artists (not surprisingly) did not wish to show Europeans abasing themselves before Oriental potentates.

and Italians launched a surprise attack on the besiegers. It was a total success: the Ottoman field army was shattered and, in the years that followed, the Turks were driven right out of Hungary.

This victory has been much celebrated, and attention has been drawn to the military superiority of the European armies during the Hungarian wars, with their long ranks of musketeers supported by batteries of field guns throwing a continuous barrage of fire which the Turks seemed unable either to withstand or to imitate. But it did not always matter: although, as it appeared to some, the Turkish army learnt nothing and forgot nothing, their army remained a force to be reckoned with. They may have lost Hungary, but they still controlled the entire Arab world east of Libya and most of the areas that now form Greece, Albania, Bulgaria, Romania and Yugoslavia.

Apart from their role in converting to Islam substantial parts of south-eastern Europe (much of the areas which are now Albania and Yugoslavia), the Ottomans' most enduring achievements were probably in the fields of art and architecture. Perhaps the best-known form of Ottoman art is miniature painting, derived from Persian models, or the beautifully glazed pottery of Iznik. The three successive Ottoman capitals, – Bursa, Edirne, and Istanbul – are the sites of sumptuous mosques and theological colleges (or *medreses*), and important religious monuments and public buildings can still be seen in the major administrative centres of the Ottoman empire in Europe and the Arab world. Mehmed II, the conqueror of Istanbul, extended and beautified the city in the fifteenth century, and his successors Bayezid II and Suleiman continued his work. The Ottomans also constructed a network of postroads in Europe and Asia, complete with bridges and hostels for travellers.

From their capital city, Istanbul, the descendants of Mehmed the Conqueror continued to rule an empire that was substantially larger than any state in western Europe. It was not until the first decade of the twentieth century that the Ottomans were forced out of all but the furthest corner of Europe; and not until 1918 that four hundred years of Turkish rule over the Arab lands finally ceased. Turkey may have become as the British Prime Minister Gladstone used to say, 'the sick man of Europe'; but he took a long time to die.

The Turkish siege of Vienna *above* in 1683 began on 14 July. An Ottoman army of about 100,000 began to tunnel towards the 16th-century walls around the city in an attempt to plant mines beneath them. It was slow work: only on 2 September did their troops manage to capture some of the outer fortifications. Ten days later, as the Turks launched an assault on the city, a vastly superior relief army (led by John Sobieski, the King of Poland) delivered a surprise attack that drove the Ottoman army back beyond Budapest. This anonymous contemporary painting shows the battle on 12 September at its height.

Iznik pottery *right* was first developed in the late 15th century, coinciding with the first period of Ottoman expansion, and was influenced by contemporary Ming blue-and-white ware and Persian craftsmanship. The decorative motifs were largely figurative (unusual in Islamic art), often featuring floral designs or sailing vessels, although only rarely including representations of human beings.

Legend

	areas of Islamic penetration c.1500
	Ghana 8th – 12th century
	Mali 12th – 15th century
	Songhay c.1500
	Kanem Borno
	state nucleus
■	Muslim colony
M	musk
C	copper
♂	slaves
⊟	salt
∖	bananas
⊘	millet
⬮	rice
∖	ivory
◪	gold
🐂	cattle

EUROPE

Atlantic Ocean

Canary Is.

Marrakesh
Ceuta
Atlas Mts
Maghreb
Algiers
Tunis
Mediterranean Sea

Awlil
TAKRUR
9th C–11TH C
Awdaghost
Kumbi Saleh
Walata
Taodeni
Taghaza
Ghadamès
Wargla
Murzuk
Augila

Galam
Goure
Jenne
Timbuktu
Tadmekka
Ghat
Alexandr
Cairo

R. Niger
Gao
AIR
Agadès
Sahara Desert
EGYPT

MOSSI STATES
HAUSA STATES
Katsina
Kano
Bilma

AKAN
OYO
IFE
NUPE
Zaria
Ngazargumu
KANURI
WADAI
DARFUR
NUBIA
Dongola
R. Nile
MAKURRA

BENIN
KWARARAFA
Lake Chad
ALWA
Meroe
Mecca
Red Sea

YORUBA STATES
FUNJ EMPIRE
15 CENTURY
AXUM
3rd C–8th C
Adulis
ARABIA

R. Congo (Zaire)
ETHIOPIA
ADAL
Zeila
Berbera

KONGO

Sanga
Lake Victoria
Jvuna
Mombasa
Malindi
Mogadishu

Kalahari Desert
Ingombe Ilede
Kilwa Kisiwani
Pemba I.
Zanzibar

Orange R.
R. Zambezi
ZIMBABWE
Zimbabwe
Comoro Is.

Mapungubwe
Sofala
Phalaborwa

Cape of Good Hope

MADAGASCAR

Indian Ocean

40° 40° 60°

CHAPTER 15

AFRICA BEFORE THE EUROPEANS
100–1500

'I had before me a boundless forest, and a country, the inhabitants of which were strangers to civilized life; and to most of whom a white man was the object of curiosity or plunder. I reflected that I had parted from the last European I might probably behold and perhaps quitted for ever the comforts of Christian society. Thoughts like these would necessarily cast a gloom over the mind, and I rode musing along for about three miles.'

The young Scotsman, Mungo Park, as he began his solo exploration of West Africa in 1795, had good reason for gloom. Within six months he was, by his own confession, 'worn down by sickness, exhausted with hunger and fatigue, half-naked and without any article of value by which I might procure provisions, clothes, or lodging'. He also lacked a map for, in his day, the interior of Africa was 'still but a wide extended blank, on which the geographer…has traced, with hesitating hand, a few names of unexplored rivers and uncertain nations'.

Mungo Park's Africa was indeed 'the Dark Continent' to Europeans, and it long remained so. Even today, almost two centuries after Park, the history and geography of Africa are not as easy to study as those of Europe or Asia. Africa was – and, in some respects, still is – extraordinarily inaccessible. In the first place, from about 4000 BC, the once-fertile Sahara began to dry up, creating the wasteland of the earth's largest desert, stretching from the Atlantic to the Red Sea. The Sahara was not, of course, wholly impenetrable; but journeys across it were largely restricted to trading caravans, following known routes and possessing very specific objectives. To depart into the unknown was usually fatal. The Greek historian Herodotus, writing about 450 BC, tells the story of a military detachment, on patrol only seven days' march west of the Nile, that was overtaken by a sandstorm and buried while the men were taking their midday meal. Similar freak storms still afflict the area today, turning the midday sun to dusk in a matter of minutes.

Access to the interior further south, from the sea, is not much easier. Although covering almost 12 million square miles, and thus more than three times the size of the United States, incredibly enough Africa's coastline is shorter. There are few sheltered bays or natural harbours. There is no Caribbean to assist penetration and, of the great rivers, only four – the Nile, Niger, Senegal and Zambezi – are easily navigated from the sea. Much of the African interior is a vast plateau, broken by the broad interior basins, stretching in most areas almost to the coast: often, only a few miles from the sea, the traveller faces rapids and spectacular waterfalls as rivers tumble hundreds of feet down a sheer escarpment. On the Congo (Zaire) river, for example, only eighty

The great empires of Africa *left* which flourished from 900-1500 were largely interior states, often deep in the heart of the continent. A string of major states developed on the southern fringe of the Sahara, benefiting from trans-Saharan trade fostered by the Islamic states of north Africa and the Middle East; and as Islamic traders spread down the east African coast, new trading networks became established to the south. Lines of communication were limited; there are few natural harbours south of the Sahara, and the major rivers descend sharply from the plateaux of the interior, *above left* making passage impossible. Thus the history of Africa was profoundly different from that of Europe or Asia.

The career of Mungo Park (1771-1806) is a fine example of the cultural shock experienced by the first Europeans to penetrate the Africa continent. He trained as a surgeon before he was engaged by the British African Association to explore the course of the river Niger. When he left Scotland in 1795, he was still the fresh-faced young man of the oval lithograph *far left*. But by the time of his death, apparently in an accident on the Niger during his second journey, he was already in appearance an old man. Few who saw his picture *left* would have imagined him to be only 34.

Timbuktu *right* was one of the cities that thrived on the trans-Saharan trade, and which attracted Muslim merchants and missionaries southwards, beyond the desert, to the prosperous kingdoms of the upper Niger. This 19th-century European engraving of the city shows the mixture of traditional African mud-brick huts with Arabic two-storey dwellings, mosques and caravanserais that gave Timbuktu its exotic charm in Western eyes.

miles inland the cataracts begin, and there are thirty-two of them – taking the traveller a total of 1,000 feet above sea-level before the great river basin, with easy navigation, is reached. Even there, however, malarial swamps, the tse-tse fly and a host of tropical diseases complicated the task of survival. For all these reasons, until the nineteenth century, few of those from the outside world who reached the interior and made contact with its civilizations lived to tell the tale.

It is worth insisting on these points because, until recently, this absence of evidence has been interpreted as evidence of absence. Some have used the silence to argue either that pre-colonial Africa had no history, or that such history as it possessed was unworthy of study. But Africa was far from 'dark' to the teeming millions who lived there – probably equal in number, until modern times, to the population of Europe. The truth is that Africa was peopled by societies of great power and sophistication in the centuries before the Europeans arrived, especially in sub-Saharan West Africa and along the coastal plain of East Africa. Few of them, unlike those along the Mediterranean coast, developed any writing of their own, which additionally complicates the task of the historians who try to chart their rise and fall; but it is wrong to describe people without written records as people without history.

In the seventh century, followers of the Prophet Mohammed spread with great rapidity westwards from Arabia across the whole of North Africa, until they reached the Atlantic coast of what is now Morocco. There they soon heard of rich and ancient kingdoms to the south, beyond the desert in the savanna country lying on the southern edge of the Sahara.

Archaeological research has shown that, as early as about 400 BC, the cattle herders and cereal cultivators who lived in the savanna had learned how to smelt iron, and thus to apply new skills to the control of their environment. In this land of scarce resources and vast distances, trade developed on a substantial scale during the first millennium AD. States and urban centres arose through their control of the trade carried by the long trans-Saharan routes to the successive Roman and Arab settlers of North Africa. Timbuktu and Jenne were the most famous of these centres, built at the point where the river-traders of the Niger met the nomads of the desert. At about the time of Christ the

Without the camel *below* the sands of the Sahara would have prevented almost any contact between the fertile Mediterranean coast of Africa and the tropical forests to the south. Even then, guiding a train of up to 12,000 camels across the trackless wastes of the largest desert in the world, on a journey that might last three months, was a major feat of navigation. There were few landmarks, fewer oases, and the Tuareg cameleers had only the sun and the stars to guide them.

tents of the traders beside the inland delta, near Jenne, began to give way first to grass huts, and then to buildings of sun-dried bricks like the ones to be seen there today. This change was accompanied by another: the arrival of Islam. Missionaries from the north crossed the desert and carried out a highly successful campaign of conversion. Timbuktu rose to real prominence in the fourteenth century under the Islamic Sultans of Mali, whose famous ruler, Mansa Musa, went on an ostentatious pilgrimage to Mecca in 1324. On his journey he showered so much gold about him that his fame spread far and wide. He even appears, brandishing a gold coin, in the famous 'Catalan Atlas' made in Majorca in the year 1375; and the gap in the Atlas Mountains through which his gold might come to Europe was prominently displayed.

Mansa Musa died in 1332 and his empire, though vast in both extent and wealth, did not long survive. But other powerful states soon dominated the area, all of them Muslim. Some, such as the Songhay empire in the fifteenth and sixteenth centuries, derived their power from control of the gold mines of the Upper Niger. Others further east – such as Kano and Borno – grew rich from the north-south trade in other goods, including slaves.

The Catalan Atlas *right* was prepared for King Charles V of France in the late 14th century, and reflects the best information available at that time in Europe about north Africa. Although the cartographers worked in Majorca, it is surprising how little they knew about the lands to the south of the Atlas mountains, represented by the yellow-brick wall running parallel to the coast. But they were aware that, close to 'Tenbuch' (Timbuktu), lived a ruler of prodigious wealth: 'This black lord' says the legend, in Catalan 'is called Musa Mally, lord of the negroes of Guinea. The gold which is found in his country is so abundant that he is the richest and noblest lord in all the region'. On the left, a veiled Tuareg trader approaches on his camel to barter for Mansa Musa's gold.

The great mosque at Jenne *left* the trading city founded in the 13th century on the inland delta of the river Niger in Mali, is a testament to the influence of Islam. The city served as an *entrepôt* for trade between the western and central Sudan and Guinea's tropical forests. By the 17th century the city was known as the centre of Muslim learning south of the Sahara, outstripping its rival Timbuktu.

The kingdom of Benin was one of the foremost kingdoms of the West African forest region. It reached its greatest extent just as the first Europeans appeared at the mouth of the Niger, and its wealth was enhanced by considerable acumen in trading ivory, pepper, palm oil and slaves with the Portuguese. A more lasting accomplishment was sophisticated and highly naturalistic bronze-casting, and among the many examples which have survived are these 17th-century images of the *oba* (king) with his advisers *right* and wearing his ceremonial necklace and headdress *far right*.

It was not only in the West African savanna that important kingdoms arose. Further south, in the forest zone, comparable developments took place; but, because these forest states were not in direct
contact with the literate, Islamic north, most of our information about
them comes from archaeology. Nonetheless it is clear that the environment of the area dictated a life-style markedly different from that which
prevailed in the savanna. Domestic animals could rarely be kept; and
yams, not cereals, were the main food crop. Moreover, travel was slow-
er and more difficult, so the forest peoples lived in greater isolation
than their more northerly contemporaries. But the achievements were
no less impressive. Excavations in modern Ghana and Nigeria have
revealed great technological sophistication and amazing artistic
accomplishments among the yam-cultivators of the West African
forests. Some 1100 years ago, bronze-casting by the lost-wax process
reached a peak of excellence that has rarely (if ever) been equalled
anywhere in the world. In Benin, the bronze-casting tradition continued into recorded historical times, and was reported by the first
European settlers.

Far away to the east, a completely separate urban civilization arose
on the relatively flat triangle of land bordering the Indian Ocean coast
of what is now Somalia, Kenya and Tanzania. Two thousand years ago,
much of this part of East Africa was inhabited by pastoralists and
hunters, some of whom had already learned how to work iron. But by
about AD 800 they began to indulge in long-distance trade. The products of the region, including frankincense, skins, ivory and – a little
later – slaves and gold, were being brought to the cities of the coast,
whence they were transported to Arabia and to India, utilizing the

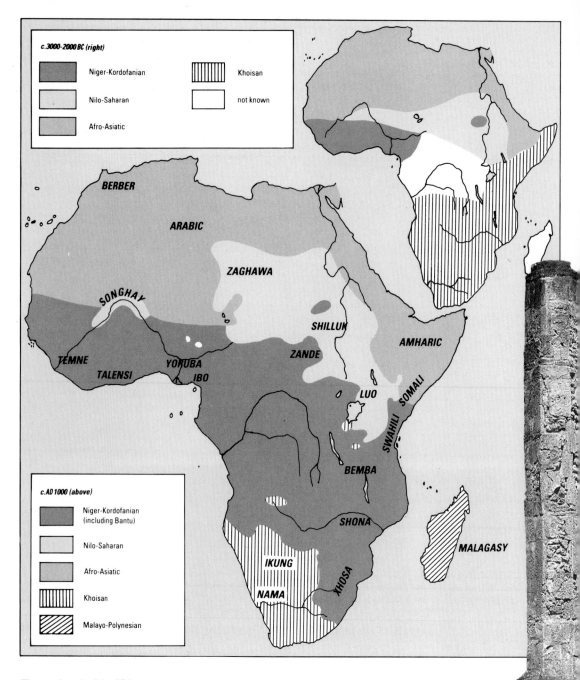

c.3000–2000 BC (right)

Niger-Kordofanian

Nilo-Saharan

Afro-Asiatic

Khoisan

not known

BERBER

ARABIC

ZAGHAWA

SONGHAY

SHILLUK

AMHARIC

TEMNE

YORUBA

TALENSI

IBO

ZANDE

LUO

SOMALI

SWAHILI

BEMBA

c.AD 1000 (above)

Niger-Kordofanian
(including Bantu)

Nilo-Saharan

Afro-Asiatic

Khoisan

Malayo-Polynesian

SHONA

MALAGASY

IKUNG

KHOSA

NAMA

The regal tomb of the 15th-century sultan of Gedi *right* stands amid the ruins of the principal mosque of what is now a ghost-city by the coast of Kenya. The port-cities of the Swahili coast, founded in the 9th century by migrants from the African interior, were once prosperous and powerful, especially after Islamic merchants came to the area in the 11th century and encouraged trading contacts with Arabia, India and even China. But when the Portuguese arrived in the 16th century, the Muslim faith of the population was taken as a sign of hostility and Gedi, like most of the other port-cities or the region, was promptly sacked.

The analysis of African languages *left* provides possible clues to unravelling much of Africa's unrecorded history, such as the spread of population across the Sudan, the problem of linking Bantu-speakers of the south with their origins north of the Congo, and the overlaying of Bantu upon earlier Khoisan cultures.

Kilwa *below* built on an island a mile from the shore, became in the 15th century the leading commercial centre of the entire east African coast between Sofala and Mombasa. Palaces, luxurious merchant houses and mosques flourished until 1505, when the Portuguese came ashore and sacked the city 'with laughter, jesting and song' (according to one of their own chroniclers). The oppressive Fort Santiago, shown here, was built at once to dominate the surviving population of Kilwa and to control its trade.

monsoon winds of the Indian Ocean to establish regular seasonal circuits. In return they imported the carpets of Isfahan and Gujerat, the ceramics of China and Persia, the horses of Arabia, and the cottons of India. An idea of their wealth can still be gathered from the extensive ruins of the palaces and mansions, once several stories high, at Gedi in Kenya or at Kilwa in Tanzania. These were city-empires, just like medieval Venice or Genoa, and their contacts spread far and wide. As early as 1071 the trading cities of East Africa sent an embassy to China, and recent excavations of the urban remains have revealed copious quantities of Chinese porcelain, especially of the early Ming period. This connection helps to explain why, in 1418 and again in 1422, they were visited by the great fleets of 'treasure ships' sent westwards by the Chinese emperor Yung-lo (chapter 13).

It used to be assumed that the native peoples of Africa did not build towns or stone houses, so that the impressive port-cities of East Africa must have been the work of Islamic immigrants from Arabia. But the archaeological record shows something quite different: Kilwa and several other cities were clearly founded in the ninth or tenth century by the ancestors of the modern Swahili people, who became both town-dwellers and traders with the interior long before they became (some time in the twelfth century) Muslims, and who preserved many essential elements of their traditional culture long after they adopted the religion and ways of Islam. Thus, for example, although they took over Arabic script, they used it to transcribe their own native language. The inscriptions of the rulers of Gedi are written in Swahili, not in Arabic.

But not long after the visit of the Chinese treasure ships, the prosperity of the cities along the Swahili coast began to decline. First, their trade with the interior waned; then, after the arrival of the Portuguese in 1498, their maritime commerce was seriously and permanently disrupted. The great port-cities, whose ruins are today so haunting, seem to have died almost overnight.

Muslim influence in East Africa did not reach far inland, nor did it extend on the coast much beyond Mozambique (probably because it was impossible to sail further south, or return, with the aid of predictable monsoon winds, in a single season). By the time Gedi and Kilwa were in their prime, most of southern Africa was the exclusive domain of the Bantu peoples. But it had not always been so. Until about the beginning of the Christian era, most of the African peoples living south of the Equator were hunters and gatherers. They had no domestic animals or cultivated crops; and they made no pottery and did not smelt iron or other metals. Their tools were made of bone, wood and stone, and they mostly lived a nomadic existence in small groups, often taking refuge in caves or rockshelters, the walls of which they sometimes decorated with fine paintings.

But about AD 100 a remarkable and sudden change took place. In many areas of sub-Equatorial Africa archaeologists have found villages of farming people which clearly date from this period: people who herded sheep, goats and cattle, who grew cereal and other crops, who made pottery and iron tools – people who followed a life-style in many respects very similar to that which has continued in rural areas of Africa into recent times. These changes were so complete and so sudden, and were associated with the introduction of so many things that were previously unknown, that they were probably linked to an expansion of farming people from elsewhere, perhaps speaking a Bantu language not unlike those still used in the area today. Gradually these Bantu-speaking farmers may have moved into lands previously inhabited only by hunter-gatherer groups, cultivating small fields cleared

Rock paintings of hunters and herdsmen *right* have been found in many parts of Africa, reflecting the importance, especially of cattle, at different times and places in Africa's history. Many have been found in the Sahara, dating from about 2000 BC, illustrating the thriving life of the region before desiccation set in and the desert was formed. This painting, from Zimbabwe, is less ancient, but the great care and detail in rendering the cattle indicate the continuing importance of livestock in the agricultural economy of that region.

Throughout history many African peoples have pursued traditional ways of life unchanged since they were first depicted in ancient cave-paintings: the passage of the centuries seems to have had little or no impact. In the Kalahari desert of south-western Africa, the San peoples still hunt game with bows and arrows as their forefathers have always done *left*; while in many parts of sub-Saharan Africa villagers continue to use digging sticks to plant their crops *below*. Similarly, the staple food crops cultivated by these farmers, including millet, sorghum and yams have remained unchanged for centuries.

from the bush on the edges of the river valleys and establishing villages. Sometimes they will have traded with the hunters, perhaps in due course intermarrying with them; and gradually some of the hunters would have adopted the life-style and technology of the newcomers. When the fields became exhausted, no doubt some of the farmers would move on and the process would be repeated.

The process of expansion was not always peaceful. For many generations, some of the hunter-gatherers were able to maintain their traditional way of life but, eventually, as the farming population expanded, competition for land and resources became such that either the hunters were finally absorbed into the society of the farmers, or they perished. Sometimes trade and mutual respect characterized relationships between farmers and hunters; on other occasions, avoidance or hostility were more common. The domesticated herds of the farmers were tempting prey for the hunters, and the vivid rock paintings of southern Africa show many examples of raids by the hunters and of retaliation by the farmers. But, however it happened, by about AD 400 the Bantu-speakers were established over most of Africa south of the Equator, and their numbers increased rapidly. So did their skills. Around 1000 years ago they began to exploit their new territory more intensively, often keeping large herds of cattle. They also discovered and worked the area's mineral resources – salt, iron, copper and, in some parts, gold. The huge size of some of the ancient mines was a source of wonder to early European prospectors: in Rhodesia (now Zambia and Zimbabwe), for example, the British South Africa Company's agents in the 1890s found few deposits not previously discovered by their African predecessors and many that had been exhausted. This is not surprising. The minerals of Zimbabwe were not to be found elsewhere in southern Africa and traders from the north had long travelled great distances to secure them.

The granite walls at Great Zimbabwe cover an area of over 100 acres, and constitute probably the largest and the most dramatic prehistoric site in sub-Saharan Africa. They lie off the southern edge of the high plateau that forms the watershed between the Zambezi and Limpopo rivers, in the fertile basin midway between gold-rich hills and extensive grass-lands. In the later 14th century, due to its prosperity from both mining and herding, Great Zimbabwe became a major political and religious centre: both the elliptical building at the centre of the main complex – 800 feet in circumference and almost certainly a royal residence *below* – and the large conical tower within it marking the major religious focus *right* – date from this period.

Here, as in West Africa in rather earlier times, the combined pressure created by a growing population and the need to control the distribution of valuable resources provided a stimulus for the growth of states. One of the best known, and by far the most spectacular, of these early southern African empires was centered on the massive stone complex at Great Zimbabwe (a name which may mean 'stone houses'). These impressive buildings were constructed with wealth derived from several sources. The fertile upland plains on which they are situated supported large herds of cattle. Copper was obtained from the north, and iron was available locally. But it was gold which enabled the rulers of Great Zimbabwe to control a lucrative long-distance trade with Sofala on the east coast, in what is now Mozambique, whence large quantities of beads, porcelain and other imported luxuries found their way inland. Some of the walls at Zimbabwe are thirty feet high, built without mortar or cement, and the site is both striking and complex. Yet there are no written records and few local traditions to explain their origin. It is only recently that archaeologists and historians have established that the ruins, and the treasures associated with them, date from the fourteenth century AD, and were the work of the ancestors of the Shona people who still live in the area. They are also fairly sure that this civilization was already in decline by the late fifteenth century. As with the Swahili port-cities, the civilization of Zimbabwe was destroyed in the main by other African peoples; the Europeans, when eventually they arrived on the scene, merely completed the task.

But the Europeans were by no means the first Christians to come to Africa. Egypt, like the rest of the Mediterranean world, formed part of the Roman Empire and of its Byzantine successor. Alexandria, Christian capital of Egypt, provided a home for intellectuals such as St Clement and Origen, served as a centre of learning, and became the hub of far-reaching commerce. By the first century AD, with 700,000 inhabitants, it was by far the largest city in Africa. But the Arab conquest in 642 laid it low (chapter 8). Christianity came later to Ethiopia – probably only around AD 300 – when it was adopted by the rulers of Axum, which had long been regarded by outsiders as one of the world's great empires; here it lasted far longer. Axum was in close contact with Sabaea across the Red Sea, the 'Sheba' whose queen enchanted King Solomon. The rulers of Axum claimed descent from Solomon and the queen of Sheba, and the title 'Lion of Judah' borne by the last emperor of their putative line, Haile Selassie of Ethiopia, also appears in the earliest records. Axum's Christianity, once her neighbours turned to Islam, gradually led to isolation, although her power and wealth continued to command respect. Visitors still came to admire the huge stelae, carved from single slabs of stone, one of them rising like some modern tower-block to a height of almost 100 feet. But Axum's power was broken about 1000 years ago by a local revolt, exploited by the Muslims who cut her off first from the Mediterranean and finally from the Red Sea. The state only survived by moving its capital south to Lalibela, named after the king who ordered ten vast churches and palaces to be cut into the rock. These have been in constant use since their construction, around the year 1200 for, although isolated from the rest of the Christian word for many centuries, Ethiopia retained her distinctive faith and her Coptic rite. The legend of 'Prester John', of a living Christian king in the heart of Africa, persisted in Europe and was confirmed when, in 1520, a Portuguese missionary reached Lalibela and managed to get a report of the country back to Portugal. The long seclusion of the Ethiopian Coptic church was over.

Giant obelisks *far left* are all that remain of the kingdom of Axum in northern Ethiopia. They were probably erected in the 4th century AD, when Axum rose to become the most powerful maritime trading state on the Red Sea. The kingdom enjoyed close relations with Byzantium and with the rich incense states of southern Arabia, and its rulers were converted to Christianity in the 4th century. In the 7th century Axum clashed with the rising power of Islam, and never recovered from the destruction of its fleet by the Arabs in 702.

The church of St. George at Lalibela **c.1200** *below* was carved out of solid volcanic rock. First, the bed-rock was hacked away to form a trench 40 feet deep; then the huge block of stone at the centre was carved into the shape of a Greek cross; and finally the structure was hollowed out and decorated. The top of the church is level with the ground. It was fashioned, along with several other similar structures, in the remote highlands of Ethiopia in the 12th century, and it has remained in use to this day.

The growth of the slave trade *far right* was phenomenal. In the 15th century a few hundred slaves were taken from west Africa to Europe and the Atlantic islands. From the 1520s, slaves began to be transported by Europeans to the New World. The trans-Atlantic trade reached its peak in the 18th century, when between six and seven million Blacks were shipped to the Americas. The trade only finally came to an end in 1870. The areas shown on the map were the principal sources of slaves, and the figures shown are for 1526-1810.

The crowded European slave-ships *below* marked a callous compromise between two competing considerations: on the one hand, the slavers wished to ferry as many Africans to America on each ship as possible, in order to maximize profits; on the other other, they needed to ensure that as many as possible of those embarked reached their destination alive, and thus preserved their value. The loading plan shows how many slaves could be crammed below decks and still survive, for despite the absence of light and sanitation, records show that by the later 18th century most ships lost less than 10 percent of their human cargoes. In earlier times, however, losses had sometimes exceed 30 percent, leading the Portuguese to refer to their slave-ships as *tumbeiros* – coffins.

The arrival of the Christians from Europe in other parts of Africa was not so benign however. Already, the advance of the Portuguese down the western coast of the continent had been marked by the taking of slaves (chapter 11). When, after 1480, the Europeans came in contact with the societies around the Bight of Benin, they encountered peoples who already practised slavery on a considerable scale. It is sometimes supposed that this institution was actually introduced by the white man, but it now seems clear that it was an integral part of Bantu Africa long before. Wars, for example, were often fought for slaves, not land, because a man's wealth was measured by the number of people he controlled, not by the amount of territory he dominated. Furthermore, many societies operated a legal system in which the commonest form of punishment – whether for theft, adultery or witchcraft – was enslavement. Some slaves were set to work for those whom they had wronged or for those who had captured them in battle; but others were sold by the state to merchants who exported them for profit, usually to the Arab world. When the Europeans arrived, these African merchants readily included the newcomers among their clients, and started shipping slaves to the coast as well. As long as the consumers required relatively few – five or six thousand a year – the demand could easily be satisfied. It was only when, in the eighteenth century, the Europeans alone demanded between sixty and seventy thousand slaves a year, that the impact on traditional societies became catastrophic, eventually causing their collapse and thereby facilitating subsequent European conquest. It was then that slavery became, in the words of a recent historian, 'the most significant and large-scale enforced movement of peoples in the pre-modern world'. And the principal cause of this transformation was not a rising demand in Europe, but the destruction by the Europeans of the peoples and social system of yet another continent: America.

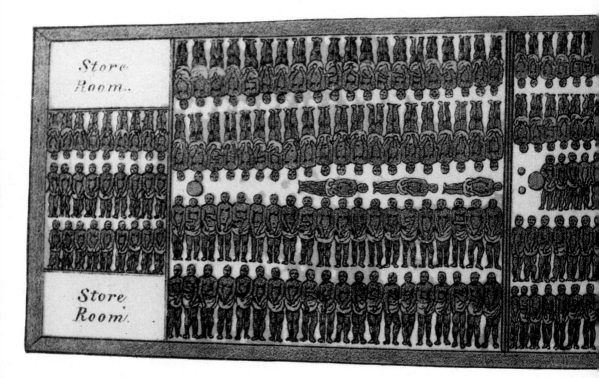

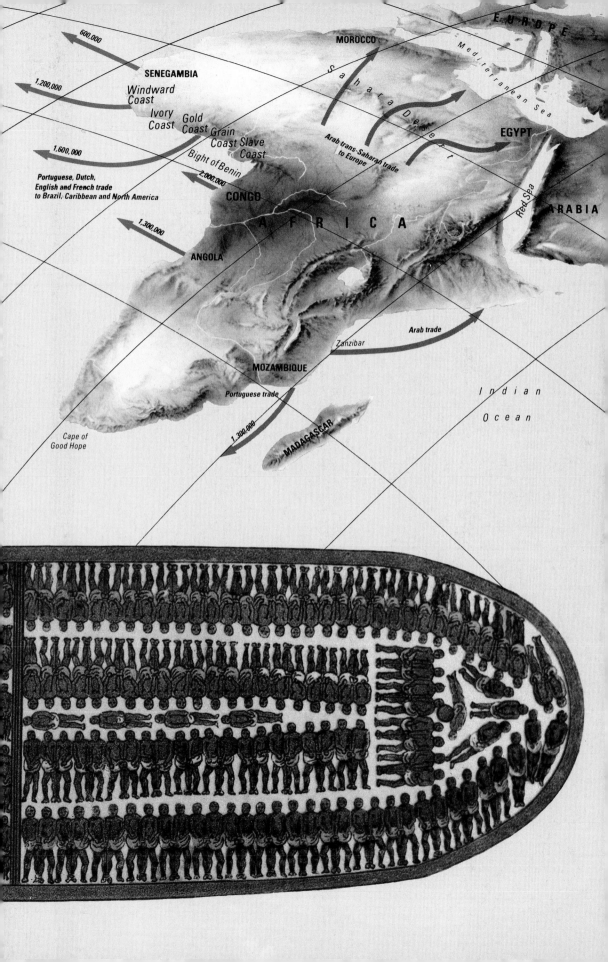

EUROPE

MOROCCO

Mediterranean Sea

600,000

SENEGAMBIA

Sahara Desert

1,200,000

Windward
Coast

EGYPT

Ivory
Coast   Gold
Coast   Grain
Coast   Slave
Coast

1,600,000

Bight of Benin

Arab trans-Saharan trade
to Europe

Red Sea

2,000,000

Portuguese, Dutch,
English and French trade
to Brazil, Caribbean and North America

CONGO

ARABIA

AFRICA

1,300,000

ANGOLA

Arab trade

Zanzibar

MOZAMBIQUE

Indian

Portuguese trade

Ocean

1,300,000

Cape of
Good Hope

MADAGASCAR

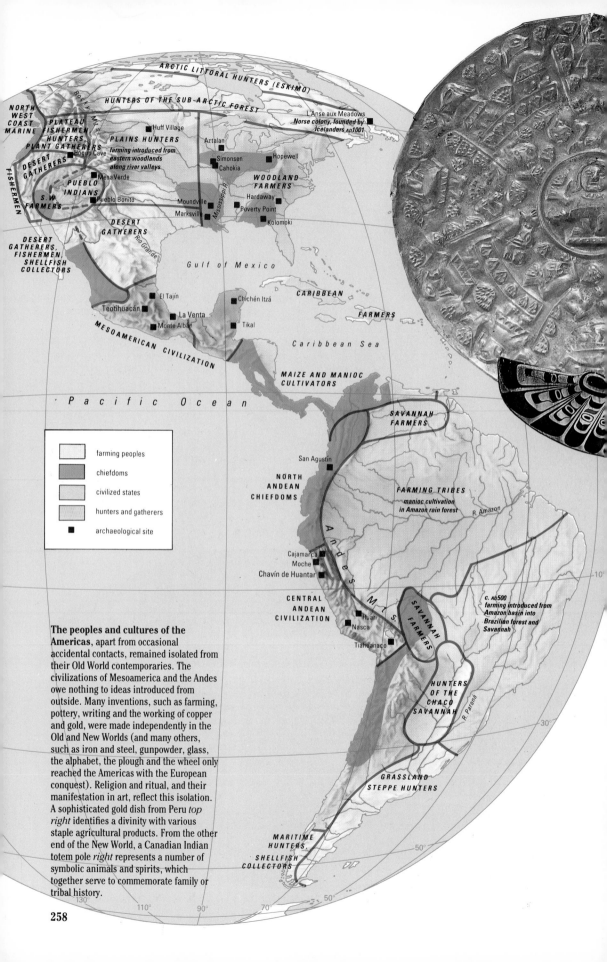

ARCTIC LITTORAL HUNTERS (ESKIMO)

HUNTERS OF THE SUB-ARCTIC FOREST

NORTH WEST COAST MARINE FISHERMEN

PLATEAU FISHERMEN, HUNTERS, PLANT GATHERERS

DESERT GATHERERS

Rocky Mts.

PLAINS HUNTERS
farming introduced from eastern woodlands along river valleys

Huff Village

Aztalan

L'Anse aux Meadows
Norse colony, founded by Icelanders AD1001

Hogup Cave

Simonsen
Cahokia

Hopewell

Mesa Verde

PUEBLO INDIANS

S.W. FARMERS

Pueblo Bonito

WOODLAND FARMERS

Moundville

Hardaway

DESERT GATHERERS

Marksville

Poverty Point

Mississippi R.

Kolomoki

DESERT GATHERERS, FISHERMEN, SHELLFISH COLLECTORS

Rio Grande

Gulf of Mexico

CARIBBEAN

FARMERS

Chichén Itzá

El Tajín

Teotihuacán

La Venta

Monte Albán

Tikal

Caribbean Sea

MESOAMERICAN CIVILIZATION

MAIZE AND MANIOC CULTIVATORS

Pacific Ocean

SAVANNAH FARMERS

San Agustín

NORTH ANDEAN CHIEFDOMS

FARMING TRIBES
manioc cultivation in Amazon rain forest

R. Amazon

farming peoples

chiefdoms

civilized states

hunters and gatherers

■ archaeological site

Cajamarca
Moche
Chavín de Huantar

Andes Mts.

CENTRAL ANDEAN CIVILIZATION

Huari
Nasca

Tiahuanaco

SAVANNAH FARMERS

c. AD500
farming introduced from Amazon basin into Brazilian forest and Savannah

HUNTERS OF THE CHACO SAVANNAH

R. Paraná

The peoples and cultures of the **Americas**, apart from occasional accidental contacts, remained isolated from their Old World contemporaries. The civilizations of Mesoamerica and the Andes owe nothing to ideas introduced from outside. Many inventions, such as farming, pottery, writing and the working of copper and gold, were made independently in the Old and New Worlds (and many others, such as iron and steel, gunpowder, glass, the alphabet, the plough and the wheel only reached the Americas with the European conquest). Religion and ritual, and their manifestation in art, reflect this isolation. A sophisticated gold dish from Peru *top right* identifies a divinity with various staple agricultural products. From the other end of the New World, a Canadian Indian totem pole *right* represents a number of symbolic animals and spirits, which together serve to commemorate family or tribal history.

GRASSLAND STEPPE HUNTERS

MARITIME HUNTERS, SHELLFISH COLLECTORS

CHAPTER 16

AMERICA BEFORE THE EUROPEANS
300–1500

The first human immigrants to America entered Alaska from Asia between 40,000 and 25,000 years ago, and by 7000 BC they had populated the entire continent. Dependent on hunting wild herds of now extinct animals such as mammoth, camels and horses, the earliest nomadic peoples had exterminated all large animals apart from bison by about 8000 BC. In response to this exhaustion of food supplies specialized gathering and hunting techniques developed. Some of these societies survived until the very recent past: the Eskimo (or Inuit) of America's sub-arctic fringe, for example, perfected methods of catching seals and other sea-mammals, while in the hot dry deserts of the south-west seed gathering provided most of the food required by the local population. Throughout North America almost all food was obtained from hunting and gathering until about AD 750, by which time squash, gourds, sunflowers and maize were cultivated (chapter 2).

Based on the slenderest agricultural economy, the native peoples of the eastern forests of what we now call Ohio, Kentucky, Pennsylvania and West Virginia achieved something very close to civilization. Massive burial mounds containing rich grave goods were built between 1000 BC and 300 BC by the Adena people who were succeeded and eclipsed by the Hopewell inhabitants of the same area during the centuries 300 BC to AD 500. The Hopewell chiefs built huge geometric monuments forming patterns of circles, squares, octagons and parallel lines, some of which cover up to four square miles. Exotic imported goods buried in the funeral mounds of Hopewell leaders include fine metalwork as well as a range of decorative luxuries traded from the Rockies, the Gulf coast and the Great Lakes. As maize cultivation increased in yield and importance, even larger earthen mounds were constructed as the foundation platforms for temples and élite residences, which formed the nuclei of the first towns in North America. The site of Cahokia, near St Louis, had a population by AD 1000 of about 40,000 people and can only be described as a city, the first in the history of the northern continent.

Further south, village and town life and the domestication of plants and animals occurred far earlier and developed more quickly. In the fertile Tehuacán valley of Mexico agriculture began in about 6000 BC, while in the Peruvian Andes it began five hundred years earlier (chapter 2). By about 1500 BC in both Mesoamerica and in the Andes numerous farming villages developed which produced pottery, textiles and tools very much like the agricultural settlements of the Old World.

But in two important respects the American story was different from that of the Old World. Firstly there was limited animal husbandry (no animals suitable for haulage were to be found in the New World);

and secondly the transition to settled village life in America, once plants and animals had been domesticated, took some 4,000 years – almost three times as long as in the Near East. Once the process was completed, subsequent developments took place at more or less the same pace on both sides of the Atlantic; but, nevertheless, a crucial disequilibrium between the Old World and the New had been created which lasted until the European invasion.

One of the most frustrating differences between Old and New World civilizations is the almost total absence of documentary records in the Americas. Only a few pre-European codices, written on paper made from bark, together with a wealth of inscriptions on walls, pillars, pots and jades are known from Mesoamerica. The enigmatic scripts have resisted almost every scholarly attempt to decipher them, though now the code is beginning to be understood. For the time being, however, in order to learn about the civilizations that existed before Columbus discovered America in 1492 – the societies that we call pre-Columbian – we are dependent for the most part upon material unearthed by archaeologists and the deductions which they make from their evidence.

The first known civilization of America is that of the Olmecs, who expanded from the tropical lowlands around the Gulf of Mexico around 1200 BC and created a culture which exemplified many of the religious, political, social and economic characteristics of all later pre-Columbian civilizations. Thus they invented both a style of hieroglyphic writing and a numerical system which spread over the entire continent; they built ceremonial centres, with platforms and pyramids positioned along a north-south axis, which became the model for subsequent cities everywhere; and they played the ceremonial ball-game, in large stone-lined courts, which became a central feature of so many later cultures.

The Olmec state, whose population numbered tens of thousands, included a priesthood, a civil service, and a hierarchy of social classes. They also employed skilled craftsmen, who fashioned works of stone ranging from ceremonial jade axe-heads to colossal likenesses of their gods. The cult of the feline, so evident in Olmec carving, subsequently appeared in the art of almost all pre-Columbian societies, continuing long after the Olmecs' main centre, at La Venta, was systematically destroyed in about the fifth century BC. The great heads were slashed and smashed; the temples were demolished and burnt. The cultural domination of the isthmus passed to the neighbouring Maya of Yucatán.

Originating in the rain forests of the tropical lowlands of Guatemala and Belize at least 2,000 years earlier, the Maya in their prime, between AD 300 and 900, came to control western Honduras, eastern Campeche, and northern Yucatán. By the beginning of the Classic phase of Maya civilization, around AD 300, enormous stone-built complexes had been built in a number of places, such as Palenque, Tikal and El Baúl. Huge, plaster-floored plazas were surrounded by massive stepped pyramids topped by temples and flanked by impressive multi-storied palaces. The vast amount of labour that must have gone into the construction of these cities indicates the existence of a very large, highly regimented population. To feed them, sophisticated agricultural techniques were developed: whole hillsides were terraced in order to provide high crop yields from small areas.

This prosperous civilization of the tropical rain forests produced some of the world's most elaborate and elegant artistic creations in what appears an unpromising environment. Their themes were remarkably consistent. Stone reliefs, wall paintings, sculptures, carved

from AD 700 Mexican influence to N. America, platform mound architecture and ritual ball game

Tzintzun
late
Post-Cla
Tarasca

Ortices

R. Balsas

Mesoamerican cultures *above* flourished for some 1200 years before the arrival of the Europeans. The Classic period in Mesoamerica is the Maya era (AD 250-900), the early Post-Classic is the Toltec era (900-1325) and the late Post-Classic is the Aztec era (1325 to the Spanish conquest). Although the Maya occupied much of Mesoamerica, their cultural heartland was the Yucatán peninsula. The Aztecs, like the Toltecs who dominated much of Mexico and Yucatán from Tula, entered central Mexico from the north. In the course of the 15th century they built up a large tribute-based empire controlled from Tenochtitlán, their capital city founded in the early 14th century.

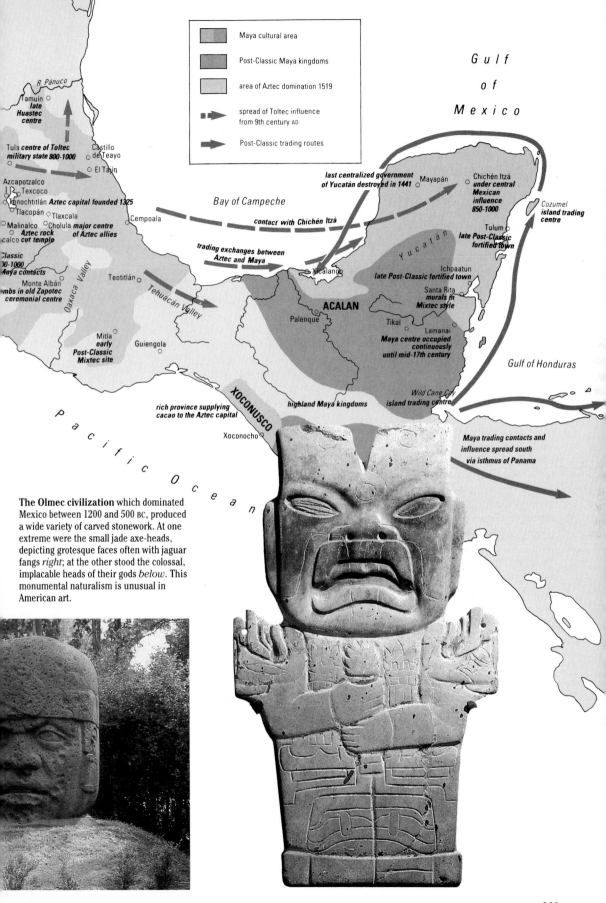

Gulf

of

Mexico

R. Pánuco

Tamuin *late Huastec centre*

Tula *centre of Toltec military state 800–1000*

Castillo de Teayo

El Tajín

Azcapotzalco
Texcoco
Tenochtitlán **Aztec capital founded 1325**
Tlacopán
Tlaxcala
Malinalco *Aztec rock calco cut temple*
Cholula *major centre of Aztec allies*

Cempoala

Bay of Campeche

last centralized government of Yucatán destroyed in 1441 Mayapán

Chichén Itzá *under central Mexican influence 850–1000*

Cozumel *island trading centre*

contact with Chichén Itzá

spread of Toltec influence from 9th century AD

Post-Classic trading routes

Maya cultural area

Post-Classic Maya kingdoms

area of Aztec domination 1519

trading exchanges between Aztec and Maya

Xicalango

Yucatán

Tulum *late Post-Classic fortified town*

Classic 00–1000 Maya contacts

Monte Albán mbs in old Zapotec ceremonial centre

Teotitlán

ACALAN

Palenque

Tehuacán Valley

Ichpaatun *late Post-Classic fortified town*

Santa Rita *murals in Mixtec style*

Mitla *early Post-Classic Mixtec site*

Guiengola

Tikal

Lamanai *Maya centre occupied continuously until mid-17th century*

Oaxaca Valley

XOCONUSCO

rich province supplying cacao to the Aztec capital

Xoconocho

highland Maya kingdoms

Wild Cane Cay *island trading centre*

Gulf of Honduras

Maya trading contacts and influence spread south via isthmus of Panama

Pacific Ocean

The Olmec civilization which dominated Mexico between 1200 and 500 BC, produced a wide variety of carved stonework. At one extreme were the small jade axe-heads, depicting grotesque faces often with jaguar fangs *right*; at the other stood the colossal, implacable heads of their gods *below*. This monumental naturalism is unusual in American art.

jade, and brilliantly painted pottery were all decorated in a distinctive style to record and illustrate events associated with Maya rulers and gods. The intellectual achievement was equally impressive. The Maya excelled in astronomical and astrological observation and calculation, developing further the Olmecs' numerical system, based on units of twenty and including the concept of zero. They elaborated and refined a 52-year cycle, intermeshing the 365-day solar year with a 260-day lunar year, and they calculated time from an arbitrary date corresponding to 3113 BC (much as Muslims date their calendar from the Hejira and Christians from the birth of Christ). The Maya were obsessed with the recording of time, and erected carved stone pillars and altars to mark the passage of set periods as well as to commemorate important events such as the accession, anniversary or death of rulers. These monuments are covered with explanatory hieroglyphic texts: but so far only the glyphs concerning numbers, dates, gods, place-names and genealogies have been decoded. Many hundreds of others remain unexplained.

Thus it is not known why, some time in the ninth century AD, this vast and sophisticated society collapsed quite suddenly, leaving its great monuments and cities totally abandoned. It may have been because population growth outran resources, coupled with land exhaustion due to over-cultivation. Alternatively, the Maya may have been laid low by epidemic disease, or by some peasant revolt caused by internal social discontent. Portraits of foreigners, seemingly from Mexico, carved on Late Classic stelae may even indicate that there was an invasion. But whatever the reason, from about the sixth century AD, the main focus of American civilization shifted southwards to the high Andean basins.

In the eastern Andes, the first great temples were built at Kotosh around 2000 BC; but they were eclipsed from about 1000 BC onwards by the religious hegemony exercised by Chavín de Huantar. The large stone platforms there, decorated with sculptures and reliefs of jaguars, eagles and caymans – or of human beings with jaguar fangs, eccentric eyes and serpentine hair – form the centre of what must have been an extraordinarily important place of religious pilgrimage, since its followers were found from the northern highlands of Peru to the Central American coast, and its religious appeal lasted until the third century BC.

The Gateway of the Sun at Tiahuanaco *below* was carved from a single block of stone at some time between AD 400 and 700, and forms part of a large complex of temples and other buildings in central Peru. Tiahuanaco's wide influence is reflected in the fact that the bird-headed staffs of the central god, like the winged figures that surround him, appear on later ceramics, sculptures and textiles found throughout the Andes.

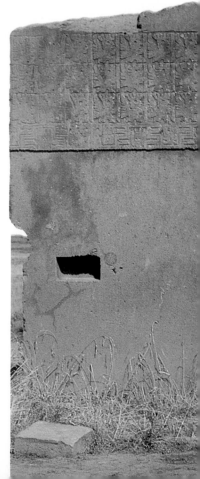

The Maya erected intricate pillars to commemorate major events in their history, and festooned them with pictures and texts *left*. But very few of the glyphs of which the text are composed can be understood today. The significance of the event depicted here, for example, which shows one Maya figure presenting a jaguar head to another, is no doubt explained in the glyphs on the T-shape between them; but the message has not been deciphered. Even the Maya's monumental architecture *far left* is hard to interpret: this vast ball-court at Chichén Itzá was presumably built for the same game played on similar courts by other pre-Columbian peoples. It involved two teams smashing the ball back and forth across a central line, using only elbows, hips and thighs. Any team who drove the ball through the ring high up on the side-wall is said to have been entitled to confiscate the property of any spectators they could catch.

There is then a gap in the record for the area until the seventh century AD when two new centres, Tiahuanaco and Huari, grew to dominate much of the central Andes, and a good part of the Pacific coast too. It is clear from archaeological evidence that the two were contemporary, and were linked by a common religion and a shared artistic style; but without written records it is impossible to be sure of their exact relationship. The site of Tiahuanaco lies on the bleak high plateau of Bolivia, near Lake Titicaca. Famous for its megalithic architecture and austere stone sculptures, it is difficult to tell whether Tiahuanaco was a populous city, or merely the pilgrimage centre for a pan-Andean cult. But clearly the stone figure, known as the 'Gateway God' because he is the central motif above the gateway of the sun, was a mythological being of great religious importance. So, presumably, were the winged running figures and feline forms which appear on so many painted vessels, multi-coloured textiles and stone monuments associated with this culture.

Huari, a Peruvian city of more than 100,000 people in the eighth century AD, was the home of a religion very similar to that of Tiahuanaco: huge painted urns from Huari also show the 'Gateway God' and his

Feline symbols *above* were a popular motif in the art of the Andean region and Mesoamerica, and may indicate considerable cultural contacts and continuity. The city of Cuzco, for example, is thought to have been laid out in the shape of a puma. The most common motif was the jaguar, which appears in many forms, from sculptures and relief carvings to pottery and, as here, tapestry.

running 'angels'. But, unlike Tiahuanaco, Huari was a powerful military state, extending from the Urubamba river basin to the middle Marañón, covering more than half of modern Peru. It was unified by a centrally-planned programme of road building and colonization, and was administered from purpose-built new towns such as Piquillacta, a regimented rectangular complex. But about the year 800 the Huari empire disintegrated, and its capital city was deserted. Tiahuanaco, too, was abandoned and the two great civilizations of the highlands, whose cultural forms had for over two centuries displaced all others, both suddenly vanished. And, once again, it is not known why.

Meanwhile, a new and powerful city-state had appeared in Mexico. Between about AD 100 and 750, Teotihuacán was the most populous city in the New World, with between 125,000 and 250,000 inhabitants. It was an important religious, commercial and manufacturing centre, and in its prime, by AD 200 it covered an area of eight square miles and included more than twenty-three temple complexes. Its main thoroughfare, on a north-south axis, later called by the Aztecs 'the Street of the Dead', was over 100 feet wide and several miles long. But this metropolis, one of the largest cities of its day anywhere in the world, has left no written records. Its violent destruction in the eighth century is one of the great mysteries of Mexican history.

No other city-state emerged as a dominant unifying force in the area for some two centuries – or perhaps even longer, for the accounts of this period are a curious mixture of fact and legend. Even they have only been preserved due to the efforts of a Franciscan missionary, Bernardino de Sahagún, who arrived in Mexico in 1529 at the age of thirty. For the remaining sixty years of his life – aided by a group of native Mexicans trained to write their Nahuatl language in Latin letters, and by a group of artists able to interpret Aztec pictures – he compiled twelve illustrated volumes entitled *A General History of the Things of New Spain*. In it, the friar tried to describe every aspect of the lands and peoples newly acquired by the Europeans. It was not, of course, a perfect history: some records had been tampered with, since each Aztec ruler tended to rewrite history in his own image, and others were lost. But Sahagún's work has made the Mexicans the best known ancient people of America.

According to the legends collected by Sahagún, between the seventh and tenth centuries AD barbarian tribes from the north invaded Mexico, conquering the more developed areas and absorbing some of their culture. In 968 one of these tribes, the Toltecs, established their headquarters at Tula in the central valley, which swiftly became both the centre of a military state and the hub of a trading network extending to Panama and Colombia. But at this point, the chronicles become intertwined with myths. At first, the Toltecs seem to have revered a god known as Quetzalcoatl, 'the feathered serpent', who had also possessed followers (and a vast temple) at Teotihuacán. But in the year 987 the high priest of Quetzalcoatl at Tula, and his disciples, were expelled by a rival religious group which advocated human sacrifices to the gods in preference to Quetzalcoatl's symbolic offerings of jade, butterflies and snakes. The defeated leader led his followers from the capital, past Lake Texcoco and the twin volcanoes, to the Gulf of Mexico where, according to one tradition, he sailed westward on a raft of serpents prophesying that he would return one day to claim his people. But, in fact, the ascendancy of the Toltecs ended about two centuries later as fresh waves of northerners, known as the Chichimecs, migrated from their increasingly arid homelands and overran the empire. Tula itself was destroyed in about 1170.

The collapse of the Toltec empire left the Mexico valley politically

The sculpture of Teotihuacán *below* shares features with the highly complex Maya compositions of figures and glyphs, and foreshadows the monumental and geometrically abstracted style of the Toltecs and Aztecs. Figures and busts such as this also give us considerable clues concerning Mesoamerican styles of dress and personal decoration which achieved a sophistication unparalleled in the Old World.

Teotihuacán in the valley of Mexico
right was a city-state that flourished at
about the same time as Tiahuanaco in
Peru; but it was far larger – larger, indeed
than imperial Rome, for the city covered an
area of eight square miles, regularly laid
out and incorporating the massive complex
of religious buildings shown here. In its
prime, in the 3rd century AD, it was the
home of perhaps 250,000 people, but its
power seems to have collapsed around 750,
at much the same time as the decline of
several Maya centres. Nevertheless, even
in Aztec times seven centuries later,
pilgrims still came to the ruins of
Teotihuacán to worship.

Monumental Toltec warriors *below*
form a group which was probably erected
around the year 1000. They stand upon one
of the numerous temples on the vast site of
Tula, the Toltec capital, in the valley of
Mexico, which was abandoned after its
destruction by invaders (probably Aztecs)
from the north in the late 12th century.

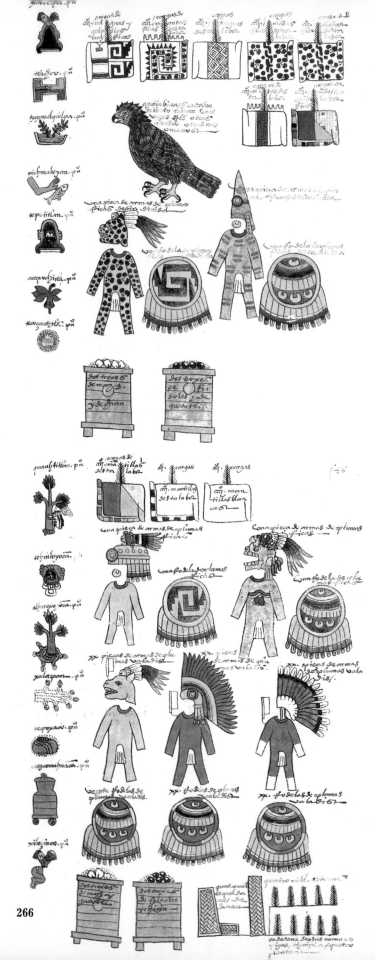

Aztec sacrificial knife *above* Although metals were widely available in Mexico, the Aztec priests preferred to work with traditional materials. This tapered blade of chalcedony, with an inlaid handle bearing delicate turquoise and lignite decoration, was no doubt used to slaughter victims in the brutal style depicted overleaf. The crouching figure is dressed as an 'eagle warrior', a member of the order dedicated to the service of the blood-thirsty sun god.

The Codex Mendoza *left* is one of the few surviving manuscript records concerning pre-Columbian America, and contains a copy of the register of tribute paid annually to the last Aztec emperor, Montezuma. Down the left-hand side of each folio are glyphs representing seven towns per sheet. Then the tribute payable by each is recorded; embroidered cloaks (the decorated squares on the top line), war dresses, shields, bins of grain, rush mats (bottom line, left) and even, in the case of one town, a live eagle. Each entry was copied from the original by an Indian painter, and an explanation in Spanish was added because the Codex was to be sent to the Emperor Charles v. It was intended to instruct the successor of Montezuma in the strange ways of his new subjects, but in effect the Codex provides an invaluable insight into the scale and diversity of the Aztec tributary economy.

fragmented, with a number of city-states building up their own political strength and ideology on Toltec foundations. Then, in the thirteenth century another Chichimec tribe from the north, the Aztecs, arrived in the valley and in 1325 settled on a group of islands in the swampy margins of Lake Texcoco, where they built their capital, Tenochtitlán – its name derived from the 'tenochtli', or cactus, of the area. Serving at first as mercenaries of nearby mainland towns, they learned much from their overlords and finally overthrew them in 1428, so becoming rulers of the entire valley. In just over a century they had transformed themselves from a tribal group into a well-organized state, headed by a priest-king and an hereditary aristocracy, and had embarked upon an ambitious programme of conquest which was still going on when the Spaniards arrived.

Warfare was fundamental to the Aztec state. Their strategy was simple: they allied themselves with neighbouring states (such as Texcoco), defeated common enemies, and then turned on their allies and defeated them as well. Their professional army was maintained by the food produced on the fertile floating gardens of Lake Texcoco, and by the heavy tributes paid to the Aztecs by all conquered peoples. The detailed lists of tribute – meticulously noting clothes, armour, even an eagle, as well as payments of maize and other foodstuffs – form a major part of the surviving Aztec records. But there was also another, more important form of tribute. Continuous warfare likewise supplied captives who could be sacrificed to the bloodthirsty gods of the tribe, Texcatlipoca and Huitzilopochtli. Tens of thousands of victims were killed each year by having their hearts ripped out of their bodies. On special occasions, the Aztecs demanded human sacrifices on an almost unimaginable scale. At the consecration of a great new temple in Tenochtitlán in 1487, two columns of victims were assembled and ordered to climb the steps in close order towards the priests at the altars. All were killed. For four days and nights the sacrifice continued. Most sources agree that, on this occasion alone, 20,000 men and women were ritually murdered. Some of them were local slaves; others were prisoners captured in the Aztecs' numerous and victorious wars; but most were victims brought along as tribute by neighbouring princes who had been defeated in the past.

The floating gardens or *chinampas below* on the five great lakes in the middle of the valley of Mexico have now almost entirely disappeared, like the lakes themselves: a few small areas are all that remain of the agricultural system that sustained the Aztec capital from the 13th century onwards. Long, narrow strips of highly fertile land, surrounded by water on at least three sides, were created in the fresh-water areas of the lakes and made to produce maize, beans and other crops for the rapidly growing metropolis of Tenochtitlán. The intervening canals which were created by this land reclamation scheme acted both as sources of irrigation and as a highly effective transport network, bringing fresh agricultural produce from outlying settlements such as Xochimilco into the heart of Tenochtitlán every day.

The rationale behind this destructive faith is obscure. Undoubtedly the victims were despatched partly in order to placate the gods, whom the Aztecs believed to be only marginally committed to their cause: they needed to be bought or bribed with constant sacrifices. But the reasons for this intensely pessimistic theology are harder to grasp. Certainly the Aztec empire faced serious problems. Twenty-five million subjects were probably too numerous for the available resources – indeed some historians have argued that human sacrifice was a form of population control – and there were frequent famines and revolts. But the pessimism seems to have struck deeper psychological roots. It was as if the Aztec leadership believed that the sacrifices, however numerous, would still not be enough to avert ultimate destruction: that they could only delay, but would never prevent, the inevitable disaster that threatened to overwhelm them and their world.

It was in an effort to improve their collective chances of survival that in 1502 the small Aztec élite chose as its new emperor not another general, but a priest from the main temple of Huitzilopochtli: Montezuma II. His reign began well: he attacked some neighbouring cities and returned with 5,000 captives to sacrifice at his coronation. But after this, Montezuma's behaviour became more autocratic. He proclaimed himself the equal of the gods; he murdered other members of the ruling élite; and he increased the tribute required from both his subjects and

The Pyramid of the Soothsayer at Uxmal, Mexico *below* was built and rebuilt by the Maya at least five times. The final version, dating from the 8th century, was made of earth faced with stone blocks, and covered with white plaster. The sanctuary on the top, reached by the massive flight of wide, steep steps, was reserved for the priests; lay worshippers had to watch the ceremonies from ground level, over 100 feet below.

Blood sacrifice was an important aspect of Mesoamerican religious activity, and such ceremonies took place on the top of the temple pyramids. The Aztecs believed that the continuation of human society and the present (fifth) creation required nourishing the sun and the earth with human blood and hearts *left*. War was necessary to provide the sacrificial victims. This illustration is taken from the *General History of the things of New Spain* by Bernadino de Sahagún, and was painted in the 1550s by Aztec artists. Among the Maya, however, human sacrifice was less common, although not unknown, as this unsophisticated *graffito, right* indicates; dogs, quail, iguana, squirrels and wildfowl were more usual offerings.

his neighbours. At the same time there were crop failures, local revolts against Aztec authority and, after 1510, some successful resistance by neighbouring states. Also in 1510 a comet was observed over Mexico, which astrologers interpreted as a warning of the return of Quetzal-coatl, the Feathered Serpent, banished five centuries before. When, not long afterwards, rumours multiplied that white-skinned, bearded strangers had appeared in the islands of the Gulf, there were many in Mexico who longed for deliverance from the arbitrary rule of Montezuma.

No sooner had Christopher Columbus returned to Europe from his first voyage of discovery than plans were laid to colonize the islands of the Caribbean. The first settlement, on Hispaniola, was established in 1493 with the aim of exploiting the island's precious metals and serving as a base for trade with China, which was still believed to be nearby (chapter 11). But further exploration revealed only more islands and the mainland of a country which was certainly not Cathay. The disease-ridden settlers soon exhausted the first easy pickings of gold, pearls and slaves; and, though profits could be made from growing sugar cane and exporting dyewood, this was not the glorious, treasure-stuffed New World they had come for. So they looked further afield. Columbus himself explored part of the South American coast. Balboa landed at Panama, crossed the isthmus, and was the first European to see the Pacific. But he too found little gold, and so the quest continued.

MEXICO.

MEXICO REGI
ET CELEBRIS
HISPANIAE No
VAE CIVITAS

The Aztec capital of Tenochtitlán *right*, renamed Mexico by the Spaniards, 'shimmered like a jewel in its watery setting' according to Hernán Cortés in 1519, when he first set eyes on it. This map, based on an original by the Spanish cartographer Alonso de Santa Cruz in 1555, shows the elaborate causeways and the canals as well as the central ceremonial walled precinct and palace. The sophisticated construction of this floating city astonished the Spanish conquerors, although they did little to preserve it after the defeat of the Aztecs.

In 1519, Hernán Cortés, the young mayor of Havana, was appointed leader of a 600-strong colonizing expedition which set sail in 1519, 'in the service of God and His Majesty Charles V, and to give light to those who sat in darkness; and also to acquire that wealth which most men covet'. He landed at Veracruz on the Gulf of Mexico and quickly crushed the opposition of the local inhabitants: Indian padded cotton armour offered little protection against the steel swords, guns and crossbows wielded by the mounted invaders, while Spanish steel armour kept out most Indian weapons of wood and flint. The defeated Indians were so impressed by Cortés and his men that they resolved to join them. Together they set off for the Aztec capital and, as they marched, many other tribes alienated by Montezuma's oppression provided supporters too. By the time they had reached the pass between the twin volcanoes that guard the valley of Mexico (retracing the route followed long before by the 'Feathered Serpent'), and gazed down upon Tenochtitlán 'which shimmered like a jewel in its watery setting', Cortés was at the head of a powerful army.

Evil omens had recently been seen in the city, predicting disaster, and many believed the white-skinned Spaniards to be Quetzalcoatl and his followers; so Montezuma, uncertain how to proceed, let them into the city, where he showered them with rich gifts. Then, news of an attack on the Spanish base at Veracruz prompted Cortés to take Montezuma captive, so that he now held both the capital and the ruler. His

The massacre at the temple *below* on 6 May 1520. When some 600 Aztec leaders gathered together at the temple complex in the centre of Tenochtitlán, the small Spanish garrison under Pedro de Alvarado, fearing a coup against them, panicked. Priests and nobles alike were massacred. This provoked a general uprising against the Spaniards in Tenochtitlán. Montezuma, totally discredited, was killed by his subjects, and Alvarado led his garrison (both Spaniards and loyal Indians) on a daring night-time escape across one of the causeways to the lake shore *centre below*. But the Aztec warriors were waiting. Attacked from boats as well as by land, most of the fugitives perished in what Cortés later called the *noche triste* or night of sorrow. These illustrations come from the *History of the Indies* by Diego Durán, a Spanish Dominican monk; he had lived in Mexico since he was a boy, and wrote in the 1580s, trying to explain to his Spanish contemporaries the tragic history of the extinguished Indian civilization. It is not surprising that he failed to find a publisher.

success seemed complete. But at this triumphant moment, Cortés was suddenly recalled to the coast and during his absence, the 200 Spaniards in Tenochtitlán panicked and massacred the celebrants at a religious service. The Aztecs rose against them.

Although Cortés at once hurried back to relieve his besieged men in the capital, their situation was impossible. Montezuma was killed while pleading with his former subjects for peace, and the Spaniards made a daring pre-dawn escape along one of the causeways linking Tenochtitlán to the shores of the lake. But the Aztecs had been warned and were waiting: three-quarters of the fugitives, weighed down by their loot, were killed before they reached safety.

It was here, in the midst of defeat, that Cortés showed his true mettle. Instead of abandoning the enterprise, he planned a new campaign with his surviving Indian allies. First they subdued the provinces around the great lake in which the capital lay and set up a close blockade; then they built a small fleet in order to protect their advance simultaneously along the three causeways leading to the city. The Aztecs still put up a desperate fight but, after weeks of fighting, worn down by famine and disease, the defenders surrendered in August 1521. Cortés had won the whole of Mexico, which was renamed New Spain, from the Pacific to the Caribbean – an area larger than the Iberian peninsula itself – for his master, the Emperor Charles V. Next it was the turn of Peru.

271

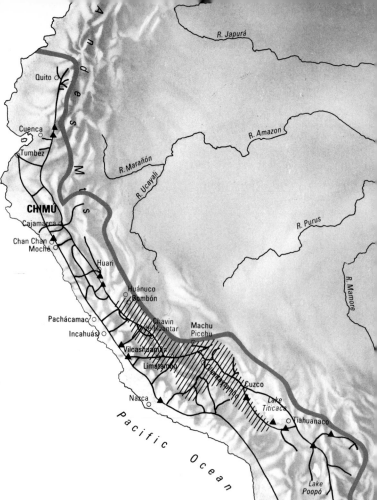

The Inca empire in Peru expanded rapidly in the 15th century. At its widest extent it included modern Peru, Ecuador, Bolivia, northern Argentina and northern Chile. From Cuzco, the emperor, or Inca, exerted rigid control over this extensive territory by means of a highly trained bureaucracy, a state religion, a powerful army (which operated on a sophisticated method of conscription) and, most remarkably, an advanced communications network. An elaborate system of paved roads linked every part of the empire, making even remote parts of the Andes and the Atacama desert accessible. The system was serviced by a series of state-run inns, or *tampu*, placed approximately one day's travel from each other. The final phase of expansion, under Huayna Capac, put all these institutions under great strain, and civil war divided the empire immediately before the arrival of the Spaniards.

Inca empire under Pachacuti 1438-63

extent of Inca empire under Huayna Capac 1493-1525

imperial roads

▲ *tampu* (roadside lodgings)

The most famous of South American civilizations, the Inca empire was also one of the briefest, taking shape less than a century before its destruction. Until the early fifteenth century the Incas played only a minor role in Andean history, being one of the many small highland tribes intermittently at war with neighbouring groups. But in 1438 Pachacuti Inca came to the throne and began a series of conquests which, over the next twenty years, extended Inca control from Lake Titicaca to Lake Junín. His son, Topa Inca, pushed the boundary much further north, and then turned on the only rival civilized state in Peru, the coastal kingdom of Chimor. Chimor was defeated in 1476, after which the empire was enlarged southwards to include much of present day Chile and parts of Argentina. In forty years an empire had been created which stretched for 2,000 miles along the Andes and included the Pacific coast and parts of the Upper Amazon.

This meteoric growth was only possible because of extraordinarily thorough social and political organization. Inca society was strictly hierarchical and rigidly ordered. An absolute, 'divine' Inca topped the social pyramid, while landless peasants toiled at the bottom. State control of labour and resources maintained the well-trained army, and provided the workforce and materials needed to carry out the schemes of professional architects, engineers and administrators. 9,000 miles of paved roads, bridges and tunnels linked Cuzco, the capital, with the distant fringes of the empire, exemplifying Inca ability and efficiency. But a fatal flaw existed in this quasi-welfare state: all power devolved from one man, the Supreme Inca. In 1525 Huayna Capac died, leaving two rival claimants to the throne, Huáscar and Atahuallpa. Internal dissent split the empire and a bloody civil war began.

The murder of Atahuallpa *right* in November 1532 set the seal on Spain's conquest of the Inca empire. Although there were perhaps only 180 Europeans in Peru, most of them young men in their twenties, their brutal murder of the 'divine Inca' broke the resistance of the Peruvian peoples. This vigorous illustration of the deed comes from the *Royal Commentaries* published between 1609 and 1616 by Garcilaso de la Vega, the son of a conquistador and an Inca princess.

CONQVISTA
CORTALE·LACAVESA·A
ATAGVALDA·INGA·VMATACVCHV

At precisely this moment, the Spaniards arrived. Led by the fifty-year-old Francisco Pizarro, the invaders only numbered about 180 men: but they were all motivated by consuming worldly ambition and fanatical religious zeal. They also possessed the great advantages of horses, steel weapons and armour; and in Mexico they had learnt how to use them to maximum effect against the Indians. But at first they scarcely needed to fight. When they reached the highlands of Peru in 1532, Atahuallpa had recently defeated his brother Huáscar and was encamped with his army of over 40,000 men near the town of Cajamarca. Remembering how useful the kidnapping of Montezuma had been to Cortés in Mexico, Pizarro seized Atahuallpa during a parley, and held him hostage for an enormous ransom in gold and silver. When it had been paid, Pizarro had him murdered. Without their divine leader, weakened by civil war, and scourged by epidemics of European disease, the peoples of Bolivia, Peru and Chile soon succumbed to the conquistadors. Pizarro finally took the Inca capital, Cuzco, on 15 November 1533.

But the pre-European civilizations of the Americas did not entirely disappear with the Spanish invasion and conquest. There are, even today, many survivals, especially outside the towns (where westernization has virtually obliterated all alternative cultures). The one ubiquitous inheritance of the past is, of course, the appearance of the people themselves: almost everybody has some Indian blood, as revealed in their copper-coloured skins and aquiline features, and there are still many millions of pure-blooded Indians living in Latin America. Some have also preserved the most fundamental aspects of their ancient indigenous cultures. The Maya language is still spoken by more than two million people; and Nahuatl, the language of the Aztecs, is used in highland central Mexico. Use of Quechua, the *lingua franca* of the Inca empire, has even spread: today twenty-eight varieties of the language are spoken by some ten million people in South America. Even the Christian missionaries had to learn it for their work.

Dress, food and farming also retain many pre-Columbian elements, Although peasant costume in South America has been heavily influenced by regional Spanish styles (such as the full, multi-layered skirts and the European-style hats favoured by Andean women), in Peru and Bolivia the *poncho* is still worn, woven on traditional backstrap looms to designs which have changed little in a millennium. Nor has there been any major revolution in the basic diet of rural Latin Americans

The Aymara people *far left* who live around the shores of Lake Titicaca are still unmistakably Amerindian, yet they have adopted many of the ways of their Spanish conquerors. Along with the traditional poncho, Aymara women wear a curious hat modelled on the steel morions of the conquistadors. There are, however, pure-blooded Indians in Latin America, and the blending of Indians and Iberians has produced a unique hybrid culture.

The remains of Inca architecture *below* point to a remarkable technical facility. The outstanding quality of the drystone masonry remains near Cuzco remains unequalled in either the Old or New World. The massive interlocking blocks, laid for the most part regularly, are exquisitely dressed and fitted, a remarkable achievement for a culture which used neither iron nor the wheel. Many of the modern buildings in Cuzco are built on original Inca foundations.

since the arrival of the conquistadors, apart from the introduction of European domestic animals. Potatoes, oca, quinoa remain major crops in the Andes; llamas are herded; and guinea pigs still scuttle about hut floors. The old-fashioned foot-plough used by the Incas remains more efficient on steep, terraced terrain than tractor- or oxen-pulled ploughs, while peasant farmers practise slash-and-burn agriculture in the tropical forests in the footsteps of their ancestors. Maize, potatoes, squash and beans still account for their basic diet, and they and their families continue to live in single-room pole and thatch houses set on low mounds, identical to those built by the ancient Maya.

Most of the really important changes in everyday life in Latin America since 1500 have been wrought by the Roman Catholic church, whose teachings and festivals now permeate most Indian cultures. Extreme religious devotion is widespread. Nevertheless, in many places Christian dogma has been adopted and mixed with pre-Columbian religious beliefs. Thus the thirteen sky gods of Maya tradition are now conflated with Christian saints, and in Peru the ancient belief in *huacas*, natural objects such as rocks or trees with supernatural power, continues in tandem with devout Christian behaviour. Politically, however, pre-Columbian America died in the first half of the sixteenth century. The destiny of the entire continent thenceforth lay, for better or worse, in the hands of the European settlers and their governments (chapter 18).

Machu Picchu *right* an Inca mountain fortress, stands 2000 feet above the Urubamba river in the Andes. Its vast terraced hillsides and massive ruined buildings cover an area of 5 square miles and contain over 3000 steps linking the various levels. Although only 50 miles from Cuzco, it was never discovered by the conquistadors and was therefore one of the few urban centres of pre-Columbian America to be found intact by modern archaeologists when it was rediscovered in 1911.

In 1500 the strong states of Europe *below* lay at the extreme east and west of the continent. Muscovy and the Ottomans were poised to turn the weaker states of eastern Europe into their satellites, while France and the Habsburg Netherlands were ready to make inroads into Germany, and Spain was encroaching on the Italian peninsula. The economy was still broadly agricultural. The villagers in Pieter Bruegel's *Haymaking*, painted in the Netherlands in the 1550s *lower right* were fortunate: they lived in an area where crop yields were among the highest in Europe. It was in the Netherlands and Britain that more efficient agricultural methods were gradually pioneered, including land reclamation, drainage, crop rotation, fertlization and experimentation with new field crops such as the potato, first imported from the Americas in 1525.

Habsburg territory
Ottoman territories
Muscovy and territories
Venetian territories
Empire of Casimar IV 1447-92
1453   date of conquest

NORWAY
SWEDEN
Union of Kalmar 1397
1526

SHETLAND
to Scotland 1468

ORKNEY
to Scotland 1468

SCOTLAND

North Sea

KINGDOM OF IRELAND 1542

WALES
to England 1536

ENGLAND
London

Calais
to Habsburgs 1477
1477

DENMARK

SCANIA

HOLSTEIN 1460

Teutonic Kn...
secular... 1526
to Poland 1466

NETHERLANDS 1523-43

HOLY ROMAN EMPIRE

Hohenzollern BRANDENBURG

Wettin SAXONY

PALATINATE
Wittelsbach

BOHEMIA 1526

SILESIA 1526

MORAVIA 1526

POLAND

BRITTANY 1491

ANJOU 1481

BOURBON

LA MARCHE

F R A N C E

BURGUNDY 1477

LORRAINE
to Habsburgs 1493

SWISS CANTONS

SAVOY

TYROL

BAVARIA
Wittelsbach

SALZBURG

STYRIA

AUSTRIA

to Habsburgs 1526

HUNGARY

MILAN
to Habsburgs 1535

REPUBLIC OF VENICE

AUVERGNE 1527

Avignon
to the Papacy

PROVENCE 1481

Genoa

G E N O A

LUCCA

PISA

FLORENCE

Venice

PAPAL STATES

Adriatic Sea

1463

1459

15...

NAVARRE
to Spain 1512

(CASTILE) AND (ARAGON)
to Habsburgs 1504   to Habsburgs 1516

ROUSSILLON
to Spain 1493

S P A I N

PORTUGAL

SIENA

Rome

GRANADA
conquered 1482-92

Balearic Is.

SARDINIA
to Aragon 1291

to Habsburgs 1516

NAPLES
to Aragon 1504

1478

MELILLA   ORAN

BONA

M e d i t e r r a n e a n   S e a

TUNIS
to Habsburgs 1535

SICILY
to Aragon 1283

MORE...
14...

On the map:

FINLAND

acquired by
Ivan III 1462-1505

M U S C O V Y 1462

ESTONIA

PSKOV

LITHUANIA

acquired by
Vassily III
1505-33

MOLDAVIA 1504

1504

...LLACHIA

Tartars

Black Sea

1453 Constantinople

...1451

OTTOMAN EMPIRE

Lesbos 1462

EA Chios (Genoese)

Aegean Sea

Rhodes 1522

CRETE (Venetian)

CHAPTER 17

EUROPE: STATE AND POWER
1453–1700

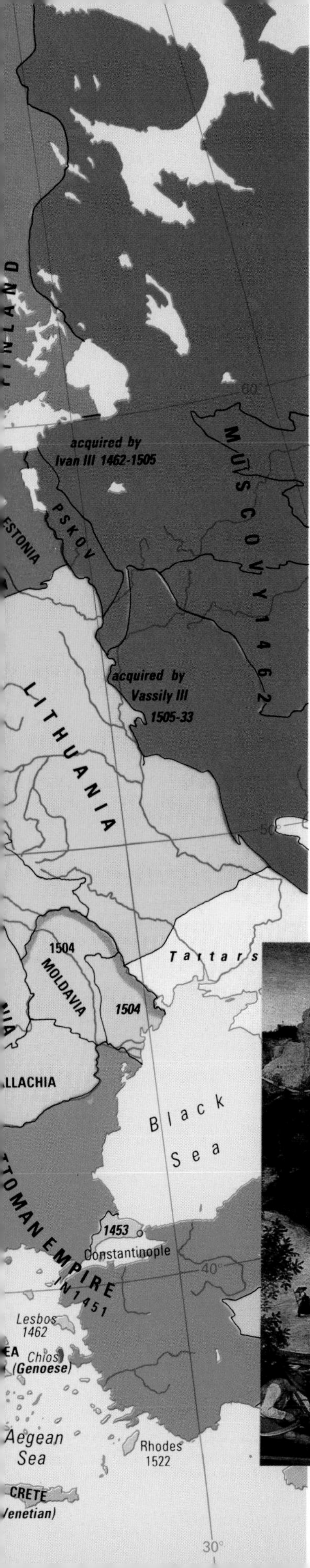

In the aftermath of the Turkish capture of Constantinople in 1453 (chapter 14), few observers would have considered Christian Europe likely to acquire the political, economic and technological strength required to dominate the globe. Her states were numerous, small and weak, forever dissipating their energies in internecine wars, her economy was comparatively backward, and 90 percent of her population lived in the countryside and made their living from subsistence agriculture. However, by 1700 this war-torn, beleaguered and relatively underdeveloped continent proved able to gain control of a large part of the globe: all of Siberia; much of the Americas; parts of southern and south-east Asia; and numerous enclaves around the coast of Africa.

The explanation for this is to be found in the emergence of the modern state. Europe was only able to expand because her meagre resources were marshalled and maximized with ruthless efficiency by a small number of centralized, bureaucratic, entrepreneurial states: the city-states of Italy and Germany in the fifteenth century; Portugal and Spain in the sixteenth century; and France, Britain, Sweden, Prussia, the Dutch Republic and (eventually) Russia in the seventeenth. Needless to say, however, the chronology of state-building was not uniform.

279

Developments in the West came earlier, so that by 1700 Louis XIV's France, a fully-fledged absolutist state, stood at one end of the spectrum while Peter the Great's Russia, just about to embark upon a programme of modernization (chapter 21), stood at the other. And in between lay governments of every imaginable political complexion.

The key to strong government in early modern times was the combination of two skills: the ability to utilize effectively the resources of both subjects and neighbours; and the power to build up irresistible naval and military strength. Naturally, the two were not unrelated – waging war required a state to become proficient at collecting taxes, mobilizing supplies, and recruiting troops – and improvements in governmental organization were often introduced in response to the pressures induced by war.

But this was not always the case. The rapid expansion of the central administration in England during the 1530s, for example, was carried

As well as agriculture, primary industries such as mining remained the principal source of national wealth for many of the countries of northern Europe. The production of silver at Kutná Hora in Bohemia involved many processes. Underground, in the 15th-century miniature *lower left*, miners clad in white (because of the darkness in the galleries) hack out the silver ore which was raised to the surface to be crushed, washed and smelted. After their shift, the miners were given a close body-search while, at the top of the picture, the mine owners looked on.

SCOTLAND
Covenanters' uprisings

Tippermuir 1644 ✕   Dur

Edinburgh
Philiphaugh 1645 ✕

IRELAND
Catholic uprising 1641, 1649

Antrim 1641 ✕

ULSTER

Pres

PRESIDENCY OF
CONNAUGHT
1569

✕ Drogheda 1649   1

Dublin
Irish Sea

THE PALE
Kilkenny

Nantwi
16

PRESIDENCY OF
MUNSTER 1571

✕ Wexford
1649

Worce
1

Edgehill

Bris

Lostwithiel 1644 ✕

En

'Nu-pieds' of Normandy 163

Ligue
1588-9

Atlantic Ocean

revolts of the Huguen
1568-89, 1621-

——	boundary of Netherlands 1548
⊂⊃	revolts of the later 16th century in France
/////	revolts of the later 17th century in France
Abbeville **1639**	date of revolt
✕	battle in English Civil War

Ormée revolt of the j
and people of Bord
1648-55, 1641,

S P A I N

The city of Augsburg in Germany was one of a number which owed its prosperity to trade rather than industry. It was poised on a key route linking Europe's two richest areas, Flanders and the Rhineland and northern Italy. It was also the seat of the Fugger family, a new generation of entrepreneurial bankers who were largely responsible for financing the Holy Roman Emperor, Charles V (1500-1558). In 1500 the city's leading citizens *right* were carefully portrayed in all their finery.

The states of north-west Europe *below* were plagued by rebellion between 1500 and 1650. There were over a dozen major rebellions in England, culminating in full-scale civil war between Parliament and the King (1642-46). The victory of the former led to the establishment of a republic which lasted until 1660, when monarchy was restored. In the Netherlands there was continuous revolt from 1572 – 1648 and in France over 500 popular risings culminated in the *Fronde* of 1648. After 1688, however, the internal tensions subsided and the three governments took to fighting each other, above all for control of the seas about them.

out in peacetime: here the stimulus seems to have been Henry VIII's determination to take over the lands, revenues and duties of the church throughout England, following his breach with the Pope. The existing bureaucracy, based on the king's immediate entourage, could not cope with the sudden influx of new business – above all that caused by the dissolution of over 800 monasteries, which brought all monastic lands under direct royal administration for a time – so new councils and boards had to be created. Yet still the civil service remained relatively small. As late as 1600, the Tudor monarchy governed its four million subjects in England and Wales with less than 1,500 full-time officials. It was the same elsewhere. In Castile, considered by many observers to be the best-run state in Europe and the heart of the empire of Philip II (1556-1598), supreme power was exercised by no more than 500 civil servants; and yet Castile remained well-governed and orderly, the envy of Europe.

The maintenance of law and order was a function that all early modern rulers took extremely seriously. When a collection of all current laws in Castile was printed, at the king's command, in 1569, it filled two fat volumes and included no less than 4,000 separate acts of legislation. But Castile was exceptional, in that the same code of laws was observed all over the kingdom. Philip II was also the ruler of Aragon, Catalonia, Valencia and Navarre within the Iberian peninsula, and of Naples, Sicily and Milan in Italy, each of which had their own legal heritage. The Netherlands, which he also governed, possessed some 700 different legal codes, many of them enacted by semi-autonomous representative assemblies and enforced by quasi-independent local law-courts. It was much the same in France, where some 60 major and 300 minor legal codes operated in the seventeenth century, most of them in provinces with their own structure of local government and a strong sense of local identity. New laws – including new tax laws – could only be introduced there with the express consent of the local institutions.

Understandably, the central government came to resent bitterly the existence of these restrictions on its authority, and made attempts to diminish them.

Equally understandably, such attempts usually provoked opposition. In the Netherlands, Philip II's decision to raise new taxes in spite of the resolute opposition of the local representative assemblies fuelled support for a major insurrection in 1572, known as the Dutch Revolt; in France, a concerted effort in 1629 by the chief minister of Louis XIII, Cardinal Richelieu, did indeed secure the suspension of the local institutions in most provinces, but the resulting uprisings so terrified the government that it abruptly dropped its proposals.

Richelieu was more successful, however, in introducing agents of the central government (known as *intendants*) into the provinces. The new officials enforced unpopular legislation, supervised the collection of taxes, and commanded the local forces of law and order; gradually each administrative region had an *intendant* of its own, creating a degree of centralization and uniformity that France had never previously known. However, when France was engulfed in a major rebellion, shortly after Richelieu's death, their narrow power base made them an easier target for removal. The revolt – the Fronde – which lasted from 1648 until 1653, caused a major hiatus in the progress of absolute royal power in France.

The public execution of Charles I of England *above* in 1649 caused a sensation throughout Europe, for it was the first time that a European monarch had been formally tried by his subjects. The warrant for the King's execution, on a charge of high treason, was signed by members of the House of Commons *left* (including Oliver Cromwell, the third signature in the left-hand column). The king was led onto a public scaffold erected in front of the banqueting hall of his palace at Whitehall, in the centre of London. There his head was cut off and exhibited, causing some in the audience to faint while others dipped their handkerchiefs in his blood. Although Charles's son was restored in 1660 his brother and successor, James II was driven into exile in 1688, ensuring that the power of the crown in England would never again be absolute.

The Fronde began in Paris, with the refusal of the supreme courts to enforce a new series of unpopular taxes decreed by the government. The courts, in effect, declared the taxes to be unconstitutional, and a ham-fisted attempt to arrest the judges provoked a major popular uprising in the capital. The king's Court fled. This proved to be the signal for which the regime's other numerous enemies had been waiting: nobles, provincial law courts, town oligarchs and peasants seized the opportunity to withdraw their obedience. It took five years and several full-scale military campaigns before the government could restore its authority.

But the 1640s seems to have been a decade during which major political disorders were unusually common. Catalonia, Portugal, Naples and Sicily all rebelled against the authority of their Habsburg ruler Philip IV; there were coups or attempted coups in Russia, Sweden and the Dutch Republic; there was a major revolt in the Ukraine against the union with Poland. Like the Fronde, all these uprisings were provoked by a combination of economic hardship, increased tax demands to finance war, and resistance to constitutional innovation. Put simply, the states were attempting to take more from those who had less, and to do so by new methods. But the 1640s also saw almost simultaneous revolts in England, Scotland and Ireland against the government of Charles I, leading to a bitter civil war which only ended with the king's public trial and execution in 1649. Here the motive was not so much economic or fiscal, but rather the defence of traditional liberties against a thrusting monarchy. Thus, war, economic dislocation, constitutional dispute and religious passion were the four principal destabilizing forces in early modern Europe, against which even powerful states were often impotent.

The greatest of these was war. There were, in fact, only five years of complete peace in Europe during the entire sixteenth century, and only

The wooden warship *right* was the capital symbol of power for the modern states of north-west Europe. A ship-of-the-line such as this 84-gun man-of-war was considerably larger than a country house. This illustration, showing a recommended launching procedure, appeared in Colbert's *Atlas*. J.B. Colbert (1619-83) was Louis XIV's chief minister, an outstanding statesman who was responsible for the construction of a modern French navy, a first step in the development of commerce and colonization.

four in the seventeenth. War was more the norm than peace and, as time passed, it became both more complex and more general. The crucial development, both by land and sea, was the increasing use of artillery. Both gunpowder and the gun were Chinese inventions but, by the early fifteenth century, small cannon were in use in Europe on both ship and shore. Gradually they became larger and more powerful, and their role in warfare became greater. At sea, starting with the Portuguese, specialized sailing ships were designed which sought to destroy their adversaries by gunfire, instead of by ramming and boarding. The tactic of delivering a broadside from a fleet sailing in single file was to remain the basic technique of European naval warfare until the twentieth century. By 1714, the British navy possessed 247 large warships (known as 'capital ships' or 'ships of the line'), weighing a total of 167,000 tons and carrying 10,603 guns.

DEVENTER

European warfare by land was dominated in the 16th and 17th centuries by sieges. The invention of powerful artillery, capable of smashing down the tall, thin walls erected during the Middle Ages, forced military engineers to build defensive systems that were lower but deeper. Following the capture of the city of Deventer *above* by Dutch troops in 1591, the city was equipped with elaborate bastions and ravelins, and a redesigned moat *right* to prevent anyone from repeating the exercise. This kind of fortification can still be traced today around many European cities.

If naval warfare thus came to be dominated by the capital ship, the key to European land warfare in this period was the bastion. From about 1450, Italian military engineers became concerned that traditional defensive fortifications were no longer effective against the gun. Walls and towers that had been built high and thin, in order to avoid being scaled by the besiegers, now presented an exposed and vulnerable target to artillery bombardment. Now designs were required that increased the width and lowered the height of walls, with vast arrow-shaped bastions, broad moats, and further outworks beyond, all bristling with heavy defensive cannon. Finally, some fortifications were almost as large as the towns they defended. Artillery could not get near them, so that the only way of ensuring their capture was by a pro-

DAVENTRIA DEVENTER.

longed blockade. Sieges came to be the most common form of European warfare and could last months, if not years, requiring armies of up to 50,000 men to complete the blockade. During the Spanish struggle to suppress the Dutch Revolt, for example, the siege of Haarlem (1572-73) took seven months, that of Antwerp (1584-85) took eleven months, and that of Ostend (1601-04) took three years. All of them tied down between 40,000 and 60,000 Spanish troops.

This development gave rise to a change in the art of war which has been hailed as 'the military revolution'. European field armies in the fifteenth century normally consisted of 10,000 men or less, made up of heavy cavalry armed with lances, supported by great phalanxes of pikemen pushing at each other rather like a rugby scrum, aided by loose formations of archers. From the late sixteenth century, however, European armies included fewer cavalry units; for what besieging armies needed was more infantry, most of them armed with muskets rather than with pikes or bows. In the 1590s, starting with the Dutch army, field training and firing drill were developed: musketeers formed long ranks, each line firing their weapons in unison and then retiring to the back to reload while the other ranks, in equally precise manner, followed suit. A continuous hail of shot could thus be directed at the enemy and every man brought into action: the full potential of the army was thus maximized, and even a small force, if properly drilled, could engage and defeat far larger numbers deployed in the traditional fashion. Also, the open formations pioneered by the Dutch allowed an almost infinite number of troops to be involved simultaneously in action. The major battles of Louis XIV's wars in the 1700s involved as

Cavalry, of little use in siege warfare, remained important in open countryside, or where no bastions had been built. In his *Art of War for Cavalry*, Johan Jacob von Wallhausen showed how detachments of horse should manoeuvre both for the charge *below* and for the march (on which they were accompanied by numerous carts and camp followers).

The illustrated drill manual became very popular in 17th-century Europe, starting with Jacob de Gheyn's *Exercise of Arms* of 1607 which showed how the Dutch army used their muskets and pikes *above*. Considerable attention was devoted to ensuring that whole regiments should act in unison, so the process of loading and firing a musket, or of holding the pike, was broken down into numerous stages, each one separately numbered and illustrated for ease of imitation. These training techniques have formed the basis of military drill down to the present day.

many as 100,000 per army; the total armed forces of the various combatants often approached 1,000,000.

Not surprisingly, military changes on this scale affected far more than the art of war. To begin with, there was the increased cost of supporting such large standing armies. The only way in which a small state could afford to go to war in the age of gunpowder was in alliance with a more powerful partner: Venice could only take on the Ottoman empire in the 1570s in tandem with Spain; the Dutch Republic could only oppose Louis XIV in the 1690s with the aid of a Grand Alliance that included Britain, Spain, Sweden, Savoy and many of the larger states of Germany.

Even then, the financial pressures caused by the military revolution could only be absorbed by the rapid and sustained growth of the European economy during the sixteenth century. The population in all areas seems to have risen strongly and almost continuously: in some areas it doubled. There was also a striking increase in the percentage of the population living in towns, and thus fully participating in the market economy: in the maritime provinces of the Netherlands more than half the total inhabitants were urban dwellers by 1600, and the situation in northern Italy was not much different. Both of these highly urbanized zones were centres not only of industrial production and consumption, but also of capital accumulation. Further, both areas played a key role in the emergence of modern finance in Europe.

The Muslim invention of banking, letters of credit and cheques were copied by Italian merchants in the fourteenth century, but at first they remained confined to private firms. Not until the 1580s do we find major public banks, guaranteed by the state: the Banco di San Giorgio of Genoa (1584) and the Rialto Bank of Venice (1587) in Italy; and, somewhat later in northern Europe, the Exchange Bank of Amsterdam (1609), the Bank of Hamburg (1619) and the Bank of England (1694). The amount of money handled by these institutions was colossal. The Genoese banks between them by the 1580s dealt with well over £11 million sterling every year – roughly thirty times the size of the total annual revenues of Elizabethan England, and six times that of Philip II's Spain, the richest European state of its day. By contrast, the initial capital of the Amsterdam bank was equivalent to a mere £250,000, while even that of the Bank of England amounted to only £1.3 million.

The great wealth of sixteenth-century Italy is surprising, for historians used to believe that the peninsula plunged into economic catastrophe as soon as the direct sea-route to India was opened by the Portuguese in 1498 (chapter 11). But until a cycle of disastrous plagues

and wars began in the 1630s, Italy remained a prosperous centre of trade, industry and banking, and nowhere was its wealth more apparent than in the luxury and splendour of its art and architecture. There was, of course, a long artistic tradition in Italy. The Florentine painter Giotto (1260-1327), for example, set new standards of realism in his depiction of the human form: the figures in his surviving work (mostly frescoes) had a new naturalism and immediacy (chapter 9). But the technique of perspective painting only came about a century later with a series of outstanding artists – like Piero della Francesca (c.1410-1492), Andrea Mantegna (1431-1506), Michelangelo Buonarroti (1475-1564) and Raphael (1483-1520) – who mastered the problems of pers-

pective, light, tone, and the representation of human anatomy in both painting and sculpture. They were followed by others – Titian (1490-1576), Tintoretto (1518-94), Caravaggio (1573-1610) and many more – who all developed a distinctive repertory of styles and techniques which were widely imitated elsewhere in Europe.

The great paintings, sculptures and architectural projects of the Renaissance seem to resemble those of ancient Greece and Rome, rather than those of the Middle Ages; this was deliberate. There was, from the mid-fourteenth century onwards, an increasing search for the manuscripts of classical authors, and their writings and opinions became the subject of detailed analyses and wholesale emulation by scholars, who called themselves 'humanists'. Some studied the writings of Aristotle, and went on to write philosophy, like Marsilio Ficino (1433-99) or Giovanni Pico della Mirandola (1463-94); others rediscovered the architectural principles of imperial Rome and went on to build classical structures, like Filippo Brunelleschi (1377-1446), who first demonstrated the rules of perspective and showed, in his great dome on the cathedral of Florence, that the monumental architectural feats of the Romans could be successfully imitated. Throughout the two centuries following his death, many Italian cities were beautified along

Perspective, the device of representing space accurately, was invented in Florence in the early 15th century, and the painter Piero dello Francesca (1420-92) was one of its finest exponents. He painted the *Flagellation of Christ, lower right*, at Urbino in 1457-8, using the columns and the checkerboard pattern of the floor to create a strong illusion of depth. The monumental solidity of his figures lends a further dimension to the mathematically precise construction of the painting.

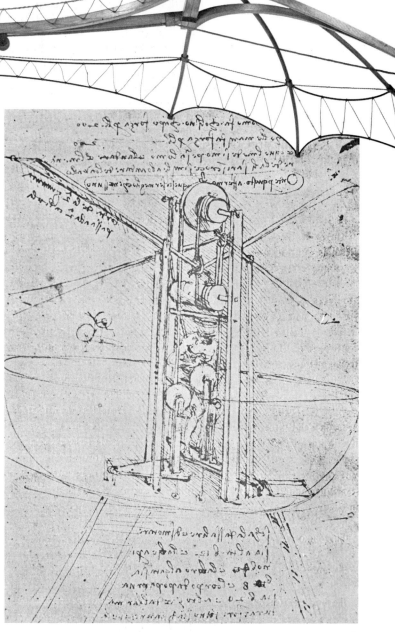

Leonardo da Vinci began life as a painter in Florence but in 1482, at the age of 30, he moved to Milan and served the duke as a musician and (in his own words) 'an artificer of instruments of war'. But his interests stretched far beyond art, music and defence to schemes of applied science, such as machines to make men fly. A page from his extensive notebooks *right* shows a sketch for a man-powered helicopter, annotated in Leonardo's famous mirror writing, intended to conceal his ideas from prying eyes. The reconstruction of an alternative scheme *above* is also based on his notebooks, and demonstrates Leonardo's knowledge of anatomy, based on dissection.

classical lines, and Italian artists and craftsmen found employment throughout Europe as prime protagonists in the rebirth of classical European culture.

There were also significant advances in science and learning, many of them years ahead of their time. Not all of them succeeded: even Leonardo da Vinci (1452-1519) – painter, architect, sculptor, military technician, anatomist, botanist, physicist and meteorologist – the epitome of the 'universal man', failed to design a machine that could make men fly. But enormous progress was made in the observation and measurement of the natural world: the telescope (1609), the microscope (1618), the slide rule (1622), the thermometer (1641) and the barometer (1644) all enabled men to understand the mysteries of the world in which they lived. Perhaps the most dramatic results were achieved by turning the telescope towards the heavens. In 1610 Galileo Galilei, a professor at the university of Padua, published his

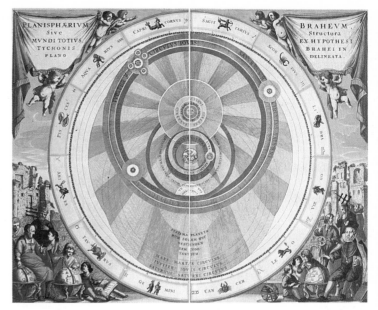

The discovery that the planets rotated round the sun and that the moon rotated round the earth was one of the most important scientific advances of the European Renaissance. The Danish astronomer Tycho Brahe (1564-1601) *right* – shown seated in the right hand corner – deduced from his observation of the heavens (without the benefit of a telescope) the orbit of each planet. Shortly afterwards, the Italian Galileo Galilei (1564-1642) sketched in his notebook *below* the phases of the moon seen through his primitive telescope in 1609-10, and gave names to the various lunar features which, for the first time in history, could be identified from Earth.

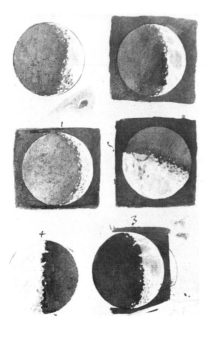

observations of the moon and the planets, drawing the inescapable conclusion that they, like the earth, rotated around the sun, his findings contradicting the view of the Catholic church that the earth was at the centre of the universe. The Pope formally condemned the theory, and all books containing it were ordered to be withdrawn from circulation. Galileo himself was made to promise that he would never publish his astronomical theories again. This was only one instance of the clash between the new humanist/classicist empirical tradition and the massed forces of religious orthodoxy: there were many others.

At the beginning of the sixteenth century, almost everyone in western and central Europe accepted the authority of the Pope in Rome. There had been important groups of dissenters in the past – the Cathars or Albigensian heretics in southern France; the Hussites of Bohemia; and the Jews, who continued to find toleration in most areas of continental Europe. But by 1520, persecution had sapped the strength of these heterodox minorities: the Cathars were to be found only in a few Alpine valleys; the Hussites remained confined to Bohemia; the Jews had been expelled from Spain and Portugal. And yet, fifty years later, almost half the continent – including all the northern states – had established rival Christian churches of their own. This sensational development was the work of two forces: the first, an attack on the papacy by a group of remarkably talented critics; the second the availability, for the first time in Europe, of a medium of mass communication – the printing press.

The idea of printing images from blocks of wood or metal was not new, but the idea of moving individually crafted letters around to create the various pages of text was revolutionary. It was first introduced to Europe by Johannes Gutenberg of Mainz in Germany in the 1450s. Although it might require 50,000 pieces of type to create a large book, such as the Bible, once set the same work could be reproduced thousands of times. By 1520, there were more than 200 different printed editions of the Bible, in several separate languages, representing in all perhaps 50,000 individual copies of the work. But though printing was already well established in Europe, the religious upheavals of the Reformation transformed the trade into a major industry: a total of 150 separate publications appeared in Germany in 1518, 570 in 1520, and 935 in 1523, their combined sales totalling perhaps 500,000 copies.

The character of the Popes on the eve of the Reformation did much to discredit the Roman church. The Spaniard Rodrigo Borgia, who reigned as Alexander VI (1492-1503) *above*, became a Cardinal in 1456 at the age of 25, but nevertheless fathered several children and amassed a huge fortune — with which he bribed his way to election as pope. He did nothing to reform abuses in the church, devoting his energies instead to aggrandizing his family's possessions. This portrait of him by Pinturicchio, in the Borgia apartments of the Vatican, also shows that he spared no expense on personal adornment.

The printing press was the essential tool of the Reformation, because Protestantism called for ordinary people to know the Scriptures for themselves. The title page of the 'Great Bible' of 1539 *right*, printed in English, shows King Henry VIII (watched approvingly by Christ) handing out the Word of God to Archbishop Cranmer and Thomas Cromwell, the king's Vicar General, for distribution to a grateful populace. But the mechanics of early printing took time and patience. In the ideal printer's shop *top right*, at one side compositors gather individual pieces of type with which to copy the manuscript page in front of them. In the centre, a proof-reader dictates the changes to be made and, on the far side, reams of paper are brought in to feed the presses while a small boy piles up the printed sheets ready for binding.

Moreover, although some of them were in Latin, the traditional language of scholarly debate, the majority were in the vernacular. They could be read, or heard, and understood by almost everyone.

A considerable number of these new works were written by one man – Martin Luther. Of the 935 books published in Germany in 1523, 183 were from his pen, and some of his later publications were issued in runs of 100,000 each. Luther, a monk from the powerful German state of Saxony, did not set out to divide the church: on the contrary, he wished to reform and strengthen it. But his criticisms of papal policies, initially mild in tone and limited in scope, such as the *Ninety-five theses* of 1517, were ignored. Indeed, every attempt was made to stifle him, so Luther's complaints became both more strident and more general, appealing directly to other believers (over the head of the Pope) to support his call for reform of the church. Since the Pope still would not listen, Luther exhorted princes and lay rulers to carry out a Reformation of their own instead. As this opened the door for the secularization of much church property, many accepted his summons. Henry VIII of England, Gustavus Vasa of Sweden, and most princes and cities of northern Germany protested the authority of the Pope, introduced a more or less reformed church order, and took charge of all monastic property in their realms.

Martin Luther (1483-1546) painted *above* by Lucas Cranach, was a professor of theology at the university of Wittenberg in Saxony. In 1517 he issued a condemnation of papal claims to be able to dispense sinners from some of the pains of purgatory. The dispute, however, rapidly got out of hand, and Luther soon found himself the leading theologian of an independent Protestant church with adherents all over northern Europe *below*. Even Spain, Portugal and Italy — which ultimately remained wholly Catholic — were affected by Protestantism. France and Poland, two of the largest states of the continent, although eventually brought back to Roman Catholicism, seemed in 1560 to be well on the way to a Protestant takeover, with organized churches spread over most of their territory. Only the Orthodox believers in the east remained indifferent to the message of Luther, Zwingli, Calvin and other leading Protestant reformers.

At the same time, in Switzerland and south-western Germany, other Protestant Reformers – notably Huldreich Zwingli in Zurich and John Calvin in Geneva – introduced a new theology of their own, guaranteed by the civil government and independent of the Pope. Later, many Christians in France, Poland and the Habsburg lands were won over by Calvin's teaching and the governments of Scotland, the Dutch Republic, and several German states made Calvinism their official religion.

Despite these hammer blows, for forty years the Papacy steadfastly refused to see any merit in the Reformers' criticisms. Only in 1562-63, after two false starts, did the bishops and theologians of the Roman church spell out the precise beliefs and behaviour expected of a Catholic. A general council of the church, meeting at the little town of Trent in the Alps, passed a series of decrees on doctrine which remained in force until the next council met more than three centuries later. The Council of Trent also established an effective hierarchy of supervision to ensure that both clergy and laity observed the new standards of discipline and orthodoxy expected of them. In some states there was an Inquisition, made up of trained lawyers and theologians, who interrogated and punished all whose religious views did not coincide with those of 'Mother Church'. These measures, known as the Counter Reformation, halted the tide of Protestantism and a new enthusiasm and confidence animated the Catholics. By 1650, more than two-thirds of Europe was again obedient to the Church of Rome: the Reformation, by and large, only retained its hold in the North.

The division of Europe into two religious camps after 1520 had significant political consequences. In the first place, it destabilized international relations. True, long before differences of creed and faith appeared, European states had frequently fought each other; but after the Reformation their wars became more bitter and more general. In France, the Protestant minority (never more than 10 percent of the total population) accepted aid from England, the Dutch Republic and German sympathizers in order to gain guarantees of toleration from their monarchs: wars of religion paralyzed France between 1562 and 1598, and again between 1621 and 1629. Perhaps the greatest religious conflict – certainly the longest-running – was the Eighty Years' War between the Spanish Habsburgs, rulers of the Netherlands by hereditary right, and their Protestant subjects.

The Roman Church was very slow to accept the need for internal reform. A general council of the church met three times at Trent, a town in the Alps, in 1545-7, 1551-2 and 1562-3 *above left* and, in a series of committee discussions, reformulated the doctrines to be accepted by Catholics everywhere and laid down norms of behaviour for clergy and laity alike. These measures became known as the Counter Reformation. This re-affirmation of faith provoked considerable fervour: on the one hand in the establishment of a number of Catholic missionary orders, among them the Jesuits (founded 1540); on the other in the canonization of many modern saints, such as the Jesuit founder St. Ignatius Loyola (1491-1556, canonized 1622) and the Spanish mystic St. Teresa of Avila (1515-82, canonized 1622). New standards of religious art were also established, stressing emotion and realism and seeking to involve the spectator in the events portrayed. 'The Ecstasy of St. Teresa', a life-size marble sculpture by the leading Roman architect and sculptor Bernini (1598-1660) *above*, is a fine example of the arresting and theatrical style favoured by the Counter-Reformation church.

PARIS

After the Council of Trent Catholics all over Europe began to counterattack. In France, religious wars broke out in which the Catholic majority sought to exterminate the Protestant communities that grew up in the 1550s. On 24 August, St. Bartholomew's Day, 1572, with the blessing of the government, the Catholics of Paris massacred all the Protestants they could find – about 6000 in all *above*. Meanwhile, in the Netherlands, a revolt against Spanish rule led by Protestants produced a civil war that lasted almost 80 years and involved great brutality on both sides *upper right*. When the rebellious town of Haarlem surrendered in 1573, after a six months siege, for example, the victorious Spaniards executed the garrison, the town magistrates, and all declared Protestants.

Opposition by a Calvinist minority to the religious policies for the Netherlands decreed by Philip II in the 1560s was met resolutely with force. A huge army was sent from Spain and over 60,000 Netherlanders were forced into exile. In 1572 these refugees, with assistance from France and England, staged an invasion which captured more than twenty towns in the maritime provinces of Holland and Zeeland. Since most of these were defended by elaborate bastions, the Spanish reconquest was extremely slow; indeed, before it was completed, the besieging forces mutinied and the war became a costly stalemate. When the war finally ended in 1648, the Netherlands were partitioned into a Catholic south, the modern Belgium, and a Calvinist north, now the kingdom of the Netherlands, then known as the Dutch Republic.

This republic was no ordinary state. Although Calvinism was the official religion its clergy were never able to gain the degree of control and censorship over intellectual activity and daily life that existed almost everywhere else. There was never a Calvinist Inquisition: freedom of speech and action existed on a scale that excited amazement among all visitors – and there was much the same liberty in politics. Supreme authority in the Republic was exercised by an elected representative assembly, not by a single sovereign; although representation only extended to about 2,000 nobles and town councillors, it was still a far more democratic system than obtained elsewhere.

There were few imitators. Most seventeenth-century rulers were convinced that the key to stable government was the sovereign's exclusive control of both religion and politics. From the early days of the Reformation, Protestant monarchs like Henry VIII of England had found that extending their authority over the church greatly enhanced their power over the state. Even in the seventeenth century, the ability of the Swedish kings to intervene in continental Europe was based upon their control of the Lutheran church throughout their dominions: the pastors were mobilized to preach sermons justifying Swedish imperialism, as well as to help select conscripts for the army. By then, however, Catholic rulers, too, were willing to tap the power of the pulpit. The Thirty Years' War between the Habsburg emperors in Germany and their (mainly Protestant) enemies between 1618 and 1648, was normally presented by both sides as a religious struggle.

fAERLEM.

After 1648, however, governments became more reluctant to appeal to religious sentiment in their foreign policy. Instead, most wars in the later seventeenth century came to be fought to preserve the international settlement established between the states of Europe by the wars and revolutions of the mid-century, which contemporaries began to call 'the balance of power'. Increasingly, the chief threat to this new order was identified as the growing power of France.

The early years of Louis XIV, who ruled France from 1643 to 1715, were overshadowed by the Fronde rebellion; but after its collapse (1653), and the securing of a highly favourable peace with Spain (1659), the young king set out to impose his direct and immediate rule throughout France. In the first place, the *intendants* abolished by the Fronde were restored, and the civil service was both streamlined and increased. The provincial bureaucracy was to be found both in the areas directly governed from Paris, and in those which still preserved their own local institutions: the king could now reach out and influence the daily life of ordinary people in a way that had previously been inconceivable. Their dress, wages, behaviour and beliefs were now all subject to strict regulation. Louis XIV's power had become absolute: it was no longer shared with other groups within the state, such as the supreme court, the nobility, or the Protestants. As Louis himself put it: 'L'état, c'est moi' – 'I am the state'.

Nowhere was the new absolutism more apparent than in military affairs. Louis XIV went to war in 1667-68, in 1672-78, in 1689-97 and in 1701-14. Each time France gained a more defensible frontier, more secure against foreign invasion; but in order to achieve these gains, however modest, ever larger armies were required. By 1696, French soldiers were even more numerous than French clerics, and almost one in four of Louis XIV's subjects was mobilized. Few questioned the king's right to do this: after the Fronde there were singularly few revolts in France for over a century – none by nobles, only one by the Protestants (or 'Huguenots', many of whom fled abroad in any case during the 1680s), and very few by the peasantry. Instead the king cultivated the notion that he enjoyed semi-divine status, creating at Versailles a sumptuous setting intended to emphasize the king's superiority over

The Dutch Revolt in spite of all Spain's efforts at suppression, eventually secured independence for seven of the Northern Netherlands provinces. The Dutch Republic, as it was known, was ruled by representatives of each of the constituent provinces, known as the States-General, meeting together in the Hague on an almost daily basis *below*, beneath the numerous standards and ensigns captured from the Spanish army in the Low Countries' Wars.

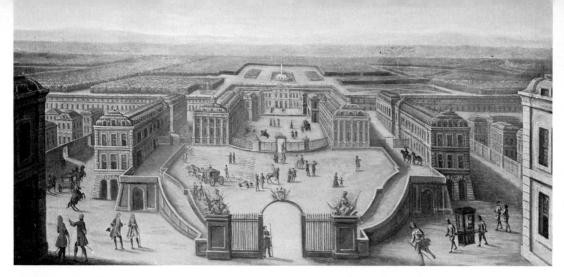

all others. By 1700, most monarchs in continental Europe regarded Louis as master of the craft of kingship, the only model worthy of emulation (chapter 20). The only exceptions were the rulers of Brandenburg-Prussia and Great Britain. Frederick William (1640-88), known as the Great Elector of Brandenburg, adopted a policy of religious toleration in order to attract settlers; abandoned the peasants to serfdom under their aristocratic landholders in order to purchase social stability; and employed the nobles as officers to lead the army. By 1740 this army was the fourth largest in Europe (although the state that supported it was only the thirteenth largest), and with its aid Brandenburg-Prussia managed to rise from obscurity until it became the dominant state on the continent (chapter 24).

The other notable contrast to Louis XIV's style of kingship was offered by William III of Orange, leader of the Dutch Republic from 1672 and king of England, Scotland and Ireland from 1688 until his death in 1702, who spent the greater part of his reign opposing French imperialism. William's great advantage lay in his fleet. In 1688, although Louis XIV's navy numbered an impressive 221 warships, that of Great Britain was 173 and that of the Dutch 102 more. Within four years, the French battle fleet was outmanoeuvred and confined to port. Even on land, William and his Habsburg allies were able to raise armies equal to that of France and, after his death, under the Duke of Marlborough in the Netherlands and Prince Eugene of Savoy in Italy, the generals of Louis XIV were repeatedly defeated. Moreover, thanks to the resources of the public banks of Amsterdam and London, even after the victories ceased the allies could mobilize enough money to go on fighting until France collapsed.

Nevertheless, the collapse was not total: Louis XIV's revolution in government was inherited intact by his descendants in France, and was introduced during the eighteenth century into Spain, where a junior branch of the French royal family was established from 1700 onwards (in spite of the bitter opposition of Britain and her allies). The Bourbon family, to which the kings of France and Spain now belonged, thus controlled half of western Europe, a wide selection of forts and territories around the coast of Africa and Asia, and the larger part of America (Mexico and Peru, together with their adjoining dependencies ruled from Madrid; Canada and Louisiana controlled from Paris). It was this very concentration of power that encouraged the Bourbons' enemies to attack them where their authority was weakest: at the periphery. To an increasing extent, the conflicts between the European powers became 'world wars', fought as much for overseas empires as for territorial advantage in Europe. Paradoxically, it was this colonial rivalry that played a leading part in the rise of the West to world domination.

Louis XIV of France, born in 1638, exercised a very different type of authority from the Dutch States-General. By the 1660s, his sole power to command was as absolute as that of a Roman emperor, to whom his flattering court artist Mignard compared him in the equestrian portrait *right*. This was amply reflected in the construction of his monumental palace at Versailles *above*. Erected in the midst of what had been a sandy waste, Versailles was a potent symbol of Louis's power and the wonder of Europe, an affirmation of the ascendency of France as the cultural and political leader of Europe.

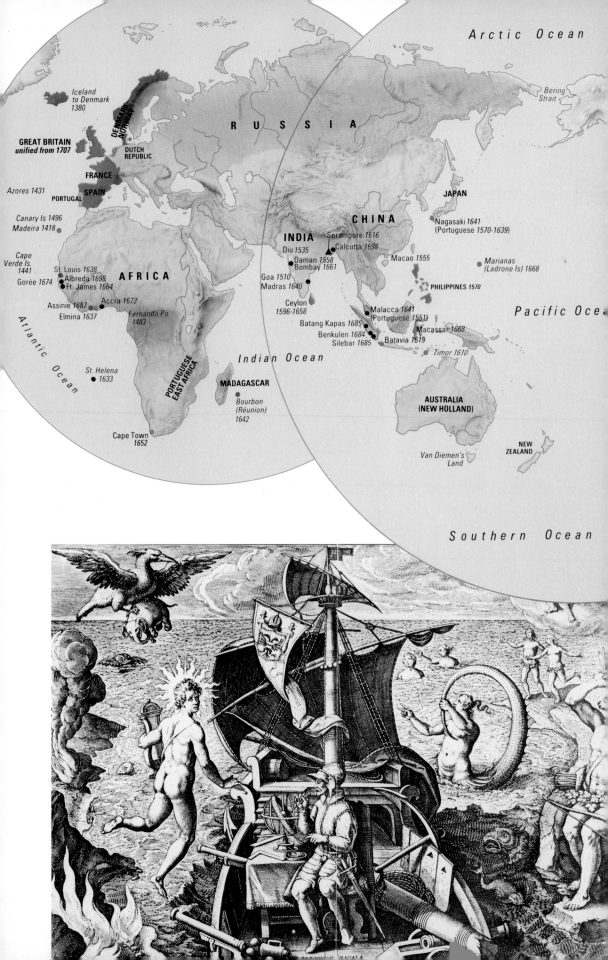

Arctic Ocean

Iceland to Denmark 1380

RUSSIA

Bering Strait

GREAT BRITAIN
unified from 1707

DUTCH REPUBLIC

DENMARK-NORWAY

FRANCE
SPAIN

PORTUGAL

Azores 1431

Canary Is 1496
Madeira 1418

Cape Verde Is. 1441

St. Louis 1638
Albreda 1698
Gorée 1674
Ft. James 1664

AFRICA

Assinie 1687
Accra 1672
Elmina 1637

Fernando Po 1483

JAPAN

CHINA

Nagasaki 1641
(Portuguese 1570-1639)

INDIA

Serampore 1616
Diu 1535
Calcutta 1698

Daman 1558
Bombay 1661

Macao 1555

Marianas (Ladrone Is) 1668

Goa 1510
Madras 1640

Ceylon 1596-1658

PHILIPPINES 1570

Pacific Oce

Malacca 1641
(Portuguese 1551)

Batang Kapas 1685
Macassar 1668

Benkulen 1684
Silebar 1685
Batavia 1619

Timor 1610

Atlantic Ocean

Indian Ocean

St. Helena 1633

PORTUGUESE EAST AFRICA

MADAGASCAR

Bourbon (Réunion) 1642

AUSTRALIA (NEW HOLLAND)

Cape Town 1652

Southern Ocean

Van Diemen's Land

NEW ZEALAND

RUPERT'S LAND
1670

NORTH
AMERICA

NEW FRANCE

Atlantic Ocean

St. Pierre and
Miquelon 1635

FLORIDA *1513*

Bermuda 1609/84

VICEROYALTY OF
NEW SPAIN
from 1535

Cuba
1511

Bahamas 1670

St. Domingue 1665

Hispaniola 1492

Puerto Rico 1493

BELIZE *1638*

Jamaica
1655

St. Thomas 1671

Guadeloupe 1635

MOSQUITO
COAST
1655

Barbados 1627

GUIANA

Cayenne *1635*

SOUTH
AMERICA

BRAZIL

VICEROYALTY OF PERU
from 1543

European overseas possessions in 1700 *left* were surprisingly limited. Spain and Portugal still possessed the largest land areas; but increasingly Holland, France and Britain controlled key strategic ports and trading emporia, often dominating essential sea-lanes. These possessions were the deciding factor in the 'game' of empire, for it was control of the seas rather than vast tracts of land which determined the winner.

European territories in 1700:

◼	Spanish possessions
◻	Portuguese possessions
⬛•	British possessions
◼	French possessions
◻	Dutch possession
▲	Danish possessions
1511	date of acquisition

The first circumnavigation of the world (1519-1522) seemed little short of miraculous to contemporaries. The engraving *left* shows the expedition's leader, Ferdinand Magellan, assisted not only by artillery and navigational instruments, but by gods and mermaids too.

CHAPTER 18

THE WEST AND THE WIDER WORLD
1500–1700

The 1490s were the most remarkable decade in the whole history of European navigation. Following Columbus's demonstration of how to sail across the Atlantic to the Caribbean (and how to get back), other explorers quickly made contact with Newfoundland, the central American isthmus, and (in 1500) Brazil; while Portuguese fleets established a direct sea-route to India (chapter 11). Over the next twenty years, further voyages of exploration revealed to the Europeans more and more of the coasts of Asia, Africa and America until it became virtually certain that all the continents were surrounded by a single sea.

This fact was demonstrated by the flotilla of five ships and 250 men, commanded by Ferdinand Magellan, which left Spain in 1519 intending to sail around the southern tip of America into the Pacific, there to establish a new trade-route to the spices of east Asia (just as Columbus had originally hoped to do). In 1519 Spanish settlements in the Caribbean seemed unrewarding, and the American mainland still appeared more of an obstacle than an opportunity. Magellan's task was therefore to establish a viable commercial route to the Moluccas – the Spice Islands. The simple fact is that he failed, for the journey proved long, arduous, and far too costly in lives and ships. There was a serious, savagely repressed mutiny before he penetrated into the Pacific by way of the Strait of Magellan; he lost his own life in battle on an island in the Philippines; and those of his men who reached the Moluccas, and bought cargoes of spices there, then found that only one of their ships was still seaworthy. Rather than return the way they had come, the survivors decided to keep sailing west. Under the command of Juan Sebastián Elcano, a former mutineer against Magellan, the *Victoria* finally rounded the Cape of Good Hope and crawled back into the harbour of San Lúcar de Barrameda in southern Spain late in the summer of 1522. Magellan had been lost, as had four of his five ships; and of the 250 men who set out only eighteen returned. In contrast, by this time Cortés had conquered Mexico for Spain and, as bullion from mainland America began to reach Spain, the Spanish Crown began to lose interest in the Moluccas which, in any case, were eventually recognized as being in the Portuguese sphere of influence.

299

At first then, this heroic, costly and disappointing circumnavigation stood alone: Spain made no further attempts to gain a share of the spice trade. But Magellan had, in the course of his voyage, made contact with another archipelago off east Asia which no Europeans had previously seen. Further Spanish attempts to reach it were made in the 1520s and 1540s; and then, in 1565, a fleet sent from America under Miguel López de Legazpi claimed the islands in the name of Philip II of Spain. In his honour they were called the Philippines.

The islands were highly unusual in south-east Asia, for they had developed no urban civilization before the arrival of the Europeans. Indeed, only in two areas had anything larger than villages emerged – around Cebu, in the centre of the archipelago, and around Manila Bay – and neither of those could boast a single community larger than 2,000 inhabitants. Nevertheless, the city of Manila was formally established by the Spaniards in 1572. By 1620 it could boast 40,000 inhabitants; by 1640 it had twice as many. Feeding this unprecedented concentration of people presented new problems, for there was no pre-existing tradition in the islands of growing a food surplus or paying tribute; but gradually the villages around Manila were coerced into increasing the yield of their crops in order to feed the metropolis. Trade, however, not agriculture, was the key to Manila's rapid expansion: by 1600 almost all Spanish residents in the archipelago lived in the great fortified city by Manila bay – the best natural harbour in all Asia – which proved to be a convenient point for Chinese traders bringing their silks and ceramics and was not too

Purpose-built warships *below* emerged in Europe in the early 16th century. Early versions had high 'castles' fore and aft, from which troops could pour a hail of small-arms fire onto their enemies; but the main armaments were the great ship-smashing cannon carried on the lower decks, fired through hinged gun-ports. This engraving from about 1520 shows a ship like Magellan's *Victoria* under full sail in the southern hemisphere, surrounded by flying fish and other exotic creatures.

far from the spices of the Moluccas. Such goods could readily be exchanged for American silver. The Spaniards had to fight off Portuguese and, later, Dutch rivals, as well as cope with a large resident Chinese population, against whom from time to time they perpetrated horrific massacres. But in spite of everything, they nevertheless established a permanent commercial link between the Far East and the Far West, and made huge profits from it: contemporaries estimated that the cargo of each one of the Manila galleons sailing between the Philippines and Mexico in the early seventeenth century was worth more than the total annual revenues of the king of England.

One reason for the speed with which the Philippines were colonized – by 1600 perhaps half the islands' population was under Spanish control – was the conquerors' previous experience in America. By the 1560s, the Spaniards had established themselves not only in the Caribbean islands, Mexico and Peru, but also in the central isthmus, along the Caribbean shore of South America, and in central Chile. They had more experience of planting colonies than any other people in the world. But their success was only achieved at a huge human cost.

It seems likely that much of Pre-Columbian America – particularly Mexico – was overpopulated on the eve of the Spanish conquest (chapter 16), and that some sort of demographic disaster was highly probable even without European intervention. But if there were too many people before the conquest, very soon after it there were too few. The 21 million Mexicans of 1519 – making up more than a third of the total

The arrival of the Dutch in the Far East after 1595 extended the European struggle between Spain and the Low Countries (chapter 17) to the other side of the globe. Wherever the possessions and ships of the king of Spain were found, the Dutch attacked. In 1610 a powerful squadron tried to capture the large new city of Manila, in the Philippines *below*; but, operating too far from their bases, and in the teeth of powerful and resolute defence, they failed. Spain retained control of the Philippines until 1898, but did not stop the Dutch establishing a lucrative trading network in the East Indies.

population of the continent – had fallen dramatically to 2.5 million by 1565, and even further to only one million by 1607. Over the same period, the 11 million native Peruvians declined to perhaps 1.5 million; and the inhabitants of other areas were similarly affected. The total population of the Americas before the European conquest was around 57 million; a century later it had fallen overall by 90 percent.

At first sight, this appears to be genocide: the extermination of one race by another. But genocide is the fruit of deliberate policy; and the depopulation of America was, to a large extent, accidental. Certainly some indiscriminate slaughter occurred during the conquest, as at the capture of Tenochtitlán, the Aztec capital (chapter 16); and, equally certainly, there was much brutality towards the vanquished Americans by their Spanish masters. Far more destructive, however, was the dislocation of traditional ways by the European invasion – especially around the towns (which constantly required labour services from the surrounding villages) and the mines (which could not be exploited without the wholesale conscription of native workers). Many of these unfortunate forced labourers died, either from the rigours of their new jobs or from despair; but their numbers were as nothing compared to the victims of the diseases imported by the Europeans. The native Americans, whom their conquerors labelled Indians, were descended from groups of Ice Age hunters who had crossed into America from eastern Asia across a land-bridge later submerged by rising sea levels (chapter 1). So, for thousands of years, they had lived in isolation. They therefore developed their own repertory of diseases and had no resistance to those which suddenly came from outside after 1492. To them, influenza, measles, and above all, smallpox were lethal. 'The natives are so sickly', wrote an unsympathetic and uncomprehending European, 'that the mere sight or smell of a Spaniard makes them give up the ghost'.

The Spanish government did its best. In 1542, in legislation known as 'the New Laws', it prohibited the enslavement of the Indians, and

Bernardino de Sahagún was one of the greatest European ethnographers. He arrived in Mexico as a young friar in 1529, and quickly mastered the Nahuatl language of the local population. In 1540 he prepared a book of sermons in their language to facilitate the spread of Christianity, and it was to improve the missionaries' understanding of their converts that in 1558 Sahagún was commanded by his superiors to compose a history of Aztec culture. The illustrated *History of the Things of New Spain* contained pictures and descriptions of traditional everyday life *right* as well as accounts of the practices of the former lords of Mexico (chapter 16). But the work of Sahagún remained unpublished and, after 1577, no further work on the 'superstitions and customs' of the Indians was permitted for the Spanish were less concerned with native traditions, and more interested in Indians as a source of slave labour with which to exploit the rich silver deposits of the New World *below left*. Spanish brutality, *below centre* illustrated in the popular *Very Brief Account of the Destruction of the Indies*, by Bartolomé de las Casas (1552) was probably exaggerated – the principal destructive agents were diseases carried to the New World by the Europeans. The majority of Spaniards were, however, quick to defend their treatment of the natives by citing atrocities perpetrated by the Indians upon Christian colonists *below right*. Lurid illustrations such as this were produced to support their argument.

commanded its officials in America to protect the native population against exploitation; but the decree was ignored in Mexico, whilst in Peru it was greeted by a major revolt which came within an ace of turning the colony into an independent republic ruled by the Pizarro family. These events sapped the government's self-confidence. In 1550-52, in an unusual exercise in 'open government', the question of how the colonies should be run was publicly debated. A flood of pamphlets

and polemics were printed, and a personal confrontation took place at Valladolid between Bishop Bartolomé de las Casas, who argued from his experiences in America that the Indians were like children who required protection and loving care, and Philip II's tutor, Juan Ginés de Sepúlveda, who (although he had never crossed the Atlantic) compared them to the natural slaves described by Aristotle. Eventually, the government retreated from the extreme position of the New Laws: in the mines, forced labour was now permitted; on the great ranches, where sheep and cattle were raised, the landlords remained a law unto themselves. The network of provincial administrators, each directly responsible to the Crown, might endeavour to enforce the laws protecting the Indians, while committed missionaries (like las Casas) might try to improve local conditions by their preaching and writing; but the majority of the colonists continued to do as they pleased. It was never easy to discipline families like the Cortés, descended from the conqueror of Mexico, whose estates included 23,000 Indian vassals.

By the mid-century, however, the fall in native numbers began to affect the prosperity of the lords. They therefore turned to an alternative source of labour: African slaves. The Portuguese had been engaged in systematic slaving to help pay for their voyages since the 1440s. A papal bull of 1455 recognized their 'right' to enslave any non-Christian people whom they might capture in the course of exploring the coast of Africa and this privilege was exercised on an ever-increasing scale (chapter 11). Then, from the 1540s, the Spanish Crown began to sell licences to Portuguese slavers to trade in Spanish America and, after the union of the Spanish and Portuguese Crowns in 1580, there was no serious obstacle to prevent Portuguese slave-traders from visiting the American colonies and selling their wares. Thanks to their efforts, by 1650 there were some 40,000 blacks in Mexico, and perhaps 30,000 in Peru. But these totals were modest compared with the slave populations of Brazil and the Caribbean islands.

Brazil was formally claimed for Portugal in 1500 by the fleet of thirteen ships under Pedro Alvares Cabral which was following up the success (two years previously) of Vasco da Gama in reaching India via the Cape of Good Hope. Cabral only left two men in Brazil where, for two generations, French and English traders were as common as Portuguese. But then, in the 1550s, the Portuguese rapidly and permanently

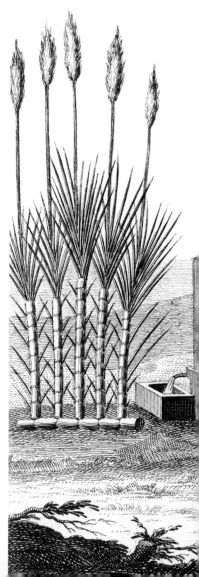

The word 'slave' originally derived from 'slav' and, in the Middle Ages, men and women from the Balkans were abducted in large numbers to labour on the sugar plantations in the islands of the eastern Mediterranean (chapter 11). When sugar-cultivation was introduced to the Americas, it was thus thought natural that slaves should be imported too, to perform the same functions. Now, however, the slaves were black Africans, and were transported across the Atlantic in appalling conditions aboard overcrowded, insanitary vessels *left*. Crude factories were installed on the plantations of the West Indies and Brazil *below*, to press and refine the sugar cane, but much of the energy and the transport was still supplied by slaves. In the words of a 17th-century governor of Brazil: 'It is not possible to effect anything here without slaves; if anyone feels this is wrong, it is a futile scruple'. In 1832 Britain took the first step towards abolition of the Atlantic slave trade, but slavery persisted in Brazil until the early 20th century.

began to settle the coastal plains. The main activity was the cultivation of sugar: in 1600, some 10,000 tons of Brazilian sugar were exported; in 1630, 20,000 tons; in 1660, 40,000 tons. But the production of sugar was extremely labour-intensive, and the labour was hard. During the seventeenth century, some 5,000 slaves were shipped annually from west Africa to Brazil alone, and the total rose inexorably in the eighteenth; between 1550 and 1800, Brazil probably absorbed some 2.5 million black slaves. And yet, by 1800, the total negro population of South America was still less than a million, because most of the slaves died within a few years – and sometimes within a few months – of their arrival. For some, malnutrition, despair and disease caused premature death; but the majority perished because their masters wished it so. Slave-owners seem to have made a callous calculation. At first, by working flat out, a slave could produce about three-quarters of a ton of sugar a year. At the prices of the period, this meant that, within two years, he would produce an amount of sugar equivalent to his purchase price and maintenance; so if the slave lived for six years, the investment of the planter would be trebled. But, thereafter, it made sense to buy a new and more vigorous replacement. There was thus little incentive to improve conditions, or to encourage the slaves to bring up families. It was cheaper and more efficient to work them to death.

The first French colonists were attracted by the possibility of a lucrative fur trade. Samuel de Champlain (1567-1635) was a leading explorer who penetrated America via the St. Lawrence river, and established the first colonies of New France, including Quebec (1608). His account of his adventures with Huron Indian war parties, attacking the Iroquois and the Onondaga tribes *left* is an example of how, in order to avoid a massed Indian attack, early colonists exploited divisions between native tribes.

The picture for the Caribbean was little better. The sugar-producing islands, whether run by French, Dutch or British entrepreneurs, were also vast consumers of slaves: in the course of the seventeenth and eighteenth centuries, perhaps two million were sent from Africa to the West Indies.

Conditions were far more favourable on the North American mainland, however, where slaves reproduced their numbers at more or less the same rate as their white neighbours. Indeed, until the later seventeenth century the bulk of the unfree labourers in England's American colonies were white: indentured or bond servants who secured an expensive (by their standards) voyage across the Atlantic to America by accepting servile status for a number of years. They were, however, treated much the same as any other slaves and it was only a shortage of these people, due to a rise in real living standards in England, that prompted the switch to black slaves after the 1660s.

The early history of the colonies planted in North America was not, in fact, one of unqualified success. The first French settlement, in Florida, was destroyed by the Spaniards in 1565; the first English attempt to colonize Virginia failed dismally; and the ultimate fate of the members of the third expedition, sponsored by Sir Walter Raleigh to make a settlement at Roanoke, is still unknown. Landing in July 1587 at the site of the two previous unsuccessful attempts, they were abandoned by their leader, the artist John White, within a month. By 1591, they had vanished. Sustained colonization in North America, backed by adequate resources only came with the seventeenth century. It began with Jamestown on the Chesapeake river in 1607 and Quebec on the St Lawrence river in 1608. Not that these towns were immediate centres of growth – on the contrary, conditions in Jamestown over the winter of 1609-10 were so adverse that the colonists were reduced to eating their own dead. But, gradually, the settlers expanded by supplying the neighbouring tribes with firearms, and then aiding their allies against the less well-armed peoples further west. It was the same story in Canada: in 1649, the French and their Iroquois allies used their combined firepower to destroy the Hurons.

The areas of European settlement thus steadily grew. Old colonies increased (there were 5,000 whites in Virginia by 1650) and new ones were added – most notably the 'Pilgrim Fathers' in Massachusetts, the Puritans in Connecticut and Rhode Island, and the Catholics and Protestants in Maryland. French and British colonists also settled further

English attempts to colonize North America were made at Roanoke in Virginia in the 1580s. One of the pioneers was John White, a cartographer and artist, who was commissioned to depict life in the New World, and his collection of pictures presents a charming and accurate picture of how the Indian population of the area lived on the eve of the European invasion. *Right* is the village of Secoton, showing the houses and corn-fields, the graveyard and religious centre, and the communal activities of the population. *Below* is another village, surrounded by an extensive palisade. The Roanoke colony was abandoned, largely because the ships carrying supplies and reinforcements were commandeered for service against the Spanish Armada.

The towne of Pomeiooc and true forme
and enclosed some with mattes, and some
about with smale poles stock thick togeth

Their rype corne

Their greene corne.

Corne newly sprong.

Their sitting at meate.

The place of solemne prayer.

wherin the Tombe of their Herounds standeth.

SEGOTON.

A Ceremony in their prayers w[th]
strange iestures and songes dansing:
abowt posts carued on the topps
lyke mens faces.

along the St Lawrence, so that by 1700 there were perhaps 250,000 white settlers in North America, living off agriculture and fishing, exporting tobacco and furs, and satisfying most of their needs from local manufactures. But none of these colonies were, as yet, either as populous or as prosperous as Latin America. The mines of Spanish America between 1500 and 1650 officially exported some 181 tons of gold and 17,000 tons of silver to Europe, and production thereafter rose even further; while in Portuguese Brazil the export of gold rose in the eighteenth century to no less than ten tons each year.

These windfalls were by no means all retained in Europe, however. Instead they continued their journey westward into Asia: most of the 'pieces of eight' minted in Mexico and Peru ended up in the state treasuries of China, India or south-east Asia. The problem was that, until the industrial revolution permitted a fall in the real price of European manufactured goods, there were very few commodities produced in the West that could be sold at a profit in the East. Imports from Asia – spices, silks and other oriental luxuries – had to be paid for in bullion; so three-quarters of the outward cargoes of most East Indiamen, whether Portuguese or Dutch or English, were therefore made up of silver. As late as 1800, the Chinese would exchange their goods for nothing else (chapter 19). Without their ability to export the cheap silver provided so copiously by the forced labour of the American Indians, therefore, Europe would have been forced to live without most of the riches of Asia.

But not all the European adventurers who went to the Indian Ocean were interested in supplying the West with silks and spices: ever since the days of Vasco da Gama, many had indulged in a vigorous 'country trade' between the various ports of Asia. In effect, the Portuguese operated two semi-independent trading systems in the Far East. The first was official, relying on the control of a few major fortresses and the direct trade between Asia and Europe. It was financed by the Crown and, on the whole, made a loss. The second, sometimes known as the 'shadow empire', was carried on unofficially by private individuals with their own ships, warehouses, and contacts – most of them in ports controlled by independent rulers – and generated high profits. But it depended absolutely on the ability of the Portuguese to rule the waves. In the sixteenth century, this presented no problem because all the

The Dutch East India Company was licensed by the States-General (1602) to expand trade and to support the war against Spain and Portugal overseas. This was only possible with a substantial and efficient fleet *left*. In 1619 its headquarters were established at Batavia, providing a base from which the British and the Portuguese were driven from the East Indies, Malaya and Ceylon, thus cornering the immensely wealthy trade of the Spice Islands. The Dutch failed however to dislodge their rivals in India. At Goa *below*, the heavily fortified administrative, commercial and spiritual headquarters of the Portuguese in the east had been established since 1510.

European ships carried artillery, whereas most native vessels of the Indian Ocean, constructed with rope and wooden pegs, lacked the strength either to withstand artillery bombardment from without or to absorb the recoil of large ordnance firing from within. Thanks to this technological edge, the Portuguese were able to regulate the seaborne commerce of their rivals: they exacted massive payments as 'protection money'; they forbade the transport of numerous lucrative goods (such as spices or horses) in any ships except their own; and they limited the amount of traffic and the destinations allowed for each local state. Any ship that disregarded these regulations was bombarded into surrender, its crew drowned, and its cargo (if captured) confiscated.

Luckily for the Portuguese, when they burst into the Indian Ocean no native state was powerful enough to challenge them single-handed. Within a few years of Vasco da Gama's arrival in India, the ports of Goa (1510), Malacca (1511) and Ormuz (1515) had been captured and fortified so that when, shortly afterwards, two strong native states emerged in the area, the Portuguese could no longer be dislodged. The Ottoman Turks (chapter 14) sent three major naval expeditions into the Indian Ocean (in 1538, 1551 and 1587), but all of them failed. The Mughal empire, established in northern India by an Afghan ruler, Babur, in 1526, was potentially more dangerous, being closer to the

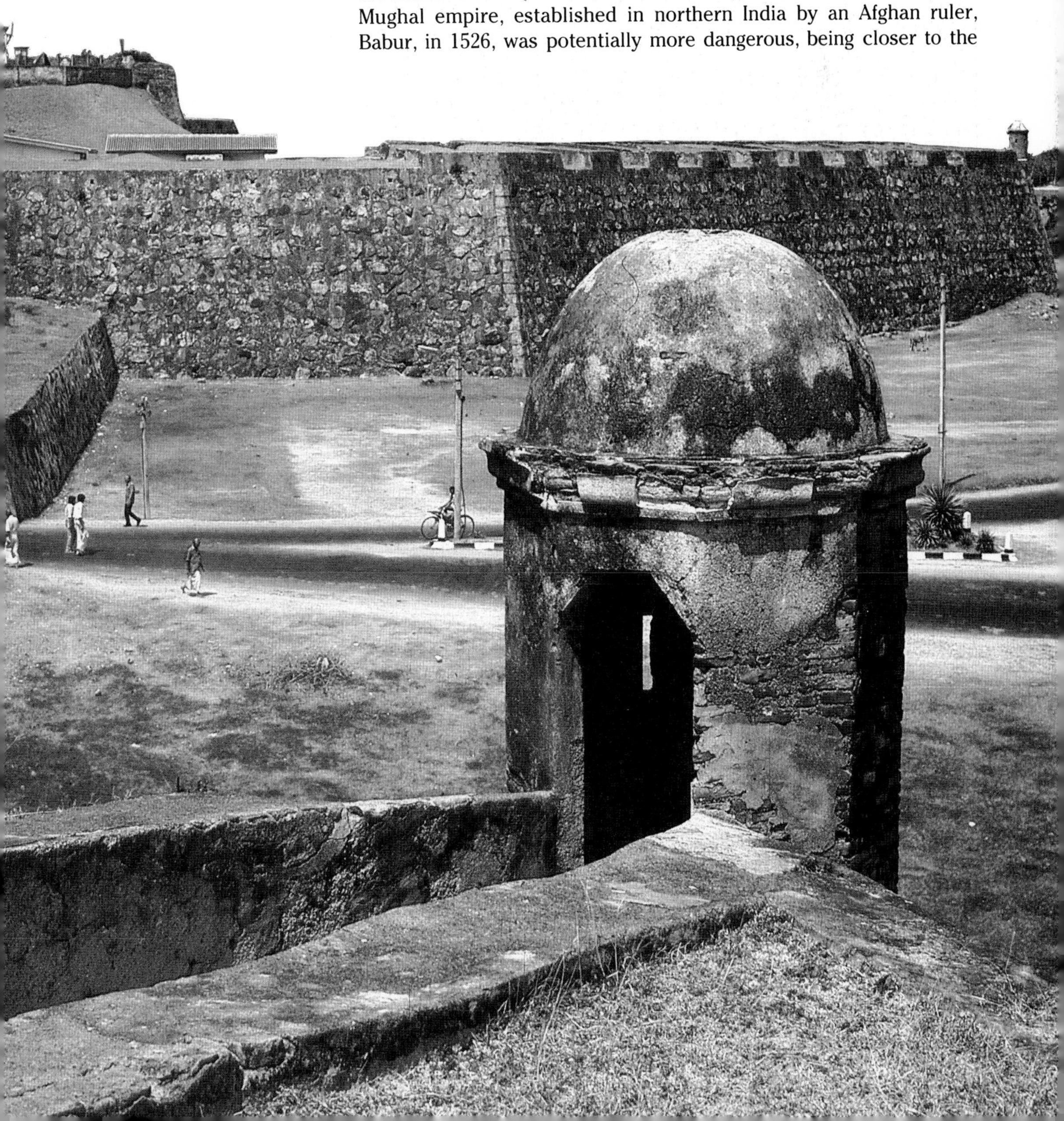

Portuguese positions. But the Mughals were not particularly interested in seapower: theirs was a land empire, and they only acquired access to the sea – at Surat – in the 1570s. Even afterwards, due to the presence at the Mughal court of Jesuit missionaries, the Portuguese were usually given good warning of any hostile intentions and could therefore place their fortresses on a war footing in good time. So secure did the Portuguese feel that in the 1590s they embarked on an ambitious new venture: the conquest of Ceylon, the world centre of cinnamon production. In this they might have succeeded, but for the simultaneous arrival in the Indian Ocean of their enemies from Europe.

For over a century, Portugal had tried to avoid involvement in the numerous wars of Europe: she had sought only to preserve intact her trade with all other countries. But in 1580 her native dynasty died out and King Philip II of Spain, claimed the succession. There was a Portuguese candidate, Dom António, Prior of Crato, whom most Portuguese clearly preferred; but Philip had no intention of yielding, and the same year he marched in and took over. Although he was careful to keep the government of his new kingdom separate from that of Spain, that was not how it appeared to the outside world: after all, when Philip launched the Spanish Armada against England and the Dutch in 1588, it sailed from Lisbon, included eleven Portuguese warships, and carried two regiments of Portuguese troops.

The Armada campaign was a turning-point in Europe's relations with Asia. On the one hand, it was accompanied by a series of measures aimed at preventing Philip II's enemies from gaining access to the

The defeat of the Spanish Armada in 1588 was a decisive event. The destruction of so many of Philip II's ships (shown in the windows behind the bejewelled and triumphant Queen Elizabeth of England *right*) opened the way to overseas expansion by both England and the Dutch Republic. Already the queen's hand rests upon North America (shown on the globe), where colonies soon sprang up; and, before long, her ships also sailed into the Indian Ocean in search of trade. The Dutch were also encouraged to attack Spanish and Portuguese bases in America and Asia; the painting *left* shows an episode from a Dutch attempt to take Goa from the Portuguese in 1639. A major factor in their general success, whether against the Armada or further overseas, was the superior naval artillery of the north Europeans: mounted on compact sea-carriages, their 24 and 36-pounder bronze guns could fire broadside salvoes rapidly and accurately at ranges of up to half-a-mile. The example *below*, salvaged in 1981 from the English warship *Mary Rose*, which sank in 1544, is the earliest example known.

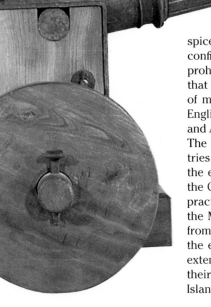

spices of the Orient: English and Dutch shipping in Iberian ports was confiscated, and trade between Iberian and north European ports was prohibited. Yet, at the same time, the defeat of the Armada revealed that Philip II – despite his conquest of Portugal – was no longer capable of maintaining a monopoly of Atlantic trade for his subjects. So the English and the Dutch mounted raids on the king's bases in America and Africa, and soon sent powerful armed fleets into the Indian Ocean. The profits of piracy were high and therefore, in 1600-02, both countries chartered an 'East India Company' to expand their own trade at the expense of the Portuguese and, wherever possible, to undermine the Catholic gains made by the numerous Iberian missionaries. But in practice it was not so simple. The English established an embassy at the Mughal court, where Sir Thomas Roe represented James VI and I from 1615 to 1618; but it was not until the dotage of Mughal power in the eighteenth century that the English East India Company secured extensive trading privileges in the Indian subcontinent. The Dutch, for their part, after some initial reverses, took over control of the Spice Islands and in the 1650s moved on to conquer Ceylon and the Malabar

coast. There they made haste to ban Catholic worship among their new subjects but were unable to put anything in its place – the shareholders of the Dutch East India Company were unwilling to spend much on missionary work which yielded no obvious profit.

It would be hard to argue that these changes did anything to increase the overall European share of the trade of Asia. The first Dutch fleets sent into the Indian Ocean were advised that destroying Portuguese assets was more important than making a profit; and, for some time, the Dutch, and to a lesser extent the English, only went where the Portuguese had been before. Their own initiatives and innovations were small-scale: the Dutch colony at the Cape of Good Hope, founded in 1652, still only had 1,200 white settlers by 1700; the English forts in India, at the same time, were manned by less than 2,000 whites. To the Mughal emperors, the Europeans must have seemed like mere fleas on the Indian elephant, even in 1750. And to the rulers of China and Japan they were scarcely even that. The Europeans may have become undisputed rulers of the seas around the other continents, but until the middle of the eighteenth century only in the New World had they acquired any significant territorial power.

The English East India Company was created in 1600 for the monopoly of trade with the East. After losing the East Indies to the Dutch, its energies were virtually limited to the Indian textile trade. By the middle of the 18th century, with British conquests in Bengal (chapter 19), its position in the sub-continent became impregnable. The Company's intervention in Indian politics upon the disintegration of the Mughal empire laid a firm foundation for the gradual absorption of Indian states within the British empire. Company traders and administrators, nicknamed 'nabobs', lived well, and the attractions of a colonial career were considerable. Johan Zoffany's elegant portrait of about 1780 *above* shows an English merchant in Calcutta, immaculate in wig and waistcoat despite the heat, pausing at his desk to give instruction to an Indian factor while a bearer looks respectfully on.

The Mughal emperor Jehangir (1605-27) *right* is shown in an allegorical study as a haggard and resigned old man, offering a book (perhaps symbolizing his life) to a Muslim holy man. Jehangir's generally just and tolerant reign carried within it the seeds of later Indian decline: he was the first Mughal emperor to receive trade emissaries from England, but his main energies were spent pursuing internal campaigns in Rajputana and the Deccan. Here he sits upon an hour-glass throne from which, although inscribed with the wish that he should live a thousand years, the sands of time have almost run out. His thoughts seem fixed on the next world, and he ignores the attentions of the Ottoman Sultan (perhaps copied from a European print), of James I of England (certainly taken from an English miniature), and even of the artist himself.

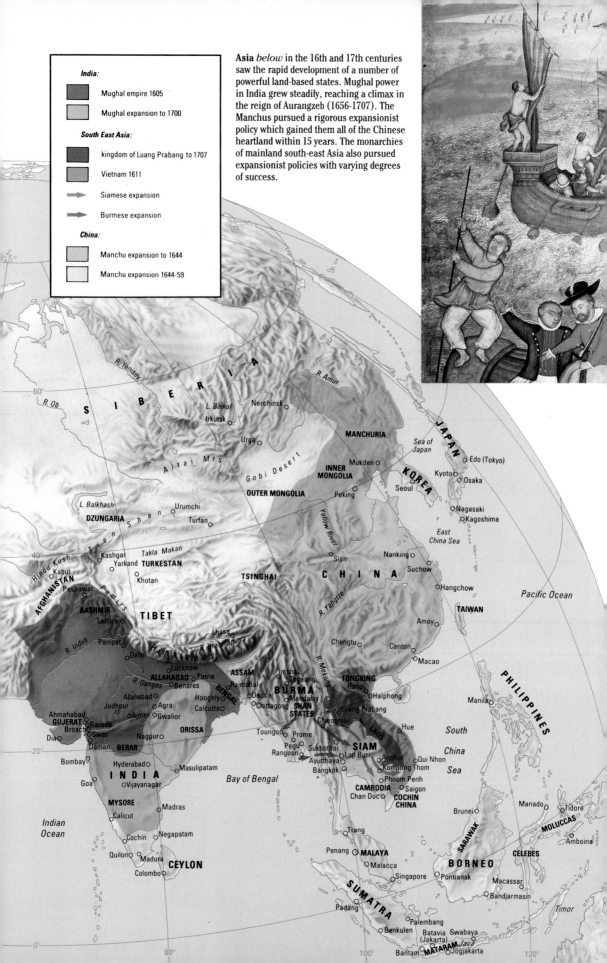

India:

Mughal empire 1605

Mughal expansion to 1700

South East Asia:

kingdom of Luang Prabang to 1707

Vietnam 1611

Siamese expansion

Burmese expansion

China:

Manchu expansion to 1644

Manchu expansion 1644-59

Asia *below* in the 16th and 17th centuries saw the rapid development of a number of powerful land-based states. Mughal power in India grew steadily, reaching a climax in the reign of Aurangzeb (1656-1707). The Manchus pursued a rigorous expansionist policy which gained them all of the Chinese heartland within 15 years. The monarchies of mainland south-east Asia also pursued expansionist policies with varying degrees of success.

R. Yenisey

R. Ob

S I B E R I A

R. Amur

L. Baikal

Nerchinsk

Irkutsk

Urga

MANCHURIA

Sea of Japan

JAPAN

Edo (Tokyo)

Mukden

Kyoto

Osaka

INNER MONGOLIA

OUTER MONGOLIA

Peking

Seoul

KOREA

Nagasaki

Kagoshima

Altai Mts

Gobi Desert

L. Balkhash

Urumchi

Turfan

DZUNGARIA

Tien Shan

Yellow River

East China Sea

Kashgar

Takla Makan

TURKESTAN

Yarkand

Khotan

TSINGHAI

Sian

Nanking

C H I N A

Suchow

Hindu Kush

Kabul

Peshawar

AFGHANISTAN

Pamirs

KASHMIR

Lahore

TIBET

Lhasa

R. Brahmaputra

Hangchow

Pacific Ocean

R. Yangtze

TAIWAN

Amoy

R. Indus

Panipat

Himalayas

Delhi

Lucknow

Chengtu

Canton

Macao

R. Ganges

Patna

ALLAHABAD

Benares

ASSAM

Rajmahal

Imphal

Tagaung

R. Mekong

TONGKING

Hanoi

Allahabad

Dacca

BENGAL

BURMA

Mandalay

Haiphong

Ahmahabad

GUJERAT

Baroda

Jodhpur

Ajmer

Agra

Gwalior

Hooghly

Calcutta

Chittagong

SHAN STATES

Luang Prabang

PHILIPPINES

Manila

Diu

Broach

Swat

Nagpur

ORISSA

Chiengmai

LAOS

Hue

Daman

BERAR

Toungoo

Prome

Pegu

Sukhothai

SIAM

Angkor

Qui Nhon

South China Sea

Bombay

Hyderabad

Masulipatam

Rangoon

Ayutthaya

Lop Buri

Kompong Thom

Bangkok

Goa

I N D I A

Vijayanagar

Phnom Penh

Saigon

CAMBODIA

COCHIN CHINA

Manado

Tidore

MYSORE

Madras

Chan Doc

Brunei

MOLUCCAS

Indian Ocean

Calicut

Bay of Bengal

Amboina

Cochin

Negapatam

Trang

SARAWAK

CELEBES

Quilon

Madura

CEYLON

Penang

MALAYA

BORNEO

Macassar

Colombo

Malacca

Singapore

Pontianak

Bandjarmasin

S U M A T R A

Timor

Padang

Palembang

Benkulen

Batavia

Swabaya

Bantam

MATARAM

Java

Jogjakarta

CHAPTER 19

ASIA 1600–1800

The appearance of European ships and traders at Asian ports caused little comment. Although Portuguese mercenaries found work in south-east Asia, Europeans were largely seen as outsiders, exotic curiosities at best. The 16th-century Mughal miniature *above* shows a Portuguese square-rigger and its crew with clinical detail. In the Japanese screen *below* foreigners are caricatured as they pay homage to the local dignatory.

If, for some reason, in the year 1750 all the European bases east of the Cape of Good Hope had been closed down, and their white populations withdrawn, Asia would scarcely have noticed. For the largest of the continents was home to some 70 percent of the world's population and, in the mid-eighteenth century, there were some 150 million Chinese and about as many Indians, as against no more than 80 million Europeans, of whom only 20,000 were scattered around the shores of south Asia at any one time. Asia also boasted levels of production and prosperity that astonished the Europeans. For the Portuguese poet Luis de Camões in 1572, India was 'the land of wealth abounding'; for the Italian political writer Giovanni Botero in 1589, 'there is no kingdom that is either greater, or more populous, or more rich, or more abundant in all good things' than China; and for the Jesuit missionaries who followed St Francis Xavier's trail to the Far East, Japan was 'the land of the gods', the probable site of paradise.

This praise was not unwarranted. Although it is very difficult to 'measure' the economic output of early modern Asia, since reliable statistics on production were rarely kept, every scrap of information that comes to light confirms a far greater scale of enterprise and profit in the East than in the West. Thus Japan, in the second half of the seventeenth century, was the world's leading exporter of silver and

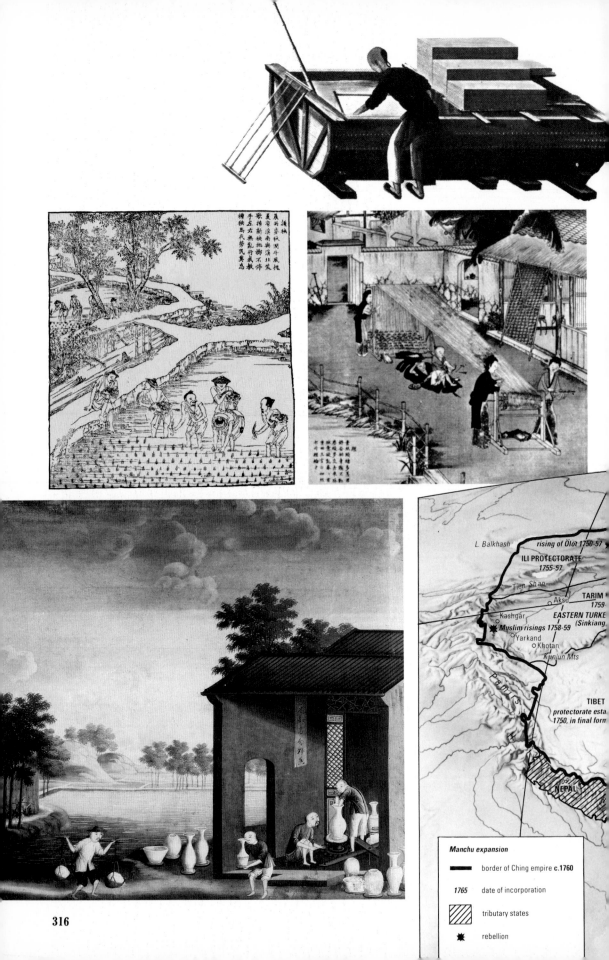

Manchu expansion

▬▬▬ border of Ching empire c.1760

1765 date of incorporation

▨▨▨ tributary states

✺ rebellion

Ch'ing imperial expansion *below* continued on a vast scale until the mid-18th century, although only a small part of these territories was settled or incorporated under Chinese administration. The campaigns were an immensely expensive attempt to stem Russian incursions in the north and British expansion in India. In the late 18th and early 19th centuries widespread peasant rebellions broke out, usually in areas affected by the economic problems arising from population pressure. The vast power of Ch'ing China rested upon her sophisticated economy. Laborious wet-rice cultivation *centre left* in some areas yielded crops of 50 grains for each one sown. Silk-weaving *centre right*, was also labour-intensive and employed large numbers of workers (especially women). So did the manufacture of 'China' pottery *lower left*. In numerous small workshops of western and central China, tens of thousands of craftsmen turned special clays into elegant vases and pots for both domestic use and export. By contrast, paper-making *top* required relatively few workers, but a good deal of expensive equipment. At the time these pictures were made (1650-1750) Chinese production of all four leading commodities far exceeded that of Europe.

copper, her 55,000 miners surpassing the output of Peru for the former and of Sweden for the latter. But most of it was exported to other parts of Asia. Although Western sources tend to stress the role of the eight or so Dutch ships which docked in Japan each year, in fact the eighty or so junks from China were far more important. It was the same in south-east Asia: the Europeans may have traded widely in the area, but their ships were normally outnumbered ten-to-one by Chinese vessels; and the Europeans' cargoes consisted, in the main, not of Western wares but of Chinese porcelain and silk.

The output of both commodities was stunning. In Nanking alone, the ceramic factories produced a million pieces of fine glazed pottery every year, much of it specifically designed for export – those for Europe bore appropriate dynastic motifs, while those for Islamic countries displayed tasteful abstract patterns. The output of textiles, which is far harder to measure, was also enormous. In India, the city of Kasimbazar in Bengal produced, just by itself, over 2 million pounds of raw silk annually during the 1680s, while the cotton weavers of Gujerat in the west turned out almost 3 million pieces a year for export alone. By way of comparison, the annual export of silk from Messina – which handled most of the output of Sicily, Europe's foremost silk producer – was a mere 250,000 pounds in the 1680s, while the largest textile enterprise in continental Europe, the Leiden 'new drapery', produced less than 100,000 pieces of cloth per year. Asia, not Europe, was the centre of world industry throughout early modern times. It was likewise the home of the greatest states. The most powerful monarchs of their day were not Louis XIV or Peter the Great, but the Manchu emperor K'ang-hsi (1662-1722) and the 'Great Mogul' Aurangzeb (1658-1707).

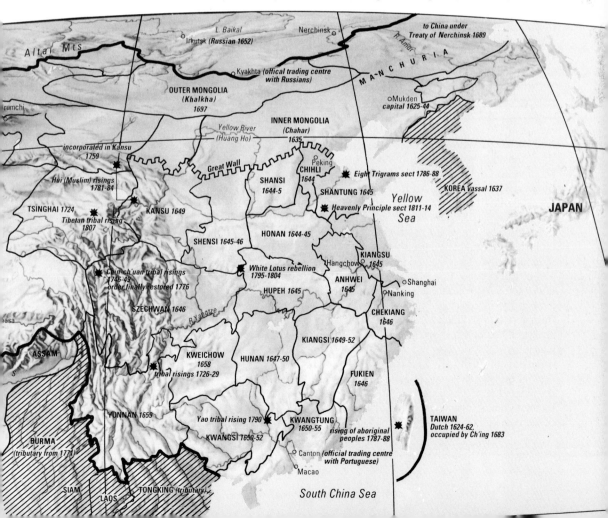

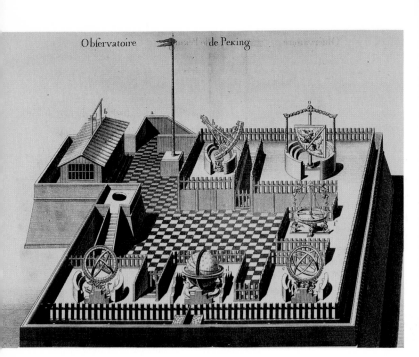

Obfervatoire de Peking

The fall of Peking in 1644, first to a rebel army and then to the forces of the Manchus (chapter 13), established a new imperial dynasty: the Ch'ing. But although their authority was quickly extended to almost the whole of China, supporters of the Ming held out on offshore islands for some years, and in 1674, before the last of them had been defeated, a major rebellion by three of the new dynasty's most powerful Chinese subjects broke out in Szechwan. The 'revolt of the three feudatories' continued until 1681. The last Ming loyalists finally surrendered two years later.

Now, at last, the empire entered a prolonged period of peace and relative prosperity, during which the Chinese population more than doubled. The growth from perhaps 130 million in 1580 to about 150 million in 1700 was modest; but during the eighteenth century the total rose rapidly to some 320 million. True, some of the increase was due to the acquisition of new territories, for the campaigns of K'ang-hsi and his grandson Ch'ien Lung (1736-95) extended Chinese authority far to the west: Outer Mongolia was annexed in 1697; Tibet and Turkestan in the 1750s. But the bulk of the population resided in the heartland of the empire, and particularly in the Yangtze river valley, where all available land was now under intensive cultivation. The introduction of new crops helped to increase productivity, but the most important harvest in almost all areas remained that of the staple food: rice. And by the end of the century, it was clear that not enough rice was being produced to feed the increasing population. Food shortages became common in the more remote upland areas, where yields were lower and transport more difficult. Social tensions increased as more people struggled for food resources: peasant revolts led by dissident gentry, which had always been common in Chinese history, now became more widespread. Eventually, in 1795, in the mountains of Szechwan, a general uprising began, led by the millenarian Buddhist sect known as the 'White Lotus'. It was only suppressed, after great effort, in 1804; and by then Chinese scholars were already beginning to prophesy the end of the dynastic cycle of the Ch'ing.

Part of the problem in coping with this rebellion was a marked deterioration in the calibre of Chinese government. Land tax was fixed:

The Peking observatory in the Imperial Palace was founded by Kublai Khan in the 13th century. Although it was maintained by the Ming emperors, their Chinese and Muslim astronomers lacked instruments accurate enough to predict important celestial events correctly. But the Jesuit missionaries who came to China in the 17th century *above right* — Matteo Ricci, Ferdinand Verbiest and (in the centre) Johan Adam Schall von Bell — quickly proved their superior skills. Although the fall of the Ming seemed for a moment to threaten their position in Peking, Schall predicted to the minute the solar eclipse of 1 September 1644 and was rewarded with control of the imperial observatory *above left*, which he filled with Western globes and instruments.

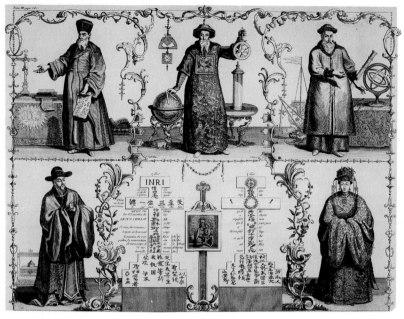

The Jesuits' influence in the imperial government of China remained confined to astronomy. The administration was firmly in the hands of the Confucian-trained bureaucracy, and culture was dominated by Confucian scholars, like the three portrayed *above*. Later attempts by the Europeans to challenge Confucian views about the outside world, such as the British embassy led to Peking by Lord Macartney in 1793 *below*, were firmly rejected. The tapestry portraying the mission's arrival is an unconscious illustration of the Chinese world-view, for it shows George III's envoys dressed like Elizabethan courtiers: it was composed from earlier pictures, not from life — no doubt because the artists wished to spare themselves any risk of contamination should they encounter the 'red-haired barbarians' in person.

it did not rise with the growth of population and, besides, money went increasingly either into the pockets of the landholding gentry or to finance westward expansion. There was still a numerous bureaucracy, which was staffed by gentry who had passed examinations in Confucian morals and deportment, but it failed to increase in step with the population. Traditional Confucianism was of little use, in any case, in coping with the difficulties of the peasant economy and the inadequacy of the food supply. The great public works – the grand canals and the major roads – were not maintained.

There is little evidence, however, that the mandarins themselves were aware of any of these basic shortcomings. Precisely as European intellectuals were becoming more flexible in their thought, and less opposed to novelty, their Chinese counterparts became more rigid and resistant to change, especially if it were suggested by outsiders. There was, it is true, a small Jesuit mission in Peking from 1601, which purveyed some Western knowledge to the Chinese court – clock- and map-making, gun-founding and clavichord-playing – but these skills remained peripheral to Chinese tradition. The only important contribution made by the Westerners was the adjustment of the Chinese calendar, thanks to the greater accuracy of their astronomical observations. The German Jesuit, Johann Adam Schall von Bell, even became Director of the Imperial Board of Astronomy in 1644, though to do so he had to adopt Chinese costume and customs.

In other respects, however, the Confucian élite of China was not interested in new ideas – wherever they might originate. Nor were they much interested in trade. They were content to permit the export of porcelain, silk and tea; but in return they would only accept bullion – silver from the Western traders and gold from the Russians. Although, following the treaty of Nerchinsk in 1689 (the first bilateral agreement ever signed by the court of Peking), Russians were allowed to trade freely in China, other Westerners were not. The precarious colony of the Portuguese in Macao, at the mouth of the Pearl river, was tolerated, and other nations were eventually allowed to sail up-river to Canton; but no direct commerce was permitted beyond. The imperial court persisted in regarding Western missions sent to negotiate trading concessions as embassies bearing gifts and homage from subject rulers. As late as 1793 the emperor Ch'ien Lung insisted on regarding Lord Macartney, the envoy of George III, as 'the ambassador bearing tribute from the king of England'; and the British diplomats were crestfallen at the 'coldness and indifference with which the court received our discoveries' – which included surgical knowledge, weaving techniques, a hot-air balloon and a battery of horse artillery.

But the Europeans never gave up. Their desire for Chinese goods, and especially tea – which quickly became the national drink in Russia as well as in Britain – was insatiable. And yet they were frustrated at every turn by the refusal of the mandarins of Canton to accept any 'trade goods' from the West except silver. In the late eighteenth century, an alternative was found at last: opium. Copious quantities of the drug were produced in southern Asia, and a demand for its narcotic and medicinal properties was carefully fostered among the Chinese who were in contact with the Europeans. Some Chinese coastal merchants and corrupt officials were only too eager to smooth the path for this illicit and damaging trade so that, by the 1820s, some 5,000 chests of opium were being annually landed at Canton, in spite of repeated imperial prohibitions. Inevitably, the inflow of silver dwindled, putting further pressure on the depleted imperial treasury. The stage was now set for a major confrontation between China and the Europeans on the

The Europeans first came to Japan in 1543 not only to trade but also to spread Christianity. After 50 years, trade was brisk and converts numbered about 300,000. But then the Japanese government, seeing the new Western faith as a challenge to its own absolute demands on its subjects, forbade the practice of Christianity and began to execute missionaries. In 1597, at Nagasaki, 6 European and 20 Japanese Christians were crucified *below*. But trade was allowed to continue. Although the Portuguese and the Spaniards were expelled, the Dutch were allowed to remain. Their base on the island of Deshima, just off Nagasaki, was an object of curiosity to their Japanese neighbours, who noted with amusement *right* the curious dress of the visitors, as well as their odd habits, such as playing billiards. There were, during the 17th century, perhaps 150 Dutch people at Deshima, but as trade with Japan began to decline in the 18th century, this total fell dramatically. By the 1780s, there were sometimes no more than 4 or 5 Dutchmen on the island.

issue of free trade – a confrontation which the greatest empire in the world, overpopulated and restless, was about to lose.

The internal history of Japan in the seventeenth and eighteenth centuries followed a very different course. After the fall of the last stronghold opposed to the rule of the Tokugawa *shogun* Ieyasu in 1615 (chapter 13), Japan enjoyed over two centuries without war. During this almost unparalleled period of peace, the area of farmland under cultivation doubled in size, its production of rice quadrupled, and the number of inhabitants trebled. But the burdens on this growing population remained extremely heavy, and peasant revolts became numerous. Yet the slightest deviation from total obedience to the orders of all superiors was punished with instant death. After the 1590s, for example, the government issued a series of edicts forbidding Christianity. The Europeans' faith was not only perceived as alien by Japan's rulers: the *shoguns* were also alarmed by the fact that Christianity had been adopted as a badge of independence by some of the great lords of the coastal regions and their dependents. Missionaries were captured and executed (often by crucifixion), and converts were tortured until they either recanted or died. Partly to prevent any encouragement of the banned faith, and partly to prevent the coastal lords becoming too rich from trade, contacts between Japan and the Europeans were kept thereafter to a strict minimum. From 1639 until 1853, only the Dutch were allowed to reside in Japan, and for most of that time even they were strictly confined to their small factory at Deshima in Nagasaki bay. Practically the only sight that ordinary Japanese had of a European was when the Dutch factor and his staff were required to travel to the *shogun's* court in order to pay homage in a humiliating public ceremony. Only the high profits of the Japan trade reconciled the Dutch East India Company to this arrangement.

Profits from the Japan trade were massive: between twenty-five and thirty tons of silver bullion were exported from Japan every year. Much of it was directed towards China, where it was used to purchase raw silk – the one major commodity which the Japanese seemed unable to produce for themselves, despite their almost insatiable demand for it. The manufacture of magnificent silk kimonos and other fabrics,

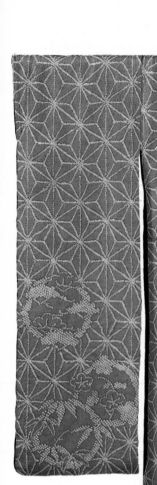

however, was entirely in Japanese hands and, by 1700, some 70,000 silk weavers were active in Kyoto alone. The government tried hard to confine the wearing of silk kimonos to the *samurai*, or warrior class, but still the habit spread, encouraged inadvertently by one of the government's own initiatives. The *shoguns* insisted that all feudal lords should spend every other year in residence at their capital, Edo (later renamed Tokyo); and that all important *samurai*, in their turn, should spend long periods living at the capital of their lord. These feudal centres were usually castle-towns, centred around a vast defensive fortification; now, residential quarters were added outside the walls, where merchants, craftsmen and shopkeepers could cater for the needs of the wealthy visitors. By 1800, as much as 20 percent of Japan's

Exquisite silk kimonos *above left* have been woven in Japan for centuries and handed down within the same family for generations. But the silk was almost all imported from China, either through Nagasaki or through Tsushima, in vast quantities. Throughout the 17th century some 200 tons of white raw silk were imported into Japan each and every year.

population lived in towns. Edo, which had been little more than a fishing village in 1600, boasted half-a-million inhabitants two centuries later. Even the countryside participated a little in the new prosperity. After 1650, when the rate of population growth began to slow down, some farmers were able to profit from supplying food to the new towns.

In time, many of these townspeople grew extremely wealthy from providing goods and services to the lords and *samurai,* and they began to imitate the lavish life-style of their social superiors. At first the *shoguns* tried to prohibit this; but after the 1650s a brilliant 'alternative culture' grew up, where the rich commoners could satisfy their vanity. It was known disparagingly as 'the floating world' – that is, a world where people could float thoughtlessly on a sea of pleasure – and it

The city of Kyoto, founded in AD 794 as the new imperial capital of Japan, still bustled with commerce and industry under the Tokugawa shogunate. The anonymous painted screen, c.1700, *above* shows noblemen and warriors parading in the city's rectilinear streets during the Gion festival; this began as a procession seeking deliverance from the plague in the 9th century and is still celebrated in Kyoto's Gion district every July.

was to be found in a special quarter of all the major cities. Restaurants, theatres, massage-parlours and brothels sprang up, where wealth could be displayed in any way its owner chose. But not all the prosperity of the middle class was dissipated in entertainment: there was also a lively book-trade and a heavy investment in education – by 1850 it has been estimated that 40 percent of all Japanese males could read (a figure that few European societies of the day could match). And some of the literature was by then Western in origin. In Nagasaki, a group of interpreters and scholars acquired Dutch books from the factory at Deshima and translated them into Japanese. The country may still have lacked the power-driven machines and scientific knowledge of the West, but it possessed superbly skilled craftsmen, an efficient financial and commercial system, and a moderate degree of prosperity in town and country, sufficient to respond successfully to the challenge of Westernization when it came in 1853, with the arrival of an American naval squadron determined to 'open' Japan to Western trade.

The islands of South-East Asia came under Western domination far earlier than the mainland. There were two separate reasons for this. Some islands, most notably Taiwan and the Philippines, were relatively

'**Ships trading in the East**' was one of several paintings commissioned by the Dutch East India Company in the early 17th century from the marine artist Hendrick Cornelisz Vroom. Here, European traders on a jetty admire from beneath their parasols the huge East Indiamen riding at anchor. One, flying a tricolour at the mainmast, is Dutch; another, flying the St. George's cross, is English. The picture was painted in 1614, during the brief period when the English and Dutch Companies were prepared to co-operate in Asian waters. The Asiatic landscape is completely imaginary.

Kabuki, *right* a highly stylized and melodramatic form of theatre, was created to entertain the emerging middle class of Japan's cities from the 17th century onwards. Many of the plots were devised specifically for their audience, showing clever commoners outwitting their wicked, stupid and vain social superiors — the *samurai* — either in love or in combat.

Tokugawa Ieyasu (1542-1616) *below right* founded a dynasty of *shoguns* early in the 17th century which ruled until 1868. He was cautious and patient in the pursuit of his political aims and built upon the progress made by his predecessors, Oda Nobunaga and Toyotomi Hideyoshi, in bringing Japan under a single authority. As a Japanese proverb puts it: 'Nobunaga made the cake, Hideyoshi baked it, but Ieyasu ate it'. This portrait is executed in the traditional Japanese style, with a stiff pose and drapery, but a realistic face.

underdeveloped and could offer no resistance to more organized invaders who were determined to settle (chapter 18). But neither Taiwan
nor the Philippines had much to offer the Europeans except the labour
and tribute of their people; they produced no spices. The islands of the
Indonesian archipelago, however, were entirely different. Almost all the
spices desired by the Europeans – pepper, cloves, nutmeg and so on –
grew there in profusion, but their production was controlled by powerful Muslim states. The Europeans therefore established western-style
walled cities in the tropics at strategic places – the Portuguese at
Malacca in 1511 (until the Dutch took it in 1641); the Dutch at Batavia
in 1619 – from which the garrisons of outlying forts and factories could
be supported, and a powerful fleet for trade and war maintained. These
were not, until the late eighteenth century, territorial empires, but
rather commercial networks, their power resting less upon the troops
in the forts than upon the guns of the fleets. From the quarterdecks of
their elegant East Indiamen, the Europeans may not have been able to
wield power effectively inland, but they could certainly prevent anyone
else from doing so.

**The arrival of Commodore Matthew C.
Perry** of the US Navy in 1853 *above*
confronted Tokugawa Japan with the
Western world after over 200 years of
relative seclusion. The American squadron
came to Tokyo Bay, instead of to Nagasaki
(the only port where foreign trade was
permitted) and demanded the right to free
commerce. Perry's four warships, clearly
visible in this contemporary painting, made
refusal virtually impossible.

**The Muslim Mughal dynasty (from
1526)** in India fostered a great flowering of
Indian civilization, particularly in painting
and architecture. In this miniature
painting Shahjahan, the builder of the Taj
Mahal, is being weighed against gold,
silver and other precious metal on his 16th
birthday, in 1607. The balance was
distributed to the fakirs and the needy.

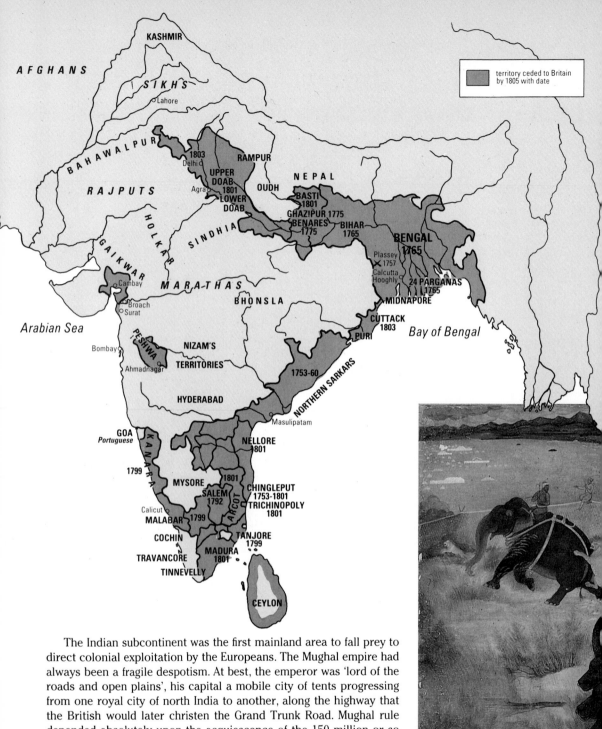

The Indian subcontinent was the first mainland area to fall prey to direct colonial exploitation by the Europeans. The Mughal empire had always been a fragile despotism. At best, the emperor was 'lord of the roads and open plains', his capital a mobile city of tents progressing from one royal city of north India to another, along the highway that the British would later christen the Grand Trunk Road. Mughal rule depended absolutely upon the acquiescence of the 150 million or so Hindu peasant farmers and petty landlords who paid the emperor's military commanders a tax on agricultural produce in silver rupees. It was a delicate balance: if the peasants and landlords were overtaxed, they would revolt; and if the grandees were not rewarded with office and wealth, they would desert the court.

In the later seventeenth century, the emperor Aurangzeb pushed his armies to the south, swallowing up the remaining independent Muslim states, but intensifying the fiscal pressure on his Hindu vassals in order to pay for this increase in his empire. It could not last. After Aurangzeb's death in 1707 the powerful Muslim governors of the provinces of Oudh, Hyderabad, Bengal and the Carnatic gradually became

Aurangzeb, son of Shahjahan, was an avid hunter. In 1670 *below* he is shown, accompanied by one of his sons and some court officials, in the *howdah* of an elephant, hunting lions, preceded by beaters mounted on buffaloes. Aurangzeb was the last Mughal ruler to wield absolute power. Infiltration by the European powers (here he is armed with a Western matchlock) and confrontation with the Hindu Maratha states led to a rapid disintegration of centralized authority after Aurangzeb's death. For a while the Marathas seemed poised to succeed the Mughals, but defeat by the Afghans and the growing power of the British in Bengal and on the eastern seaboard *left* effectively contained them.

independent of the emperor in Delhi, while revolts by the Sikhs in the Punjab and incursions by the Hindu Marathas from western India sapped the empire's strength. Then, in 1739 Nadir Shah, ruler of Iran, descended across the Hindu Kush, defeated the Mughals and slaughtered 30,000 people on the streets of Delhi. Even the Peacock Throne of the emperors was carried off to Persia. The Mughal emperors lingered on until 1857, but real power now resided in the provinces and localities.

A graver threat, however, lurked in the wings. Wishing to protect their commerce from the demands of the new regional rulers, the British merchants gathered in the trading towns of Calcutta, Madras and Surat gradually penetrated and suborned the courts of the new Indian states which emerged out of the wreck of Mughal rule. In the south, the British supported Mohammed Ali Wallajah against his French-backed rivals in the wars of 1739-60 in the Carnatic. Dependent on the British for military and naval support, he quickly fell in debt to his European architects, soldiers and doctors. They all made enormous fortunes from his troubles.

A greater prize still was the flourishing eastern province of Bengal. Here in 1757 Robert Clive, son of a petty squire from Shropshire, staged a momentous coup against the local viceroy of the Mughal empire, now effectively an independent ruler. Nawab Siraj-ud Daulah, enraged by the pretensions of the British merchants, had captured the city of Calcutta the previous year, and imprisoned all the European residents

he could find in a storeroom of the fort, later called the 'Black Hole', where many died of suffocation. The British retook Calcutta easily enough. But then Clive went on to bribe a number of the nawab's supporters, including his military commander Mir Jafar, and furthermore obtained the support of Bengal's great indigenous financiers, the Jagat Seth. On 23 June 1757, at the battle of Plassey, a small British force, assisted by the nawab's enemies, prevailed over their adversaries. Siraj-ud Daulah was captured and executed; Mir Jafar replaced him. But only at a price: Clive secured for the East India Company the income from the land-tax of all Bengal, worth perhaps £2 million a year. In addition the European adventurers were loaded with personal presents, indemnities and perquisites valued at £3 million. Clive later declared, 'I stood astonished at my own moderation'.

Although the fortunes made by Clive and his friends attracted great attention (most of it unfavourable), the 'Bengal settlement' was the real jewel: with the taxes of that vast province, the East India Company was able to support an army capable of intervening in any part of the subcontinent and, eventually, beyond. In 1740, the British forces in India still totalled less than 2000 men; but by 1782, they stood at 115,000. Of course they were not all British. Instead, the officers of the East India Company managed to train native Indian troops, known as sepoys, to fight in the European manner: they were drilled exhaustively in the use of the musket, disciplined to fire their weapons in volleys, and taught to reload while the other ranks fired in turn. By the end of the century, these tactics had proved so successful that independent Indian princes began to copy them. But it was too late: the sepoys were better trained, and they served a political authority unaffected by internal revolt and debilitating faction. They were bound to prevail. In the 1790s, the last independent ruler of the south, Tipu Sultan of Mysore,

was crushed; in the 1800s it was the turn of the Marathas of the central Deccan. With their final defeat, in 1806, almost all the wealth and the military manpower of the vast subcontinent lay in European hands. It was not long before they were used to open up the other realms of Asia to Western influence: first Burma, then Malaya, and finally China. The combination of European industrial technology with Indian troops and taxes was to prove irresistible.

So, almost inevitably, Asia finally entered the era of European domination. Yet it is important to remember that European power rested not only on military force but also on the support and compliance of important bodies of Asians – soldiers, merchants and administrators. Asia was bowed but not prone. It should not be forgotten that, in the later nineteenth century, it was from among those Asians working closest to the colonial rulers that the first generation of nationalists was to come.

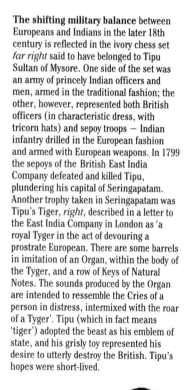

The shifting military balance between Europeans and Indians in the later 18th century is reflected in the ivory chess set *far right* said to have belonged to Tipu Sultan of Mysore. One side of the set was an army of princely Indian officers and men, armed in the traditional fashion; the other, however, represented both British officers (in characteristic dress, with tricorn hats) and sepoy troops – Indian infantry drilled in the European fashion and armed with European weapons. In 1799 the sepoys of the British East India Company defeated and killed Tipu, plundering his capital of Seringapatam. Another trophy taken in Seringapatam was Tipu's Tiger, *right*, described in a letter to the East India Company in London as 'a royal Tyger in the act of devouring a prostrate European. There are some barrels in imitation of an Organ, within the body of the Tyger, and a row of Keys of Natural Notes. The sounds produced by the Organ are intended to ressemble the Cries of a person in distress, intermixed with the roar of a Tyger'. Tipu (which in fact means 'tiger') adopted the beast as his emblem of state, and his grisly toy represented his desire to utterly destroy the British. Tipu's hopes were short-lived.

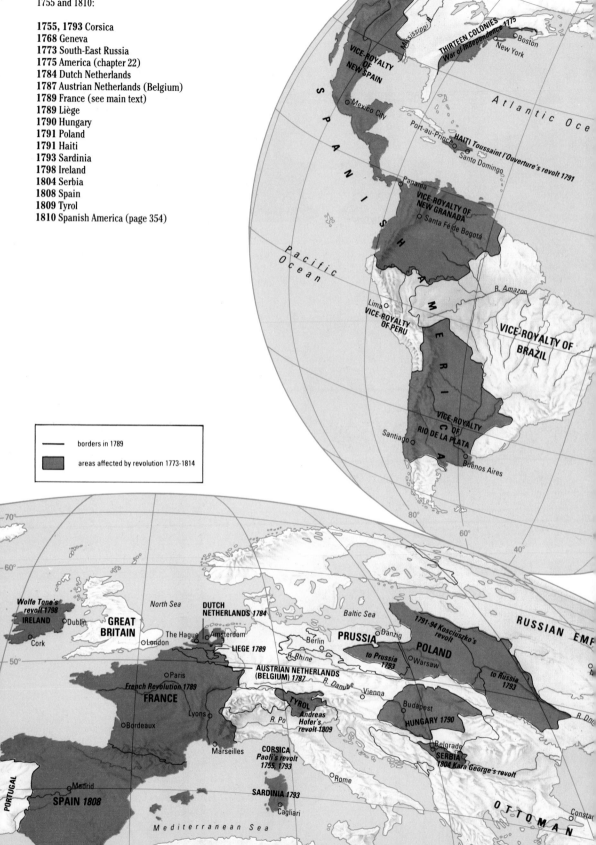

The late 18th century was a time of upheaval in many parts ot the western hemisphere *below*. Risings and rebellions took place in the following areas between 1755 and 1810:

1755, 1793 Corsica
1768 Geneva
1773 South-East Russia
1775 America (chapter 22)
1784 Dutch Netherlands
1787 Austrian Netherlands (Belgium)
1789 France (see main text)
1789 Liège
1790 Hungary
1791 Poland
1791 Haiti
1793 Sardinia
1798 Ireland
1804 Serbia
1808 Spain
1809 Tyrol
1810 Spanish America (page 354)

borders in 1789

areas affected by revolution 1773-1814

THIRTEEN COLONIES *1775*
War of Independence
Boston
New York

VICE-ROYALTY OF NEW SPAIN

Mexico City

Port-au-Prince
HAITI Toussaint l'Ouverture's revolt 1791
Santo Domingo

Panama

VICE-ROYALTY OF NEW GRANADA
Santa Fé de Bogotá

R. Amazon

Lima
VICE-ROYALTY OF PERU

VICE-ROYALTY OF BRAZIL

VICE-ROYALTY OF RIO DE LA PLATA
Santiago
Buenos Aires

Atlantic Oce

Pacific Ocean

S P A N I S H   A M E R I C A

80°
60°
40°

70°
60°
50°

Wolfe Tone's revolt 1798
IRELAND
Dublin
Cork

North Sea
GREAT BRITAIN
London

DUTCH NETHERLANDS *1784*
Amsterdam
The Hague
LIÈGE *1789*
R. Rhine
Berlin

Baltic Sea
Danzig
PRUSSIA

1791-94 Kosciuszko's revolt
POLAND
Warsaw
to Prussia 1793
to Russia 1793

RUSSIAN EMP

Paris
French Revolution 1789
FRANCE
Lyons
Bordeaux

AUSTRIAN NETHERLANDS (BELGIUM) *1787*
R. Danube
Vienna

TYROL Andreas Hofer's revolt 1809
R. Po

Budapest
HUNGARY *1790*
Belgrade
SERBIA *1804* Kara George's revolt

R. Dn

Marseilles
CORSICA Paoli's revolt 1755, 1793

Rome

PORTUGAL
Madrid
SPAIN *1808*

SARDINIA *1793*
Cagliari

Mediterranean Sea

OTTOMAN
Constan

10°
20°

THE AGE OF
REVOLUTIONS
1776–1848

The extraordinary prosperity of the 18th century was reflected in architecture. Even an unremarkable German ruler, like the Prince-Bishop of Würzburg, could afford patronage on a scale never equalled before or since. In 1750 the Prince-Bishop commissioned the leading Italian painter Tiepolo to paint the ceiling of this vast hall *below* – an explosion of colour and geometry which depicts 'the four continents'. Würzburg itself was only a sleepy German town; when similar techniques are applied in Catherine the Great's St. Petersburg, they produced the Winter Palace. But such ostentatious displays emphasized the anomalous position of a wealthy and powerful minority in an increasingly 'enlightened' age.

The eighteenth century was the great age of absolute monarchy in Europe. From their glittering courts and their splendid palaces, the sovereigns of this era seemed quite literally to be masters of all they surveyed; and, as if to celebrate the fact that their power rivalled that of the Roman emperors, they built their capitals on massive, neo-classical lines, and attracted to them the leading intellectuals of what became known as the 'Age of Enlightenment'. The Berlin of Frederick the Great, the St Petersburg of Catherine the Great, the Vienna of Joseph II could all boast a galaxy of native and foreign talent. Some became salaried courtiers, advisers or apologists, lending respectability to the arbitrary regimes they served, and enabling the rulers to call themselves 'the Enlightened Despots'.

Somewhat lower down the scale, the nobility also enjoyed, at this time, almost unprecedented wealth and power. They, too, built palaces that were often enormous, and they reigned over estates that seemed endless. One Hungarian nobleman, Prince Eszterhazy, was said to

possess more sheep than the king of England had subjects. But gone
were the days when these great noblemen would challenge the power
of the monarchies: now they served the crown as soldiers and bureaucrats, or concentrated on developing their own lands, often placing
heavy burdens on their tenants and subjects.

For this was the golden age of privilege – a word that itself means
'private law'. One was born into a particular place in society, tightly
circumscribed by its own rights and obligations, its own codes and
laws, which varied, sometimes quite bewilderingly, from place to place.
All over Europe, there were degrees of privilege. In France, Prussia and
Spain, for example, nobles were entirely exempt from direct taxation,
on the grounds that those who served their king in person should not
also have to serve him with their purse. In the Dutch Republic, however, most revenue was raised by indirect taxes which fell equally on
everyone; while in Great Britain the landowning classes voted, from
time to time, to tax themselves heavily in order to pay for their government's wars. There were also social differences between countries.
Thus French nobles were not expected to enter industry or trade: if
they did so, they forfeited their status. In Italy, on the other hand, many
nobles did little else – the Genoese aristocracy in 1785, for example,
had only 18 percent of their total assets in real property, as against 69
percent in business, loans, stocks and shares, and 13 percent in cash.

At the other end of the social scale, the status of those without
privilege also varied from country to country. In western Europe, many
of the burdens imposed on the peasants had disappeared. But in eastern Europe, the lot of the peasantry had deteriorated seriously since
the sixteenth century: in Russia, some peasant families had to provide
seven days' labour per week on their landlord's domain; in Brandenburg, all children of the unfree peasants (known as 'serfs') could be

Baroque civilization saw the world as
God's theatre: I act, therefore I am. The
static, ceremonial-bound world of the 17th
century was softened in the 18th century in
the work of Watteau (1684-1721) *above* into
an intelligent fantasy land.
Anyone from this world of strained
elegance knew that the peasant, in the
words of the Frenchman Boileau, was ' a
sort of animal' living in the fields and not
distinguishable from his own farmyard
animals. The popular print *right* shows,
however, the stirrings of social conscience.
The agricultural labourer is neither
picturesque nor romanticized but rather
'born to toil'.

compelled to work as unpaid servants for their lord for up to four years; in Hungary, there was in fact no limit to the services the lord could require of his peasants. By 1800, according to one observer, the landlords of eastern and central Europe had created 'the den of a predator which lays waste everything around it and surrounds itself with the silence of the grave'. This was a social order designed for a very stable, if not for a totally static, world. All criticism of the *status quo* was energetically silenced, either by the royal bureaucracy or by the church.

And yet, in spite of all the apparent stability, changes were underway. In the first place, the system had evolved in a modestly populated, essentially rural world; but, in the eighteenth century, for reasons that are still not entirely understood, the population of most European countries began to increase rapidly. There were, for example, 19 million Frenchmen in the 1690s, but 25 million in the 1780s – an overall growth of some 28 percent; and in some of the provinces of the north and east, the increase was between 100 and 200 percent. It was the same in Italy (where the total population rose during the eighteenth century from 13 million to almost 19 million), and elsewhere.

Not surprisingly, demographic growth on this scale was often difficult to absorb, even though there were sometimes innovations in agricultural technique which raised the productivity of many estates. A better use of fertilizers, improved rotation of crops, and new methods and technology in farming could increase harvests significantly. In England and Wales, wheat yields rose from around eleven bushels per acre in 1600 to roughly twenty in 1700 and to twenty-two by 1800. Other countries also managed to enhance their agricultural performance by cultivating other crops, above all the potato, which would grow on land too poor to support regular grain harvests and which

NE POUR LA PEINE

337

proved more resistant to climatic extremes. 'A year of scarcity is rare since potatoes were cultivated in such quantities,' wrote a Scottish observer in 1799; and the same was true of Ireland, Scandinavia and the Low Countries. Nevertheless, many parts of continental Europe still failed to produce enough to feed their entire population. In such areas, better transport often made it possible to import additional food supplies. Roads and canals snaked across lands which had previously been virtually impassable. But, in spite of all this, some communities still remained unable to support all their people, and many therefore took to the road in order to search for a living elsewhere, often in a town. This was important in two ways: on the one hand, it reduced rural overpopulation; on the other, it enabled towns to grow despite the high mortality rates that prevailed there. Thanks to sustained, high immigration, the size of many towns and cities more than doubled in the course of the eighteenth century, some of them reaching unprecedented levels: by 1800, Paris and London could each boast around one million inhabitants.

In the short run, these developments increased the power of Europe's rulers: there were now more volunteers to enlist in their armies and navies, and more subjects to pay taxes. But, as the process continued, it began to strain the structures of tradition, privilege and hierarchy. The first unmistakable signs of a new sort of tension between government and the governed appeared in the most advanced of the world's economies: Great Britain.

Formed by the legislative union of 1707 between England and Scotland, and including Ireland and the North American colonies, Britain was a hereditary monarchy, and the power of her monarchs – on paper at least – was formidable. In practice, however, that power was severely circumscribed. In 1649 Charles I, who had alienated his subjects, was publicly tried and executed (chapter 17); in 1688 his son, James II, was driven into exile when he, in turn, tried to enforce policies of which the

George III's attempt to re-establish royal authority was opposed not only by American colonists (chapter 22) but by many of his British subjects as well. In the 1760s his policies were openly criticized by John Wilkes (*below right*, engraved by Hogarth), editor of the satirical newspaper *The North Briton*. In 1763 an outspoken attack on the king and his government in issue 45 led to Wilkes's arrest and the newspaper's suppression; but popular opinion was so enraged that Wilkes was released and freedom of the press upheld. Satirical prints now multiplied. One of 1775 *right* shows the King's carriage driving over Magna Carta and the Constitution, while the coachman (Bute, George's First Minister, a Scotsman) bribes the onlookers, bishops look on in silence, and the American colonies burn.

The 17th-century European nobility continually had themselves painted except in Holland, where the 'rise of the middle classes' had actually happened, and pictures there became a middle-class matter. In 18th-century England, the spread of Dutch agricultural techniques meant that middle-class people, such as Gainsborough's Mr and Mrs Andrews *below*, could more profitably exploit land and spend money on having themselves recorded for posterity. The Andrews, painted here in the setting of their tidy estate, established their title to land by putting walls and hedges round their property – a novelty at the time.

majority of his subjects disapproved. Power was now effectively in the hands of the landowning aristocracy and gentry, and of the richer merchants, who controlled Parliament. When, in due course, George III (1760-1820) tried to reassert monarchical influence, especially his right to appoint ministers even if they lacked support in Parliament, he failed; similarly, his over-enthusiastic backing for the efforts of his ministers and Parliament to dictate to his American colonial subjects produced the first revolution of modern times (chapter 22).

The terms in which the American colonists proclaimed their cause could stand for every one of the upheavals that rocked Europe over the next two generations:

'We hold these truths to be self-evident, that all men are created equal; that they are endowed by their Creator with certain inalienable rights; that among these are life, liberty and the pursuit of happiness. To ensure these rights, governments were instituted among men, deriving their just powers from the consent of the governed.'

In Britain itself, these words struck many chords; yet there was no revolution. The British landed classes in Parliament were able to check any increase in monarchical power as well as to resist demands for a role in the political system from radicals such as John Wilkes; and the unified Common Law (in both England and Scotland) continued to guarantee the basic rights of property and personal inviolability against all comers, providing an appearance of equality in what was an essentially aristocratic system.

At the same time, Britain was fast becoming prosperous on a scale that no other European state could match. The population of the United Kingdom increased from 5 million in 1700 to more than 10 million a century later – a growth rate of roughly one percent per annum; while the

Textile manufacture was traditionally the work of women at home and, even after methods of mass-production were introduced in the 18th century, many stages in the process were still performed outside the factory. *The complete dictionary of arts and sciences*, published at London in 1764, for example, *below* showed how wool

The first industrial revolution harnessed the power of coal, water and steam to drive heavy machinery. At Coalbrookdale in Shropshire, *right* the coke-fired ironworks of Abraham Darby produced cheaper, better and more iron than elsewhere in Europe. Among the products manufactured here were the iron shells produced for the rotary steam-engine *below* developed in 1782 by James Watt. Although not an original idea, Watt produced a more efficient and economic design. By 1800, 200 steam pumps and 300 rotary engines had been constructed.

was washed, rinsed and dried before being sent to the factories for spinning and weaving. This mixture of machine and traditional artisan was very successful and English cloth dominated world markets. Intensive mechanization only occurred on a large scale in the mid-19th century.

gross national product, between 1760 and 1830, rose by an average of two percent per annum. This, of course, represented a substantial improvement in living standards from which, in spite of the markedly unequal distribution of national income, almost all social groups derived some benefit.

The main growth stemmed from Britain's increasing dominance of world trade and from the expansion of her domestic industry; and it took place above all in textiles (flannel, linen and later cotton from Lancashire; stockings from Nottingham; worsteds from Norfolk and Yorkshire), and in mining (especially coal and iron). The output of both industries increased spectacularly until, by the 1770s, 54 percent of Britain's exports were textiles and 44 percent were metals and other manufactured goods. The country had already become (in the contemporary phrase) 'the workshop of the world'. Thanks to her efficient agriculture, her comprehensive network of canals and roads, and her captive colonial markets in America and Asia, demand steadily rose and new, more efficient techniques of production were constantly found. Coke-smelting for iron (patented by Abraham Darby in 1709); Newcomen's steam-engine for drainage (1705; later adapted to other uses by James Watt); Hargreaves' 'spinning jenny' (capable of handling eighty spindles at once by 1784); Arkwright's water-powered spinning frame (used in his factory at Cromford in Derbyshire from 1771) – these were just some of the crucial innovations that enabled British manufacturers to increase their output while cutting their costs, usually associated with a concentration of production in a few large factories rather than in many small workshops: a process which has been termed the 'Industrial Revolution'.

Of course there was opposition to these changes in some quarters. In the Midlands and the north there were riots against the mechanization of industry and disorders caused by the social distress associated with

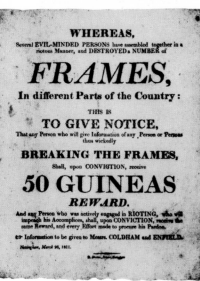

FRAMES,

In different Parts of the Country:

THIS IS

TO GIVE NOTICE,

That any Person who will give Information of any Person or Persons thus wickedly

BREAKING THE FRAMES,

Shall, upon CONVICTION, receive

50 GUINEAS

REWARD.

And any Person who was actively engaged in RIOTING, who will impeach his Accomplices, shall, upon CONVICTION, receive the same Reward, and every Effort made to procure his Pardon.

☞ Information to be given to Messrs. COLDHAM and ENFIELD.

Nottingham, March 26, 1811.

Mass production of goods by machines may have lowered prices, but they also, in the first instance, reduced jobs. Several hundred textile knitting-frames were smashed in English Midland towns, such as Nottingham, by rioters calling themselves 'Luddites'. Rewards were offered to those who betrayed the Luddites *above*, but to little avail. First troops were brought in and then, in 1812, an Act of Parliament made machine-breaking a capital offence.

industrialization; elsewhere, disturbances and demonstrations were prompted by the lack of political representation for the new middle classes. Perhaps the most dangerous time for the traditional ruling élite came in the 1810s, when social unrest among the new industrial workers coincided with these middle-class political demands. But in 1832, the 'Great Reform Act' damped down the middle-class political agitation by redistributing many Parliamentary seats to the new industrial centres and doubling the number of men entitled to vote. The landowners had agreed to share power with the representatives of industry and commerce; and, although subsequent working-class pressure for universal suffrage, annual elections and equal electoral districts (the Chartist movement) won enormous popular support between 1838 and 1848, it produced no practical concessions and no revolution. As the enlightened conservative, Edmund Burke, had said some years before, in Britain 'We go from light to light: we compromise, we reconcile, we balance'.

It was quite different in France. Her kings had been the most splendid in Europe for over a century, and Louis XIV (chapter 17) had set the standards of absolute monarchy by which other rulers measured themselves. His successor Louis XV (1715-74) was less successful, however. Although the splendour of his Court remained undimmed and his manipulation of absolute power was unchecked, most of his foreign policy initiatives failed. Above all, he found himself fighting unsuccessfully against Britain in 1740-48 (the 'War of the Austrian Succession') and in 1756-63 (the 'Seven Years' War'): two bitter conflicts that were waged in the European colonies as well as in Europe, and resulted in the loss of France's empire both in India and in North America.

The humiliation of these defeats was only partially redressed by France's successful support for the American Revolution between 1778 and 1783: for the independence of the former English colonies did nothing to restore those lost by France in 1763 (chapter 22). Still less

Le DEFECIT

The bankruptcy of the French government in the 18th century was known to all Europe. In the cartoon of 1788 *left*, with captions in execrable French, the English satirist Isaac Cruikshank celebrated Louis XVI's recall of the finance minister he had dismissed 7 years previously. 'M.Necker', the portly king complains, as he eyes the empty chest, 'there's no money there'. 'But I know I left some ....' replies Necker. Nevertheless, Louis XVI – as in the official portrait by J.S. Duplessis *above* – continued to think of himself as the Vicar of God, after the style of Louis XIV.

did it help to solve the pressing economic problems faced by the government in a country which lagged far behind Britain in agricultural and industrial development. Firstly, the population boom served to force up prices, and especially food prices (which rose fourfold, in some areas, in the course of the eighteenth century). Secondly, partly due to the loss of so many colonies, France faced a growing balance of payments deficit after 1770. Finally, the government's expenditure on liberating the American colonists vastly increased the national debt.

To fend off bankruptcy, the government of Louis XVI (1774-93) called in a succession of experts and advisers, who recommended a wide variety of expedients for raising taxes (which fell chiefly on the peasants and middle class), or reducing spending; but still the budget could not be balanced. So, in the end, the government reluctantly appealed to those social groups which were largely exempt from taxation but controlled the majority of the kingdom's wealth: the nobles, the church and the office-holders. When, in 1788, it became clear that they would refuse to vote taxes without acquiring direct political control over the monarchy, it was decided to throw caution to the winds and summon the old representative assembly of France, the States General. This met, for the first time in nearly 200 years, in May 1789, at Versailles; and it did so in an atmosphere of general despair and widespread famine, caused by the failure of the harvests in 1787 and 1788. Almost at once, the Crown lost control. For six weeks there was a squabble among the three estates – lords, clergy and commons – over their powers (did each deputy have a vote, or should each estate have one corporate vote?), until in June, the Third Estate (the commons), assisted by some sympathetic clerics and noblemen, declared itself the 'National Assembly' and demanded effective guarantees for basic human rights, a constitutional monarchy with a representative assembly, and other sweeping reforms which would abolish noble and clerical privilege.

These concepts had become deeply entrenched among French intellectuals in the course of the eighteenth century and were the common currency of educated Frenchmen. Jean-Jacques Rousseau, in his influential *Social Contract* of 1764, called for the overthrow of all governments that were morally repugnant: 'Man is born free, but everywhere he is in chains', he wrote. Other 'enlightened' writers – Diderot and Voltaire among them – popularized the view that governments should be just, responsible, rational and humane. Their great manifesto, the *Encyclopédie* (published in thirty-five illustrated volumes between 1751 and 1786 and filled with articles on a wide variety of topics contributed by over 150 writers) criticized with such eloquence so much that the eighteenth century took for granted, that the entire social order was called into question. It was the greatest publishing enterprise of the century: it cried out stridently for reform.

Nevertheless, Louis XVI was reluctant to comply. Early in July 1789 he dismissed those of his ministers who favoured concessions, and prepared to disperse the National Assembly with force. The Paris populace, known as *sans-culottes* (because they wore trousers rather than the knee-breeches favoured by the upper-classes), now rioted. Their grievance was the most basic of all – lack of food – and, to preserve order, the city of Paris established a National Guard, made up of men with substantial property who could pay for their own uniforms and weapons. But the National Guard took the side of the *sans-culottes* and, on 14 July 1789, together they seized the great royal fortress that dominated the eastern side of Paris: the Bastille. It marked the end of

The States General of France had not met since 1614. On 5 May 1789, the three estates assembled at Versailles in order to solve the financial problems facing Louis XVI's government *below left*. It was a large gathering – 300 nobles, 300 clerics and 600 commoners – and within a month they had formed progressive and conservative factions. On 17 June, the members of the Third Estate unilaterally declared themselves a 'National Assembly' and when, three days later, the government tried to suspend their meetings, the delegates assembled in the nearby indoor tennis court *right* and took an oath not to separate until they had given the realm a constitution. This painting by J.L. David, later a leading figure of the Revolution, gives the incident a heroic grandeur.

The Age of Reason was the first to challenge religion and leading the challenge was Jean-Baptiste Voltaire (1694-1778), here seen addressing a gathering of philosophers (mostly anti-clericals) including Diderot and d'Alembert, chief figures in the making of the *Encylopédie*, a massive conspectus of empirical knowledge which dared to suggest that the Bible was not the last word in wisdom and history. Voltaire was a funny man, and you did well to avoid becoming his enemy. Louis XVI, not a funny man, failed this test.

the old order. In the course of August, the Assembly passed a series of momentous decrees which abolished tax-exemptions, tithe-collection, the aristocratic monopoly on office-holding, and (most important of all) the entire feudal system. It also promulgated a *Declaration of the Rights of Man and of the Citizen*, which proclaimed liberty, equality and the respect for life and property as the foundation of the new state. It established equality before the law, careers open to talent, equality of taxation, and freedom of speech. The declaration was a manifesto for the middle classes which controlled the Assembly, and for all European liberals in the next century.

At first, however, much of this legislation went unheeded. In the autumn of 1789, rumours of a counter-attack by royalist supporters, perhaps aided by foreign troops, provoked a wave of savage peasant uprisings against their landlords, while in Paris a crowd of women marched on Versailles and brought the royal family back to the capital, where their actions could be more strictly monitored. For the time being the monarchy was allowed to continue, but the king became a cypher: he was powerless to prevent the proclamation in 1791 of a new constitution, which ended absolutism and virtually abolished the

The French Revolution really began with
the storming of the royal prison known as
the Bastille on 14 July 1789 *left*. The
fortress, built in the 14th century, had no
strategic importance, but the failure of the
government to intervene and prevent the
release of the few political prisoners within
marked the end of its authority.

During the Revolution, those suspected
of being hostile to the government were
publicly decapitated by means of a new
machine, invented by a Scottish doctor,
called the guillotine *below*. One of the
advantages of the new instrument was held
to be that everyone was equal before it.
Previously, different social groups had been
executed in separate ways — nobles were
beheaded; thieves hanged; witches burnt.
Now, in a practical demonstration of the
new republican slogan: Liberty, Equality,
Fraternity, all offenders were guillotined.

powers of the monarchy. It also effected the reorganization of France
into the *départements* and *cantons* that persist to this day. The previous year the 'Civil Constitution of the Clergy' had broken the power of
the church and ordered the sale of its land to lay proprietors.

The royal family and the nobles, many of whom went into exile after
the fall of the Bastille, deeply resented the decline in their authority
and schemed ceaselessly to reverse the process. But at first they were
unable to interest the other rulers of Europe in their plight: the
Austrian Habsburgs were faced with rebellions in both the Netherlands
and Hungary, while Russia and Prussia were more interested in the
partition of Poland (chapter 21). In 1792, however, the French Assembly responded to growing foreign support for the Crown by declaring
war on Austria and Prussia. Even though the eventual invasion of
France by these foreign powers in support of the Old Regime failed, the
state of national emergency that it caused brought to power a radical
and republican faction in Paris. Firstly, all those suspected of opposing
the regime were rounded up; then, in September 1792, they were massacred in their gaols by the Paris mob; finally the king, whose powers
had already been declared null and void, was publicly tried and executed in January 1793. Meanwhile a 'decree of fraternity and assistance' promised French aid to all peoples who desired to overthrow
their oppressors and, before the year was out, the bayonets of the new
Republic had 'liberated' parts of the Rhineland and the Austrian
Netherlands, and had annexed several independent enclaves along the
frontiers. Moreover, the government in Paris proclaimed that France
had a historic right to occupy all the territory bounded by her 'natural
frontiers': the Alps, the Rhine and the Pyrenees.

These developments constituted a political threat that the rest of
Europe could scarcely ignore. In 1793, therefore, France found herself
at war with most of her neighbours, led by Great Britain, whose most
effective measure was to prevent the import of foodstuffs into France.
Shortages of grain, coupled with the fear of counter-revolutionaries
active within the Republic, created a climate of acute tension within
the country, while in Paris a new war government emerged, dominated
by a 35-year-old lawyer from Arras, Maximilien Robespierre: the Committee of Public Safety. For more than a year, the Committee, which
claimed to base its rule on universal suffrage, followed extreme policies and waged the first 'total' war on its external and internal enemies:
it raised a massive conscript army; it tried to regulate the economy by

Popular enthusiasm for the Revolution remained high in certain quarters. A series of contemporary watercolours by the Le Sueur brothers, *left and right* show groups of citizens in the streets clamouring for 'Liberty or Death', and the departure of a citizen volunteering for the army amid the good wishes of his wife (who holds his musket) and family. The inspiring national anthem the *Marseillaise* was written to accompany such scenes.

The empire of Napoleon *below* By 1812 Napoleon controlled the greater part of western Europe, exacting men and money for his armies but bringing great opportunities for men of talent. Only Spain, supported by Britain, was in rebellion against him. In 1812, however, his invasion of Russia met with disaster. Driven back into France, he was obliged to abdicate (1814). His empire was destroyed, but many of his ideas lived on.

Napoleonic empire c.1812

other dependent states c.1812

✕ French victory

✕ French defeat

1812➔ Napoleon's major campaigns

NORWAY

SWEDEN

Stockholm

St Pet

Baltic Sea

Tilsit R. Niemen

Be

Cross

DENMARK Copenhagen Danzig ✕ Friedland 1807

Lübeck ✕ Eylau 1807

North Sea Hamburg R. Elbe Berlin PRUSSIA R. Vistula Warsaw

Bremen Leipzig (Battle of the Nations) 1813 GRAND DUCHY OF WARSAW

UNITED KINGDOM Amsterdam WESTPHALIA Lützen 1813 ✕✕ Bautzen 1813

Antwerp Jena Auerstädt ✕1806 Dresden 1813 ✕ Austerlitz 1805

London Brussels Frankfurt CONFEDERATION Prague Wagram 1809 ✕✕

Waterloo 1815 ✕ Ligny 1815 Hohenlinden 1800 ✕ Ratisbon 1809 Aspern/Essling 1809

Hanau 1813 OF THE RHINE Vienna

Laon 1814 ✕ ✕ Rheims 1814 Zurich 1799 Ulm 1805 Munich Eckmühl/Ebersberg 1809 A U S

Château Thierry 1814 ✕ ✕ Champaubert 1814 Lonato 1796 Rivoli 1797

Channel Islands ✕ Paris 1814 ✕ La Fère-Champenoise 1814 Bassano 1796 R. Sava R.

(British) R. Loire Montereau 1814 Montmirail/Vauchamps 1814 Castiglione 1796 ✕ ✕ Arcole 1796 ILLYRIAN PROVINCES

Geneva Lodi 1796 ✕ Venice

Atlantic Ocean F R A N C E Dego 1796 ✕ Marengo 1800 KINGDOM OF ITALY Adriatic Sea Cataro (French)

R. Rhône Lyons Mondovi 1796 ✕ Montenotte 1796 ✕✕ Florence Ragusa (French)

1808 Marseilles Toulon Genoa PIOMBINO KINGDOM OF NAPLES

CATALONIA Barcelona 1808 Corsica Elba Rome Corfu

✕ Corunna 1809 Vitoria 1813 ✕ R. Ebro Ajaccio ✕ Naples (French)

Saragossa (captured) 1809 ✕

Salamanca 1812 ✕ Madrid (captured) 1808 Sardinia Palermo Ionian

R. Tagus ✕ Valencia 1808 ✕ Balearic Is. Sicily (Britis

Vimeiro S P A I N ✕ Talavera 1809 M e d i t e r r a Malta (British)

1808 ✕✕ Badajoz (captured) 1812 ✕ Bailén 1808 n e a n

Lisbon PORTUGAL

1809 Seville

Trafalgar (sea) 1805 Gibraltar (British) Melilla (Spanish)

Ceuta (Spanish)

18th-century revolutionaries appealed to classical models and had themselves painted in togas as exemplars of republican virtue. J.L. David perfected the classical style of French painting and was employed as painter of the Republic and of Napoleon – portrayed *left* striking an historical attitude as he crosses the Alps. He is compared to Hannibal and Charlemagne. For many, Napoleon fulfilled the role of Romantic hero – an idealistic, youthful visionary, successful and yet inevitably doomed to failure.

In 1804, the year of his coronation as emperor, Napoleon introduced the *Code Napoléon*, *below right* as a means of consolidating some of the achievements of the Revolution. It confirmed legal equality and property rights, and members of the old nobility were allowed to share the benefits of this legislation provided they accepted the new regime. This achievement outlived the emperor and now a large part of the world now operates under the 'Napoleonic Code' of law — the most substantial legacy of the French Revolution.

methods of considerable brutality; and it executed all who would not co-operate with the regime, in what became known as 'the reign of terror'. Possibly 40,000 died; but France was saved. In 1794 and 1795 the revolutionary armies defeated all their enemies and annexed not only the rest of the Austrian Netherlands and the Rhineland, but also turned the Dutch Republic into a satellite 'sister' Batavian Republic. Spain and Prussia hastened to make peace, leaving Austria isolated until, in 1797, by the Peace of Campo Formio, the Habsburg emperor was forced to surrender Belgium directly to France, while most of northern Italy was transformed into a further 'sister' republic. Only Britain remained at war.

These spectacular achievements, which expanded French rule almost to the bounds of Charlemagne's empire a millennium before, were due in part to the ineptitude and divisions of the Republic's enemies. But they also owed much to the military ability of her generals – especially Napoleon Bonaparte. Under the Bourbons, men of military talent, unless of noble birth, had usually been prevented from rising to high command. The Revolution changed that: swashbuckling military adventurers (like Napoleon, the son of a Corsican outlaw) were free to rise to the top. By attaching himself to various winning sides in the politics of the Revolution, Napoleon had risen to high places: in 1796, aged only twenty-six, he was made commander of the army of Italy.

The French army was no ordinary fighting force. The decision of the Committee of Public Safety, in August 1793, to impose universal conscription on France produced a military establishment of unprecedented size. The French armed forces in 1789 had totalled 160,000 men; now they stood at 750,000. The early victories of the conscript

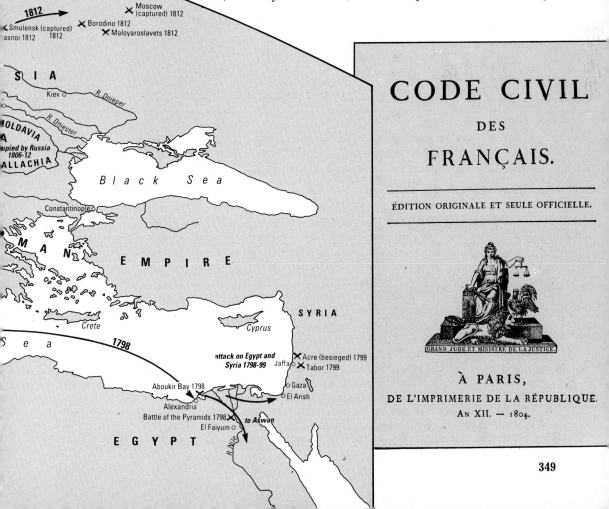

CODE CIVIL

DES

FRANÇAIS.

ÉDITION ORIGINALE ET SEULE OFFICIELLE.

GRAND JUGE ET MINISTRE DE LA JUSTICE.

À PARIS,
DE L'IMPRIMERIE DE LA RÉPUBLIQUE.
AN XII. — 1804.

1812 →
× Moscow (captured) 1812
× Smolensk (captured) 1812
asnoi 1812
× Borodino 1812
× Maloyaroslavets 1812

S I A
Kiev ○
R. Dnieper
R. Dniester
MOLDAVIA
upied by Russia 1806-12
ALLACHIA

B l a c k   S e a

Constantinople ○

M
A
N
E M P I R E

Crete
Cyprus

S Y R I A

S e a
1798
attack on Egypt and Syria 1798-99
Jaffa ○ × Acre (besieged) 1799
× Tabor 1799
Aboukir Bay 1798 ×
○ Gaza
○ El Arish
Alexandria
Battle of the Pyramids 1798 ×
El Faiyum ○
to Aswan
R. Nile

E G Y P T

Great Britain, the leading opponent of revolutionary France, was relatively safe from attack due to the proven strength of her navy. The French Republic elected therefore to attack Britain's Indian empire (a long-standing bone of contention between the two nations), by way of Egypt. An army was sent in July 1798 under Bonaparte, which easily forced a landing at Aboukir Bay near Alexandria *above*. The following month, however, the British navy under Nelson destroyed the French fleet at its anchorage (the battle of the Nile), leaving the French force stranded.

army were largely the combined result of massive numerical superiority and great enthusiasm for revolutionary principles; but as their enemies recovered, it was clear that better tactical techniques would be called for. Napoleon's greatest gift was his ability to manoeuvre rapidly: even against more powerful adversaries, he could still concentrate enough troops and guns together in one place to win a decisive battle.

His run of spectacular victories abroad, however, made him much feared at home. After the conquest of northern Italy (1796-97), Napoleon was sent to invade Egypt and the Holy Land. There, he was less successful and in 1799 he returned unexpectedly to stage the first military coup d'état of modern times. He joined with a group of dissident Paris politicians in order to depose the revolutionary government which had become increasingly dominated by corrupt politicians and war profiteers. In its place, he set up, first, a semi-dictatorial consulate (in accordance with Roman models) and then, in 1804 (still more in accordance with Roman models), an empire.

It was an empire in the classic tradition: a military monarchy which

created order at home, but which was later devoted to conquest abroad. Its domestic achievements were both real and lasting. In place of the economic dislocation, the terror and the social upheaval of the various revolutionary regimes, Napoleon imposed a new legal code (which is still the basis of French law), a national educational network, a centralized administration, and a stable financial system anchored on the new Bank of France. His rule was autocratic but efficient; and, although there were some ardent royalists and extreme republicans who remained irreconcilable, the majority of France's people at first welcomed the new government and demonstrated their support in plebiscites. Its popularity only waned as the cost of Napoleon's continual foreign wars mounted. Between 1803 and 1815 some 2 million soldiers entered the French army; some 900,000 of them never came back. The monetary and material costs were likewise high, as Napoleon's armies fought all of the other European powers in turn. But the successes were breathtaking. At Austerlitz (1805), Austria and Russia were humiliatingly defeated; many of the lands of the Austrian empire were amputated and distributed to France and her satellites (now kingdoms under Napoleon's relatives rather than 'sister' republics). After Jena (1806), Prussia lost vast territories and Germany was re-shaped into a French-dominated assemblage of client states. After the defeat of another Russian army at Friedland (1807), Tsar Alexander met Napoleon at Tilsit and came to an agreement that divided the Eurasian landmass between France in the west and Russia in the east. Once again it was only Britain, secure behind her fleets in the Channel, which held out.

The victorious French now reshaped continental Europe in their own image: serfdom was abolished, the Church's power abated, ancient laws and customs abrogated, all privilege ended. In their efforts, it is true, the 'liberators' were usually assisted by those middle-class 'patriots' who had opposed the privileged nobles and church of the old regime; but they rarely enjoyed popular support, because of the substantial tribute in men and money imposed by France. So Napoleonic Europe came to be run by a vast, sometimes corrupt, and often cruel bureaucracy of collaborators under French tutelage. It was unlikely to endure unchallenged.

The first rent in the fabric of Napoleon's empire came in 1808 when his troops invaded Spain and deposed the legitimate monarch, provoking widespread popular opposition, fostered by nobles and priests. The

Napoleon invaded Spain in 1808, deposing a Spanish Bourbon dynasty whose king spent his time knitting jumpers for statues of saints. He introduced emancipation of the serfs, progressive taxation, literacy and clean drains. But this incursion was not very popular. There was a great uprising, for which the Spanish *guerrilla* (little war) was used. As in all such wars since, the fighting was bitter, and the civil population bore the brunt of it; but the French, assailed by the *guerrilleros* and by the British who supported them, eventually retired after endless defeats. The etching *right* by Spain's leading artist Goya is one of a passionate series, *The Disasters of War*.

British, having established decisive naval superiority over the French and Spanish fleets at the battle of Trafalgar (1805), made haste to send forces over to support the Spanish irregulars and to preserve Portugal from invasion. At first they failed, but a second attempt, led this time by Sir Arthur Wellesley, later Duke of Wellington, was far more successful. By 1813, the French had been driven out of the peninsula. Wellington's triumph, however, was due in large measure to Napoleon's decision to reduce his army in Spain and commit the bulk of his forces, in 1812, to the invasion of Russia, with a view to forcing the Tsar to support him in imposing the Continental System against British trade with Europe. This was his grandest and greatest blunder, for an army of 600,000 men, drawn from all of the satellite countries, vanished into the steppe and the snow. Once Napoleon had lost that campaign the rest of Europe, encouraged by British subsidies and diplomacy, joined hands against him in a way that had not happened before. He was defeated by a coalition army at a great battle outside Leipzig (October 1813), and then finally (following a brief period of exile) in June 1815, at the battle of Waterloo.

Europe had undergone a convulsion, almost a generation in length, which left nothing unaffected. Old states and institutions had been abolished; the world of the *ancien régime* had gone for ever. When the representative of the victorious powers met, at the Congress of Vienna, to establish the terms of peace, they were at a loss as to how to proceed. They had already agreed that Napoleon should be deposed and exiled (he was sent first to Elba and then, after his final defeat at Waterloo, to St Helena, in the South Atlantic, where he died in 1821). But beyond that, the Congress was irresolute. The central architect of the new order, the Europe of the Restoration, was an Austrian states-man, Prince Metternich. He, like conservatives everywhere, regarded the Revolution as a disaster, the root of all evil. His riposte was coun-ter-revolution, exercised by police, Church, army; or, as his enemies said, 'a standing army of soldiers, a kneeling army of priests, and a creeping army of officials'. There were to be no parliaments; there was to be no talk of human rights; above all, the new doctrine of national-ism, which the French had launched, was firmly to be crushed and political boundaries were to be re-drawn regardless of nationalities. There were, admittedly, Germans and Italians, particularly intellectuals and the middle classes, who wished to set up their own nations, as independent republics in defiance of traditional legitimacy; but Metter-nich retorted that 'Italy is just a geographical expression', and his agents and satellites likewise thwarted the students and professors who advocated a national Germany. Only in France did the solution seem obvious: the restoration of Louis XVI's brothers – broken, tired old men who had 'learnt nothing and forgotten nothing' – to the French throne, although too much had happened over the past generation for them not to grant a constitution.

However, the reactionaries were fighting a hopeless battle. Metter-nich himself recognized this when he stated, 'I have spent my life in shoring up rotten buildings'. The Napoleonic reforms had produced shock-waves that none of the ancient structures could resist. Mass education and a popular press, coupled with the improvement in roads and the spread (after 1830) of railways, gradually created an integrated political nation in each country. In the towns, especially, where the spread of industrial production created a new wealthy and professional middle class, the landed aristocracy's attempts to preserve a monopoly of power created resentment and anger.

After 1815, these classes looked back increasingly to the days of the French Revolution and Napoleon. The great events of the recent past were now veiled in sentimentality and nostalgia: the horrors tended to

The first large battle that Napoleon lost was at Leipzig in mid-October 1813. It was called the Battle of the Nations because Napoleon was, for the first time, opposed by the rest of Europe – Austrians, Prussians, Russians, British, and even Swedes: his only allies were the Saxons, who were quite remarkable, over centuries, at choosing the wrong side. On this occasion, a small group of nationalistic German civilians were recruited in the Prussian army – they were not representative, but they were the first expression of German nationalism. Napoleon, who had given them the nationalistic example to follow, was driven back to France, with Death staring him – as in the Rowlandson cartoon *above* – in the face. By April 1814 it was all over: Napoleon abdicated.

Francisco de Goya (1746-1828) was one of Europe's outstanding Romantic artists, whose work reflected almost every aspect of contemporary life. In *Los Caprichos*, a series of 80 prints published in 1799, he condemned religious, social and political abuses. The frontispiece of the collection, *The sleep of reason produces phantoms, left*, set the general tone, and individual plates satirized well-known public figures and institutions. Not surprisingly, the collection had to be withdrawn from sale after a few days.

be forgotten. Then, the French had shown the way both to a new social order at home, and to national assertion abroad.

The old order now faced one challenge after another. In the 1820s, there were rebellions in Serbia and Greece against the Turks, and in Latin America against the Spanish and Portuguese colonial regimes. The British on the whole supported these liberal and nationalist causes – since they were in parts of the world where British political and strategic interests were not involved but where British trade could be expected to benefit – and the Royal Navy offered support to the 'liberator' of Latin America, Simon Bolívar, and to others, in their efforts to create independent states. Then in 1830 there were revolutions in Paris (which deposed the last of Louis XVI's brothers) and Brussels (which secured the creation of an independent Belgium). The disorders ended with the establishment of limited monarchies with parliaments, but were as nothing compared to the upheavals of 1848, 'the year of revolutions'. These followed a generation of increasing population growth and urbanization and a year of harvest failure and economic collapse. Another king of France – Louis Philippe – lost his throne in February 1848. News travelled to every capital in Europe by telegraph and rebellion broke out in response: in Vienna, where Metternich fell from power; in Milan; in Rome; and throughout the various capitals of Germany. Only the two fully industrialized states, Belgium and Britain, did not experience political revolution in 1848, for there the political structures had been adapted to the new age; by contrast, in Russia the processes of modern change had not gone far enough for revolution to stand much chance of success (chapter 21).

The year 1848 was hailed as 'the spring-time of the nations', but in practice things did not work out at all as the liberal middle-class rebels had intended. In the first place, the various new nations quarrelled with

Latin America's main wars of liberation *below* against Spain lasted until 1826. They involved two major forces: one, led by the Venezuelan Bolívar *below right* and Sucre, converging on Peru, the central Spanish bastion; the other, the Army of the Andes, with San Martín's Argentines and Bernardo O'Higgins's Chileans attacking the Peruvian capital Lima. Latin American nationalists fought not only Spain and Portugal, but also each other; except for Brazil, fragmentation swiftly followed emancipation, leading to the emergence of today's 20 republics.

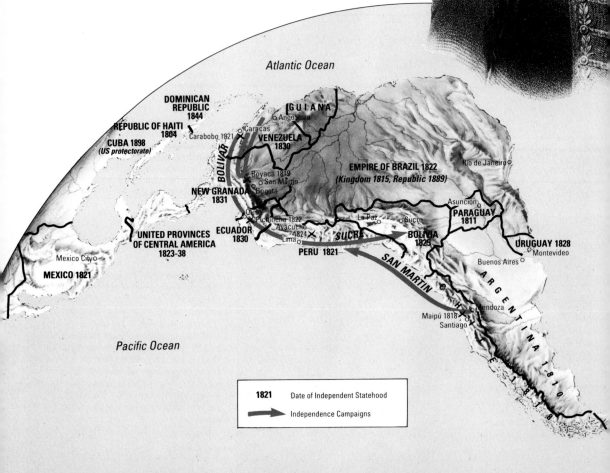

each other just as bitterly as they had quarrelled with the old order: Germans fought Poles, Czechs and Italians; Hungarians fought Croats and Romanians. Then again, although the bulk of the rural classes sympathized with the Revolution to begin with, they did so only with the object of securing an end to the remains of serfdom. Once that was achieved, they lost interest; indeed, at the behest of the priests who looked after them in troubled times, they swung back to the support of the old dynasties and showed hostility to the towns, the centres of revolution. The famous Italian revolutionary and democrat, Giuseppe Garibaldi, remarked that he could find support in Italy from nobles, townsmen, and the urban poor – from everyone but the peasants.

The most enduring result of the year of revolutions, however, was the publication of the *Communist Manifesto* by Karl Marx and Friedrich Engels, because it gave birth to a new and lasting ideology. It reflected an idea of class war and Utopian progress which was derided at the time; but it sowed the seeds of future upheavals. The proletariat, or working classes, had increased mightily in the past generation of industrial and urban growth; many of them faced terrible hardships, exacerbated in the 1840s by famine and cholera, and they blamed not only the old order of crowned heads and noblemen, but also the newly rich townspeople for their plight. In France, for instance, the middle-class revolutionaries of February 1848 introduced a scheme whereby the unemployed poor laboured on public works. When this caused wages and taxes to rise, however, the decision was rescinded. So in June 1848 those who were thus deprived of their jobs and faced by starvation revolted, threw up barricades, and demanded political rights for all citizens, whatever their economic position. Some of these radicals and democrats also appealed to a new creed altogether: socialism. Where liberalism had emphasized the individual and his rights, but in

practice had limited them to the property owners, socialism stressed the community and its collective welfare. The liberals advocated the freedom of the individual and the need for a laissez-faire economy; but the socialists, believing that human welfare could best be advanced by legislation and economic levelling, sought to change society by promoting collective well-being rather than individual liberty.

The democratic doctrine that all citizens should participate in the political process, and the socialists' demands for social and economic reform under threat of a class war, naturally alarmed the middle class. Almost everywhere, continental liberals swung round to support a return of the *ancien régime*, provided that it made sufficient concessions, so that by 1850, an uneasy alliance had come about between a reformed old order and repentant liberals prepared to tolerate its ways. Every state acquired parliaments representing the landed and middle classes: but these bodies were as determined to keep out the delegates of the lower classes as the old aristocracies had been. The inheritance of the French Revolution therefore passed to the masses: the Red Flag, which had originally been used by Paris revolutionaries in 1790, became the symbol for democrats and especially for socialists everywhere; and the last sentences of the *Communist Manifesto* became a slogan to make all men of property tremble: 'The workers have nothing to lose but their chains. They have a whole world to win. Workers of the world, unite!'.

The French Revolution of 1830 did not produce a republic, but a more liberal monarchy under a junior member of the Bourbon dynasty, Louis Philippe. In 1848, however, following a major agricultural and industrial recession, the political opposition demanded electoral reform and an end to parliamentary corruption. When these were refused, there was rioting in the streets of Paris. Louis-Philippe abdicated and a republic was proclaimed: the Bourbon throne was ceremonially burnt *above* and the monarchy abolished.

1848 – the 'Springtime of Revolutions' – announced that a new spectre was haunting Europe: a movement of the working class, hoping for the abolition of private property and the wage-system. The Communists in 1848 published their manifesto *right* – produced in London, not by working people, but by a middle-class intellectual, Karl Marx (1818-83) and a successful businessman, Friedrich Engels (1820-95). In 1848 it was little noticed, and after the failure of the socialist revolution in Germany (1848), both Marx and Engels returned in exile to England (1850). However, in later years, the *Communist Manifesto* inspired countless works of theory and history. Translated into many languages, it has probably been read by very few. Nevertheless, half of the world's population now lives under regimes that take it as their bible.

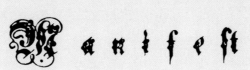

Manifest

der

Kommunistischen Partei.

———

Veröffentlicht im Februar 1848.

———

Proletarier aller Länder vereinigt Euch!

London.

Gedruckt in der Office der „Bildungs-Gesellschaft für Arbeiter"
von J. E. Burghard.

46, LIVERPOOL STREET, BISHOPSGATE.

Russia was divided, following the Tartar or Mongol conquest, into West Russia, or Lithuania, and East Russia, dominated by Moscow *below*. The latter expanded during the 16th century, absorbing Lithuania, linking the Black Sea and the Baltic, thrusting east into Siberia – with the help of the huge rivers – and establishing strategic forts and trading posts.

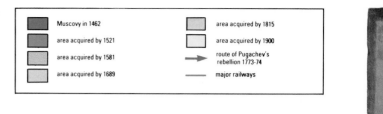

Muscovy in 1462	area acquired by 1815
area acquired by 1521	area acquired by 1900
area acquired by 1581	route of Pugachev's rebellion 1773-74
area acquired by 1689	major railways

ALASKA
Bering Sea
Pacific Ocean
KAMCHATKA
Sea of Okhotsk
Kurile Is.
Sakhalin
JAPAN
Sea of Japan
Vladivostok
KOREA
Okhotsk
MANCHURIA
Port Arthur
R. Amur
Peking
Yakutsk
Nerchinsk
Chita
R. Lena
L. Baikal
Irkutsk
Arctic Ocean
MONGOLIA
Altai Mts
Krasnoyarsk
R. Yenisey
Novaya Zemlya
Obdorsk
Semipalatinsk
Berezov
R. Ob
Tobolsk
Omsk
L. Balkhash
PECHORA
Ural Mts
Yekaterinburg
KAZAKHSTAN
Murmansk
Perm
Tashkent
Archangel
Vyatka
Chelyabinsk
Syr Darya
White Sea
Northern Dvina
KOKAND
Samarkand
L. Onega
Kazan
Orenburg
Aral Sea
Bukhara
FINLAND
NOVGOROD
Nizhniy Novgorod
Bolgar
Samara
Amu Darya
Vyborg
L. Ladoga
Yaroslavl
AFGHANISTAN
St Petersburg
Novgorod
Suzdal
Vladimir
MUSCOVY
TURKMENISTAN
KINGDOM OF SWEDEN
Pereyaslavl
Saratov
ESTONIA
Pskov
Moscow
Guryev
LIVONIA
Polotsk
Voronezh
R. Don
Tsaritsyn
Astrakhan
Riga
R. Volga
Baltic Sea
LITHUANIA
Kursk
Caspian Sea
Vilnius
Minsk
Derbent
Baku
Kaliningrad
Chernigov
Kharkov
Azov
Stavropol
Caucasus Mts
POLAND
Kiev
Pereyaslavl
Donets
Tiflis
Vladimir
Poltava
Sea of Azov
GEORGIA
Warsaw
UKRAINE
R. Dnieper
Kerch
Poti
Kamenets
R. Dneister
Kherson
CRIMEA
Kolomyya
BESSARABIA
Odessa
Sevastopol
Carpathian Mts
Black Sea
ROMANIA
TURKEY

CHAPTER 21

THE MAKING OF RUSSIA
1480–1860

Russian Christian artistic styles have remained remarkably consistent across space and time. Western Christianity dealt in the coin of this world, and Popes became secular rulers. Eastern Christianity was different: it regarded the secular world with horror, and retreated into mystic spirituality. Byzantine Greek art — unrepresentational and non-narrative — put its stamp on a whole world from Minsk to Vladivostok, whether in church architecture or painting. The remarkable wooden church of the Transfiguration *below* on Kizhi island is a miniature Kremlin. Our Lady of Vladimir, painted in Constantinople c.1130, provided a model for endless imitation *above*, and remains the most popular, and most reproduced, work in Russian history.

The Soviet Union today has almost 250 million inhabitants, divided among almost 100 different nationalities. From its capital, Moscow, the direct power of the USSR spreads into eleven of the twenty-four time zones of the world and comprises over one-sixth of the world's landmass. Yet before AD 850, there were only scattered Slavonic tribes, originally from eastern Europe, in the area, widely distributed over a barren landscape of marshes, forests and steppe. There were few towns, and most of them were mere villages protected by a stockade. Moscow did not even exist. Only Novgorod and Kiev stood out as places of importance, for they dominated the overland trade route which linked the Baltic with the Black Sea.

In the middle of the ninth century, however, two new external influences transformed the situation. From the south came the Byzantine missionaries, St Cyril and St Methodius (chapter 9), who introduced Greek Orthodox Christianity to the Slavs. From the north, at much the same time, came Vikings: Scandinavian raiders known as 'Varangians' or 'Rus'. Some pushed as far south as Constantinople, where many of them took service in the Byzantine army (in a unit known as the Varangian Guard); but the majority settled along the great trade route between Novgorod and Kiev. Both towns, and the others that grew up along the way, became the seats of Scandinavian princes, each one fiercely independent; there was no single, unifying authority for more than a century. Vladimir of Kiev (980-1015), described by a contemporary chronicler as *fornicator immensus* yet later canonized by the

The Lay of the Host of Igor, first written down in 1185-7, quickly became a familiar legend to all Russians. Although it was concerned exclusively with the deeds of princes and nobles, its nationalism was taken up by the Communist Revolution, and the vigorous representation *above* of Igor's battle with the Tartars dates from 1934. But in fact the campaign was a fiasco: Prince Igor of Novgorod was defeated and captured by his enemies, although he later escaped and returned to his people.

church, was the first ruler to bring all the Rus under his authority; he also made Eastern Orthodox Christianity the official religion of his new state. This choice was to have a profound effect on the country's future for, shortly afterwards – in 1054 – a schism occurred between the Latin church of Rome and the Orthodox church of Byzantium. It was never properly healed: Russia and the rest of Europe would never kneel together at the same altar.

There were still numerous trading connections with the West, however, especially through the Baltic, and also some diplomatic contacts: one of Vladimir's granddaughters married the king of France, another the king of Hungary, and a third the king of Norway. But Kiev's days of greatness were numbered. In 1093, the city was sacked by nomads from the steppe, and many inhabitants of the area moved north and eastwards in search of safety: new towns were founded between the Oka and the Volga, such as Vladimir, Suzdal, Rostov and (about 1140), Moscow. Then, during the thirteenth century, came an even greater threat from Asia: the Mongols (chapter 10). In 1223 there was a first attack, in which an army fielded by the Russian princes was defeated at the Kalka River, and Kiev was threatened; but shortly afterwards the invaders withdrew as suddenly as they had come. But in 1237 they returned devastating all of central and southern Russia, sacking Kiev and coming within sixty miles of Novgorod before withdrawing southwards to create a powerful state on the lower Volga, with their capital at Sarai.

For the next century and a half the Khanate of the Golden Horde (the name given to the new Mongol dominion) was the most powerful state in Russia. Its armies totally controlled the grasslands around the Caspian and the Black Sea, preventing almost all contacts with Byzantium; and its Khans acted as suzerains over the surviving principalities in the north, playing off one ruler against another, exacting tribute, and levying military contingents. The effects of the Mongol conquest were not merely political, however. The fall of Kiev destroyed the cultural centre of medieval Russia, with its rich Byzantine-based literature and art. Instead, the traditions of the north, derived from sagas and legends, and incorporating many archaic ideas, prevailed; and its classic expression, *The Lay of the Host of Igor*, became the most influential tract in Old Russian literature.

By the fourteenth century, however, the power of the Golden Horde was on the wane and, increasingly, its mantle fell upon the small state of Muscovy, strategically situated near the headwaters of both the Don and the Volga. In the 1330s, the princes of Moscow were charged by the Khans with the task of collecting tribute from all the Christian states and, at the same time, the metropolitan of the Russian church made the

Muscovy gained its independence from the Mongols under Ivan III in 1480, which inauguarated a period of rapid expansion. The Tartars were eventually defeated, but their long rule in southern Russia made a lasting impact. Many Tartar words survive in the Russian language and even in the 16th century, as the German woodcut *below* shows, Russian nobles still wore leather armour and carried composite bows just like the invaders from the steppe.

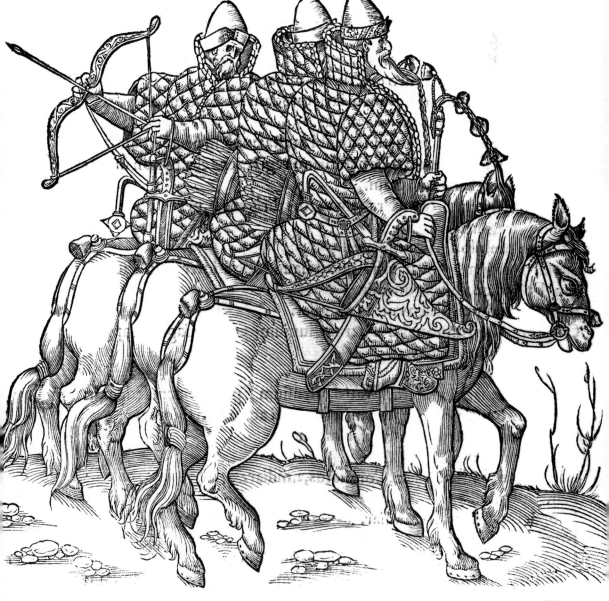

The Victory of Prince Dimitri of Moscow at Kulikovo on the river Don in 1380 came to be seen as a turning point in the rise of Muscovy. It ended the Tartars' levy of tribute from central Russia, and earned Dimitri the epithet *Donskoi* ('of the Don'). In this 16th century illustration *left*, the prince – with halo, sceptre and white horse – is depicted as a supreme ruler, the ancestor of the tsars.

Ivan the Terrible *right* came to the throne of Russia at the age of three, in 1533, and ruled until his death 51 years later. He enjoyed some success in foreign wars, but his domestic policies were marked by brutal excesses. Occasionally he suffered bursts of intense remorse and repentance, as after he swung his steel-tipped staff in a fit of temper and smashed the skull of his son and heir (1581); but the killing never stopped for long. By the time of his death in 1584, much of central Russia was depopulated, thanks largely to the efforts of the *oprichniki* (derived from the Russian word *oprichny* meaning 'apart'). This special core of civil servants was created by Ivan in 1565 in a successful attempt to break the hereditary power of the nobility. They were the tsar's personal servants, responsible to him alone and, as the engraving by a Danish visitor in 1627 *far right* shows, they even dressed in the same uniform. However in reality it was not white, but black.

city his residence. In 1380, Prince Dimitri Donskoi routed the Khan's army at Kulikovo, and he and his successors patiently extended their authority into the neighbouring principalities. The size of Muscovy grew from 31,000 square miles in about 1300 to 290,000 in 1462.

The reign of Ivan III (1462-1505) opened another phase of expansion. In 1478 he annexed the large state of Novgorod giving Muscovy, simultaneously, access to the Baltic, the White Sea and the Urals; and in 1480 he rejected Mongol suzerainty and declared himself 'Tsar of all the Russias' (using the Slavonic version of the Latin word Caesar). Since Constantinople had fallen to the Turks some years earlier (chapter 14), Ivan – married to the niece of the last Byzantine ruler – further claimed to be heir to the Roman empire and protector of the entire Orthodox

The Moscow Kremlin *right* is a fortified triangular enclosure covering 90 acres in the centre of the city, beside the Moskva river. Its stone walls were renewed in the Renaissance style during the 15th century, and a series of fine churches and palaces were soon erected or rebuilt within. But clearly visible from the exterior are the gilded domes of the Annunciation Cathedral, built in the 1480s, and the fairytale tower and multicoloured domes of St. Basil's Cathedral, built in the 1550s to celebrate Ivan the Terrible's victories over the Tartars on the lower Volga.

church. 'Moscow is the third Rome,' thundered the monk Philotheus, 'and a fourth shall never be'. As if to prove the point, Ivan brought in Italian architects to rebuild his capital: the Uspenski (Assumption) Cathedral was erected and the Kremlin (which means 'fortress') was rebuilt in the best Renaissance style with a new crenellated wall and twenty towers, covering some ninety acres.

By the time Ivan's grandson, Ivan IV (also known as 'the Terrible') succeeded in 1533, Muscovy had expanded to 1.7 million square miles, and the new tsar was to double that, extending his rule to perhaps 12 million subjects. In the 1550s his forces conquered the whole of the Volga valley from the descendants of the Mongols, bringing Muscovite power down to the Caspian, while adventurers spread Muscovite influence eastwards to the Urals. But Ivan's single most important act was the creation, in 1565, of the *oprichina*, the tsar's 'private domain', virtually a 'state-within-a-state'. This was a large area around Moscow which was directly administered by the tsar through a new, secret police force which was given absolute and arbitrary power over everyone. All noble landowners in the *oprichina* were dispossessed – and either murdered or exiled – and their lands and serfs given to the new officials on a personal, not a hereditary, basis. This development was crucial for two reasons. First, it broke the power of the nobility and thus removed a force which, in some Western states, protected civil liberties and private rights. Second, it rendered intolerable the condition of the peasantry in large parts of Russia: tied to the soil and burdened with heavy labour services, the only escape from the arbitrary rule of the *oprichniki* was flight. And hundreds of thousands fled, leaving much of central Muscovy depopulated. Some went to the Muslim states, whose regimes seemed less oppressive; others settled in the new lands along the Don and Volga, where they could live by hunting or ranching without interference from Moscow. These refugees were known as Cossacks, and it was from their numbers that, just before Ivan's death in 1584, the first conquerors of Siberia were drawn.

363

There was nothing new in moving east: Russians had been doing it for centuries, crossing the trackless miles of tundra and forest in search of game and mineral deposits. They had encountered some native tribes as they advanced, such as the Mari and the Samoyeds; but these were easily subjugated. However, when the Russians reached the Urals, in the 1570s, they came into contact with the more powerful Khanate of Sibir, beyond the mountains. For a time, further advance was halted by the raiders from the steppe; but then, in 1581, the Stroganovs (a powerful merchant family with extensive concessions in the Urals) hired the services of a band of Cossacks from the Volga to defend their interests. Led by an escaped criminal, Yermak, the Cossacks scored an immediate success: with 840 musketeers, supported by artillery, Yermak stormed and captured the Khan's capital, Sibir (from which the entire area takes its name: Siberia in English).

Expansion eastwards now became very rapid. Whereas the English landed in Virginia in the 1580s, but sixty years later had still not reached the Appalachian mountains, the Russians over the same period managed to cross the entire Asian continent. From Sibir they descended the Irtysh and Ob rivers until they came within portage of the Yenisey, where they built a fortified village at Turukhansk (1604). Thence they reached the Lena river system, where they built Yakutsk (1632); and while some continued north-eastwards down the Kolyma, others struck out towards the Pacific. Othotsk was founded in 1649; it was 6,000 miles east of Moscow.

There were several reasons for this remarkably rapid progress. First, the geography of Siberia favoured the explorers: plains stretched as far as the Yenisey and plateaux as far as the Lena, all of them intersected by broad, navigable rivers. Second, the area was sparsely peopled by unwarlike tribes who offered little opposition to the invaders: there

The conquest of Siberia was essentially a result of the quest for furs. Like the contemporary fur trappers of French Canada, the Russians courageously beat off the attacks of native archers *left* and doggedly dragged their boats between the broad rivers *top* constantly moving eastwards. The furs were sent west to be sewn together *above* into the hats, coats and boots *right* without which life in the Russian winter was impossible.

were no Iroquois or Algonquin in Siberia. Yet the entire sub-continent, though deficient in people, was abundant in animals, hundreds of thousands of whose fur coats (especially sables) were exported annually to Muscovy. The 'fur rush' swiftly boosted the area's population: the 23,000 Russians in Siberia in 1622 had grown to 105,000 in 1662 and 230,000 in 1709.

Life for these early colonists, however, was harsh, for Siberia produced very little food of its own. After a while, this led to attempts to find a new source of supply in the south: in the 1640s bands of Cossacks began to move into the Amur basin, where they built fortified posts and began to plant crops and pillage the local population. For a while the settlements prospered, but in 1658 the Chinese emperor – whose territory this was – sent in an army to dislodge the interlopers. When this effort failed, he sent another in 1689. This time, an agreement was reached whereby the Russians promised to evacuate the Amur basin in return for the freedom to trade each year with China. The treaty of Nerchinsk brought peace to Russia's eastern frontier and allowed Moscow to consolidate her control over an area far larger than the European colonies in North America.

But at first Siberia was left very much alone, for Muscovy underwent a major political and social crisis following the death of Ivan the Terrible, known as the 'Time of Troubles'. In 1561, the tsar had made a desperate attempt to gain direct access to the Baltic by invading Livonia and capturing the port of Narva. This, however, attracted counter measures by two other powers also interested in the region – Sweden and Poland – and a war broke out that lasted more than twenty years. The burdens laid upon Ivan's subjects increased dramatically: the taxes paid by an average noble estate rose from 8 roubles in the 1550s to 151 in the 1580s. Small wonder that so many Russians moved

Michael Romanov *above* was chosen tsar in 1613. His election owed less to any innate ability than to his distant descent from the ancient line of Rurik tsars. He came to the throne reluctantly at the end of the Time of Troubles, but he nonetheless gave his new subjects peace, and founded a dynasty that was to last for over three centuries. During that period, Russia was introduced to numerous western techniques and ideas. Under Michael's grandson, Peter the Great (1682-1725), even the newspaper made its appearance in St. Petersburg: the script may have looked unfamiliar to Westerners, but the format and the function were the same. This page *below* describes a diplomatic meeting between George I of England and the King of Prussia.

САНКТЪПІТЕРБУРХЪ.

ВѢДОМОСТИ.

Изъ БЕРЛІНА 16 Октября.

Въ прошлои Вторнікъ Король Велі-кобрітанскіи, простілся въ Шарло-тенбургѣ съ Королевою Прускою, и со всею Королевскою Фамілїею, съ велікіми доказателствы усердія и дружбы. На завтреѣ его Велíче-ство, поѣхалъ отъ туль съ Королемъ
14   Прускімъ

beyond the Urals; small wonder, too, that those who remained became desperate. In the prophetic words of an English ambassador to Russia, Dr Giles Fletcher, written in 1591:

'The late Tsar's tyrannous practices…have so troubled that countrey, and filled it so full of grudge and mortal hatred ever since, that it will not be quenched (as it seemeth now) till it burn againe into a civill flame…The desperate state of things at home, maketh the people for the most part to wishe for some forreine invasion which they suppose to bee the onely meanes to rid them of the heavy yoke of this tyrannous government.'

They did not have long to wait. In 1605, Moscow was occupied by a Pretender, known as 'the False Dimitri' (because he claimed to be Ivan the Terrible's dead son of that name), aided by a Polish army. Then, after his defeat, in the year 1610, first a Swedish and then a Polish army occupied the Russian capital. The Kremlin remained in Polish hands until the end of 1612. The election of the only surviving relative of Ivan IV, Michael Romanov, as tsar in 1613 scarcely improved matters: although his descendants were to rule Russia for just over three centuries, his early years were both precarious and inglorious. First, Sweden invaded again, and had to be placated with the Baltic provinces (1617); then Poland, which had taken Smolensk in 1611, came within an ace of retaking Moscow and had to be bought off with more concessions (1619). By the time peace returned, perhaps half the villages in the heartland of Muscovy were deserted, especially the larger settlements and those along the major roads. It has been suggested that the average community in Muscovy by the 1620s consisted of a mere five wooden tenements.

The road to recovery was slow. The Poles invaded again in 1632-34; there was a major rebellion against the government in Moscow in 1648; then war broke out once more with Poland in the 1650s over the transfer of the Ukraine to Russia following a rising by the Don Cossacks. Only after the peace of Andrusovo in 1667, which confirmed Russian possession of Smolensk and the Ukraine, could the Romanov dynasty breathe easy.

The union of the Ukraine with Russia brought about a marked increase in the influx of western ideas to Muscovy. Kiev had been the capital of the Orthodox part of Poland, and had become influenced by the religious changes taking place in the west (chapter 17). In 1631, a new theological college, modelled on Roman Catholic schools, was opened there: the staff, some of them trained by Jesuits, taught in Latin and used textbooks adapted from the works of Catholic theologians. In 1645 a short Orthodox catechism was printed in Kiev, unashamedly based on the standard Catholic version. By the end of the century, a further 200 Western works had been translated into Russian, compared with only thirteen between 1600 and 1650.

But the main impetus for Westernization came later, under Russia's most famous tsar, Peter the Great. But he was only nine years old when he came to the throne in 1682 and the temporary removal of strong central control provoked a palace revolution. The Moscow garrison, incensed by the government's attempt to subordinate them to the Western system of discipline and command, marched on the Kremlin and spent three days murdering every relative and friend of Peter's mother they could lay their hands on. Peter himself, and his mother, were spared; but the massacre planted in Peter a loathing for Moscow which would stay with him throughout his life. It was in a spirit of revenge that he ordered a vast new capital city to be built by the Baltic: St Petersburg. Over 150,000 serfs died in the fetid swamps by the banks of the Neva in order to fulfil Peter the Great's dream of a capital that would rival Versailles in its scale and splendour. His principal residence, the Winter Palace, eventually came to

Peter the Great stood 6 feet 8 inches tall, and this full-length portrait of him as a young man testifies to his regal bearing on official occasions. But at other times it could be very different. During the tsar's 'incognito' visit to England in 1697-8, for example, he and his entourage virtually destroyed the house in Deptford where they lodged. After their departure, all the floors were found to be covered in grease, ink and vomit; all paintwork, wall-hangings and bedlinen were fouled; all paintings were vandalized; all chairs – originally 50 in number – were either missing (presumed burnt) or broken; and 300 window panes were smashed. Despite this remarkable behaviour Peter was responsible for single-handedly modernizing Russia. The visit to England was in order to study techniques of naval construction, only one of many innovations which he introduced, rapidly forcing his nation onto the stage of European politics. The spacious palaces of his new capital, St. Petersburg, epitomized Peter's wish to be seen as a modern European monarch; but the Summer Palace *below*, built between 1710 and 1714 by the Italian architect Trezzini, was both simple and durable. It has survived to our day.

occupy an area of some 400,000 square feet, and was about one-third of a mile wide. Peter had moved his court to the western edge of his vast empire: it was almost as though he wished to announce his arrival to the emperors and kings of Europe, proclaiming that Russia was now truly a part of the West.

The architects of St Petersburg were foreigners. They were not the only ones imported by Peter the Great: Dutch experts were brought in to drain marshes and build ships and Germans were imported to train the army – so numerous were they that drill manuals for the tsar's army had to be composed in German as well as in Russian, and even now the rank-titles of the Red Army are straight translations from German. In Moscow, foreign craftsmen and technicians lived in their own special quarter, the Arbat, which was a corruption of the German word *Arbeit* (meaning 'work'); and many technical terms in Russian were imported from German.

But the foreigners were not very popular with most Muscovites, especially the old boyar nobility. 'Let us not,' said one, 'imitate the odd and difficult cleanliness of the Germans, who so often wash the floors of their houses, and where a guest may not so much as spit or vomit on the floor…' However, this articulate Muscovite, who spoke up so eloquently for the leisured classes of seventeenth-century Russia, did not impress the tsar. Until his death in 1725, Peter made every effort to Westernize his world. The most famous instance was his enforced removal of the beard. The Russian people thought that beards, being traditional, had been modelled on those of the saints and were therefore holy. As a contemporary said:

'Nothing but the terror of having them pulled out by the roots could ever have persuaded the Russes to part with them… Some shaven

Westernization under Peter the Great was more successful in the naval sphere. Previously, Russia had scarcely possessed a fighting fleet, yet by 1714 Peter's navy, consisting mainly of galleys capable of operating close inshore among the islands of the Baltic *right*, was able to win a crushing victory over Sweden's men-of-war. Peter realized that access to European waterways via the Baltic Sea was crucial. His new capital at St. Petersburg was sited virtually on the Gulf of Finland, and between 1704 and 1721 he gained Ingermanland, Estonia, Livonia and southern Finland from the Swedes, creating a huge Baltic seaboard.

workers in St Petersburg kept their beards in their pockets, to show to St Nicholas on Judgement Day.'

But the tsar got his way and, gradually, these and other Western ideas caught on at Court. It was said in the eighteenth century that the Russian nobles 'went to Paris little piglets and came back perfect swines'. They spoke French in preference to Russian – even in the 1860s, long passages of Tolstoy's *War and Peace* were written in French because that was the language used by the Russian upper class at home. They also began to despise the Orthodox church and its practitioners. But not all the old ways were abandoned. A German diplomat in the eighteenth century reported, of a memorable audience in St Petersburg:

'After having gulped down a dozen bumpers of Hungarian wine at dinner, the Vice-Tsar gave me, with his own hands, a full quart of brandy which I had to empty in two draughts. I soon lost my senses, though I had occasion to observe that the rest of the guests, asleep already on the floor, were in no condition to make reflections on my little skill in drinking.'

But if life in the palaces of St Petersburg was at least as debauched and splendid as in any other European court, in the villages of 'Holy Russia' little had changed. Peter the Great's empire was a place where 'First-class batteries of horse artillery galloped through mud villages'. Scarcely any iron was used in agriculture – ploughs had wooden mould-boards and harrows had wooden teeth – while windmills and watermills were rare. To some extent natural factors were to blame for all this. The growing season around Novgorod was (and still is) only four months, and around Moscow only five (as against eight or nine in France), which limited the impact of any innovation. And the high, thick forests and slow, meandering rivers did not favour the introduction of mills. But other countries, similarly disadvantaged by nature, nevertheless managed to improve agricultural

Peter the Great's zeal to eradicate traditional ways, for example by cutting off the beards of religious fanatics – of which there were many – *above*, caused widespread resentment. In 1698, while Peter the Great was on his tour of the West, the Moscow garrison staged a major revolt *left*. Although it was suppressed by loyal foreign and native troops, led by the Scotsman Patrick Gordon, the challenge to his authority brought the tsar back to Russia in haste. He did not leave it again. Work began on building a new capital, St. Petersburg, shortly afterwards.

Russian rural life *above* was unaffected by the 'capitalism' of the rural property-owners in the West. It was far more egalitarian, and conservative in every way, relying on tools that the Middle Ages would have known. But from 1497 Russian peasants had been tied to the land. Initially they had two weeks of free movement every November. This was withdrawn under Boris Godunov in 1593, and in 1648 a decree removed all limits to forcible reclamation of runaway serfs. By the beginning of the 19th century the Russian population had reached over 40 million, only 4 percent of which was urban. Inevitably, during the 19th century Russian peasant life was romanticized, but real reform only occurred under Alexander II with the emancipation of the serfs in 1861.

output in the eighteenth century. The problem in Russia was the oppressive social system. Serfs were required to work so long on their lords' land, and were so effectively tied to their village, that neither they nor their masters had much incentive to change the traditional ways. Ninety-seven percent of the tsar's subjects lived, and long continued to live, in what Trotsky later called 'the Russia of icons and cockroaches'.

Not surprisingly, there were revolts against the system, particularly among the Cossacks of the south who had already shown their dissatisfaction and independence by flight. The revolts led by Stenka Razin (1670-71) and Emelyan Pugachev (1773-75) were merely the biggest and best known: popular uprisings were almost an annual event in Tsarist Russia, even though they were always suppressed ruthlessly with public executions and an ingenious array of tortures. There were also palace revolutions. The imperial guard mutinied against Peter the Great in 1698; the brains of Peter III were dashed out with a footstool by his wife's lover in 1762; and Paul I was murdered, with a curtain cord, by noble conspirators acting with the connivance of his son and heir, Alexander, in 1801.

So the strictest rule of the tsarist court came to be that any relaxation of the severities of the system was fatal. It was a lesson fully absorbed by Peter's most powerful successor Catherine, also called 'the Great', who ruled the empire with an iron hand from 1762 to 1796. The least infraction of court etiquette, or the slightest disobedience, was punished by public flogging or worse, and no opposition was allowed to her policy of importing Westerners and Western fashions wholesale. Under her patronage, St Petersburg began to look even more like a Western capital. The original wooden buildings were now largely finished in stone. She also employed the resourceful merchants and nobles from the newly acquired Baltic provinces, wrested from Sweden during the Great Northern War (1700-21), to develop the resources of the Ukraine; with these, Russia's army was expanded until it was a match for those of its western

Catherine the Great *right* began life in
1729 as the daughter of a minor German
ruler. But in 1745 she married the Russian
tsarevich and, soon after his deposition in
1761, made herself ruler of the greatest
state in Europe. In domestic policy she was
ruthless: courtiers who vexed her were
summarily flogged; peasant unrest was
suppressed without mercy. Abroad she
advanced Russian power both against the
Ottoman empire, gaining much new
territory around the Black Sea and against
the kingdom of Poland, from which she
eventually acquired all of Lithuania and the
Ukraine. Such was her success that
envious foreigners saw in it the work of the
Devil *below*.

CONSTANTINOPLE

WARSAW

QUEEN CATHERINES DREAM,

London Pub by W.Holland N°50 Oxford St November 4 1791

The reorganization of the Russian army in the 18th century created a force that could match even the greatest military genius of the age. Although an English cartoon of 1813 might make fun of the somewhat primitive tactics of 'The Cossack extinguisher' *right*, there was no mistaking the advantages conferred by the dogged perseverance and superior numbers of the Russian troops. The battle of Borodino, romantically portrayed by a French artist *far right*, may have delivered Moscow to Napoleon Bonaparte and his army in September 1812, but it could not safeguard his lines of communication back to France. One month later, the retreat began, and 'The extinguisher' came into his own: Cossacks, partisans and regular troops combined to attack the Grand Army which lost, in the end, 95 percent of its strength – 570,000 men, 200,000 trained horses, 1100 guns. The catastrophe made the collapse of Napoleon's empire inevitable.

neighbours. In 1812-14, the Russians even managed to defeat a major French invasion under Napoleon Bonaparte (chapter 20).

But perhaps the greatest gains in the west were made by diplomacy rather than by war. Although Catherine conquered some territory from the Turks, she won far more from her peaceful partitions of Poland in 1772, 1793 and 1795. With the full consent of Austria and Prussia, some 5 million new subjects were added to the Russian empire, and its frontier was advanced almost to the river Oder. And yet neither Catherine nor her successors did much to improve the conditions of their subjects. Although Alexander II declared rhetorically, in a momentous speech of 1857, 'It is better to abolish serfdom from above than to wait for it to abolish itself from below', he soon found that it was one thing to declare all serfs to be free (as was finally done in 1861), and quite another to feed, clothe and educate them. Since the task of modernizing the agriculture of their vast empire seemed impossible, the tsars decided instead to introduce industry on a large scale, and so take the people away from the land. However, capital for industrialization could only come from abroad; and so huge Western investment in Russia was permitted, both to develop railways and oilwells and to construct very large factories. But this created as many problems as it solved, for to an impoverished and discontented peasantry was now added a poorly-paid and ill-fed urban workforce, toiling (so it seemed) for the sole benefit of foreign investors and the tsarist autocracy. Time was running out for the Romanovs.

The first European settlers in North America — whether French, Dutch, English or Swedish — were few in number and could only establish themselves with the goodwill of the native population. For example, in 1681 the Quaker William Penn was granted by the British Crown the American seaboard between 40 and 43 degrees north, which he named Pennsylvania. But to take up his new possession, he had to make a formal treaty with the Indian leaders in the area *left*.

CHAPTER 22

THE MAKING OF THE USA 1776–1890

Early French settlers colonized the lands along the St. Lawrence river eventually settling the inland waterways of the Great Lakes and the Mississippi, whereas British colonies were concentrated on the Atlantic seaboard. Inevitably, the two communities were repeatedly drawn into the European wars between France and Britain until, in 1759, the capture of Quebec *below* by a large British army, and of Montreal the following year, delivered all French Canada to its rivals, creating a British America that stretched from Hudson's Bay almost to the Caribbean. The development of the United States as we know them today *left* was a long and often heroic story. Although the United States gained vast tracts of land on paper from the European powers during the first half of the 19th century, the settlement of these areas, and the formalization of their status as states took over a century.

In the year 1775, most of the North American continent was legally subjected to the authority of four European states. In the west, Russian traders from Siberia busily established trading settlements along the Pacific coast. By 1819 nineteen of them stretched from the Aleutian islands to the Russian river in California. There they confronted the friars and priests from Spanish Mexico, who had created a chain of mission stations along the coast as far north as San Francisco. They had also colonized Florida, Texas and much of New Mexico. In the east, the British possessed thirteen separate colonies along the Atlantic seaboard (some of them formerly Dutch and Swedish settlements) from Georgia up to New Hampshire and inland as far as the Allegheny mountains. They also held the thinly-populated lands around Hudson Bay, known as Rupert's Land. And in between these two segments of British North America, and largest of all, lay 'New France'.

Since the foundation of Quebec in 1608 (chapter 18), French traders and missionaries had pushed onwards down the St Lawrence river, explored the Great Lakes and (from the 1680s) the Mississippi river. They established forts and settlements as they went – Montreal was founded in 1642, Fort Frontenac in 1673, Detroit in 1701, New Orleans in 1718 – and organized the colony of Louisiana in 1699. This encirclement of Britain's possessions inevitably led to tension, and to competition between French and British settlers to occupy the strategic lands lying between them: Nova Scotia and the Ohio Valley. The former was secured by military and naval force in the 1740s, and attention thereafter focused on the latter. In 1753 a French army was sent to occupy the upper valley, and the following year a force of British colonists (with the young George Washington second-in-command) was sent in to challenge them. In 1755 general hostilities commenced all along the common border, in which the French were generally successful. But the whole situation changed when Austria, Russia and France declared war on Prussia in June 1756, initiating the general conflict known as the Seven Years' War. Britain sided with Prussia, and ruthlessly exploited France's preoccupation with the struggle in Europe in order to occupy French possessions overseas. By the Peace of Paris in 1763, France lost not only her empire in India (chapter 19) but also her colonies in America. Louisiana was ceded to Spain, which brought the frontier of Latin America to the Mississippi; while Quebec and Florida became part of a British empire which now stretched from Hudson Bay down to the Caribbean.

Seen in retrospect, the revolt of the thirteen British colonies along the Atlantic seaboard in 1776 seems inevitable; but that is not how it appeared at the time. The colonists and the British government felt pride in equal measure over their joint defeat of France and Spain. Furthermore, in

The Boston Tea Party (1773) *above* was provoked by the British government's decision to reduce the excise duty on tea at home, but not in the American colonies (the Tea Act). Inhabitants of Boston, one of America's principal early ports, boarded British East India Company ships in the harbour, disguised as Indians, and jettisoned their cargoes of tea overboard; excise men were tarred and feathered, and had tea forced down their throats. This early 19th-century print identifies the rebellion with the independence movement by showing the Liberty Tree; in fact greater unrest resulted from the British government's punitive measures (the Intolerable Acts) which included an embargo on Bostonian trade until compensation for the cargo was paid.

blood, language, religion, culture and economic organization, the British and the white Americans were essentially one people: the individual colonies had always looked towards London, rather than towards each other, for political support, political identity, and commercial opportunity. However, the magnitude of the gains made by the Peace of Paris created new problems at the same time as it solved old ones. On the one hand, once the threat of French attack was removed, the colonists became more resentful of British interference in their affairs: they looked for a greater measure of self-government. On the other, the acquisition of so much new territory encouraged the government in London to take steps to tighten its imperial organization. New taxes were imposed on the colonies to pay for the defence of the new lands; yet legislation was also passed to prohibit individual settlers from spreading west – the ministers in London intended to sell rights over the new lands to the highest bidder.

The colonies had a venerable tradition of disobedience and even resistance to government edicts. All of them had their own elective assemblies, most of which had a long record of clashes with the governors and other officials sent out from London. But the quarrels of the past were as nothing compared to the opposition that greeted the new measures decreed by Britain in the decade after 1763. There were stormy assembly meetings; there were angry court decisions condemning the taxes; there were violent popular demonstrations. In the end, the British government responded with severe measures designed to restore order, and the Americans countered by calling a congress of representatives from all the colonial assemblies (September 1774) and organizing an embargo on British imports. Tension mounted, and in April 1775 an armed confrontation between local demonstrators and British troops at Lexington in Massachusetts ended in bloodshed. A second continental congress met at Philadelphia the following month and searched anxiously for a compromise.

Only as each formula for reconciliation was rebuffed by London did a faction of radical colonists find widespread support for the idea of breaking with Britain. On 4 July 1776, after much debate, a unilateral Declaration of Independence, drafted by Thomas Jefferson of Virginia, was adopted. On 2 August the members of Congress signed it one by one: John Hancock, President of Congress, signed first, with an enormous, bold signature to make sure (he said) that King George could read it without his spectacles. When the text reached the American commander-in-chief, George Washington, he had it read out to every company of his troops so that they might be sure why they were fighting. In this way a new nation,

The War of Independence was the culmination of several years of colonial unrest. A limitation on the westward movement of settlers (the Proclamation Line, 1763) and a series of heavy taxes, imposed in order to fund wars against the Indians and the French, caused bitter resentment among the colonists. By 1770 reinforcements were brought to New England to quell increasing violence there. Agitators such as Paul Revere made much of relatively minor incidents such as the shooting of 5 rioters in Boston in 1770 *below*. Of the 8 soldiers involved, only 2 were found guilty of manslaughter. Organized fighting broke out in Massachusetts in April 1775, and the British response was initially effective, culminating in the capture and burning of New York *near left* in September 1776.

the United States of America, was born: a republic committed to Jefferson's proposition that 'all men are created equal'.

But in 1776 this new nation patently lacked the organization to survive. Congress was little more than a recurrent diplomatic conference of sovereign states. The army which it raised with much difficulty and supported inadequately would have collapsed altogether but for the courage, wisdom and iron fortitude of General Washington. And, even then, there were many defeats: New York was lost in 1776, Philadelphia in 1777, Savannah in 1778, Charleston in 1780. But the British commanders seemed to possess an uncanny knack of snatching defeat from the jaws of victory. In 1777 a British army, pressing south from Canada, advanced too far from its supply bases, was cut off, and had to surrender ignominiously at Saratoga. This event persuaded the French, still smarting from their humiliation in the Seven Years' War, to declare war on Great Britain. In 1781, bottled up on the Yorktown Peninsula by a French fleet and a Franco-American army, the last British field army surrendered.

The British soldiers are said to have marched off into captivity playing a tune called *The world turned upside down*. And so it must have

The BLOODY MASSACRE perpetrated in King-Street BOSTON on March 5th 1770 by a party of the 29th Regt.

seemed to them; for Yorktown marked the defeat of the greatest empire in the world – a defeat formalized in 1783 by a peace treaty which explicitly recognized American independence. But still the victors had no adequate corporate constitution. This was finally provided in 1787, by a special convention meeting at Philadelphia where, during several months of hard and secret negotiation, the Constitution that has governed the United States ever since was devised.

It is a document full of wise practical detail, which in part explains its survival; but its success was chiefly due to its three governing principles. First, the republic was deemed to be a nation. The opening words of the preamble are: 'We, the People of the United States, in order to form a more perfect Union…'. The logic of the revolt against Britain was thus admitted: Britain had driven the Americans together in resistance to its oppression; they would not now let themselves be put asunder. But, second, they remained a confederation. The thirteen states were too well-established to be abolished or entirely subjected to the new central government; besides, with a vast continent to explore and settle, it was common sense to allow the greatest possible freedom to local governments. It took weeks to ride the stage-coach route from Charleston to Boston, and even longer to cross the wilderness from the north of Maine, or from the Mississippi. So the union was called 'federal', meaning that it would join the states loosely, not tightly, and treat them all equally (in the United States Senate every state – however large or small – is still represented by two Senators).

The new Constitution also embodied the famous principle of the

General George Washington (1732-99) a Virginian land-owner and statesman, had extensive military experience during the French and Indian Wars (1754-63), and became commander of the colonial forces in 1775. He gained military advantage over the British at Christmas 1776 when he crossed the Delaware river by night *left* and launched surprise attacks on isolated British forces before they had time to concentrate. He proved to be a forceful leader, ending hostilities with the surrender of the British troops at Yorktown (1781). He was a popular choice for first President of the Republic (1789), enjoying two terms in office.

Anglo-American hostility continued in
one form or another for some decades after
the peace of 1783. Confrontation usually
occurred at sea, and in the War of 1812 the
Americans, avoiding a British attempt to
bottle the United States Navy in port,
defeated British warships on five
successive occasions *above*. By 1813,
however, the Royal Navy had succeeded in
its original aim, but a British attempt to
invade America was bloodily defeated in
1814, bringing a more lasting peace.

'separation of powers': federal authority was divided between the executive (headed by a president chosen for only four years at a time), a
legislature (the bicameral Congress), and a judiciary (the Supreme
Court). All had different methods of election or appointment, which
made it virtually impossible for a single person, or even a small group
of people, to gain control of all three branches of the federal government simultaneously. Finally, the Constitution, in its first ten amendments, guaranteed certain basic rights of the individual – such as the
right of all citizens to bear arms, to enjoy freedom of religion and
freedom of speech. These amendments, known collectively as the Bill
of Rights, helped to prevent the presidents (of whom the first was
George Washington), the Congress or the states from abusing their
power, as had the British king and prime minister against whom the
colonists had rebelled.

The Constitution came into effect in 1789, and at once began to show
its worth. Poor men felt that it safeguarded their rights, and their
loyalty was thus renewed. Rich men felt new confidence in the country's future, and were readier to invest in it (especially since, for a long
time, the government did not tax them very heavily). This public confidence made possible the next great event in United States history: the
Louisiana Purchase of 1803. By that date much of the land east of the
Mississippi, west of the Appalachians, and south of the Great Lakes had
been organized into new states and admitted to the union (Kentucky in
1792, Tennessee in 1796, Ohio in 1803). Now France (which had recovered Louisiana from Spain shortly before) sold all its claims to the
area between the Mississippi and the Rocky Mountains for $15 million,
thereby doubling the size of the United States. As soon as news of the
purchase became known, settlers crossed the Mississippi in large numbers, searching for the better lands, greater wealth and larger freedom
that always seemed to lie towards the sunset. This great movement of
population continued unabated until the end of the nineteenth century.
The country which numbered thirteen states in 1783, and seventeen in
1803, with a combined population of 4 million, had grown to thirty-five

states by 1861 with a population of 31 million, and to forty-seven states by 1900 with a population of 90 million.

The Louisiana Purchase was not the last such acquisition. Parts of Florida were conquered from Spain, and the rest secured by compulsory purchase, in 1819; Oregon was secured by agreement with Britain in 1846; New Mexico and California were annexed, after a bloody two-year war against Mexico, in 1848; Alaska was purchased from Russia in 1867. But most of the territory west of the Appalachians also had to be wrested by brute force from its original inhabitants.

The Indian tribes of the Great Plains were far more formidable foes of the white man in the nineteenth century than they had been in the days of Hernán Cortés or Captain John Smith. From the Spaniards in Mexico they had acquired the horse; from the French and English in the northeast they had taken up the gun; and by the mid-eighteenth century some tribes, such as the Apache and the Sioux, had learnt to combine the two. But it was no longer enough. The firepower of the white settlers was, usually, far superior to that of the tribes. The white men therefore behaved as they wished, forcibly removing the Indians with great cruelty – and no legal justification – from any lands that they

The Continental Congress and other early assemblies had met at Philadelphia, and the first Congress held under the United States Constitution met at New York in 1789. But the following year it was resolved to build a new federal capital, on a site by the Potomac river personally selected by President Washington. It was named after him, and from 1800 served as the seat of the President, Supreme Court and, in the Capitol building, the Senate and House of Representatives *right*. This structure, and most others in Washington, was burnt down by the British during the War of 1812. The present, classical, white-domed structure replaced it.

desired. In the 1830s, for example, 50,000 Cherokees from Georgia were collected into concentration camps and then sent on a winter march to 'reservations' in Oklahoma. Many of them died. A similar fate befell the other tribes of the south-east. Few indeed were the tribal leaders who, like Chief Seattle in the Pacific Northwest, played the white man at his own game and won: in 1851 he sold a stretch of land by Puget Sound for a large sum of money, on condition that the town to be built on the site should bear his name. It still does. Most other chiefs lost their lands without compensation or memorial; and any attempt to break out of the arbitrary 'reservations' was mowed down by the Gatling guns of the United States army. In 1500, there had been perhaps 4.5 million 'Red' Indians living north of the Rio Grande; by 1890, after the final defeat of the Sioux at the battle of Wounded Knee, there were probably less than 500,000. It was a man-made human disaster almost on the scale of the Spanish destruction of Aztec Mexico.

The victors in the earlier Indian wars were mostly of white, English, Protestant farming stock; and most of them long remained farmers. It is true that the urban population of the United States expanded, in the first half of the nineteenth century, at a rate that has never been equalled since (in seventy years it leaped from around 200,000 to well over 5 million). But elsewhere the forests were felled, the prairies were ploughed, and the immense abundance of the virgin lands of America began to make itself felt: by 1850 the United States was exporting

The winning of the West is a story that can be told in many different ways. For the white population of the eastern states, the West was presented as a land of boundless opportunity, wide open for settlement and exploitation *above*. In fact, of course, the Great Plains were already settled: the Indian population had lived there for generations, and the white man could only move in if the red men were driven off first. As the frontier moved westward, so the Indian struggle became more bitter and desparate. On the plains the economic base of Indian culture was finally broken when the buffalo herd was cut in two by the railroad (1869). An attempt to settle the Black Hills of Dakota by force (following the discovery of gold) provoked violent resistance by the Sioux Indians of the area, who in 1876 destroyed a US army detachment under Colonel George Custer at the Little Big Horn *far left*. The massacre caused public outrage and a vicious backlash. Twenty years later the Indians, like the buffalo, survived only in protected reservations *below*.

annually 1 million bushels of wheat, 146 million pounds of leaf tobacco, and no less than 635 million pounds of raw cotton. At the same time the American population was rising so rapidly that a vast home market developed, hungry not just for the produce of American farms and plantations, but also for the products of the growing American factories. Prosperity was thus assured, and one of the outstanding themes of American history was announced: the high standard of living which prosperity made possible for a large percentage of the population, and which has become one of the chief components of the 'American way of life'.

These linked phenomena of continental expansion, growing production and a rising population were the work of an energetic, intelligent and well-trained people. The Americans were not only enthusiastic democrats and boastful nationalists; they were also the best-educated people in the world, and took care to maintain that advantage. Almost everybody believed that schooling was necessary and desirable for both men and women. And since, in most states, all white males were franchised, the poor voters were able to use their political power in order to force the rich to pay for education. Primary schooling was almost universal in the Northeast and Midwest (though not in the South) by the middle of the nineteenth century. In the years that followed, higher education was also extended. The first university college in North America was Harvard, founded in 1636. Many others followed in the colonial period and, after independence, a public university was founded in each new state, for the practice moved westwards with the people. A university opened in Iowa in 1855, at Iowa City; in Washington in 1861, at Seattle; in Illinois in 1867, at Champaign-Urbana; in Oregon in 1872, at Eugene; and so on. Admittedly – because they

In the wake of the first settlers the railway, stage coach and covered wagon brought reinforcements. The lithograph *lower left*, from a painting of 1872 by John Gast, shows the figure of Progress (clasping a schoolbook under her arm and looping telegraph wires behind her) leading settlers westwards, where they drive darkness, buffaloes and Indians alike before them with peaceful but firm resolution. The lithograph poster *lower right* of the Illinois Central Railroad, dates from the time (10 years later) when transcontinental lines had linked the entire continent. The American steam locomotives appear larger than their European counterparts (even though many of them were made in Glasgow) because they were designed to burn wood rather than coal, a less compact source of energy which required a larger boiler and a larger tender. For farmers, however, agricultural

uses for the steam engine still lay far in the future. Only the most prosperous could afford even horse-drawn equipment, such as the mechanical reaper invented by Cyrus H. McCormack in 1834. However this new machine, shown *below* in a fresco in the Capitol building in Washington, made it possible to harvest, with minimal labour, the enormous acreages of cereals grown in the Midwest.

created fewer jobs – these foundations were seen as less beneficial to the local community than the state penitentiary (which was usually bought at public auction by the largest town) or the state legislature (which went to the second largest); but, even so, higher education soon became far more generally available in the United States than in any European country.

The high level of general education goes some way towards explaining the success and ingenuity of Americans. The industrial revolution was embraced early by the young republic: a power-driven cotton mill was operating in Rhode Island from 1791, and two years later Eli Whitney introduced his cotton gin, which made possible the large-scale cultivation and marketing of short-staple cotton (the only sort which would grow properly in the uplands of the interior). Whitney also pioneered the manufacture of machinery with interchangeable parts, later known as 'the American system', which greatly facilitated mass-production. Food output was revolutionized by the introduction of a mechanical reaper in the 1820s (and a full combine harvester after 1840), and a steam-driven plough in 1858; while food preservation was made possible by Appert's canning process (using tin cans from 1811) and Lowe's mechanical method of refrigeration (from the 1860s).

But undoubtedly the greatest impact on agricultural production, as on so much else, was made by the railways (chapter 23) which made it possible to market the new surpluses. The first American steam railroad opened in 1830; fifty years later, the rail network in the United States was larger than that of all Europe (including Britain and Russia). The railways lowered overland freight costs in the United States by 500 percent, and travel time by 900 percent, during their first twenty years of operation. Without them, the West could hardly have been won.

But there was a high price to pay for all these accomplishments. The Americans had called up forces which they could not control. The political system which gave so much scope to individual enterprise was democratic, and it grew more so as the population expanded, since white male suffrage was almost universal. Power therefore had to be shared by more and more people. The English Protestant community, though prolific, was not large enough to do all that needed to be done by itself; so it encouraged an enormous tide of other peoples – Catholic, or non-English-speaking, or both – to come to America. Although less than 1 million persons emigrated to the United States between 1821 and 1840, the total over the next two decades exceeded 4.5 million – the majority of them German and Irish.

There was, naturally enough, some hostility to the immigrants – especially the Catholic Irish – in the 1850s; but in most areas the similarities between the old and new Americans outweighed the differences. In the first place, they were all equally dedicated to the ruthless exploitation of the continent's resources (whether human, animal, mineral or vegetable). Second, they were all socially and geographically mobile. And third, they were all conditioned to expect good times and plenty just around the corner, whether through trade, speculation, or a gold rush; the first California gold strikes date from 1848. All these trends led to the erosion of traditional values and the atomization of society: respect for authority, never a strong suit in the colonies, was undermined. As Alexis de Tocqueville wrote in his celebrated essay *Democracy in America* (1835), the American child had become:

Life for the early settlers on the western plains was primitive and harsh. Those who survived the arduous and exposed journey by ox-drawn wagon *below* had to work long and hard before they could afford anything better than a turf cabin *left*. Simply built, using any materials that were available, these dwellings were nevertheless verminous and dangerous, tending to collapse on their inhabitants when rain-sodden. The delights of a 'home on the range' were a long time coming.

For many in Europe and elsewhere America seemed a land of limitless opportunity and guaranteed wealth. But, by the 1850s, concern was expressed in some quarters that the continent was becoming overpopulated, and measures were

'a sort of domestic dictator from infancy; the first notion he acquires in life is that he was born to command, and the first habit he contracts is that of ruling without resistance.'

Virtually every European traveller in the nineteenth century remarked on the unrestrained egotism of American children:

'The lad of fourteen… struts and swaggers and smokes his cigar and drinks rum; treads on the toes of his grandfather, swears at his mother and sister, and vows that he will run away.'

But the nation faced a number of problems in the 1840s and '50s which could only be solved satisfactorily by patience, goodwill and cool calculation: the organization of the new lands in the West, the war with Mexico, and above all the role of slavery. 'Individualism' could only, and did only, make these problems worse.

The cultivation of cotton and tobacco in the Southern states rested upon the exploitation of blacks through the system of plantation slavery (chapter 18). This system had grown up in the seventeenth century, but it owed its survival in the nineteenth century to immense profits made from the growth of cotton consumed by the prosperous mills of Lancashire and New England. The whites of the cotton states could not bring themselves to discard a system which made them so much money, despite the growing sense of outrage among whites outside the South at this flagrant violation of basic Christian and democratic principles.

contemplated to halt the flow of immigrants. The *Puck* cartoon *above* satirized the newly-respectable citizens who sought controls. In the event, no effective limits to immigration were set until 1921.

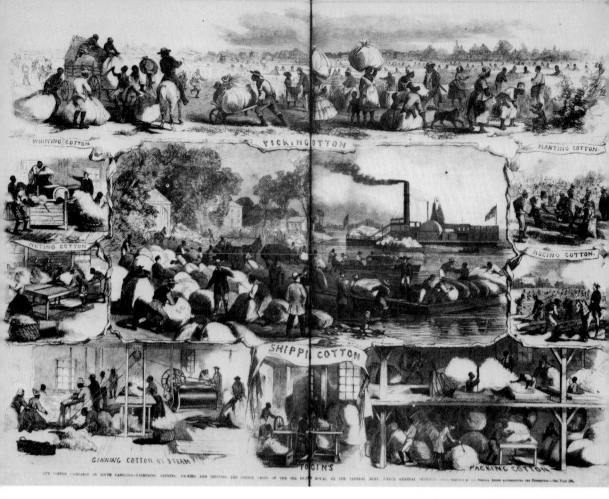

Gradually, the dispute came to dominate and poison American politics.

Fittingly enough, matters came to a head over the lands stolen from the Indians. The northern and western states were determined that the new lands of Kansas, Nebraska and elsewhere should only be developed by free labour; yet they were afraid that, in open economic competition with the slave system, the free farmers might lose, having less capital and higher overheads. The Southern states, for their part, feared that, unless slavery were allowed to expand into the new territories, they would grow too weak in the Union to be able to resist the northern anti-slavery faction. Each side began to grow violent in defence of what it saw as its essential interests.

By 1860 a breaking-point had been reached. The election of a determined anti-slavery President, Abraham Lincoln of Illinois, in November of that year, convinced the Southern leaders that their interests were no longer safeguarded by the Union. South Carolina passed an ordinance of secession on 20 December, and six more states had followed suit by the time of Lincoln's inauguration in January 1861. In February they formed a new, Southern republic: the Confederate States of America. Impatient to be done with the North, they fired on Fort Sumter in Charleston harbour, compelling its surrender (13 April 1861). The Northern states and the United States government, however, intent on preserving the political system to which most of the success of the past eighty years was attributed, determined to suppress the rebellion by force. This drove the states of the Upper South, Virginia foremost among them, to join the Confederacy, and America was plunged into a great civil war.

The economy of the Southern states rested essentially on the profitable cultivation of cotton by black slaves. Even the apparently impartial newspaper article *above*, which sought to explain the various stages by which the crop was prepared for export, testified to the massive involvement of slaves at every point. The exploitation of unfree labour, however, was a source of profound embarrassment and distress to the liberals of the north. A vast anti-slavery literature developed in the 1850s and '60s, which contrasted *right* the evils of the plantation with the virtues of emancipation. In the centre is the anti-slavery President Lincoln .

The North held great advantages. It was three times as wealthy as the South, outproducing it in manufactured goods by ten to one (in firearms by thirty-two to one) and in merchant shipping by nine to one; furthermore, it enlisted 2,200,000 men in the course of the war, as against 800,000 in the South. But the South had sufficient resources to stave off defeat for four years, and indeed at times came tantalizingly close to victory. For it only had to break the Northern will to continue, whereas the object of the North had to be to reconquer every foot of Southern soil. It was a close-run thing.

The Union armies suffered over 600,000 casualties, as against under 400,000 for the Confederacy, for the Southerners were better led for much of the war – their principal general, Robert E. Lee, was one of the ablest military commanders of the century. Only gradually did Abraham Lincoln emerge as the greatest of American presidents, able to

Many modern aspects of warfare made their appearance during the American Civil War. The sheer scale of the conflict (see map page 388) was appalling. This was the first war in history in which railways played a vital role, transporting men, ammunition and supplies. Field telegraphs facilitated communication, and press and photographic coverage was extensive. The Union armies also established large-scale concentration camps for corralling prisoners in which poor sanitary conditions caused many further casualties. Most notable was the invention, by the Union General William T. Sherman, of the 'scorched earth policy'. An advocate of bringing hostilities to an end by inflicting devastation on the civil population, his March to the Sea through Georgia (1864) razed Atlanta *left* and destroyed crops, goods, buildings and factories across a 60-mile wide path.

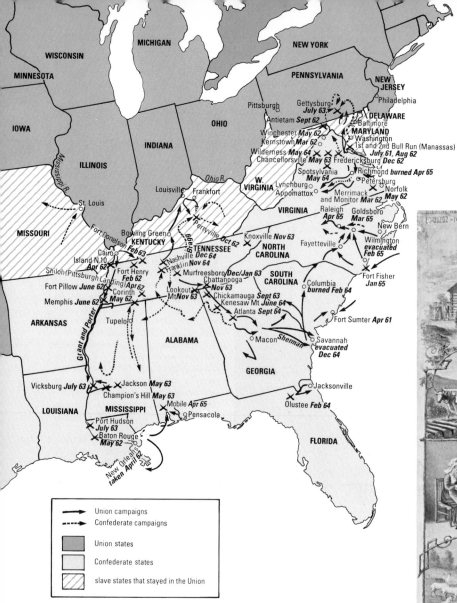

convince the world that this was a war to ensure the survival of democracy and the extinction of slavery. But it was the Northern strategy of attrition, as much as superior propaganda, which defeated Lee. After General Sherman's 'march to the sea' through Georgia and General Grant's bloody campaigns in Virginia in 1864-65, the South was a desert and half its army lay dead: the superior resources of the North in the end prevailed. The Union was preserved and slavery, the immediate cause of the war, was abolished.

The settlement which followed the Civil War left American blacks, on the whole, still at the mercy of the dominant whites; and for this, too, a terrible price would eventually have to be paid. But by the first centenary of the Revolution, in 1876, a rising standard of living, founded in hard work and high output, was restoring prosperity to the nation; and thereafter the process gathered momentum. Between 1877 and 1892, America's factories tripled their production. The population of the United States, at 90 million, was larger than that of any European nation except Russia; its economy was the most productive (and enjoyed the fastest growth rate) in the world; and its republican government had become strong, centralized and highly stable. In a little over a hundred years, the young nation had become a giant.

The Civil War 1861-65 *left* began when the Confederate States of America fired on US troops at Fort Sumter in April 1861, and ended when the main Confederate armies surrendered in April 1865. Nearly three million Americans served in the war, and 200,000 of the Union troops were black. More than 21 percent of the participants were killed, a much higher proportion than any of the armies in the First World War. In the Civil War armies about twice as many men died of disease as were killed in battle.

During the first century of independence and in spite of the economic and moral destruction of the South, the United States became a prosperous and populous nation. The commemorative poster *below* tried to measure the progress achieved in various spheres – from seamstress to sewing-machine, from sailing ship to steamer – a continuing vision of progress which carried the United States forward into the 20th century.

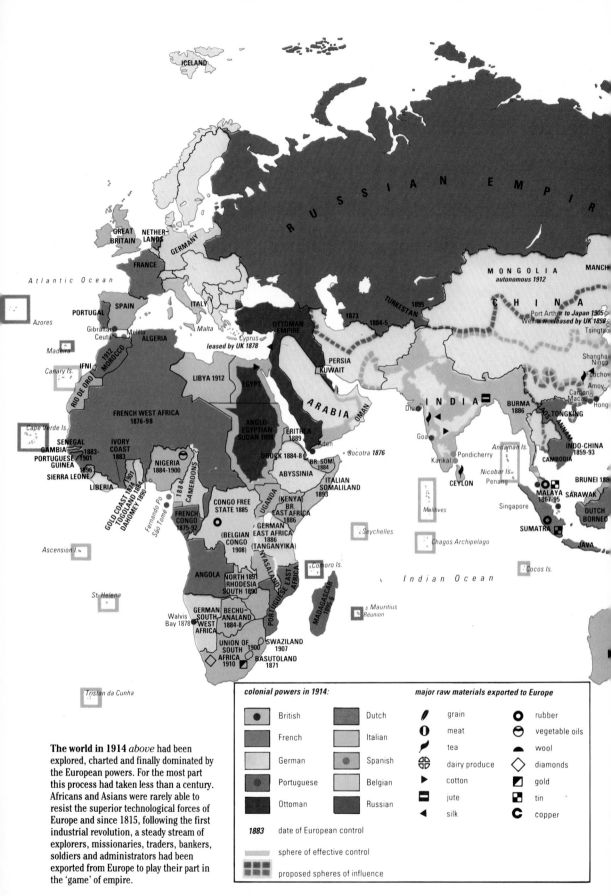

ICELAND

RUSSIAN EMPIRE

Atlantic Ocean

GREAT
BRITAIN

NETHER-
LANDS

GERMANY

FRANCE

MONGOLIA
autonomous 1912

MANCH

PORTUGAL

SPAIN

ITALY

TURKESTAN 1895

CHINA

Azores

1873

Port Arthur **to Japan 1905**
Welhaiwei *leased by UK 1898*

Tsingta

Gibraltar
Ceuta

Melilla

Malta

OTTOMAN
EMPIRE

Cyprus
leased by UK 1878

1884-5

Shangha
Ningp

Madeira

ALGERIA

Canary Is.

IFNI
MOROCCO
1912

PERSIA
KUWAIT

INDIA

Fobcho

RIO DE ORO

LIBYA 1912

EGYPT

ARABIA

OMAN

BURMA
1886

TONGKING

Amo
Canton
Macao

Hong

FRENCH WEST AFRICA
1876-98

ANGLO-
EGYPTIAN
SUDAN 1898

ERITREA
1889

Diu

Goa

INDO-CHINA
1859-93

Cape Verde Is.

SENEGAL

IVORY
COAST
1883

Aden

Socotra 1876

Karikal

Pondicherry

Andaman Is.

CAMBODIA

GAMBIA
PORTUGUESE
GUINEA

1883-
1901

1896

NIGERIA
1884-1900

DBOCK 1884-8

BR. SOM.
1884

Nicobar Is.
Penang

CEYLON

BRUNEI 188

SIERRA LEONE

ABYSSINIA

MALAYA
1867-95

SARAWAK

LIBERIA

GOLD COAST 1874
TOGOLAND 1884
DAHOMEY 1890

CAMEROONS 1884

Fernando Po
São Tomé

FRENCH
CONGO
1875-92

CONGO FREE
STATE 1885

UGANDA

ITALIAN
SOMALILAND
1893

(KENYA)
BR.
EAST AFRICA
1886

Maldives

Singapore

DUTCH
BORNEO

SUMATRA

JAVA

Ascension I.

(BELGIAN
CONGO
1908)

GERMAN
EAST AFRICA
1886
(TANGANYIKA)

Seychelles

Chagos Archipelago

Cocos Is.

St. Helena

ANGOLA

NORTH 1891
RHODESIA
SOUTH 1890

NYASALAND

EAST
AFRICA

PORTUGUESE

Comoro Is.

MADAGASCAR
1885-6

Indian Ocean

Mauritius
Réunion

Walvis
Bay 1878

GERMAN
SOUTH
WEST
AFRICA

BECHU-
ANALAND
1884-8

SWAZILAND
1907

UNION OF
SOUTH
AFRICA
1910

1900

BASUTOLAND
1871

Tristan da Cunha

The world in 1914 *above* had been
explored, charted and finally dominated by
the European powers. For the most part
this process had taken less than a century.
Africans and Asians were rarely able to
resist the superior technological forces of
Europe and since 1815, following the first
industrial revolution, a steady stream of
explorers, missionaries, traders, bankers,
soldiers and administrators had been
exported from Europe to play their part in
the 'game' of empire.

colonial powers in 1914:

● British

French

German

Portuguese

Ottoman

Dutch

Italian

Spanish

Belgian

Russian

major raw materials exported to Europe

grain

meat

tea

dairy produce

cotton

jute

silk

rubber

vegetable oils

wool

diamonds

gold

tin

copper

1883 date of European control

sphere of effective control

proposed spheres of influence

CHAPTER 23

INDUSTRY AND EMPIRE
1870–1914

In 1800, the Europeans and the North Americans between them dominated 35 percent of the world's land surface, and by 1914 they controlled 84 percent. The key to this extraordinary extension of white imperialism was industrial power (chapter 20); but the process of industrialization among the imperial powers was far from uniform. At the time of the American Civil War, Great Britain was the world's leading industrial and trading nation, a place it had gained and held since the beginning of the nineteenth century. But between 1870 and 1914, although Britain remained the major trading power, her industrial supremacy was challenged by both Germany, united in 1871 under Prussian leadership, and the United States.

Part of the explanation for this shift lies precisely in the fact that Britain had been first in the field: her industrial plant was geared to the traditional sources of energy – water and coal – and she found it difficult to adapt to the newer ones. Although British inventors were the first to discover cheaper methods of mass-producing steel (the Bessemer and Gilchrist-Thomas processes), these were first exploited in Europe; and the major developments in new industries (especially the production of chemical compounds for agriculture, dyes, drugs and, eventually, plastics) were also made elsewhere. Then, in the 1860s efficient electric dynamos were perfected in Germany, and swiftly harnessed to drive machinery, to light streets and factories, and to power trams. In the 1870s, also in Germany, an internal combustion engine was developed which ran on petroleum and could drive machines, automobiles and ships. Britain's manufacturing rivals needed the advantages bestowed by these developments; yet to be fully competitive they also needed protection. So tariffs were introduced almost

Coal provided the power that moved machines in the first industrial revolution, and the profits derived from selling the crucial fuel gave many miners a standard of living that was high for manual workers. By 1813, when George Walker produced a series of studies of local fashions and customs in northern England *right*, a profitable landscape was one dominated by pit-heads, factories and the first railways.

everywhere, except in Britain, bringing to an end the brief era of Free Trade and encouraging greater economic nationalism.

The combination of tariffs and new products brought great dividends. Although the British economy doubled its industrial output between 1870 and 1914, output in the United States trebled, in Germany quadrupled, and in Russia increased nine-fold. Of course, to some extent such spectacular gains merely reflected the degrees of backwardness which had prevailed in many European countries, for there was much ground to be made up: even as late as 1896 British industry employed 13 million horse power of energy, against Germany's 8 million, and Russia's mere 3 million. But inevitably, as slack resources were brought into production, Britain's relative position declined in favour of economies with greater natural riches and larger populations.

These variations in the 'pecking order' of the industrial giants were important for European history (chapter 24); but, in a global context, the crucial factor was the stunning increase in their combined output. Annual coal production in Europe rose from 170 million tons in the

Industrial technology developed at a breathless rate during the 19th century, and changed the everyday life of Europeans in different ways. The wrought-iron lattice of the Eiffel Tower *below left* (built in Paris in 1889 to commemorate the first centenary of the French Revolution), initiated a new style of civil engineering and architectural design. The steel bicycle had by then come into mass-production *below* and dramatically extended the horizons of ordinary people: those unable to afford a horse, or living far from the railways, could now travel fairly extensively, whether for business or pleasure. For those wishing to journey further afield, the successful construction of iron ships by Isambard Kingdom Brunel (pictured *right* beside the enormous anchor chains of his ship, the *Great Eastern* in 1858) provided fast and reliable transport across the oceans. Shortly afterwards, the invention first of wireless telegraphy in 1895 and then of the radio in 1920 by Giuseppe Marconi *lower right* brought news and ideas from all around the world into every home.

1860s to 594 million in the 1890s, and in the United States from 43 million to 281 million tons. World steel output rose from 540,000 tons in 1870 to 14 million in 1895; world steam engine capacity, over the same period, from 18 million horse-power to 66 million. This unprecedented and unparalleled growth in crude output was accompanied by a seemingly endless stream of new inventions: the automatic loom-and-spindle, the telephone, the camera, the sewing machine, the typewriter, the bicycle, the motor car.

There were several reasons for this rapid expansion. In the first place, Europe's population soared, and with it, domestic demand. During the course of the nineteenth century, the inhabitants of the continent multiplied from 190 million to 423 million, while a further 40 million emigrated, mainly to the Americas, between 1850 and 1914 (19 million from Britain, 6 million from Germany). This demographic revolution had two immediate causes. On the one hand, the birth rate increased rapidly, largely because more people were earning good wages and so could afford to marry at a younger age and raise a larger

'The Last of England' by Ford Madox Brown *left* was undoubtedly a romantic view, but it depicted a common enough experience – emigration. During the 19th century the population of Europe increased from 190 million to 423 million. Many were tempted to improve their lot in the less-populated colonial possessions or in America. Between 1821 and 1920 over 36 million immigrants entered North America from Europe; a further 2 million emigrated to Australia and New Zealand, and over 3 million to Latin America.

Oil was to the second phase of industrialization what coal had been to the first. The photograph *below left* was taken in 1865 in Western Pennsylvania, USA, not far from where the strike was made in 1858 which ushered in the modern petroleum industry. Closely-packed wooden derricks of various companies jostle for a share of the deposits below the barely-cleared forest valley in the race to extract as much oil as quickly as possible.

family. On the other, the death rate fell, mainly due to a marked reduction in the virulence and extent of the major epidemic diseases, better nutrition (particularly the potato), and improvements in public health and sanitation. Although population growth on the whole preceded industrialization, and indeed was highest in the least wealthy parts of Europe (Spain and Russia), industrial growth ensured that the burgeoning populations could be employed, and fed. Living standards rose everywhere, though living conditions improved more slowly.

To speed up and secure the process of economic improvement on the Continent required encouragement from above as well as growing demand from below. Governments throughout Europe believed that industrial power was now the key to international power; so in the great states with weak economies (Russia, Austria, and Germany, though not in the Ottoman empire), industrialization took place with full government backing. But it also enjoyed the full support of the trading, banking and manufacturing communities, which saw indus-

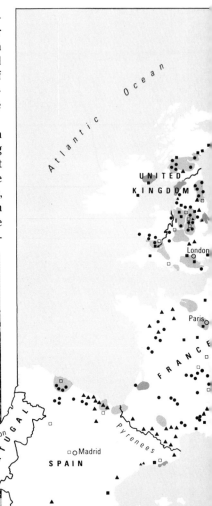

In Europe between 1870 and 1914
below the industrial regions which had been developed in the early 19th century – notably Britain, the Ruhr, the Saar and northern France – continued to expand; but they were now joined by new industrial areas which were opened up when railways were developed. Also, after 1870, the old-established industries (coal, iron, textiles) were joined by new branches of manufacture such as the chemical and electrical industries.

trialization as the best way to emulate the prosperous, free-trading middle classes of Britain. An early area of co-operation between government and governed was the provision of a stable and safe financial system. There were, by now, parliaments in almost every industrial nation, usually elected by wide (if not universal) manhood suffrage, to ensure that governments did not arbitrarily steal the public's money; and there was a Gold Standard to make sure that currencies kept, or increased, their values. The Pound Sterling and the Franc Germinal offered a fixed rate of exchange, valid all over the world. Furthermore, after 1850 there was a solid and rapidly-expanding private banking system in every industrial nation. Large international banking houses, like the Rothschilds or Barings, oiled the wheels of world trade and investment. New mortgage and investment banks, particularly in Germany, the United States and France, helped to channel funds directly from savers to domestic industry. And finally, as the developing economies grew richer, an increasing flow of capital found its way overseas, to develop new markets and new sources of raw materials. By 1914 the United States had £534 million invested abroad, while Germany had £1,200 million, France £1,700 million and Great Britain £4,000 million.

The return on these foreign investments, both in the form of cheaper raw materials and in enhanced profits, favoured a concentration of enterprises at home, for the bigger the factory or the mine, the bigger the savings and the greater the profit. As the successful firms grew, they looked around for other businesses to buy up, and giant firms emerged, like Standard Oil in America. Founded by the Rockefeller family, Standard Oil rapidly grew by taking over its smaller rivals.

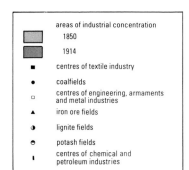

areas of industrial concentration
- 1850
- 1914
- ■ centres of textile industry
- ● coalfields
- □ centres of engineering, armaments and metal industries
- ▲ iron ore fields
- ◑ lignite fields
- ◔ potash fields
- ı centres of chemical and petroleum industries

By 1905 it controlled 85 percent of all American oil production and 95 percent of all oil trade. The remarkable American financier, John Pierpont Morgan, built up the largest trust in the world in iron and steel, in banking, in railroads and in shipping. Although from the 1890s legislation was passed which sought to prevent further mergers which might substantially lessen competition, the small family firm steadily lost ground to the public company under expert managerial control.

The coming of industry transformed western society, a process which historians have called 'modernization': the development of new forms of economic and institutional life, of better education, of a larger state apparatus. But above all it meant urbanization. In the 1860s, most people in the United States and western Europe lived in villages and on farms; by 1914 the majority lived in towns and cities. The greatest transformation came in England, where the rural population declined to a mere 10 percent of the total workforce in the course of the nineteenth century. In Germany much the same shift was squeezed into a single generation: in 1871 it was still largely a country of small towns and villages; but by 1914 there were thirty cities whose populations exceeded 100,000. When Alfred Krupp set up his armaments works in the 1840s, Essen was a small Ruhr village; yet by 1914, the Ruhr had become the power-house of European industry, transforming the traditional, small-farming region of Westphalia beyond recognition.

The rapid growth of cities was accompanied by a revolution in Europe's social structure. Not only did more people now share urban life; most of them became part of the new proletariat thrown up by industrialization. The traditional working class of artisans and master-craftsmen was joined by an army of unskilled and semi-skilled

Industrialization and urbanization went hand in hand. Towns which had been mere villages, or had not even existed, sprang to life as great centres of industry, commerce or mining. When Friedrich Krupp (1787-1826) built a small steel plant in the village of Essen, in the Ruhr valley, West Germany, in about 1810, his family had been manufacturing military weapons in the area for over two centuries. But it was his son Alfred (1812-87) who made Krupp a household name. In the 1840s, his factory *below left* began to make armaments of cast steel. They proved highly effective, and bulk orders soon came in from the Prussian army, the Russians, and others, leading to an enormous extension of the Essen factory complex (*right* in the 1870s), the building of many houses for workers, and to the installation of massive machinery (like the great steam hammer known as 'Fritz', *below right*, in 1861). After the Franco-Prussian War of 1870-1, which was won partly through the superior quality of the German weaponry, Krupps increasingly specialized in the production of guns, and the firm remained the principal supplier of armaments to the German armed forces until 1945. The Ruhr region remains one of Europe's great industrial centres.

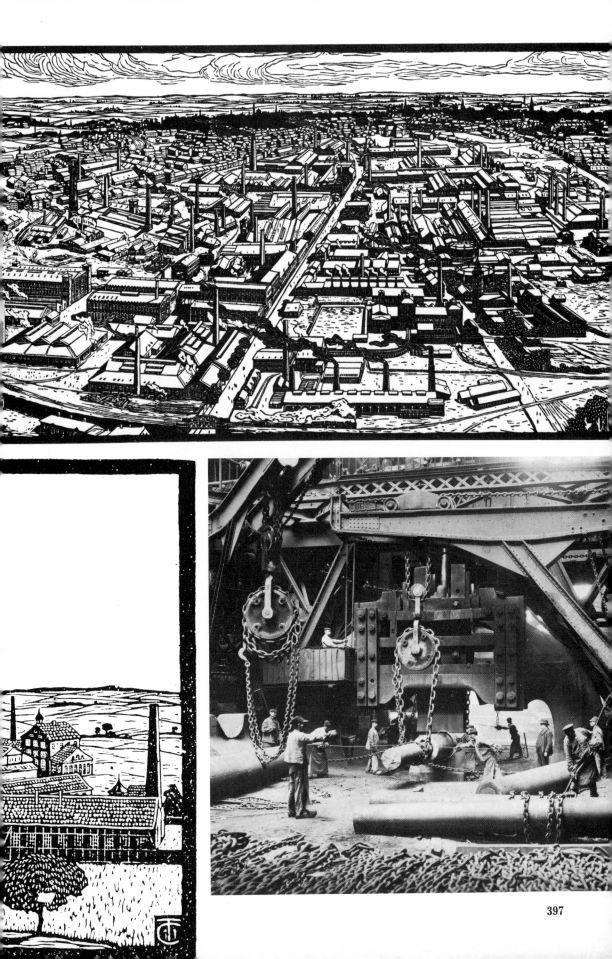

397

Population growth was not spread evenly over urban and rural districts. The expansion of old cities and the founding of new towns were characteristic features of the industrial age. The expansion of some cities with a history going back to medieval times – London, Cologne, Lyons, Moscow and many others – often brought the greatest problems. The hasty erection of small, cheap, closely-packed houses in already heavily-populated centres led rapidly to slum conditions; the incursions made by new roads and railways only added to the problems of urban pollution. In 1872 the French artist Gustave Doré engraved a series of scenes from the everyday life of London *below*; some of his views of metropolitan life were so gloomy and squalid that they were used in evidence in government reports on urban conditions.

labourers in building, transport and factories. Thrown together by the new economic system, workers began to combine in unions and political movements which aimed to improve wages and working conditions. A new middle class emerged as well, committed to servicing and managing modern industry and trade, anxious to rise up the social scale, and keen to improve and modernize the cities. This new middle class gradually came to supplant both the old educated townsmen (the clergy, lawyers and teachers) and the old aristocracy (which rapidly switched from loss-making agriculture to shrewd investments in transport or industry, good bourgeois marriages, and a seat on the board).

Cities signalled other changes, too. Education was now both easier to manage and more necessary to obtain, thanks to the demand for a literate working class and a trained bureaucracy. In most countries, compulsory education for young children was introduced by law (in Britain after 1870; in France after 1882 and so on); and the number of children going to secondary schools increased dramatically (in France, it doubled between 1850 and 1910). The acquisition of the basic skills of reading, writing and arithmetic came to be seen as a desirable goal by intellectuals, clerics, government and working-class leaders alike:

education was held to promote economic and technical improvement, to provide the key to social opportunity and, in an age of liberal enlightenment, to show the path to a virtuous and rational life. This was the age of self-improvement, of an optimistic conviction that 'progress' was now the natural condition of mankind.

And optimisim was not out of order for most Europeans. Though poverty and deprivation were widespread (leading to the growing fear and distrust of the working class by the new rich), the thirty years before 1914 witnessed a major improvement in living standards, opportunities and expectations. Whether seen through the popularity of new

BRITISH STEEL SMELTERS AMALGAMATED ASSOCIATION

Estd 1886

Like a rib of steel

Then, join you with them

To make strength stronger

AMALGAMATED ASSOCIATION

UNITED WE STAND DIVIDED WE FALL

This is to Certify that
was admitted a Member of the above Association
on the   day of   19
John Hodge
General Secretary

daily newspapers, or the bicycle craze, or the rise of popular theatre and revue, industrial and urban growth had ushered in the age of mass consumption and mass culture. For the first time, Europeans were, for the most part, free from want. They could feed themselves adequately and still have money in their pockets for pleasure and amusement, for holidays and housing, for clothes and ornaments. The cost of food, which had previously absorbed a very large part of the weekly income of the working classes, now fell dramatically: in Britain, the price of a loaf of bread dropped from 1 shilling and 5 pence (7p) in 1870 to 4 pence (2p) in 1904.

Organized labour was a concomitant of the industrial revolution. Although guilds had existed since medieval times, repressive laws against industrial labour movements were introduced in England following the French Revolution. Their repeal (1824) inaugurated a rapid growth in trade unions, but legal recognition and full emancipation did not come until the first decades of the 20th century. The membership certificate *above* dates from the 1890s.

The key to this cheaper food lay in the creation of a new, fast and reliable transport network which was capable of carrying bulk cargoes over long distances. The adoption of the steam engine in shipbuilding during the early nineteenth century revolutionized sea transport. The early steamships operated mainly on narrow inland waterways (the first plied along the Hudson from 1807), where sailing ships had always experienced the greatest difficulty; but before long, ocean-going steamers were being built, at first of wood but later of iron. This made it possible to increase the size as well as the speed of ships: the *Great Eastern*, built in England in 1857-58, weighed 27,000 tons (whereas the largest wooden ships weighed only 2,000). World steamship tonnage rose dramatically from 1.4 million in 1870, to 8 million in 1890, and to 19 million (10 million of it British) in 1910.

By land, the steam engine made possible the railways. Some 400 miles of track already existed by the 1820s in England, but most of them were used by horse-drawn wagons to transport coal for short distances from a colliery to a waterway. In 1825, however, a commercial line for steam locomotives was opened between Stockton and Darlington, and several other 'commuter routes' were in operation by 1838, when Birmingham and London were at last linked by rail. In 1840 there were still only 4,700 miles of track in the world, mostly in Britain, Belgium and the United States; but by 1900, there were 490,000 miles – 176,000 in Europe, 223,000 in North America, and the rest scattered throughout the world. The Trans-Siberian rail link was completed in 1905, making it possible to travel in a few weeks by train all the way from Ostend on the North Sea to Vladivostok on the Pacific.

Transport and communication by land and sea was vastly improved in the later 19th century. The first trans-continental railway in North America was completed in 1869 and, in the same year, the Suez Canal *above* was opened, linking the Red Sea with the Mediterranean and cutting the sea journey from Europe to India by almost half. It soon became one of the world's most heavily used shipping lanes and, by the 1950s, handled about 15 percent of the world's sea traffic. In 1891 work commenced on the Trans-Siberian Railway *right*. Progress was slow because of the immense distance to be covered and the variety of natural obstacles in the way. In the western section, for example, between Chelyabinsk in the Urals and Irkutsk, 8 bridges of 300 yards or more were required. The line was only completed in 1905 with a loop around Lake Baikal, which included 38 tunnels in 43 miles. Covering 4600 miles, the Trans-Siberian Railway is the longest continuous stretch of track in the world.

The transport revolution entered its second phase at the turn of the 19th century. The invention of the aeroplane *above* was the culmination of many experiments with gliders and powered model planes. When; in 1903, Orville and Wilbur Wright succeeded in flying a machine (powered by an internal combustion engine) that was heavier than air at Kittyhawk, North Carolina, few people – including the Wright brothers – would have suggested that their mechanical monstrosity would, within 30 years, change the face of international travel. The more mundane motor car had been growing in popularity since the 1890s. Soon popular demand made it possible to introduce techniques of mass-production. In 1908, Henry Ford of Michigan, USA, decided to launch his Model T *below*, and over the next twenty years 15 million of them rolled off a continuous assembly line – the first in the world – making Ford the largest automobile producer in the world.

By 1914 it was even possible for the determined traveller to fly to his destination. In 1900 the first airship, pioneered by Count Zeppelin, rose above Germany and, by 1910, regular passenger services by airship had begun to operate. In 1903, in America, the Wright brothers made their first successful trip in a flying machine that was heavier than air, powered by a 12-horsepower petrol engine. Meanwhile, in Europe, Louis Blériot flew across the Channel by aeroplane and Henri Farman made the first 100-mile flight in 1909. But mass transportation of goods or passengers by air remained a thing of the future. The petrol engine, at this stage, was more successfully applied to road vehicles.

The first motor cars were patented in the 1880s. Within ten years they were being produced in every industrialized country as playthings for the rich, often built by those same craftsmen who made horse-drawn carriages; but after twenty years, small specialized production gave way to mass-production in large factories. Ford in the United States, Renault in France and Morris in Britain pioneered motoring for the masses. By 1914 there were over one million cars in the United States and a quarter of a million in Britain. Motor-bus services began in England (ironically, at the initiative of railway companies) in 1903; motor-driven fire-engines followed in 1905; taxi-cab services in 1907. On the eve of war the first armoured cars appeared.

This transport revolution had many effects. In the first place, it completed the integration of the various advanced economies. In Britain, it permitted (for example) the soft fruit growers of Blairgowrie in Scotland to sell their perishable produce in London: every night in July, a special train was loaded with raspberries, which the next morning

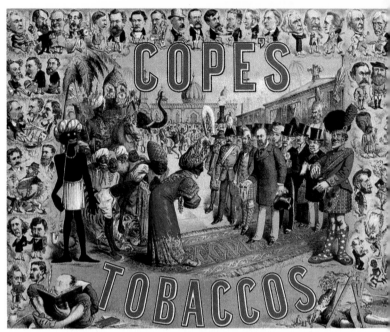

Advertisements often unconsciously reflect the assumptions on which societies operate. The Victorian tobacco advert *right* shows the wealthy European manufacturers receiving the raw material from crudely parodied native growers, to whom the finished product will eventually be resold. But European exploitation of the colonies was not always detrimental. Roads were built, education and medicine provided, harbours improved, and *below* topographical surveys carried out. Nevertheless, the notion of white racial superiority was rarely, if ever, questioned.

were on sale in Covent Garden, 500 miles to the south. In America, according to the proud boast of steel baron Andrew Carnegie, integration, profit and public utility marched hand-in-hand:

'Two pounds of ironstone mined upon Lake Superior and transported 1900 miles to Pittsburgh; one pound and one-half of coal, mined and manufactured into coke, and transported to Pittsburgh; one-half pound of lime, mined and transported to Pittsburgh; a small amount of manganese ore mined in Virginia and transported to Pittsburgh – and these four pounds of materials manufactured into one pound of steel, for which the consumer pays one cent.'

But transport of these commodities did not stop at national frontiers. Cheap food and raw materials began to flood into Europe and America from Australia, Asia and Africa; and expensive manufactured goods began to pour back. So, in the 1880s the people of Scotland ate bread made from North American wheat brought to them by locomotives made at the Springfield works outside Glasgow and steamships built on the Clyde, and packaged in sacks made in Dundee from jute brought there from Calcutta. Trade had become the fibre that held the world economy together.

That fibre, however, could constrict as well as connect, especially abroad. The scramble for raw materials and commodities overseas gave rise to a race to control and monopolize the areas from which supplies were drawn. Even the most unpromising terrain, like Kenya or Nigeria, could now be transformed by railways and modern irrigation into new plantation colonies. Here, crops such as tea, coffee, cotton, tobacco, sisal and cocoa could be grown at great profit. These were relatively backward areas which had little resistance to European technology – they had avoided becoming colonies before only because the white man had lacked adequate defences against tropical disease (especially malaria) until the mass-production of quinine in the 1830s. Any attempt to oppose the Westerners, whether by the Zulus in the south or by Muslim zealots in the north, was ruthlessly crushed: the rifles and machine guns of the Europeans were rarely defeated.

Of course imperialism was not new in Europe: the old colonial empires (Spanish, Portuguese, Dutch, French and British) stretched back over three centuries. But after 1870 the scramble for empire rapidly caught the imagination of populations eager for new opportunities and fed on a new diet of popular papers and cheap nationalist fiction. Empire became a mark of national virility, sometimes justified by ideas of mission ('the White Man's Burden': to bring civilization and enlightenment to the native societies they ruled) but more usually assumed to be a God-given reward for innate racial superiority. As Cecil Rhodes, the richest man in southern Africa, used to tell his friends: to be born British was to win first prize in the lottery of life. But to be born Belgian, German or French was not much worse. In 1884 Leopold II of Belgium took over the entire Congo basin, which he exploited with great cruelty as his private domain. Shortly afterwards, Germany laid claim to African territory in four different areas (Togoland, the Cameroons, South-West Africa and East Africa) covering nearly 1 million square miles and containing some 14 million people; while France, which had invaded Algeria as early as 1830, by the end of the century ruled Madagascar and the greater part of West and North Africa, an empire of some 4 million square miles and 47 million people. Other areas of the continent were claimed by Italy, Spain and Portugal so that, by 1914, there was scarcely a flagpole in Africa from which some European flag did not fly.

The tides of empire flowed no less strongly in Asia. Tsarist Russia began in the 1820s to push forward against the Muslim Khanates of the steppe, survivals of the empires of Genghis Khan and Timur the Lame. One

Cecil John Rhodes (1853-1902) *above* moved to South Africa at the age of 17 to recover from tuberculosis, but soon made a fortune from diamonds. His wealth and openly imperialist views made him an effective political figure and, in 1890, he became Prime Minister of Cape Colony. He dreamed of planting the British flag all the way from Cape Town to Cairo but, in the event, although he brought much of southern Africa (including Rhodesia, named after him) into the empire, he failed in his attempt to topple the government of the Boer Republics in 1895 and was forced to resign.

Charles George 'Chinese' Gordon (1833-85) *left* was another sort of imperial hero. Outspokenly Christian, sexually repressed, unswervingly duty-bound and charmingly naive he remains a symbol of British stoicism and bravery. After a distinguished career in the Far East where he helped supress the Taiping rebellion (page 406), Gordon was sent to the Sudan in 1884 to prevent a charismatic Islamic leader, the Mahdi, from threatening British bases in Egypt. Although under orders to retreat, Gordon decided to confront the Mahdi, but Gordon's forces were too small to cope either with the sheer number of the Mahdi's followers, or with their fanaticism. They besieged Khartoum for ten months and on 26 January 1885 they stormed it, massacring Gordon and the entire garrison. Gordon immediately became a hero in Britain, but Khartoum was not regained until 1898.

COPY OF MEMO FROM ABOVE
WRITTEN IN MISS LINDSAY HANDWRITING
MRS JACKSON & HER DAUGHTERS WERE
IN THIS HOUSE HERE.

THE HOUSE (NATIVE) IN WHICH OUR WOMEN WERE SLAUGHTERED BY ORDER OF NANA SAHIB.
ON 16TH JULY, 1857. From A DRAWING ON THE SPOT BY LIEUT. CRUMP, RA.

The Indian Mutiny began among the sepoys (native troops) of the British East India Company garrisoned at Meerut, just north of Delhi, in May 1857 and quickly spread to other sepoy regiments. Until the recapture of Delhi *above* by loyal forces in September, there were many popular risings and revolts by native princes anxious to throw off British rule. Europeans were massacred wherever they were found (*left*: an emotive print of the scene at Cawnpore, where 211 British women and children were massacred, made to fan the flames of vengeance). Despite their skill with European weapons, once regular troops arrived in the subcontinent in sufficient numbers, the Indian mutineers were defeated as easily as the troops of Mysore and the Marathas half-a-century before.

by one they fell – Tashkent in 1865, Samarkand and Bukhara in 1868, Merv in 1884 – taking the Russian frontier down to the Himalayas and the borders of India. There, following the defeat of the ruler of Mysore and the Maratha confederation (chapter 19), British power had expanded steadily both by war (in the Punjab, Afghanistan and Sind to the west, and in Burma to the east) and by the 'doctrine of lapse' (which brought native states without a clear successor under direct British rule). But a major uprising occurred in May 1857. Known as the Indian Mutiny, because it began among the native sepoy regiments of the British army in India, in fact it involved many princes and landowners in the north who resented British interference and encroachment. When the rebellion was finally suppressed, after fourteen months of bitter fighting, numerous concessions were thought necessary in order to placate the surviving native princes (over 500 of them). First, the government of British India was transferred from the East India Company to the Crown: the governor-general in Delhi was now directly responsible to the Secretary of State for India who sat in the British Cabinet. Second, the 'doctrine of lapse' was abandoned, and the British promised not to interfere with India's religions. Third, the legal administration was overhauled, the civil service was partially opened to qualified Indians, and a programme of public works was undertaken (most notably, the construction of a massive rail network). By such means, British rule in India was preserved for another ninety years.

For Asia, however, perhaps the greatest significance of the Indian Mutiny was that it temporarily distracted Britain from tightening her grip on China. The British had been allowed, along with other European nations, to trade at Canton with imperial permission. But the Chinese government only welcomed the westerners for their money: so long as Chinese goods were purchased with silver, which was needed to pay the emperor's taxes, there was no real problem. Early in the nineteenth century, however, the Europeans managed to persuade the merchants and mandarins of Canton to accept opium in lieu of silver; and then they began to introduce a much stronger variant of the drug, which (for the first time) caused addiction among those who took it (chapter 19). The imperial court debated for many years how to respond to the reduction in silver inflow, and at last (and with some reluctance) in 1839 decided to use force to halt the import of opium. But their troops and ships were routed, and in 1842 Hong Kong was ceded to Britain as a sovereign colony and five other ports were opened to western traders. The disruption of the Chinese economy was thereby accelerated.

Already in the eighteenth century there had been numerous rebellions against the Ch'ing dynasty; but they had almost all occurred in

From 1793 the British, anxious to secure the Chinese market for their manufactures, tried to make China open normal diplomatic relations, without success. The British encouraged the production and export of Indian opium *above* because its medicinal qualities were appreciated in China, making it a desirable commodity. Chinese attempts to halt this illicit trade led to war in 1839-42. The Chinese forces were decisively defeated, and the cession was made of Hong Kong (to the British) and the opening of five Treaty Ports in which foreign residents could trade. Colonial incursions were, however, carefully resisted and by the 1850s European influence in China was still confined to the coast. Although the waterfront at Canton (one of the Treaty Ports) *below* was dominated by Western trade factories, and the Chinese junks dwarfed by European steamships, no foreigners were allowed inland. Challenges to European power elsewhere – above all the Indian Mutiny – helped to prolong this state of affairs until the 1890s.

the frontier provinces. Now, however, they erupted in the heartland of the empire. Shortage of silver caused massive dislocation of local markets, as well as widespread confiscations for tax-arrears, all over China. Agrarian unrest reached a crescendo in the 1850s, with the outbreak of the Taiping rebellion which eventually involved 17 provinces and may have cost 20 million lives. Led by Christian converts, a rebel army perhaps a million strong captured Nanking in 1853 and threatened both Peking and Shanghai. Although Nanking was recaptured in 1864, the Ch'ing dynasty was so weakened by the rebellion that it never again managed to establish effective control over the country.

Naturally, the Europeans exploited these grave disorders: an Anglo-French army (including large numbers of Indian troops) marched on Peking and secured more trading concessions in 1860; while the Russians occupied the entire Amur basin and founded the port-city of Vladivostok (a name meaning, significantly, 'Queen of the East'). However, had Britain not been preoccupied by the pacification of India, far more could have been gained. Instead, the Great Powers began to concentrate on picking off China's tributary states: during the 1880s, the British consolidated their hold on Burma, the French occupied large areas of Indo-China, Korea was first opened to foreign trade and then (1894-5) occupied by Japan.

This string of humiliating defeats encouraged the domestic enemies of the Ch'ing to come into the open again. Secret anti-government societies moved into opposition. In 1900 one of these, the I-ho-tuan (or 'Boxers'), began to attack Christian communities and property. When imperial troops moved against them, the Boxers launched a determined assault upon the railways which were being built by Westerners near Peking, destroying all the Western goods they could find: stations, tracks, suits, even umbrellas ... For a moment the Ch'ing supported them, and sent troops to sack the western legations in Peking; but the armies of eight foreign powers, led by Japan, soon marched into the capital, suppressed the Boxers, and organized the partition of the empire into spheres of influence.

Such a striking display of impotence by the imperial government could not go unremarked by its subjects. Nevertheless it was not until 1911 that an effective challenge to Ch'ing authority was made. It began with a small-scale army mutiny in Wuchang; but within two months almost every province in the empire had proclaimed its independence and in February 1912 the last Ch'ing emperor abdicated. China swiftly disintegrated into a series of semi-independent states ruled by different warlords. The only areas of stability and prosperity were the Treaty Ports of the foreign powers and their hinterlands (chapter 25).

Although many other parts of Asia succumbed to Western imperialism no less speedily – Malaya to the British, the East Indies to the Dutch – there were other areas in which the European imperialists met their match. The first was in South Africa. The transfer of Cape Colony, founded in 1652 (chapter 18), from Dutch to British rule during the Napoleonic Wars led to conflicts between the new colonial administration and the Dutch settlers known as 'Boers' (farmers). Eventually, the discontented Boers left the Cape and travelled northwards into the interior, where they founded independent republics: the Transvaal (1852) and the Orange Free State (1854). For most of the time they were left alone, but the importance of the republics was transformed in the 1880s by the discovery of gold on the Witwatersrand: the Dutch farmers now possessed an asset that excited the cupidity of the British.

The British tried at various points to compel the republics to recognize their suzerainty, but these were defeated. Then in 1899, it seemed to the Boers that another, more serious attempt to subjugate them was

China under the Ch'ing dynasty suffered numerous foreign incursions during the later 19th century, gradually losing territory to Britain, France and Japan. But far more damaging to imperial authority was the wave of internal rebellions which disrupted many provinces in the 1850s and 1860s and resulted in over 25 million deaths. The most serious of these was the Taiping Tienkuo ('Heavenly Kingdom of Great Peace', which began in Kwangsi province in the south, in 1850, drawing inspiration from elements of Protestant Christianity). The rebels captured Nanking in 1853. At first the European powers sympathized but then sided with the dynastic power when chaos loomed and trade concessions were threatened. They assisted in its suppression and the rebellion collapsed in 1864. The crude but effective Taiping propaganda print *above* shows the rebel army besieging an imperial city.

The prosperity and enterprise of the British empire was at the heart of the outburst of national pride which occurred in London at the time of Queen Victoria's

Diamond Jubilee in 1897 *left*. Large numbers of native colonial troops appeared in the parade. Two years later, however, the outbreak of the Boer War showed how fragile the whole imperial structure was.

Although the defeat of the Boers of South Africa in 1902 was celebrated enthusiastically in Britain – with many souvenirs like the fan *above* showing all the victorious commanders – it had strained the empire's resources to the limit. It took up to 300,000 imperial troops almost three years to deal with no more than 75,000 Boers. British losses were as high as America's in Vietnam, about 50,000.

407

in preparation. They therefore decided to make a pre-emptive strike before the British could build up irresistible strength. Although, in the event, they failed, their brilliant guerrilla tactics forced the British to fight for over five years, and concentrate 300,000 regular troops, before the war was ended in 1902.

Even more of a challenge to European hegemony was posed by Japan. At first it seemed that the island empire would be laid open to western exploitation just like India and China: in 1853 the Americans forced trading concessions, and in 1858 the European nations followed suit. A forlorn attempt to repulse the Western embrace was repressed by naval bombardment in 1863. But then Japan changed course. It was not difficult. China and India were ruled by dynasties founded by foreigners and exploiting the native peoples, so that popular revolts against the government tended to aid the Europeans. But political authority in Japan had been exercised since the early seventeenth century by a native dynasty of military autocrats: the Tokugawa shoguns (chapter 19). It was their failure to stand up to the West which provoked popular opposition; and when in 1866 the shoguns turned to the Westerners for support against their domestic enemies, political unrest became so serious that in 1868 the Emperor Meiji in person was forced to take charge. Feudalism was abolished in 1871; a national education system was introduced a year later; and a conscript army, financed by a new tax system, was created the following year. The Meiji settlement nonetheless lacked widespread popular support and the emperor opposed any move towards liberalizing the regime (the Japanese Liberal Party was suppressed in 1884). Instead, Japan sought to exploit the rivalries of the colonial powers abroad, in order to avoid becoming a colony itself; while at home, factories were set up on western lines, and the energies of Japan's skilled craftsmen were harnessed to produce exports. Gradually, the empire became a major

The Sino-Japanese war (1894-5), arising from disputes in Korea, provided Japan with an opportunity to test her new Western-style armed forces, and her victory was a major stepping stone in imperial expansion. From then on, Russia and Japan were in continual rivalry for control of their respective interests in Korea and Manchuria, which culminated in the war of 1904-5. *Above* a Japanese print shows foreign newspaper reporters carefully noting the success of the imperial army. Support for the Japanese divided the Western powers.

The Boers' fighting strength depended on their excellent armament and on their development of guerrilla tactics. When the war began, in October 1899, their field army was equipped with the latest German Krupp and French Le Creusot artillery, and their troops were armed with highly accurate long-range European rifles such as Martinis, Mannlichers and Mausers *left*. They often operated in small strike forces, relying on excellent horsemanship, mobile bases and an intimate knowledge of the terrain. Even after the British assumed the offensive in March 1900, these tactics successfully prolonged the war for a further 18 months.

industrial nation. Her population grew from 35 million in 1873 to 55 million in 1918; and her exports soared from 30 million yen in 1878-82 (only 7 percent of them manufactured goods) to 932 million yen in 1913-17 (40 percent of them manufactures). Japan even tried to gain colonies of her own. In 1879 she annexed the Ryukyu islands; in 1895, after a war with China, she acquired Taiwan and a claim to the Liaotung peninsula. The latter, however, was vetoed by Russia; Japan therefore prepared for a trial of strength with her western neighbour. In 1904 her army attacked, capturing Port Arthur, and the next year, a major Russian battlefleet sent from Europe to redress the balance in the east was destroyed by the Japanese in the Tsushima straits. Liaotung and Korea were annexed; Manchuria was claimed.

The Russo-Japanese war has often been seen as a turning-point in world history, for it marked the first major defeat of an industrial European empire by a non-Western power. Certainly it was important, both specifically in weakening the Tsarist regime in Russia and more generally in encouraging the peoples of Asia to question the myth of Western invincibility. But, even after the battle in the Tsushima Straits, the power of the white men remained unquestioned over four-fifths of the globe. And it is unlikely that their grip would have weakened significantly for many decades to come had they not found themselves required to squander their wealth and reputations on the bloody battlefields of the First World War.

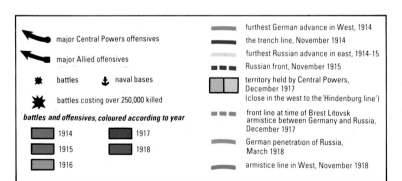

major Central Powers offensives

major Allied offensives

★ battles ⚓ naval bases

✸ battles costing over 250,000 killed

battles and offensives, coloured according to year

1914	1917
1915	1918
1916	

furthest German advance in West, 1914

the trench line, November 1914

furthest Russian advance in east, 1914-15

Russian front, November 1915

territory held by Central Powers, December 1917 (close in the west to the 'Hindenburg line')

front line at time of Brest Litovsk armistice between Germany and Russia, December 1917

German penetration of Russia, March 1918

armistice line in West, November 1918

410

Two major new states had emerged in Europe shortly before the First World War, due largely to the efforts of two remarkable individuals. In 1860, Giuseppe Garibaldi (1807-82) *far right* took Sicily and Naples, (with his 'Thousand Volunteers') driving out the governments restored by the Congress of Vienna (chapter 20). By popular vote, Victor Emmanuel II of Piedmont became king of a united Italy. Otto von Bismarck (1815-98) *right*, chief minister of Prussia, defeated Denmark (1864) and Austria (1866) and formed the North German Confederation in 1867 under Prussian leadership. In 1871, after defeating France in a swift campaign, he proclaimed all Germany to be an empire under the rule of William I of Prussia.

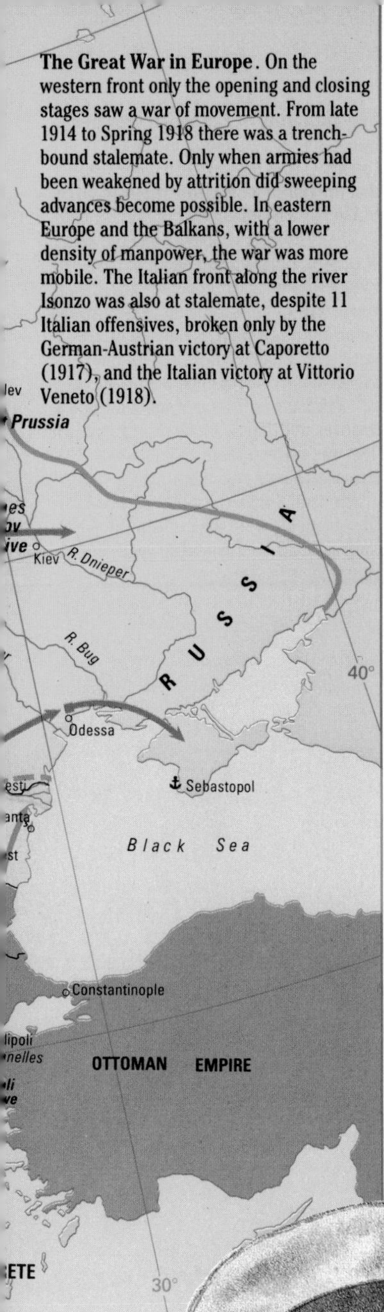

CHAPTER 24

THE END OF THE OLD ORDER
1914–1929

The Great War in Europe. On the western front only the opening and closing stages saw a war of movement. From late 1914 to Spring 1918 there was a trench-bound stalemate. Only when armies had been weakened by attrition did sweeping advances become possible. In eastern Europe and the Balkans, with a lower density of manpower, the war was more mobile. The Italian front along the river Isonzo was also at stalemate, despite 11 Italian offensives, broken only by the German-Austrian victory at Caporetto (1917), and the Italian victory at Vittorio Veneto (1918).

Prussia

Kiev

R. Dnieper

R. Bug

R U S S I A

40°

Odessa

Sebastopol

Black   Sea

Constantinople

OTTOMAN   EMPIRE

CRETE

30°

Between 1871 and 1908, Europe was at peace. Admittedly there were moments of tension (between Britain and Germany in 1896 over southern Africa; between Britain and France in 1898 over Egypt; between France and Germany in 1905 over Morocco); but, on each occasion, hostilities were avoided. Much of the credit for this generation of peace belongs to the close dynastic links between many of the rulers of Europe. The emperors of Russia and Germany, who were cousins, used to meet on each other's yachts in the Baltic; the emperor of Germany and the king of Great Britain often shared the same carriage at state occasions; and almost all the crowned heads of Europe attended the funeral of Queen Victoria in London in 1901, for they were almost all her relatives. On such occasions, policy disagreements could be – and were – discussed and resolved. But after the death of Victoria's son and heir, the genial Edward VII, in 1910, this dynastic diplomacy was less successful. In particular it could no longer paper over the enmity felt by France towards Germany.

Under the expert guidance of Otto von Bismarck, the kingdom of Prussia had completed the political unification of Germany and, in three short wars between 1864 and 1871, defeated Denmark, Austria and France. The gains from the Franco-Prussian war (1870-71) extended Germany's frontiers beyond the Rhine to include Alsace and Lorraine. After that, again under Bismarck's direction, she embarked

upon a rapid course of industrialization, acquired an overseas empire (chapter 23), and created a complex system of international alliances designed to preserve her new territorial gains. But these alliances never included France. The humiliating defeat in the war of 1870-71 and the loss of Alsace-Lorraine were hard enough for France to swallow, but far worse was the loss of her primacy in Europe. Between 1870 and 1914, Germany's population doubled (from 33 to 65 million, while that of France and Britain both hovered around 40 million), and her industrial output quadrupled. She also built up impressive armed forces. Her army, at 95 divisions, was twice the size of the French army and twelve times the size of Britain's; her navy, with twenty modern battleships by 1912, was large enough to rival the British fleet (which only had thirty in European waters) and heavily outnumbered the French.

This rapid yet decisive shift in the balance of power within Europe had serious diplomatic repercussions. The growing military power of Germany caused France and Russia to become nervous allies from 1894, while her naval build-up led a reluctant Britain to form the 'Entente cordiale' with France ten years later. In 1907, finally, the three powers buried their differences and signed the 'Triple Entente' to assure their mutual defence in case of German attack. But in Berlin, these measures of alleged self-defence seemed like encirclement: Germany now faced declared enemies to the east and to the west. She therefore drew closer to Austria, which was already seriously at odds with Russia.

Here, the chief bone of contention was the Balkans, which had been under Ottoman rule for more than four hundred years (chapter 14). During the nineteenth century, however, various parts of the Ottoman empire in Europe secured their independence: much of Greece in 1830; Bulgaria, Serbia, Montenegro and Romania by 1878. The Ottoman, Austrian and Russian empires, however, all desired to extend their territories and influence in the area, and exploited every opportunity both to destabilize the new independent states and to occupy disputed frontier areas. In 1908, for example, Austria annexed the Turkish provinces of Bosnia and Herzegovina, almost provoking war, and leading the independent states to jostle for advantage. This highly unstable situation suddenly become critical in 1911-13, when the minor Balkan powers fought first against the Turks and then amongst each other, resulting in considerable gains for Austria's principal enemy, Serbia.

Austria searched anxiously for an excuse to redress the balance: the assassination of the Austrian crown prince in the Serbian capital, on 28

June 1914, offered just such a pretext. Extreme demands for reparations were made to the Serbian government on 23 July and when, as expected, they were rejected, Austria declared war. Less expected was the Russian response to this: on 30 July, instead of ordering just a mobilization against Austria, the tsar ordered a general mobilization. Germany viewed this as a hostile act and sent an ultimatum requiring Russia to cease concentrating her forces along the German frontier. When this was ignored, Germany too called up all her forces and on 1 August declared war on Russia. But the German armies did not move east: instead they moved west. The Berlin government believed that the sudden crisis offered a golden opportunity to destroy the Triple Entente by launching a pre-emptive strike on Russia's unsuspecting western allies. On 3 August, Germany declared war on France and the following day invaded Belgium, as the first stage in a march on Paris. The rival alliances now came into play: Britain promptly declared war on Germany and Austria declared war on Russia. The First World War had begun.

The civilized world threw itself into war with eager expectations and great enthusiasm. Everyone, in every country, looked forward to a

The First World War began in old-fashioned, romantic style. Following the brief wars of the Bismarck era, everyone expected a rapid, decisive conflict and all armies mobilized large cavalry formations. *Below* British lancers, in confident mood, travel towards the front in northern France. There they had to exchange their horses for trenches, and there the horse cavalry as a tool of modern warfare very suddenly became redundant.

For most of the war the armies on the western front spent their time in the trenches *left* which, by the end of 1914, extended from the Channel to the Swiss border. Cold, damp, verminous and prone to collapse the trenches provided some protection from machine-gun fire and snipers, but little from gas, mortars or artillery bombardment. The notion of warfare as glorious rapidly dissolved in a sea of mud, pestilence and corpses. Morale was difficult to maintain and news from the front was carefully censored in order to maintain recruitment and the war effort in general at home.

rapid victory. 'The war,' all governments confidently prophesied, 'will be over by Christmas'. And in 1914 it almost happened. While a small German force and Austria's main army held the eastern front, confident that Russia's mobilization would be slow, some 1.5 million German troops hastened through Belgium to cross the relatively undefended northern frontier of France. By early September they were on the river Marne and threatened Paris. The French government, following the precedent of 1870 (when the Germans had last invaded), fled ignominiously to Bordeaux.

But, this time, Paris did not fall. A small but well-trained British army joined the French; reinforcements were brought up from Paris (a bizarre sight, for they all came by taxis); and a counter-attack drove the over-stretched invaders back to the Aisne. For the rest of the year, both sides tried to turn the other's flank, but their efforts only succeeded in extending the opposing front lines from the Swiss border to the North Sea, a distance of some 400 miles.

There now began a new type of conflict. The campaigns of the first four months had been a war of manoeuvre, fought in much the same way as the Napoleonic wars – except that the casualties were appallingly high. Between August and November 1914, 90,000 British, 700,000 German and 850,000 French troops were killed or wounded, most of them by artillery, mines and machine-gun fire; both the generals and the private soldiers tragically underestimated the effectiveness of modern firepower. But by the end of 1914, almost by accident, the Germans on the western front discovered a new, battle-winning weapon: the spade. Against infantry in trenches, artillery was at first powerless because it was too inaccurate; but against advancing troops, the fire from the trenches was lethal. Trench warfare now became the characteristic form of conflict on the western front.

In the early years of the war the armed forces of the major combatants were filled by volunteers. Some joined to escape unemployment or domestic problems; others enlisted out of a sense of duty (*top right* an early British recruiting poster) or patriotism (*bottom* a German invitation to 'Help our victory'). Those who did not respond were liable to public humiliation (such as posters which showed children asking 'What did you do in the war, daddy?' or women dispensing white feathers in the street to any young man not in uniform); and conscientious objectors were often imprisoned (and, in Britain, also disenfranchised for five years after the war). But conscription, and the heavy losses at the front which made it necessary, began seriously to deplete the labour force. By 1916, 1.6 million women were working in Britain, half of them in engineering plants producing (among other things) munitions *above*. Yet still there were not enough workers to keep production levels up, so in the end recruiting posters began to be directed at women too *centre right*. During the Second World War, Britain went even further and introduced conscription for women.

Some areas along the front changed hands several times over the next four years; but others were defended tooth and nail, such as Ypres in Flanders, where the Menin Gate war memorial records the names of no less than 70,000 British officers and men who died there with no known grave.

Who will remember, passing through this gate,
The unheroic dead who fed the guns?

asked the war poet Siegfried Sassoon. The French army lost even more men in the defence of Verdun on her eastern border: perhaps half a million Frenchmen were killed and wounded there in 1916 alone. It was military slaughter on an almost unprecedented scale.

Not surprisingly, many soldiers tried to desert from such appalling conditions (and were usually shot), and in 1917 there was a major mutiny among the French troops at the front; but, by and large, men did their duty and replacements for the fallen were often volunteers. Perhaps they knew no better, for the reporting of the war was heavily censored so that little or no news of defeats or losses ever reached the home front. On the whole, newspapers filled their pages with 'atrocity stories' about the enemy and other items designed to encourage young men to join up, and the hoardings were covered with a barrage of recruiting posters which appealed to patriotism, filial piety, or shame. Every belligerent nation used propaganda to the full, although by 1916 all of them had found it necessary to back it up with conscription.

By then the war on the western front had been recognized by both sides as a costly stalemate, and victory was sought elsewhere. In 1915 the German army switched its major effort to the east and launched a devastating campaign against Russia. By the end of the year, the Russians had lost most of Poland, and two million of their men had been

415

taken prisoner. The Tsarist regime had been dealt a blow from which it would never recover. Meanwhile, the Turks (who had entered the war on Germany's side) repulsed an allied attempt to invade via the Dardanelles (the disastrous Gallipoli campaign); while Italy entered the war on the side of the Triple Entente, but quickly became bogged down on the frontier with Austria.

In 1916 the Germans once again made a major thrust in the west, but it failed; so, too, did the allied counter-attack on the Somme. Accordingly, in 1917, the Germans withdrew slightly to a heavily fortified chain of trenches and redoubts known as the Hindenburg Line, to await and repel allied attack, while their main energies were channelled in two other directions. First, major resources were used to equip a submarine fleet which could destroy all shipping – whether allied or neutral – carrying supplies to Britain and France. Second, a new offensive was launched against Russia, since it was noted that enthusiasm there for the war was fast waning. Both campaigns were successful, but were swiftly overtaken by events. Thus, although the unrestricted U-boat campaign succeeded in destroying 25 percent of all shipping leaving British ports, it also provoked the United States into declaring war on Germany. At almost the same time, and even before the new German offensive got underway on the eastern front, riots and strikes broke out in the Russian capital. The Russian revolution, seen by many historians as the most important single event of the twentieth century, was about to begin.

Mechanized warfare came of age during the Great War. Submarines destroyed shipping and aeroplanes were used for reconnaissance and bombing for the first time. Land warfare was transformed by poison gas and machine guns *above left*. With guns firing up to 600 rounds a minute, an entrenched infantryman could inflict devastating damage on a massed attack. The tank *above*, introduced in the closing stages of the Somme battle, provided some protection, but the early models were cumbersome, slow and prone to mechanical failure.

The Gallipoli campaign (1915). After the failure of an attempt by the British and French navies to force a passage through the Dardanelles, a force of six Australian and British divisions was landed on the Gallipoli peninsula. The Turks, forewarned and reinforced, pinned the invaders down on the shore *below*. After severe losses, the survivors were evacuated at the end of the year having achieved nothing.

Tsarist Russia generally had a dreadful press. For a time, following the emancipation of the serfs in 1861 (chapter 21), a genuine programme of reforms was undertaken: a new system of local self-government was created under administrative boards (*zemstva*, comprising representatives of all social classes) and the entire judicial hierarchy was reorganized on French lines (1864). But before long, liberal and radical elements became dissatisfied that more was not conceded, and began to oppose the regime. Some tried to stir up peasant resistance; others adopted a policy of terror (in 1881 the tsar himself was assassinated). Meanwhile, the government's efforts to industrialize, which increased the number of factory workers from 385,000 in 1865 to 3 million in 1898, created one more group of discontented subjects; and it was for them that a new revolutionary organization, the Social Democrats, was founded in 1898.

The new party was unashamedly Marxist in its policies, dedicated to the proposition that social progress was only to be achieved through the class struggle – in this case, the struggle of workers against capitalists (chapter 20). But the capitalists themselves also wanted change. A wave of strikes in the cities, mutinies among the armed forces, and revolts by the peasants in the spring of 1905 gave them their chance. The liberals used the disorders to force Tsar Nicholas II to concede a measure of democracy, symbolized by a national assembly (or *Duma*) for representatives of the middle classes. The Social Democrats refused to have anything to do with this body, however, which they regarded as the plaything of the bourgeoisie, and instead formed a workers' council (*soviet*) in the capital to co-ordinate strikes and industrial action aimed at bringing the whole system down. But in this they were largely unsuccessful, thanks to the efficiency of the tsarist police and the loyalty of the army. The 1905 uprising was brutally crushed, and its surviving leaders driven into exile. They were still there in 1914, quarrelling about the best way to foment revolution from abroad. In the event, the revolution began without them.

On 8 March 1917, in protest against military defeats at the front and economic chaos at home, the workers of Petrograd (as St Petersburg was now called) staged a general strike. The streets filled with demonstrators. But this time, unlike 1905, the troops were sympathetic;

Attempts to modernize Tsarist Russia met with only partial success. Each village was given its own governing council (*above* pictured in 1910), but their powers were limited. Without the strain of war, perhaps this rural society would have continued to live in peace and poverty; but three years in the army exposed the peasants both to radical propaganda and to the worst excesses of government inefficiency. When, early in 1917, the supply system broke down and bread riots occurred in the leading cities, the disillusioned troops *top* refused to obey orders to fire on the rioters. Instead, as the slogans on the banners show, they supported them.

indeed, many of the army's rank-and-file joined the strikers. The tsar was away from his capital at the time and, when his initial measures for restoring order were disobeyed, he started out for Petrograd in person to direct the repression. But he came by rail, and the railway workers held up his train. Nothing could have illustrated more clearly the total collapse of the whole machinery of imperial government. Only the telegraph system seemed still to work, and so when Nicholas II decided to abdicate on 15 March, he prosaically sent the news by cable. A few days later he was placed under arrest.

Power in the capital was now claimed by two groups. On the one hand, the *Duma* had appointed a 'Provisional Committee' of moderate reformers to handle the administration left behind by the tsar; after his abdication they called themselves the Provisional Government. On the other hand, the workers' Soviet in the capital, which had organized the general strike, also claimed the right to govern. Wisely, its executive committee decided to include representatives of the armed forces: it now became the 'Soviet of Workers' and Soldiers' Deputies', and its Order No. 1 (dated 14 March 1917) deprived all officers of authority, except for strategic operations, and placed military affairs under the control of committees elected by officers and men. In effect, the Petrograd Soviet, which soon gave orders to Soviets in other cities, had become an alternative government; and its voice became far more radical and effective with the arrival in mid-April of a group of Social Democratic exiles known as the Bolsheviks, led by the balding 47-year-old Vladimir Ulyanov, better known by his underground alias: Lenin.

Lenin had fled from Russia in 1900, after a three-year sentence in Siberia for revolutionary activities, and he was still in exile in Switzerland when news of the general strike and the tsar's abdication reached him. But he lost no time in exploiting the unexpected advantage: he set out immediately for Russia. Within minutes of his arrival at Petrograd, on 16 April, he declared his aims: 'The people need peace; the people need bread; the people need land'. And this message was repeated time after time, and amplified: Lenin consistently called for an immediate end to the war, for the redistribution of all land to the peasants, for the Soviets to seize absolute power. It was an extreme position, and at first it did not even command the support of all Bolsheviks. But the failure of the Provisional Government's campaign against Germany in the summer of 1917, and its failure to improve the supply of food and fuel to the capital, gave Lenin his great chance. On 7 November (25 October by the Julian calendar used then in Russia), the Bolsheviks seized strategic points in Petrograd, arrested the Provisional Government, and assumed power in the name of the Soviets. The very next day they issued a Land Decree which ordered the immediate redistribution of all large landed estates among the peasants, and nationalized all banks (confiscating all private accounts). A stream of further socialist acts

The Russian Revolution did not at first affect the war with Germany. For almost a year after the abdication of the tsar, in March 1917, Russian armies fought on – encouraged by the Bolshevik leaders Lenin (1870-1924) *top left* and Trotsky (1879-1940) (standing to the right of the podium; later versions of this photograph, however, cut him out after he had fallen from favour). In Russia, as in the West, women were employed in factories and munitions plants *above*, and the war effort was partly underwritten by public subscription to government bonds. The 'emancipation' of the masses required to make the war effort succeed helped in large part to politicize the workers, providing fuel for the Revolution.

followed: workers were given control over their factories (but lost the right to strike); all church property was confiscated; the national debt was repudiated.

Equally important, the new regime, firmly under Lenin's control, immediately started discussions with Germany and Austria to end the war. At first the Russian negotiators called for a return to the frontiers of 1914. This, however, Germany understandably rejected and, since Russia rejected Germany's terms, the war recommenced. Russia's demoralized forces were driven back on all fronts and, when peace was eventually signed at Brest-Litovsk on 3 March 1918, the Soviets were forced to abandon Finland, the Baltic provinces, Poland and (above all) the Ukraine – all of which briefly became independent nations. Russia thus lost all the western acquistions of the Romanovs: an area of more than a million square miles containing 62 million people, three-quarters of Russia's coal and steel resources, one-half of her factories, and one-third of her crops. By deliberately delaying a final agreement, Germany thus ensured that revolutionary Russia would be unable to intervene effectively in the west; but in fact those same delays cost Germany the final victory.

Germany's decision on 1 February 1917 to engage in unrestricted submarine warfare in the Atlantic was a calculated risk. It was realized that the sinking of neutral American shipping would almost certainly lead to an eventual declaration of war by the United States; but it was 'reckoned that Britain would be forced to surrender before American aid had time to arrive. The gamble nearly paid off. Although America did indeed declare war in April 1917, a year later there were still only

America joined the war in 1917. In February, President Woodrow Wilson (1856-1924) broke off diplomatic relations with Germany in protest at the campaign of unrestricted submarine warfare; two months later, the USA declared war, closely followed by several Latin American countries. Medical volunteers *right* had already tended the wounded of the Allied armies. Eventually a million American soldiers would serve in France. This gave America, in spite of her late entry into the war, a decisive voice in the conclusion of peace. The eventual armistice was agreed on the basis of the 'Fourteen Points' put forward by President Wilson.

85,000 American soldiers in France; while between January 1917 and March 1918, almost 8 million tons of allied and neutral shipping was sunk (as against less than 4 million constructed). But Britain did not surrender, and it was not until early in 1918 that the German and Austrian forces freed by the peace of Brest-Litovsk became available for deployment in the west. The able German Chief-of-Staff, General Ludendorff, immediately decided to launch a new all-out offensive to win the war. The attacks began on 21 March with a sudden bombardment of 6,000 guns against the British lines at St Quentin. Surprise was total. Within a month the British stood (in the phrase of their commander) 'with their backs to the wall' and the Germans were within forty miles of Paris. But it was too late.

The German advance was halted by the rapid build-up of fresh American forces: 306,000 men were in France in July, and just over a million by November. This represented irresistible force, and when the allied armies counter-attacked in August, the Germans fell back. At first it was

In the last year of the war improvements in artillery bombardment made it possible to cause more thorough and total destruction to selected areas than ever before. Sectors deemed to be of strategic importance, like Passchendaele wood *below left*, were turned into a bizarre wilderness of tree stumps and waterlogged craters, in which there was as great a risk of death by drowning in the mud as from direct enemy action. Numerous towns near the front were likewise devastated. Ypres *below* and countless other centres became the target of incessant shellfire which swiftly reduced them to rubble.

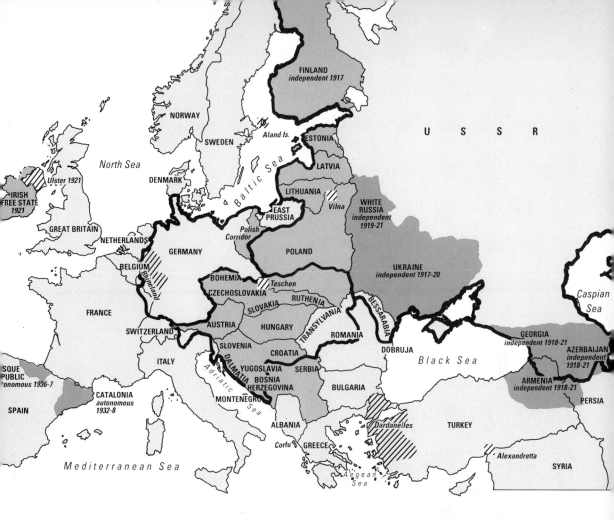

frontiers of Germany, Austria-Hungary and Russia in 1914

post-settlement frontiers

new states

areas temporarily autonomous or independent

areas of dispute

The peace treaties of 1919 created as many problems as they tried to solve *above*. A belt of new states were established: in the north territories were freed from Russia, and in the south new states were created from the empire of Austria. Poland was restored after 120 years of partition. Numerous border disputes were settled, sometimes satisfactorily, by plebiscite or unilateral action, but elsewhere often without consideration of the ethnic problems involved. Some national groups achieved independence or autonomy, only to lose it by force to those whose temporary weakness had made it possible.

an orderly withdrawal, but as news arrived of reverses in other areas – the surrender of Bulgaria and the retreat of the Turks in Palestine in September; the defeat of the Austrians on the Italian front in October – the Germans lost their nerve. Mutinies broke out among both soldiers and sailors; masses of troops lay down their arms or deserted; there were riots in Munich and other German cities. Demoralized by this clear evidence of moral collapse, and by the surrender of Turkey (30 October) and Austria (3 November), Emperor William II abdicated on 9 November and the German republic that replaced him authorized a cease-fire on the western front, to take effect two days later.

As the trenches were emptied of the wounded and dead, and the losses began to be counted (the latest estimates put the total number of casualties at 30 million, including over eight million dead), representatives of the thirty sovereign states involved in the war assembled at Versailles to work out the conditions of peace. A separate treaty was made with each of the defeated governments, but there were certain important features common to all of them. First, the principle of 'self-determination' was applied within Europe. This meant that 'historic peoples' – such as the Hungarians, the Poles and the Finns – were to be given independence as nation states. It also meant that ethnic minorities should be reunited wherever possible with their own nation state (Thrace was transferred to Greece, and so on). In fact this principle was not enforced in all cases – for example the Sudetan Germans remained part of Czechoslovakia and the Tyrolean Germans became part of Italy – but at least there were fewer ethnic minorities after Versailles than there had been before. The idea of 'self-determination'

421

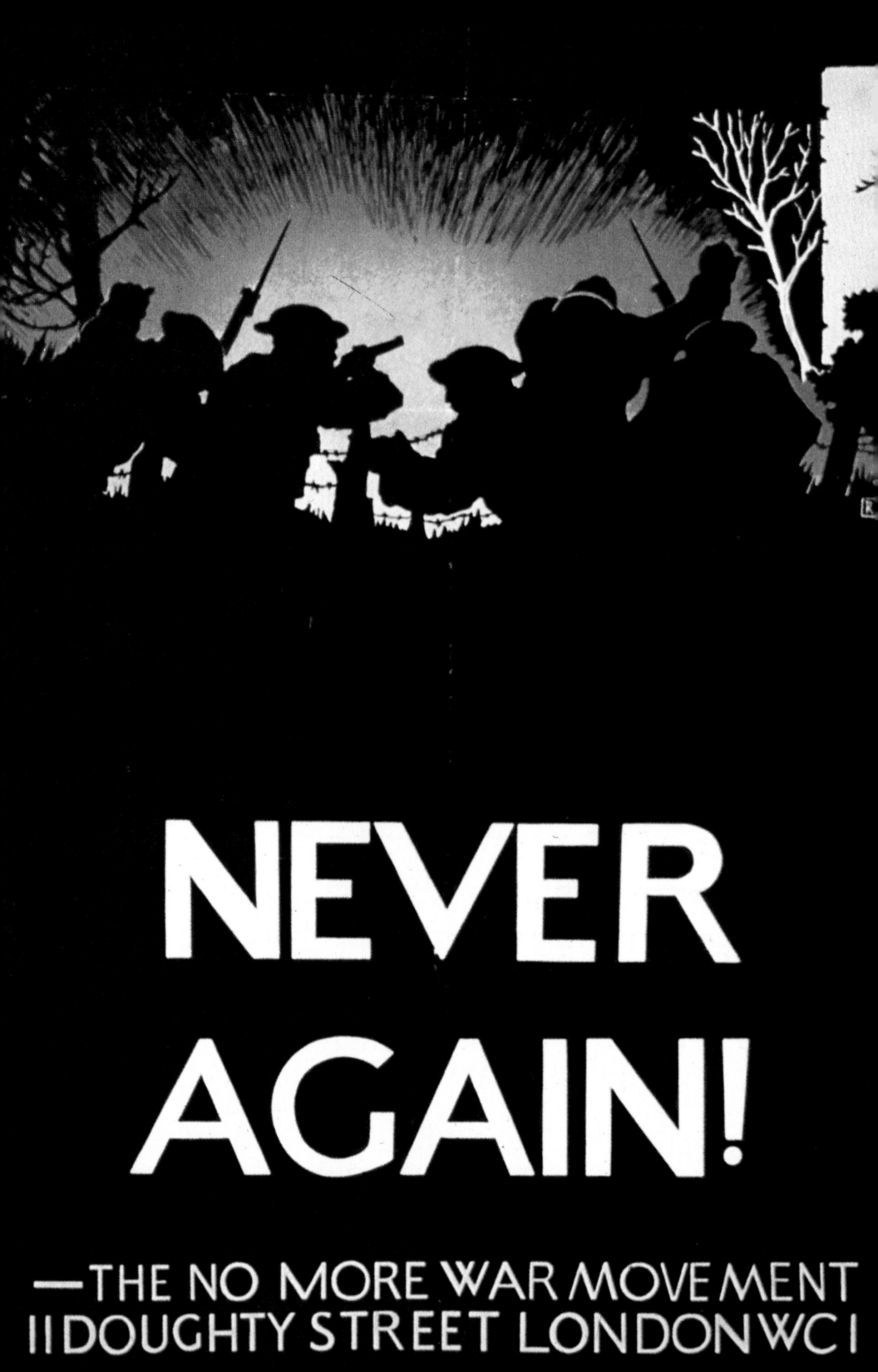

NEVER
AGAIN!

—THE NO MORE WAR MOVEMENT
11 DOUGHTY STREET LONDON WC 1

Opposition to rearmament became widespread in Britain during the 1920s. It was reflected in the almost simultaneous publication of several harrowing literary works about what trench warfare had really been like (*Journey's End* by R.C. Sherriff in 1928; *Good-bye to All That* by Robert Graves in 1929; *Memoirs of an Infantry Officer* by Siegfried Sassoon in 1930). It was closely linked to the Labour movement in Britain and it also gave rise to various organizations dedicated to preserving peace at almost any price. Some, like the 'Peace Pledge Union', were Christian in inspiration; others, like the 'No More War Movement' *left* were Communist dominated. But as first Japanese, then Italian and finally German agression increased in the 1930s, pacifism gradually lost support.

was not, however, applied at all outside Europe. Many former colonies of the defeated powers in Africa (mainly German) and the Middle East (mainly Turkish) were liberated; but the politicians at Versailles determined that these were inhabited by 'peoples not yet able to stand by themselves under the strenuous conditions of the modern world'. So they were transferred to the 'tutelage' of one of the victors, who treated the nationalist aspirations of their new subjects with contempt. Naturally, this led to problems, especially in the Middle East. The transfer of Lebanon and Syria to French 'tutelage' and of Palestine and Mesopotamia to Britain (who thereby acquired Middle Eastern influence beyond her wildest dreams) caused widespread resentment and several revolts in the 1920s and '30s. In east Asia, most former German colonies were transferred to Australia, New Zealand and Britain; the Japanese, despite their support of the allied cause, received only 1,400 tiny Pacific islands with a total area of 836 square miles, scattered over an immense area (which was to prove a costly misjudgement by the allies in subsequent years).

In theory, however, all these areas were not colonies but 'Mandates'. They were regarded as 'nations on the road to independence' and, as such, they were only administered by a Great Power as the mandated agent of a new international body created by the Versailles peace conference: the League of Nations. This was the first worldwide association in the history of governments dedicated to the resolution of disputes by non-violent methods. There were forty-two original member states, each with one vote in a General Assembly; and a Council of nine (five of them permanent, and provided by the victors in the war; four of them rotating among the other states). The League was intended, on the one hand, to preserve peace and (as the phrase went) 'to make the world safe for democracy'; and, on the other, to improve general health and safety standards, as well as social and economic conditions throughout the world. Considerable successes were scored by the specialized bodies created to discharge the latter functions (the Health Organization; the International Labour Organization), but these tended to be obscured by the repeated failures of the League to preserve peace, either in Europe through its arbitration, or overseas through its Mandates.

The Versailles settlement was founded on a number of illusions. There was, first of all, the illusion that the United States would continue to be present in Europe. But 150 years of isolation could not be abandoned so easily: participation in the World War had not been popular in all quarters of America, and the pressure for total withdrawal from the horrors of Europe now became irresistible. The United States never joined the League of Nations. Further, as the European powers sought to salvage some dignity from the ruins of the old order, the United States had her own sphere of influence to service and maintain. A series of populist revolutions in neighbouring Mexico (1910–20) made the United States firm in their wish to have a controlling interest in Central and Latin American affairs; with the opening of the Panama canal in 1914 (leased to the USA in perpetuity) they established a hold on the area, and gained a further stepping stone towards the final forum of empire – the Pacific.

And then there was the disintegration of Russia, which also did not join the League. In December 1917, scarcely a month after the Bolshevik revolution, many groups opposed to the new regime began to mobilize forces against it. There were revolts by the Don cossacks; separatist movements in the Ukraine, Azerbaijan, Armenia and the Baltic provinces; and rebellions in eastern Siberia and White Russia. All these movements attracted some support from those foreign powers

opposed to Communism: Japanese forces intervened in Siberia; the Poles invaded the Ukraine; Western armies assisted the White Russians. In the event all of them failed – as much through their own disunity and economic weakness as through the strength of the Bolsheviks – but they forced Lenin to retreat somewhat from the purity of Communist economics. The effectiveness of Soviet commitment to world revolution (Comintern, founded 1919) was severely limited. In 1921, the government announced a 'New Economic Policy', which reintroduced a measure of private enterprise for both agriculture and industry. In effect, a limited market economy was restored. By the time of Lenin's death, in January 1924, Russia had been reorganized as the Union of Soviet Socialist Republics (Russia, the Ukraine, White Russia and Transcaucasia), and the new state had been officially recognized by the international community. Domestically, the enemies of the state had been defeated and the country was at peace; by 1929, industrial production had regained pre-war levels.

But as Russia appeared to become more stable, disorders among her western neighbours increased. The venerable Habsburg monarchy, which dominated central Europe, had never managed to overcome the division of interests among the nationalities subjected to its rule. When the imperial army mobilized in 1914, for example, recruiting posters were required in fifteen different languages. But the redistribution of empire in 1919 among seven different states, all of them fairly weak, did little to improve either the social conditions or the political equilibrium of central Europe. There was a Communist revolution in Hungary

The Bolshevik Revolution was by no means popular outside the major cities. Even before the end of the war against Germany, rebellious and separatist movements sprang up on the periphery of the former empire, drawing support from those loyal to the tsar (the White Russians) and the foreign powers hostile to Communism. Eventually they were all defeated; opponents of the Moscow regime were executed or exiled. *Above* White Russian refugees await evacuation by the French navy at Odessa in southern Russia.

War was not the sole agent in the demolition of the established European order. Sigmund Freud (1856-1939) *far right*, from Austria, pioneered scientific psychoanalysis and offered evidence that men are driven principally by unconscious instincts rather than rational calculation. Meanwhile Albert Einstein (1879-1955) *right*, from Switzerland, demonstrated that space and time are not absolute and universal, as earlier scientific theories had supposed, but in fact varied according to the position of the observer (the 'theory of relativity'). Both ideas although apparently technical and specific, undermined popular confidence in a fixed, rational and predictable world.

in 1919, and in its wake the government there fell under a military dictatorship. Elsewhere, more moderate left-wing governments likewise fell to military coups in the course of the 1920s: Bulgaria in 1923; Poland and Greece in 1926; Yugoslavia in 1929.

In Italy, too, there was chaos. She had gained very little from her three years of war against Austria, and her government and economy were severely weakened. In part this was due to structural causes – Italy, like Germany, was a recently unified state; the process was only completed in 1870. But part of the trouble was also a determined Communist offensive: a wave of strikes broke out, organized by left-wing activists anxious to create a Soviet republic in the peninsula. By 1919, leading industrialists and landowners, alarmed by the growing threat of anarchy and revolution, lent financial support to (among others) Benito Mussolini, editor of a strident nationalist newspaper in Milan and the guiding hand behind numerous right-wing protection squads who (for a fee) broke up strikes and protected capital assets. In 1921, thanks to subsidies from industrialists like the Pirelli and Fiat companies, Mussolini and his party, known as the Fascists (after the *fasces* used as a symbol of authority in the Roman republic) won a number of seats in parliament. The left wing now played right into Mussolini's hands: they organized more disorders and more protests, culminating in a general strike in August 1922. The capitalists, the church, the armed forces and even the Freemasons, all of them afraid of a Communist take-over, encouraged the Fascists to make a bid for power and Mussolini prepared his supporters for a march on Rome. It proved unnecessary: in October, the king called on Mussolini to become his prime minister, and Italy quickly became a one-party state.

Germany managed to avoid a dictatorship during the 1920s, but only just. The abdication of the emperor in November 1918 was followed (as in Russia eighteen months before) by simultaneous bids for power from the parliamentary Liberals and the revolutionary Communists: as Philip Scheidemann proclaimed the foundation of a democratic republic from the balcony of the Reichstag, one mile away Karl Liebknecht announced the creation of a Soviet Germany from the balcony of the imperial palace. For three months the two groups manoeuvred for an advantage, but when the Communists staged an open revolt in Berlin in

The process of dissolution was most keenly reflected in the arts. Long-established traditions of academic painting, initially questioned in the 19th century by the Romantics and the Impressionists, were dealt a *coup de grace* with the work of Cubist painters Pablo Picasso (1881-1973) and George Braque (1882-1963). The latter's *Still Life* (c.1912) *above right* demonstrates their disregard for traditional representational painting. Revolutionary Russia, in the early years, fostered extreme abstraction – a direct appeal to the masses untrammelled by tradition and history. The poster *above left* designed by El Lissitzky (1890-1941) during the Civil War, is overt in its message: *The Red Wedge Divides the Whites* (1919). In Germany, the absurdist Dada movement (a forerunner of Surrealism) broke down traditional barriers of taste and subject matter. By the 1920s artists like George Grosz (1893-1959) were

producing forthright (and often obscene) social and political criticisms such as The Owners (*above* 1920). By the mid-1930s Grosz, and many of his contemporaries, had been forced to leave Germany.

One of the domestic achievements of Mussolini, Europe's first Fascist dictator, was to restore relations between the Italian Kingdom and the Papacy in the Concordat of 1929, which established the Vatican City as a sovereign state. This picture *right* shows the dictator on the right with King Victor Emmanuel III, on the left, flanking Pope Pius XI.

January 1919, the republicans were able to call in the army to suppress them. Those who were not killed in the streets were subsequently dispatched to prison. A national assembly met shortly afterwards at Weimar (since the capital seemed unsafe) and devized a constitution for the new state.

The survival of the 'Weimar Republic' (as the new state was called) was always precarious, however. Throughout its short life it had to beat off challenges, often violent, from extreme groups of both the left and the right. In 1920 the monarchists tried to topple the regime; then, in 1922, an unlikely alliance between discontented army officers, led by General Ludendorff, and an extreme right-wing party led by Adolf Hitler, tried to take over the regional government of Bavaria in the Munich *putsch* of 1923. They too were defeated. As long as the German economy continued to offer reasonably full employment, the Weimar experiment functioned fairly well. But when material circumstances worsened, the appeal of those who promised to restore the prosperity through firm government and tighter regulation was greatly enhanced.

It was, in fact, the Western allies who ultimately undermined the German economy. Each of them had suffered grave damage during the war. All had run up large public debts and incurred heavy casualties; France had, in addition, suffered great devastation in the war zone, while Britain had lost millions of tons of shipping. Furthermore, both had reorganized their economies to produce war materials rather than exports and, through this and other factors (most notably the Russian revolution), had therefore lost many of their traditional overseas markets. By March 1921, there were 2 million unemployed in Great Britain. Not surprisingly, there was some urgency to suggestions that Germany should be 'made to pay' for all this and in 1921, after long deliberations, a Reparations Committee announced that the total sum payable to the allies was $32 billion. This was bad enough for Germany, whose economy had also suffered serious dislocation during the war, but the problem reached catastrophic proportions with the collapse of her currency: the mark, which stood at 25 US cents in 1914, fell to 2 cents by July 1922 and thereafter became virtually worthless – 2.5 trillion to the dollar by 1924.

Britain believed that the collapse of the mark was caused by the burden of reparations, and proposed that repayments should be frozen. But in return, she asked that her own debts, and those of the other European powers, to the United States – totalling some $8 billion – should also be suspended. This, America refused. Instead, in 1924, a committee of economic experts, headed by the American banker Charles L. Dawes, laid down a fixed time-table (stretching ahead to 1988) for paying the agreed reparations, and money began to pour into the United States faster than ever. A massive imbalance was created in the international economy, as more and more of the resources of Europe were diverted to debt repayment and interest, reducing the market for industrial goods. The stage was set for the 'Great Depression', which was finally to complete the process begun by the Great War: the destruction of the old order in Europe.

Europe, ruined by the Great War, in the 1920s underwent galloping inflation that was, for many families, far worse. In Germany at the height of devaluation late in 1923, even everyday items cost thousands and even millions of marks *right*. Those on fixed incomes were ruined. It was to these despairing members of the working and middle classes that the young ex-soldier and political orator, Adolf Hitler (1889-1945), appealed. He already had a small political following, the National Socialist Party (Nazis), and he made his base in Munich. Hitler, aided by some German army officers (including General Ludendorff), decided to attempt a 'march on Berlin'. However, they did not get far beyond the steps of the Munich beer hall where their plot was hatched in October 1923 *below*, and Hitler spent much of the next year in prison, where he wrote *Mein Kampf*.

Kaufe:
Stampfpapier 20,000
Lumpen: 50,000 Mark.
Knochen: 5,000 Mark.

FRICK KRIEBEL LUDENDORFF   HITLER BRÜKNER RÖHM WAGNER

Legend:

- Axis territory 1 September 1939
- Axis satellites
- Axis occupied
- Soviet occupied territory 1939-40
- British Empire
- neutral powers

- German advances
- Italian advances
- Soviet forces
- Allied forces
- retreat and withdrawal
- ▲ concentration camps

The expansion of the Fascist powers 1939-42. In September 1939 Hitler invaded Poland; in 1940, Denmark, Norway and the Low Countries. The defeat of France followed. Great Britain, its army in France evacuated from Dunkirk, rejected Hitler's peace offers and defeated his *Luftwaffe*. Mussolini's abortive attack on Greece, British intervention and an anti-Axis coup in Yugoslavia led to German occupation of Yugoslavia, Greece and Crete (May 1941). In June 1941 Hitler attacked the Soviet Union, reaching Leningrad, Moscow and Kiev. In 1942 his armies crossed the lower Don and reached the Caucasus, but failed to take Stalingrad. The limit of the German expansion had been reached.

GREAT BRITAIN
Belfast
Glasgow
Liverpool
Manchester
Hull
Birmingham
Coventry
Bristol
Plymouth
Southampton
London
North Sea

Apr. 1940
NORWAY
Narvik
Namsos
Trondheim
Andalsnes
Bergen
Oslo
Stavanger
Apr. 1940
Apr. 1940

SWEDEN
Stockholm
Helsinki
Gulf of Finland
FINLAND

DENMARK
Copenhagen
Baltic Sea
Danzig
Konigsberg
E. PRUSSIA

ESTONIA
Riga
LATVIA
LITHUANIA 1939
Wilno
Mir

withdrawal of British army May-June 1940
NETHERLANDS
Rotterdam
Dunkirk
Brussels
Cologne
BELGIUM
Paris
Sedan
May 1940
GERMANY
Hamburg
Berlin
Leipzig
Prague
Stuttgart
Munich
Linz
Sept. 1939
Kutno
Warsaw
POLAND
Cracow
1939
to Hungary 1940

Châlons-sur-Marne
Dijon
FRANCE
Bordeaux
Vichy
Lyon
VICHY FRANCE
(under Vichy government 1940-42)
June 1940
SWITZERLAND
Milan
Venice
Genoa
SLOVAKIA
Bratislava
Vienna
Budapest
HUNGARY
R. Dniester

PORTUGAL
Madrid
SPAIN
Balearic Is.
Gibraltar (British)
SP. MOROCCO
Mers-el-Kebir
MOROCCO
ALGERIA
(under Vichy government 1940-42)
TUNISIA
Tunis
Mediterranean Sea

Corsica
Sardinia
Rome
ITALY
Taranto
Sicily
Malta (British)

Marseilles

Zagreb
Sarajevo
Belgrade
Ragusa
YUGOSLAVIA
ROMANIA
Ploesti
Bucharest
Adriatic Sea
Sofia
BULGARIA
ALBANIA
Oct. 1940
Thessalonika
GREECE
Apr. 1941
Aegean Sea
Corinth
Athens
20 May 1941
Maleme
Canea
Crete
1 Feb 1941

Tripoli
Afrika Korps
14 Feb – 1941
LIBYA
Benghazi
Tobruk
Sidi Barrani
Apr. 1941
under Br. occupa...
EGYPT

CHAPTER 25

THE WORLD IN CONFLICT
1929–1945

The Great Depression began with a spectacular fall in share prices on the New York stock exchange in the course of 1929, followed by the collapse of banks all across America: between 1929 and 1932, more than 5,000 closed their doors, destroying the savings of innumerable investors. But first, the doomed American banks called in their short-term foreign loans, thus spreading the effects of the 'Wall Street Crash' far beyond the United States. In May 1931 the largest Austrian bank declared itself bankrupt and many others in continental Europe soon followed suit.

Inevitably, other forms of economic activity were severely affected by the lack of capital and credit; international trade slumped by 60 percent; world industrial production (excluding the Soviet Union) fell by 40 percent. Equally inevitably, this decline in output and sales led to unemployment of a corresponding magnitude: by March 1933, the number of people out of work in Britain (3 million) and the United States (14 million) approached 25 percent of the workforce. Even the liberal, energetic Franklin D. Roosevelt, who became US President in January 1933 and pushed through a series of measures designed to create jobs and restore business confidence, met with only limited success. Strikes became more common (in 1934 some 20 billion days were lost through industrial action) and many men remained unemployed through the 1930s (in 1938 there were still over 10 million Americans out of work). But, at least, there was no major upheaval: Roosevelt's 'New Deal' managed to preserve the social and political order relatively intact.

Events took a very different course in Europe. In France, Britain and Germany, the Depression came at a time when Left-wing governments were in power. All three were faced by the stark alternatives of either increasing relief to the unemployed (in the hope of stimulating demand and therefore, eventually, production), or cutting public expenditure in the hope of restoring business confidence. All three chose the former, but were driven from office when their policies failed to bring an immediate return of prosperity. In Britain, a National Government took office in 1931, dominated by the Conservative party; in France, the Right gained power in 1934. Both transfers of power were peaceful; and so was the transfer of power to the Right in Germany. But there the similarities ended.

Adolf Hitler was an Austrian who moved to Munich in the years before the First World War. He served with distinction in the 1914-18 war. After demobilization, he joined one of the small parties founded in post-war Germany, the National Socialist Workers Party, of which he soon became leader (*Führer*). But his following was small. His attempt

431

LINE FOR
1¢ RESTAURANT
20 MEALS FOR 1¢
DONATIONS INVITED
HELP FEED THE HUNGRY
1¢ WILL FEED 20
1¢ RESTAURANT
107 W 43rd ST.

The Great Depression 1929-1939 threw the industrialized West into disarray. In Europe protest movements of the Left and Right arose in almost every country. Where democratic institutions were weak, the Right tended to gain the upper hand. Here the charismatic appeal of strong personalities preaching a reactionary doctrine, and producing popular ideologies in powerful military fancy-dress won the day. Mussolini in Italy, Franco in Spain and Hitler in Germany *below* formed a triumvirate of posturing dictators. In America, the land of promise and bastion of democracy, massive unemployment and the sight of food queues *left* also undermined the social fabric; but here (as in France) the election of Left or liberal administrations provoked waves of strikes, stimulated trade union organization, and encouraged a variety of reform efforts. President Roosevelt's New Deal, involving financial and economic reform, emergency relief and large-scale public works projects, was a partial solution. However, it ultimately required a second World War to pull the US economy out of depression.

to seize power in the Munich *putsch* of 1923 was a fiasco (chapter 24), and his party obtained only twelve seats in the National Assembly in the 1928 elections. The Great Depression changed all that. By 1930, no less than 40 percent of the German workforce was unemployed, and Hitler's programme (which remained largely unchanged) gained widespread support. His promise to liberate Germany from the humiliation of the peace settlements appealed to German pride; although Left-wing in part of its programme, especially in its earlier years, his party espoused race-war rather than class-war and his identification of the Jews as the unacceptable face of both Capitalism and Communism offered a convenient scapegoat for the prevailing economic and political chaos; Hitler's call for the abolition of unearned income and usury, together with the nationalization of all major companies (and the introduction of profit-sharing in others), seemed to hold out some prospect of escape from the crisis.

In the elections of 1930, although the Nazis (as the party was commonly known) polled only 18 percent of the popular vote, they gained 107 seats in the Assembly, with which they held the balance of power. In 1932, when fresh elections were held, they gained 37 percent of the votes and 230 seats. In January 1933, after other Right-wing leaders had failed to assert their authority, Adolf Hitler became prime minister of a government composed of Nazi Party members. The Communists were eliminated from the Assembly almost at once, and the activities of the other parties were restricted. The trade unions, news media, and schools were brought under control. Economic affairs were closely regulated and, through public works programmes (the most famous of

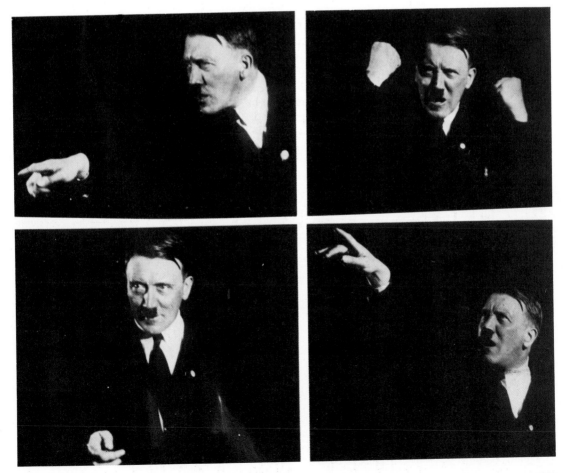

Hitler's policy of Nazification
(*Gleichschaltung*) subjected all major
German institutions – universities,
schools, professions, youth organizations –
to Nazi control. Only the armed forces, the
Catholic church and some dissenting
Lutheran congregations resisted takeover.
Trade unions were abolished. In 1934 the
German parliament (*Reichstag*) voted its
powers to Hitler through the Enabling Law.
Popular support for Nazism was mobilized
by the dramatization of the leader cult
(*Führerprinzip*) and through mass
political spectacles *right*, of which the
annual highlight was the Party rally at
Nuremberg. A strong appeal to Germanic
traditions and folk culture was also a major
element in Hitler's programme. Mountains,
pine forests and peasant costumes were
favoured elements of his propaganda
photographs *below*.

which was the autobahn system) and carefully directed investment,
unemployment began to fall and prosperity began to return. Few Germans seem to have felt strong opposition to Hitler's assumption of
absolute power in August 1934.

It was a curious irony that, just as the industrial production of the
West was collapsing, that of Soviet Russia was increasing. Already by
1926 industrial and agricultural production had reached pre-war levels.
In 1928 Joseph Stalin, Lenin's successor as leader of the Communist
party, produced the first of a series of five-year plans, which laid down
objectives for every sector of the economy. The details were worked
out by a new agency known as the State Planning Commission (*Gosplan*): three volumes, containing 1,600 pages of text, statistics and
tables, were issued to explain the exercise, and a stream of directives
followed on how different factories and farms should operate.

Thus, at a time when the Western governments floundered in an
economic morass, without any clear idea of what had caused the Depression or how to cure it, the Soviets adopted a blueprint of unprecedented complexity for the total reorganization and regulation of the
largest state economic sector in the world, and also created a mechan-
ism to monitor and control the changes. Under the first five-year plan

alone (1928-32), Russia managed to double its industrial output, rising from fifth to second largest producer of manufactured goods in the world and increasing its share in global industrial output from under 2 percent in 1921 to 10 percent in 1939.

But an economic transformation on this scale could only be achieved through a ruthless regimentation of resources. Firstly, all whom the state defined as 'subversive' or as opponents of its policies, were liable to be arrested and sent to slave labour camps, most of them in Siberia. Furthermore, within the industrial sector, the production of capital goods was favoured at the expense of consumer goods (which remained in short supply and of inferior quality), while much of the profit from production was subject to compulsory reinvestment on Gosplan's instructions. However, state intervention in industry was as nothing compared with state intervention in agriculture. Here the problem was less tractable, because the government's plans to secure cheap and copious supplies of food for the cities ran counter to the interests of the prosperous peasant farmers (*kulaks*), whose farms supplied a large part of the food consumed by the cities. They aimed to secure the best price for their produce. The *kulaks*, not surprisingly, bitterly opposed the new agricultural policy introduced by Stalin, which ordered all peasant holdings to be amalgamated into collective farms, each with its own production quota and its own state-appointed management committee. Although each farmer was permitted a small private plot, the produce of which might be sold on the open market, the crops grown on the main farm were sold to the government at artificially low prices for redistribution to the cities.

The opposition of the *kulaks* to 'collectivization' swiftly reduced the food supplied to all major cities, and thus presented a challenge that Stalin could not ignore. Accordingly, hundreds of thousands of *kulaks* were either massacred or sent to labour camps in Siberia for 're-education'. By 1934, at an appalling cost, over 200,000 collective farms were in operation, and the Soviet Union seemed set for a period of comparative calm after two decades of upheaval. In September of that year she even joined the League of Nations.

At precisely this moment, however, Stalin embarked upon a sustained purge of his own Communist Party followers. At first, in 1935, he arrested a relatively small number of senior opponents; then in 1936, a

Myths similar to those favoured by the Fascists were used to promote Joseph Stalin (1879-1953) in Russia. A man of many guises, his popular image drew on his 'peasant' background (he was the son of a Georgian cobbler) to create the image of an earthly patriarch, uncle of his people *below*. In fact, ruthless elimination of political rivals following the death of Lenin, brutal depopulation, consequent on his collectivization of agriculture, and his construction of a police state broke more eggs and produced fewer omelettes than all the Fascist regimes in the rest of Europe.

Stalin, originally an insignificant member of the Bolshevik Party, steadily worked his way to its top by his skill at manipulating its organizational machinery. By 1939, as a result of ruthless purging of the Party hierarchy, the army, the government and industry, he exercized complete power over the Central Committee *above*, and so over the whole of the Soviet Union, power as great as that possessed by Hitler in Germany.

group of former critics were accused of treason and put on trial. Finally, after 1937, the purges were extended to officers of the armed forces, diplomats, industrial managers, and local party officials. In all, between 1935 and 1939, in an appalling holocaust, more than 7 million Russians were arrested, of whom some 90 percent died – either by execution before or after trial, or in the Siberian labour camps. These upheavals produced a catastrophic weakening of Russia's domestic and international position. On the one hand, the loss of so many experienced administrators and professionals from every walk of life reduced efficiency and stunted growth. On the other, the show trials of the accused, which often involved ridiculously fanciful and improbable crimes (to which many nonetheless confessed), widely discredited the Soviet system abroad. Above all, the elimination of half the senior officers throughout the armed forces fatally weakened Russia's military position against the growing power of both Germany to the west and Japan to the east.

The Paris peace settlements (chapter 24) offered few rewards to Japan. She had hastened to declare war in 1914 on Germany and had taken a large (if self-interested) part in 'liberating' German possessions in China and the Pacific. But much of these were either transferred to Australia and Britain, or handed back to China. She had also intervened during the civil war in Russia 1919-20, in the hope of gaining some territory there; but again she failed. Yet the need for expansion into the Asian mainland became more pressing with the passage of time. The Meiji revolution (chapter 23) had made Japan into a great trading nation, exporting her manufactures all over the world; and the 1914-18 War, with its opportunities for providing munitions and merchant shipping to the belligerents, increased Japan's overseas trade even further – from a value of under 1 billion yen in the period 1913-17 to almost 2 billion in 1918-22. But the Great Depression in the West caused a savage fall: between 1929 and 1931, Japanese foreign trade was halved.

This was not Japan's only economic problem. There were also natural disasters (especially the great earthquake of 1923 which destroyed three-quarters of Tokyo), and an acute population problem (the total number of Japanese was increasing at 1.5 percent – almost 1 million people – every year). In some government circles the view gained ground that a solution to all these problems might be found by carving out an empire which would make Japan self-sufficient and, therefore, economically independent of the rest of the world.

The contemporary condition of China offered the Japanese imperialists, mainly army and navy officers, both the temptation and the opportunity for expansion. Ever since the collapse of the Ch'ing dynasty in 1911, China had declined steadily into disunity. The provinces fell into the hands of various warlords who spent most of the 1920s fighting each other, at a high cost in casualties and dislocation. In Canton, however, a new Nationalist party was organized: the Kuomintang. With help from both Chinese and Russian Communists, the Kuomintang general, Chiang Kai-shek, waged a campaign in 1926-7 which secured

The struggle for power in China, between the Nationalist Kuomintang and the Communists reached a crucial phase with the Long March (1934-35) when Mao Tse-tung *below right* led the Communist forces from their southern bases in Kiangsi and Hunan (where they had been under constant attack) to a new base area in the north west. An unsatisfactory truce was reached enabling both factions to form a united front against the increasing threat of Japanese expansion. The Japanese response was to invade China in force; by the end of 1939, in a campaign which involved heavy civilian loss of life, often by the bombing of cities such as Shanghai *below left*, they had occupied most of north and central China, gaining all of the main industrialized areas. The Nationalists made a fighting retreat to the mountains of the south west, while the Communists sustained a guerrilla war within Japanese-occupied territory.

Nanking as his capital and established control over the lower Yangtze basin. But Chiang now turned on his Communist allies, whom he forced to withdraw into the mountainous western provinces, and then destroyed several other warlords in the east. By 1930, Chiang's regime had received international recognition and seemed poised to reunite China.

If the Japanese were ever to establish their power on the mainland, they would have to strike sooner rather than later. Thus, in 1931, Japanese forces stationed in Manchuria took control of the province, with its rich industrial resources. Chinese protests to the League of Nations failed to mobilize effective international action, and Japan went on in 1933 to annex the province Jehol, and in 1937 launched a full-scale invasion of northern China. Within a year, most of the northern and central areas, containing almost all the major cities, were in Japanese hands. The Kuomintang, like the Communists before them, were forced to retreat westwards.

It was clear to China's neighbours that Japanese expansion would continue: the only questions concerned the direction it would take. Russia feared a northward thrust, and so in the summer of 1939 her army (under the able General Zhukov) began hostilities along the Manchurian border in order to deter further Japanese aggression. The United States, fearing a southwards attack on the Philippines (which

Mussolini's pretensions to an enlarged colonial empire first found an outlet in the Ethiopian campaign in 1935. Italy already possessed Libya, Eritrea and Italian Somaliland. He intervened in Spain (1936), and turned to Hitler for support in the Rome-Berlin Axis (celebrated *above* in 1941). Thereafter imitation of Hitler inspired him to claim European territories (part of France 1938, Albania 1939 and Greece 1940). Military and economic weakness tied him to Hitler in the Pact of Steel (1939), and by 1941 Germany was forced to bail him out in Greece and Libya.

Japan's expansion in Asia was designed to eliminate British, American and Soviet influence and to maximize economic and industrial resources there, its final aim being to construct a 'Greater East Asia', a self-sufficient, defensible empire. In the 1943 poster *left* a Japanese soldier tramples Westerners; the chain-links A, B and D stand for American, British and Dutch.

The Spanish Civil War 1936-39 grouped the Right, the military and the Catholic Church (with German and Italian 'volunteers' and military aid) against the Popular Front government, republicans, anti-clericals, anarchists, socialists and Communists. Against superior weaponry and numbers, the Left fought desperately and capitalized on Nationalist atrocities, such as the bombing of civilian areas *below*. The Left were, however, equally guilty of appalling crimes.

she had governed since the Spanish-American war in 1898), restricted iron and steel exports to Japan, threatened to cut off her supplies of oil, froze Japanese credit in America, and stepped up aid to Chiang Kai-shek. Once again, it seemed to those Japanese who favoured expansion that time was not on their side: after some debate, it was decided to expand southwards, into the areas held by the United States and the Europeans, rather than northwards into Russian-held territory. Accordingly a non-aggression pact was signed with the Soviet government on 13 April 1941, and Japanese forces began to move southwards. It was to prove the salvation of the Soviet system.

In his autobiographical polemic *Mein Kampf*, composed in prison during 1923, Hitler had made clear his loathing of Communism and his desire to see Soviet Russia destroyed. On this point he never wavered. But before this cardinal aim could be achieved, certain other obstacles had to be overcome. The first was German rearmament, which the peace settlements had forbidden. In 1935, therefore, universal military service was reintroduced, and a programme of rearmament for land, sea and air initiated, causing a marked revival in heavy industry. In 1936, taking advantage of the international crisis caused by Italy's unprovoked invasion of Ethiopia, Hitler ordered his new army to occupy those areas of the Rhineland placed under League of Nations occupation. His action went unopposed.

For the next three years, the political focus of Europe shifted to Spain, where a Left-wing government, elected in 1931, had introduced a sweeping programme of social and economic reforms. In 1936 a revolt by the army, supported by Right-wing politicians, began a desperate civil war in which the Soviet Union and Left-wing groups in Europe and America supported the government in Madrid, while Germany and Italy provided vital aid to the rebels. Eventually the latter, led by General Francisco Franco, were victorious on all fronts; but the Spanish Civil War possessed significance far beyond the peninsula. Firstly, it revealed the unwillingness (or inability) of the Western democracies to use armed force to achieve their foreign policy objectives: even the Left-wing Popular Front government elected in France in 1936 could neither provide effective help to the Republicans nor prevent aid from other quarters reaching the rebels. Secondly, it provided (like the Ethiopian crisis of 1936) a distraction while Hitler's forces occupied

Hitler's anti-Semitic policy, implicit in his early political testament *Mein Kampf* (1925), was first effectively instituted in the racial Nuremberg Laws of 1935. The Laws deprived Jews of their civil and commercial rights. In 1941 the Nazi state proceeded to what became known as the 'Final Solution' of the Jewish problem, the deliberate extermination of Jewish communities throughout occupied Europe. Most of the victims were transported by rail *above* to extermination camps in Poland, though many were massacred near their homes, sometimes *above right* being forced to dig their own graves beforehand. Exact figures are unavailable, but about 6 million Jews are known to have been killed by the Nazis.

neighbouring territories in central Europe: Germany annexed Austria and large areas of Czechoslovakia in 1938.

Not everyone deplored these blatant violations of the 1919 peace settlements, nor were the tough measures adopted by totalitarian governments of the Left and the Right universally condemned. To many Western observers, both the Fascist and the Communist dictators appeared to be dealing with their economic and social problems in a similar fashion, with considerably more success than their own governments and both ideologies enjoyed a substantial body of support in most Western countries. The authoritarian methods used against opponents of the regime – summary imprisonment, show trials, and the labour and concentration camps – were certainly known about; but they were excused by many on the ground that 'you can't make an omelette without breaking eggs' – that wholesale social improvement could not be achieved without hardships and sacrifices for some. Those who called for action against Communism, or against aggression by Hitler or Mussolini, were branded as war-mongers; and those who publicly criticized the policies of the dictators were placed under official pressure to moderate their tone. When, in September 1938, the prime ministers of France and Britain (Edouard Daladier and Neville Chamberlain respectively) approved the annexation of parts of Czechoslovakia in return for a promise from the dictators that there would be no more expansion (the 'Munich agreement'), they were hailed by their electors as national heroes. But in March 1939, Hitler proceeded to occupy the rest of Czechoslovakia and seized the port of Memel from Lithuania; in April, Mussolini swiftly overran Albania.

These new acts of unprovoked aggression totally discredited the policies that had led to Munich. Both Britain and France, faced with the prospect of limitless Fascist expansion in central Europe, promptly issued pledges to Poland, Greece and Romania, promising military assistance if any of them were attacked. A crash programme of military spending was initiated – conscription was re-introduced into Britain on 27 April 1939 – and approaches were made to Russia with the intention of creating a 'peace front' to the east of Germany. But it was too late. On 23 August Germany, despite her declared hostility towards Communism, signed a non-aggression pact with the Soviet Union, which

Concentration camps, introduced in 1933, were the means by which the Nazi state sequestered and punished its enemies. They were places of cruelty, starvation, and widespread killing. By the end of the war, degradation and disease had made them places, such as Belsen *above*, indistinguishable from extermination camps like Auschwitz.

By 1936 Hitler's government had effectively eliminated the restrictions imposed on Germany at Versailles: rearmament was in top gear, the Saar restored by plebiscite, the Rhineland had been re-militarized, and the Locarno treaties (1925), guaranteeing European frontiers, denounced. Many could see a threatening future emerging; one was David Low, the British political cartoonist, *above*. Nevertheless Hitler managed to annex Austria and partition Czechoslovakia (1938) before his invasion of Poland (1939) *below* provoked the outbreak of war with Britain and France.

provided not only that neither side would attack the other, but also that either party would remain neutral if the other were attacked by a third power. The Nazi-Soviet pact was one of the most controversial events of the decade. Supporters of Russian Communism explained it away by pointing out that Britain and France had spurned Russian approaches for a collective security pact – but the fact was that the pact effectively partitioned Poland between Germany and Russia. With this guarantee in his pocket, Hitler's forces – some 1.7 million men strong – invaded Poland on 1 September. Britain and France demanded that Germany withdraw, but the ultimatum was ignored, and they declared war on Germany.

This sudden firmness, after so many years of appeasement, took Hitler somewhat by surprise. However, since neither France nor Britain was in a position to attack, he continued his successful eastern campaign. By 17 September, when Russian forces also began to invade Poland, the process was almost concluded. Organized resistance ended a week later and, on 29 September, the German and Russian governments partitioned Poland.

Hitler now had to deal with his new western enemies before they had time to build up their strength. Despite its successes in the east, Germany was still relatively weak after the Depression, and her economy was not equipped to provide armament in depth: too many resources diverted to military production might lead to shortages at home which would cause unrest. So Hitler prepared for a short but decisive 'lightning campaign' (*Blitzkrieg*). In April 1940 his forces unexpectedly but efficiently overran Denmark and Norway, and on 10 May they suddenly opened a devastating offensive against Holland, Belgium and France which met with immediate success. The French and British armies moved by pre-arrangement to Belgium's rescue; German tanks appeared across their rear, swept away the forces left to defend it and reached the Channel coast on 19 May. Precipitately, the remnants of the British army withdrew to Dunkirk and were evacuated.

On 27-28 May the British Cabinet, badly shaken, debated whether to seek peace terms. Chamberlain (the former prime minister) and Halifax (the foreign secretary) were in favour, believing (correctly) that Germany would be generous; but they were outvoted by their colleagues,

"Of course there's no harm in your knowing!"

CARELESS TALK COSTS LIVES

Britain, the first country ever to undergo a sustained air offensive against its people and economy, was also to become the most fully mobilized of the Second World War. The Blitz *above right* failed to bring London to a stand-still. Churchill, the Prime Minister, here inspects some bomb damage. Children were evacuated from the major targets, women were conscripted with men, female- substituted for male-labour in many sectors of the economy, civilians organized into home defence and welfare organizations and the whole country alerted to enemy subversion *above left*. As a result of the latter, German intelligence infiltration in Britain was practically non-existent.

led by the new premier Winston Churchill. But, at first, it seemed that Churchill had miscalculated. The Germans pressed on inexorably towards Paris; Italy declared war on France and Britain; and on 22 June the French government surrendered. The northern half of France was placed under German occupation and the rest was governed from the town of Vichy by an administration made up largely of Right-wingers driven from office by the Popular Front in 1936. In the early years of the occupation, the Nazis enjoyed considerable local support, particularly in France and Belgium, and Britain stood alone.

By July 1940, when Hitler held victory celebrations in Berlin, Germany and Italy – known as the 'Axis' – were masters, directly or indirectly, of the whole of the western and central, and much of eastern Europe. Russia, it is true, had made use of Hitler's western offensive in order to occupy Finland and the Baltic states; but the difficulties experienced by the Soviet army in attaining these objectives suggested that it posed no threat to Germany. Likewise, although the Royal Air Force had managed to defeat a major air offensive designed either to prepare the way for an invasion by German ground forces or to bomb Britain into surrender (the Battle of Britain), Britain was manifestly in no position to counter-attack for as long as the United States (however sympathetic emotionally) refused to embrace her cause openly and actively.

Thus on 28 September 1940, when it was clear that the bombing offensive against Britain had failed, Hitler ordered his armaments factories to cease producing landing craft and planes and instead to concentrate on tanks and armoured cars. The invasion of Russia, known as Operation Barbarossa, was scheduled for 7 May 1941, with 3 million

The German-occupied nations of Europe suffered varying fortunes. The comprehensive supervision of government and administrative functions by the Nazi police state – the Gestapo and SS – ensured, for the most part, acquiescent collaboration. Of course, many actively sympathized. For others, open resistance was a dangerous and morally questionable activity. The Nazis relied on a 'ministry of fear' and grossly callous reprisals as effective security measures. Passive resistance, for instance in Denmark where King Christian X *left centre* chose to wear the yellow star which the Nazis obliged Jewish subjects to display, was widespread. Active resistance was only waged where geographical conditions favoured it, as in Yugoslavia.

The British North African offensive of October 1942 reversed the tide of German victory in the west.
The massed artillery and tank battle at El Alamein *above right* just preceded Operation Torch, the Anglo-American invasion of French North Africa. Within six months the Germans had lost the whole of North Africa and a quarter of a million men. The victory coincided with the Soviet breakthrough at Stalingrad. All at once, the New Order seemed to be on the run, but the promise of the optimistic Russian poster *below* celebrating the alliance of Great Britain, the USSR and the USA would not be fulfilled for another 2½ years.

men due to advance on a 2,000 mile front. 'When Barbarossa begins,' Hitler informed his general staff, 'the world will hold its breath'.

But it did not begin on 7 May. Late in 1940, having successfully occupied Albania, Italian forces launched an unprovoked attack on Greece. It met with stout resistance, and with a counter-attack in Albania; before long, British troops from Egypt arrived in Greece to assist. Then in March 1941 a coup d'état in Yugoslavia replaced the pro-German government with one more favourable to Britain and, at the same time, the British forces in Egypt invaded Italian Libya. These reverses were serious, and Hitler took seriously Mussolini's appeal for aid. On 3 April a small but highly-trained German army (the *Afrikakorps*) under General Rommel launched a strong counter-attack in Libya which the British army, having sent 60,000 men to Greece, was powerless to resist. Then on 6 April, a much larger German force under Field Marshal List poured into the Balkans. Both campaigns had succeeded within six weeks: Rommel reached the borders of Egypt on 29

May and a German airborne landing captured Crete two days later. Resistance in the Balkans was henceforth carried on by relatively small numbers of guerrillas.

Hitler's army had scored another triumph; but it came too late for the original Barbarossa schedule. List's tanks had travelled to the Peloponnese and back: they needed repairs and their crews needed rest. So the invasion of Russia began six weeks late, on 22 June. But it was still a fantastic success: Smolensk, a heavily-defended city 400 miles behind the Russian frontier, fell within a month, and in late November, having taken three million prisoners and destroyed or captured 18,000 tanks and 20,000 planes, the Germans stood at the gates of Leningrad and Moscow. But there they remained as the Russian winter set in: those six weeks lost in the Balkans had cost Hitler his victory. On 7 December 1941, amid sub-zero temperatures that disabled the German tanks and planes (but not those of the winter-wise Russians) a massive counter-attack was launched outside Moscow. The troops, commanded by General Zhukov, were fresh, for they had come from Manchuria on the Trans-Siberian railway in the course of the summer, freed by the Russo-Japanese non-aggression pact signed in April. The intervention of the new troops was crucial for, although their casualties were heavy, they drove the Germans back more than a hundred miles, giving Stalin six months in which to reorganize his shattered defences.

On the other hand, the rout of Russia's forces in the summer and autumn of 1941 convinced the Japanese that they had nothing to fear from that quarter. And so, on 7 December, the same day as the Moscow counter-attack, the Japanese air force carried out a devastating surprise attack on Pearl Harbor, Hawaii, sinking the battleships of the American Pacific fleet at anchor; on the Philippines, where most American planes were destroyed on the ground; and on British colonial outposts in Malaya and Hong Kong.

These events turned the European war into a world war. On 8 December, the United States declared war on Japan; three days later, Germany and Italy declared war on the United States. The latter was a

Stalingrad marked the furthest eastward limit of German penetration of the Soviet Union. Besieged in the autumn of 1942, the city became the focus of the bitterest fighting of the war *below*. The city was flattened, and the surviving forces resorted to a street-by-street defence. In November, the Red Army successfully staged a counter-offensive which encircled the German attackers, making them the besieged, leading to the humiliating German capitulation in February 1943. Twenty German divisions were destroyed and the defeat terminated the course of German victory which had continued uninterrupted since 1939.

surprising strategic blunder on Hitler's part. President Roosevelt was already selling munitions to Britain and Russia with payment deferred until after the war (the 'Lend-lease' agreement of March 1941), but he had not been able to convince the US Congress to authorize a declaration of war on Germany. Now Hitler forced his hand – and for no apparent reason, except perhaps to shame Japan into attacking Russia; but, with her forces now fully committed in east Asia and in the Pacific, there was no incentive for the Japanese to do that. Instead, Roosevelt allocated the lion's share of America's ground and air forces to the European theatre of operations, in preparation for an attack on Hitler's 'Fortress Europe'.

But little was achieved by the Western Allies in 1942. A landing at Dieppe was repulsed with heavy losses, and the liberation of North Africa over the winter of 1942-43 involved the loss of relatively few

Hitler's failure to defeat Great Britain in the Blitz and the Atlantic, and to overthrow Stalin's regime in the Soviet Union made his own defeat inevitable, as their irreconcilable ideologies ruled out a compromise peace. The German armies were defeated in detail on the eastern front; the British and Americans were victorious in North Africa, invaded Sicily, Italy and then France. In sum this made German collapse under attack from east, west and south only a question of time.

German troops or resources. When Germans spoke about 'the war', they meant operations on the eastern front. Four million troops (most of them Germans, but with Italian, Romanian, Spanish and Hungarian contingents sent to aid the crusade against Communism) surged forward to the Volga in the summer of 1942 and thrust down into the Caucasus occupying Russia's agricultural heartland, the Ukraine, and all but gaining her oil reserves at Baku. But they did not take the key city on the lower Volga: Stalingrad. As winter closed in once more, 500,000 Axis troops struggled for control of the Russian city; but by February 1943, despite the airlifts which Air Marshal Goering had falsely promised could fly in everything the troops might require, the battle had been lost. The starving survivors of twenty German divisions surrendered. It had been the greatest battle in history, claiming 1,000,000 military casualties.

At last, Hitler was forced to abandon his guns-and-butter economy. Consumer spending in Germany in 1942 had been as high as in 1937; but now certain items were rationed and forced labour was required from the occupied countries to an increasing extent. Between January 1942 and July 1944, Germany's armaments production trebled. By now, however, even this was no longer enough to win the war. In an attempt to reverse the verdict of Stalingrad, Hitler resolved to launch a massive attack on Kursk: one million men and 2,700 tanks were to be committed. The German units rolled forward on 5 July; within the first week, half of them had been lost; within another week, the Germans had begun to retreat. Hitler still commanded 2.5 million men, 2,300 tanks and 8,000 field guns on the eastern front; but Stalin could throw against them 5.5 million, 8,400 and 21,000 respectively. In early 1944, the Russian forces outnumbered their enemies by six to one and a steady westward advance began – although at a staggering cost. Russia lost 15,000 men – the equivalent of a whole division – each and every day of the war. Nevertheless by June 1944, the Russian army was standing at the gates of Warsaw.

What were the Western Allies doing during these climactic years to encompass the defeat of Germany? To Russian eyes, it seemed, very little. Admittedly, valuable convoys of supplies and equipment were sent by sea to Archangel and Murmansk (despite heavy losses from German submarines), and by rail through Persia to the Caspian; in addition, British and American bombers raided numerous German towns, destroying munitions factories and supply trains (although not until late in 1944 was the production of critical war materials such as gasoline, coal or armaments significantly reduced). Then, in July 1943, having occupied North Africa and destroyed the *Afrikakorps*, 160,000 Allied troops occupied Sicily and, in September, they crossed to Italy and caused the collapse of Mussolini's regime. Italy surrendered unconditionally. However, the German forces in the peninsula fought on with great courage and skill, giving way only slowly and inflicting heavy losses. Rome did not fall until June 1944, and the Allies only reached Lombardy in April 1945. It was not really until the invasion of France in June 1944, with Operation Overlord (the D-Day landings) in Normandy, that a decisive blow was struck against Hitler's grip on western Europe

– and even then, despite the fact that most élite units of the German army were in the east, progress was slow. The Germans fought tenaciously and, by the end of 1944, only France and parts of Belgium had been regained: the Allies could not yet cross the Rhine.

However, by then it was clear that Hitler's Germany was on the brink of collapse. Poland had been reconquered; Finland, Bulgaria and Romania had realigned themselves with Russia; Greece and southern Yugoslavia had been evacuated by Axis forces. In the west, Hitler's last offensive in the Ardennes (the Battle of the Bulge) had failed, and his secret weapons programme – the VI and V2 rockets – proved insufficient to halt the Allied advance. The Anglo-American strategic bombing offensive, by contrast, mounted now from recaptured continental airfields, was at last bringing Germany's industry close to collapse, her population close to desperation, and her armed forces close to disintegration. As the Russian army fought its way towards Berlin, the Western Allies crossed the Rhine. Hitler anticipated the outcome of this final offensive by committing suicide; on 7 May the Nazi leadership surrendered unconditionally. The following day, the Allied leaders declared the war in Europe to be over.

But the war in Asia continued. Between December 1941 and May 1942, Japan had conquered all the British, Dutch and American islands in south-east Asia, and had overrun the entire mainland as far as the Indian border. It was a spectacular achievement, and even three years later, when the war in Europe ended, only Burma, the Philippines and some smaller offshore islands had been recovered. There were still one million undefeated Japanese troops in China, with 585,000 more in Malaya, Thailand, Indonesia and Indo-China. Of the Japanese archipelago itself, only parts of Okinawa – invaded on 1 April 1945 – were in Allied hands, and resistance there continued until 21 June. Clearly, to continue the war by the same conventional means would take years rather than months, involving the loss of countless more troops and munitions. So, although plans were laid for the invasion of Java in the autumn of 1945, and although Russia was offered many inducements (largely in the shape of surrendered prisoners and lands in Europe) to persuade her to break her 1941 non-aggression pact with Japan, an alternative strategy was actively pursued.

First, from May until the end of July 1945, almost all major Japanese cities were subjected to an American aerial bombardment of unprecedented ferocity. And then, suddenly, it ceased. For a week there was a lull. The Allies had prepared a new secret weapon: they wanted to use it with maximum psychological effect. Experiments with nuclear fission had been going on since 1942, and by the summer of 1945 there were three atomic bombs capable of being used, each with an explosive

Operation Overlord, the Allied landings in Normandy on 6 June 1944 (D-Day, *above left*) was the largest amphibious operation in history, involving 100,000 assault troops, 5000 ships and 14,000 aircraft. Allied air attack on German communications prevented a German counter-attack and artificial 'Mulberry' harbours turned the beaches into readymade ports to maintain the flow of supplies and reinforcements. After a fierce battle to establish a foothold, the Allies defeated the German defenders of Normandy by relentless attrition and then broke out to liberate Paris (August 25) and Brussels (September 3). By September 14 the US 1st Army had crossed the German frontier, but revived German resistance was then to prolong the war until the spring of 1945, which saw the Allied strategic bombing offensive against German industrial cities reach its greatest intensity, culminating in the destruction of Dresden, (February 13-14 *above right*).

Secret work on a nuclear weapon was sanctioned by Churchill and Roosevelt in 1942. In July 1945 a special commission recommended to President Truman that the bomb be used against Japan. The Potsdam Declaration, apppealing to the Japanese to surrender, was rejected, and the Japanese cities of Hiroshima and Nagasaki were subjected to the new weapon *right*. Russia immediately declared war on Japan, invading Manchuria, and at an imperial conference the Japanese emperor decided to surrender unconditionally to the Allies.

force equal to 20,000 tons of TNT. The first was used at a test site in New Mexico on 16 July: it worked. The other two were therefore transported to the Pacific theatre of the war and dropped on Japan on 6 August (at Hiroshima) and 9 August (at Nagasaki). Between them, the two bombs killed 150,000 people and devastated the targets. The Japanese were not to know that this terrifying demonstration of power temporarily exhausted America's nuclear arsenal. All they could see was an unprecedented force of destruction, against which they had no defence; and they could not overlook, in addition, Russia's declaration of war on 8 August, and her whirlwind conquest of Manchuria in the following week. Accordingly, on 14 August 1945, Japan unconditionally surrendered. With the conclusion of peace in the Far East, and in the shadow of the mushroom cloud of nuclear power, a new age in world history took shape.

Pacific Ocean

Arctic Ocean

Atlantic Ocean

US 1st fleet

ALASKA

UNITED STATES OF AMERICA

CANADA

GUATEMALA
★ 1954

PANAMA

CUBA
1961-2
★

DOMINICAN
REPUBLIC
★

Puerto Rico

US 2nd fleet

Baffin Island

GREENLAND

Iceland

SOVIET UNION

HOLLAND

BELGIUM

NORWAY

DENMARK

UNITED
KINGDOM

EG C

FRANCE

ITALY

PORTUGAL

SPAIN

WEST GERMANY

MOROCCO

P

H

ROMANIA

YUGOSLAVIA
★ 1948-53

BULGARIA

ALBANIA

GREECE
★ 1946-49

TURKEY
★ 1945-47

LIBYA

US 6th fleet

ISRAEL
★

IRAQ

KOREA
1950-

JAP

abbreviations

C	CZECHOSLOVAKIA
	★ 1948
	● 1968
EG	EAST GERMANY
	★ Berlin 1948-49, 1958-62
	● Berlin 1953
H	HUNGARY
	★ 1956
	● 1956
P	POLAND
	★ 1956
	● 1956

USA and allies

USSR and allies

↓ Soviet ICBM bases (7000 mile range)

↓ other Soviet missile sites

▲ principal Soviet military airfields

↓ US ICBM bases (5500 mile range)

▲ US heavy bomber bases
(capable of reaching USSR
with airborne refuelling)

■ US nuclear and other
major bases (Oct. 1962)

⬸ strategic US fleets

★ points of conflict in the Cold War

● uprisings in the Communist world

CHAPTER 26
THE MODERN WORLD FROM 1945

One of Hitler's favourite pieces of military music was the Prussian Army's Torgau March. Ironically, it was at Torgau, on the river Elbe, that Soviet and American troops first met up, towards the end of the Second World War, as the two fronts closed on Germany. At that time, everyone hoped that the Soviet-American alliance would continue into peacetime, to bring order to the world; as a sign of it, the United Nations was created, at a conference in San Francisco in summer, 1945. The plan was that the five Great Powers – the United States and its ally Great Britain, the Soviet Union, France and China – would run the world's affairs, acting as a sort of central committee.

But almost within a few weeks of Hitler's suicide, the Russians and the Americans had begun to disagree very deeply as to the shape of the post-war world, and by 1947 they had effectively divided Europe into rival spheres of influence. There was a prodigious war of words, virtually no trade, and a great stock-piling of weaponry on both sides; there was almost open warfare on several occasions. However, the 'Cold War', as it was called, never became a hot war. This was the first, and easily the most important, feature that marked off the period after 1945 from the rest of the history of mankind. War, at all previous times, had been the final arbiter. Now, war, which in the past had dictated the fate of empires and peoples, was ruled out because neither America nor Russia, the 'super-powers', could afford to risk it.

The decisive event of the Second World War occurred, in effect, after it was over in Europe, and several months after Hitler had killed himself. The deployment of the Western Allies of the atomic bomb, bringing the war against Japan to an end, was a display of explosive power

With the explosion of the first nuclear weapon in warfare, over Hiroshima, in 1945 *left* and with the meeting of the 'Big Three' Allied leaders – Churchill, Stalin and Roosevelt – at Yalta, on the Black Sea *right* earlier that year, two major steps in the formation of the divided post-war world were made. At Yalta, the Western Allies granted Stalin post-war control of eastern Europe. The heart of the Cold War was Germany, which by 1947 was partitioned between a democratic western and a communist eastern state; to defend this a Western military alliance (NATO, 1949) was formed to which the Russians responded with the Warsaw Pact (1955).

that went far beyond anything hitherto used. 150,000 people were killed, many thousands horribly maimed and the after-effects of the radiation, in the development of various cancers, lasted for decades. The mushroom-cloud of the atom bomb has haunted the imagination of the world ever since; but it became clear that, however just the cause, war could not bring victory in any meaningful sense to anyone. On the contrary, it would result only in universal disaster. In 1945 the Americans had a monopoly of atomic weapons, but – partly because of efficient espionage – the Soviet Union soon caught up. By 1949 the two super-powers were engaged in endless nuclear research and development, producing an ever more fearsome collection of weapons: hydrogen bombs in the early 1950s; intercontinental ballistic missiles (ICBMs) and nuclear-powered, and armed, Polaris submarines in the 1960s; neutron bombs and a prolific new generation of intermediate and short-range ballistic missiles (IRBMs) – Cruise and Trident – in the 1970s; by 1985 there were some 20,000 thermo-nuclear weapons in existence. Against them there was no known defence, although towards the end of the period the Americans alarmed the world with their research into 'Star-Wars' – a system of defence by which Soviet missiles could be detected as they were fired, and destroyed by lasers based in space on special satellites. This research threatened to disturb the balance of 'mutually-assured destruction', or MAD, as it was known in the ghoulish technocratic parlance of nuclear strategists.

From time to time, the expense and sheer destructive potential of the new weaponry prompted the two sides to discuss possible disarmament – the more energetically when it was shown that testing weapons in the atmosphere could create a widespread radiation with, in the long-term, lethal effects. The round of strategic arms limitation talks (SALT) which began in 1972 did produce agreements on limitation, though they were never very far-ranging: after all, each side could test nuclear weapons underground, often undetectably, and neither trusted the other nor could agree to an open monitoring system. The fact is that MAD, though unimaginably terrible, was effective in securing a *de facto* balance of power, and hence peace between the two super-powers. Then again, the sheer expense of it all ensured that nuclear weaponry would be confined to countries with a very large economy, so that lesser countries could not compete. There were small British and French contributions; the Chinese and Indians eventually also produced their own nuclear technology. But, in general, the lesser powers'

In 1945 the victorious Allies had separate zones in Germany, and Berlin was similarly divided, though it lay in the centre of the Russian zone. By 1948, relations had worsened between West and East, and the Russians tried to drive the Western powers from Berlin by imposing a blockade of all land transport from the West to Berlin. The West responded with an air-lift *below* – a fantastic piece of organization with planes landing at Tempelhof airport every four minutes: there was only one accident. The population survived, and the Russians lifted the blockade in 1949 after 5 months. Berlin continued to be a battlefield: as Western prosperity flooded into the western sector of the city, it attracted millions of emigrants from the East German state. In 1961, a huge wall was constructed to stop the emigration, which was ruining the East German economy; many people were gunned down for trying to scale it. In 1981 the East German state celebrated the 'Twenty Years of the Anti-Fascist Protection Rampart'.

role in a nuclear world was best summed up by a Danish politician who said that his country's defence policy was to broadcast a gramophone record repeating 'We surrender' in Russian over the radio.

Still, all of this weaponry produced the paradoxical result that there were no great wars. True, it all became expensive. By 1985, the British defence budget, at over £18 billion, swallowed almost £4 billion more than education, and £2 billion more than 'social expenditure', including health and pensions; the Soviet Union devoted almost a fifth of its resources to defence, the United States almost a tenth (figures which do not include all aspects of defence); perhaps a third of American industry depended on defence contracts. There was seldom anything very dramatic to show for all of this money: and, to make it more exciting to the public at large, both the Soviet Union and the United States embarked on complicated space-exploration. Rocket technology was developed by the Germans during the Second World War; and in 1957 the Russians put the first satellite into space, *Sputnik I.* In 1961 they put the first man in space. This caused alarm in the United States, which then devoted more to space research and, in 1969 won the race

Just as Russians and Americans quarrelled over Germany's inheritance in the West, they fought over Japan's possessions in the East. By 1949, the Chinese civil war had ended with the Communists victorious. Korea, a former Japanese protectorate, had been partitioned between Russians and Americans, who withdrew their forces in 1950. The Communist North and the anti-Communist South then went to war *above*, and US forces, with a contingent from the United Nations, intervened to stop the North from conquering. The propaganda machine went into action *right* and US General MacArthur threw the North Koreans back, invading North Korea; and this prompted Chinese intervention in October 1950. The world, used to American military superiority, was surprised when the Chinese retook all of the North and a large part of the South, including the capital, Seoul. A successful counter-attack in 1951 brought the front further north to the 38th parallel, and in July 1953 the stalemate was sealed by the armistice of Panmunjom. The two Koreas then went separate ways – the South to an extraordinary spurt of industrial progress, the North to crypto–Stalinism under the long-lived Kim Il-sung.

to place the first man on the Moon. This was, as propaganda made him say, 'a giant step for mankind'; but the Moon only turned out to consist of rock and the only tangible benefits that mankind experienced were largely accidental and indirect – new photographic films and a saucepan to which ingredients did not stick, even when burned. But the placing of a man on the moon and the subsequent sending of pieces of complicated machinery to take photographs of even further-flung pieces of rock may prove to be of greater significance. By the 1980s the deployment of unmanned satellites was an everyday event, transforming communications, surveying and surveillance; many of these were launched and serviced by a commercial US 'shuttle' system, while the Russians were constructing ever larger orbiting laboratories and space stations. Inevitably the strategic significance of space, as a war zone and as a place of refuge, could not be ignored. Would these achievements, in the future, count as a second version of 1492?

The 'Balance of Terror' echoed, in a curious way, the world of 1870-1914. Then, too, powers had shrunk from war because of its expense and destructiveness although, when new technology threatened to up-set the balance, war came just the same. Before 1914, as after 1945, the Great Powers' rivalries had been confined to the periphery – the game of imperialism as it was called. There were a number of small wars, fought between clients of the Great Powers after 1945.

Most of these wars arose as a consequence of the disintegration of European empires. The Second World War had destroyed the old conti-nent, nowhere more so than in Germany, many of whose cities resem-bled a moonscape after the great bombing raids, and whose popula-tion, in 1945-47, lived at starvation level. The only European country with pretentions to Great-Power status was Great Britain, whose prime ministers, Winston Churchill and Clement Attlee, could claim a third-share in the re-making of the world in 1945. But war had put her hopelessly in debt to the much richer Americans, and one price that had to be paid was co-operation on American terms. These included, in principle, the acceptance of free trade within a huge dollar area, which led to the devaluation of the pound sterling; they also included, in the small print, the dismantling of the British empire. In any case, many, perhaps most, people in the British Isles were already bored with empire, saw only problems in it, and shrank from the expense of fighting for it. Accordingly, that quarter of the globe which, in 1945, was coloured pink on British school-children's maps, was handed away. India became independent in 1947, most of Africa during the early 1960s; by then a certain choreography could be set up for decolonization: a native prime minister, one usually jailed at some previous time as a colonial agitator, would inspect a guard of British troops in the company of some, frequently junior, member of the Royal Family while the Union Jack was ceremonially hauled down and a new flag, designed for the occasion, would wobble up the flag-staff, to the singing of a national anthem, also designed for the occasion. Then, all too frequently, mayhem would begin. Nowhere was this worse than in the Uganda of Idi Amin who slaughtered virtually all of the educated Ugandans and exiled the Indian community, confiscating their property. Even India, whose struggle for emancipation was one of the greatest progressive causes, gained independence only at the price of a civil war between Hindus and Muslims that killed off millions, including the outstanding architect of Indian independence, Mahatma Gandhi.

The French were more reluctant to decolonize their huge tracts of world territory. This was partly because French civilization was much more universalist than British: since the French Revolution, and even in some ways before, France had claimed that all natives were entitled

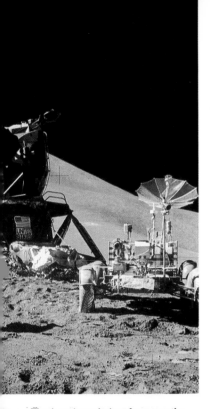

The American placing of a man on the Moon in August 1969, *above right* was only the most spectacular stage of a process that had begun with Russia putting a satellite Sputnik I, into orbit in 1957. The Russians also launched the first man, Yuri Gagarin, into space in 1961. Russian development of space technology and exploration has been less spectacular and more programmatic than that of the Americans. The *Soyuz* series of the 1970s and 1980s *left* concentrated on long-duration experiments and the construction of manned space laboratories and stations. At the same time the Americans concentrated on the shuttle service and also developed a proliferation of orbiting space satellites. They could be used for countless purposes – providing a photographic record of the world's weather, *above left*; allowing instant telephonic signals between continents; providing defence and industrial intelligence; monitoring earth and ocean resources; finally supplying the possibility, not as yet developed, of defence against nuclear weapons, in that missiles in flight may be destroyed by computerized laser-beams. This thrust into space was part of an acceleration of techological change which altered medicine, transport, finance, the media, and the monetary system in ways that have yet to be fully understood.

Nigeria was one of the first and most successful of the African states to become independent of Britain in 1960 *right*. Nevertheless, within 7 years the country was divided by a bitter separatist civil war which lasted until 1970.

The hero of Indian independence from the British, and the greatest figure in decolonization, was Mahatma Gandhi (1869-1948) *above*. He was not only a nationalist agitator; he also supplied an anti-modern ideology, with fasting and spinning-wheels, which was supposed to make the new India a model of peace and love. He himself was a conundrum, being a highly-educated barrister, with perfect English and an exceedingly acute brain; with the help of very able lieutenants such as Jawaharlal Nehru (1889-1964), he kept together his 'Congress Party' which eventually secured Indian independence in 1946. But peace and love were hard work in an India torn between Hindu and Muslim; decolonization led to civil war, and the emergence of a separate Muslim Pakistan. Gandhi himself was assassinated by a fanatic from his own camp.

The French empire proved far less easy to decolonize than the British, partly because there were so many French settlers. In Algeria *left* the Algerian Liberation Front (FLN) waged a vicious guerrilla war in the country and in the cities. The French responded with torture and search-and-destroy methods, but by 1958 the cost and divisiveness of the war brought the French Fourth Republic to an end. De Gaulle returned to power, and to the horror of the settlers, gave Algeria independence in 1961. In south-east Asia, their prestige broken by 3 years of Japanese occupation, the French again hung on tenaciously. The Communist Viet Minh dominated nationalist resistance and were backed by China, and their mastery of guerrilla tactics gave them the upper hand. French defeat at Dien Bien Phu (1954) led to their withdrawal, leaving a Communist North Vietnam, and a non-Communist South Vietnam, Laos and Cambodia. Almost immediately North Vietnam invaded the South; by the end of the 1960s US forces were actively involved, bringing new techniques (saturation and napalm bombing, chemical defoliation and helicopter mobility *above*) designed to

combat guerrilla strategies. In this they failed. The troops were badly led and demoralized, and the war-effort undermined: this was the first instantly-televized war, which inevitably brought home to the public the price of such a conflict. One of the few times in which Communist guerrilla warfare was successfully combatted was by the British during the Malayan emergency (1948-59 *above right*). Mass resettlement of poor Chinese was organized, and they were granted Malayan citizenship. Army and police patrolled the deep jungle; bombardment of civilians was avoided and ruthless use of bribery, coercion and psychological warfare effectively eliminated the problem.

to be considered French, and equality in principle was more rigorously asserted than in the British case; it was far more fun to be a black African in Paris than in London. There were also a great many French settlers in North Africa. As the Fourth Republic struggled into strife-ridden existence after the Liberation of 1944, the question of the colonies became a political football match in which even the French Communists sometimes took the nationalist side. Thus, France became hopelessly embroiled in Algeria, fighting a guerrilla war of appalling intensity; it divided France, and led to de Gaulle's being appointed virtual dictator of the country in 1958. He set up the Fifth Republic, and acted as conservative statesmen in Europe tended to do after 1945, stabbing his own followers in the back: he granted Algeria independence and hundreds of thousands of French settlers withdrew in 1962.

Two other areas of former European predominance suffered equally bloody decolonization: south-east Asia and the Middle East. The French had had colonies in south-east Asia since the 1880s. In the Second World War, they became discredited by defeat; the Japanese had fostered anti-Western feeling, and by 1945 the ground was set for a nationalist uprising. In Vietnam there were two separate elements – French-educated Vietnamese middle and upper-class people on the one hand, and Communists on the other, led by Ho Chi Minh. The peculiar terrain of Vietnam gave the nationalist resistance a good chance of survival and the French were peculiarly obstinate in fighting on. In 1954, after a savage defeat at Dien Bien Phu, they ultimately agreed to hand over the north of the country to Communists, and the south to anti-Communist nationalists. The Communists inevitably began to invade the south, which the Americans decided in 1957 to defend, and a long, cruel war resulted. Despite saturation bombing and the commitment of over half a million ground troops, it ended in American humiliation. American troops did not see why they were fighting in Vietnam, and fought badly, under generals who appear to have been desperately incompetent. The leaders of their local allies seem to have been more interested in their Swiss bank accounts than in prosecuting the war; a widespread and often misguided opposition to the war built up in the United States, and in 1969 the new Republican president, Richard M. Nixon, promised to reduce, and finally (1973) to withdraw US ground troops from Vietnam. By 1975, the South Vietnamese state was overrun; within a few years, much of the population was in prison camps, and another substantial proportion fled for the sea in leaky boats, to find such refuge as it could. The American fear of a 'domino

effect' in the region was partly realised when Laos and Cambodia also succumbed to Communism.

War between the United States and the Soviet Union was never a likely outcome of the south-east Asian imbroglio. However, in the Middle East, it was a different matter. This area mattered above all because it contained such a very large proportion of the world's oil – a commodity on which the entire economic system of the post-war world was based. Between the Wars, Great Britain and France had exercized control, directly or indirectly. In 1917, the British had promised to help create a Jewish Home in Palestine, and by 1945 about a million Jews, fleeing from the Nazi holocaust in Central Europe, had emigrated there. They became concentrated in certain oddly-shaped areas, but were much out-numbered by an Arab population, some of whom had also immigrated to take advantage of the superior circumstances of a British mandate and Jewish settlement. In one sense, the Jewish cause, and the state of Israel, was the first of the national liberation movements. In another sense, it was the last of the European imperialisms, for the Jewish, or Israeli, claim was partly that of a superior civilization: democratic, medical, efficient in agriculture, more open to women's emancipation. In 1947-48 the British, despairing of producing any solution, and criticized by everyone, simply withdrew, and in the resulting war the state of Israel was created.

The vastly more populous Arab world responded, at one level, with united condemnation for this incursion of a dollar-paid outsider, and there were wars between Israel and her Arab neighbours – in 1948, again in 1956, again in 1967 and again in 1973. On each occasion the Israelis' superior weaponry, and the courage of desperation, brought victory of a sort. Yet, after each war, a solution seemed to be further off than before, and Israel became dominated by extremists, who took the view that the country needed bastions far into Arab territory to survive, and would have to control its Arab population very strictly. The West Bank of the river Jordan, for instance, occupied in 1967, became open

The horrors of south-east Asia, terrible in Vietnam, became unimaginable in Cambodia, where millions of people were worked and starved to death by a crazed ultra-Communist, Pol Pot. Cambodia strove to remain neutral in the Vietnam war, but US planes bombed the jungle routes by which Vietnamese Communists infiltrated the South. This devastated much of the country and the disruption was accompanied by the rise of very young, fanatical Communists called Khmer Rouge, who allied the Left-wing doctrines of Paris intellectuals with ferocious peasant nationalism. Pol Pot, taking over the country, decided that 'the towns' were the enemy, and slaughtered their inhabitants, surviving elements being forced to work in the fields *above*.

In Iran, oil revenues were substantial, and when the Shah asserted control of them by successful defiance of the Westerners who had run the industry, he embarked on full-scale modernization: education, technology, urbanization, medicine. He kept power through a secret police, but by the later 1970s his rule was challenged by opponents of hectic change – especially the mullahs (Shi'ite priests) inspired by the exiled and aged Ayatollah Khomeini. The Shah was overthrown after enormous demonstrations, his Western supporters being driven out or murdered. There was an extreme religious reaction against American influence, and American diplomats were seized as hostages, and a wave of violent anti-Americanism swept the country *far right*.

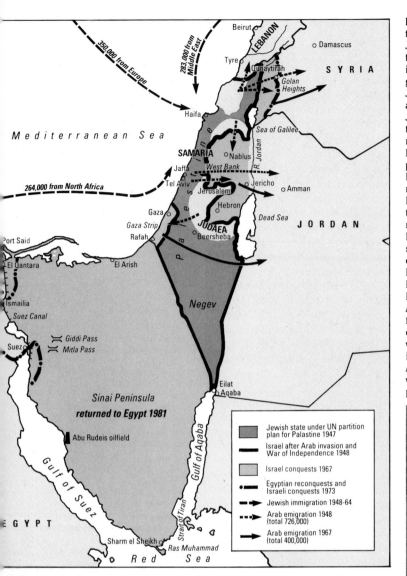

Beirut
LEBANON
○ Damascus

350,000 from Europe

283,000 from Middle East

Tyre
Qunaytirah
Golan Heights
SYRIA

Haifa
Sea of Galilee

Mediterranean Sea

SAMARIA ○Nablus
Jaffa West Bank
Tel Aviv R. Jordan
Jerusalem ○Jericho ○Amman
Hebron
264,000 from North Africa
Gaza
Gaza Strip
Rafah JUDAEA Dead Sea JORDAN
○Beersheba

Port Said
El Qantara
El Arish

Ismailia
Suez Canal
Negev

Suez Giddi Pass
Mitla Pass

Sinai Peninsula
returned to Egypt 1981

Abu Rudeis oilfield

Eilat
Aqaba

Gulf of Suez
Gulf of Aqaba
Strait of Tiran

EGYPT

Sharm el Sheikh
Ras Muhammad
Red Sea

	Jewish state under UN partition plan for Palestine 1947
	Israel after Arab invasion and War of Independence 1948
	Israel conquests 1967
	Egyptian reconquests and Israeli conquests 1973
	Jewish immigration 1948-64
	Arab emigration 1948 (total 726,000)
	Arab emigration 1967 (total 400,000)

Israel and Palestine *left*. For many years there was increasing pressure to create a Jewish National State. Jewish immigration to Palestine from Europe increased sharply in the 1930s and '40s. The British government, under pressure from Arabs, Jews and the US, withdrew from Palestine, and a plan to partition the territory into a Jewish and an Arab state was adopted by the United Nations (1947). This was rejected by the Arabs and on the day of British withdrawal the state of Israel was proclaimed; in the ensuing war the Palestinian Arabs, supported by neighbouring Arab states, were defeated. During and after the fighting, two-thirds of the Arabs left their homes and became refugees in Jordan, Gaza, Syria and Lebanon. After the war of 1948, the Jewish soldiers *below left* celebrated the establishment of the first Jewish state in Palestine since the Roman conquest. But Israel's refusal to acknowledge Palestinian claims, and the refusal of the Arab states to recognise Israel led to 3 further wars, in 1956, 1967 and 1973. In each case superior Israeli tactics and weaponry won the day, and resulted in increasing the areas of occupied territory. A degree of détente was reached by 1981 when Israel agreed to return the Sinai peninsula to Egypt.

to Israeli settlements, heavily subsidized by the government; the Golan Heights, along the Israeli/Syrian border, captured by a brilliant stroke in 1967, were permanently garrisoned. But the only real hope for Israel, apart from eventual peace with its neighbours, lay in American support on the one hand, and Arab disunity on the other.

Arab disunity was certainly forthcoming. The Arab world stretches from the former French territories of the Maghreb in North Africa to the borders of Iran. Hatred of Western colonizers had produced nationalist revolts in areas that had been colonized, whereas in others, notably Saudi Arabia, attitudes to the West were reasonably friendly. In Egypt and Syria, there was great tension between nationalists and Muslims; the nationalists, mostly in the army, tended to want secularization and Westernization. In Iran, the Shah promoted Western modernization, and transformed his country in two decades; Saudi Arabia, paradoxically more friendly to the West, remained more traditionally Muslim. The strangest outcome of all was in Libya, where a synthesis of desert puritanism and Westernization produced the violently anti-Western regime of Colonel Gaddaffi. In all of this, hatred between Arab and Arab grew, all the more when the British and French withdrew from the area after a final display of gunboat diplomacy when they tried to retain control of the Suez Canal Company, after it had been nationalized by the Egyptians in 1956. Instability between and within Arab countries, at its worst during the Lebanese civil war (from 1975) which pitted countless groups against each other, made the Middle East an impossible area to govern, or even to understand; Arab unity could only occur over Israel.

Towards the end of this period, a new and possibly far-reaching phenomenon came about – Muslim revivalism. The Arab states had been self-consciously 'modernist', determined to catch up. Colonel Nasser, a nationalist who seized power in Egypt in the early 1950s, was strongly anti-religious, and took all the nostrums of the then doctrines of progress – nationalization, for instance, plus short-sighted land reform and widespread punitive taxation. In the Maghreb and in Syria, much the same occurred, though under far less charismatic leaders. Defeat in war caused Nasser to be discredited; more particularly, the failure of his economic programme in Egypt, a country with a strong mercantile, Mediterranean personality, caused some re-thinking. His successor, Anwar Sadat, made peace with Israel. Even so, Egyptian politics have a constant Muslim undertone, and Sadat's assassination by Muslim fanatics was a testimony to this. In the same way, the overthrow of the Shah of Iran in 1979, by Muslim fundamentalists headed by the aged Ayatollah Khomeini, set a strange pattern of religious nationalism, far more difficult for Westerners to understand than the Communist, or socialist, nationalism that had gone before. In all of this, the two super-powers were involved – sometimes reluctantly, sometimes, eagerly. The Middle East remained a powder-keg, and the process of disintegration was furthered in 1982, when the Israelis invaded the Lebanon in pursuit of Arab terrorists, and in 1980, when Iraq invaded Iran, fearing the spread of Muslim fundamentalism. The resulting war froze in a bloody stalemate along their shared frontier, costing several hundred thousand lives.

The two super-powers, ever shadow-boxing in the glare of these outbreaks, also became involved in conflicts that were less acute. The European decolonization of Africa was confused, and left highly unstable states in which the Soviet Union, sometimes to its demonstrable embarrassment, was involved. South Africa remained in white hands, controlling a huge proportion of the continent's disposable resources, and ruled by a system of literal-minded racial separation, *Apartheid*,

One of the characteristic images of the modern world was that of a politicized peasant armed with a sophisticated gun. After 1950, and the withdrawal of direct Western control, the economically and strategically important Middle East became one of the most unstable and 'politicized' areas of the world. Libya and Egypt, Syria and (part-Christian) Lebanon, Iraq and Iran were often enemies. Only war against the alien Israel, allegedly the pawn of the United States, occasionally united the Arabs. The Palestinian exiles and refugees from Israel formed the Palestine Liberation Organization, (PLO), (*inset, above right*) led by Yassir Arafat, which endorsed international terrorism as a means to an end. In 1973 the Arabs used oil prices, quadrupling them in a matter of months to inflict economic damage to Israel's friends in the West. But there were endless problems beyond these frontiers, most of all in the Lebanon which, originally an island of peace amidst the Middle Eastern storms, disintegrated into warring factions in 1976. Beirut became a nightmare in which religious and political factions disputed control of the country *above* and of the drug-running to which more and more Lebanese and Palestinians had recourse. The Israeli invasion in 1982 solved nothing.

which revolted outsiders in its pettiness and cruelty. At the same time, it was by far the most prosperous and ordered state on the continent, and so attracted hundreds of thousands of African immigrants. It lasted for an astonishing length of time, given the unanimity with which its racial practices have been condemned; only by the mid–1980s was there any serious indication of change.

In Latin America, as in Africa, a persistent problem was population: whatever the progress made by various states, they were threatened by the sheer fact of having too many mouths to feed. In Africa, this produced famine; in Latin America, political instability, as the gap between rich and poor grew. Since the Great Depression of the 1930s, many of these states had become military dictatorships: Argentina, under Perón, virtually became a Fascist state in the 1940s; Chile's own well-established parliamentary system was challenged, first of all by the

In Latin America population growth was so rapid that neither modernization of agriculture nor expansion of industry were able to absorb the increasing multitude. Agrarian reform did not succeed in transforming conditions in the countryside or halting the migration of rural people to the cities. Urban over-population, notably in Mexico City and São Paulo *below*, making these 2 cities among the most populous in the world, was only the most obvious symptom of the problem.

'The Chinese giant' – easily, with 1000 million people, the greatest country on earth – became Communist, after a lengthy civil war, in 1949. Her leader, Mao Tse-tung (chapter 24), reigned until 1976. He ruled, at first, through Stalinist prescriptions: heavy industry, a large war-effort, collectivization of agriculture, and the cult of personality *right*. The *Thoughts of Chairman Mao*, a collection of sayings that, when translated from Chinese, turned out to contain sentiments such as 'It never rains but it pours', was supposed to be one of the great revolutionary texts. Unfortunately, the Chinese revolution outdid its Stalinist model in offering tyranny, inefficiency, and isolation on a colossal scale. 50 million people died in the course of the characteristically-named Great Leap Forward (1958-9) to collectivize agriculture; the Cultural Revolution (from 1966, *below*) also killed off millions. By 1960, Chinese relations with the Soviet Union had developed very badly, and there was a split, to the point where Peking in 1971 took up détente with the United States. By the later 1970s, the Chinese, seeing the great economic success of their non-Communist neighbours in Japan, South Korea, Taiwan and Hong Kong, began to dismantle Communism in economic affairs.

Allende regime, (which threatened, for a time, to become a Left-wing dictatorship) and then by General Pinochet, an exponent of the Right. In Nicaragua, there was a similar vacillation between Left and Right, which by the early 1980s produced civil war, in which the super-powers were covertly involved. The greatest instances of Latin America's various problems were two Caribbean islands, only a few miles apart. Haiti, under the dictator 'Papa Doc' Duvalier, became almost the poorest country in the globe, ruled by black magic and terror from 1957 to 1972. Cuba, next door, became Communist under Fidel Castro, in 1959, and a thorn in the Americans' flesh. Soviet threats to place missiles on Cuban soil provoked the single greatest clash of the super-powers in the post-war era, in 1962, when American naval ships set up a blockade of Cuba which, if tested, would have resulted in seizure of Soviet ships. The Soviet Union backed down from confrontation but exacted from US president Kennedy the promise that the USA would not invade. The Castro regime survived. Its jails were overflowing, and its public life was highly regimented; on the other hand, there was undeniable social progress. People were literate, even if censorship deprived them of much to read. Was this a price worth paying for 'social progress'? Opinions differed.

This dilemma came up throughout the Communist world after 1945 as it had done since 1917 in the Soviet Union. Broadly speaking, Communism had seized control in backward countries, whether the Balkans, or China, in the later 1940s. War had shaken the original social structures of these countries to their foundations; in China the Communists under Mao Tse-tung had emerged in the inter-war anarchy, had spearheaded the fight against the Japanese and, by 1949, had taken power. China, with a population four times larger than that of the Soviet Union, now put Stalinist modernization plans into action: collectivizing agriculture during the Great Leap Forward and attempting helter-skelter industrialization based on iron, coal and steel, much as

在毛澤東的勝利旗幟下前進

Stalin had done. The results were heralded, in some quarters, as brilliant, and the Chinese eventually also produced their own nuclear industry. As had happened in Stalin's Russia, the social turmoil produced a tremendous, to outsiders virtually inexplicable, series of purges, known as the Cultural Revolution (1966): after Mao's death in 1976, the facts concerning these events came out. It emerged for instance, that thousands of intellectuals had been tortured to death in the basements of the Ministry of Culture. Apologists for Mao looked foolish when his successor, Deng Xiaoping, dismantled most of the Maoist economic system on the grounds that it had produced fifty million deaths from famine.

The Soviet Union had undergone a not dissimilar process in the 1930s; and after 1945 'Progressives' everywhere expected it to settle down. In reality, Stalin after 1945 reverted to methods of unspeakable tyranny, both at home and in Hungary, Poland, Czechoslovakia, Romania and Bulgaria, the principal satellite countries of eastern Europe that were forcibly brought within the Soviet sphere of influence after Germany's collapse; the facts of this again came out in 1956, when Stalin's successor, Nikita Khrushchev, revealed them at a Party Congress. Thereafter, Soviet Russia and her satellites made a better effort

Communists in Europe managed a modest degree of prosperity. In comparison with the West, however, the benefits of the modern world were limited, and communal (rather than individual) values were emphasized. The inhabitants of an agricultural commune *above* share their produce and their tables. Russia and Romania, still very tightly controlled, did not revolt. But there were revolts in other parts of the Communist world. Hungary erupted in 1956, and order was restored only when the Red Army brought up tanks to bombard tenements *below left*. A satellite regime under János Kádár was installed, and it surprised the world by pioneering ways in which the original Communist prescriptions would be profitably adulterated with capitalism. East Germany accepted West German money, and became relatively prosperous. Poland, with a large, semi-controlled, private sector, also took Western money, suffered a huge inflation of black-market prices, and saw the disintegration of the Communist Party. A free trade union, *Solidarity*, developed in the late 1970s and in the end military dictatorship, under General Jaruzelski, had to restore order in place of the discredited Communist Party. In Czechoslavakia in 1966-7 *above left* a liberal Communist, Alexander Dubček, introduced 'Socialism with a human face' – free from shortages and secret police. His reign inevitably came to an end with the arrival of Russian tanks in August 1968, ironically at a time when Left-wing student demonstrations broke out in West Germany, Paris, London and the USA.

World population *right* grew at an alarming rate after the Second World War. In spite of infant mortality 8 times higher and a life expectancy one-third lower, the population of the poor countries grew 3-4 times as fast as that of the rich countries.

to observe 'social legality'; and there was at least some concern for the well-being of the consumer. Largely on the basis of endless floods of fresh peasant labour, industrial growth, of an old-fashioned sort, went ahead, and in the 1970s the influx of Western bankers' money brought significant change in the eastern European satellites. By the end of the 1970s, however, the Soviet Union itself was running out of fresh labour, and her industrial system, with its inflexible planning, seemed unable to compete in terms of new technology with the Western countries. There was crisis throughout the Soviet bloc, best shown in the revolt of a significant part of the Polish working class, under the guidance of priests, in 1976-1985. A military coup in December 1982 restored 'order'; many commentators asserted that, since the old-style Communist parties were clearly disintegrating, such military juntas could well represent the future governments of the Communist world. By the middle of the 1980s a new Soviet leader, Mikhail Gorbachov, was talking the language of serious reform, and retiring a great number of the tired old men whom he inherited.

The strongest argument advanced for Communism was that it would lead to mass prosperity. In practice, though it secured in most cases a minimum of prosperity, its achievements were far behind those of the

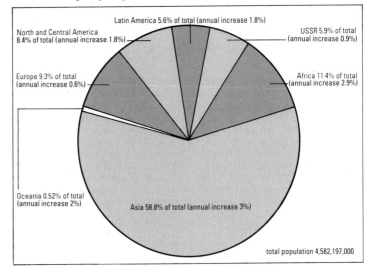

Latin America 5.6% of total (annual increase 1.8%)

North and Central America 8.4% of total (annual increase 1.8%)

USSR 5.9% of total (annual increase 0.9%)

Europe 9.3% of total (annual increase 0.6%)

Africa 11.4% of total (annual increase 2.9%)

Oceania 0.52% of total (annual increase 2%)

Asia 58.8% of total (annual increase 3%)

total population 4,582,197,000

'capitalist' West. Western Europe and the United States, with their outposts in other continents, and their imitators in Japan, underwent after 1945, and especially in the 1950s, a degree of mass prosperity such as had never been seen in any previous stage of history. Cheap power, free trade, an agreed international medium of exchange – the dollar – labour mobility and – though opinions vary as to its effectiveness – government planning for full employment made for an economic miracle in the West. Western Germany made a spectacular recovery; so, later, did France and Italy, the three states bound together in an economic community (EEC) which eventually expanded to include most of the western European nations. Japan astonished the world with her feats of mass quality production and ruthless marketing, so that the world of the 1970s and 1980s saw endless inventions which transformed everything, from telephone to medicine. The older Western powers, Great Britain and the United States, fell behind in this race, though after the recession of the later 1970s both made efforts to catch up. The problems of the West were mainly those of prosperity – self-indulgence, an erosion of authority, and a flight from the past. In French schools, History – the great staple of the Republics, and the foundation of their political culture – was replaced by 'awareness studies'. Although education became available to more people than ever before, the range of reference and literacy of people in the West generally declined from its peak in 1914, and it became a common complaint in matters of education and culture that the specialists pursued their specialism to the point of incomprehensibility, whereas the masses were fobbed off with a cultural diet of pop music and television. Even these, however, remained the privileged few. For most of the world's burgeoning population education remained fairly rudimentary.

The Polish writer, Czesław Milosz, remarked that 'the Europe of shop-keepers and *midinettes* brewed up the poison that killed it': namely, that the prosperity of the European middle classes before 1914 both depended on, and provoked, a degree of class-tension which created Communism and the terrible slaughter which followed its arrival. Were the rich countries now provoking much the same problem, on a world-wide scale? Their own advances in medicine allowed populations in what was known as the Third World to grow and grow, creating pressures on land and food that created famine. Historically, the prosperity of the city-state usually ended in invasion from hungry outsiders, combined with internal division, and/or war between rival city states. The West after 1945 consisted even more demonstrably of shop-keepers and *midinettes* than ever before. Is its poison the nuclear arms-race, the advance of uncontrolled technology, the down-trodden minorities within, or the down-trodden majorities without? Or is there not really any poison at all, and can we look forward to infinite progress? To these questions, the historian has no answer.

All previous ages in world history knew too many children meant too little food *right*. All previous ages were at the mercy of climate and soil-exhaustion. Until 1950, the world's population had been relatively stable, its growth small and unpredictable. Agricultural populations tended to breed children in great numbers, knowing that many would die early, and that the survivors would be, in effect, a guarantee of security for the parents in their old age. After 1945, these habits of reproduction persisted, whereas infant mortality, partly due to Western medicine, declined dramatically. The result in Africa, and much of Asia, was a population explosion.

Faulty development economics, frequent civil wars, bureaucracy and corruption also interfered with African and Asian populations' age-old ways of dealing with land. These problems only added to the gross imbalances in the world economy, setting poor nations against rich nations. With 5 billion out of an anticipated world population of 6 billion in the year 2000 crowded in impoverished Third World countries, imbalances of this magnitude could give rise, if nothing were done to correct them, to an explosion capable of tearing the world apart as we know it. But the signs of anything being done are few.

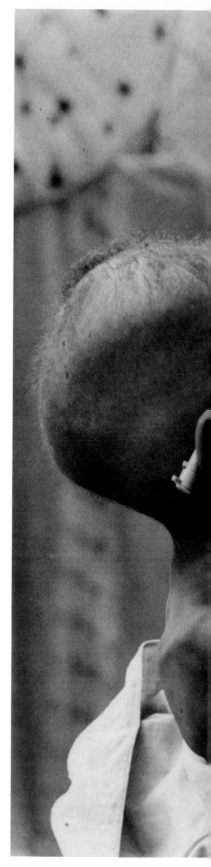

BIBLIOGRAPHY

Among the large number of works consulted by the contributors, the following contain information which has proved particularly useful, and may be recommended for further reading or research.

GENERAL BOOKS AND HISTORICAL ATLASES

Barraclough, G. (ed.) *The Times Atlas of World History*, London 1984
Barraclough, G. (ed.) *The Times Concise Atlas of World History*, London 1986
Brice, W.C. *An Historical Atlas of Islam*, Leiden 1981
Cambridge Ancient History vols 1–11 (various eds., from 1970)
Chang, Kwang-chih *The Archaeology of Ancient China*, New Haven 1977
Darby, H.C., Fullard H. (eds.) *The New Cambridge Modern History vol XIV: Atlas*, Cambridge 1970
Engel, J. (ed.) *Grosser Historischer Weltatlas*, 3 vols, Munich 1953–1978
Fontana History of the Ancient World vols 1–6 (various eds.)
Geelan, P.J.M., Twitchett, D.C. (eds.) *The Times Atlas of China*, London 1974
Hammond, N.G.L. *History of Greece to 323 BC*, Oxford 1959
Langer, W.L. *An Encyclopaedia of World History*, London 1972.
McNeill, W.H. *A World History*, New York 1971
Schwartzberg, J.E. (ed.) *Historical Atlas of South Asia*
Shepherd, W.R. *Historical Atlas*, New York 1964
Sherratt, A. (ed.) *The Cambridge Encyclopaedia of Archaeology*, Cambridge 1980
Stavrianos, L.S. *The World to 1500*, Englewood Cliffs, N.J. 1975
Stavrianos, L.S. *The World since 1500*, Englewood Cliffs, N.J. 1975
Toynbee, A.J., Myers, E.D. *A Study of History, Historical Atlas and Gazetteer*, Oxford 1959
Van der Heyden, A.M., Scullard, H.H. *Atlas of the Classical World*
Westermann *Grosser Atlas zur Weltgeschichte*, Brunswick 1976

CHAPTER 1
Klein, R. *Ice Age Hunters of the Ukraine*, Chicago 1973
Leakey, R. *The Making of Mankind*, London 1981
Leroi-Gourhan, A. *The Dawn of European Art*, Cambridge 1982
Pfeiffer, J.E. *The Emergence of Man*, New York 1978
Sieveking, A. *The Cave Artists*, London 1979

CHAPTER 2
Clark, G. *Mesolithic Prelude*, Edinburgh 1980
Dennell, R. *European Economic Prehistory*, New York
Megaw, J.V.S. (ed.) *Hunters, Gatherers and First Farmers Beyond Europe*, Leicester 1977
Mellaart, J. *The Neolithic of the Near East*, London 1975
Mellaart, J. *Çatal Hüyük*, London 1967
Oates, D. & J. *The Rise of Civilization*, Oxford 1976
Redman, C.R. *The Rise of Civilization*, San Francisco 1978
Reed, C. (ed.) *The Origins of Agriculture*, The Hague 1977

Struever, S. *Prehistoric Agriculture*, New York 1971

CHAPTER 3
Adams, R.McC. *The Evolution of Urban Society*, 1966
Allchin, B. & R. *The Rise of Civilisation in India and Pakistan*, Cambridge 1982
Chang, Kwang-chin *Shang Civilization*, New Haven 1980
Edwards, I.E.S. *The Pyramids of Egypt*, Harmondsworth 1980
Gelb, I.J. *A Study of Writing*, Chicago 1978
Postgate, N. *The First Empires*, Oxford 1977
Trigger, B.G., Kemp, B.J., O'Connor, D., Lloyd, A.B. *Ancient Egypt: A Social History*, Cambridge 1983
Whitehouse, R. *The First Cities*, Oxford 1977

CHAPTER 4
Collis, J. *The European Iron Age*, London 1984
Cook, J.M. *The Persian Empire*, London 1983
Cotterell, A. *The First Emperor of China*, London 1981
Roux, G. *Ancient Iraq*, Harmondsworth 1980
Saggs, H.W.F. *The Might That Was Assyria*, London 1984
Sandars, N.K. *The Sea Peoples*, London 1978
Thapar, R. *Asoka and the Decline of the Mauryas*, Oxford 1973
Wheeler, M. *Flames over Persepolis*, London 1968

CHAPTER 5
Balsdon, J.P.V.D. *Rome, the Story of an Empire*, London 1970
Burn, A.R. *History of Greece*, Harmondsworth
Bury & Meiggs *A History of the Greek World*
Cary, M., Scullard, H.H. *A History of Rome down to the Reign of Constantine*, London 1975
Cornell, T. & Matthews, J. *Atlas of the Roman World*, Oxford 1982
Ehrenberg, V. *From Solon to Socrates*, London 1968
Ferguson, J. *The Heritage of Hellenism*, London 1973
Finley, M.I. *Studies in Ancient Society*, London 1974
Levi, P. *Atlas of the Greek World*, Oxford 1980
Rostovtzeff, M. *The Social and Economic History of the Roman Empire*, Oxford 1957
Scullard, H.H. *From the Gracchi to Nero*, London & New York 1959
Snodgrass, A. *Archaic Greece*, London 1980

CHAPTER 6
Basham, A.L. *The Wonder that was India*, 1955
Boyce M. *Zoroastrians: Their Religious Beliefs and Practices*, London 1979
Bultmann, R. *Primitive Christianity in its Contemporary Setting*, 1956
Chadwick, H. *The Early Church*, Harmondsworth 1967
Conze, E. *Buddhism*, Oxford 1957
Dood, C.H. *The Founder of Christianity*, London 1971
Epstein, I. *Judaism: A Historical Presentation*, Harmondsworth 1959
Ferguson, J. *Religions of the World*, Guildford & London 1978
Fingarette, H. *Confucius*
Kedourie, E. *The Jewish World*, London 1979
Ling, T. *A History of Religion, East and West*, London 1968
Ling, T. *The Buddha*, 1973
Morgan, K.W. *The Religion of the Hindus*, New York 1953
Parrinder, E.G. *Man and his Gods*, London 1971

Smart, N. *The Religious Experience of Mankind*, London 1971
Zaehner, R.C. *The Concise Encyclopaedia of Living Faiths*
Zaehner, R.C. *The Dawn of Twilight of Zoroastrianism*, 1961

CHAPTER 7
Brown, P. *The World of Late Antiquity*, London 1971
Chambers, M. *The Fall of Rome: Can it be explained?*, New York 1963
Dilli, S. *Roman Society in the Last Century of the Western Empire*, London 1898, rep. 1958
Gibbon, E. *Decline and Fall of the Roman Empire*, (ed. J.B. Bury 7 vols), London 1909–14)
Jones, A.H.M. *The Late Roman Empire*, (3 vols), Oxford 1964
Loewe, M. *Imperial China*, 1966
Mazzarino, S. *The End of the Ancient World*, London 1966
Moss, H.St.L.B. *The Birth of the Middle Ages*, Oxford 1935
Musset, L. *The Germanic Invasions*, 1975
Thompson, E.A. *A History of Attila and the Huns*, 1948
Ure, P.N. *Justinian and his Age*, Harmondsworth 1951
Walbank, F.W. *The Awful Revolution*, Liverpool 1969

CHAPTER 8
Ahmed, Azia *An Intellectual History of Islam in India*, Edinburgh 1969
Ashtor, E. *A Social and Economic History of the Near East in the Middle Ages*, London 1976
Hodgson, M.G.S. *The Venture of Islam: Conscience and History, in a World Civilization*, (3 vols), Chicago 1974
Lewis, B. *The World of Islam: Faith, People, Culture*, London 1967
Lewis, B. *The Arabs in History*, London 1968
McNeill, W.H. and Waldman, M.R. *The Islamic World*, New York 1973
Rodinson, M. *Mohamed*, Harmondsworth 1971
Saunders, J.J. *A History of Medieval Islam*, London 1965
Von Grunebaum, G.E. *Medieval Islam: a Study in Cultural Orientation*, Chicago 1946
Watt, W.M. *Muhammad, Prophet and Statesman*, Oxford 1976
Watt, W.M. *The Formative Period of Islamic Thought*, Edinburgh 1973

CHAPTER 9
Barraclough, G. *The Crucible of Europe*, London 1976
Brooke, C.N.L. *The Twelfth-Century Renaissance*
Cipolla, C. (ed.) *Fountana Economic History of Europe*, 1972
Clanchy, M.T. *From Memory to Written Record*, 1979
Duby, G. *The Age of Cathedrals*
Keen, M.H. *Chivalry*, Yale and London 1984
Lopez, R.S. *The Birth of Europe*
Lopez, R.S. *The Commercial Revolution of the Middle Ages*, 1971
Painter, S. *A History of the Middle Ages 284–1500*, 1974
Southern, R.W. *The Making of the Middle Ages*, 1953
Wallace-Hadrill, J.M. *The Barbarian West 400–1000*

CHAPTER 10
Dawson, D. (ed.) *The Mongol Mission*, London 1955 (reprinted as *Mission to Asia*, USA 1966)

Fox, R. *Genghis Khan*, London 1935
Juvaini *History of the World Conqueror*, (trans. J.A. Boyle, 2 vols), London 1972
Rashid al-Din *The Successors of Genghis Khan*, (trans. J.A. Boyle), London 1972
Saunders, J.J. *History of the Mongol Conquests*, London 1972
Spuler, B. *History of the Mongols*, (trans. H. & S Drummond), London 1972

CHAPTER 11
Boxer, C.R. *The Portuguese Seaborne Empire*, 1969
Chambers, D.S. *The Imperial Age of Venice*, London 1970
Lane, F. *Venice, a Maritime Republic*, Baltimore 1971
McNeill, W.H. *Venice, the hinge of Europe*, *1081–1797*, Chicago 1974
Morison, S.E. *The European Discovery of America*, (2 vols) 1971–1974
Olschki, L. *Marco Polo's Asia*, Berkeley 1960
Scammell, G.V. *The World Encompassed*, London & Berkeley 1981

CHAPTER 12–13
Blunden, C. Elvin, M. *Cultural Atlas of China*, Oxford 1983
Herrmann, A. *An Historical Atlas of China*, Edinburgh 1966
Papirot, E. *Historical and Geographical Dictionary of Japan*, Rutland, Vt. and Tokyo 1972
Smith, B. *Japan: a History in Art*, London 1965
Smith, B., Weng, Wan-go *China: A History in Art*, London 1973
Wiethoff, B. *Introduction to Chinese History*, London 1975

CHAPTER 14
Holt, P.M. *Egypt and the Fertile Crescent 1516–1922*, London 1966
Inalcik, H. *The Ottoman Empire: the Classical Age 1300–1600*, London 1973
Itzkowitz, N. *Ottoman Empire and Islamic Tradition*, New York 1972
Karpat, K. *The Ottoman State and its Place in World History*, Leiden 1974
Pitcher, D. *An Historical Geography of the Ottoman Empire*, Leiden 1972
Shaw, S.J. *Empire of the Gazis: the Rise and Decline of the Ottoman Empire, 1280–1808*, New York and London 1976
Sugar, P.F. *Southeastern Europe under Ottoman Rule, 1354–1804*, Seattle 1977

CHAPTER 15
Fage, J.D. *A History of Africa*, London 1978
Fage, J.D. *An Atlas of African History*, London 1958
Garlake, P.S. *Great Zimbabwe*, London 1973
Inskeep, R.R. *The Peopling of Southern Africa*, London 1978
Oliver, R., Fagan, B.M. *Africa in the Iron Age*, Cambridge 1975
Phillipson, D.W. *African Archaeology*, Cambridge 1985
Shaw, C.T. *Nigeria*, London 1978

CHAPTER 16
Bankes, G. *Peru Before Pizarro*, Oxford 1977
Hammond, N. *Ancient Maya Civilization*, Cambridge 1982
Hemming J. *The Conquest of the Incas*, London 1972
Weaver, M.P. *The Aztec, Maya and their Predecessors*, New York 1972 (rev. ed. 1981)
Willey, G.R. *An Introduction to American Archaeology*, (2 vols) Englewood Cliffs, N.J. 1968/71

Zubrow, E.B., Fritz, M.C., Fritz, J.M. *New World Archaeology*, New York 1974

CHAPTER 17
Clark, G.N. *The Seventeenth Century*, Oxford 1945
Davies, R. *The Rise of the Atlantic Economies*, London 1973
Hale, J.R. *Renaissance Europe*, London 1970
Israel, J.I. *The Dutch Republic and the Hispanic World 1606–1661*, Oxford 1982
Kamen, H. *The Iron Century 1560–1660*, London 1971
Parker, G. *The Dutch Revolt*, Harmondsworth 1977

CHAPTER 18
Bower, C.R. *The Dutch Seaborne Empire*, London 1965
Boxer, C.R. *The Portuguese Seaborne Empire*, London 1969
Parry, J.H. *The Age of Reconnaissance*, London 1963
Parry, J.H. *The Spanish Seaborne Empire*, London 1966
Quinn, D.B., Ryan, A.N. *England's Sea Empire*, London 1983
Rawley, A. *The Trans-Atlantic Slave Trade: A History*, New York 1981

CHAPTER 19
Chandhuri, K.N. *Trade and Civilization in the Indian Ocean*, Cambridge 1985
Elvin, M. *The Pattern of the Chinese Past*, Stanford 1972
Habib, I., Raychaudhuri, T.P. *Cambridge Economic History of India* vol 1, Cambridge 1981
Lehmann, J.P. *The Roots of Modern Japan*, London 1982
Ricklefs, M.C. *A History of Modern Indonesia*, London 1983

CHAPTER 20
Anderson, M.S. *Europe in the 18th Century*, London 1961
Andrews, S. *The Eighteenth Century*, London
Behrens, C.B.A. *The Ancien Régime*
Furet, F., Richet, D. *The French Revolution*, (2 vols)
Henderson, W.O. *The Industrialization of Europe 1780–1914*, London 1969
Hobsbawm, E.J. *The Age of Revolution*, London 1962
Perkin, H. *The Origins of Modern English Society 1780–1800*, London
Rudé, G. *Revolutionary Europe*, London 1972
Tulard, J. *Napoleon*, London 1984

CHAPTER 21
Blum, J. *Lord and Peasant in Russia*, Princeton 1981
Florinsky, M.T. *Short History of Russia*, New York 1953
Klyuchevski, V. *History of Russia*, 1968
Parker, W.H. *An Historical Geography of Russia*, London 1968
Riasanovski, N.V. *History of Russia*, Oxford 1963
Seaton, A. *The Cossacks*, 1985
Sumner, B.H. *Survey of Russian History*, London 1944
Wallace, D.M. *Russia*, London 1905
West, T. *Russian Orthodoxy*, Harmondsworth
Wittram, R. *Peter the Great*

CHAPTER 22
Brogan, H. *History of the United States*, London 1985
Christie, I. *Crisis of Empire*, London 1966

Collins, B. *Origins of America's Civil War*, London 1981
Concise Dictionary of American History, New York & Oxford 1963
Harvard Guide to American History, Cambridge, Mass. 1974
Makesy, P. *The War for America*, Princeton 1965
Van Alstyne, R.W. *The Rising American Empire*, Oxford 1960

CHAPTER 23
Fieldhouse, D. *The Colonial Empires*, London 1982
Hope-Simpson, J. *The Making of the Machine Age*, Heinemann 1978
Kemp, T. *Industrialisation in Nineteenth Century Europe*, London 1969
Kim, Key-Hiuk *The Last Phase of the East Asian World Order*, Berkely, 1980
Langhorne, R. *The Collapse of the Concert of Europe*, London 1981
May, E.R. *Imperial Democracy: the Emergence of America as a Great Power*, 1961
Stone, N. *Europe Transformed*, London 1983

CHAPTER 24
Craig, G. *History of Modern Germany*
Ferro, M. *The Great War*
Ferro, M. *The Russian Revolution* (2 vols.)
Galbraith, J.K. *The Great Crash*, New York 1955
Grenville, J.R. *World History in 20th Century*, (2 vols)
Liddell Hart, B. *History of First World War*, London 1934, 1970
Smith, D. *Mussolini*
Taylor, A.J.P. *The First World War*, London 1963
Trotsky, L. *The Russian Revolution*, (3 vols)
Westwood, J.N. *Short History of the USSR*

CHAPTER 25
Arnold-Forster, M. *The World at War*, London 1973
Bullock, A. *Hitler*, London 1952
Calvocoressi, P., Wint, G. *Total War*, Harmondsworth 1972
Collier, B. *A Short History of the Second World War*, London 1967
Erickson, J. *The Road to Berlin*, London 1983
Erickson, J. *The Road to Stalingrad*, London
Liddell Hart, B. *History of the Second World War*, London 1970
Speer, A. *Inside the Third Reich*, London, New York, 1970

CHAPTER 26
Alison, G. *Essence of Decision: Explaining the Cuban Missile Crisis*, 1971
Brown, C., Monney P.J. *Cold War to Detente 1945–1980*, 1981
Critchfield, R. *Villages*, 1981
Halle, L. *The Cold War as History*, 1967
Hauser, P.M. *World Population Problems (Headline series No. 174)*, 1975
Low, A.D. *The Sino–Soviet Dispute*, 1978
McDougall, W.A. *The Heavens and the Earth: A Political History of the Space Age*, 1985
Poole, P. *The United States and Indochina from FDR to Nixon*, 1973
Safran, N. *From War to War: The Arab–Israeli Confrontation 1948–1969*, 1969
Tucker, R.W. *The Inequality of Nations*, 1977
Ulam, A.B. *The Rivals: America and Russia since World War II*, 1971
Whiting, A. *China Crosses the Yalu*, 1960

PICTURE CREDITS

We have pleasure in acknowledging the following museums, picture agencies and publishers. The abbreviations below indicate t: top, b: bottom, l: left, r: right, c: centre.

INDEX

The references in italics refer to maps.